THEATRE PROFILES 9

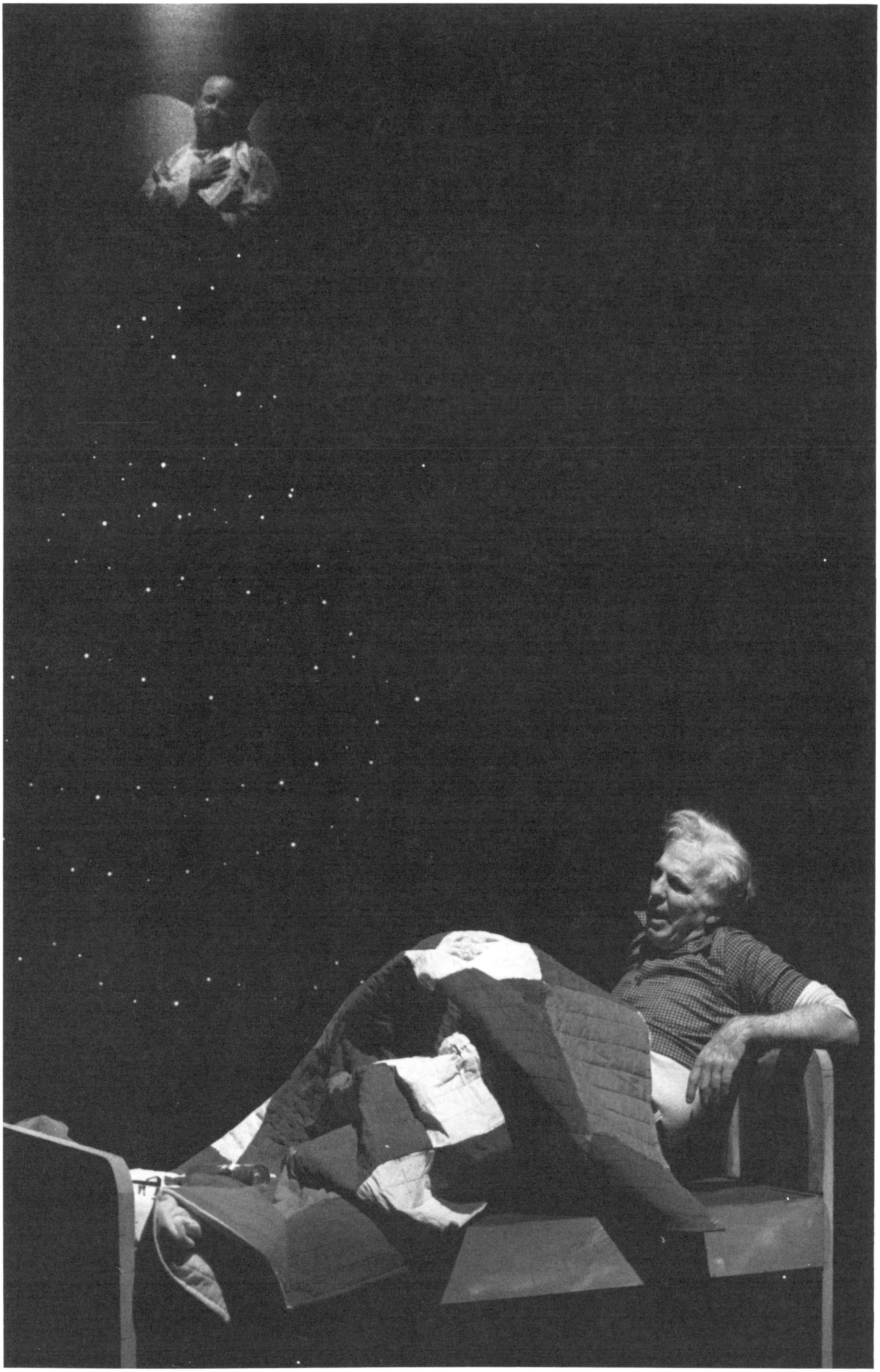

THEATRE PROFILES 9

THE ILLUSTRATED REFERENCE GUIDE
TO AMERICA'S NONPROFIT
PROFESSIONAL THEATRE

THEATRE COMMUNICATIONS GROUP
NEW YORK • 1990

TCG gratefully acknowledges public funds from the National Endowment for the Arts and the New York State Council on the Arts, in addition to the generous support of the following foundations and corporations: Alcoa Foundation; Ameritech Foundation; ARCO Foundation; AT&T Foundation; Beatrice Foundation; Center for Arts Criticism; Citicorp/Citibank; Common Wealth Fund; Consolidated Edison Company of New York; Eleanor Naylor Dana Charitable Trust; Dayton Hudson Foundation; Exxon Corporation; Ford Foundation; Jerome Foundation; Andrew W. Mellon Foundation; Metropolitan Life Foundation; National Broadcasting Company; New York Community Trust; New York Times Company Foundation; Pew Charitable Trusts; Philip Morris Companies; Scherman Foundation; Shell Oil Company Foundation; Shubert Foundation; Lila Wallace-Reader's Digest Fund; Xerox Foundation.

Copyright © 1990 by Theatre Communications Group, Inc., 355 Lexington Ave., New York, NY 10017.

All rights reserved. No part of this book may be reproduced in any manner whatsoever without written permission from the publisher, except in the case of brief quotations embodied in critical articles and reviews.

TCG would like to thank the following staff members and individuals who helped with the massive job of preparing this volume: Joanna Adler, Jonathan Brandt, Winifred Breckenridge, Cathy Cole, Robert Gilman, Scott Graham, M. Elizabeth Osborn, Nancy Walther, George Wolfe and Howard Zisser.

On the cover, Arena Stage's 1988 production of *The Cherry Orchard* with Shirley Knight, Tana Hicken and Rebecca Ellens, photograph copyright © 1988 by Joan Marcus. Arena Stage is celebrating its 40th anniversary this year.

Design and composition by the Sarabande Press

ISBN 1-55936-007-0

First Edition, April 1990

**Frontis. Great North America History Theatre. Graham Thatcher in *Tree of Memory*.
Photo: Gerald Gustafson.**

CONTENTS

USING THIS BOOK	vi
THEATRES	viii
THEATRE PROFILES	1
THEATRE CHRONOLOGY	168
REGIONAL INDEX	170
INDEX OF NAMES	172
INDEX OF TITLES	193
ABOUT TCG	203

USING THIS BOOK

All the theatres included in *Theatre Profiles* 9 are constituents of Theatre Communications Group, the national organization for the nonprofit professional theatre. Information was requested in the spring and summer of 1989. The text of this volume is based on the materials submitted by the 233 theatres included. The following notes provide a guide to the elements of the book.

Personnel

Each theatre's current artistic and managerial leaders are included. This information was updated through December 1, 1989. If there had been a change in the artistic leadership of the theatre within the past two seasons, the former artistic head is noted following the artistic statement, with an indication of the season(s) for which he or she was responsible.

Contact Information

The mailing address of each organization is included, which is not necessarily the address of the theatre. Where two telephone numbers are listed, the first is for the administrative or business "(bus.)" office and the second for the box office "(b.o.)."

Founding Date and Founders

The founding date represents the beginning of public performances, or in a few cases, the conceptual or legal establishment of the organization. The names of all founders are listed under the date in alphabetical order.

Season

The season information is included as a general guide to the annual performance dates of each theatre. The months listed indicate the opening and closing of each theatre's season. "Year-round" designates companies that perform continuously throughout the year; "variable" indicates irregular or varying schedules.

Facilities

The facilities are the theatre space(s) in which each company regularly performs. The seating capacity and type of stage are included for each facility. The name of the space is provided if it differs from the organization's name. The information is current as of July 1989 and doesn't necessarily indicate the performance venues of the seasons highlighted in the book. The following terminology is used in describing each facility:

Trinity Repertory Company. Richard Kavanaugh in *Mensch Meier.* Photo: Mark Morelli.

PROSCENIUM: The traditional, picture-window stage separated from the auditorium by a proscenium arch, so that the audience views the action from a single "fourth wall" perspective.

THRUST: All types of facilities wherein the stage juts into the audience and is thereby surrounded on three sides. A "modified thrust" or "modified proscenium" protrudes less, often utilizing a fan-shaped apron on which action can take place.

ARENA: Also called "theatre-in-the-round." The audience completely surrounds the stage.

FLEXIBLE: All types of theatre space which can be altered or converted from one category to another.

CABARET: A simple performance platform, with the audience usually seated at tables.

USING THIS BOOK   vii

LORT: League of Resident Theatres contract
SPT: Small Professional Theatre contract
TYA: Theatre for Young Audiences contract
U/RTA: University/Resident Theatre Association contract

The letters enclosed in parentheses following the contract abbreviations designate the contract type, based on the size of theatre and scale of payment. Please note that members of the League of Resident Theatres (LORT) also operate under agreements with the Society of Stage Directors and Choreographers (SSDC) and United Scenic Artists (USA), which are referenced to the LORT Equity contracts. For more specific information on these contracts, please contact the unions directly.

Artistic Director's Statement

All artistic heads were invited to submit a statement describing the artistic philosophy governing the work at their respective institutions from their personal perspective. While all have been edited for style, every attempt has been made to retain the individuality of each statement.

Production Lists

Productions from the 1987–88 and the 1988–89 seasons (1988 and 1989 for theatres with summer operations) are listed, most often in the chronological order in which they were produced. The title of each production is immediately followed by the name of the playwright and, where applicable, the adapter, translator and/or source of literary adaptation if such information was provided by the theatre. In the case of musicals, all composers, librettists and lyricists are included. The director and set, costume and lighting designers follow, designated by a bold-faced letter in parentheses directly preceding the name—(**D**), (**S**), (**C**), (**L**). Choreographers, sound/video designers and musical directors are not included.

Photographs

A photograph from one of each theatre's listed productions accompanies each entry. The photos help convey the range and diversity of production activity and were generally selected for clarity of image from those submitted for possible inclusion by the theatre. Actors' names are included in the caption when there are five or fewer actors pictured.

Finances

Operating expenses are included to provide a general sense of the overall size of each theatre's operation. Most often the financial figures are from calendar year 1988 or fiscal year 1988–89, the most recent year available at the time information was gathered for *Theatre Profiles*.

Actors' Equity Contracts

The following AEA abbreviations are used:

BAT: Bay Area Theatre contract
CAT: Chicago Area Theatre contract
COST: Council on Stock Theatres contract
CORST: Council on Resident Stock Theatres contract

Regional Index

A geographical, state-by-state listing of every theatre is included to readily identify theatres by region.

Theatre Chronology

The "time line" history of the nonprofit professional theatres included in this volume is intended to demonstrate the growth pattern of the decentralized nonprofit professional theatre movement in the United States.

Name/Title Indices

Playwrights, composers, artistic and management heads, directors, designers and founders appear in the index of names. For convenience, a separate index includes titles of all dramatic works listed in this book.

THEATRES

Academy Theatre
A Contemporary Theatre
The Acting Company
Actors Theatre of Louisville
Actors Theatre of St. Paul
Alabama Shakespeare Festival
Alley Theatre
Alliance Theatre Company
AMAS Musical Theatre
American Conservatory Theatre
The American Place Theatre
American Repertory Theatre
American Stage
American Stage Festival
American Theatre Company
American Theatre Works
Arena Stage
Arizona Theatre Company
The Arkansas Arts Center Children's Theatre
Arkansas Repertory Theatre
Asolo Theatre Company
A Traveling Jewish Theatre
Attic Theatre
The Back Alley Theatre
Barter Theatre
The Bathhouse Theatre
Berkeley Repertory Theatre
Berkeley Shakespeare Festival
Berkshire Theatre Festival
Bilingual Foundation of the Arts
Bloomsburg Theatre Ensemble
BoarsHead: Michigan Public Theater
The Body Politic Theatre
Brass Tacks Theatre
Bristol Riverside Theatre
Caldwell Theatre Company
California Theatre Center
Capital Repertory Company
The CAST Theatre
Center Stage
Center Theater
The Changing Scene
The Children's Theatre Company
Child's Play Touring Theatre
Cincinnati Playhouse in the Park
Circle Repertory Company
City Theatre Company
Clarence Brown Theatre Company
The Cleveland Play House
Cornerstone Theater Company
Creation Production Company
Creative Arts Team
The Cricket Theatre
Crossroads Theatre Company
CSC Repertory Ltd.—The Classic Stage Company

Cumberland County Playhouse
Dallas Theater Center
Delaware Theatre Company
Dell'Arte Players Company
Denver Center Theatre Company
Detroit Repertory Theatre
East West Players
El Teatro Campesino
Emmy Gifford Children's Theater
Empire State Institute for the Performing Arts
The Empty Space Theatre
Ensemble Studio Theatre
Eureka Theatre Company
First Stage Milwaukee
Florida Shakespeare Festival
Florida Studio Theatre
FMT
Ford's Theatre
Free Street Theater
Fulton Opera House
George Street Playhouse
Germinal Stage Denver
GeVa Theatre
Gloucester Stage Company
Goodman Theatre
Goodspeed Opera House

Great Lake Theater Festival
Great North American History Theatre
Grove Shakespeare Festival
The Guthrie Theater
Hartford Stage Company
Heritage Artists, Ltd.
Hippodrome State Theatre
Honolulu Theatre for Youth
Horse Cave Theatre
Hudson Guild Theatre
Huntington Theatre Company
Illinois Theatre Center
Illusion Theater
The Independent Eye
Indiana Repertory Theatre
INTAR Hispanic American Arts Center
Intiman Theatre Company
Jean Cocteau Repertory
Jewish Repertory Theatre
Jomandi Productions
La Jolla Playhouse
Lamb's Players Theatre
L.A. Theatre Works
Lincoln Center Theater
Living Stage Theatre Company

Long Island Stage
Long Wharf Theatre
Los Angeles Theatre Center
Mabou Mines
Madison Repertory Theatre
Magic Theatre
Manhattan Punch Line Theatre
Manhattan Theatre Club
Marin Theatre Company
Mark Taper Forum
McCarter Theatre Center for the Performing Arts
Merrimack Repertory Theatre
Milwaukee Repertory Theater
Missouri Repertory Theatre
Mixed Blood Theatre Company
Musical Theatre Works
Music-Theatre Group
National Jewish Theater
Nebraska Theatre Caravan
New American Theater
New Dramatists
New Federal Theatre
New Jersey Shakespeare Festival
New Mexico Repertory Theatre
New Stage Theatre
New York Shakespeare Festival

Hartford Stage Company. Patricia Conolly and Richard Thomas in *Peer Gynt*. Photo: T. Charles Erickson.

New York Theatre Workshop
North Carolina Shakespeare
    Festival
Northlight Theatre
Oakland Ensemble Theatre
Odyssey Theatre Ensemble
The Old Creamery Theatre
    Company
Old Globe Theatre
Omaha Magic Theatre
O'Neill Theater Center
Ontological-Hysteric Theater
The Open Eye: New Stagings
Oregon Shakespeare Festival
Organic Theater Company
Pan Asian Repertory Theatre
Paper Mill Playhouse
PCPA Theaterfest
Pennsylvania Stage Company
The Penumbra Theatre
    Company
The People's Light and Theatre
    Company
Periwinkle National Theatre for
    Young Audiences
Perseverance Theatre
Philadelphia Drama Guild
Philadelphia Festival Theatre for
    New Plays

The Philadelphia Theatre
    Company
Ping Chong and Company/The Fiji
    Company
Pioneer Theatre Company
Pittsburgh Public Theater
Players Theatre Columbus
Playhouse on the Square
Playmakers at the Ritz
PlayMakers Repertory Company
The Playwrights' Center
Playwrights Horizons
Portland Repertory Theater
Portland Stage Company
Puerto Rican Traveling Theatre
Remains Theatre
Repertorio Español
The Repertory Theatre of St.
    Louis
River Arts Repertory
The Road Company
Roadside Theater
Roudabout Theatre Company
Round House Theatre
Sacramento Theatre Company
The Salt Lake Acting Company
Saltworks
San Diego Repertory Theatre
San Jose Repertory Company

Seattle Children's Theatre
Seattle Group Theatre
Seattle Repertory Theatre
Second Stage Theatre
Seven Stages
Shakespeare Repertory
The Shakespeare Theatre at the
    Folger
Snowmass/Aspen Repertory
    Theatre
Society Hill Playhouse
Soho Repertory Theatre
South Coast Repertory
Stage One: The Louisville
    Children's Theatre
Stage West
StageWest
Steppenwolf Theatre
    Company
St. Louis Black Repertory
    Company
The Street Threater
Studio Arena Theatre
The Studio Theatre
Syracuse Stage
Tacoma Actors Guild
The Tampa Players
The Theater at Monmouth
Theatre de la Jeune Lune

Theatre for a New Audience
Theater for the New City
Theatre IV
Theatre Project
Theatre Project Company
Theatre Rhinoceros
TheatreVirginia
TheatreWorks
Theatreworks/USA
Theatre X
Theatrical Outfit
Touchstone Theatre
Trinity Repertory Company
Unicorn Theatre
Victory Gardens Theater
Vineyard Theatre
Virginia Stage Company
Whole Theatre
Williamstown Theatre Festival
The Wilma Theater
Wisdom Bridge Theatre
The Women's Project and
    Productions
The Wooster Group
Worcester Foothills Theatre
    Company
WPA Theatre
Yale Repertory Theatre
Young Playwrights Festival

THEATRE PROFILES 9

American Repertory Theatre. Cherry Jones and Tom Hewitt in *Life is a Dream.* Photo: Richard Feldman.

Academy Theatre

FRANK WITTOW
Producing Artistic Director

MARGARET FERGUSON
Managing Director

Box 77070
Atlanta, GA 30357
(404) 873-2518 (bus.)
(404) 892-0880 (b.o.)

FOUNDED 1956
Frank Wittow

SEASON
Sept.-June

FACILITIES
The Phoebe Theatre
Seating Capacity: 383
Stage: thrust

The Phoenix Theatre
Seating Capacity: 200
Stage: flexible

The Genesis Theatre
Seating Capacity: 75
Stage: flexible

FINANCES
July 1, 1988-June 30, 1989
Expenses: $1,125,500

CONTRACTS
AEA letter of agreement

The Academy Theatre is a resident theatre company whose mission is to serve the community through three interdependent programs: subscription series of plays for adults, outreach programs and plays for young audiences and special populations, and a new play program for the development of new work by students and established playwrights. Our resident acting ensemble serve as the core performers in our plays, teach classes, direct and develop new plays, and facilitate our outreach programs. Our burgeoning program of new play development includes classes, conferences, workshops, readings and a three-play series which has its own subscriber base. From our Theatre for Youth's issue-oriented, original plays to the dramatic classics and modern literature we produce for adults, we strive to stimulate our audiences to fresh awareness. We utilize the varied and considerable talents of our resident actors, playwrights, directors, designers, technicians, administrators and craftspeople to achieve artistic excellence and to enrich the community we serve.
—*Frank Wittow*

PRODUCTIONS 1987–88

Animal Farm, adapt: Peter Hall, from George Orwell; lyrics: Adrian Mitchell; music: Richard Peaslee; (D) Frank Wittow; (S) Stephen Found and Michael Stauffer; (C) Chris Cook; (L) Paul R. Ackerman
A Christmas Carol, adapt: John Stephens, from Charles Dickens; (D) John Ammerman; (S) Karen Whipple; (C) Carrie L. Stockard; (L) Paul R. Ackerman
The House of Bernarda Alba, Federico Garcia Lorca; (D) Frank Wittow; (S) Michael Halpern; (C) Judy Winograd; (L) Paul R. Ackerman
A Touch of the Poet, Eugene O'Neill; (D) John Stephens; (S) Gary Jennings; (C) F. Elaine Williams; (L) Robert Corin

New Play Program:
Greasepaper, Terry Cawley; (D) John Stephens; (S) George Oswald; (C) Cindy Reno; (L) Robert Corin
The Love Talker, Deborah Pryor; (D) Kerrie Osborne; (S) Robert Corin; (C) Heather Heath; (L) Kevin Crysler
Local Menace, Marc Honea; (D) Dale Lyles and Kevin Crysler; (S) Holly Elliott; (C) Cindy Reno; (L) Robert Corbin

Theatre for Youth:
Heart of the Nation, Beverly Trader; (D) John Forrest Ferguson; (S) John Forrest Ferguson; (C) Chris Cook; (L) Robert Corin
Headlines, adapt: John Stephens, from Frank Wittow; (D) John Stephens; (S) John Stephens; (C) Christine Cook
In the Memory of Trees, John Forrest Ferguson; (D) John Forrest Ferguson; (S) Gary Weatherly; (C) Gary Weatherly; (L) Robert Corin

PRODUCTIONS 1988–89

Les Liaisons Dangereuses, adapt: Christopher Hampton; (D) Frank Wittow; (S) Gary Jennings; (C) Gary Jennings; (L) Paul R. Ackerman
The Keepers, Barbara Lebow; (D) Barbara Lebow; (S) Michael Halpern; (C) Chris Cook; (L) Paul R. Ackerman
A Christmas Carol, adapt: Levi Lee, from Charles Dickens; (D) Levi Lee; (S) Gary Jennings; (C) Gary Jennings; (L) Paul R. Ackerman
The American Century, Murphy Guyer; (D) Murphy Guyer; (S) Patricia Martin; (C) Chris Cook; (L) Jeffrey Nealer
The Realists, Murphy Guyer; (D) Murphy Guyer; (S) Patricia Martin; (C) Chris Cook; (L) Jeffrey Nealer
Sally's Gone, She Left Her Name, Russell Davis; (D) Barbara Lebow; (S) Patricia Martin; (C) Chris Cook; (L) Jeffrey Nealer
A Lie of the Mind, Sam Shepard; (D) Frank Wittow; (S) Buck Newman; (C) Chris Cook; (L) Paul R. Ackerman
Three Postcards, book: Craig Lucas; music and lyrics: Craig Carnelia; (D) Frank Wittow; (S) Gary Jennings; (C) Gary Jennings; (L) Paul R.. Ackerman

New Play Program
Samantha, Linda Anderson; (D) Gregory Blum; (S) Bryan Thompson; (C) Gregory Blum; (L) Kevin Crysler
Bait Shop, Ed Brock, Jr.; (D) Haynes Brooke; (S) Haynes Brooke; (C) Haynes Brooke

Theatre for Youth:
In the Memory of Trees, John Forrest Ferguson; (D) John Forrest Ferguson; (S) Gary Weatherly; (C) Gary Weatherly
Runaways, company-developed; (D) Bill Johns; (S) Bill Johns; (C) Bill Johns

A Contemporary Theatre

JEFF STEITZER
Artistic Director

SUSAN T. MORITZ
Managing Director

Box 19400
Seattle, WA 98109
(206) 285-3220 (bus.)
(206) 285-5110 (b.o.)

FOUNDED 1965
Gregory A. Falls

SEASON
May-Dec.

FACILITIES
Mainstage
Seating Capacity: 449
Stage: thrust

FINANCES
Jan. 1, 1988-Dec. 31, 1989
Expenses: $1,837,250

CONTRACTS
LORT (C), and AEA TYA

Academy Theatre. Carol Mitchell-Leon, Frank Wittow and Ruth Reid in *The Keepers*. Photo: Alan David.

A Contemporary Theatre. John Aylward and R. Hamilton Wright in *A Chorus of Disapproval*. Photo: Chris Bennion.

Celebrating its 25th anniversary, A Contemporary Theatre is dedicated, more than ever, to offering our audiences the most provocative, engaging and theatrical contemporary plays available—in productions that represent the most vibrant collaborations among actors, directors and designers that we can assemble. At ACT, the playwright is the predominant point of focus, with a new priority on generating work by commissioning writers whose efforts we want to support on a long-term basis. ACT vigorously seeks out dramatists with lively, unique voices: playwrights whose work examines issues that are socially pertinent to our audience; whose writing appeals to the head, heart and soul; and whose aesthetic is informed by the imaginative possibilities that can occur only on the stage. Our professsional theatre for young audiences, the Young ACT Company, is one year younger than our mainstage. It has produced more than 30 plays, 14 of which were original scripts, performed for hundreds of thousands of young people throughout Washington State.
—*Jeff Steitzer*

Note: During the 1987-88 season, Gregory A. Falls served as producing director.

PRODUCTIONS 1987–88

March of the Falsettos, book, music and lyrics: William Finn; (D) Jeff Steitzer; (S) Scott Welden; (C) Sarah Campbell; (L) Rick Paulsen
*A **Lie of the Mind***, Sam Shepard; (D) Gregory A. Falls; (S) Karen Gjelsteen; (C) Sally Richardson; (L) James Verdery
The Diary of a Scoundrel, adapt: Erick Brogger, from Alexander Ostrovsky; (D) Jeff Steitzer; (S) Scott Weldin; (C) Michael Olich; (L) Rick Paulsen
The Marriage of Bette and Boo, Christopher Durang; (D) Anne Denise Ford; (S) Robert Gardiner; (C) Sally Richardson; (L) Jennifer Lupton
Glengarry Glen Ross, David Mamet; (D) David Ira Goldstein; (S) Jerry Hooker; (C) Rose Pederson; (L) Phil Schermer
Biloxi Blues, Neil Simon; (D) Gregory A. Falls; (S) William Forrester; (C) Rose Pederson; (L) William Forrester
*A **Christmas Carol***, adapt: Gregory A. Falls, from Charles Dickens; (D) Jeff Steitzer; (S) William Forrester; (C) Nanrose Buchman; (L) Jody Briggs

PRODUCTIONS 1988–89

Merrily We Roll Along, book: George Furth; music and lyrics: Stephen Sondheim; (D) Jeff Steitzer; (S) Scott Weldin; (C) Rose Pederson; (L) Jennifer Lupton
Mrs. California, Doris Baizley; (D) Lee Shallat; (S) Scott Weldin; (C) Rose Pederson; (L) Paulie Jenkins
*A **Chorus of Disapproval***, Alan Ayckbourn; (D) Jeff Steitzer; (S) Michael Olich; (C) Laura Crow; (L) Rick Paulsen
God's Country, Steven Dietz; (D) David Ira Goldstein; (S) Shelly Henze Schermer; (C) Frances Kenny; (L) Phil Schermer
Principia Scriptoriae, Richard Nelson; (D) Jeff Steitzer; (S) Michael Olich; (C) Michael Olich; (L) Rick Paulsen
The Voice of the Prairie, John Olive; (D) David Ira Goldstein; (S) William Forrester; (C) Sally Richardson; (L) Rick Paulsen
*A **Christmas Carol***, adapt: Gregory A. Falls, from Charles Dickens; (D) Jeff Steitzer; (S) William Forrester; (C) Nanrose Buchman; (L) Jody Briggs

The Acting Company

MARGOT HARLEY
Executive Producer

JAMES F. PRIEBE
Acting Managing Director

Box 898, Times Square Station
New York, NY 10108
(212) 564-3510

FOUNDED 1972
John Houseman, Margot Harley

SEASON
Aug.-May

FINANCES
July 1, 1988-June 30, 1989
Expenses: $2,026,600

CONTRACTS
LORT (B) and (C)

The Acting Company's mission has remained constant since our founding in 1972. It is to give talented, trained American actors an opportunity to grow and develop through touring in a repertory ensemble over a season or more, and to provide first-rate performances of a classical and contemporary theatre repertoire to audiences across the nation, especially those with limited access to live professional theatre. A major focus of The Acting Company in the 1989-90 season will be on education in the arts through performances and workshops. As the touring arm of the John F. Kennedy Center for the Performing Arts, the company participates in the Imagination Celebration, a series of nationwide festivals that celebrate young people and the arts. Also in 1985-90, The Acting Company hosted an exchange of Soviet and American theatre students, to be followed in 1991 by an exchange of The Acting Company with its counterpart from the Moscow Art Theatre School.
—*Margot Harley*

Note: During the 1987-88 season, Michael Kahn served as artistic director. During the 1988-89 season, Gerald Gutierrez served as artistic director.

PRODUCTIONS 1987–88

Five by Ten, Tennessee Williams; (D) Michael Kahn; (S) Derek McLane; (C) Ann Hould-Ward; (L) Dennis Parichy
Kabuki Macbeth, adapt: Karen Sunde, from William Shakespeare; Karen Sunde; (D) Shozo Sato; (S) Shozo Sato; (C) Shozo Sato; (L) Dennis Parichy
Much Ado About Nothing, William Shakespeare; (D) Gerald Gutierrez; (S) Douglas Stein; (C) Ann Hould-Ward; (L) Pat Collins

PRODUCTIONS 1988–89

Boy Meets Girl, Bella Spewack

The Acting Company. Oni Faida Lampley and Oliver Barreiro in *This Property is Condemned*. Photo: Bob Marshak.

and Samuel Spewack; (D) Brian Murray; (s) Derek McLane; (C) Jennifer vonMayrhauser; (L) Stephen Strawbridge
The Phantom Tollbooth, adapt: Susan Nanus, from Norton Juster; (D) Jennifer McCray; (s) Russell Parkman; (C) Constance Romero; (L) Stephen Strawbridge
Love's Labour's Lost, William Shakespeare; (D) Paul Giovanni; (s) Robert Klingelhoefer; (C) Jess Goldstein; (L) Stephen Strawbridge

Actors Theatre of Louisville

JON JORY
Producing Director

ALEXANDER SPEER
Administrative Director

MARILEE HERBERT-SLATER
Associate Director

316-320 West Main St.
Louisville, KY 40202-2916
(502) 584-1265 (bus.)
(502) 584-1205 (b.o.)

FOUNDED 1964
Ewel Cornett, Richard Block

SEASON
Sept.-June

FACILITIES
Pamela Brown Auditorium
Seating Capacity: 637
Stage: thrust

Victor Jory Theatre
Seating Capacity: 159
Stage: thrust

Downstairs at Actors
Seating Capacity: 100
Stage: cabaret

FINANCES
June 1, 1988-May 31, 1989
Expenses: $4,800,000

CONTRACTS
LORT (B) and (D)

Actors Theatre of Louisville has three primary areas of emphasis which constitute an artistic policy. The first is the discovery and development of a new generation of American playwrights. In the last 17 years Actors Theatre has produced the work of over 200 new writers. This work, strongly backed by a commissioning program, is central to our aesthetic. Our second area of emphasis is an interdisciplinary approach to the classical theatre combining lectures, discussions, films and plays through the annual Classics in Context Festival. Working under a different umbrella theme each year, this festival provides new insights into the classial repertoire, both for our company and our resident audience. Last year's Victorian Festival attracted scholars and theatre people from around the world. Actors Theatre is also beginning a decade long examination of America's forgotten repertoire called the 20th Century Project and a four-year series of Shakespeare's masterworks called the Bingham Signature Shakespeare.
—*Jon Jory*

PRODUCTIONS 1987–88

Classics in Context Festival:
Camille, adapt: Barbara Field, from Alexandre Dumas; (D) Michael Maggio; (s) Paul Owen; (C) Lewis D. Rampino; (L) Ralph Dressler
Caprices of Marianne, adapt: Peter Meyer, from Alfred de Musset; (D) Jon Jory; (s) Paul Owen; (C) Lewis D. Rampino; (L) Ralph Dressler

Ring Round the Moon, Jean Anouilh; (D) Jon Jory; (s) Paul Owen; (C) Lewis D. Rampino; (L) Ralph Dressler
A Christmas Carol, adapt: Barbara Field, from Charles Dickens; (D) Frazier W. Marsh; (s) Paul Owen; (C) Lewis D. Rampino; (L) Ralph Dressler
The Gift of the Magi, book adapt, music and lyrics: Peter Ekstrom; (D) Bob Krakower; (s) Paul Owen; (C) Hollis Jenkins-Evans; (L) Ralph Dressler
The Real Thing, Tom Stoppard; (D) Frazier W. Marsh; (s) Elmon Webb and Virginia Dancy; (C) Lewis D. Rampino; (L) Ralph Dressler
Faith Healer, Brian Friel; (D) Ray Fry; (s) Paul Owen; (C) Hollis Jenkins-Evans; (L) Ralph Dressler
Tomfoolery, Cameron Mackintosh and Robin Raymusic; lyrics: Tom Lehrer; (D) William Roudebush; (s) Paul Owen; (C) Hollis Jenkins-Evans; (L) Ralph Dressler

Actors Theatre of Louisville. Lizbeth Mackay and Jan Leslie Harding in *Tales of the Lost Formicans*. Photo: Richard Trigg.

Humana Festival
The Queen of the Leaky Roof Circuit, Jimmy Breslin; (D) George Ferencz; (s) Paul Owen; (C) Marie Anne Chiment; (L) Ralph Dressler
Whereabouts Unknown, Barbara Damashek; (D) Barbara Damashek; (s) Paul Owen; (C) Lewis D. Rampino; (L) Ralph Dressler
Lloyd's Prayer, Kevin Kling; (D) Ken Washington; (s) Paul Owen; (C) Marie Anne Chiment; (L) Ralph Dressler
Alone at the Beach, Richard Dresser; (D) Gloria Muzio; (s) Paul Owen; (C) Lewis D. Rampino; (L) Ralph Dressler
Channels, Judith Fein; (D) Jon Jory; (s) Paul Owen; (C) Marie Anne Chiment; (L) Pavel Dobrusky
The Metaphor, Murphy Guyer; (D) Murphy Guyer; (s) Paul Owen; (C) Marie Anne Chiment; (L) Pavel Dobrusky
Sarah and Abraham, Marsha Norman; (D) Jon Jory; (s) Paul Owen; (C) Lewis D. Rampino; (L) Ralph Dressler

Taking Steps, Alan Ayckbourn; (D) John Going; (s) Paul Owen; (C) Lewis D. Rampino; (L) Ralph Dressler
The Rocky Horror Show, Richard O'Brien; (D) Edward Stone; (s) David Potts; (C) Lewis D. Rampino; (L) Ralph Dressler

PRODUCTIONS 1988–89

Classics in Context Festival
Peter Pan, James M. Barrie; (D) Jon Jory; (s) John Conklin; (C) Merrily Murray-Walsh; (L) Ralph Dressler
Engaged, William S. Gilbert; (D) Gloria Muzio; (s) Paul Owen; (C) Lewis D. Rampino; (L) Ralph Dressler
The Whore and the h'Empress, adapt: Jonathan Bolt, from Henry Mayhew; (D) Alex Dmitriev; (s) Paul Owen; (C) Lewis D. Rampino; (L) Ralph Dressler

The Nerd, Larry Shue; (D) Ray Fry; (s) Paul Owen; (C) Hollis Jenkins-Evans; (L) Ralph Dressler
A Christmas Carol, adapt: Barbara Field, from Charles Dickens; (D) Frazier W. Marsh; (s) Paul Owen; (C) Lewis D. Rampino; (L) Ralph Dressler
The Gift of the Magi, book adapt, music and lyrics: Peter Ekstrom; (D) Bob Krakower; (s) Paul Owen; (C) Hollis Jenkins-Evans; (L) Ralph Dressler
Harvey, Mary Chase; (D) Frazier W. Marsh; (s) Paul Owen; (C) Hollis Jenkins-Evans; (L) Ralph Dressler
Les Liaisons Dangereuses, adapt: Christopher Hampton, from Choderlos de Laclos; (D) Laszlo Marton; (s) Paul Owen; (C) Lewis D. Rampino; (L) Ralph Dressler
Beehive, Larry Gallagher; (D) Fran Soeder; (s) Paul Owen;

(C) Lewis D. Rampino;
(L) Ralph Dressler

Humana Festival:
God's Country, Steven Dietz;
(D) Steven Dietz; (S) Paul
Owen; (C) Lewis D. Rampino;
(L) Ralph Dressler
Autumn Elegy, Charlene Redick;
(D) Gloria Muzio; (S) Paul
Owen; (C) Lewis D. Rampino;
(L) Ralph Dressler
Tales of the Lost Formicans,
Constance Congdon;
(D) Roberta Levitow; (S) Paul
Owen; (C) Lewis D. Rampino;
(L) Ralph Dressler
Stained Glass, William F.
Buckley, Jr.; (D) Steven
Schachter; (S) Paul Owen;
(C) Lewis D. Rampino;
(L) Ralph Dressler
The Bug, Richard Strand;
(D) Jules Aaron; (S) Paul Owen;
(C) Michael Krass; (L) Victor En
Yu Tan
Blood Issue, Harry Crews; (D) Jon
Jory; (S) Paul Owen; (C) Michael
Krass; (L) Victor En Yu Tan
Bone-the-Fish, Arthur Kopit;
(D) James Simpson; (S) Paul
Owen; (C) Michael Krass;
(L) Victor En Yu Tan

Steel Magnolias, Robert Harling;
(D) Charles Karchmer;
(S) Robert T. Odorisio;
(C) Lewis D. Rampino;
(L) Ralph Dressler
The Tempest, William
Shakespeare; (D) Jon Jory;
(S) Ming Cho Lee; (C) Marcia
Dixcy; (L) Allen Lee Hughes

Actors Theatre of St. Paul

MICHAEL ANDREW MINER
Artistic Director

MARK LIGHT
Executive Director

28 West Seventh Place
St. Paul, MN 55102
(612) 297-6868 (bus.)
(612) 227-0050 (b.o.)

FOUNDED 1977
Michael Andrew Miner

SEASON
Oct.–June

FACILITIES
Actors Theatre
Seating Capacity: 350
Stage: proscenium

FINANCES
July 1, 1988–June 30, 1989
Expenses: $950,000

CONTRACTS
LORT (D)

Actors Theatre of St. Paul is committed to the cohesive ensemble production of stylistically and thematically varied plays. At the heart of the theatre's aesthetic is an ongoing resident company of actors, playwrights, composers, designers and directors whose collective interests and talents are strong determinants of the direction, change and growth of the theatre from season to season. From its inception, Actors Theatre eagerly embraced responsibility for the generation of new works for the stage. Actors Theatre's long-term interest in other cultures has been demonstrated in the past by exchanges with Trinidad and Tobago, Surinam, Ireland and South Africa. An important milestone was reached in 1989, when Michael Andrew Miner directed *Awake and Sing* at Moscow's Yermolova Theatre, with scenic designs by Nayna Ramey, believed to be the first American to design for the Soviet stage. The exchange was reciprocated when Yermolova artistic director Valerie Fokin and designers Olga Tvardovskaya and Vladimir Makushenko collaborated with the Actors Theatre company on the American professional premiere of Alexander Vampilov's *Last Summer in Chulimsk*.
—*Michael Andrew Miner*

PRODUCTIONS 1987–88

Breakfast with Strangers, Vladlen
Dozortsev; trans: Elise Thoron;
(D) Michael Andrew Miner;
(S) Nayna Ramey; (C) Rich
Hamson; (L) Nayna Ramey
Ten November, Steven Dietz;
(D) Steven Dietz; (S) Lori
Sullivan; (C) Sandra Nei Schulte;
(L) Nayna Ramey
*Why the Lord Come to Sand
Mountain*, Romulus Linney;
(D) Louis Schaefer; (S) Dick
Leerhoff; (C) Nayna Ramey;
(L) Nayna Ramey
Second Sheperd's Play,
Anonymous; (D) Louis Schaefer;
(S) Dick Leerhoff; (C) Nayna
Ramey; (L) Nayna Ramey

**Minnesota One-Act Play
Festival:**
Mickey's Teeth, Amlin Gray;
(D) John Seibert; (S) Dick
Leerhoff; (C) Nayna Ramey and
Rich Hamson; (L) Doug Pipan
The Zoo Story, Edward Albee;
(D) Michael Andrew Miner;
(S) Dick Leerhoff; (C) Nayna
Ramey and Rich Hamson;
(L) Doug Pipan
Fire in the Basement, Pavel
Kohout; trans: Peter Stenberg
and Marketa Goetz-Stankiewicz;
(D) James Cada; (S) Dick
Leerhoff; (C) Nayna Ramey and
Rich Hamson; (L) Doug Pipan
Hughie, Eugene O'Neill;
(D) James Cada; (S) Dick
Leerhoff; (C) Nayna Ramey and
Rich Hamson; (L) Doug Pipan
A Betrothal, Lanford Wilson;
(D) David M. Kwiat; (S) Dick
Leerhoff; (C) Nayna Ramey and
Rich Hamson; (L) Doug Pipan
The Business at Hand, Martha
Boesing; (D) D. Scott Glasser;
(S) Dick Leerhoff; (C) Nayna
Ramey and Rich Hamson;
(L) Doug Pipan
Gurley and the Finn, David
Brunet; (D) Michael Andrew
Miner; (S) Dick Leerhoff;
(C) Nayna Ramey and Rich
Hamson; (L) Doug Pipan
Elsie's Kitchen, Rich Foster;
(D) Michael Andrew Miner;
(S) Dick Leerhoff; (C) Nayna
Ramey and Rich Hamson;
(L) Doug Pipan
The Lost Colony, Wendy
MacLeod; (D) D. Scott Glasser;
(S) Dick Leerhoff; (C) Nayna
Ramey and Rich Hamson;
(L) Doug Pipan

Ten November, Steven Dietz;
(D) Steven Dietz; (S) Lori
Sullivan; (C) Sandra Nei Schulte;
(L) Nayna Ramey
A Day in the Death of Joe Egg,
Peter Nichols; (D) Michael
Andrew Miner; (S) Chris
Johnson; (C) Rich Hamson;
(L) Todd Hensley
Blue Window, Craig Lucas; (D) B.
Rodney Marriott; (S) Nayna
Ramey; (C) Nayna Ramey;
(L) Nayna Ramey

PRODUCTIONS 1988–89

Noises Off, Michael Frayn; (D) D.
Scott Glasser; (S) Dick Leerhoff;
(C) Rich Hamson; (L) Nayna
Ramey
Four Our Fathers, Jon Klein;
(D) Michael Andrew Miner;
(S) Nayna Ramey; (C) Rich
Hamson; (L) Nayna Ramey
The Gift of the Magi, book adapt,
music and lyrics: Peter Ekstrom;
(D) Kent Stephens; (S) Steve
Kennedy; (C) Nayna Ramey;
(L) Doug Pipan

**Minnesota One-Act Play
Festival:**
Intelligent Life, David Babcock;
(D) John Seibert; (S) Dick
Leerhoff; (C) Rich Hamson;
(L) Doug Pipan
Silent Night, Jon Klein; (D) D.
Scott Glasser; (S) Dick Leerhoff;
(C) Rich Jamson; (L) Doug
Pipan
Water Torture, Beverly Smith-
Dawson; (D) Dawn Renee Jones;
(S) Dick Leerhoff; (C) Rich
Hamson; (L) Doug Pipan
Icarus's Mother, Sam Shepard;
(D) Kent Stephens; (S) Dick

Actors Theatre of St. Paul. Jim Ridge and Allan Hickle-Edwards in *Getting the Hell Out of Dodge*. Photo: Kerry Jorgensen.

Leerhoff; (C) Rich Hamson; (L) Doug Pipan

The American Dream, Edward Albee; (D) Peter Cantwell; (S) Dick Leerhoff; (C) Rich Hamson; (L) Doug Pipan

Confessions of an Actor, David M. Kwiat; (D) Michael Andrew Miner; (S) Dick Leerhoff; (C) Rich Hamson; (L) Doug Pipan

Chinamen, Michael Frayn; (D) David M. Kwiat; (S) Dick Leerhoff; (C) Rich Hamson; (L) Doug Pipan

If I'm Traveling on a Moving Train . . ., Norah Holmgren; (D) Dawn Renee Jones; (S) Dick Leerhoff; (C) Rich Hamson; (L) Doug Pipan

Fellow Travellers, Jeffrey Hatcher; (D) Kent Stephens; (S) Dick Leerhoff; (C) Rich Hamson; (L) Doug Pipan

Getting the Hell Out of Dodge, Gary Amdahl; (D) John Seibert; (S) Dick Leerhoff; (C) Rich Hamson; (L) Doug Pipan

Not I, Samuel Beckett; (D) Kent Stephens; (S) Dick Leerhoff; (C) Rich Hamson; (L) Doug Pipan

The Road to Mecca, Athol Fugard; (D) Michael Andrew Miner; (S) Nayna Ramey; (C) Nayna Ramey; (L) Nayna Ramey

Last Summer in Chulimsk, Alexander Vampilov; trans: Paulina Shur; (D) Valerie Fokin; (S) Vladimir Makushenko and Olga Tvardovskaya

Noises Off, Michael Frayn; (D) D. Scott Glasser; (S) Dick Leerhoff; (C) Rich Hamson; (L) Nayna Ramey

Alabama Shakespeare Festival

KENT THOMPSON
Artistic Director

JIM VOLZ
Managing Director

1 Festival Dr.
Montgomery, AL 36117
(205) 272-1640 (bus.)
(205) 277-2273 (b.o.)

FOUNDED 1972
Martin L. Platt

SEASON
Sept.-Aug.

FACILITIES
Festival Stage
Seating Capacity: 750
Stage: proscenium

The Octagon
Seating Capacity: 225
Stage: flexible

FINANCES
Oct. 1, 1987-Sept. 30, 1988
Expenses: $4,164,206

CONTRACTS
LORT (C) and (D)

In an age of constant change and frequent turmoil, the classics, including those of this century, provide us with historical and cultural perspective. The Alabama Shakespeare Festival is first and foremost committed to artistic excellence in the production and performance of classics and contemporary plays, with the works of Shakespeare forming the core of the repertoire. We believe this is best achieved through a commitment to a company of resident artists, for only through the development and growth of an entire company can the Festival achieve the sustained creative output necessary to produce these challenging plays. As the Alabama State Theatre, we believe that the future of arts in Alabama depends upon a commitment to education, including training future theatre professionals, introducing schoolchildren to theatre, and educating our audiences through support programs such as Theatre in the Mind. We are also dedicated to producing outstanding new plays, especially those dealing with southern issues. When classics are combined and contrasted with the works of excellent contemporary writers, we can begin to see ourselves as we are. That vision will help us understand our past, accept our present and change our future.

—*Kent Thompson*

Note: During the 1987-88 and 1988-89 seasons, Martin L. Platt served as artistic director.

PRODUCTIONS 1987-88

Hay Fever, Noel Coward; (D) Stephen Hollis; (S) David M. Crank; (C) Kristine Kearney; (L) Karen S. Spahn

Long Day's Journey into Night, Eugene O'Neill; (D) Martin L. Platt; (S) David M. Crank; (C) David M. Crank; (L) Karen S. Spahn

Little Shop of Horrors, book and lyrics: Howard Ashman; music: Alan Menken; (D) Diana Baffa-Brill; (S) Michael Stauffer; (C) Kristine Kearney; (L) Michael Stauffer

Wild Honey, Anton Chekhov; adapt and trans: Michael Frayn; (D) Martin L. Platt; (S) David M. Crank; (C) Kristine Kearney; (L) Judy Rasmuson

Painting Churches, Tina Howe; (D) William Partlan; (S) Michael Stauffer; (C) James B. Greco; (L) Michael Stauffer

As You Like It, William Shakespeare; (D) Martin L. Platt; (S) David M. Crank; (C) Kristine Kearney; (L) Karen S. Spahn

Hamlet, William Shakespeare; (D) Stephen Hollis; (S) David M. Crank; (C) Alan Armstrong; (L) Paul Ackerman

You Never Can Tell, George Bernard Shaw; (D) Richard Russell Ramos; (S) Michael Stauffer; (C) Kristine Kearney; (L) Michael Stauffer

A Bold Stroke for a Wife, Susanna Centlivre; (D) Martin L. Platt; (S) David M. Crank; (C) Alan Armstrong; (L) Paul Ackerman

A Streetcar Named Desire, Tennessee Williams; (D) Edward Stern; (S) Michael Stauffer; (C) Kristine Kearney; (L) Michael Stauffer

The Sea, Edward Bond; (D) Will York; (S) Michael Stauffer; (C) Jim Greco; (L) Karen S. Spahn

The Playboy of the Western World, John Millington Synge;

Alabama Shakespeare Festival. Greta Lambert and Daniel Kern in *The Taming of the Shrew*. Photo: Scarsbrook.

(D) Christopher Schario; (S) Patrick J. Scully; (C) Alice Sullivan; (L) Karen S. Spahn

A Month in the Country, Ivan Turgenev; trans: Earle Edgerton; (D) Edmond Williams; (S) Charles J. Kilian, Jr.; (C) Greg A. West; (L) Lorin Blane Knouse

PRODUCTIONS 1988-89

A Christmas Carol, adapt: Martin L. Platt, from Charles Dickens; (D) Martin L. Platt; (S) David M. Crank; (C) Alan Armstrong; (L) Karen S. Spahn

Steel Magnolias, Robert Harling; (D) Bill Gregg; (S) Bill Clarke; (C) James B. Greco; (L) Karen S. Spahn

Candida, George Bernard Shaw; (D) Tony Van Bridge; (S) Bill Clarke; (C) Kristine Kearney; (L) F. Mitchell Dana

Romeo and Juliet, William Shakespeare; (D) Richard Russell Ramos; (S) David M. Crank; (C) Lowell Detweiler; (L) Karen S. Spahn

Les Liaisons Dangereuses, adapt: Christopher Hampton, from Choderlos de Laclos; (D) Martin L. Platt; (S) David M. Crank; (C) David M. Crank; (L) F. Mitchell Dana

Much Ado About Nothing, William Shakespeare; (D) Richard Ouzounian; (S) Bill Clarke; (C) Kristine Kearney; (L) Karen S. Spahn

On the Verge or The Geography of Yearning, Eric Overmyer; (D) Kent Thompson; (S) Charles Caldwell; (C) Lois Carren; (L) F. Mitchell Dana

Cyrano de Bergerac, Edmond Rostand; trans: Brian Hooker; (D) Martin L. Platt; (S) Lowell Detweiler; (C) Kristine Kearney; (L) Karen S. Spahn

The Road to Mecca, Athol
Fugard; (D) Will York;
(S) Charles Caldwell; (C) James
B. Greco; (L) F. Mitchell Dana
Pericles, Prince of Tyre, William
Shakespeare and George
Wilkins; (D) Martin L. Platt;
(S) Lowell Detweiler; (C) Alan
Armstrong; (L) Karen S. Spahn
The Beggar's Opera, John Gay;
(D) Martin L. Platt;
(S) Catherine Dixon; (C) Alice
Sullivan; (L) Karen S. Spahn
Titus Andronicus, William
Shakespeare; (D) Will York;
(S) Catherine Dixon; (C) James
B. Greco; (L) Chris Eicher
The Winter's Tale, William
Shakespeare; (D) Susan Willis;
(S) Catherine Dixon; (C) Alice
Sullivan; (L) Chris Eicher

Alley Theatre

GREGORY BOYD
Artistic Director

MARY LOU ALESKIE
General Manager

615 Texas Ave.
Houston, TX 77002
(713) 228-9341 (bus.)
(713) 228-8421 (b.o.)

FOUNDED 1947
Nina Vance

SEASON
Jan.-Dec.

FACILITIES
Large Stage
Seating Capacity: 824
Stage: thrust

Hugo V. Neuhaus
Seating Capacity: 296
Stage: arena

FINANCES
June 30, 1988-July 01, 1989
Expenses: $5,419,894

CONTRACTS
LORT (B) and (C)

The Alley Theatre has recently taken major steps in its evolution, and has reaffirmed its commitment to a repertoire that is shared by newly interpreted classic plays, side by side with new American plays and contemporary works from other cultures, in the firmly held belief that the great plays of the past inform our work on contemporary writing and vice versa. The theatre is committed to an "extended family" of artists, some in residence, others with an ongoing relationship to the work at the Alley over a period of several seasons. Dedicated to creating a place for playwrights and a "home" for actors that serves as a catalyst for continued development and imagination, the Alley supports programs that cultivate and train young talent, develop new and diverse audiences, and foster national and international interchange through touring.

—Gregory Boyd

Note: During the 1987-88 season, Pat Brown served as artistic director. During the 1988-89 season, Jim Bernhard served as the interim artistic director.

PRODUCTIONS 1987–88

The Last Flapper, William Luce;
(D) Charles Nelson Reilly;
(S) Patrick Hughes and
Christopher Mandich; (C) Noel
Taylor; (L) Patrick Hughes and
Christopher Mandich
Henceforward . . ., Alan
Ayckbourn; (D) Alan Ayckbourn;
(S) Charles S. Kading;
(C) Howard Tsvi Kaplan;
(L) James Sale
Self Defense, Joe Cacaci; (D) Pat
Brown; (S) Elva Stewart;
(C) Patricia E. Doherty;
(L) James Sale
Stepping Out, Richard Harris;
(D) James Martin; (S) Elva
Stewart; (C) Howard Tsvi
Kaplan; (L) Pamela Gray Bones
Hunting Cockroaches, Janusz
Glowacki; (D) Joan Vail Thorne;
(S) Michael A. Ryan and Patrick
Hughes; (C) Lauren K. Lambie;
(L) Pamela Gray Bones
The Miracle Worker, William
Gibson; (D) Beth Sanford;
(S) William Bloodgood;
(C) Patricia E. Doherty;
(L) Pamela Gray Bones
Sharon and Billy, Alan Bowne;
(D) George Anderson; (S) Elva
Stewart; (C) Howard Tsvi
Kaplan; (L) John E. Ore
The Lucky Spot, Beth Henley;
(D) Robert Straine; (S) Charles
S. Kading; (C) Patricia E.
Doherty; (L) Pamela Gray Bones
A Shayna Maidel, Barbara
Lebow; (D) Beth Sanford;
(S) Michael Ryan; (C) Patricia E.
Doherty; (L) Pamela Gray Bones
A Class 'C' Trial in Yokohama,
Roger Cornish; (D) Burry
Fredrik; (S) Charles S. Kading;
(C) Howard Tsvi Kaplan;
(L) James Sale
The Nerd, Larry Shue; (D) James
Martin; (S) Michael A. Ryan;
(C) Patricia E. Doherty; (L) John
E. Ore
Tomfoolery, book: Cameron
Mackintosh and Robin Ray;
music and lyrics: Tom Lehrer;
(D) Charles Abbott; (S) Elva
Stewart; (C) Howard Tsvi
Kaplan; (L) Pamela Gray Bones

PRODUCTIONS 1988–89

The Road to Mecca, Athol
Fugard; (D) Beth Sanford;
(S) Elva Stewart; (C) Lauren K.
Lambie; (L) John E. Ore
*Frankie and Johnny in the
Claire De Lune*, Terrence
McNally; (D) Sidney Berger;
(S) Jay Michael Jagim;
(C) Lauren K. Lambie; (L) John
E. Ore
*The Merry Wives of Windsor,
Texas*, adapt: John Haber, from
William Shakespeare; music and
lyrics: Tommy Thompson, Jack
Herrick, Bland Simpson and Jim
Wann; (D) Thomas Bullard;
(S) Charles S. Kading;
(C) Donna Kress; (L) John E.
Ore
The Voice of the Prairie, John
Olive; (D) James Martin; (S) Jay
Michael Jagim; (C) Lauren K.
Lambie; (L) John E. Ore
A View from the Bridge, Arthur
Miller; (D) Beth Sanford;
(S) William Bloodgood;
(C) Lauren K. Lambie; (L) John
E. Ore
Alfred Stieglitz Loves O'Keefe,
Lanie Robertson; (D) Eberle
Thomas; (S) Jay Michael Jagim;
(C) Lauren K. Lambie;
(L) Pamela Gray Bones
Heaven's Hard, Jordan Budde;
(D) Allen R. Belknap; (S) Keith
Belli; (C) Lauren K. Lambie;
(L) John E. Ore
The Waltz of the Toreadors, Jean
Anouilh; trans: Lucienne Hill;
(D) James Martin; (S) Jay
Michael Jagim; (C) Lauren K.
Lambie; (L) James Sale
Steel Magnolias, Robert Harling;
(D) Beth Sanford; (S) Jay
Michael Jagim; (C) Lauren K.
Lambie; (L) Robert Jared

Alley Theatre. Robin Moseley and John Spencer in Frankie and Johnny in the Claire de Lune. Photo: Mark Navarro.

Alliance Theatre Company

ROBERT J. FARLEY
Artistic Director

EDITH H. LOVE
Managing Director

Robert W. Woodruff Arts Center
1280 Peachtree St NE
Atlanta, GA 30309
(404) 898-1132 (bus.)
(404) 892-2414 (b.o.)

FOUNDED 1969
Atlanta Arts Alliance

SEASON
Sept.-Jun.

FACILITIES
Alliance Theatre
Seating Capacity: 826
Stage: proscenium

Studio Theatre
Seating Capacity: 200
Stage: flexible

FINANCES
Aug. 1, 1988-July 31, 1989
Expenses: $6,292,000

CONTRACTS
LORT (B) and (D)
AEA TYA

As it enters its third decade with new leadership firmly in place, the Alliance Theatre aims to be a unique voice in the South, for artists and audiences alike. Through staff collaboration and the nurturing of our outstanding trustees, we are committed to reexploring the theatrical experience and its engagement with the communities of Atlanta. This exploration requires an awareness of the diverse society in which we work, and the belief that people hunger for a dimension that awakens new thinking, stimulates us to lead better lives and encourages the chance to dream. Emphasizing the importance of artists working together through extended collaboration, the theatre seeks to provide a full canon of work specifically rewarding to the region we serve.
—*Robert J. Farley*

PRODUCTIONS 1987–88

All My Sons, Arthur Miller; (D) Robert J. Farley; (S) Karen Gjelsteen; (C) Susan E. Mickey; (L) Victor Becker
End of the World with Symposium to Follow, Arthur Kopit; (D) Dan Bonnell; (S) James Wolk; (C) Deborah Shaw; (L) William B. Duncan
Carnival!, book: Michael Stewart; music and lyrics: Bob Merrill; (D) Larry Carpenter; (S) John Falabella; (C) Lowell Detweiler; (L) Jason Kantrowitz
The Road to Mecca, Athol Fugard; (D) Robert J. Farley; (S) Karen Gjelsteen; (C) Susan E. Mickey; (L) Judy Rasmuson
Steel Magnolias, Robert Harling; (D) Clayton Corzatte; (S) Michael Stauffer; (C) Sally Richardson; (L) Paul R. Ackerman
Candide, book Hugh Wheeler; music: Leonard Bernstein; lyrics: Richard Wilbur; add'l lyrics: Stephen Sondheim and John Latouche; (D) Fran Soeder; (S) James Leonard Joy; (C) Mariann Verheyen; (L) Jeff Davis
American Dreams: Lost and Found, adapt: John Hirsch, from Studs Terkel; (D) John Hirsch; (S) Michael Stauffer; (C) Susan E. Mickey; (L) Michael Tauffer
The Immigrant: A Hamilton County Album, Mark Harelik; conceived: Mark Harelik and Randal Myler; (D) Michael Bloom; (S) Scott Bradley; (C) Susan E. Mickey; (L) Liz Lee
T Bone N Weasel, Jon Klein; (D) Kenneth Leon; (S) Johnny Thigpen; (C) Yvonne Lee; (L) P. Hamilton Shinn
The Normal Heart, Larry Kramer; (D) Charlie Hensley; (S) Michael Stauffer; (C) Jeff Cone. David; (L) David O. Traylor
A Wrinkle in Time, adapt: Sandra Deer, from Madeleine L'Engle; (D) Skip Foster; (S) Victor Becker; (C) Susan Hirschfeld; (L) William B. Duncan
The Secret Garden, adapt: Thomas W. Olson, from Frances Hodgson Burnett; (D) Walton Jones; (S) Chris Barreca; (C) Pamela Peterson; (L) Judy Rasmuson

PRODUCTIONS 1988–89

Animal Crackers, book: George S. Kaufman and Morrie Ryskind; music and lyrics: Bert Kalmer and Harry Ruby; (D) Larry Carpenter; (S) James Leonard Joy; (C) Lindsay W. Davis; (L) Marcia Madeira
Double Double, Eric Elice and Roger Rees; (D) Munson Hicks; (S) John Falabella; (C) Susan E. Mickey; (L) Michael Stauffer
Peter Pan, book: James M. Barrie; music: Mark Charlap; lyrics: Carolyn Leigh; (D) Fran Soeder; (S) James Leonard Joy; (C) Lindsay W. Davis; (L) Marcia Madeira
Joe Turner's Come and Gone, August Wilson; (D) Kenneth Leon; (S) Michael Olich; (C) Susan E. Mickey; (L) Ann G. Wrightson
Noises Off, Michael Frayn; (D) Robert J. Farley; (S) Michael Stauffer; (C) Susan E. Mickey; (L) Victor Becker
Amadeus, Peter Shaffer; (D) Fran Soeder; (S) James Leonard Joy; (C) Mariann Verheyen; (L) Marcia Madeira
Driving Miss Daisy, Alfred Uhry; (D) Robert J. Farley; (S) Michael Stauffer; (C) Michael Stauffer; (L) Michael Stauffer
Treasure Island, adapt: Levi Lee and Larry Larson, from Robert Louis Stevenson; (D) Levi Lee; (S) Michael Stauffer; (C) Jeff Cone; (L) Michael Stauffer
Beauty and the Beast, Sandra Deer; (D) Skip Foster; (S) Victor Becker; (C) Susan E. Mickey; (L) Victor Becker
Cotton Patch Gospel, Tom Key and Russell Treyz; (D) Russell Treyz; (S) John Falabella; (C) Carol Hammond; (L) Pete Shinn

Alliance Theatre Company. *Candide.* Photo: Jonathan Burnette.

AMAS Musical Theatre

ROSETTA LENOIRE
Artistic Director

JEFFREY SOLIS
Managing Director

1 East 104th St.
New York, NY 10029
212-369-8000 (bus.)
212-36534-6080 (b.o.)

FOUNDED 1968
Rosetta LeNoire, Mara Kim, Gerta Grunen

SEASON
Oct.-Aug.

FACILITIES
Mainstage
Seating Capacity: 99
Stage: thrust

Eubie Blake Children's Theatre
Seating Capacity: 75
Stage: proscenium

FINANCES
July 1, 1988-June 30, 1989
Expenses: $325,000

CONTRACTS
AEA Funded Non-Profit Theatre code and letter of agreement

AMAS Repertory Theatre is a multiracial theatrical organization dedicated to the development of new American Musicals and bringing all people—regardless of race,

AMAS Musical Theatre. *Step Into My World.* Photo: Gilbert Johnson.

creed, color, religion or national origin—together through the performing arts. Since the American musical combines influences from every nationality and culture, spans all age groups and includes within it virtually every other aspect of artistic creativity—drama, music, dance, painting—AMAS's multiracial commitment is embodied in its dedicatioin to this uniquely American art form. AMAS sponsors five major programs: the mainstage musical theatre, the AMAS Eubie Blake Children's Theatre, an adult workshop, a summer tour, and a Musical Lab series for staged readings of new musicals.

—Rosetta LeNoire

PRODUCTIONS 1987–88

Conrack, book: Granville Burgess and Anne Croswell; book and music: Lee Pockriss; lyrics: Anne Croswell; (D) Stuart Ross; (S) Richard Block; (C) Debra Stein; (L) Donald Holder
Struttin', book, music and lyrics: Lee Chamberlin; (D) Lee Chamberlin; (S) Jeffrey Miller; (C) Bernard Johnson; (L) Shirley Pendergast
Robin's Band, book: Jerome Eskow and Anthony Abeson; lyrics and music: Maija Kupris; (D) Anthony Abeson; (S) Jeffrey Miller; (C) David Mickelsen; (L) Kathy Kaufmann

PRODUCTIONS 1988–89

Blackamoor, book: Joseph George Caruso; book and lyrics: Helen Kromer; music: Ulpio Minucci; (D) Kent Paul; (S) Steve Caldwell; (C) Jana Rosenblatt; (L) Phil Monat
Step into My World, music and lyrics: Micki Grant; (D) Ronald G. Russo; (C) Mary Ann Lach; (L) Jeffrey Hubbell
Prizes, book: Raffi Pehlivanian; music and lyrics: Charles DeForest; (D) Lee Minskoff; (S) Jane Sablow; (C) Robert Mackintosh; (L) Beau Kennedy

American Conservatory Theater

EDWARD HASTINGS
Artistic Director

JOHN SULLIVAN
Managing Director

450 Geary St.
San Francisco, CA 94102
(415) 749-2200 (bus.)
(415) 749-2ACT (b.o.)

FOUNDED 1965
William Ball

SEASON
Oct.-May

FACILITIES
Geary Theatre
Seating Capacity: 1,396
Stage: proscenium

Playroom
Seating Capacity: 49
Stage: flexible

FINANCES
June 1, 1988-May 31, 1989

Expenses: $8,300,000

CONTRACTS
LORT (A)

The American Conservatory Theatre of San Francisco is a national center for the theatre arts, dedicated to the revelation of the truths of human experience through the exploration of the dramatic literature of all ages and nations. We affirm the principle that the growth of individual creativity is the essential component of cultural progress, and that this growth and its expression in the theatre reach their fullest realization when repertory performance and professional training are concurrent and inseparable. We advocate the inherent right of the company member to participate in the formation of institutional policy, and are committed to the development of artists and audiences from all sectors of the ethnically diverse community that we serve.

—Edward Hastings

PRODUCTIONS 1987–88

King Lear, William Shakespeare; (D) Edward Hastings; (S) Richard Seger; (C) Robert Fletcher; (L) Derek Duarte
A Lie of the Mind, Sam Shepard; (D) Albert Takazauckas; (S) Barbara J. Mesney; (C) Beaver D. Bauer; (L) Derek Duarte
A Christmas Carol, adapt: Dennis Powers and Laird Williamson, from Charles Dickens; (D) Laird Williamson; (S) Robert Blackman; (C) Robert Morgan; (L) Derek Duarte
The Floating Light Bulb, Woody Allen; (D) Albert Takazauckas; (S) Ralph Funicello; (C) Beaver D. Bauer; (L) Derek Duarte
The Immigrant: A Hamilton County Album, Mark Harelik; conceived: Randal Myler and Mark Harelik; (D) Sabin Epstein; (S) Ralph Funicello; (C) Cathleen Edwards; (L) Derek Duarte
Diamond Lil, adapt: Paul Blake and Dennis Powers, from Mae West; (D) Powers Dennis; (S) Douglas W. Schmidt; (C) Robert Fletcher; (L) Derek Duarte
End of the World with Symposium to Follow, Arthur Kopit; (D) Laird Williamson; (S) Richard Seger; (C) Fritha Knudsen; (L) Derek Duarte

Golden Boy, Clifford Odets; (D) Joy Carlin; (S) Jesse Hollis; (C) Warren Travis; (L) Derek Duarte
Feathers, adapt: Stanley R. Greenberg, from Aristophanes; (D) John C. Fletcher; (S) Barbara J. Mesney; (C) Beaver D. Bauer; (L) Derek Duarte

PRODUCTIONS 1988–89

Marco Millions, Eugene O'Neill; (D) Joy Carlin; (S) Ralph Funicello; (C) Jovita Chow; (L) Derek Duarte
Woman in Mind, Alan Ayckbourn; (D) Sabin Epstein; (S) Barbara J. Mesney; (C) Lydia Tanji; (L) Derek Duarte
A Christmas Carol, adapt: Dennis Powers and Laird Williamson, from Charles Dickens; (D) Laird Williamson; (S) Robert Blackman; (C) Robert Morgan; (L) Derek Duarte
Side by Side by Sondheim, music and lyrics: Stephen Sondheim; music: Leonard Bernstein, Mary Rogers, Richard Rogers and Jule Styne; (D) Paul Blake; (L) Derek Duarte
Joe Turner's Come and Gone, August Wilson; (D) Claude Purdy; (S) Scott Bradley; (C) Pamela Peterson; (L) Derek Duarte
When We Are Married, J.B. Priestley; (D) Edward Hastings; (S) Joel Fontaine; (C) Robert Fletcher; (L) Derek Duarte

American Conservatory Theatre. Andrea Marcovicci in *Saint Joan*. Photo: Mary Sohl.

Saint Joan, George Bernard Shaw;
(D) Michael Smuin; (S) Ralph
Funicello; (C) Sandra Woodall;
(L) Derek Duarte
Nothing Sacred, George F.
Walker; (D) Robert Woodruff;
(S) George Tsypin; (C) Susan
Hilferty; (L) Derek Duarte
A Funny Thing Happened on the Way to the Forum, book: Burt
Shevelove and Larry Gelbart;
music and lyrics: Stephen
Sondheim; (D) Albert
Takazauckas; (S) Ralph
Funicello; (C) Beaver D. Bauer;
(L) Derek Duarte

The American Place Theatre

WYNN HANDMAN
Director

STEPHEN LISNER
General Manager

111 West 46th St.
New York, NY 10036
(212) 840-2960 (bus.)
(212) 840-3074 (b.o.)

FOUNDED 1964
Michael Tolan, Myrna Loy,
Sidney Lanier, Wynn Handman

SEASON
Sept.-June

FACILITIES
Mainstage
Seating Capacity: 299
Stage: thrust

Subplot Cafe
Seating Capacity: 74
Stage: flexible

First Floor Theatre
Seating Capacity: 74
Stage: flexible

FINANCES
July 1, 1988-June 30, 1989
Expenses: $700,000

CONTRACTS
AEA Special Production and Mini

The American Place Theatre is currently in its 25th Anniversary Season of producing new American plays by living American writers. Its continuing purpose is to be a force for the advancement of theatre by actively responding to the contemporary theatre's needs. Toward that end, the American Place provides talented writers with a creative environment free of commercial considerations. Our innovative, original programming opens the way for increased public awareness and enrichment of the mainstream of the nation's theatre. In order to promote and encourage new work of various genres with differing production needs, the American Place has several ongoing programs in addition to its Venture Plays Series. These include The American Humorists' Series and the JUBILEE! Festival Celebrating Ethnic America.
—*Wynn Handman*

PRODUCTIONS 1987–88

That Serious He-man Ball,
Alonzo D. Lamont, Jr.;
(D) Clinton Turner Davis;
(S) Charles McClennahan;
(C) Julian Asion; (L) William H. Grant
Roy Blount's Happy Hour & a Half, Roy Blount, Jr.; (D) Wynn
Handman; (S) Marc D.
Malamud; (C) Marc D.
Malamud; (L) Marc D. Malamud
Celebration, Shauneille Perry;
(D) Shauneille Perry; (S) Marc
D. Malamud; (C) Marc D.
Malamud; (L) Marc D. Malamud
At The Back of My Head,
Stephanie Silverman; (D) Wynn
Handman; (S) Marc D.
Malamud; (C) Marc D.
Malamud; (L) Marc D. Malamud
Odd Jobbers, Michael Heintzman,
Terry Hempleman and
Marguerite Kuhn; (D) Wynn
Handman; (S) Marc D.
Malamud; (C) Marc D.
Malamud; (L) Marc D. Malamud
The Boob Story, Jane Gennaro;
(D) Wynn Handman; (S) Marc
D. Malamud; (C) Marc D.
Malamud; (L) Marc D. Malamud
Tallulah Tonight, book and lyrics:
Tony Lang; music: Bruce W.
Cole; (D) Wynn Handman;
(S) Marc D. Malamud; (C) Marc
D. Malamud; (L) Brian
MacDevitt
Splendid Mummer, Lonnie Elder,
III; (D) Woodie King, Jr.;
(S) Charles McClennahan;
(C) Edi Giguere; (L) Brian
MacDevitt

PRODUCTIONS 1988–89

Calvin Trillin's Uncle Sam,
Calvin Trillin; (D) Wynn
Handman; (S) John M. Lucas;
(C) John M. Lucas; (L) John M. Lucas
A Burning Beach, Eduardo
Machado; (D) Rene Buch;
(S) Donald Eastman;
(C) Deborah Shaw; (L) Anne Militello
The Unguided Missile, David
Wolpe; (D) Fred Kolo; (S)
Holger; (C) Gail Cooper-Hecht;
(L) Holger
A. Whitney Brown's The Big Picture, A. Whitney Brown;
(D) Wynn Handman; (L) Brian MacDevitt
The Blessing, Clare Coss;
(D) Roberta Sklar; (S) Donald
Eastman; (C) Sally J. Lesser;
(L) Frances Aronson
Zora Neale Hurston, Laurence
Holder; (D) Wynn Handman;
(S) Terrance Chandler;
(L) Terrance Chandler

American Repertory Theatre

ROBERT BRUSTEIN
Artistic Director

ROBERT J. ORCHARD
Managing Director

64 Brattle St.
Cambridge, MA 02138
(617) 495-2668 (bus.)
(617) 547-8300 (b.o.)

The American Place Theatre. Liann Pattison, Ivonne Coll, George Lundoner and Lillian Garrett in *A Burning Beach*. Photo: Martha Holmes.

FOUNDED 1979
Robert Brustein

SEASON
Nov.-June

FACILITIES
Loeb Drama Center
Seating Capacity: 556
Stage: flexible

ART/New Stages
Seating Capacity: 353
Stage: proscenium

FINANCES
Aug. 1, 1988-July 31, 1989
Expenses: $4,755,000

CONTRACTS
LORT (B)

The American Repertory Theatre, founded as a professional producing organization and a theatrical training conservatory, is one of a very few companies in this country with a resident acting ensemble performing in rotating repertory. The company has presented 67 productions, including over 40 premieres, new translations and adaptations. Our productions, which have increasingly involved artists of national and international stature from a wide variety of disciplines, generally fall into three distinct categories: newly interpreted classical productions, new American plays, and neglected works of the past, frequently involving music. ART has toured extensively in this country and abroad, including performances in Avignon, Paris, Venice, Edinburgh, Tel Aviv, Belgrade, London and Amsterdam; at the 1984 Olympic Arts Festival in Los Angeles; and most recently at Madrid's Teatro Espanol. In the fall of 1987, the American Repertory Theatre Institute for Advanced Theatre Training at Harvard began formal instruction under the direction of Richard Riddell. ART received the 1985 Jujamcyn Theatre Award and a special Tony Award in 1986 for continued excellence in resident theatre.

—Robert Brustein

PRODUCTIONS 1987–88

Six Characters in Search of an Author, adapt: Robert Brustein, from Luigi Pirandello; (D) Robert Brustein; (S) Michael H. Yeargan; (C) Michael H. Yeargan; (L) Jennifer Tipton

The Good Woman of Setzuan, Bertolt Brecht; trans: Eric Bentley; (D) Andrei Serban; (S) Jeff Muskovin; (C) Catherine Zuber; (L) Howell Binkley

Gillette, William Hauptman; (D) David Wheeler; (S) Loy Arcenas; (C) Catherine Zuber; (L) Howell Binkley

Right You Are (If You Think You Are), adapt: Robert Brustein, from Luigi Pirandello; (D) Robert Brustein; (S) Michael H. Yeargan; (C) Christine Joly de Lotbiniere; (L) Richard Riddell

Quartet, Heiner Muller; trans: Carl Weber; (D) Robert Wilson; (S) Robert Wilson; (C) Frida Parmegianni; (L) Howell Binkley and Robert Wilson

The Fall of the House of Usher, music: Philip Glass; book Arthur Yorinks; (D) Richard Foreman; (S) Richard Foreman; (C) Patricia Zipprodt; (L) Richard Riddell

Tis Pity She's a Whore, John Ford; (D) Michael Kahn; (S) Derek McLane; (C) Catherine Zuber; (L) Frances Aronson

Life and Fate, adapt: Frederick Wiseman, from Vasily Grossman; (D) Frederick Wiseman; (C) Elizabeth Perlman and Jane Perry; (L) Alan P. Symonds

Big Time: Scenes from a Service Economy, Keith Reddin; (D) Steven Schachter; (S) Bill Clarke; (C) Ellen McCartney; (L) Thom Palm

Uncle Vanya, adapt and trans: David Mamet, from Anton Chekhov; (D) David Wheeler; (S) Bill Clarke; (C) Catherine Zuber; (L) Thom Palm

PRODUCTIONS 1988–89

The King Stag, Carlo Gozzi; trans: Albert Bermel; (D) Andrei Serban; (S) Michael H. Yeargan; (C) Julie Taymor; (L) Jennifer Tipton

The Serpent Woman, Carlo Gozzi; trans: Albert Bermel; (D) Andrei Serban; (S) Setsu Asakura; (C) Setsu Asakura; (L) Victor En Yu Tan

Platanov, Anton Chekhov; trans: Mark Leib; (D) Liviu Ciulei; (S) Liviu Ciulei; (C) Smaranda Branescu; (L) Richard Riddell

Mastergate, Larry Gelbart; (D) Michael Engler; (S) Philipp Jung; (C) Candice Donnelly; (L) James F. Ingalls

The Miser, Moliere; trans: Albert Bermel; (D) Andrei Serban; (S) Derek McLane; (C) Judith Anne Dolan; (L) Howell Binkley

Life Is A Dream, Pedro Calderon de la Barca; trans: Edwin Honig; (D) Anne Bogart; (S) Loy Arcenas; (C) Catherine Zuber; (L) Richard Riddell

Fun, Howard Korder; (D) David Wheeler; (S) Derek McLane; (C) Karen Eister; (L) Peter West

Nobody, Howard Korder; (D) David Wheeler; (S) Derek McLane; (C) Karen Eister; (L) Peter West

In Twilight: Tales from Chekhov, adapt: Tina Landau, from Anton Chekhov; (D) Tina Landau; (S) Derek McLane; (C) Christine Joly de Lotbiniere; (L) John Malinowski

American Repertory Theatre. Alvin Epstein in *The Miser*. Photo: Richard Feldman.

American Stage

VICTORIA L. HOLLOWAY
Artistic Director

JOHN A. BERGLUND
Producing Director

Box 1560
St. Petersburg, FL 33731
(813) 823-1600 (bus.)
(813) 822-8814 (b.o.)

FOUNDED 1979
Bobbie Seifer, Richard Hopkins

SEASON
Oct.-July

FACILITIES
Mainstage
Seating Capacity: 120
Stage: thrust

Deman's Landing
Seating Capacity: 1,500
Stage: flexible

FINANCES
July 1, 1988-June 30, 1989
Expenses: $545,723

CONTRACTS
AEA SPT and TYA

Tampa Bay is home. We own a house, we pay local taxes, we're concerned with who's on city council. We read the city/state section of our newspaper first. What happens here in this community affects our daily lives most, and consequently affects our work on stage. For the past decade we have sought the perfect union between personal artistic expression and realistic programming. We have responded on the one hand to our artistic needs, and on the other to the needs of our community. The balance between the two has insured our success. Our commitment is to artists, to language, to all segments of our community, and to ourselves. At this time, our future is here: green benches, mirrored towers, growth management, transitory populations, Mouseketeers, high school dropouts, crack cocaine, manatees and lots of sand.

—Victoria L. Holloway

PRODUCTIONS 1987–88

Broadway, Philip Dunning and George Abbott; (D) Victoria L. Holloway; (S) David Malcolm Bewley; (C) David Malcolm Bewley; (L) Bill Lelbach

Side by Side by Sondheim, Stephen Sondheim; (D) Cathey Crowell Sawyer; (S) K. Edgar Swados; (C) Mary Beth Sprankle; (L) Michael Newton-Brown

The Early Girl, Caroline Kava; (D) Victoria L. Holloway; (S) K. Edgar Swados; (C) Mary Beth Sprankle; (L) Joe Oshry

Vikings, Stephen Metcalfe; (D) John Berglund; (S) K. Edgar Swados; (C) David Malcolm Bewley; (L) William Langley, Jr.

The Mystery of Irma Vep, Charles Ludlam; (D) Bruce Siddons; (S) K. Edgar Swados;

American Stage. *The Artificial Jungle.* Photo: Joe Walles.

(C) Mary Beth Sprankle;
(L) Ewin Stone
The Tempest, William
Shakespeare; (D) Victoria L.
Holloway; (S) Jimmy Humphries;
(C) David Malcolm Bewley;
(L) Michael Newton-Brown

PRODUCTIONS 1988–89

Les Liaisons Dangereuses, adapt:
Christopher Hampton, from
Choderlos de Laclos; (D) Bruce
Siddons; (S) Jimmy Humphries;
(C) Abby Lillethun; (L) Bill
Lelbach
The Artificial Jungle, Charles
Ludlam; (D) Bruce Siddons;
(S) Jimmy Humphries; (C) Mary
Beth Sprankle; (L) Robert
Wenck
Independence, Lee Blessing;
(D) Victoria L. Holloway;
(S) Jimmy Humphries; (C) Anne
Hull; (L) Richard Sharkey
Miss Edwina, Patrick Brafford;
(D) Patrick Brafford; (S) Scott
Kirkham; (C) Mary Beth
Sprankle; (L) Joe Oshry
So Long on Lonely Street,
Sandra Deer; (D) Cathey
Crowell Sawyer; (S) Jimmy
Humphries; (C) Joanne Johnson;
(L) Richard Sharkey
The Mystery of Irma Vep,
Charles Ludlam; (D) Bruce
Siddons; (S) K. Edgar Swados;
(C) Mary Beth Sprankle; (L) Joe
Oshry
The Comedy of Errors, adapt:
Victoria L. Holloway, from
William Shakespeare; music and
lyrics: Lee Ahlin; (D) Victoria L.
Holloway; (S) Jimmy Humphries;
(C) Susan Kelly; (L) Robert
Wenck

American Stage Festival

RICHARD ROSE
Producing Director

AUSTIN TICHENOR
Assoc. Director/Literary Manager

Box 225
Milford, NH 03055
(603) 673-4005 (bus.)
(603) 673-7515 (b.o.)

FOUNDED 1975
Terry C. Lorden

SEASON
May-Sept.

FACILITIES
American Stage Festival
Seating Capacity: 496
Stage: proscenium

Nashua Center for the Arts
Seating Capacity: 350
Stage: flexible

FINANCES
Nov. 1, 1987-Oct. 31, 1988
Expenses: $760,805

CONTRACTS
LORT (C) and (D)

The artistic mission of the American Stage Festival is to expand the spectrum of theatre art by presenting rewarding and challenging theatrical material, with particular attention to pieces that reflect the concerns of southern New Hampshire; to invigorate audiences with work that is emotionally fulfilling and intellectually stimulating; to discover, develop and produce new theatrical works; to further the education of young theatre artists by serving as a bridge between training programs and the "real world"; to entertain and educate the young people of our area through the performances and workshops of our Young Company; to further enrich our audiences through the presentation of works from the entire realm of live performance, including dance and music; and, finally, to raise our standards and those of our audience so that the limits of regional resources do not limit expectation or imagination.
—*Richard Rose*

Note: During the 1987-88 season, Larry Carpenter served as artistic director.

PRODUCTIONS 1987–88

I'm Not Rappaport, Herb
Gardner; (D) Munson Hicks;
(S) John Falabella; (C) John
Falabella; (L) Marcia Madeira
The Voice of the Prairie, John
Olive; (D) Sheldon Epps;
(S) John Falabella; (C) John
Falabella; (L) Stuart Duke
Woody Guthrie's American Song,
Peter Glazer; (D) Peter Glazer;
(S) Philipp Jung; (C) Deborah
Shaw; (L) David Noling
Starmites, book: Stuart Ross and
Barry Keating; music and lyrics:
Barry Keating; (D) Larry
Carpenter; (S) Lowell Detweiler;
(C) Susan Hirschfeld; (L) Jason
Kantrowitz
Sherlock Holmes, adapt: William
Gillette, from Arthur Canan
Doyle; (D) Israel Hicks;
(S) Mark Wendland; (C) Mark
Wendland; (L) Stuart Duke

Young Company:
The Miracle Worker, adapt:
Austin Tichenor, from William
Gibson; (D) Austin Tichenor;
(S) John Falabella; (C) Jeff
Boring; (L) Darren Clarke
Cinderella, Barbara Richards;
(D) Robert Richards; (S) John
Falabella; (C) Jeff Boring;
(L) Scott Pegg
Alice Through The Looking Glass, Austin Tichenor; (D) Eve
Muson; (S) John Falabella;
(C) Jeff Boring; (L) Darren
Clarke
The First Olympics, Eve Muson

American Stage Festival. Michael Lynch and Liz Larsen in *Starmites*. Photo: Jim Witek.

and Austin Tichenor; (D) Mimi McGurl; (S) Charles Morgan; (C) Jeff Boring; (L) Scott Pegg
Tom Sawyer, Eve Muson; (D) Eve Muson; (S) Charles Morgan; (C) Jeff Boring; (L) Scott Pegg
The Emperor's New Clothes, book: David Saar and Debra Stevens; music and lyrics: Jeff Payne; (D) Scott Pegg; (S) Lowell Detweiler; (C) Jeff Boring; (L) Scott Pegg

PRODUCTIONS 1988–89

West Side Story, book: Arthur Laurents; music: Leonard Bernstein; lyrics: Stephen Sondheim; (D) Richard Rose; (S) Gary English; (C) Dawna Gregory; (L) Ken Smith
Heaven Can Wait, Harry Segall; (D) Gregory Hurst; (S) Atkin Pace; (C) Barbara Forbes; (L) Don Holder
The Foreigner, Larry Shue; (D) Austin Tichenor; (S) Charles Morgan; (C) Dianne Tyree; (L) Sid Bennett
The Rainmaker, N. Richard Nash; (D) Charles Morey; (S) Gary English; (C) Dianne Tyree; (L) Ken Smith
Dracula, Hamilton Dean and John A. Balderston; (D) Richard Rose; (S) Charles Morgan; (C) Amanda Aldridge; (L) Ken Smith

Young Company
Storybook Theatre, Eve Muson; (D) Eve Muson; (S) Charles Morgan; (C) Jeff Boring; (L) Kace Christian
Ozma of Oz, Eve Muson; (D) Eve Muson; (S) Charles Morgan; (C) Jeff Boring; (L) Kace Christian
Little Red Riding Hood, Bruce Goldstone; (D) John Tichenor; (S) Charles Morgan; (C) Jeff Boring; (L) Kace Christian
Beauty and the Beast, Austin Tichenor; (D) John Tichenor; (S) Charles Morgan; (C) Jeff Boring; (L) Kace Christian
The Princess and the Pea, Scott Pegg; (D) Scott Pegg; (S) Charles Morgan; (C) Jeff Boring; (L) Kace Christian
Dancing on the Ceiling, adapt: Austin Tichenor, from Franz Kafka; (D) Denise Ryan; (S) Charles Morgan; (C) Jeff Boring; (L) Kace Christian
The Pushcart War, Gregory A. Falls; (D) Eve Muson; (S) Charles Morgan; (C) Jeff Boring; (L) Kace Christian
The Lone Ranger, John Tichenor; (D) John Tichenor; (S) Charles Morgan; (C) Jeff Boring; (L) Kace Christian
Rumplestiltskin, Eve Muson; (D) Scott Pegg; (S) Charles Morgan; (C) Jeff Boring; (L) Kace Christian

American Theatre Company

KITTY ROBERTS
Producing Artistic Director

LISA SWIGGART
Manager

Box 1265
Tulsa, OK 74101
(918) 747-9494 (bus.)
(918) 596-7111 (b.o.)

FOUNDED 1970
Kitty Roberts

SEASON
Jan.–Dec.

FACILITIES
John Williams Theatre
Seating Capacity: 429
Stage: proscenium

Studio One
Seating Capacity: 293
Stage: flexible

Brady Theatre
Seating Capacity: 1,200
Stage: proscenium

FINANCES
July 1, 1988-June 30, 1989
Expenses: $320,000

CONTRACTS
AEA Guest artist

Oklahoma's pioneer spirit arises from a life shared together at the edge of recent American history—the forced resettlement of Native Americans from 1820 on, the land rush by European settlers in 1889, statehood in 1907, the oil boom from 1912 to 1920, the Dustbowl depression of the 1930s, the expansion of military bases during World War II, the energy crisis and oil embargo of 1973. As Oklahoma's only resident professional theatre company, the American Theatre Company can persuade Oklahomans that their frontier viewpoint is mirrored in the traditions of world drama, and that their frontier voices can be expressed in a unique dramatic idiom. Therefore, our goal is to play a leading role in shaping a common public vision for the economic, political, educational, religions and artistic life of Oklahoma. ATC presents six main-stage productions, two summer productions, and conducts an ongoing statewide education program.

—*Kitty Roberts*

American Theatre Company. *Biloxi Blues*. Photo: Rabbit Hare.

PRODUCTIONS 1987–88

The 1940's Radio Hour, Walton Jones; (D) Kitty Roberts; (S) Richard Ellis; (C) Gene Barnhart; (L) Jim Queen
A Christmas Carol, adapt: Robert Odle, from Charles Dickens; (D) Claudia Winters; (S) Richard Ellis; (C) Gene Barnhart; (L) Jim Queen
A Coupla White Chicks Sitting Around Talking, John Ford Noonan; (D) Rebecca Nesbitt Bones; (S) Richard Ellis; (C) Gene Barnhart; (L) Jim Queen
All My Sons, Arthur Miller; (D) Jim Queen; (S) Richard Ellis; (C) Gene Barnhart; (L) Christina Coleman
Steel Magnolias, Robert Harling; (D) Kitty Roberts; (S) Richard Ellis; (C) Randy Blair; (L) Jim Queen
Biloxi Blues, Neil Simon; (D) Jim Queen; (S) Richard Ellis; (C) Randy Blair; (L) Jim Queen
Eddie and the Ecclectics, company-developed; (D) Kitty Roberts; (S) Richard Ellis; (C) Jo Wimer; (L) Larry McKinney

PRODUCTIONS 1988–89

Sherlock's Last Case, Charles Marowitz; (D) Jim Queen; (S) Richard Ellis; (C) Randy Blair; (L) Richard Wilson
A Christmas Carol, adapt: Robert Odle, from Charles Dickens; (D) Randy Blair; (S) Richard Ellis; (C) Jo Wimer; (L) Christina Coleman
I'm Not Rappaport, Herb Gardner; (D) Jim Queen; (S) Richard Ellis; (C) Randy Blair; (L) Jim Queen
The Road to Mecca, Athol Fugard; (D) Randy Blair; (S) Curt Selby; (C) Randy Blair; (L) Jim Queen
Is There Life After High School?, book: Jeffrey Kindley; music and lyrics: Craig Carnelia; (D) Randy Blair; (S) Richard Ellis; (C) Randy Blair; (L) Richard Wilson
Broadway Bound, Neil Simon; (D) Jim Queen; (S) Richard Ellis; (C) Randy Blair; (L) Pat Sharp
Eddie and the Ecclectics, company-developed; (D) Marilyn Neal and Ken Nelson; (S) Curt Selby; (C) Jo Wimer; (L) Richard Wilson

American Theatre Works

JILL CHARLES
Artistic Director

JOHN NASSIVERA
Producing Director

Box 519
Dorset, VT 05251
(802) 867-2223 (bus.)
(802) 867-5777 (b.o.)

FOUNDED 1976
John Nassivera, Jill Charles

SEASON
June-Sept.

FACILITIES
The Dorset Playhouse
Seating Capacity: 218
Stage: proscenium

FINANCES
Jan. 1, 1988-Dec. 31, 1988
Expenses: $340,000

CONTRACTS
AEA SPT

American Theatre Works, Inc. produces the Dorset Theatre Festival at the Dorset Playhouse, a season of five or six contemporary American and British plays as well as revivals of American classics and at least one new play. Over the past 14 seasons, the company has built up a pool of New York-based directors, designers, technicians and actors to draw from, and new talent is added each year. American Theatre Work's educational arm serves the theatre profession in two ways: through its outstanding apprentice program, offering Actors' Equity membership credit and a focus on career development, and through publication of two annual employment resources, Summer Theatre Directory and Regional Theatre Directory, as well as the Directory of Theatre Training Programs. Also, American Theatre Works operates the Dorset Colony from September through May, a resident artists' colony, offering writers (particularly playwrights) a retreat for intensive periods of work.

—*Jill Charles*

PRODUCTIONS 1987–88

Mass Appeal, Bill C. Davis; (D) Mark S. Ramont; (S) William John Aupperlee; (C) Mary Marsicano; (L) Jeffrey A. Bernstein
Without Apologies, Thom Thomas; (D) Edgar Lansbury; (S) William John Aupperlee; (C) Mary Marsicano; (L) Jeffrey A. Bernstein
A Thousand Clowns, Herb Gardner; (D) Jill Charles; (S) William John Aupperlee; (C) Mary Marsicano; (L) Jeffrey A. Bernstein
Taking Steps, Alan Ayckbourn; (D) John Morrison; (S) William John Aupperlee; (C) Mary Marsicano; (L) Jeffrey A. Bernstein
My Three Angels, Bella Spewack and Sam Spewack; (D) John Morrison; (S) William John Aupperlee; (L) Jeffrey A. Bernstein

PRODUCTIONS 1988–89

Crossing Niagara, Alonso Alegria; (D) Mark S. Ramont; (S) William John Aupperlee; (C) Eric Hansen; (L) Jeffrey A. Bernstein
Painting Churches, Tina Howe; (D) Edgar Lansbury; (S) Wade Battley; (C) Eric Hansen; (L) Jeffrey A. Bernstein
Steel Magnolias, Robert Harling; (D) Jill Charles; (S) William John Aupperlee; (C) Eric Hansen; (L) Jeffrey A. Bernstein
Country Cops, Robert Lord; (D) John Morrison; (S) Wade Battley; (C) Eric Hansen; (L) Jeffrey A. Bernstein
All the Queen's Men, John Nassivera; (D) Edgar Lansbury; (S) William John Aupperlee; (C) Eric Hansen; (L) Jeffrey A. Bernstein

Arena Stage

ZELDA FICHANDLER
Producing Director

DOUGLAS WAGER
Associate Producing Director

6th and Maine Ave., SW
Washington, DC 20024
(202) 554-9066 (bus.)
(202) 488-3300 (b.o.)

FOUNDED 1950
Edward Mangum, Zelda Fichandler, Thomas C. Fichandler

SEASON
Oct.-Jun.

FACILITIES
The Arena
Seating Capacity: 827
Stage: arena

The Kreeger Theater
Seating Capacity: 514
Stage: thrust

The Old Vat Room
Seating Capacity: 180
Stage: flexible

FINANCES
July 1, 1988-June 30, 1989
Expenses: $7,800,000

CONTRACTS
LORT (B+), (C) and (D),

Arena Stage embodies the concept of achieving artistic excellence by means of a resident ensemble of actors, directors, technicians, administrators, craftspeople and associate artists who create together in an ongoing, evolving process. Our repertoire is aggressively eclectic, spanning national and international dramatic literature, both classic and modern. We explore subjects that express an involvement with the human condition through a variety of dramatic forms. Most important, the actor stands at the center of our work as the primary embodiment of the art itself, the instrument of highest communication and communion, bringing life to life by means of word, gesture, intelligence, imagination and passion. Arena is a deeply spiritual and spirited artistic home for a family of creative theatre professionals dedicated to enriching the cultural life of our human community.

—*Zelda Fichandler*

PRODUCTIONS 1987–88

Joe Turner's Come and Gone, August Wilson; (D) Lloyd Richards; (S) Scott Bradley; (C) Pamela Peterson; (L) Michael Giannitti
All the King's Men, adapt: Adrian Hall, from Robert Penn Warren; (D) Douglas C. Wager; (S) Douglas Stein; (C) Marjorie Slaiman; (L) Allen Lee Hughes
From Off the Streets of Cleveland Comes...American Splendor, adapt: Lloyd Rose, from Harvey Pekar; (D) James C. Nicola; (S) Michael Franklin-White; (C) Noel Borden; (L) Nancy Schertler
Light Up the Sky, Moss Hart; (D) James C. Nicola; (S) Andrew Jackness; (C) Marjorie Slaiman; (L) Nancy Schertler
Enrico IV, Luigi Pirandello; trans: Robert Cornthwaite; (D) Mel Shapiro and Zelda Fichandler; (S) Douglas Stein; (C) Marjorie Slaiman; (L) Allen Lee Hughes
Les Blancs, adapt: Robert Nemiroff, from Lorraine Hansberry; (D) Harold Scott; (S) Karl Eigsti; (C) Marjorie Slaiman; (L) Allen Lee Hughes
The Rivers and Ravines, Heather McDonald; (D) Douglas C. Wager and Paul Walker; (S) David M. Glenn; (C) Marjorie Slaiman; (L) Nancy Schertler
Checkmates, Ron Milner; (D) Woodie King, Jr.; (S) Karl Eigsti; (C) Noel Borden; (L) Allen Lee Hughes
The Cocoanuts, book: George S. Kaufman; music and lyrics: Irving Berlin; (D) Douglas C. Wager; (S) Thomas Lynch; (C) Martin Pakledinaz; (L) Allen Lee Hughes
The Cherry Orchard, Anton Chekhov; trans: Jean-Claude van Itallie; (D) Lucian Pintilie; (S) Radu Boruzescu; (C) Miruna Boruzescu; (L) Beverly Emmons

American Theatre Works, Inc. Barry Lynch and Suzanne Grodner in *Educating Rita*. Photo: Wm. John Aupperlee.

16 ARENA STAGE

Arena Stage. Six Characters in Search of an Author. Photo: Joan Marcus.

PRODUCTIONS 1988–89

The Tale of Lear, adapt: Tadashi Suzuki, from William Shakespeare; (D) Tadashi Suzuki; (S) Arden Fingerhut; (C) Tadashi Suzuki; (L) Arden Fingerhut
Abyssinia, book and music: Ted Kociolek and James Racheff; (D) Tazewell Thompson; (S) James Leonard Joy; (C) Amanda J. Klein; (L) Allen Lee Hughes
Six Characters in Search of an Author, Luigi Pirandello; trans: Robert Cornthwaite; (D) Liviu Ciulei; (S) Liviu Ciulei; (C) Smaranda Branescu; (L) Allen Lee Hughes
Ring Round the Moon, adapt: Christopher Fry, from Jean Anouilh; (D) Douglas C. Wager; (S) George Tsypin; (C) Marjorie Slaiman; (L) Frances Aronson
Playboy of the West Indies, Mustapha Matura; (D) Tazewell Thompson; (S) Adrianne Lobel; (C) Marjorie Slaiman; (L) Nancy Schertler
A Chorus of Disapproval, Alan Ayckbourn; (D) Mel Shapiro; (S) Karl Eigsti; (C) Marjorie Slaiman; (L) Allen Lee Hughes
Briar Patch, Deborah Pryor; (D) Max Mayer; (S) David M. Glenn; (C) Betty Siegel; (L) Christopher Townsend
A Lie of the Mind, Sam Shepard; (D) Douglas C. Wager; (S) Douglas Stein; (C) Marjorie Slaiman; (L) Nancy Schertler
Nothing Sacred, George F. Walker; (D) Garland Wright; (S) John Arnone; (C) Marjorie Slaiman; (L) Nancy Schertler
On the Town, book and lyrics: Betty Comden and Adolph Green; music: Leonard Bernstein; (D) Douglas C. Wager; (S) Zack Brown; (C) Zack Brown; (L) Allen Lee Hughes
A Walk in the Woods, Lee Blessing; (D) Paul Weidner; (S) John Arnone; (C) Marjorie Slaiman; (L) Nancy Schertler

Arizona Theatre Company

GARY GISSELMAN
Artistic Director

Box 1631
Tucson, AZ 85702
(602) 884-8210 (bus.)
(602) 622-2823 (b.o.)

17 East Thomas Road, Suite 15
Phoenix, AZ 85012
(602) 234-2892 (bus.) (602) 279-0534 (b.o.)

FOUNDED 1966
Sandy Rosenthal

SEASON
Oct.–June

FACILITIES
Herberger Theatre Center
Seating Capacity: 800
Stage: proscenium

Temple of Music and Art
Seating Capacity: 625
Stage: proscenium

FINANCES
July 1, 1988-June 30, 1989
Expenses: $2,713,998

CONTRACTS
LORT (C)

The Arizona Theatre Company is in a constant state of rediscovering itself. Tucson and Phoenix are growing and changing so rapidly that ATC is at once a part of, as well as a reflection of, that growth and change. Our two-city operation will be artistically enriched by moving into new peformance facilities in both cities over the next two years. The population moving to Arizona is from all over the U.S., Europe, Central and South America, so the process of discovering our community and our audience is a dynamic one. We are trying to be our own model and discover our own uniqueness as a regional theatre in the Southwest. We aim to provide an exciting and nurturing creative atmosphere for all theatre artists. To that end, our repertoire is eclectic, drawing from classical and contemporary work. All is enhanced by the exotic embrace of the desert, which provides an operating metaphor for ATC: not how little grows, but how much grows on so little.
—*Gary Gisselman*

PRODUCTIONS 1987–88

Candide, adapt: Hugh Wheeler, from Voltaire; music: Leonard Bernstein; lyrics: Stephen Sondheim, John LaTouche and Richard Wilbur; (D) Gary Gisselman; (S) Tom Butsch; (C) David Kay Mickelson; (L) Don Darnutzer
Great Expectations, adapt: Barbara Field, from Charles Dickens; (D) John Clark Donahue; (S) Tom Buderwitz; (C) David Kay Mickelson; (L) Don Darnutzer
Sizwe Bansi Is Dead, Athol Fugard, John Kani and Winston Ntshona; (D) Edward Payson Call; (S) David Potts; (C) Bobbi Culbert; (L) Don Darnutzer
On the Verge or The Geography of Yearning, Eric Overmyer; (D) John Clark Donahue; (S) David Potts; (C) Gene Davis Buck; (L) Michael Murnane
The Tempest, William Shakespeare; (D) Gary Gisselman; (S) Kent Dorsey; (C) Jared Aswegan; (L) Don Darnutzer
Taking Steps, Alan Ayckbourn; (D) Edward Payson Call; (S) Vicki Smith; (C) Bobbi Culbert; (L) Don Darnutzer
Dreamers of the Day, adapt: Michael Grady, from Studs Terkel; (D) John Clark Donahue and Gary Gisselman; (S) Greg Lucas; (C) David Kay Mickelson; (L) Don Darnutzer

PRODUCTIONS 1988–89

Cat on a Hot Tin Roof, Tennessee Williams; (D) Gary Gisselman; (S) Tom Butsch; (C) David Kay Mickelson; (L) Don Darnutzer
Under Milk Wood, Dylan Thomas; (D) Gary Gisselman; (S) Greg Lucas; (C) David Kay Mickelson; (L) Don Darnutzer
I'm Not Rappaport, Herb Gardner; (D) David Ira Goldstein; (S) Jeff Thomson; (C) Gene Davis Buck; (L) Don Darnutzer
Arms and the Man, George Bernard Shaw; (D) Edward Payson Call; (S) Kent Dorsey; (C) Gene Davis Buck; (L) Don Darnutzer
Steel Magnolias, Robert Harling; (D) Libby Appel; (S) Kent Dorsey; (C) Gene Davis Buck; (L) Don Darnutzer
A Walk in the Woods, Lee Blessing; (D) Gary Gisselman; (S) Greg Lucas; (C) Cathie McClellan; (L) Don Darnutzer

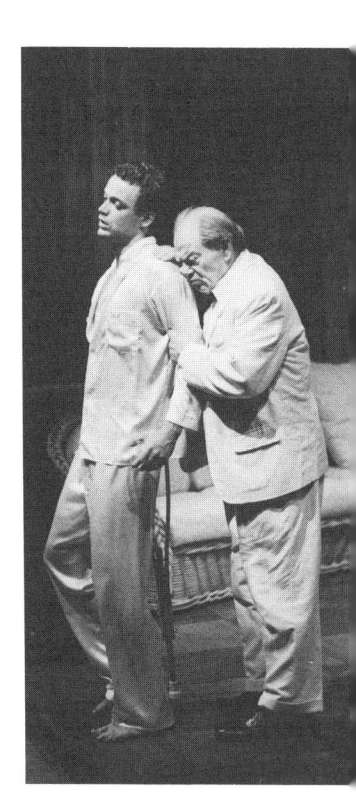

Arizona Theatre Company. Ray Chambers and George Murdock in Cat on a Hot Tin Roof. Photo: Tim Fuller.

The Arkansas Arts Center Children's Theatre

BRADLEY D. ANDERSON
Artistic Director

P. J. POWERS
Theatre Administrative Manager

Box 2137
Little Rock, AR 72203
(501) 372-4000

FOUNDED 1963
Museum of Fine Arts, The Junior League of Little Rock, The Fine Arts Club

SEASON
Sept.-May

FACILITIES
The Arkansas Arts Center Theatre
Seating Capacity: 389
Stage: proscenium

The Arkansas Arts Center Theatre Studio
Seating Capacity: 200
Stage: flexible

FINANCES
July 1, 1988-June 30, 1989
Expenses: $398,832

The Arkansas Arts Center Children's Theatre exists to provide high quality theatre experiences for young people and their families. We provide a master/apprentice education where children work alongside professional actors, all sharing in the common goal of excellence. Our best work can be experienced on at least three distinct levels: for the young child there is simply a great story and lots of sensory pleasure; the older child enjoys more of the subtleties in the language and in the art form; adults appreciate the more sophisticated humor or irony and see the symbolism that moves beyond the immediate story itself to the world at large. A dedicated ensemble of actors, directors and designers produce a mainstage season, three touring productions, an experimental lab studio and teach in an intensive summer theatre academy that brings children into direct working contact with the creative process. We attempt to educate young audiences through artistic observations of the human condition, while trying to heighten the quality of theatre experiences for children.
—*Bradley D. Anderson*

PRODUCTIONS 1987–88

The Voyage of Sinbad the Sailor, Curt L. Tofteland; (D) Alan Keith Smith; (S) James E. Lyden; (C) Mark Hughes; (L) Alan Keith Smith and James E. Lyden
The Starcleaner Reunion: Tales of Wonder, book: Bradley D. Anderson; music and lyrics: Lori Loree; (D) Bradley D. Anderson; (S) James E. Lyden; (C) Jeff Kinard; (L) Alan Keith Smith
Beauty and the Beast, book and lyrics: Marc French; music: Robert F. Clark; (D) Bradley D. Anderson; (S) Alan Keith Smith; (C) Jeff Kinard; (L) James E. Lyden
The Three Little Pigs and Three Billy Goats Gruff, the acting company; (D) Bradley D. Anderson; (S) James E. Lyden; (C) Burton Curtis and Jeff Kinard; (L) Alan Keith Smith
Lord of the Flies, adapt: Thomas W. Olson, from William Golding; (D) Bradley D. Anderson; (S) James E. Lyden; (C) Jeff Kinard; (L) Alan Keith Smith
Tales of a Fourth Grade Nothing, adapt: Bruce Mason, from Judy Blume; (D) Ron MacIntyre-Fender; (S) James E. Lyden; (C) Jeff Kinard; (L) Alan Keith Smith

PRODUCTIONS 1988–89

Charlotte's Web, adapt: Joseph Robinette, from E.B. White; (D) Bradley D. Anderson; (S) Alan Keith Smith; (C) Jeff Kinard and Mark Hughes; (L) James E. Lyden
Dracula, adapt: Thomas W. Olson, from Bram Stoker; (D) Bradley D. Anderson; (S) James E. Lyden; (C) Jeff Kinard; (L) Alan Keith Smith
Cinderella, adapt: John B. Davidson; add'l material: company (D) Alan Keith Smith; (S) James E. Lyden; (C) Jeff Kinard; (L) Daniel Grace
The Astonishing World of Benjamin Franklin, Bradley D. Anderson and Phyllis Finton Anderson; music and add'l lyrics: Lori Loree; (D) Bradley D. Anderson; (S) Alan Keith Smith; (C) Jeff Kinard; (L) James E. Lyden
Jack and the Beanstalk, adapt: Burton Curtis and Rich Gerdes; (D) Bradley D. Anderson; (S) Burton Curtis and Rich Gerdes; (C) Burton Curtis and Rich Gerdes; (L) James E. Lyden
Robin Hood of Sherwood Forest, adapt: Marc French; (D) Alan Keith Smith; (S) Alan Keith Smith; (C) Jeff Kinard; (L) James E. Lyden

The Arkansas Arts Center Children's Theatre. Burton Curtis and Jay Johnston in *Tales of Wonder*. Photo: Art Meripool.

Arkansas Repertory Theatre

CLIFF FANNIN BAKER
Producing Artistic Director

712 East 11th St.
Little Rock, AR 72202
(501) 372-0715 (bus.)
(501) 378-0405 (b.o.)

FOUNDED 1976
Cliff Fannin Baker

SEASON
Jan.-Dec.

FACILITIES
MainStage Theatre
Seating Capacity: 354
Stage: proscenium

SecondStage Theatre
Seating Capacity: 99
Stage: flexible

CONTRACTS
AEA letter or agreement

Arkansas Rep's 14th season represents the diversity of our audiences and our outreach goals, while exhibiting a prevailing interest in contemporary scripts and American playwrights. Our mission at The Rep has remained a constant: to provoke, educate and entertain our audiences while providing meaningful experiences for the professional artistic company. The Rep is still best described as "emerging." We moved into a new performing arts center while entering the third year on a new letter of agreement with Actors' Equity Association. Our subscription base has doubled in the past few years, our company is growing and our programming is challenging both artists and audiences. We are proud of the theatre's regional reputation, national support and local impact. Our programs include an eight-play mainstage season, a three-play second stage season, a lunchtime performance series, play readings and "Talkbacks," a professional intern program, a 12-year-old arts-in-education program and a six-state regional tour.
—*Cliff Fannin Baker*

PRODUCTIONS 1987–88

Marry Me a Little, book: Craig Lucas and Norman Renee; music and lyrics: Stephen Sondheim; (D) Terry Sneed; (S) Mike Nichols; (C) Mark Hughes; (L) Robert A. Jones
Biloxi Blues, Neil Simon; (D) John Vreeke; (S) Mike Nichols; (C) Mark Hughes; (L) Kathy Gray
Kiss of the Spider Woman, Manuel Puig; trans: Allan Baker; (D) Cliff Fannin Baker; (S) Mike Nichols; (C) Mark Hughes; (L) Kathy Gray
The Club, Eve Merriam; (D) John Vreeke; (S) Mike Nichols; (C) Mark Hughes; (L) Kathy Gray
Pageant, book: Cliff Fannin Baker, Jack Heifner, Romulus Linney, Kent R. Brown, Hank Bates and Mary Rhode; music and lyrics: Michael Rice; (D) Cliff Fannin Baker; (S) Mike Nichols; (C) Mark Hughes; (L) Kathy Gray
The Mousetrap, Agatha Christie; (D) Terry Sneed; (S) Mike Nichols; (C) Mark Hughes; (L) Robert A. Jones
Educating Rita, Willy Russell; (D) John Vreeke; (S) Charles Carr; (C) Don Bolinger; (L) Kathy Gray
The Foreigner, Larry Shue; (D) Cliff Fannin Baker; (S) Mike Nichols; (C) Mark Hughes; (L) Kathy Gray
Talking With . . ., Jane Martin; (D) Cathy Crowell Sawyer; (S) Charles Carr; (C) Mark Hughes; (L) Kathy Gray
Tomfoolery, adapt: Cameron Mackintosh and Robin Raybook; music and lyrics: Tom Lehrer; (D) Cliff Fannin Baker; (S) Charles Carr; (C) Mark Hughes; (L) Kathy Gray

PRODUCTIONS 1988–89

Steel Magnolias, Robert Harling; (D) Cathy Crowell Sawyer; (S) Mike Nichols; (C) Mark Hughes; (L) Robert A. Jones
The Mystery of Edwin Drood, book adapt, music and lyrics: Rupert Holmes; (D) Cliff Fannin Baker; (S) Keith Belli; (C) Mark Hughes; (L) Kathy Gray
A Walk in the Woods, Lee Blessing; (D) Pat Brown; (S) Mike Nichols; (C) Mark Hughes; (L) Kathy Gray
The Golden Shadows Old West Museum, adapt: Larry L. King, from Michael Blackman; (D) Cliff Fannin Baker; (S) Mike Nichols; (C) Mark Hughes; (L) Kathy Gray
On the Verge or The Geography of Yearning, Eric Overmyer; (D) Veronica Brady; (S) Mike Nichols; (C) Mark Hughes; (L) Kathy Gray
Romeo and Juliet, William Shakespeare; (D) John Vreeke; (S) Mike Nichols; (C) Huang Qizhi; (L) Kathy Gray
Greater Tuna, Jaston Williams, Joe Sears and Ed Howard; (D) Cliff Fannin Baker; (S) Mike Nichols; (C) Mark Hughes; (L) Robert A. Jones
Noises Off, Michael Frayn; (D) Terry Sneed; (S) Nels Anderson; (C) Mark Hughes; (L) Robert A. Jones
The Nerd, Larry Shue; (D) Mark DeMichele; (S) Mike Nichols; (C) Don Bolinger; (L) Robert A. Jones
Danny and the Deep Blue Sea, John Patrick Shanley; (D) Mark DeMichele; (S) Charles Carr; (C) Don Bolinger; (L) Kathy Gray
The Early Girl, Caroline Kava; (D) Debbie Weber; (S) Charles Carr; (C) Mark Hughes; (L) Kathy Gray
Sister Mary Ignatius Explains It All for You, Christopher Durang; (D) Mark DeMichele; (S) Charles Carr; (C) Mark Hughes; (L) Kathy Gray
L'Histoire du Soldat, adapt: Earl McCarroll, Jr., from C.F. Ramuz; music: Igor Stravinsky; (D) Cliff Fannin Baker; (S) Mike Nichols; (C) Mark Hughes; (L) Kathy Gray

Arkansas Reperatory Theatre. Jean Lind and Macon McCalman in *The Golden Shadows Old West Museum*. Photo: Barry Arthur.

Asolo Center for the Performing Arts

JOHN ULMER
Artistic Director

LEE WARNER
Executive Director

5555 N. Tamaimi Trail
Sarasota, FL 34243
(813) 351-9010 (bus.)
(813) 351-8000 (b.o.)

FOUNDED 1960
Eberle Thomas, Robert Strane, Richard G. Fallon, Arthur Dorland

SEASON
Dec.-July

FACILITIES
Mainstage
Seating Capacity: 499
Stage: proscenium

Second Stage
Seating Capacity: 175
Stage: flexible

Bette Oliver Theatre
Seating Capacity: 138
Stage: flexible

FINANCES
Sept. 1, 1988-Aug. 31, 1989
Expenses: $3,300,000

CONTRACTS
LORT (C)

The Asolo Center for the Performing Arts is the new home to the Asolo Theatre Company as well as to M.F.A. conservatories in actor training, and film and television, administered by Florida State University. The Asolo is a service institution producing its own local seasons, as well as professional school tours and a national tour of one mainstage offering. Though located in a non-metropolitan area, Asolo is a major theatre attraction for the state of Florida, and so presents an eclectic selection of plays with broad audience appeal. As we are a subsidized theatre, our season must add up to theatre art. We strive for a quality of acting and directing that brings the plays to stage life by detailing organic human behavior in all its dazzling variety.
—*John Ulmer*

PRODUCTIONS 1987–88

Nunsense, Dan Goggin; (D) John Ulmer; (S) Keven Lock; (C) Catherine King; (L) Martin Petlock
First Time Anywhere!, Leo B. Meyer; (D) John Ulmer; (S) Leo B. Meyer; (C) Christina Weppner; (L) Pat Simmons
Philadelphia, Here I Come!, Brian Friel; (D) Jamie Brown; (S) Holmes Easley; (C) Ainslie G. Brumeau; (L) Martin Petlock
Mass Appeal, Bill C. Davis; (D) Garry Allan Breul; (S) Keven Lock; (C) Vicki S. Holden; (L) Tenna Matthews
The Heiress, Ruth Goetz and Augustus Goetz; (D) Tony Tanner; (S) Bennet Averyt; (C) Ainslie G. Bruneau; (L) Martin Petlock
Of Mice and Men, John Steinbeck; (D) John Ulmer; (S) John Ezell; (C) Ainslie G. Bruneau; (L) Martin Petlock
Ladies in Retirement, Edward Percy and Reginald Denhan; (D) Jamie Brown; (S) Bennet Averyt; (C) Ainslie G. Bruneau; (L) Martin Petlock
Pump Boys and Dinettes, John Foley, Mark Hardwick, Debra Monk, Cass Morgan, John Schimmel and Jim Wann; (D) Robert Miller; (S) Jeffrey Dean; (C) Ainslie G. Bruneau; (L) Joseph Oshry and Martin Petlock
I'm Not Rappaport, Herb Gardner; (D) Jamie Brown; (S) Keven Lock; (C) Ainslie G. Bruneau; (L) Joseph Oshry
Berlin to Broadway with Kurt Weill, book: Gene Lerner; music: Kurt Weill; (D) John Ulmer; (S) Ken Kurtz; (C) Vicki S. Holden; (L) Martin Petlock
Why Can't You Be Him?, John Ford Noonan; (D) John Gulley; (S) Rick Cannon; (C) Vicki S. Holden; (L) Martin Petlock

Asolo Theatre Company. Kimberly King, Mary Fogarty and Candace Dian Leverett in *Eleemosynary*. Photo: Alan Ulmer.

PRODUCTIONS 1988–89

Side by Side by Sondheim, lyrics and music: Stephen Sondheim; music: Leonard Bernstein, Mary Rodgers, Richard Rogers and Jule Styne; (D) Rob Marshall; (S) Jeffrey W. Dean; (C) Ainslie G. Bruneau; (L) Martin Petlock
Towards Zero, Agatha Christie; (D) John Gulley; (S) Keven Lock; (C) Ainslie G. Bruneau; (L) Martin Petlock and Tenna Matthews
The Boys Next Door, Tom Griffin; (D) John Ulmer; (S) Bennet Averyt; (C) Ainslie G. Bruneau; (L) Martin Petlock
As You Like It, William Shakespeare; (D) John Gulley; (S) Bennet Averyt; (C) Ainslie G. Bruneau; (L) Martin Petlock
Burn This, Lanford Wilson; (D) Pat Brown; (S) Bennet Averyt; (C) Ainslie G. Bruneau; (L) Martin Petlock
Medea, adapt: Robinson Jeffers, from Euripides; (D) John Ulmer; (S) Keith Anderson; (C) Howard Tsvi Kaplan; (L) Martin Petlock
Frankie and Johnny in the Clair de Lune, Terrence McNally; (D) John Gulley; (S) Jeffrey W. Dean; (C) Howard Tsvi Kaplan; (L) Martin Petlock
Eleemosynary, Lee Blessing; (D) Jamie Brown; (S) Keven Lock; (C) Howard Tsvi Kaplan; (L) Martin Petlock
Cyrano de Bergerac, Edmond Rostand; (D) John Ulmer; (S) Keven Lock; (C) Howard Tsvi Kaplan; (L) Martin Petlock
Quarry, Ronald Bazarini; (D) Garry Allan Breul; (S) Rick Cannon; (C) Howard Tsvi Kaplan; (L) Martin Petlock and Rick Cannon
Driving Around the House, Patrick Smith; (D) John Gulley; (S) Rick Cannon; (C) Howard Tsvi Kaplan; (L) Martin Petlock and Rick Cannon

A Traveling Jewish Theatre

COREY FISCHER
Funding Member
Co-Artistic Director

NANCY LEVIDOW
Managing Director

Box 421985
San Francisco, CA 94142
(415) 861-4880

FOUNDED 1978
Naomi Newman, Albert Greenberg, Corey Fischer

SEASON
variable

FACILITIES
Blake Street Hawkeyes
Seating Capacity: 70
Stage: flexible

New Performance Gallery
Seating Capacity: 200
Stage: flexible

Tiffany Theatre
Seating Capacity: 99
Stage: proscenium

Potrero Hill Neighborhood Theatre
Seating Capacity: 125
Stage: proscenium

FINANCES
July 1, 1988-June 30, 1989
Expenses: $300,000

CONTRACTS
AEA special contract

A Traveling Jewish Theatre was born out of a desire to create a contemporary theatre that would give form to streams of visionary experience that run through Jewish history, culture and imagination. Since its founding, the company has created eight original works whose concerns have included the legends of the Hasidim, the necessity of reclaiming the feminine, the world of the Yiddish poets, images of God, the nature of healing, assimilation, isolation, exile, Germany, Israel and America. We have used music, masks, puppets, bare stages, naked faces, English, Yiddish, Hebrew, Ladino, silence and sound in various combinations as tools to share what we feel needs to be shared. Now celebrating our 10th anniversary season, we have performed in Oslo, New York, Berlin, Chicago, Jerusalem and more than 60 other cities in the United States, Canada, Europe and Israel.
—*Corey Fischer*

PRODUCTIONS 1987–88

The Last Yiddish Poet, company-developed; (D) Naomi Newman; (C) Jane Pollack; (L) Jim Quinn
Dance of Exile, company-developed; (D) Naomi Newman; (S) Jim Quinn; (C) Jane Pollack; (L) Jim Quinn
Berlin, Jerusalem and the Moon, company-developed; (D) Michael Posnick; (S) David Brune; (C) Eliza Chugg; (L) David Brune
Snake Talk: Urgent Messages from the Mother, Naomi Newman; (D) Martha Boesing; (S) David Brune; (L) David Brune

PRODUCTIONS 1988–89

Snake Talk: Urgent Messages from the Mother, Naomi Newman; (D) Martha Boesing; (S) David Brune; (L) Joelle Serban
Dybbuk, S. Ansky; Bruce Meyers; (D) Mark Samuels; (S) Mark Samuels; (C) Eliza Chugg; (L) Jim Quinn
Heart of the World, Albert Greenberg, Helen Stoltzfus and Martha Boesing; (D) Martha Boesing; (S) Alan Droyan and Bruce Hasson; (C) Michelle Jacobs; (L) Jim Quinn

Attic Theatre

LAVINIA MOYER
Artistic Director

TERRANCE S. HILL
Managing Director

Box 02457
Detroit, MI 48202
(313) 875-8285 (bus.)
(313) 875-8284 (b.o.)

A Travelling Jewish Theatre. Naomi Newman in *Snake Talk: Urgent Messages From the Mother*. Photo: Valerie Haimowitz.

Attic Theatre. Loretta Higgins, Roy Dennison and Henry Hoffman in *A Moon for the Misbegotten*. Photo: Bobbie Hazeltine.

FOUNDED 1975
Nancy Shayne, Lavinia Moyer, James Moran, Herbert Ferrer, Divina Cook, Curtis Armstrong

SEASON
Sept.-July

FACILITIES
New Center Theatre
Seating Capacity: 299
Stage: proscenium

FINANCES
Sept. 1, 1988-Aug. 31, 1989
Expenses: $815,000

CONTRACTS
AEA SPT

We are dedicated to providing artists an environment that produces the highest professional standards. We offer contemporary American works, regional and world premieres, and the classics—focusing on themes and issues that "speak" to the region. Our special educational and outreach programs make a strong impact on this community: artist residencies in the schools, student matinees with study guides and post-performance discussions, internships for gifted students and in-service teacher training; a senior-citizen touring company that serves both old and young; master classes and workshops for the ensemble and the public; and American Sign Language-interpreted performances for the hearing-impaired. Our Writers' Unit, which serves playwrights in developing new theatre pieces, was recently recognized by a Rockefeller Foundation playwright fellowship grant.

Our artistic rationale is based on a professionally trained ensemble, engaging both audience and artist in theatre that is challenging, innovative and compelling.
—*Lavinia Moyer*

PRODUCTIONS 1987–88

Dogman's Last Stand, Rick Cleveland; (D) Lavinia Moyer; (S) Gary Decker; (C) Anne Saunders; (L) Gary Decker
The Lusty and Comical History of Tom Jones, adapt: John Morrison, from Henry Fielding; (D) Ronald Martell; (S) Eric M. Johnson; (C) Heidi Hollman; (L) Kendall A. Smith
Holiday Cabaret: Expectations, book: Daniel Yurgaitis; lyrics: Douglas Braverman; (D) Daniel Yurgaitis; (S) Sam Bagarella; (C) Anne Saunders; (L) Reid Downey
Tamer of Horses, William Mastrosimone; (D) Von H. Washington; (S) Rolfe Bergsman; (C) Mary Lou Olszewski; (L) Paul Epton
Knock Knock, Jules Feiffer; (D) Wayne David Parker; (S) Eric M. Johnson; (C) Anne Saunders; (L) Paul Epton
Learn to Fall, James Burnstein; (D) Stephen Rothman; (S) Peter Harrison; (C) Peter Harrison; (L) Paul Brohan
Lady Day at Emerson's Bar and Grill, Lanie Robertson; (D) Lavinia Moyer; (S) Melinda Pacha; (C) Melinda Pacha; (L) Reid Downey

PRODUCTIONS 1988–89

Woody Guthrie's American Song, adapt: Peter Glazer, from Woody Guthrie; (D) Peter Glazer; (S) Philipp Jung; (C) Deborah Shaw; (L) David Noling
Ten November, Steven Dietz; (D) Lavinia Moyer; (S) Eric M. Johnson; (C) Catherine Woerner; (L) Paul Epton
The Gift of the Magi, adapt., music and lyrics: Peter Eckstrom; (D) Gordon Reinhart; (S) Sam Bagarella; (C) Laurie Danforth; (L) Kendell A. Smith
Bopha, Percy Mtwa; (D) Von H. Washington; (S) Felix E. Cochren; (C) Felix E. Cochren; (L) Paul Epton
Measure for Measure, William Shakespeare; (D) Ronald Martell; (S) Eric M. Johnson; (C) Sharon Sprague; (L) Reid Downey
A Moon for the Misbegotten, Eugene O'Neill; (D) Anthony Schmitt; (S) Sam Bagarella; (C) Catherine M. Woerner; (L) Paul Epton
House of Correction, Norman Lock; (D) David Regal; (S) Melinda Pacha; (C) Catherine M. Woerner; (L) Paul Epton

The Back Alley Theatre

ALLAN MILLER
LAURA ZUCKER
Producing Directors

15231 Burbank Blvd.
Van Nuys, CA 91411-3590
(818) 780-2240 (bus.)

FOUNDED 1979
Laura Zucker, Allan Miller

SEASON
Jan.-Dec.

FACILITIES
Seating Capacity: 93
Stage: proscenium

FINANCES
Jan. 1, 1988-Dec. 31, 1988
Expenses: $353,162

CONTRACTS
AEA 99-seat Theatre Plan and SPT

PRODUCTIONS 1987–88

Sand Mountain, Romulus Linney; (D) John Schuck; (S) Jack Forrestel; (C) Hilary Sloane; (L) Ken Lennon
Jacques Brel Is Alive and Well and Living in Paris, adapt: Eric Blau and Mort Schuman; music and lyrics: Jacques Brel; (D) Allan Miller; (S) Rich Rose; (C) Sylvia Moss; (L) Leslie Rose
The Early Girl, Caroline Kava; (D) Allan Miller; (S) Derek McLane; (C) Meg Gilbert; (L) Ken Lennon
What's Wrong with this Picture?, Donald Margulies; (D) Stuart Damon; (S) Don Gruber; (C) Bob Miller; (L) Lawrence Oberman

PRODUCTIONS 1988–89

Amazing Grace, Sandra Deer; (D) Allan Miller; (S) Don Gruber; (C) Cathy Crane; (L) Lawrence Oberman
Bittersuite, Elliot Weiss and Michael Champagne; (D) Rick Roemer; (S) Don Gruber; (L) Lawrence Oberman
A Walk on the Wild Side, adapt: Will Holt, from Nelson Algren; (D) Allan Miller and Patricia Birch; (S) Don Gruber; (C) Bob

The Back Alley Theatre. Rachel Babcock, Barry Gordon and Ronny Cox in *The Voice of the Prairie*. Photo: Ed Krugir.

Miller; (L) Lawrence Oberman
The Fox, adapt: Allan Miller, from D.H. Lawrence; (D) Allan Miller; (S) Rich Rose; (C) Hilary Sloane; (L) Lawrence Oberman
The Voice of the Prairie, John Olive; (D) Bob Clark; (S) Don Gruber; (C) Bob Miller; (L) Lawrence Oberman
Gloria Duplex: An Erotic Worship Service for Theatre, Rebecca Wells; (D) Teri Ralston; (S) Deborah Raymond and Dorian Vernacchio; (C) Scott Lane; (L) Lawrence Oberman

Barter Theatre

REX PARTINGTON
Artistic Director/Producer

Box 867
Abingdon, VA 24210
(703) 628-2281 (bus.)
(703) 628-3991 (b.o.)

FOUNDED 1933
Robert Porterfield

SEASON
Apr.-Oct.

FACILITIES
Barter Theatre
Seating Capacity: 394
Stage: proscenium

Barter Playhouse
Seating Capacity: 150
Stage: thrust

FINANCES
Nov. 1, 1987-Oct. 31, 1988
Expenses: $855,741

CONTRACTS
LORT (D)

Barter is the oldest, longest-running professional repertory theatre in the U.S. It is our desire that the plays we produce, in addition to entertaining our patrons, will give them something to think about. We do not intend that each play must impart a profound message; but we do feel the productions we present, whether they are classical or contemporary or brand new, should be provocative. They should reflect and comment on the times and on the human race. As a pioneer of regional theatre, we are dedicated to quality—whether it's on our main-stage Barter Theatre, in the Playhouse, on our Youth Stage, or in our touring productions. Our diversified audiences can expect to see the finest in classical and contemporary comedy and drama as well as worthwhile new plays.
—*Rex Partington*

PRODUCTIONS 1987–88

Relatively Speaking, Alan Ayckbourn; (D) Ken Costigan; (S) Daniel Ettinger; (C) Lisa Micheels; (L) Al Oster
The Prince and the Pauper, adapt: Richard Kinter, from Mark Twain; (D) Richard Kinter; (S) Russ Bralley; (C) Kathryn K. Conrad; (L) Timothy M. Chew
Dear Liar, adapt: Jerome Kilty, from Richard Kinter; (D) Geoffrey Hitch; (S) M. Lynne Allen; (C) Cyndi Orr; (L) Timothy M. Chew
Steel Magnolias, Robert Harling; (D) Frank Lowe; (S) Daniel Gray; (C) Karen Brewster; (L) Timothy M. Chew
Under Milk Wood, Dylan Thomas; (D) Richard Major; (S) Christopher W. Carter; (C) Karen Brewster; (L) Timothy M. Chew
Twelfth Night, William Shakespeare; (D) Ken Costigan; (S) Daniel Ettinger; (C) Cyndi Orr; (L) Timothy M. Chew
Jacques Brel Is Alive and Well and Living in Paris, adapt: Eric Blau and Mort Shuman; music and lyrics: Jacques Brel; (D) William Van Keyser; (S) Gary Aday; (C) Karen Brewster; (L) Timothy M. Chew
Greater Tuna, Jaston Williams, Joe Sears and Ed Howard; (D) Trip Plymale; (S) M. Lynne Allen; (C) Karen Brewster; (L) Timothy M. Chew
Special Occasions, Bernard Slade (D) Ken Costigan; (S) M. Lynne Allen; (C) Cyndi Orr; (L) Timothy M. Chew
You Never Can Tell, George Bernard Shaw; (D) Frank Lowe; (S) Daniel Ettinger; (C) Cyndi Orr; (L) Timothy M. Chew
The Unexpected Guest, Agatha Christie; (D) Ken Costigan; (S) Daniel Ettinger; (C) Cyndi Orr; (L) Timothy M. Chew

PRODUCTIONS 1988–89

Blithe Spirit, Noel Coward; (D) Ken Costigan; (S) Daniel Ettinger; (C) Karen Brewster; (L) Tony Partington
Tom Sawyer, adapt: Richard Kinter, from Mark Twain; (D) Richard Kinter; (S) Christopher Carter; (C) Pamela Hale; (L) Tony Partington
Noises Off, Michael Frayn; (D) Geoffrey Hitch; (S) Daniel Ettinger; (C) Karen Brewster; (L) Tony Partington
Voices of the Prairie, John Olive; (D) Ken Costigan; (S) Rex Partington; (C) Pamela Hale; (L) Tony Partington
Taking Steps, Alan Ayckbourn; (D) Ken Costigan; (S) Dan Gray; (C) Pamela Hale; (L) Tony Partington
Offstage Voices, Stephanie Correa; (D) Joe Warik; (S) Daniel Ettinger; (C) Karen Brewster; (L) Tony Partington
Wait Until Dark, Frederick Knott; (D) Ken Costigan; (S) Daniel Ettinger; (C) Pamela Hale; (L) Tony Partington
Don Juan In Hell, George Bernard Shaw; (D) Geoffrey Hitch; (C) Pamela Hale; (L) Tony Partington
La Ronde, Arthur Schnitzler; (D) Richard Major; (C) Karen Brewster; (L) Tony Partington
Berlin To Broadway with Kurt Weill, adapt: Gene Lerner; music: Kurt Weill; (D) William Van Keyser; (S) Rex Partington; (C) Pamela Hale; (L) Tony Partington

Barter Theatre. Richard Bowden and Katherine Carlson in *Dear Liar*.

The Bathhouse Theatre

ARNE ZASLOVE
Artistic Director

MARY-CLAIRE BURKE
Producing Director

7312 West Greenlake Drive, N.
Seattle, WA 98103
(206) 524-3608 (bus.)
(206) 524-9108 (b.o.)

FOUNDED 1980
Arne Zaslove, Mary-Claire Burke

SEASON
Jan.-Dec.

THE BATHHOUSE THEATRE

The Bathouse Theatre. G. Valmont Thomas and Timothy Threlfall in The Comedy of Errors. *Photo: Fred Andrews.*

FACILITIES
Seating Capacity: 140
Stage: thrust

FINANCES
Jan. 1, 1988-Dec. 31, 1988
Expenses: $683,607

CONTRACTS
AEA SPT

Maintaining a permanent resident theatre company with high artistic standards since 1980 has taken some doing—especially given the Bathhouse's 140-seat house and earned income running from 76 to 80 percent of total revenues. Year-round operation has been an economic necessity, as well as a tremendous professional challenge for us. Extensive touring and the mounting of major productions at large downtown theatres tax our resources but, by working together as a team over the years, our core company has developed remarkable strength and versatility. The company system also adds an extra element to play selection: I ask myself not only "Does this script show real dramatic value?" and "Will it appeal to our audience?" but also "How will it stretch the particular talents of individual company members?" We at the Bathhouse take greatest pride in our company's ability to develop new original material such as *The Big Broadcast*, tackle rarely produced scripts like Priestley's *Johnson over Jordan* and create distinctive Shakespeare interpretations.
—*Arne Zaslove*

PRODUCTIONS 1987–88

The Three Sisters, Anton Chekhov; trans: Jennie Covan; (D) Martha Boesing; (S) Patti Henry; (C) Mark Mitchell and Shauna Frazier; (L) Judy Wolcott
The Playboy of the Western World, John Millington Synge; (D) Arne Zaslove; (S) Patti Henry; (C) Shauna Frazer; (L) Judy Wolcott
Little Murders, Jules Feiffer; (D) Ted D'Arms; (S) Lynn Graves; (C) Mark Mitchell; (L) Judy Wolcott
Shall We Dance?, company-developed; (D) Daniel Levans; (S) Shelley Henze Schermer; (C) Mark Mitchell and Shauna Frazier; (L) Judy Wolcott
The Comedy of Errors, William Shakespeare; (D) Arne Zaslove; (S) Greg Carr; (C) Bary Allen Odom; (L) Judy Wolcott
When the Wind Blows, Raymond Briggs; (D) Caroline Eves; (S) Patti Henry; (C) Shauna Frazier; (L) Judy Wolcott
The Best of the Big Broadcast, company-developed; (D) Allen Galli; (S) S.H. Schermer; (C) Shauna Frazier; (L) Judy Wolcott

PRODUCTIONS 1988–89

Much Ado about Nothing, William Shakespeare; (D) Michael Addison; (S) S.H. Schermer; (C) Nancy Jo Smith; (L) Jody Briggs
Twelfth Night, William Shakespeare; (D) Arne Zaslove; (S) S. H. Schermer; (C) Sarah Campbell; (L) Judy Wolcott
The Contrast, Royall Tyler; (D) Richard Edwards; (S) Dee Torrey; (C) Sarah Campbell; (L) Judy Wolcott
Say It with Music, company-developed; (D) James Lortz; (S) S.H. Schermer; (C) Sarah Campbell; (L) Judy Wolcott
U.S.A., Paul Shyre and John Dos Passos; (S) Patti Henry; (C) Sarah Campbell; (L) Judy Wolcott
Anna Christie, Eugene O'Neill; (D) Marjorie Nelson; (S) Patti Henry; (C) Sarah Campbell; (L) Judy Wolcott

Berkeley Repertory Theatre

SHARON OTT
Artistic Director

MITZI SALES
Managing Director

ANTHONY TACCONE
Associate Artistic Director

2025 Addison St.
Berkeley, CA 94704
(415) 841-6108 (bus.)
(415) 845-4700 (b.o.)

FOUNDED 1968
Michael W. Leibert

SEASON
Sept.-July

FACILITIES
Mark Taper Mainstage
Seating Capacity: 401
Stage: thrust

Addison Stage
Seating Capacity: 150
Stage: flexible

FINANCES
Sept. 1, 1988-Aug. 31, 1989
Expenses: $3,200,000

CONTRACTS
LORT (B)

Berkeley Repertory Theatre is dedicated to an ensemble of first-rate artists—including actors, playwrights, directors, artisans and designers. We intend the theatre to be a place where plays are created not just produced, communicating a distinct attitude about the world

Berkeley Repertory Theatre. Robin Goodrin Nordli in What the Butler Saw. *Photo: Ken Friedman.*

of the play and about the world around us. Our repertoire includes plays chosen from the major classical and contemporary dramatic literatures, specifically works that emphasize the cultural richness that makes American art so dynamic and vital. BRT's programming is expanding from the main stage to more flexible local venues in, our concurrent Parallel Season, focusing on new plays, adaptations from other sources, collaborations, multimedia pieces and commissioned works. Young artists and artisans are trained through Company Too, an affiliated group of non-Equity actors, and in our production internship program. Each spring we tour two productions to Bay Area schools.
—Sharon Ott

PRODUCTIONS 1987–88

Ah, Wilderness, Eugene O'Neill; (D) Ron Lagomarsino; (S) Vicki Smith; (C) Deborah M. Dryden; (L) Peter Maradudin
Long Day's Journey into Night, Eugene O'Neill; (D) Jackson Phippin; (S) Vicki Smith; (C) Deborah M. Dryden; (L) Peter Maradudin
The Rivals, Richard Brinsley Sheridan; (D) Anthony Taccone; (S) Sam Kirkpatrick; (C) Sam Kirkpatrick; (L) Dan Kotlowitz
The Road to Mecca, Athol Fugard; (D) Sharon Ott; (S) Kate Edmunds; (C) Susan Hilferty; (L) Dennis Parichy
What the Butler Saw, Joe Orton; (D) Albert Takazauckas; (S) Carey Wong; (C) Beaver D. Bauer; (L) Kurt Landisman
The Tale of Lear, adapt: Tadashi Suzuki, from William Shakespeare; (D) Tadashi Suzuki; (S) Arden Fingerhut; (C) Tadashi Suzuki; (L) Arden Fingerhut
The Hairy Ape, Eugene O'Neill; (D) George Ferencz; (S) George Ferencz; (C) Sally J. Lesser; (L) Peter Maradudin
Yankee Dawg You Die, Philip Kan Gotanda; (D) Sharon Ott; (S) Kent Dorsey; (C) Lydia Tanji; (L) Kent Dorsey

PRODUCTIONS 1988–89

Hedda Gabler, Henrik Ibsen; trans: Gerry Bamman and Irene B. Berman; (D) M. Burke Walker; (S) John Bonnard Wilson; (C) Robert Blackman; (L) Peter Maradudin
Prelude to a Kiss, Craig Lucas; (D) Norman Rene; (S) Loy Arcenas; (C) Walker Hicklin; (L) Debra J. Kletter
Waiting for Godot, Samuel Beckett; (D) Anthony Taccone; (S) Kate Edmunds; (C) Lydia Tanji; (L) Peter A. Kaczorowski
The Misanthrope, Moliere; trans: Richard Wilbur; (D) Irene Lewis; (S) Kate Edmunds; (C) Catherine Zuber; (L) Pat Collins
A View from the Bridge, Arthur Miller; (D) Richard Seyd; (S) Ralph Funicello; (C) Cathleen Edwards; (L) Peter Maradudin
Serious Money, Caryl Churchill; (D) Anthony Taccone and Sharon Ott; (S) Kent Dorsey; (C) Dunya Ramicova; (L) Peter Maradudin
In Perpetuity Throughout the Universe, Eric Overmyer; (D) Sharon Ott; (S) Kent Dorsey; (C) Beaver D. Bauer; (L) Kent Dorsey
The Stick Wife, Darrah Cloud; (D) Anthony Taccone; (S) Karen Gjelsteen; (C) Cathleen Edwards; (L) Robert Wierzel

Berkeley Shakespeare Festival

MICHAEL ADDISON
Artistic Director

SUSAN G. DUNCAN
Managing Director

Box 969
Berkeley, CA 94701
(415) 548-3422 (bus.)
(415) 525-8844 (b.o.)

FOUNDED 1974
Mikel Clifford, Bay Area actors

SEASON
July-Nov.

FACILITIES
John Hinkel Park (outdoor)
Seating Capacity: 350
Stage: thrust

Julia Morgan Theatre
Seating Capacity: 380
Stage: thrust

Siesta Valley Amphitheatre
Seating Capacity: 450
Stage: thrust

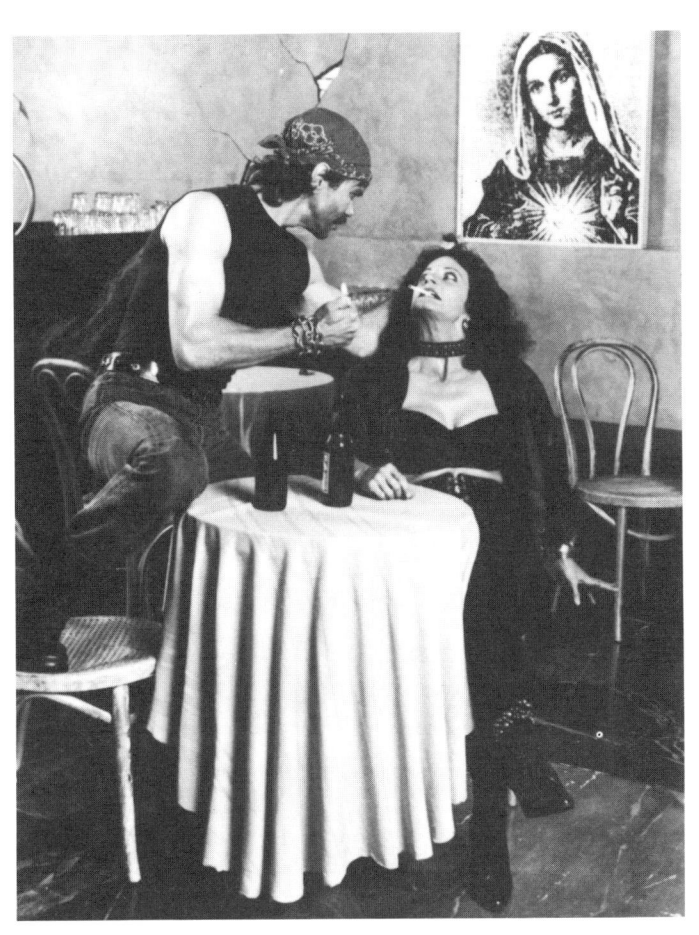

Berkeley Shakespeare Festival. Charles Shaw Robinson and Lura Dolas in *The Taming of the Shrew*. Photo: David Allen.

FINANCES
Jan. 1, 1988-Dec. 31, 1988
Expenses: $800,000

CONTRACTS
LORT (D)

The Berkeley Shakespeare Festival completes its 16th season with a renewed commitment to productions that are conceived in vividly contemporary terms but rooted in a rigorous exploration of Shakespeare's texts and the Renaissance milieu. The Festival continues to tap into the artistic energies of a core of artists who have been at the center of the work for the past decade, but also seeks out new artists each season to reinvigorate the process. The expanded season now includes three productions in repertory in an outdoor amphitheatre, a forth in the handsomely renovated Julia Morgan Theatre, and a fall tour throughout California and the West. The rigors of playing in repertory, performing in both outdoor and indoor spaces, and touring extensively all demand particularly resilient artists who are creatively adaptive to the shifting realities of the moment. We embrace this as a theatre company, convinced that our artistic reflexes and vision are sharpened by our need to maintain one constant: direct and immediate contact with our audience.
—Michael Addison

PRODUCTIONS 1987–88

The Comedy of Errors, William Shakespeare; (D) Ken Grantham; (S) Gene Angell and Ron Pratt; (C) Kate Irvine; (L) Theodore M. Dolas
Julius Caesar, William Shakespeare; (D) Oskar Eustis; (S) Victoria Petrovich; (C) Jeff Struckman; (L) Scott Stewart
Timon of Athens, William Shakespeare; (D) Julian Lopez-Morillas; (S) Michael Cook; (C) Marie Chesley; (L) T.M. Dolas
Troilus and Cressida, William Shakespeare; (D) Michael Addison; (S) Eric Sinkkonin; (C) Nancy Jo Smith; (L) T.M. Dolas

PRODUCTIONS 1988–89

The Taming of the Shrew, William Shakespeare; (D) Peggy Shannon; (S) Joel Fontaine; (C) Nancy Jo Smith; (L) Kurt Landisman
Romeo and Juliet, William Shakespeare; (D) Julian Lopez-Morillas; (S) Eric Sinkkonin; (C) Eliza Chugg; (L) Kurt Landisman
Measure for Measure, William Shakespeare; (D) Richard E.T. White; (S) Barbara Mesney; (C) Barbara Bush; (L) Kurt Landisman
Much Ado About Nothing, William Shakespeare; (D) Michael Addison; (S) Jeff Struckman; (C) Warren Travis; (L) Scott Stewart

Berkshire Theatre Festival

RICHARD DUNLAP
Artistic Director

CAROL DOUGHERTY
Managing Director

Box 797
Stockbridge, MA 01262

(413) 298-5536 (bus.)
(413) 298-5576 (b.o.)

FOUNDED 1928
Three Arts Society

SEASON
June-Aug.

FACILITIES
Berkshire Playhouse
Seating Capacity: 427
Stage: proscenium

Unicorn Theatre
Seating Capacity: 100
Stage: thrust

Children's Theatre
Seating Capacity: 100
Stage: arena (tent)

FINANCES
Oct. 1, 1987-Sept. 30, 1988
Expenses: $1,048,163

CONTRACTS
LORT (B)

From its inception, the Berkshire Theatre Festival has had two major goals: to provide thought-provoking, professional summer entertainment to its audiences, and to provide quality educational programs to aspiring theatre artists. Our playhouse houses the mainstage Equity company, performing great plays from around the world, supported by our apprentices and interns. The Unicorn Theatre is an alternative space for new and experimental works, with a non-Equity company of young actors. The Children's Theatre in the tent presents plays written by local grade school students in our Young American Playwrights Program performed by our acting interns. In 1989 the complementary nature of our professional work and our training programs was exemplified by two young actors who progressed through the ranks of our educational programs to become members of the Unicorn Company, and then to star on the mainstage. It is a trend that we hope will continue in the future.
—*Richard Dunlap*

PRODUCTIONS 1988

Stepping Out, Richard Harris; (D) Marge Champion; (S) Jim Noone; (C) Barbara Forbes; (L) Jeff Davis
The Price, Arthur Miller; (D) Gordon Edelstein; (S) Hugh Landwehr; (C) David C. Woolard; (L) Pat Collins
Tusitala, James Prideaux; (D) George Schaefer; (S) Ed Wittstein; (C) Noel Taylor; (L) Jeff Davis
The Chalk Garden, Enid Bagnold; (D) Richard Dunlap; (S) John Falabella; (C) Fran Blau; (L) Jeff Davis
The Return of Pinnochio, Richard Nelson; (D) Fritz Ertl; (S) Jim Youmans; (C) Lynda Salsbury; (L) Ken Posner
The Water Engine, David Mamet; (D) R.J. Cutler; (S) Carl Sprague; (C) Lynda Salsbury; (L) Ken Posner
No Mercy, Constance Congdon; (D) Gordon Edelstein; (S) Jim Youmans; (C) Lynda Salsbury; (L) Ken Posner

PRODUCTIONS 1989

Lute Song, adapt: Sidney Howard and Will Irwin; music: Raymond Scott; lyrics: Bernard Hanighen; (D) Marge Champion; (S) Jim Noone; (C) Gail Brassard; (L) Jeff Davis
The Middle Ages, A.R. Gurney, Jr.; (D) Richard Dunlap; (S) John Falabella; (C) David Murin; (L) Jeff Davis
Betrayal, Harold Pinter; (D) Gordon Edelstein; (S) Hugh Landwehr; (C) David C. Woolard; (L) Jeff Davis
Tete a Tete, Ralph Burdman; (D) Robert Rooney; (S) Ed Wittstein; (C) David Murin; (L) Jeff Davis
Cloud 9, Caryl Churchill; (D) Michael Greif; (S) Carl Sprague; (C) Lynda Salsbury; (L) Ken Posner
The Wedding, Bertolt Brecht; trans: Martin Kasner and Rose Kasner; (D) R.J. Cutler; (S) Jim Youmans; (C) Caryn Neman; (L) Ken Posner
Baby With the Bathwater, Christopher Durang; (D) Kim Rubinstein; (S) Jim Youmans; (C) Danielle Hollywood; (L) Ken Posner
Morocco, Allan Havis; (D) Fritz Ertl; (S) Jim Youmans; (C) Lynda Salsbury; (L) Ken Posner

Bilingual Foundation of the Arts

MARGARITA GALBAN
Artistic Director

CARMEN ZAPATA
President/Producing Director

JIM PAYNE
General Manager

421 North Ave. 19
Los Angeles, CA 90031
(213) 225-4044 (bus.)

FOUNDED 1973
Carmen Zapata, Estela Scarlata, Margarita Galban

SEASON
Jan.-Dec.

FACILITIES
Little Theatre
Seating Capacity: 99
Stage: arena

FINANCES
Jan. 1, 1988-Dec. 31, 1988
Expenses: $475,252

CONTRACTS
AEA 99-seat Theater Plan

The Bilingual Foundation of the Arts creates theatre for both the Hispanic and non-Hispanic communities. Each of these communities varies widely. To serve them all, BFA must have an artistic philosophy that can best be characterized by three words: pluralism, diversity and eclecticism. BFA's Theatre/Teatro meets this challenge by presenting a diversity of material drawn from our rich Hispanic heritage in English one

Berkshire Theatre Festival. *Stepping Out*. Photo: Walter H. Scott.

Bilingual Foundation for the Arts. Rodrigo Catalan and Annette Cardona in *A Cry in the Distance*. Photo: M. Galban.

night and Spanish the next. We present the classics of the Golden Age of Spain, contemporary Latin American plays and new plays by Hispanic-Americans. In 1987 BFA established a workshop for new plays. *Lorca Child of the Moon*, a contemporary opera, and *The Rape of Maria Perez* by Joe Morella came out of this workshop. BFA has represented the USA in Spain's foremost festival, Encuentro de 3 Continentes, and at Festival Iberoamericano in Colombia. Our Theatre for Children (Teatro Para Los Ninos) has played to more than 250,000 underprivileged elementary school children, building future audiences.
—*Margarita Galban*

PRODUCTIONS 1987–88

A Rose with Two Aromas, Emilio Carballido; trans: Margaret Peden; (D) Margarita Galban; (S) Estela Scarlata; (L) Robert Fromer

Le Senorita Margarita, trans and adapt: Dolores Prida, from Roberto Athayde; (D) Dolores Prida; (S) Estela Scarlata; (L) Robert Fromer

Mariana Pineda, Federico Garcia Lorca; trans: Michael Dewell and Carmen Zapata; (D) Margarita Galban; (S) Estela Scarlata; (C) Rene Tobar; (L) Robert Fromer

PRODUCTIONS 1988–89

Our Lady of the Tortilla, Luis Santeiro; (D) Margarita Galban; (S) Estela Scarlata; (L) Robert Fromer

A Cry in the Distance, Jorge Diaz; trans: Margarita Stocker; (D) Margarita Galban; (S) Estela Scarlata; (C) Pilar Revuelta; (L) Robert Fromer

Bloomsburg Theatre Ensemble

A. ELIZABETH DOWD
Ensemble Director

CATHY HARDMAN
Administrative Director

Box 66
Bloomsburg, PA 17815
(717) 784-5530 (bus.)
(717) 784-8181 (b.o.)

FOUNDED 1978
ensemble

SEASON
Oct.-May

FACILITIES
The Alvina Krause Theatre
Seating Capacity: 369
Stage: proscenium

FINANCES
Sept. 1, 1988-Aug. 31, 1989
Expenses: $453,510

The Bloomsburg Theatre Ensemble is entering its 12th season with the resident collective still responsible for its artistic destiny. The ensemble as a whole selects its season and directors, determines its membership and elects its leadership. The deliberately eclectic seasons of plays are chosen with the belief that a rural audience deserves a professional theatre which investigates the privileges and challenges of contemporary American life through the perspective of drama from all cultures and all times. In the face of world events, the ensemble lives and works in a rural region because it needs a home where dialogue with an audience is possible, and where the impact of its theatre on the community is positive and demonstrable. The small town of Bloomsburg and its environs has embraced BTE with financial support, dedicated trustees and volunteers, and enthusiastic attendance. The five-play mainstage season is presented in the Alvina Krause Theatre, named for the acting teacher who was the guiding spirit behind the founding of the ensemble. The annual Theatre Arts in the Classroom tour brings original, group-created pieces to schools statewide, and the BTE Theatre School offers classes for all age groups.
—*A. Elizabeth Dowd*

PRODUCTIONS 1987–88

Tartuffe, Moliere; trans: Richard Wilbur; (D) Laurie McCants; (S) Lyle Baskin; (C) Steven Bras; (L) Richard Latta

A Christmas Carol, adapt: Whit MacLaughlin, from Charles Dickens; (D) Whit MacLaughlin; (S) John Rodriguez; (C) Jonathan Bixby; (L) Mark Mongold

The Suicide, Nikolai Erdman; trans: Richard Nelson; (D) Laura Johnson; (S) Dan Bartlett; (C) Sue Ellen Rohrer; (L) Douglas Cox

The Nest, Franz Xaver Kroetz and Roger Downey; (D) Leigh Strimbeck; (S) Dan Bartlett; (C) Steven Bras; (L) Richard Latta

A Streetcar Named Desire, Tennessee Williams; (D) Gerard

Bloomsburg Theatre Ensemble. *Awake and Sing*. Photo: Marlin Wagner.

Stropnicky; (s) Tom Sturge; (c) Jonathan Bixby; (L) Tom Sturge
One Laugh to Live, company-developed; (D) Rand Whipple; (s) Jim Dixon and Steve Jankousky; (L) Jim Dixon and Steve Jankousky
The Voice of the Praire, John Olive; (D) Laurie McCants; (s) Peter Waldron; (c) Kathleen Egan; (L) Kendall Smith

PRODUCTIONS 1988–89

Light Up the Sky, Moss Hart; (D) Gerard Stropnicky; (s) James A. Bazewicz; (c) Jonathan Bixby; (L) Mark Mongold
Fools Rush In, Rand Whipple; (D) Leigh Strimbeck; (s) Linda A. Sechrist; (c) Malgorzata Komorowska; (L) Richard Latta
The Adventures of Huckleberry Finn, adapt: The Organic Theater Co., from Mark Twain; (D) Laurie McCants; (s) Peter Waldron; (c) Jonathan Bixby; (L) Kendall Smith
Who's Afraid of Virginia Woolf?, Edward Albee; (D) Mark Ramont; (s) James A. Bazewicz; (c) Jimm Halliday; (L) Wendall S. Hinkle
Awake and Sing!, Clifford Odets; (D) Martin Shell; (s) James A. Bazewicz; (c) Jonathan Bixby; (L) Richard Latta
Passage to America, Laurie McCants; (D) Tori Truss; (s) Jonathan Bixby

BoarsHead: Michigan Public Theater

JOHN PEAKES
Artistic Director

JUDITH GENTRY
Managing Director

425 South Grand Ave.
Lansing, MI 48933
(517) 484-7800 (bus.)
(517) 484-7805 (b.o.)

FOUNDED 1970
Richard Thomsen, John Peakes

SEASON
Sept.-Apr.

FACILITIES
Seating Capacity: 249
Stage: thrust

FINANCES
June 1, 1988-May 31, 1989
Expenses: $500,000

CONTRACTS
AEA SPT

BoarsHead: Michigan Public Theater is a center for theatre in our region. Our goal is the presentation of a high-standard professional theatre chosen from the classic and modern repertoires. BoarsHead had a strong commitment to the staging of new plays, and the support of emerging playwrights is manifest in its seasons. The resident company remains dedicated to the idea of an expanding theatre, reaching into both the community and the state. Plays tour statewide, new pieces are developed by area writers, and designs are commissioned from area artists. The effort to involve new audiences is central. The theatre exists for the company as well, providing time and space for artists' individual growth and development. Our focus remains the audience. Productions must be accessible, must address the concerns of the time and then, hopefully, remain with our audiences beyond the moment.
—*John Peakes*

PRODUCTIONS 1987–88

A Midsummer Night's Dream, William Shakespeare; (D) John Peakes; (s) John Peakes; (c) Charlotte Deardorff; (L) Gordon Phetteplace
Cat's Paw, William Mastrosimone; (D) Judith L. Gentry; (s) Gary Decker; (c) Charlotte Deardorff; (L) Gordon Phetteplace
Habeas Corpus, Alan Bennet; (D) John Peakes; (s) John Peakes; (c) Charlotte Deardorff; (L) James Peters
Reduced for Quick Sale, Kent R. Brown; (D) Judith L. Gentry; (s) Kyle Euckert; (c) Charlotte Deardorff; (L) James Peters
Living Skills, Jurgen Wolff; (D) Frederick Hill; (s) Gary Decker; (c) Betty Monroe; (L) James Peters
Bombshells, Kim Carney; (D) Judith L. Gentry; (s) Kyle Euckert; (c) Charlotte Deardorff; (L) James Peters
Bulldog and the Bear, Richard Gordon and Irvin S. Bauer; (D) Kyle Euckert; (s) Kyle Eukert; (c) Charlotte Deardorff; (L) James Peters
Master Harold ... and the boys, Athol Fugard; (D) John Peakes; (s) Kyle Euckert; (c) Charlotte Deardorff; (L) James Peters

PRODUCTIONS 1988–89

Little Footsteps, Ted Tally; (D) Kyle Euckert; (s) Kyle Euckert; (c) Charlotte Deardorff; (L) James Peters
Sisters, Andrew Johns; (D) Judith L. Gentry; (s) Kyle Euckert; (c) Katherine Hudson; (L) James Peters
The Importance of Being Earnest, Oscar Wilde; (D) B. Rodney Marriott; (s) Kyle Euckert; (c) Katherine Hudson; (L) James Peters
Theater, Jules Tasca; (D) Suann Pollock; (s) Kyle Euckert; (c) Katherine Hudson; (L) James Peters
Sweet-Talker, Larry Atlas; (D) Kent R. Brown; (s) Kyle Euckert; (c) Cathi Jones; (L) James Peters
Krapp's Last Tape, Samuel Beckett; (D) Judith L. Gentry; (s) Kyle Euckert; (c) Cathi Jones; (L) James Peters
No Exit, adapt: Paul Bowles, from Jean-Paul Sartre; (D) Judith L. Gentry; (s) Kyle Euckert; (c) Katherine Hudson; (L) James Peters
A ... My Name is Alice, Joan Micklin Silver and Julianne Boyd; (D) Kyle Euckert; (s) Gordon Phetteplace; (c) Katherine Hudson; (L) James Peters

BoarsHead: Michigan Public Theatre. John Bowman, Mark McKinney and John W. Hard in *Master Harold... and the Boys*. Photo: Connie Peakes.

The Body Politic Theatre

PAULINE BRAILSFORD
Artistic Director

JOHN MUSZYNSKI
Managing Director

2261 North Lincoln Ave.
Chicago, IL 60614
(312) 348-7901 (bus.)
(312) 871-3000 (b.o.)

FOUNDED 1966
Community Arts Foundation

SEASON
Sept.-June

FACILITIES
SEATING CAPACITY: 192
STAGE: THRUST

FINANCES
Aug. 1, 1988-July 31, 1989
Expenses: $570,000

CONTRACTS
AEA CAT

The Body Politic Theatre is an ensemble dedicated to presenting the work of playwrights who cherish the richness of our language and the resilience of the human spirit. We present a four-play subscription season on the mainstage. In addition, our new studio performing space will soon house experimental works, the Discovery Project of staged readings, and

guest appearances by small professional groups seeking a performing venue. A recently formed partnership with Roosevelt University lays the foundation for an exciting new phase of development: Ensemble members serve on the faculty of the university, and internships with the professional company prepare Roosevelt graduates for a career in the theatre. The 1989-90 season will mark the 20th year of production in our own theatre facility.
—*Pauline Brailsford*

PRODUCTIONS 1987–88

Moonlight Daring Us to Go Insane, E. Eugene Baldwin; (D) Pauline Brailsford; (S) Linda L. Lane; (C) Susan Bonde; (L) Michael Rourke
Rough Crossing, adapt: Tom Stoppard, from Ferenc Molnar; (D) Pauline Brailsford; (S) Jeff Bauer; (C) Kerry Fleming; (L) Michael Rourke
The Royal Family, George S. Kaufman and Edna Ferber; (D) Joseph Sadowski; (S) Thomas M. Ryan; (C) Kerry Fleming; (L) Michael Rourke
A Whistle in the Dark, Tom Murphy; (D) Tom Murphy; (S) Jeff Bauer; (C) Renee S. Liepins; (L) Michael Rourke

PRODUCTIONS 1988–89

Coastal Disturbances, Tina Howe; (D) Pauline Brailsford; (S) Jeff Bauer; (C) Kerry Fleming; (L) Michael Rourke
Sherlock's Last Case, Charles Marowitz; (D) Roger Mueller; (S) Linda L. Lane; (C) Lynn Sandberg; (L) Michael Rourke
King Lear, William Shakespeare; (D) Terry McCabe and Linda L. Lane; (S) Jeff Bauer; (C) Kerry Fleming; (L) Michael Rourke
Wenceslas Square, Larry Shue; (D) Tom Mula; (S) Brian Traynor; (C) Kerry Fleming; (L) Michael Rourke

The Body Politic Theatre. James O'Reilly and Tom Mula in *King Lear*. Photo: Jennifer Girard Studios.

Brass Tacks Theatre

PATTY LYNCH
Artistic Director

401 N. Third St - Suite 450
Minneapolis, MN 55401
612-341-8207

FOUNDED 1980
Patty Lynch

SEASON
variable

FACILITIES
Minneapolis Theatre Garage
Seating Capacity: 155
Stage: flexible

Southern Theater
Seating Capacity: 155
Stage: proscenium

FINANCES
July 1, 1988-June 30, 1989
Expenses: $118,717

CONTRACTS
AEA SPT

Brass Tacks is dedicated to developing and producing the work of its founder, Patty Lynch, and of a handful of core artists. This work is socially engaged, rich in language and visual metaphor, and seeks to affirm essential values in a rapidly changing culture. The Brass Tacks creative process proceeds from the vitality of concepts engendered by individual artists, who are supported through commissions. The work is then explored in discussions and workshops, and realized in full productions before live audiences. Brass Tacks is committed to the production of a body of work developed with its core artists over an arc of time. We do not have a season or develop work according to a producer's mentality. Occasionally the work will take the form of a discovery project, introducing a new artist to the theatre and the community.
—*Patty Lynch*

PRODUCTIONS 1987–88

The Stick Wife, Darrah Cloud; (D) Jim Stowell; (S) Michael Sommers; (C) Katie Maurer; (L) Michael Murnane
Wreck of the Hesperus, Patty Lynch; (D) Liz Diamond; (S) Jim Muirhead; (C) Katie Maurer; (L) Michael Murnane
Talking Pictures, Jim Stowell; (D) Patty Lynch
Cleveland, Mac Wellman; (D) Jim Simpson; (S) Lori Sullivan; (C) Kathleen Schuetz; (L) Michael Murnane

Brass Tacks Theatre. Buffy Sedlachek in *The Stick Wife*. Photo: Larsh Ansen.

PRODUCTIONS 1988–89

Foolin' Around with Infinity, Steven Dietz; (D) Steven Dietz; (S) Lori Sullivan; (C) Katie Maurer; (L) Michael Murnane
Talking Pictures, Jim Stowell; (D) Patty Lynch
Dr. M. Kurtz's Christian Radio Hour, Patty Lynch; (D) Kent Stephens; (S) Lori Sullivan; (C) Katie Maurer; (L) Michael Murnane

Bristol Riverside Theatre

SUSAN D. ATKINSON
Artistic Director

ROBERT K. O'NEILL
Managing Director

Box 1250
Bristol, PA 19007
(215) 785-6664 (bus.)
(215) 788-7827 (b.o.)

FOUNDED 1987
Susan D. Atkinson, Robert K. O'Neill

SEASON
Sept.-May

BRISTOL RIVERSIDE THEATRE

FACILITIES
Main Stage
Seating Capacity: 302
Stage: proscenium

Second Stage
Seating Capacity: 80
Stage: flexible

FINANCES
Sept. 1, 1988-Aug. 31, 1989
Expenses: $500,000

CONTRACTS
AEA letter of agreement

Bristol Riverside Theatre is a professional, nonprofit regional theatre company dedicated to the development of new plays and playwrights, and to freshly interpreting vintage plays, musicals and classics. Ideally, the manner in which we develop a new play or reexamine an overlooked work from the past is to: 1) give the work a staged reading and determine the necessary period of time to make appropriate revisions, so that 2) a workshop production can be given, and 3) if that is successful, further develop the work so that the fullest possible artistic merit can be shared with our audiences in a main stage production. Our primary concern is maintaining artistic integrity and pursuing excellence in our efforts to affirm the rich cultural heritage of Bucks County and the entire region, the legacy of American theatre, the betterment of the quality of life and the sharing of high-quality, affordable entertainment.

—*Susan D. Atkinson*

PRODUCTIONS 1987–88

The Good Earth, adapt: Owen Davis and Donald Davis, from Pearl S. Buck; (D) Susan D. Atkinson; (S) Wolfgang Roth; (C) Michael Sharp; (L) Wolfgang Roth
The Gift of the Magi, book adapt and lyrics: Mark St. Germain; music: Randy Courts; (D) Susan D. Atkinson; (S) Nels Anderson; (C) Helen Clark; (L) G. Todd Vaules
The Middle Passage, Dan Rustin; (D) Susan D. Atkinson; (S) George Black; (C) Helen Clark; (L) Dan Gitomer
Knock, Knock, Jules Feiffer; (D) Michael Ladenson; (S) George Black; (C) Michael Vogt; (L) Jerold R. Forsyth
The Robber Bridegroom, book and lyrics: Alfred Uhry; music: Robert Waldman; (D) Peter Webb; (S) Joseph Varga; (C) Debra Stein; (L) Scott Pinkney

PRODUCTIONS 1988–89

The Majestic Kid, Mark Medoff; (D) Derek Wolshonak; (S) Lewis Folden; (C) Debra Stein; (L) Scott Pinkney
Happy Ending, Garson Kanin; (D) Garson Kanin; (S) Joseph Varga; (C) Debra Stein; (L) Scott Pinkney
Wintertime, John Liam Joyce; (D) Susan D. Atkinson; (S) Nels Anderson; (L) John Culbert
The Philadelphia Story, Philip Barry; (D) Peter Webb; (S) Joseph Varga; (C) Beverly Bullock; (L) Scott Pinkney
A Day in Hollywood/A Night in the Ukraine, book and lyrics: Dick Vosburgh; music: Frank Lazarus; (D) Edward Earle; (S) Barry Axtell; (C) Isabel Rubio; (L) Jerry Jonas

Caldwell Theatre Company

MICHAEL HALL
Artistic/Managing Director

PATRICIA BURDETT
Company Manager

Box 277
Boca Raton, FL 33429
(407) 241-7380 (bus.)
(407) 241-7432 (b.o.)

FOUNDED 1975
Michael Hall, Frank Bennett

SEASON
Oct.-May

FACILITIES
Seating Capacity: 270
Stage: proscenium

FINANCES
Oct. 1, 1988-Sept. 30, 1989
Expenses: $1,650,000

CONTRACTS
LORT (C)

Caldwell Theatre Company. Jackie Lowe in *Lady Day at Emeron's Bar and Grill*. Photo: Joyce Brock.

The Caldwell Theatre Company, a state theatre of Florida, was founded as an ensemble group that has two goals: to produce socially relevant contemporary plays, and to revive American and European classics from 1890-1940, while striving to develop the Caldwell as an alternative to the commercial houses in the surrounding Ft. Lauderdale-Palm Beach area. Each spring, Caldwell's annual Mizner Festival highlights plays, musical cabarets and events that relate to the 1920s and '30s—the period when architect Addison Mizner introduced a style of living that made Boca Raton famous. Caldwell's other programs include classes for children and teenagers, a conservatory for professional actors, a touring musical cabaret and special plays and programs for young audiences.

—*Michael Hall*

PRODUCTIONS 1987–88

Candida, George Bernard Shaw; (D) Michael Hall; (S) Frank Bennett; (C) Bridget Bartlett; (L) Mary Jo Dondlinger
The Chopin Playoffs, Israel Horovitz; (D) Michael Hall; (S) James Morgan; (C) Bridget Bartlett; (L) Mary Jo Dondlinger
Something's Afoot, book, music and lyrics: James McDonald, David Vox and Robert Gerlach; (D) Michael Hall; (S) Frank Bennett; (C) Bridget Bartlett;

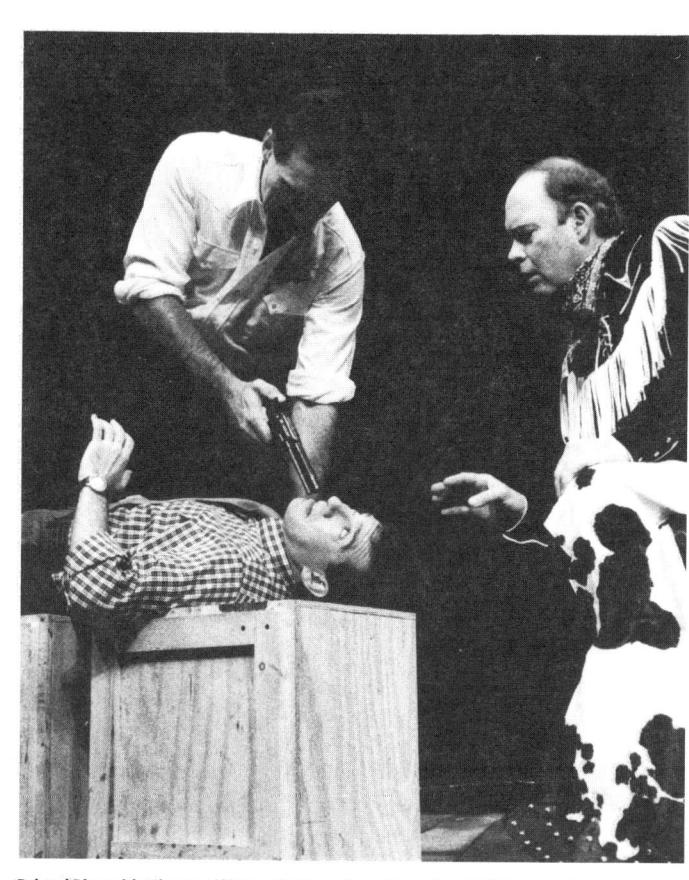

Bristol Riverside Theatre. Michael Cullen, Stuart Zagnit and William Frankfather in *The Majestic Kid*. Photo: Milton Klein.

(L) Mary Jo Dondlinger
Look Homeward Angel, adapt: Ketti Frings, from Thomas Wolfe; (D) Michael Hall; (S) Frank Bennett; (C) Bridget Bartlett; (L) Mary Jo Dondlinger
Lady Day at Emerson's Bar and Grill, Lanie Robertson; (D) Michael Hall; (S) James Morgan; (C) Bridget Bartlett; (L) Mary Jo Dondlinger

PRODUCTIONS 1988–89

The Importance of Being Earnest, Oscar Wilde; (D) Michael Hall; (S) Rick Rasmussen; (C) Bridget Bartlett; (L) Mary Jo Dondlinger
That Championship Season, Jason Miller; (D) Michael Hall; (S) Frank Bennett; (C) Bridget Bartlett; (L) Mary Jo Dondlinger
Over Here!, book: Will Holt; music and lyrics: Richard M. Sherman and Robert B. Sherman; (D) Michael Hall and Oliver Woodall; (S) James Morgan; (C) Bridget Bartlett; (L) Mary Jo Dondlinger
Another Antigone, A.R Gurney, Jr.; (D) Michael Hall; (S) James Morgan; (C) Bridget Bartlett; (L) Mary Jo Dondlinger
Fallen Angels, Noel Coward; (D) Michael Hall; (S) Frank Bennett; (C) Bridget Bartlett; (L) Mary Jo Dondlinger

California Theatre Center

GAYLE CORNELISON
General Director

Box 2007
Sunnyvale, CA 94087
(408) 245-2979 (bus.)
(408) 245-2978 (b.o.)

FOUNDED 1976
Gayle Cornelison

SEASON
Sept.–Aug.

FACILITIES
Sunnyvale Performing Arts Center
Seating Capacity: 200
Stage: proscenium

FINANCES
July 1, 1988-June 30, 1989
Expenses: $760,000

CONTRACTS
AEA Guest Artist

The California Theatre Center is a company with three major programs: a resident company that performs primarily for students and families from October to May; a resident company that performs primarily for adults in the summer; and touring companies that perform regionally, nationally and internationally. The performing artist is the focal point of CTC. Since our society fails to recognize the value of performers, it is essential that their worth be fully appreciated in our theatre. We attempt to provide the performing artist with the best possible environment so that he or she can be as creative as possible. At CTC we believe it is important for us to think of excellence as a process rather than a product. Our company strives toward the goal of outstanding theatre. As we grow and mature our concern is with the future, not the past. What we are attemping in the present is always far more exciting than our past successes. We are passionately driven by our search for excellence.
—*Gayle Cornelison*

PRODUCTIONS 1987–88

What Part Will I Play, Mary Hall Surface; (D) Mary Hall Surface; (S) Tom Butts; (C) Mary Hall Surface; (L) Michael T. Essad
Most Valuable Player, Mary Hall Surface; (D) Mary Hall Surface; (S) Paul Vallerga; (C) Colleen Troy Lewis; (L) Michael T. Essad
Ancient Memories, Modern Dreams, Gayle Cornelison; (D) Pat Patton; (S) Michael Cook; (C) Colleen Troy Lewis; (L) Michael T. Essad
Jack and the Beanstalk, Gayle Cornelison; (D) Will Huddleston; (S) Michael T. Essad; (C) Jane Lambert; (L) Michael T. Essad
Dracula, adapt: Gayle Corneilson, from Bram Stoker; (D) Bruce Williams; (S) Tom Dyer; (C) Jane Lambert; (L) Michael T. Essad
Just So Stories, adapt: Gayle Cornelison, from Rudyard Kipling; (D) Gayle Cornelison; (S) Michael T. Essad; (C) Colleen Troy Lewis; (L) Michael T. Essad
Celebrate the Pacific Basin, Mary Hall Surface; (D) Will Huddleston; (S) Michael T. Essad; (C) Colleen Troy Lewis; (L) Michael T. Essad
A Christmas Carol, adapt: Mary Hall Surface, from Charles Dickens; (D) Gayle Cornelison; (S) Michael Cook; (C) Jane Lambert; (L) Michael T. Essad
The Emperor's New Clothes, Gayle Cornelison; (D) Gayle Cornelison; (S) Ralph J. Ryan; (C) Colleen Troy Lewis; (L) Michael T. Essad
The Tempest, William Shakespeare; (D) Gayle Cornelison; (S) Brian Alan Reed; (C) Colleen Troy Lewis; (L) Michael T. Essad
Tales of Brer Rabbit, adapt: Gayle Cornelison, from Joel Chandler Harris; (D) Will Huddleston; (S) Michael T. Essad; (C) Jane Lambert; (L) Michael T. Essad
A New Age Is Dawning, Will Huddleston; (D) Christina Yao; (S) Michael Cook; (C) Colleen Troy Lewis; (L) Michael T. Essad
Imagine, Clayton Doherty; (D) Shannon Edwards; (S) Michael T. Essad; (C) Colleen Troy Lewis; (L) Michael T. Essad
Cinderella, adapt: Gayle Cornelison; (D) Julian Lopez-Morillas; (S) Keith Snider; (C) Jane Lambert; (L) Michael T. Essad
Amelia Earhart: Flights of Fancy, Will Huddleston; (D) Laurie Cole; (S) Michael T. Essad; (C) Colleen Troy Lewis; (L) Michael T. Essad
The Nightingale, Gayle Cornelison; (D) Mary Hall Surface; (S) Ralph J. Ryan; (C) Colleen Troy Lewis; (L) Michael T. Essad
Tales of the Holiday, Gayle Cornelison; (D) Shannon Edwards; (S) Tom Dyer; (C) Jane Lambert and Colleen Troy Lewis; (L) Michael T. Essad
Sea Marks, Gardner McKay; (D) Tom Ramirez; (S) Michael Cook; (C) Colleen Troy Lewis; (L) Tom O'Neil
Servant of Two Masters, Carlo Goldoni; (D) Gayle Cornelison; (S) Michael Cook; (C) Jane Lambert; (L) Tom O'Neil
The Rainmaker, N. Richard Nash; (D) Maureen O'Reilly; (S) Michael Cook; (C) Colleen Troy Lewis; (L) Tom O'Neil
Jamie 22, Gayle Cornelison; (D) Will Huddleston; (S) Michael Cook; (C) Michael Cook; (L) Tom O'Neil
Stories of the Golden West, Gayle Cornelison and Joe Bostick; (D) Joe Bostick; (S) Tom Butts; (C) Jane Lambert and Colleen Troy Lewis; (L) Michael T. Essad
Under One Sun, Gayle Cornelison and Shannon Edwards; (D) Shannon Edwards; (S) Michael T. Essad; (C) Jane Lambert and Colleen Troy Lewis; (L) Michael T. Essad

PRODUCTIONS 1988–89

A New Age Is Dawning, Will Huddleston; (D) Will Huddleston; (S) Michael Cook; (C) Colleen Troy Lewis; (L) Paul Vallerga
Apollo to the Moon, Mary Hall Surface; (D) Mary Hall Surface; (S) Kevin Reese; (C) Kevin Reese; (L) Paul Vallerga

California Theatre Center. *Jamie 22*. Photo: Carl Ballou.

Imagine, Clayton Doherty; (D) Mary Hall Surface; (S) Michael Essad; (C) Colleen Troy Lewis; (L) Paul Vallerga
The Brave Little Tailor, Gayle Cornelison; (D) Will Huddleston; (S) Tom Hird; (C) Jane Lambert; (L) Paul Vallerga
The Miser, adapt: James Keller, from Moliere; (D) Albert Takazauckas; (S) Paul Vallerga; (C) Colleen Troy Lewis; (L) Paul Vallerga
An Old Fashion Holiday, Gayle Cornelison; (D) Will Huddleston; (S) Paul Vallerga; (C) Colleen Troy Lewis; (L) Paul Vallerga
Tales of the Holiday, Gayle Cornelison; (D) Shannon Edwards; (S) Tom Dyer; (C) Jane Lambert and Colleen Troy Lewis; (L) Paul Vallerga
A Christmas Carol, adapt: Mary Hall Surface, from Charles Dickens, (D) Gayle Cornelison; (S) Michael Cook; (C) Jane Lambert; (L) Paul Vallerga
Santa's Secret, Clayton Doherty and Mary Gibboney; (D) Shannon Edwards; (S) Clayton Doherty; (C) Jane Lambert and Colleen Troy Lewis; (L) Paul Vallerga
The Nightingale, Gayle Cornelison; (D) Mary Hall Surface; (S) Ralph J. Ryan; (C) Colleen Troy Lewis; (L) Paul Vallerga
Seagirl, Frances Elitzig; (D) Shannon Edwards; (S) Paul Vallerga; (C) Colleen Troy Lewis; (L) Paul Vallerga
Beach of Dreams, Graziano Melano; (D) Graziano Melano and Luca Valentino; (S) Paul Vallerga; (C) Jane Lambert; (L) Paul Vallerga
Jack and the Beanstalk, adapt: Gayle Cornelison; (D) Will Huddleston; (S) Tom Hird; (C) Colleen Troy Lewis; (L) Paul Vallerga
Ancient Memories, Modern Dreams, Gayle Cornelison; (D) Art Manke; (S) Michael Cook; (C) Colleen Troy Lewis; (L) Paul Vallerga
An Old Time Movie, Gayle Cornelison; (D) Will Huddleston; (S) Paul Vallerga; (C) Colleen Troy Lewis; (L) Paul Vallerga
Beauty and the Beast, adapt: Gayle Cornelison; (D) Andrew J. Traister; (S) Paul Vallerga; (C) Jane Lambert; (L) Paul Vallerga
Prince Free from Sorrows, Per Lysander and Suzanne Oster; (D) Marten Harrie; (S) Kent Wendel; (C) Kent Wendel; (L) Paul Vallerga
Rapunzel and the Witch, adapt: Gayle Cornelison; (D) Shannon Edwards; (C) Jane Lambert; (L) Paul Vallerga
The Importance of Being Earnest, Oscar Wilde; (D) Gayle Cornelison; (S) Russell Whaley; (C) Jane Lambert; (L) Dinna Myers
Time and the Conways, J.B. Priestley; (D) Will Huddleston; (S) Russell Whaley; (C) Colleen Troy Lewis; (L) Dinna Myers
Hay Fever, Noel Coward; (D) Raye Birk; (S) Russell Whaley; (C) Colleen Troy Lewis; (L) Dinna Myers
Sherlock Holmes and the Shakespeare Solution, Barney Gould and Peter Donat; (D) Megs Booker; (S) Russell Whaley; (C) Colleen Troy Lewis; (L) Dinna Myers

Capital Repertory Company

**BRUCE BOUCHARD
PETER CLOUGH
Producing Directors**

**PETER KINDLON
General Manager**

Box 399
Albany, NY 12201-0399
(518) 462-4531 (bus.)
(518) 462-4534 (b.o.)

FOUNDED 1980
Michael Van Landingham,
Oakley Hall, III

SEASON
Oct.-May

FACILITIES
Market Theatre
Seating Capacity: 258
Stage: thrust

FINANCES
July 1, 1988-June 30, 1989
Expenses: $1,300,000

CONTRACTS
LORT D

Capital Repertory Company. Michael Marcus, Michael Fischetti, Terry Rabine and Alan Swift in *Glengarry Glen Ross*. Photo: Joseph Schuyler.

The work of Capital Repertory Company examines the human spirit in transition, grappling with an ever-changing social and cultural climate—from the joyous to the tragic. Premieres, second productions of new plays, works developed outside New York and seen solely by regional audiences, and pertinent plays from the commercial arena comprise our repertoire. Additionally, our long-held dream of an annual venture into the classics will begin with the 1989-90 season. As we approach our second decade, we have developed an association with a body of artists who continue to return to Capital Rep as their "artistic home"—to stretch and evolve their craft, free from commercial pressure.
—*Bruce Bouchard, Peter Clough*

PRODUCTIONS 1987–88

The Search for Signs of Intelligent Life in the Universe, Jane Wagner; (D) George Boyd; (S) Dale F. Jordan; (C) Lynda L. Salsbury; (L) Dale F. Jordan
Like Them That Dream, Edgar White; (D) Basil Wallace; (S) Ray Recht; (C) Martha Hally; (L) Jackie Manassee
Mrs. California, Doris Baizley; (D) Peter H. Clough; (S) Robert Thayer; (C) Lynda L. Salsbury; (L) John Ambrosone
Thursday's Child, Julie Jenson; (D) Gordon Edelstein; (S) Ray Recht; (C) David C. Woolard; (L) Dan Kinsley
The Big Knife, Clifford Odets; (D) Bruce Bouchard; (S) Rick Dennis; (C) Lynda L. Salsbury; (L) Jackie Manassee
The Nerd, Larry Shue; (D) Michael J. Hume; (S) Dale F. Jordan; (C) Martha Hally; (L) David Yergan

PRODUCTIONS 1988–89

Saint Florence, Elizabeth Diggs; (D) Jules Aaron; (S) Rick Dennis; (C) James Scott; (L) Victor En Yu Tan
Round and Round the Garden, Alan Ayckbourn; (D) Michael J. Hume; (S) Dale F. Jordan and Michael Hume; (C) Lynda L. Salsbury; (L) David Yergan
The Voice of the Prairie, John Olive; (D) Gloria Muzio; (S) Pat Woodbridge; (C) Martha Hally; (L) Jackie Manassee
Glengarry Glen Ross, David Mamet; (D) Gordon Edelstein; (S) Hugh Landwehr; (C) David Murin; (L) Pat Collins
The Immigrant: A Hamilton County Album, Mark Harelik; conceived: Mark Harelik and Randal Myler; (D) Howard J. Millman; (S) Kevin Rupnik; (C) Mimi Maxmen; (L) Phil Monat
Biloxi Blues, Neil Simon; (D) John Pynchon Holms; (S) Leslie Taylor; (C) Lynda L. Salsbury; (L) Andi Lyons

The CAST Theatre

TED SCHMITT
Artistic Director

MICHAEL AQUILANTE
Managing Director

804 North El Centro
Hollywood, CA 90038
(213) 462-9872 (bus.)
(213) 462-0265 (b.o.)

FOUNDED 1974
Ted Schmitt, Kathleen Johnson

SEASON
Jan.-Dec.

FACILITIES
The CAST Theatre
Seating Capacity: 65
Stage: proscenium

The CAST-at-The-Circle
Seating Capacity: 99
Stage: proscenium

FINANCES
Oct. 1, 1988-Sept. 30, 1989
Expenses: $235,050

CONTRACTS
AEA 99-seat Theatre Plan

The CAST Theatre generates new American plays and serves emerging American playwrights by developing their original scripts. CAST plays illuminate the human condition—particularly relationships and the indomitability of the human spirit. The CAST is one of the most playwright-accessible, high-profile, intimate, professional theatres in southern California and is a supportive, embracing, award-winning environment for new works that illuminate the wide variety of experiences in our diverse cultural landscape. Musicals are a theatrical form in which the CAST also excels. In the past 10 years, of the 203 plays presented, 129 were world premieres and 38 were musicals. The CAST uses an intensive three-step process to develop material. First, scripts are screened by the literary staff; some then pass into our Foundry Series of public readings. Selected scripts may then move into the third step, the Safe Harbor—staged, script-in-hand, work-in-progress, non-reviewed presentations that lead ultimately to a mainstage production.

—Ted Schmitt

PRODUCTIONS 1987–88

Teamsters Basement, Thomas G. Carter; (D) Andrew Deangelo; (S) Steve Chase
A Fine Line, Judy Romberger; (D) Guy Giarizzo; (S) Steven T. Howell; (L) Steven T. Howell
Behind You, John Pappas; (D) Laurence Braude
Savage In Limbo, John Patrick Shanley; (D) Roxanne Rogers; (S) Nina Ruscio; (C) Alison Gail Bixby; (L) Steven T. Howell
White Death, Daniel Therriault; (D) Charles Davis; (S) Kevin Adams; (C) Martha Ferrara; (L) Brian Gale
Liars Poker, Bernard Velinsky; (D) William Lanteau
Canned Laughter, Jeanette Collins and Mimi Friedman; (D) Michael P. King
Rounds, Sean Michael Rice; (D) John DiFusco; (S) Steven T. Howell
October 22, 4004 B.C., Saturday, Suzanne Lummis; (D) Robert Schrock; (S) Steven T. Howell; (C) Eleanor Hedge
Reduced Shakespeare, Jess Borgeson, Adam Long and Daniel Singer; (D) Jess Borgeson and Adam Long
Danny and the Deep Blue Sea, John Patrick Shanley; (D) Robert Berlinger; (S) Fred Duer; (L) Kathy Perkins
Mine Enemies, Greg Suddeth; (D) Brian Reise; (S) Ronnie World
Man Without A Contra, Gross National Product; (D) Comedy Improvisation
Journey Into The Whirlwind, adapt: Rebecca Schull, from Thomas G. Carter; (D) Rebecca Schull
The Little Prince, adapt: David Zuker; (D) Esquire Jauchem
Apartment/Across The Way, Mark Mawtell; (D) Mark Mawtell
The Figure and Other Short Works, Clifton Campbell; (D) Gina Wendkos; (S) Kevin Graves
Marriage Gambol, Enid Rudd; (D) Peter Flood; (S) Steven T. Howell; (C) Viveca Price; (L) Kathi O'Donohue
Dinosaurs, Gina Wendkos; (D) Gina Wendkos
Some Golden States, Tim Miller; (D) Tim Miller; (L) Rand Ryan
Buddy Systems, Tim Miller; (D) Tim Miller; (L) Rand Ryan

PRODUCTIONS 1988–89

Quirks, Leslie Ray; (D) Paul Kreppel; (S) Jimmy Cuomo; (C) Kate Bergh; (L) Steven T. Howell
Standard of the Breed, John Steppling; (D) John Steppling; (S) Lance Crush; (C) Lance Crush; (L) Erica Bradberry
Malcolm X, Damone Paul Jackson; (D) Ricky Pardon; (S) Ricky Pardon and Lance Crush; (L) Kevin Graves
Gingerale Afternoon, Gina Wendkos; (D) Gina Wendkos
Secret of Body Language, Kelly Stuart; (D) Robert Glaudini; (S) J. Phillips; (C) Lance Crush; (L) John Fisher
Big Boy, Michael Sargent; (D) Lee Kissman; (S) Erik Hanson; (C) Erik Hanson; (L) Tina Luster
Taproot, David Hall; (D) Robert Schrock
American Pie, Michael Lynch; (D) Peter Tripp; (S) Steven T. Howell; (L) Steven T. Howell
Don't Quit Your Day Job, David Allen, David Higgins and Steve Higgins; (D) David Allen and David Higgins
Omalingwo, Nkeonye Nwankwo; (D) Romell Foster Owens
Terminal Bar, Paul Selig; (D) Ken Biller; (S) Steven T. Howell; (L) Steven T. Howell
Toe to Toe, Greg Suddeth; (D) Greg Suddeth; (S) Tim Ryan; (L) Erica Bradberry
June 8, 1968, Anna Theresa Cascio; (D) Jonathan Emerson
Appetite, David Michael Erickson; (D) Anne Drecktrah; (S) Mike Chapman; (L) Laurence Oberman
Today's Special, Judd Lear Silverman; (D) Mary Lou Belli; (S) Mike Chapman; (L) Laurence Oberman

Center Stage

STAN WOJEWODSKI, JR.
Artistic Director

PETER W. CULMAN
Managing Director

700 North Calvert St.
Baltimore, MD 21202
(301) 685-3200 (bus.)
(301) 332-0033 (b.o.)

FOUNDED 1963
Community Arts Committee

SEASON
Oct.-June

FACILITIES
Seating Capacity: 541
Stage: thrust

FINANCES
July 1, 1988-June 30, 1989
Expenses: $3,273,467

CONTRACTS
LORT (B)

The CAST Theatre. *A Gang of Girls*. Photo: Ed Krieger.

Center Stage. Laila Robinson in *The Lady From the Sea*. Photo: Richard Anderson.

At Center Stage we have grown restless as a consequence of our concern over a variety of issues: the limited range of producible repertoire, the subscription audience as a source of subsidy, the level of artist compensation, the scarcity of working structures tailored to individual projects. On all these fronts we are engaged in vigorous, artistically driven planning. A major campaign is underway to create an additional, flexible performance space (scheduled to open in 1991) and a substantial addition to the theatre's endowment, in order to create an environment in which the demands of the traditional "season" do not become de facto artistic policy. Ours is a vision of one theatre with two stages, and the freedom to suit the project to the venue, the idea to the space. Its profile will be eclectic and bold; its goal to push the stylistic, thematic, formal and temporal frontiers of the American theatre as far outward as possible.
—*Stan Wojewodski, Jr.*

PRODUCTIONS 1987–88

Hamlet, William Shakespeare; (D) Stan Wojewodski, Jr.; (S) Hugh Landwehr; (C) Robert Wojewodski; (L) Pat Collins
Aunt Dan and Lemon, Wallace Shawn; (D) Irene Lewis; (S) John Conklin; (C) Catherine Zuber; (L) Pat Collins
The Colored Museum, George C. Wolfe; (D) L. Kenneth Richardson; (S) Brian Martin; (C) Nancy L. Konrardy; (L) Victor En Yu Tan
Paradise Lost, Clifford Odets; (D) Michael Engler; (S) Loren Sherman; (C) Robert Wojewodski; (L) Jennifer Tipton
The Lady from the Sea, Henrik Ibsen; trans: Rolf Fjelde; (D) Stan Wojewodski, Jr.; (S) Christopher Barreca; (C) Catherine Zuber; (L) Stephen Strawbridge
In Perpetuity Throughout the Universe, Eric Overmyer; (D) Stan Wojewodski, Jr.; (S) Christopher Barreca; (C) Robert Wojewodski; (L) Stephen Strawbridge
A Temporary Place, Frederick Gaines; (D) Irene Lewis; (S) Christopher Barreca; (C) Robert Wojewodski; (L) Stephen Strawbridge
Judgment Day, Odon von Horvath; trans: Martin Esslin and Renata Esslin; (D) Jackson Phippin; (S) Christopher Barreca; (C) Robert Wojewodski; (L) Stephen Strawbridge

PRODUCTIONS 1988–89

The Importance of Being Earnest, Oscar Wilde; (D) Stan Wojewodski, Jr.; (S) Derek McLane; (C) Catherine Zuber; (L) Pat Collins
Fool for Love, Sam Shepard; (D) William Foeller; (S) Christopher Barreca; (C) Del W. Risberg; (L) James F. Ingalls
Joe Turner's Come and Gone, August Wilson; (D) Irene Lewis; (S) Anita Stewart; (C) Candice Donnelly; (L) Pat Collins
The Tempest, William Shakespeare; (D) Stan Wojewodski, Jr.; (S) Alexander Okun; (C) Alexander Okun; (L) Stephen Strawbridge
There's One in Every Marriage, trans and adapt: Suzanne Grossman and Paxton Whitehead, from Georges Feydeau; (D) Stan Wojewodski, Jr.; (S) Derek McLane; (C) Catherine Zuber; (L) Stephen Strawbridge
The Broken Pitcher, Heinrich von Kleist; trans: Jon Swan; (D) Michael Engler; (S) Derek McLane; (C) Catherine Zuber; (L) James F. Ingalls
The Increased Difficulty of Concentration, Vaclav Havel; trans: Vera Blackwell; (D) Stan Wojewodski, Jr.; (S) Derek McLane; (C) Catherine Zuber; (L) Robert Wierzel

Center Theater

DAN LaMORTE
Artistic Director

ELIZABETH BURKE
General Manager

1346 West Devon
Chicago, IL 60660
(312) 508-0200 (bus.)
(312) 508-5422 (b.o.)

FOUNDED 1984
Eileen Manganaro, Dan LaMorte, Carole Gutierrez, Dale Calandra, Mark Vann

SEASON
Oct.–July

FACILITIES
Playhouse
Seating Capacity: 99
Stage: thrust

Studio
Seating Capacity: 30
Stage: flexible

FINANCES
Sept. 1, 1988–Aug. 31, 1989
Expenses: $100,000

CONTRACTS
AEA CAT

The Training Center for the Working Actor was developed to create a coherent and unified lifelong approach to the art and science of acting—Center Theater was born out this dedication. Our repertory company presents both new and established material in a deliberately bold, imaginative manner, and explores all the elements of production to realize the potential of every individual work. Each is dealt with specifically—discovering the play's quality, molding it, designing it with concept and color, bringing it to life for the "first time." Our theatre and training progam focus on the actor and the acting process to create exciting and risky theatre. The dream is to build an ensemble of talent—actors, directors, designers, writers—capable of bringing theatre to levels that are truthful and rare, so that risks can be taken to inspire artists and audiences alike.
—*Dan LaMorte*

Center Theatre. Gus Buktenica and Judy McLaughlin in *Two Many Bosses*. Photo: Jennifer Girard.

PRODUCTIONS 1987–88

The Scarecrow, Percy MacKaye;
(D) Dale Calandra; (S) Rob
Hamilton; (C) Rob Hamilton;
(L) Chris Phillips
Miss Lulu Bett, adapt: Peter
Burnell, from Zona Gale;
(D) Dan LaMorte; (S) John
Murbach; (C) Margaret
Fitzsimmons; (L) Chris Phillips
The Marriage of Bette and Boo,
Christopher Durang; (D) Dale
Calandra; (S) John Murbach;
(C) E. Hugh Manning; (L) Chris
Phillips
*The Lusty and Comical History
of Tom Jones*, adapt: John
Morrison; (D) Dan LaMorte;
(S) John Murbach; (C) E. Hugh
Manning; (L) Chris Phillips
Texarkana, Elizabeth Shepherd;
(D) Dan LaMorte; (S) Kevin
Rigdon; (C) Jennifer Ona Jacobs;
(L) Kevin Rigdon

PRODUCTIONS 1988–89

Labor Relations, Nancy Beckett;
(D) Dan LaMorte; (S) John
Murbach; (C) John Murbach;
(L) Chris Phillips
Two Many Bosses, book: Dan
LaMorte; music and lyrics:
Donald Coates; (D) Dan
LaMorte and Dale Calandra;
(S) Sheryl Nieman; (C) Lynn
Sandberg; (L) Jeff Schroeter
Measure for Measure, William
Shakespeare; (D) Jack Wetherall;
(L) Mary Badger
The Night of the Tribades, Per
Olov Enquist; trans: Ross
Shideler; (D) Randi Collins Hard
and Phillips Chris; (S) Rob
Hamilton; (C) Renee Starr-
Liepins; (L) Mary Badger

The Changing Scene

ALFRED BROOKS
President

MAXINE MUNT
Vice President

1527 ½ Champa St.
Denver, CO 80202
(303) 893-5775 (bus.)
(303) (303) 893-5775 (b.o.)

FOUNDED 1968
Maxine Munt, Alfred Brooks

SEASON
Jan.-Dec.

FACILITIES
Seating Capacity: 76
Stage: flexible

FINANCES
Jan. 1, 1988-Dec. 31, 1988
Expenses: $108,724

Since its founding, the Changing Scene has remained true to its philosophy that the theatre is the natural forum for all the arts to come together and that the company would produce only new work. More than 250 plays have been given world-premiere productions, along with many weeks of dance, music, films, video works, poetry and performance art, always with a visual art show in the lobby gallery. Among our foremost concerns are the growing number of mature artists who have sold out and the fact that younger artists coming out of school have been much more impressed with their business training than with their exposure to the arts. As a result, many submitted scripts seem to aspire to a commercial acceptance rather than a contribution to the theatre arts. Why duplicate sitcoms? When comes the realization that naturalism is no longer a theatrical province? Innovative freshness in new forms is the crying need.

—*Alfred Brooks*

PRODUCTIONS 1987–88

Shoes, Danny Kerwick;
(D) Christine MacDonald;
(S) Bill Gian; (C) Holly J.
Kennedy; (L) Hugh Graham
Muscles of Hands, Bill Gian;
(D) Christine MacDonald;
(S) Bill Gian; (C) Holly J.
Kennedy; (L) Hugh Graham
Dust, Danny Kerwick and Bill
Gian; (D) Christine MacDonald;
(S) Bill Gian; (C) Holly J.
Kennedy; (L) Hugh Graham
Jog, Kevin Kelly; (D) Tom Rowan;
(S) Craig Williamson; (L) Craig
Williamson
The Monkey Man, James Kiefer;
(D) Tom Rowan; (S) Craig
Williamson; (L) Craig
Williamson
Torture, Lee Patton; (D) Tom
Rowan; (S) Craig Williamson;
(L) Craig Williamson
Urges, Molly Newman; (D) Dan
Heister; (S) Dennis Lockhart;
(C) Margaret Sjoberg; (L) Craig
Williamson
Hot for You, Baby, Frank X.
Hogan; (D) Dan Heister;
(S) Dennis Lockhart;
(C) Margaret Sjoberg; (L) Craig
Williamson
Does This Hurt?, Robin
Chotzinoff; (D) Christine
MacDonald; (S) Dennis
Lockhart; (C) Margaret Sjoberg;
(L) Craig Williamson
Redmoon Waxing, Teresa M.
Marffie; (D) Kay Kuhlmann;
(S) Dennis Lockhart;
(C) Margaret Sjoberg; (L) Craig
Williamson
Gospel According to Gramps,
Marty Ann Durlin; (D) Peter
Hackett; (S) Dennis Lockhart;
(C) Margaret Sjoberg; (L) Craig
Williamson
Parenting Class, Scene 4, Frank
X. Hogan; (D) Dan Heister;
(S) Dennis Lockhart;
(C) Margaret Sjoberg; (L) Craig
Williamson
Shelter Me, Larry Bograd;
(D) Paul Jefferson; (S) Dennis
Lockhart; (C) Margaret Sjoberg;
(L) Craig Williamson
Providing, Coleen Hubbard;
(D) Dan Heister; (S) Dennis
Lockhart; (C) Margaret Sjoberg;
(L) Craig Williamson
Two Lous, Jacob Clark; (D) Kevin
Bartlett; (S) Dennis Lockhart;
(C) Margaret Sjoberg;
(L) Stephen Kramer
Break, Marie Cartier; (D) Andrea
Edwards; (S) Dennis Lockhart;
(C) Margaret Sjoberg;
(L) Stephen Kramer
Dinner with the Undertaker, Lee
Patton; (D) Robin Harwood;
(S) Dennis Lockhart;
(C) Margaret Sjoberg;
(L) Stephen Kramer
Orange Pentheus, Richard Horell;

The Changing Scene. Jeff Hess, Vincent Robinson and Tupper Cullum in *The Malignancy of Henrietta Lacks*. Photo: Nissim Levy.

(D) Claudia Newcomb;
(S) Dennis Lockhart;
(C) Margaret Sjoberg;
(L) Stephen Kramer
Flight, Terry Dodd; (D) Pamela
Clifton; (S) Dennis Lockhart;
(C) Margaret Sjoberg;
(L) Stephen Kramer
Johnny Got His Gun, adapt:
Bradley Rand Smith; (D) Lue
Douthit; (S) Jeff Hess; (C) Jeff
Hess; (L) Peter Neilson
*Dramatization of Richard
Warren*, Michael Vetrie;
(D) Dennis Bontems; (S) Dennis
Bontems; (C) Carol Kimball;
(L) C.J. Wilkerson
*Lady I & Lady II Talk Like
Pigeons, They Dooooo . . .They
Dooooo . . .*, Arnold Rabin;
(D) Pamela Clifton; (C) Margaret
Sjoberg; (L) Lisa M. Scott
The Summer of the Dance,
Michael McGuire; (D) Tom
Rowan; (S) Renye Ress; (C) Lisa
Mumpton; (L) Phillippe Heister
Feu la Mere de Madame, Georges
Feydeau; (D) Dan Heister;
(S) Rod Thompson; (C) Penny
Stames; (L) Phillippe Heister
Une Heureuse Rencontre, Jean
Tardieu; (D) Dan Heister;
(S) Rod Thompson; (C) Penny
Stames; (L) Phillippe Heister
Transitions in Time and Space,
Charles Parson; (D) Charles
Parson; (S) Charles Parson;
(C) Charles Parson; (L) Peter
Nielson
Marvels of Modern Medicine,
Trista Conger; (D) David
Kottenstett and Dan Murray;
(S) David Kottenstett and Dan
Murray; (C) David Kottenstett

and Dan Murray; (L) Dan Murray
- ***The Rosewood Bed***, Trista Conger; (D) Sallie Baker; (S) Jay Shaffer; (C) Margaret Sjoberg; (L) Jay Shaffer
- ***French Delights***, Eugene Ionesco, David Greenspan, Roger Vitrac and Kurt Schwitters; (D) John W. Wilson; (S) Steven Eagleburger; (C) Sara Crow; (L) Steven Eagleburger

PRODUCTIONS 1988-89

- ***Signs***, Susan Kirkman-Beck; (D) Jennifer Thero; (S) Bill Curley; (C) Laurie Klapperich and Linda Morken; (L) Lisa M. Scott
- ***The Irresistible Urge***, Michael Gitter; (D) Archie Smith; (S) Bill Curley; (C) Laurie Klapperich and Linda Morken; (L) Lisa M. Scott
- ***Passing Through***, Gregory Lee; (D) Stephen R. Kramer; (S) Bill Curley; (C) Laurie Klapperich and Linda Morken; (L) Lisa M. Scott
- ***A Myth of Consequence***, Rick Lawson; (D) Katie Morgan; (S) Bill Curley; (C) Laurie Klapperich and Linda Morken; (L) Lisa M. Scott
- ***Cost of Living***, L.J. Clark; (D) Jeffrey Nicholson; (S) Bill Curley; (C) Laurie Klapperich and Linda Morken; (L) Bryan Billings
- ***The Contents of Her Purse***, Coleen Hubbard; (D) Jim Hunt; (S) Bill Curley; (C) Laurie Klapperich and Linda Morken; (L) Bryan Billings
- ***Space and Light***, Seth Wilson; (D) Dennis Beck; (S) Bill Curley; (C) Laurie Klapperich and Linda Morken; (L) Bryan Billings
- ***The Goat Singers***, Mark Allen Peterson; (D) Scott Lewis; (S) Bill Curley; (C) Laurie Klapperich and Linda Morken; (L) Bryan Billings
- ***Playgroup***, Mary M. Connelly; (D) Susan Kirkman-Beck; (S) Bill Curley; (C) Laurie Klapperich and Linda Morken; (L) Dan Murray
- ***Shelter***, Pamela Stross Kenney; (D) Richard Morell; (S) Bill Curley; (C) Laurie Klapperich and Linda Morken; (L) Dan Murray
- ***Tom's Coffee Dog***, Jerry Ellis; (D) Sallie Diamond; (S) Bill Curley; (C) Laurie Klapperich and Linda Morken; (L) Dan Murray
- ***Shadow***, Kenneth Dean Brown; (D) Jay Levitt; (S) Bill Curley; (C) Laurie Klapperich and Linda Morken; (L) Dan Murray
- ***Kleinhoff Demonstrates Tonight***, Andrew Glaze; (D) Lee Traveler; (S) Jay Shaffer; (C) Margaret Sjoberg; (L) Jay Shaffer
- ***The Malignancy of Henrietta Lacks***, August Baker; (D) J.L. Abramo; (S) Joseph Abramo; (C) Holly J. Kennedy; (L) Diana Linger
- ***Takedown***, Eugene Barber; (D) Stephen R. Kramer; (S) Stephen R. Kramer; (C) Terri Edelen; (L) Stephen R. Kramer
- ***Boyle***, David Kibble; (D) Al Brooks; (S) Jay Shaffer; (C) Holly J. Kennedy; (L) Jay Shaffer
- ***Le Mariage de Figaro***, Pierre Augustin Caron du Beaumarchais; (D) Dan Heister; (S) Dennis Bontems; (C) Penny Stames; (L) Kevin Bartlett
- ***Walking Fire***, Trista Conger; (D) Carolyn Byrne; (S) George Stevenson; (C) Diana Linger; (L) Diana Linger
- ***The Names Have Been Changed to Protect the Innocent***, Christine MacDonald; (D) Al Brooks; (S) Stephen R. Kramer; (C) Christine MacDonald; (L) Stephen R. Kramer

The Children's Theatre Company

JON CRANNEY
Artistic Director

BILL CONNER
Executive Director

2400 Third Ave., South
Minneapolis, MN 55404
(612) 874-0500 (bus.)
(612) 874-0400 (b.o.)

FOUNDED 1961
Beth Linnerson

SEASON
Sept.-June

FACILITIES
Mainstage
Seating Capacity: 746
Stage: proscenium

Studio Theatre
Seating Capacity: 150
Stage: flexible

Ordway Music Theatre
Seating Capacity: 315
Stage: proscenium

FINANCES
July 1, 1988-June 30, 1989
Expenses: $3,869,398

CONTRACTS
AEA Guest Artist contract

The Children's Theatre Company is dedicated to the creation and presentation of new adaptations and original plays for young people and families, inspired by classic and contemporary sources. A rotating repertory season of seven mainstage productions is comprised by fullscale musicals, children's classics and literary dramas, created by its resident artists and artisans (80 fulltime staff), and complemented by numerous guest artists. National touring and international cultural exchanges enhance CTC's understanding and its influence within the world theatre community. CTC also provides classroom/workshop training for children and adolescents, as well as intern-apprentice positions for young adults, culminating in appropriate performance opportunities with CTC's resident company. To maintain an artistic sanctuary and wellspring that is resourceful, responsive and responsible, and to provide an honest, reverent, relevent and challenging artistic experience for the young and youthful artist and audience, is the legacy and continuing quest of the Children's Theatre Company.
—*Jon Cranney*

The Children's Theatre Company. Billy Olson and J. C. Cutler in *Rembrandt Takes a Walk*. Photo: Giannetti Studio.

PRODUCTIONS 1987-88

- ***The Adventures of Tom Sawyer***, adapt: Timothy Mason, from Mark Twain; (D) Howard Dalin; (S) Dahl Delu; (C) Ricia Birturk; (L) James F. Ingalls
- ***Raggedy Ann and Andy***, adapt: Constance Congdon, from Johnny Gruelle; (D) Myron Johnson; (S) William Schroder; (C) William Schroder; (L) James F. Ingalls
- ***Merry Christmas, Strega Nona***, book adapt and lyrics: Thomas W. Olson; music and lyrics: Alan Shorter; (D) Tomie dePaola and Jon Cranney; (S) Steven Kennedy; (C) Tomie dePaola; (L) Michael Murnane

Young Jane Eyre, adapt: Marisha Chamberlain, from Charlotte Bronte; (D) Jon Cranney; (S) Desmond Heeley and Robert Perdziola; (C) Ricia Birturk; (L) John Michael Deegan
Harriet the Spy, adapt: Leslie Brody; (D) Kyle Donnelly; (S) Evelyn Sakash; (C) Jessica Hahn; (L) Barry Browning
The Troubles: Children of Belfast, Thomas W. Olson and company; (D) Jon Cranney; (S) Carey W. Thornton; (C) Ricia Birturk; (L) Barry Browning
The 500 Hats of Bartholomew Cubbins, adapt: Timothy Mason, from Dr. Seuss; (D) Alan Shorter; (S) Jack Barkla; (C) Judith Cooper; (L) Barry Browning
Little Women, adapt: Marisha Chamberlain, from Louisa May Alcott; (D) Jon Cranney; (S) Don Yunker; (C) Christopher Beesly; (L) Michael Murnane

PRODUCTIONS 1988–89

Robin Hood, book and lyrics: Thomas Poole; music and lyrics: Michael Koerner; (D) Jon Cranney; (S) Pavel Dobrusky; (C) Pavel Dobrusky; (L) Michael Murnane
The Velveteen Rabbit, adapt: Thomas W. Olson, from Margery Williams; (D) Myron Johnson; (S) Tom Butsch; (C) Gene D. Buck; (L) Michael Murnane
Beatrix Potter's Christmas, Thomas W. Olson; (D) Myron Johnson; (S) Jack Barkla and Laura Hohanshelt; (C) Christopher Beesley and Ricia Birturk; (L) Barry Browning
The Secret Garden, adapt: Thomas W. Olson, from Frances Hodgson Burnett; (D) Thomas W. Olson; (S) Jack Barkla and Laura Hohanshelt; (C) Christopher Beesley and Thomas Dunn; (L) Barry Browning
Sherlock Holmes and the Baker Street Irregulars, Thomas W. Olson; (D) Alan Shorter; (S) Tom Butsch; (C) Ann Sheffield; (L) Dawn Chiang
Rembrandt Takes a Walk, adapt: Constance Congdon, from Mark Strand; (D) Jon Cranney; (S) Lowell Detweiler; (C) Lowell Detweiler; (L) Barry Browning
Pippi Longstocking, Astrid Lindgren; trans and lyrics: Thomas W. Olson; trans: Truda Strockenstrom; music and lyrics: Roberta Carlson; music: Anita Ruth; (D) Myron Johnson; (S) Jack Barkla; (C) Marsha Weist-Hines; (L) Michael Murnane
Rumplestilskin & Kalulu and His Money Farm: Two African Tales, adapt: Timothy Mason; (D) Richard D. Thompson; (S) Steven Kennedy and Carey Thornton; (C) Ricia Birturk; (L) Barry Browning

Child's Play Touring Theatre

VICTOR PODAGROSI
Artistic Director

JUNE PODAGROSI
Executive Director

2650 W Belden Ave - 2nd Floor
Chicago, IL 60647
(312) 235-8911

FOUNDED 1979
Victor Podagrosi, June Podagrosi

SEASON
Sept.-June

FINANCES
Sept. 1, 1988-Aug. 31, 1989
$332,279

Child's Play Touring Theatre is a professional theatre for young audiences, dedicated to performing stories and poems written by children. The upcoming 1989-90 season will mark the 11th year that our theatre has been dedicated to elevating our audience's appreciation of their own literary abilities. By recognizing and encouraging the most talented young writers we discover, Child's Play strives to inspire and empower the next generatioin of American authors. We travel nationally and have been presented at such prestigious venues as the Brooklyn Academy of Music, the Smithsonian Institution, the Detroit Institute of Arts, the McCarter Theatre and literally thousands of schools, theatres, libraries, museums and community centers across the U.S. and in Canada. In recogniton of our responsibilities to educate as well as entertain, Child's Play offers a variety of workshop and residency activities in addition to performances.

—*Victor Podagrosi*

PRODUCTIONS 1987–88

Child's Play!, company-developed; (D) Victor Podagrosi; (C) Debra Miller
Write On!, company-developed; (D) Victor Podagrosi; (C) Debra Miller
Write On, Chicago!, company-developed; (D) Victor Podagrosi; (C) Debra Miller
Fun!, company-developed; (D) Victor Podagrosi; (C) Debra Miller
New Voices, company-developed; (D) Victor Podagrosi; (C) Debra Miller
If I Had a Dinosaur For a Pet, company-developed; (D) Victor Podagrosi; (C) Debra Miller
Writing Is...Child's Play!, company-developed; (D) Victor Podagrosi; (C) Debra Miller
One Monster After Another, company-developed; (D) Victor Podagrosi; (C) Debra Miller
Rudolph Goes Hollywood, company-developed; (D) Victor Podagrosi; (C) Debra Miller

PRODUCTIONS 1988–89

Kids for President, company-developed; (D) Victor Podagrosi; (C) Debra Miller
Animal Tales and Dinosaur Scales, company-developed; (D) Victor Podagrosi; (C) Debra Miller
Child's Play, company-developed; (D) Victor Podagrosi; (C) Debra Miller
Write On!, company-developed; (D) Victor Podagrosi; (C) Debra Miller
Write On, Chicago!, company-developed; (D) Victor Podagrosi; (C) Debra Miller
Fun!, company-developed; (D) Victor Podagrosi; (C) Debra Miller
New Voices, company-developed; (D) Victor Podagrosi; (C) Debra Miller
If I Had a Dinosaur for a Pet, company-developed; (D) Victor Podagrosi; (C) Debra Miller
Writing Is...Child's Play!, company-developed; (D) Victor Podagrosi; (C) Debra Miller
Santa & Company, company-developed; (D) Victor Podagrosi; (C) Debra Miller

Child's Play Touring Theatre. Michael Thomas and Victor Podagrosi in *Salami Again*. Photo: Jennifer Girard.

Cincinnati Playhouse in the Park

WORTH GARDNER
Artistic Director

KATHLEEN PANOFF
Managing Director

Box 6537
Cincinnati, OH 45206
(513) 421-5440 (bus.)
(513) 421-3888 (b.o.)

FOUNDED 1960
Community Members

SEASON
Sept.-Aug.

FACILITIES
Robert S. Marx Theatre
Seating Capacity: 629
Stage: thrust

Thompson Shelterhouse Theatre
Seating Capacity: 220
Stage: thrust

FINANCES
Sept 1, 1986, 19-Aug. 31, 1987
Expenses: $2,730,000

CONTRACTS
LORT (B) and (D)

The Cincinnati Playhouse in the Park is dedicated to expanding the theatrical experience for both the artists and audiences through provocative, mysterious works that reawaken the imagination through the language of drama and that recognize theatre's potential to liberate our dreams, reflect our pretenses, celebrate our differences and challenge our prejudices. With the recent establishment of a resident ensemble of actors, the personal creative development of all our artists—playwrights, directors, designers and technicians—is nurtured and encouraged to stretch and redefine its limits. One- or two-year acting internships are offered to talented young individuals, who become an integral part of the Playhouse productions and receive classroom training and alternate performance opportunities. The Playwright's Fund offers an annual fellowship to an emerging playwright, and the annual Rosenthal New Play Prize rewards a superior new work with a full-staged world premiere production and its creator with an extended residency during rehearsal. These ensure that the process of playmaking can happen in the most encouraging environment.

—*Worth Gardner*

PRODUCTIONS 1987–88

Frankenstein: The Modern Prometheus, adapt: David Richmond and Bob Hall, from Mary Shelley; (D) Barbara Carlisle; (S) Paul Shortt; (C) D. Bartlett Blair; (L) Kirk Bookman
Max and Maxie, James McLure; (D) D. Lynn Meyers; (S) Eduardo Sicangco; (C) Eduardo Sicangco; (L) Kirk Bookman and David Neville
Clear Liquor and Coal Black Nights, Thomas M. Atkinson; (D) Sam Blackwell; (S) Joseph P. Tilford; (C) D. Bartlett Blair; (L) Kirk Bookman
Burkie, Bruce Graham; (D) Richard Harden; (S) Charles Cosler; (C) Rebecca Senske; (L) Kirk Bookman
Ma Rainey's Black Bottom, August Wilson; (D) Israel Hicks; (S) Lawrence Casey; (C) Lawrence Casey; (L) Kirk Bookman
American Buffalo, David Mamet; (D) Sam Blackwell; (S) Jay Depenbrock; (C) Rebecca Senske; (L) Kirk Bookman
On the Verge or The Geography of Yearning, Eric Overmyer; (D) Worth Gardner; (S) Eduardo Sicangco; (C) Eduardo Sicangco; (L) Kirk Bookman
The Blood Knot, Athol Fugard; (D) Alex Dmitriev; (S) Scott Chambliss; (C) Rebecca Senske; (L) Kirk Bookman
Stepping Out, Richard Harris; (D) Paul Moser; (S) Jay Depenbrock; (C) Rebecca Senske; (L) Kirk Bookman
Tapestry, music and lyrics: Carole King; (D) Worth Gardner; (S) Paul Shortt; (C) D. Bartlett Blair; (L) Kirk Bookman

PRODUCTIONS 1988–89

I'm Not Rappaport, Herb Gardner; (D) Sam Blackwell; (S) Scott Chambliss; (C) D. Bartlett Blair; (L) Kirk Bookman
Long Day's Journey into Night, Eugene O'Neill; (D) Sam Blackwell; (S) Joseph P. Tilford; (C) Steven Jones; (L) Kirk Bookman
Candide, book adapt: Hugh Wheeler; music: Leonard Bernstein; lyrics: John Latouche, Stephen Sondheim; (D) Worth Gardner; (S) Scott Chambliss; (C) Eduardo Sicangco; (L) Kirk Bookman
Equus, Peter Shaffer; (D) Jonathan Eaton; (S) Paul Shortt; (C) Rebecca Senske; (L) Jay Depenbrock
Cloud Nine, Caryl Churchill; (D) Worth Gardner; (S) Scott Chambliss; (C) Scott Chambliss; (L) Kirk Bookman
Steel Magnolias, Robert Harling; (D) D. Lynn Meyers; (S) Joseph P. Tilford; (C) Rebecca Senske; (L) Kirk Bookman
Invention for Fathers and Sons, Alan Brody; (D) Jay E. Raphael; (S) Charles Caldwell; (C) Rebecca Senske; (L) Kirk Bookman
Much Ado About Nothing, William Shakespeare; (D) John Russell Brown; (S) Marjorie Bradley Kellogg; (C) D. Bartlett Blair; (L) Kirk Bookman
The Colored Museum, George C. Wolfe; (D) Luther Goins; (S) Jay Depenbrock; (C) Rebecca Senske; (L) Kirk Bookman
The Rocky Horror Show, book, music and lyrics: Richard O'Brien; (D) Worth Gardner; (S) Paul Shortt; (C) Eduardo Sicangco; (L) Kirk Bookman
Miss Margarida's Way, Roberto Athayde; (D) Sam Blackwell; (S) Bob Fetterman; (C) Bob Fetterman; (L) Amy Merrell

Cincinatti Playhouse in the Park. *The Rocky Horror Show.* Photo: Sandy Underwood.

Circle Repertory Company

TANYA BEREZIN
Artistic Director

CONNIE L. ALEXIS
Managing Director

161 Ave. of the Americas
New York, NY 10013
(212) 691-3210 (bus.)
(212) 924-7100 (b.o.)

FOUNDED 1969
Lanford Wilson, Robert Thirkield, Marshall W. Mason, Tanya Berezin

Circle Repertory Company. Robin Bartlett, John Dossett and Welker White in *Reckless*. Photo: Gerry Goodstein.

SEASON
Sept.-June

FACILITIES
Seating Capacity: 160
Stage: flexible

FINANCES
July 1, 1988-June 30, 1989
Expenses: $2,003,575

CONTRACTS
AEA Off Broadway

Circle Repertory Company comprises a family of more than 200 theatre artists who share a commitment to excellence, and a vision of truth and humanity in the theatre. Now in its third decade, Circle Rep has become a national resource of new plays, producing more than 100 that have subsequently been presented at scores of professional theatres in all 50 states and many foreign countries. Dedicated to developing American works for the stage, Circle Rep continues to expand its definition of a lyric realistic style to include a multiplicity of American voices and world visions. Our developmental process, which includes a writers and directors lab, as well as three series of staged readings, allows us to challenge our mature theatre artists to explore new areas of their art while proceeding with an active search for new talent. It is this collaboration by an ensemble of artists to create a vibrant and vital theatrical experience that has become the source of growth and creative achievement for the company over the last two decades.
—*Tanya Berezin*

PRODUCTIONS 1987–88

El Salvador, Rafael Lima;
   (D) John Bishop; (S) David
   Potts; (C) Jennifer von
   Mayrhauser; (L) Dennis Parichy
Only You, Timothy Mason;
   (D) Ron Lagomarsino; (S) John
   Lee Beatty; (C) Ann Emonts;
   (L) Dennis Parichy
Cave Life, David Steven
   Rappoport; (D) Paul Lazarus;
   (S) William Barclay; (C) Nancy
   Konrardy; (L) Phil Monat
Borderlines, John Bishop;
   (D) Robert Bailey; (S) John Lee
   Beatty; (C) Jennifer von
   Mayrhauser; (L) Dennis Parichy
V & V Only, Jim Leonard;
   (D) Marshall W. Mason; (S) John
   Lee Beatty; (C) Susan Denison
   Geller; (L) Dennis Parichy

PRODUCTIONS 1988–89

Reckless, Craig Lucas;
   (D) Norman Rene; (S) Loy
   Arcenas; (C) Walker Hicklin;
   (L) Debra J. Kletter
Dalton's Back, Keith Curran;
   (D) Mark Ramont; (S) William
   Barclay; (C) Susan Lyall;
   (L) Dennis Parichy
Brilliant Traces, Cindy Lou
   Johnson; (D) Terry Kinney;
   (S) John Lee Beatty; (C) Laura
   Crow; (L) Dennis Parichy
*Amulets Against the Dragon
   Forces*, Paul Zindel; (D) B.
   Rodney Marriott; (S) David
   Potts; (C) Walker Hicklin;
   (L) Dennis Parichy
Florida Crackers, William S.
   Levingood; (D) John Bishop;
   (S) John Lee Beatty; (C) Connie
   Singer; (L) Dennis Parichy

City Theatre Company

MARC MASTERSON
Producing Director

ANNE MARIE TRISTAN
General Manager

B-39 Cathedral of Learning
University of Pittsburgh
Pittsburgh, PA 15260
(412) 624-1357 (bus.)
(412) 624-PLAY (b.o.)

FOUNDED 1973
City of Pittsburgh

SEASON
Jan.-Dec.

FACILITIES
New City Theatre
Seating Capacity: 120
Stage: thrust

*Hartwood Acres Summer
Theatre*
Seating Capacity: 275
Stage: thrust

FINANCES
July 1, 1988-June 30, 1989
Expenses: $388,563

CONTRACTS
AEA SPT

City Theatre is interested in developing new American plays, and in producing works of substance and ideas relevant to contemporary values and cultures. The company has developed an ongoing relationship with a loosely defined ensemble of actors, directors and designers over the last nine years. In 1987 City Theatre instituted a policy of nontraditional casting which has resulted in greater ethnic diversity both on stage and in

City Theatre Company. Lori Cardille and David Butler in *Talk Radio*. Photo: Suellen Fitzsimmons.

the audience. City Theatre produces programming for all ages and socioeconomic backgrounds. It is founded in deep respect for the artist, as well as the audience, and attempts to join the needs of both through the art form. City Theatre's programs include a four-play subscription series; an active new script development program including workshops, staged readings and full productions of new plays; the Playworks street theatre program which commissions new scripts each year for performances in city housing projects, parks and schools; and a summer season at Hartwood Acres Park in Allegheny County.
—Marc Masterson

PRODUCTIONS 1987–88

Danger: Memory!, Arthur Miller; (D) Jed Allen Harris and Marc Masterson; (S) Diane Melchitzky; (C) Gaye Hockenberry; (L) Norman Russell
Rose Cottages, Bill Bozzone; (D) Gordon McDougall; (S) William O'Donnell; (C) Peter Harrigan; (L) Bob Vukich
Principia Scriptoriae, Richard Nelson; (D) Marc Masterson; (S) Dennis Kennedy and John Donnelly; (C) Lorraine Venberg; (L) Bob Steineck
Tamer of Horses, William Mastrosimone; (D) Jed Allen Harris; (S) Tony Ferrieri; (C) Peter Harrigan; (L) Matt Shaffer
Tomfoolery, adapt: Cameron Mackintosh and Robin Ray; book, music and lyrics: Tom Lehrer; (D) Jed Allen Harris; (S) William O'Donnell; (C) Gaye Hockenberry; (L) William O'Donnell
The House of Blue Leaves, John Guare; (D) Marc Masterson; (S) Tony Ferrieri; (C) Tere Eglar-Bilsky; (L) Matt Schaffer

PRODUCTIONS 1988–89

Frankie and Johnny in the Clare de Lune, Terrence McNally; (D) Marc Masterson; (S) Diane Melchitzky; (C) Peter Harrigan; (L) Bob Steineck
Talk Radio, Eric Bogosian; (D) Jed Allen Harris; (S) Linda Sechrist; (C) Peter Harrigan; (L) William O'Donnell
Painting It Red, book: Steven Dietz; music: Garry Rue; lyrics: Leslie Ball; (D) Steven Dietz; (S) Tony Ferrieri; (C) Sue O'Neill; (L) Bob Steineck
The Voice of the Praire, John Olive; (D) Conrad Bishop;

(S) Henry Heymann; (C) Peter Harrigan; (L) Rick Martin
Blues in the Night, Sheldon Epps; (D) Tome Cousin; (S) Tony Ferrieri; (C) M.A. Eshelman; (L) William O'Donnell
True West, Sam Shepard; (D) Marc Materson; (S) Tony Ferrieri; (C) Dian Collins; (L) Bob Steineck

Clarence Brown Theatre Company

THOMAS P. COOKE
Producing Director

DORIS SINKS
General Manager

UT Box 8450
Knoxville, TN 37996
(615) 974-6011 (bus.)
(615) 974-5161 (b.o.)

FOUNDED 1974
Anthony Quayle, Ralph G. Allen

SEASON
variable

FACILITIES
Clarence Brown Theatre
Seating Capacity: 604
Stage: proscenium

Studio Theatre
Seating Capacity: 100
Stage: thrust

Carousel Theatre
Seating Capacity: 375
Stage: arena

FINANCES
July 1, 1988-June 30, 1989
Expenses: $544,500

CONTRACTS
LORT D

The Clarence Brown Theatre Company is the professional component of the theatre program of the University of Tennessee and is intended to provide the university community and the American Southeast region with theatre of the highest caliber. The company has a distinguished tradition of presenting the finest professional

actors in challenging classic roles and is committed to the development of new plays. It has brought to regional audiences such performances as Anthony Quayle in *Macbeth*, Simon Ward in Isherwood's *A Meeting by the River*, and Zoe Caldwell and Dame Judith Anderson in *Medea*. During the past two seasons, the company has participated in the development of an International Theatre Research Center at UT. It was one of the sponsors of Teatro del Sur's production of *Warsaw Tango* and brought Nicolai Vagin of the Moscow Art Theatre to design *Uncle Vanya* in the 1988-89 season.
—Thomas P. Cooke

PRODUCTIONS 1987–88

Master Harold . . .and the boys, Athol Fugard; (D) Peter DeLaurier; (S) Leonard Harman; (C) Marianne Custer; (L) L.J. DeCuir
Pygmalion, George Bernard Shaw; (D) Gavin Cameron-Webb; (S) Robert Cothran; (C) Marianne Custer; (L) John Horner
The Man of Mode, George Etheredge; (D) Gavin Cameron-Webb; (S) Robert Cothran; (C) Bill Black; (L) L.J. DeCuir

PRODUCTIONS 1988–89

Amadeus, Peter Shaffer; (D) Thomas P. Cooke; (S) Darwin L. Payne; (C) Bill Black; (L) Beth LaJoie
Uncle Vanya, Anton Chekhov; trans: Sergei Ponomarov; (D) Sergei Ponomarov; (S) Nicolai Vagin; (C) Mindy Mathis; (L) Beth LaJoie
Deja Vu, Maurice Lasaygues and Jean-Jacques Bricaire; trans: John MacNicholas; (D) Richard Block; (S) Constanza Romero; (C) Marianne Custer; (L) John Horner

The Cleveland Play House

JOSEPHINE R. ABADY
Artistic Director

DEAN R. GLADDEN
Managing Director

Box 1989
Cleveland, OH 44106
(216) 795-7010 (bus.)
(216) 795-7000 (b.o.)

FOUNDED 1915
Raymond O'Neill

SEASON
Sept.-May

FACILITIES
Kenyon C. Bolton Theatre
Seating Capacity: 612
Stage: proscenium

Francis E. Drury Theatre
Seating Capacity: 499
Stage: proscenium

Charles S. Brooks Theatre
Seating Capacity: 160
Stage: proscenium

Clarence Brown Theatre Company. Tamara Daniel and Alison Lyons in *Man of Mode*. Photo: Eric Smith.

The Cleveland Play House. *On the Waterfront.* Photo: Paul Tepley.

FINANCES
July 1, 1988-June 30, 1989
Expenses: $5,500,000

CONTRACTS
LORT (C)

The Cleveland Play House is experiencing a renaissance. With emphasis on new works and new ways of presenting the classics, and with our concentration on American works, over half of our resources are allocated to new plays. The Play House is a cultural leader in the revitalization of its surrounding neighborhood. But physical recovery is only one part of the solution—theatre begins and ends with people. One of our strongest imperatives is to offer work that appeals to all segments of our community, strengthening the bonds with our supporters while reaching out to new and lost audiences. Our obligation to the artists who work here is to provide them with an environment that fosters creativity and experimentation, participation and commitment, and an audience that is ready to be an active partner in creating theatre. For as we sit together in the dark—laughing, crying and experiencing live performance—we discover the best that we are as human beings.
—*Josephine R. Abady*

Note: During the 1987-88 season, William Rhys served as resident artistic director.

PRODUCTIONS 1987–88

Taking Steps, Alan Ayckbourn; (D) Sue Lawless; (S) Richard Gould; (C) Estelle Painter; (L) Richard Gould
K2, Patrick Meyers; (D) Evie McElroy; (S) Keith Henery; (C) Richard Gould; (L) Richard Gould
The Fantasticks, book and lyrics: Tom Jones; music: Harvey Schmidt; (D) Jack Eddlerman; (S) Charles F. Morgan; (C) Estelle Painter; (L) Paul Mathieson
Deathraft, Harold Mueller; trans: Roger Downey; (D) George Ferencz; (S) Bill Stabile; (C) Estelle Painter; (L) Beverly Emmons
Much Ado About Nothing, William Shakespeare; (D) Nicholas Pennel; (S) Richard Gould; (C) Estelle Painter; (L) Richard Gould
Exit the King, Eugene Ionesco; (D) William Rhys; (S) Charles Berliner; (C) Charles Berliner; (L) Richard Gould
The Common Pursuit, Simon Gray; (D) Kenneth L. Albers; (S) Keith Henery; (C) Estelle Painter; (L) Richard Gould
The Immigrant: A Hamilton County Album, Mark Harelik; (D) Dudley Swetland; (S) Richard Gould; (C) Richard Gould; (L) Richard Gould
A Christmas Carol, adapt: Doris Baizley, from Charles Dickens; (D) William Rhys; (S) Charles Berliner; (C) Charles Berliner; (L) Richard Gould
Kids in the Dark, Rick Cleveland and David Breskin; (D) Evie McElroy; (S) Keith Henery and Deborah Malcolm; (C) Dawna Gregory; (L) Anthony Sutowski and Beth Wolfe

PRODUCTIONS 1988–89

Bovver Boys, Willy Holtzman; (D) Michael Breault; (S) Jefferson Sage; (C) Kay Kurta; (L) Clifton Taylor
The Boys Next Door, Tom Griffin; (D) Josephine Abady; (S) David Potts; (C) C.L. Hundley; (L) Clifton Taylor
Born Yesterday, Garson Kanin; (D) Josephine Abady; (S) David Potts; (C) Ann Roth; (L) Jeff Davis
Breaking the Code, Hugh Whitemore; (D) Bob Baker; (S) Stancil Campbell; (C) Leslie Frankish; (L) Stancil Campbell
Carnival!, book: Michael Stewart; music and lyrics: Bob Merrill; (D) Jack Hofsiss; (S) David Jenkins; (C) William Ivey Long; (L) Natasha Katz
The Cemetery Club, Ivan Menchell; (D) Josephine Abady; (S) David Potts; (C) Jane Greenwood and David Charles; (L) Dennis Parichy
A Christmas Memory, adapt: Beth Sanford, from Truman Capote; (D) Roger Danforth; (S) Jefferson Sage; (C) Kay Kurta; (L) Clifton Taylor
The Glass Menagerie, Tennessee Williams; (D) Tazewell Thompson; (S) Jefferson Sage; (C) Kay Kurta; (L) John Hastings
Italian-American Reconciliation, John Patrick Shanley; (D) Michael Breault; (S) Loy Arcenas; (C) Jim Bluff; (L) Clifton Taylor
Les Liaisons Dangereuses, trans and adapt: Christopher Hampton; (D) Robert Berlinger; (S) Hugh Landwehr; (C) Mimi Maxman; (L) Mark Weiss
On the Waterfront, Budd Schulberg and Stan Silverman; (D) Josephine Abady; (S) David Potts; (C) Julie Weiss; (L) Richard Winkler
As Is, William Hoffman; (D) Michael Breault; (S) Jefferson Sage; (C) Kay Kurta; (L) Clifton Taylor
Real Dreams, Trevor Griffiths; (D) David Esbjornson; (S) Jefferson Sage; (C) Kay Kurta; (L) Clifton Taylor

Cornerstone Theater Company

BILL RAUCH
Artistic Director

JAMES BUNDY
Managing Director

1303 Timberly Lane
McLean, VA 22102-2503
(703) 556-0353

FOUNDED 1986
Bill Rauch, Alison Carey

SEASON
Aug.-June

FINANCES
July 1, 1988-June 30, 1989
Expenses: $225,000

Cornerstone Theater Company works alone as a professional ensemble, and in collaboration with ethnically and economically diverse communities across the United States. All of our productions are epic interactions between classics of dramatic literature and specific American communities: Moliere's disintegrating and combative families in the Kansas farmland, Shakespeare's civil strife in the segregated streets of Mississippi, Aeschylus' ancient rituals on the modern American Indian reservation. By writing local concerns into the script, by sewing local color into the costumes, by rehearsing local actors into the roles, we work to open people's minds and hearts to plays which have been traditionally closed to them. We work to build a new, inclusive American theatre. Company members are Amy Brenneman, James Bundy, Alison Carey, Benajah Cobb, Peter Howard, Mary-Ann Greanier, Lynn Jeffries, Christopher Moore, Catherine Patterson, Bill Rauch, David Reiffel and Ashby Semple.
—*Bill Rauch*

PRODUCTIONS 1987–88

The Dog Beneath the Skin: An Epidemic Epic, adapt: company, from W.H. Auden and Christopher Isherwood; music and lyrics: David Reiffel; (D) Bill Rauch; (S) Lynn Jeffries;

Cornerstone Theater Company. Amy Brenneman in *Romeo and Juliet*.

(C) Lynn Jeffries; (L) Betsy P. Cardwell
Tartoof, or an Imposter in Norcatur—and at Christmas!, adapt: company, from Moliere; (D) Bill Rauch; (S) Lynn Jeffries; (C) Lynn Jeffries; (L) Mary-Ann Greanier
A Midsummer Night's Dream, adapt: company, from William Shakespeare; (D) Bill Rauch; (S) Lynn Jeffries; (C) Sal-Thomas Taschetta; (L) Benajah Cobb
The House on Walker River, adapt: company, from Aeschylus; trans: Robert Fagles; (D) Bill Rauch; (S) Lynn Jeffries; (C) Lynn Jeffries and Sal-Thomas Taschetta; (L) Mary-Ann Greanier
I Can't Pay the Rent, company-developed; (D) Bill Rauch; (S) Lynn Jeffries; (C) Lynn Jeffries; (L) Benajah Cobb

PRODUCTIONS 1988–89

The Good Person of Long Creek, adapt: company, from Bertolt Brecht; trans: Ralph Manheim; (D) Bill Rauch; (S) Lynn Jeffries; (C) Lynn Jeffries; (L) Loren Brame
Romeo and Juliet, adapt: company, from William Shakespeare (D) Bill Rauch; (S) Lynn Jeffries; (C) Lynn Jeffries; (L) Mary-Ann Greanier
A Midsummer Night's Dream, adapt: company, from William Shakespeare; (D) Bill Rauch; (S) Lynn Jeffries; (C) Lynn Jeffries; (L) Benajah Cobb
I Can't Pay the Rent, company-developed; (D) Bill Rauch; (S) Lynn Jeffries; (C) Lynn Jeffries; (L) Benajah Cobb
Slides of Our Trip, company-developed; (D) Bill Rauch; (S) Lynn Jeffries; (C) Lynn Jeffries; (L) Benajah Cobb

Creation Production Company

MATTHEW MAGUIRE
SUSAN MOSAKOWSKI
Co-Artistic Directors

JENNIFER MCDOWELL
Administrative Director

127 Greene St.
New York, NY 10012
(212) 674-5593

FOUNDED 1977
Susan Mosakowski, Matthew Maguire

SEASON
Jan.-Jan.

FINANCES
July 1, 1988-June 30, 1989
Expenses: $140,000

CONTRACTS
AEA letter of agreement

Creation Production Company is advancing a new vision of theatre by fusing the iconoclastic with traditional stagecraft. The company aesthetic generates new forms of music theatre; site-specific work; the confrontation of political issues through formal structures; radical experiments with language; and the seamless integration of the visual arts, music, dance, video and architecture. A highly visual and conceptual performance style has been forged with an ongoing ensemble. Creation has produced 32 new works in Washington, Philadelphia, Baltimore, Minneapolis, Seattle, Berlin and Amsterdam, as well as in New York.
—*Matthew Maguire*

PRODUCTIONS 1987–88

Visions of Don Juan, Matthew Maguire; (D) Matthew Maguire; (S) Jim Clayburgh; (C) Richard Curtis; (L) Jim Clayburgh
The Rotary Notary and His Hot Plate, Susan Mosakowski; (D) Susan Mosakowski; (S) Elizabeth Diller and Ricardo Scofidio; (C) Richard Curtis; (L) Pat Dignan
The Cabinet of Dr. Caligari, adapt: Susan Mosakowski; (D) Susan Mosakowski; (S) Tom Keever; (C) Richard Curtis; (L) Pat Dignan
Wipeout, Jeffrey M. Jones; (D) Jeffrey M. Jones
Cities Out of Print, Susan Mosakowski; (D) Susan Mosakowski; (S) Tom Keever; (L) Pat Dignan

PRODUCTIONS 1988–89

The Tower, Matthew Maguire; (D) Matthew Maguire; (S) Dean Holzman and Matthew Maguire; (C) Katherine Maurer; (L) Jeff Bartlett

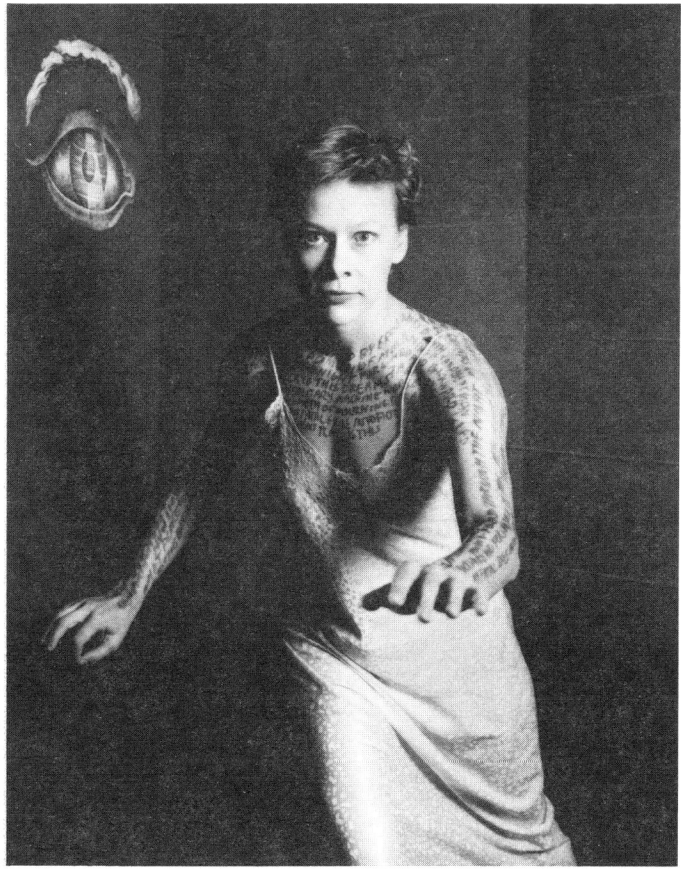

Creation Production Company. Susan Mosakowski in *The Bachelor Machine*.

Wipeout, Jeffrey M. Jones;
(D) Jeffrey M. Jones; (S) Jeffrey
M. Jones; (C) Sally J. Lessor;
(L) Pat Dignan
Bride/Bachelor Trilogy, Susan
Mosakowski; (D) Susan
Mosakowski; (S) Elizabeth Diller
and Ricardo Scofidio;
(C) Richard Curtis; (L) Pat
Dignan and Jeff Bartlett
The Tower, Matthew Maguire;
(D) Matthew Maguire; (S) Joe
Fyfe; (L) Pat Dignan
Babel on Babylon, Matthew
Maguire; (D) Matthew Maguire;
(C) Claudia Brown

Creative Arts Team

LYNDA ZIMMERMAN
Executive Director

MARSHALL JONES
Managing Director

MARK RIHERD
Program Director

N.Y. University, Gallatin Div.
715 Broadway, 5th Fl.
New York, NY 10003
(212) 998-7380

FOUNDED 1974
Lynda Zimmerman

SEASON
variable

FINANCES
July 1, 1988-June 30, 1989
Expenses: $950,000

The Creative Arts Team is the professional educational theatre company in residence at New York University. Since 1974, CAT has pioneered a combination of original theatre productions and participatory drama workshops designed to address social and curricular issues for today's youth. Recent original productions have examined child abuse (*I Never Told Anybody*), substance abuse (*Home Court*) and race relations (*The Divider*). CAT's drama workshops confront students with such topics as AIDS, prejudice and racism, teen pregnancy and sexuality, employment, illiteracy, peer pressure, self-esteem, socialization and critical reasoning skills. CAT's work has received national and international recognition and has been featured on such television programs as Good Morning America, Main Street and The Today Show. Additionally, for the past two years CAT has performed at the National Basketball Association's Rookies Conference and recently participated in the Vancouver International Children's Festival.
—*Mark Riherd*

PRODUCTIONS 1987–88

Home Court, Jim Mirrione;
(D) Achim Nowak
The Divider, Jim Mirrione;
(D) Achim Nowak

PRODUCTIONS 1988–89

Getting Through, book: Nona
Shepard; music: Helen Galvin;
add'l lyrics: Byrony Lavery;
(D) Achim Nowak
The Divider, Jim Mirrione;
(D) Michael Littman
Home Court, Jim Mirrione;
(D) Eugene Key

Creative Arts Team. Sudi Khosropur, Danny Carlton, Man Ching Tom and Eugene Key in *The Divider*. Photo: Johan Elbers.

The Cricket Theatre. Dawn Renee Jones, Karen Esbjornson, Allan Hickle-Edwards, James R. Stowell and Chuck McQuary in *The Angels of Warsaw*.

The Cricket Theatre

WILLIAM PARTLAN
Artistic Director

9 West 14th St.
Minneapolis, MN 55403
(612) 871-3763 (bus.)
(612) 871-2244 (b.o.)

FOUNDED 1971
William Semans

SEASON
Sept.-June

FACILITIES
Seating Capacity: 213
Stage: proscenium

FINANCES
July 1, 1988-June 31, 1989
Expenses: $517,582

CONTRACTS
AEA SPT

The Cricket is a playwright-oriented producing theatre. I believe our playwrights are among our most important visionaries; they create imagined worlds which contain a people, a language and a code of interaction all their own. I look for inventively-peopled theatrical worlds; for intensively interactive plays with muscular language. As theatre artists, we explore the boundaries of these worlds with the writers and together we give them a theatrical life which reaches for resonance in our audiences' lives. The Cricket provides developmental and production resources for a number of local, national and international playwrights in our new, intimate theatre facility. We do not employ a fulltime company but hire the best artists and technicians available to create the world of each project. The Cricket has emerged from economic hard times as a leaner, more flexible organization —attempting to create a vital theatrical proving ground for theatre artists.
—*William Partlan*

PRODUCTIONS 1987–88

The Deal, Matthew Witten; (D) William Partlan; (S) Chris Johnson; (C) Nayna Ramey; (L) Tina Charney
Eleemosynary, Lee Blessing; (D) Jeanne Blake; (S) Rick Polenek; (C) Rick Polenek; (L) Chris Johnson
Red Hot Holidays, John Richardson; (D) William Partlan; (S) Chris Johnson; (C) Deidra Whitlock; (L) Tina Charney
Three Postcards, Craig Lucas; music: Craig Carnelia; (D) Kent Stephens; (S) Jack Barkla; (C) Nayna Ramey; (L) Tina Charney
Savage in Limbo, John Patrick Shanley; (D) George Sand; (S) Jack Barkla; (C) Jack Barkla; (L) Tina Charney
Lady Day at Emerson's Bar and Grill, Lanie Robertson; (D) William Partlan; (S) Jack Barkla; (C) Richard Hamson; (L) Chris Johnson

PRODUCTIONS 1988–89

The Downside, Richard Dresser; (D) William Partlan; (S) Vera Mednikov; (C) Vera Mednikov; (L) Tina Charney
Frankie and Johnny in the Clair de Lune, Terrence McNally; (D) Howard Dallin; (S) Colin Tugwell; (C) Colin Tugwell; (L) Tina Charney
Diamond Cut Diamond, Jeff Wanshel; (D) William Partlan; (S) G.W. Mercier; (C) Lynn Farrington; (L) Tina Charney
Alfred Stieglitz Loves O'Keefe, Lanie Robertson; (D) Julia Carey; (S) Jack Barkla; (C) Jack Barkla; (L) Tina Charney
All God's Dangers, Theodore Rosengarten, Michael Hadley and Jennifer Hadley; (D) William Partlan; (S) G. W. Mercier; (C) G. W. Mercier; (L) Tina Charney
Red Hot Holidays, John Richardson; (D) William Partlan; (S) Chris Johnson; (C) Mark Caligiuri; (L) Tina Charney

Crossroads Theatre Company

RICK KHAN
Founder/Artistic Director

ANDRE ROBINSON, JR.
General Manager

320 Memorial Pkwy.
New Brunswick, NJ 08901
(201) 249-5581 (bus.)
(201) 249-5560 (b.o.)

FOUNDED 1978
L. Kenneth Richardson, Rick Khan

SEASON
Sept.–May

FACILITIES
Seating Capacity: 150
Stage: thrust

FINANCES
July 1, 1988-June 30, 1989
Expenses: $1,417,540

CONTRACTS
LORT (D) and AEA letter of agreement

Crossroads Theatre Company is dedicated to upholding the highest standards of artistic excellence and innovation in professional black theatre, and has successfully promoted multiracial appreciation and support for the honest portrayal of black life and culture on stage. The theatre mounts five productions annually, tours nationally and internationally, supports a multifaceted education program and conducts the much-acclaimed New Play Rites program, designed to develop new works for the main stage and for the New Play Rites Festival: Genesis. Crossroads has effectively recognized black theatre as world theatre, for our work has its roots in Africa, in the West Indies, in Latin America and Europe. These very roots, if cultivated, can provide us with a rich network of cultural resources and an expanded artistic vocabulary that is at once artistically stimulating, culturally informing and spiritually uplifting—a vocabulary that can move us successfully through the 1990s and into the 21st century.
—*Rick Khan*

During the 1987-88 season, L. Kenneth Richardson served as co-artistic director.

PRODUCTIONS 1987–88

Spell #7, Ntozake Shange; (D) A. Dean Irby; (S) Daniel Proett; (C) Alvin Perry; (L) Victor En Yu Tan
Woza Albert!, Percy Mtwa, Mbongeni Ngema and Barney Simon; (D) Richard Gant and Duma Ndlovu; (S) Daniel Proett; (C) Alvin Perry; (L) William H. Grant, III
Sophisticated Ladies, Duke Ellington; (D) Bernard J. Marsh; (S) Felix E. Cochren; (C) Bernard Johnson; (L) William F. McDaniel
Lady Day at Emerson's Bar and Grill, Lanie Robertson; (D) Bette Howard; (S) Charles McClennahan; (C) Judy Dearing; (L) Shirley Prendergast
West Memphis Mojo, Martin Jones; (D) Rick Khan; (S) Charles McClennahan; (C) Judy Dearing; (L) Shirley Prendergast
Wet Carpets, Marian Warrington; (D) Bette Howard; (S) Charles McClennahan; (C) Alvin Perry; (L) Susan A. White

PRODUCTIONS 1988–89

To Gleam it Around, To Show My Shine, Bonnie Lee Moss Ratner; (D) Rick Kahn; (S) Daniel Proett; (C) Judy Dearing; (L) Shirley Prendergast
The Mojo and the Sayso, Aishah Rahman; (D) George Ferencz; (S) Bill Stabile; (C) Sally J. Lesser; (L) Blu
Late Great Ladies of Blues and Jazz, Sandra Reave-Phillips; (D) Rick Kahn; (S) Daniel Proett; (C) Michael Hannah; (L) Shirley Prendergast
The Rabbit Foot, Leslie Lee; (D) Walter Dallas; (S) Charles McClennahan; (C) Nancy Konrardy; (L) Sandra Ross
Playboy of the West Indies, Mustapha Matura; (D) Ken Johnson; (S) Daniel Proett; (C) Alvin Perry; (L) Shirley Prendergast
Spooks, Don Evans; (D) Seret Scott; (S) Daniel Proett; (C) Beth Ribblet; (L) William H. Grant, III

Crossroads Theatre Company. *Playboy of the West Indies.* Photo: Eddie Birch.

CSC Repertory Ltd.-The Classic Stage Company

CAREY PERLOFF
Artistic Director

ELLEN NOVACK
Managing Director

136 East 13th St.
New York, NY 10003
(212) 477-5808 (bus.)
(212) 677-4210 (b.o.)

FOUNDED 1967
Christopher Martin

SEASON
Oct.–May

FACILITIES
Seating Capacity: 180
Stage: flexible

FINANCES
July 1, 1988-June 30, 1989
Expenses: $445,000

CONTRACTS
AEA letter of agreement

CSC Repertory Ltd.-The Classic Stage Company, exists to rediscover and reinterpret the rich international classical repertoire often forgotten in a country voracious for new plays. Located in the East Village, one of the hottest visual and performing arts communities in America, CSC is committed to visually evocative productions of plays from every culture—from Sophocles to Pinter to Chekhov to Ezra Pound—plays that exhibit rich language, theatricality and depth of subject matter. We actively commission American playwrights to create new translations and adaptations of classic plays, which we develop in our Sneak Previews of New and Undiscovered Classics reading series. CSC seeks out imaginative artists from every race, background, gender and genre, and makes extensive use of live music and dance in production. The Conservatory at CSC trains young actors in classical theatre, and our City Stages for City Students program brings free productions to New York City students.

—*Carey Perloff*

PRODUCTIONS 1987–88

Elektra, Sophocles; trans and adapt: Ezra Pound; (D) Carey Perloff; (S) Donald Eastman; (C) Candice Donnelly; (L) Frances Aronson

Uncle Vanya, Anton Chekhov; trans: Marion Fell; (D) Maria Irene Fornes; (S) Donald Eastman; (C) Gabriel Berry; (L) Frances Aronson

The Birthday Party, Harold Pinter; (D) Carey Perloff; (S) Loy Arcenas; (C) Gabriel Berry; (L) Beverly Emmons

PRODUCTIONS 1988–89

Rameau's Nephew, Denis Diderot; trans and adapt: Shelley Berc; (D) Andrei Belgrader; (S) Anita Stewart; (C) Candice Donnelly; (L) Robert Wierzel

Phaedra Britannica, Jean Racine; adapt: Tony Harrison; (D) Carey Perloff; (S) Donald Eastman; (C) Gabriel Berry; (L) Frances Aronson

Don Juan of Seville, Tirso de Molina; trans: Lynne Alvarez; (D) Carey Perloff; (S) Donald Eastman; (C) Gabriel Berry; (L) Frances Aronson

CSC Repertory Ltd.—The Classic Stage Company. Peterr Riegert and David Strathairn in *The Birthday Party*. Photo: Tom Chargin.

Cumberland County Playhouse

JAMES CRABTREE
Producing Director

MARY CRABTREE
Consulting Producer

Box 484
Crossville, TN 38557
(615) 484-2300 (bus.)
(615) 484-5000 (b.o.)

FOUNDED 1965
Margaret Keyes Harrison, Moses Dorton, Paul Crabtree

SEASON
Mar.-Dec.

FACILITIES
Cumberland County Playhouse
Seating Capacity: 478
Stage: proscenium

Theater-in-the-Woods
Seating Capacity: 199
Stage: arena

The Adventure Theater
Seating Capacity: 199
Stage: flexible

Fairfield Dinner Theater
Seating Capacity: 165
Stage: proscenium

FINANCES
Jan. 1, 1988-Dec. 31, 1988
Expenses: $616,020

CONTRACTS
AEA Guest Artist

Our home is a town of 6,500 in a rural Appalachian county within two hours of Knoxville and Chattanooga, to which we draw over 75,000 patrons per year. We embrace the idea that the arts can be an indigenous part of rural America, not just an imported commodity. Our Fairfield Living History Series presents new plays and musicals rooted in Tennessee history. Playhouse-in-the-Schools puts company members in classrooms as teachers for the curriculum we're developing with local educators. Mainstage and shows for young audiences tour to rural schools and communities. Since 1980 we have presented a dozen world premieres, mostly of works relating to our home region. Our resident company is from Tennessee and the Southeast, and they're joined by guest artists and a strong volunteer corps. During 1989 we began a major expansion, adding a black-box theatre, classrooms, production and administrative space. We balance our budgets, own our facility and avoid deficits.

—*James Crabtree*

PRODUCTIONS 1987–88

On Golden Pond, Ernest Thompson; (D) Abigail Crabtree; (S) Martha Hill; (C) Brenda Schwab; (L) John Partyka

A Homestead Album, book and lyrics: Jim Crabtree; music: Dennis Davenport; (D) Jim Crabtree; (S) Doyle Vaden and J. Paul Nail; (C) Amelie Crabtree; (L) John Partyka

The King and I, book and lyrics: Oscar Hammerstein, II; music: Richard Rodgers; (D) Mary Crabtree; (S) Gary Harris; (C) Brenda Schwab; (L) John Horner

Children of a Lesser God, Mark Medoff; (D) Abigail Crabtree; (S) Jim Crabtree; (C) Brenda Schwab; (L) Jim Crabtree

The Robber Bridegroom, book, lyrics and adapt: Alfred Uhry; music: Robert Waldman; (D) Marilouise Michel; (S) John Partyka; (C) Brenda Schwab; (L) John Partyka

The Perils of Pinocchio, book and lyrics: Paul Crabtree; music: Mary Catherine Brennanbook; (D) Jim Crabtree; (S) Joe Varga; (C) Mary Crabtree; (L) John Partyka

Li'l Abner, book: Norman Panam and Melvin Frank; lyrics: Johnny Merer; music: Gene dePaul; (D) Marilouise Michel; (S) John Partyka; (C) Brenda Schwab; (L) John Partyka

Smoky Mountain Suite, George Clinton and Sherry Landrum; (D) Sherry Landrum; (S) John Partyka; (C) Brenda Schwab and

Cumberland County Playhouse. *The Diary of Anne Frank.*

Terry Schwab; (L) John Partyka
Brand New Beat, Jim Crabtree
and Dennis Davenport;
(D) Marilouise Michel; (S) Gary
Harris; (C) Brenda Schwab and
Terry Schwab; (L) John Partyka

PRODUCTIONS 1988–89

Shenandoah, book: James Lee
Barrett, Peter Udell and Philip
Rose; music: Gary Geld; lyrics:
Peter Udell; (D) Abigail
Crabtree; (S) John Partyka;
(C) Brenda Schwab and Terry
Schwab; (L) John Partyka
Smoky Mountain Suite, George
Clinton and Sherry Landrum;
(D) Sherry Landrum; (S) John
Partyka; (C) Brenda Schwab;
(L) John Partyka
The Nerd, Larry Shue; (D) Abigail
Crabtree; (S) Martha Hill;
(C) Brenda Schwab; (L) John
Partyka
The Music Man, book, music and
lyrics: Meredith Willson;
(D) Mary Crabtree; (S) Leonard
Harman; (C) Mary Crabtree;
(L) John Partyka
Pirates and Pinafores, Jim
Crabtree and Dennis Davenport;
(D) Jim Crabtree; (S) Amelie
Crabtree; (C) Mary Crabtree;
(L) John Partyka
The Physicists, Friedrich
Durrenmatt; (D) Jim Crabtree;
(S) Ron Keller; (C) Brenda
Schwab; (L) John Partyka
Cornstalk Wine, Jim Connor;
(D) Jim Crabtree; (C) Brenda
Schwab; (L) John Partyka
Annie, book: Thomas Meehan;
music: Charles Strouse; lyrics:
Martin Charnin; (S) Jim
Crabtree; (C) Amelie Crabtree;
(L) Scott Leathers

Dallas Theater Center

KEN BRYANT
Interim Artistic Director

JEFF WEST
Managing Director

3636 Turtle Creek Blvd.
Dallas, TX 75219-5598
(214) 526-8210 (bus.)
(214) 526-8857 (b.o.)

FOUNDED 1959
Robert D. Stecker, Sr., Beatrice
Handel, Dallas Citizens, Paul
Baker

SEASON
Sept.-May

FACILITIES
Kalita Humphreys Theater
Seating Capacity: 466
Stage: thrust

In the Basement
Seating Capacity: 150
Stage: flexible

Arts District Theater
Seating Capacity: 500
Stage: flexible

FINANCES
July 1, 1988-June 30, 1989
Expenses: $4,059,000

CONTRACTS
LORT (C) and (D)

The most important thing an institution can offer the artist is an environment in which to flower, so certain requirements become immediately apparent. I firmly believe that the notion of stability, of company, is critical to the act of creation. History teaches that meaningful, deeply personal art arises out of a fertile community of ideas, and only rarely out of isolation. In a world that overwhelmingly prefers to reward the individual over the efforts of a group, this notion of a collective places profound demands on all concerned: the commitment over time of actors, designers and directors; the willingness of our board to finance an enterprise that may not always be economically "efficient"; the active desire of a very diverse community to come together in the meeting place that is the theatre to examine the roots of who we are. The theatre is one of the last strongholds of direct, unmediated human contact. I want The Dallas Theatre Center to continue to bend our collective imagination to creating an intimate dialogue with the audience, the community. Fashionable entertainment is no longer enough.

—Ken Bryant

Note: During the 1987-88 and 1988-89 seasons, Adrian Hall served as artistic director.

PRODUCTIONS 1987–88

The Tempest, William
Shakespeare; (D) Adrian Hall;
(S) Eugene Lee; (C) Donna M.
Kress; (L) Roger Nall
Cat on a Hot Tin Roof,
Tennessee Williams; (D) Ken
Bryant; (S) Eugene Lee;
(C) Donna M. Kress;
(L) Natasha Katz
A Christmas Carol, adapt: Adrian
Hall and Richard Cumming,
from Charles Dickens; (D) Ken
Bryant; (S) Eugene Lee;
(C) Donna M. Kress; (L) Roger
Nall
Glengarry Glen Ross, David
Mamet; (D) Larry Arrick;
(S) Eugene Lee; (C) Donna M.
Kress; (L) Linda Blase
Uncle Vanya, Anton Chekhov;
trans: Robert W. Corrigan;
(D) Fred Curchack; (S) Eugene
Lee; (C) Donna M. Kress;
(L) Linda Blase and Roger Nall
The House of Blue Leaves, John
Guare; (D) Larry Arrick;
(S) Eugene Lee; (C) Donna M.
Kress; (L) Linda Blase
The Diary of a Scoundrel, adapt:
Erik Brogger, with Alexander
Ostrovsky; (D) Ken Bryant;
(S) Eugene Lee; (C) Donna M.
Kress; (L) Natasha Katz

PRODUCTIONS 1988–89

Laughing Wild, Christopher
Durang; (D) Michael Greif;
(S) Eugene Lee; (C) Donna M.
Kress; (L) Eugene Lee
Ah, Wilderness!, Eugene O'Neill;
(D) Ken Bryant; (S) Eugene
Lee; (C) Donna M. Kress;
(L) Victor En Yu Tan
Les Liaisons Dangereuses, adapt
and trans: Christopher
Hampton; (D) Adrian Hall;
(S) Eugene Lee; (C) Donna M.
Kress; (L) Natasha Katz
A Christmas Carol, adapt: Adrian
Hall and Richard Cumming,
from Charles Dickens; (D) Jack
Willis; (S) Eugene Lee;

Dallas Theater Center. Martin Rayner and Dee Hennigan in *The Idiot*. Photo: Doug Milner.

(C) Donna M. Kress; (L) Linda Blase
Aunt Dan and Lemon, Wallace Shawn; (D) Ken Bryant; (S) Eugene Lee; (C) Donna M. Kress; (L) Gregory Cohen
The Boys Next Door, Tom Griffin; (D) Neal Baron; (S) Eugene Lee; (C) Donna M. Kress; (L) Russell Champa
The Idiot, adapt: Algirdas Landsbergis, from Fyodor Dostoyevsky; (D) Jonas Jurasas; (S) Alex Okun; (C) Donna M. Kress; (L) Eugene Lee
The Birthday Party, Harold Pinter; (D) Tony Giordano; (S) Eugene Lee; (C) Donna M. Kress; (L) Russell Champa
Red Noses, book: Peter Barnes; music and lyrics: Richard Cumming; (D) Adrian Hall; (S) Eugene Lee; (C) Donna M. Kress; (L) Natasha Katz
In the Belly of the Beast, adapt: Adrian Hall, from Jack Henry Abbott; (D) Ken Bryant; (S) Michael McGarty; (C) Donna M. Kress; (L) Michael McGarty

Delaware Theatre Company

CLEVELAND MORRIS
Artistic Director

ROBERT A. GILLMAN
Managing Director

200 Water Street
Wilmington, DE 19801
(302) 594-1104 (bus.)
(302) 594-1100 (b.o.)

FOUNDED 1979
Cleveland Morris, Peter DeLaurier

SEASON
Oct.-Apr.

FACILITIES
Seating Capacity: 300
Stage: proscenium

FINANCES
Sept. 1, 1988-Aug. 31, 1989
Expenses: $820,000

CONTRACTS
AEA letter of agreement

The Delaware Company is the state's only professional theatre. We seek to offer an encompassing, diverse examination of the art of theatre through our annual programs that mix well-known classics with unknown new plays, as well as lesser-known vintage plays with familiar contemporary works. In all cases, we seek plays of lasting social and literary value, worthy of thoughtful consideration by both artist and viewer, and produced in a style designed to strengthen the force of the playwright's language and vision. Our presentations are produced in a boldly modern facility that opened in November 1985, located on Wilmington's historic riverfront. The theatre company offers a wide variety of ancillary and educational programs in an effort to assist the general public in finding in the art of theatre an ongoing and joyful addition to their lives and community.
—*Cleveland Morris*

PRODUCTIONS 1987–88

Benito Cereno, Robert Lowell; (D) Cleveland Morris; (S) Lewis Folden; (C) Marla Jurglanis; (L) Bruce Morris
The Foreigner, Larry Shue; (D) Dorothy Danner; (S) Eric Schaeffer; (C) Marla Jurglanis; (L) Bruce Morris
3 Guys Naked from the Waist Down, Jerry Coker and Michael Rupert; (D) Derek Wolshonak; (S) Lewis Folden; (C) Marla Jurglanis; (L) Bruce Morris
Cash Flow, D.B. Gilles; (D) William Woodman; (S) Eric Schaeffer; (C) Marla Jurglanis; (L) Bruce Morris
Biography, S.N. Behrman; (D) Cleveland Morris; (S) James F. Pyne, Jr.; (C) Marla Jurglanis; (L) Bruce Morris
Crossin' The Line, Phil Bosakowski; (D) Paul Hastings; (S) Eric Schaeffer; (C) Susan Trimble; (L) Curt Senie

PRODUCTIONS 1988–89

The Beggar's Opera, John Gay; (D) Cleveland Morris; (S) Eric Schaeffer; (C) Marla Jurglanis; (L) Bruce Morris
Master Harold...and the boys, Athol Fugard; (D) Jamie Brown; (S) Lewis Folden; (C) Marla Jurglanis; (L) Bruce Morriss
1918, Horton Foote; (D) Cleveland Morris; (S) Joseph A. Varga; (C) Marla Jurglanis; (L) Bruce Morriss
A Hell of a Town, Monte Merrick; (D) Richard Hopkins; (S) Alex Polner; (C) Marla Jurglanis; (L) Bruce Morriss
Rosencrantz and Guildenstern Are Dead, Tom Stoppard; (D) Rick Davis; (S) Eric Schaeffer; (C) Marla Jurglanis; (L) Bruce Morriss

Delaware Theatre Company. *The Foreigner.* Photo: Richard C. Carter.

Dell'Arte Players Company

**DONALD FOREST,
MICHAEL FIELDS
JOAN SCHIRLE**
Co-Artistic Directors

Box 816
Blue Lake, CA 95525
(707) 668-5411 (bus.)
(707) 668-5782 (b.o.)

FOUNDED 1971
Jael Weisman, Alain Schons, Joan Schirle, Carlo Mazzone-Clementi, Jane Hill, Michael Fields, Jon Paul Cook

SEASON
Jan.-Dec.

FACILITIES
Dell'Arte Studio
Seating Capacity: 100
Stage: flexible

Dell'Arte Amphitheatre
Seating Capacity: 250
Stage: thrust

FINANCES
Oct. 1, 1987-Sept. 30, 1988
Expenses: $270,400

CONTRACTS
AEA letter of agreement

The Dell'Arte Players Company is a rurally based touring theatre ensemble which performs nationally and internationally. The four core-company artists share 12 years of collaborative work on original theatre pieces. Our non-urban point of view and themes for many of our major works come from the region where we live, where we are part of a cultural renaissance that is occuring as timber resources dwindle and the arts emerge as increasingly important to the region. The creative focus of our original work is on strong textual values performed in a highly physical style; the integration of acting, text, music, movement and content is a primary goal of our ensemble process. Our unique style has brought invitations to perform with major theatres on large-scale works like Peter Barnes' Red Noses as well as many teaching residencies. Our commitment to influencing theatre through traditional popular forms is also reflected in the training we offer at the Dell'Arte School of Physical Theatre; unique in the U.S., the school offers one-year and two-year full-time programs. As world recognition of our work grows, we move toward our goal of becoming an international center for the exploration and development of physical theatre traditions and their relationship to contemporary forms.
—*Joan Schirle*

DELL'ARTE PLAYERS COMPANY

PRODUCTIONS 1987–88

The Bacchae, adapt: company, from Euripides; (D) Jael Weisman; (S) Ivan Hess; (C) Jean Young; (L) Michael Foster

Performance Anxiety, Michael Fields, Donald Forrest, Joan Schirle, Alain Schons and Jael Weisman; (D) Jael Weisman; (S) Alain Schons; (C) Mimi Mace; (L) Michael Foster

Red Noses, Peter Barnes; (D) Jael Weisman and Sam Woodhouse; (S) Nick Reid; (C) Nancy Jo Smith; (L) Peter Maradudin

PRODUCTIONS 1988–89

Malpractice or Love's the Best Doctor, adapt: Michael Fields, Donald Forrest, Michele Linfante and Jael Weisman, from Moliere; (D) Jael Weisman; (S) Andy Stacklin; (C) Mimi Mace; (L) Michael Foster

Performance Anxiety, Michael Fields, Donald Forrest, Joan Schirle, Alain Schons and Jael Weisman; (D) Jael Weisman; (S) Alain Schons; (C) Mimi Mace; (L) Michael Foster

Slowly I Turn, Michael Fields, Donald Forrest, Joan Schirle and Jael Weisman; (D) Donald Forrest (S) Alain Schons; (C) Nancy Jo Smith; (L) Michael Foster

Dell'Arte Players. Doug Jacobs and Michael Fields in *Red Noses*. Photo: Gina Leishman.

Denver Center Theatre Company

DONOVAN MARLEY
Artistic Director

SARAH LAWLESS
Executive Director

BARBARA E. SELLERS
Producing Director

1050 13th St.
Denver, CO 80204
(303) 893-4200 (bus.)
(303) 893-4100 (b.o.)

FOUNDED 1980
Donald R. Seawell

SEASON
Sept.-May

FACILITIES
The Stage
Seating Capacity: 550
Stage: thrust

The Space
Seating Capacity: 450
Stage: arena

The Source
Seating Capacity: 155
Stage: thrust

The Ricketson
Seating Capacity: 195
Stage: proscenium

FINANCES
July 1, 1987-June 30, 1988
Expenses: $4,800,000

CONTRACTS
LORT (C) AND (D)

Denver Center Theatre Company. James L. Lawless, Ann Guilbert and Jamey Roberts in *A Christmas Memory*. Photo: Ted Trainor.

The Denver Center Theatre Company is committed to producing both classic theatre and American plays, as well as to developing new works. The company's 10th season featured 12 plays and a school tour to state high schools and metropolitan-area elementary and middle schools. An integral part of DCTC is the National Theatre Conservatory, headed by Tony Church; the MFA program allows actors to work, train, develop and learn together in the nurturing atmosphere of a professional theatre, among professional theatre artists. Another important program, PrimaFacie, solicits scripts from playwrights around the country—of the hundreds of plays submitted, up to 10 are chosen for presentation as staged readings; selected plays are then fully produced during the next season's subscription series.

—*Donovan Marley*

PRODUCTIONS 1987–88

Guys and Dolls, book: Jo Swerling and Abe Burrows; music and lyrics: Frank Loesser; (D) Donovan Marley; (S) Richard L. Hay; (C) Claudia Everett; (L) Peter Maradudin

Koozy's Piece, Frank X. Hogan; (D) Randal Myler; (S) Ralph Funicello; (C) Janet S. Morris; (L) Charles Macleod

Veteran's Day, Donald Freed; (D) Laird Williamson; (S) Anrew V. Yelusich; (C) Andrew V. Yelusich; (L) Daniel L. Murray

A Child's Christmas in Wales, adapt: Jeremy Brooks and Adrian Mitchell, from Dylan Thomas; (D) Randal Myler; (S) Richard L. Hay; (C) Patricia Whitelock; (L) Charles MacLeod

A Christmas Memory, Truman Capote; (D) Randal Myler; (S) Richard L. Hay; (C) Patricia Whitelock; (L) Charles MacLeod

The Price, Arthur Miller; (D) Frank Georgianna; (S) Andrew V. Yelusich; (C) Andrew V. Yelusich; (L) Daniel L. Murray

Two Gentlemen of Verona, William Shakespeare; (D) Laird Williamson; (S) Laird Williamson and Andrew V. Yesulich; (C) Andrew V. Yelusich; (L) Rick Paulsen

Long Day's Journey into Night, Eugene O'Neill; (D) Malcolm Morrison; (S) John Dexter; (C) Andrew V. Yelusich; (L) Charles MacLeod

Trophy Hunters, Kendrew Lascelles; (D) Bruce K. Sevy; (S) Richard L. Hay; (C) Janet S. Morris; (L) Daniel L. Murray

A Lie of the Mind, Sam Shepard;

(D) Donovan Marley; (S) Pavel M. Dobrusky; (C) Janet S. Morris; (L) Pavel M. Dobrusky
Table Manners, Alan Ayckbourn; (D) Malcolm Morrison; (S) Vicki Smith; (C) Janet S. Morris; (L) Daniel L. Murray
The Colored Museum, George C. Wolfe; (D) Andre DeShields; (S) Pavel M. Dobrusky; (C) Andrew V. Yelusich; (L) Charles MacLeod
Man of La Mancha, book: Dale Wasserman; music: Mitch Leigh; lyrics: Joe Darion; (D) Donovan Marley; (S) Richard L. Hay; (C) Andrew V. Yelusich; (L) Greg Sullivan

PRODUCTIONS 1988–89

Waiting for Godot, Samuel Beckett; (D) Randal Myler; (S) Bernard Vyzga; (C) Andrew V. Yelusich; (L) Charles MacLeod
Carousel, book and lyrics: Oscar Hammerstein II; music: Richard Rogers; (D) Donovan Marley; (S) Richard L. Hay; (C) Andrew V. Yelusich; (L) Peter Maradudin
I'm Not Rappaport, Herb Gardner; (D) Frank Georgianna; (S) Vicki Smith; (C) Janet S. Morris; (L) Daniel L. Murray
The Matchmaker, Thornton Wilder; (D) Laird Williamson; (S) Andrew V. Yelusich; (C) Andrew V. Yelusich; (L) Charles MacLeod
Cat on a Hot Tin Roof, Tennessee Williams; (D) Bruce K. Sevy; (S) Richard L. Hay; (C) Janet S. Morris; (L) Charles MacLeod
Darkside, Ken Jones; (D) Jared Sakren; (S) John Dexter; (C) Patricia Whitelock; (L) Daniel L. Murray
Peter Pan, James M. Barrie; (D) Randal Myler; (S) Carolyn Leslie Ross; (C) Andrew V. Yelusich; (L) Peter Maradudin
Exclusive Circles, Kendrew Lascelles; (D) Bruce K. Sevy; (S) John Dexter; (C) Janet S. Morris; (L) Daniel L. Murray
King Lear, William Shakespeare; (D) Donovan Marley; (S) Pavel M. Dobrusky; (C) Pavel M. Dobrusky; (L) Pavel M. Dobrusky
Child of Luck, Donald Freed; (D) Laird Williamson and Andrew V. Yelusich; (S) Andrew V. Yelusich; (C) Andrew V. Yelusich; (L) Charles MacLeod
Company, book: George Furth; music and lyrics: Stephen Sondheim; (D) Bruce K. Sevy; (S) Richard L. Hay; (C) Andrew V. Yelusich; (L) Peter Maradudin

Detroit Repertory Theatre

BRUCE E. MILLAN
Artistic Director

13103 Woodrow Wilson Ave.
Detroit, MI 48238
(313) 868-1347 (bus.)

FOUNDED 1957
Bruce E. Millan, Barbara Busby, T.O. Andrus

SEASON
Nov.-June

FACILITIES
SEATING CAPACITY: 196
STAGE: PROSCENIUM

FINANCES
Jan. 1, 1988-Dec. 31, 1988
Expenses: $303,200

CONTRACTS
AEA SPT

The Detroit Repertory's purpose over the past 32 years has been to build a first-class professional theatre by assembling a resident company of theatre artists recruited from among local professionals in the field; to seed new plays, perform known plays in new ways, and bring worthwhile, forgotten plays back to life; to expand the creative possibilities of theatre by increasing the opportunities for participation of all artists regardless of their ethnic or racial origins or gender; to reach out to initiate the uninitiated; to build a theatre operation that is "close to the people" and to act as a catalyst for the revitalization of the neighborhood in which the theatre resides; and, to attract audiences reflecting the cultural and ethnic diversity of southeastern Michigan. The Repertory received the Governor's Award for outstanding achievement in May 1986.
—*Bruce E. Millan*

PRODUCTIONS 1987–88

Glengarry Glen Ross, David Mamet; (D) Barbara Busby; (S) Sharon Yesh; (C) B.J. Essen; (L) Kenneth R. Hewitt, Jr.

Detroit Repertory Theatre. Catrina Ganey in *The Colored Museum*. Photo: Burce E. Millan.

The Colored Museum, George C. Wolfe; (D) Reuben Yabuku; (S) Gary Anderson; (C) B.J. Essen; (L) Kenneth R. Hewitt, Jr.
Morning's at Seven, Paul Osborn; (D) Bruce E. Millan; (S) Gary Anderson; (C) B.J. Essen; (L) Kenneth R. Hewitt, Jr.
Invictus, Laurie H. Hutzler; (D) Dee Andrus; (S) Sharon Yesh; (C) B.J. Essen; (L) Laura S. Higle

PRODUCTIONS 1988–89

Gone to Glory, Suzanne Finlay; (D) Reuben Yabuku; (S) Bruce E. Millan; (C) B.J. Essen; (L) Kenneth R. Hewitt, Jr.
Les Blancs, Lorraine Hansberry; (D) Bruce E. Millan; (S) Bruce E. Millan; (C) B. J. Essen; (L) Kenneth R. Hewitt, Jr.
Rhinoceros, Eugene Ionesco; (D) Barbara Busby; (S) Bruce E. Millan; (C) B.J. Essen; (L) Kenneth R. Hewitt, Jr.
Enchanted Night, Slawomir Mrozek; (D) William Boswell; (S) Bruce E. Millan; (C) B.J. Essen; (L) Kenneth R. Hewitt, Jr.

Charlie, Slawomir Mrozek; (D) Ruth Allen; (S) Bruce E. Millan; (C) B. J. Essen; (L) Kenneth R. Hewitt, Jr.
Out at Sea, Slawomir Mrozek; (D) Charles A. Jackson; (S) Bruce E. Millan; (C) B. J. Essen; (L) Kenneth R. Hewitt, Jr.

East West Players

NOBU MCCARTHY
Artistic Director

MICHELE GARZA
Managing Director

4424 Santa Monica Blvd.
Los Angeles, CA 90029
(213) 660-0366

East West Players. *Mishima*. Photo: Christopher Komuro.

FOUNDED 1965
Beulah Quo, Mako, Yet Lock, Pat Li, Guy Lee, June Kim, James Hong

SEASON
Oct.–June

FACILITIES
Seating Capacity: 99
Stage: flexible

FINANCES
July 1, 1988-June 30, 1989
Expenses: $350,000

CONTRACTS
AEA 99-seat Theatre Plan

As the country's oldest Asian-American theatre, East West Players is dedicated to the development of new works by Asian-American playwrights, and to the presentation of original plays, musicals and the classics. Our theatre aims to provide a professional, as well as creative, environment for actors, directors, designers and technicians to develop their craft. Our professional theatre training program, advanced acting workshop, and a newly formed writers workshop nurture the young artists of tomorrow and allow working theatre artists a place to explore their art form. Beyond the work on our mainstage and in our workshops, East West Players' underlying goal is to serve its community by presenting creative bilingual projects that are multicultural, socially relevant, often provocative and ultimately enlightening. Future plans are being developed to organize national and international touring productions to broaden our audiences and share with them Asian-American theatre.
—*Nobu McCarthy*

PRODUCTIONS 1987–88

A Chorus Line, book: James Kirkwood and Nicholas Dante; music: Marvin Hamlisch; lyrics: Edward Kleban; (D) Shizuko Hoshi; (S) Mako; (C) Rodney Kageyama; (L) Rae Creevey
Stew Rice, Edward Sakamoto; (D) Dana Lee; (S) Yuki Nakamura; (C) Shizuko Herrera; (L) Rae Creevey
Mother Tongue, Paul Stephen Lim; (D) Paul Hough; (S) Paul Hough; (C) Eleanor Patton; (L) Rae Creevey
Mishima, Rosanna Yamagina Alfaro; (D) Shizuko Hoshi; (S) Mako; (C) Mako; (L) Rae Creevey
Where Nobody Belongs, W. Colin McKay; (D) Momo Yashima; (S) Gilbert Wong; (C) Lydia Tanji; (L) Rae Creevey
An Afternoon at Willie's Bar, Paul Price; (D) Paul Price; (S) Eugenia Butler; (C) Lydia Tanji and Dori Quan; (L) Rae Creevey

PRODUCTIONS 1988–89

The Fantasticks, book and lyrics: Tom Jones; music: Harvey Schmidt; (D) Mako and Glen Chin; (S) Gone Taa; (C) Dori Quan; (L) Rae Creevey
Laughter and False Teeth, Hiroshi Kashiwagi; (D) Robert Ito; (S) Chris Tashima; (C) Dori Quan; (L) Rae Creevey
Webster Street Blues, Warren Sumio Kubota; (D) Nobu McCarthy; (S) Rae Creevey; (C) Terence Tam Soon; (L) Rae Creevey
Vacancy, Lillian Hara and Dorie Rush Taylor; (D) Norman Cohen; (S) Rae Creevey; (C) Terence Tam Soon; (L) Rae Creevey

El Teatro Campesino

LUIS VALDEZ
Artistic Director

PHIL ESPARZA
Producer/Administrative Director

Box 1240
SanJuan Bautista, CA 95045
(408)623-2444 (bus.)
(408)6623-2444 (b.o.)

FOUNDED 1965
Luis Valdez

SEASON
Jan.–Dec.

FACILITIES
ETC Playhouse
Seating Capacity: 150
Stage: flexible

FINANCES
Oct. 1, 1987-Sept. 30, 1988
Expenses: $300,000

CONTRACTS
AEA SPT

As we approach our 25th anniversary, El Teatro Campesino continues to explore the curative, affirmative power of live performance on actors and audiences alike, through our global vision of society. We remain acutely aware of the role of theatre as a creator of community, in the firm belief that the future belongs to those who can imagine it. We thus imagine an America born of the worldwide cultural fusion of our times, and see as our aesthetic and social purpose the creation of theatre that illuminates that inevitable future. To achieve this purpose, our playhouse in San Juan Bautista continues to function as a research-and-development center, a place to explore the evolution of new works, new images and new ideas. Our aim is to maintain a dynamic crossroads for talent: a place where children can work with adults, teenagers with senior citizens, professsionals with nonprofessionals, Hispanics with Anglos, Asians, blacks and Native Americans. Once works are created and refined in San Juan Bautista, the more successful plays are produced professionally in larger urban venues. Our productions of *Corridos!* and *I Don't Have to Show You No Stinking Badges* are examples of this process. Our theatre work is simple, direct, complex and profound, but it works. In the heart, el corazon, of a way of life.
—*Luis Valdez*

PRODUCTIONS 1987–88

El Fin del Mundo, Luis Valdez; (D) Luis Valdez and Tony Curiel; (L) Rick Larsen
La Pastorela, adapt: Luis Valdez, from Mexican folklore; (D) Tony Curiel; (S) Victoria Petrovich; (C) Josie Chavez; (L) Rick Larsen

El Teatro Campesino. Janet John and George Galvan in *Passion Play*.

Dog Lady, Milcha Sanchez-Scott; (D) Tony Curiel; (S) Rene Yanez; (C) Josie Vhavez; (L) Joseph Velasco

PRODUCTIONS 1988–89

La Virgen de Tepeyaca, adapt: Luis Valdez, from Mexican folklore; (D) Tony Curiel; (S) Jim Cave; (C) Josie Chavez; (L) Rick Larsen

The Passion Play: The Way of the Cross, adapt: Luis Valdez, from Mexican folklore; (D) Luis Valdez; (S) Jim Cave; (C) Josie Chavez

The Rose of the Rancho, David Belasco and Richard Walton Tully; (D) Robert Castro; (S) Jim Cave; (L) Lisa Larice

Simply Maria/Food for the Dead, Josephina Lopez; (D) Ramon Flores; (S) Russell Parkman; (C) Suzanne Jackson; (L) Jack Carpenter

La Pastorela, adapt: Luis Valdez, from Mexican folklore; (D) Tony Curiel; (S) Victoria Petrovich; (L) Rick Larsen

Emmy Gifford Children's Theater

JAMES LARSON
Artistic Director

MARK HOEGER
Executive Director

3504 Center St.
Omaha, NE 68105
(402) 345-4852 (bus.)
(402) 345-4849 (b.o.)

FOUNDED 1949
19 child advocacy agencies, Emmy Gifford

SEASON
Sept.-May

FACILITIES
Seating Capacity: 525
Stage: proscenium

FINANCES
June 1, 1988-May 31, 1989
Expenses: $710,000

CONTRACTS
AEA guest artist

At the Emmy Gifford Children's Theatre we believe that children's theatre is an exciting and suitable performance mode for experimentation. Children have different psychological and aesthetic needs from those of adults, primarily because a child's cerebral design is synaptically more active. For children, fantasy and anti-realism are the norm. Thus, artists in children's theatre have startling freedom in the theatrical choices they can make to break out of the straight-jacket of stultifying, ossified realism—the traditional theoretical and formal style out of which most U.S. theatre artists have developed.

—*James Larson*

PRODUCTIONS 1987–88

Mother Goose, adapt: Douglas Marr; (D) James Larson; (S) Tim Hantula; (C) Sherri Geerdes; (L) Steve Wheeldon

The Legend of Sleepy Hollow, adapt: Fred Gainer; (D) James Larson; (S) Tim Hantula; (C) Sherri Geerdes; (L) Steve Wheeldon

Cinderella, book and lyrics: Oscar Hammerstein, II; music: Richard Rodgers; (D) James Larson; (S) Steve Wheeldon; (C) Sherri Geerdes; (L) Steve Wheeldon

How to Eat Fried Worms, Thomas Rockwell; (D) M. Michele Phillips; (S) Steve Wheeldon; (C) Sherri Geerdes; (L) Steve Wheeldon

Charlotte's Web, adapt: Joseph Robinette, from E.B. White; (D) Roberta Larson; (S) Tim Hantula; (C) Sherri Geerdes; (L) Steve Wheeldon

Big Bad Bruce, adapt: James Still, from Bill Peet; (D) James Larson; (S) Steve Stabenow; (C) Sherri Geerdes; (L) Steve Wheeldon

PRODUCTIONS 1988–89

Winnie the Pooh, adapt: Kristin Sergel, from A.A. Milne; (D) James Larson; (S) Steve Wheeldon; (C) Sherri Geerdes; (L) Steve Wheeldon

The Death and Life of Sherlock Holmes, Suzan Zeder; (D) Cathy Wells; (S) Steve Wheeldon; (C) Sherri Geerdes; (L) Steve Wheeldon

Oliver!, book, music and lyrics: Lionel Bart; (D) M. Michele Phillips; (S) Steve Wheeldon; (C) Sherri Geerdes; (L) Steve Wheeldon

Frog and Toad, adapt: Belinda Acosta, from Arnold Lobel; (D) Roberta Larson; (S) Steve Wheeldon; (C) Sherri Geerdes; (L) Steve Wheeldon

Emmy Gifford Children's Theater. Kathy Wheeldon and Pam Carter in *Cinderella*.

The Little Princess, adapt: Virginia Koste, from Frances Hodgson Burnett; (D) Mark Hoeger; (S) Judy Pullin; (C) Sherri Geerdes; (L) Steve Wheeldon

Jack and the Beanstalk, adapt: Robert Bly; (D) James Larson; (S) Larry Kaushansky; (C) Sherri Geerdes; (L) Steve Wheeldon

Empire State Institute for the Performing Arts

PATRICIA B. SNYDER
Producing Director

Empire State Plaza
Albany, NY 12223

(518) 443-5222 (bus.)
(518) 443-5111 (b.o.)

FOUNDED 1976
Empire State Youth Theatre Institute (State University of New York), Patricia B. Snyder, Governor Nelson A. Rockefeller Empire State Plaza Performing Arts Center Corporation

SEASON
Sept.-June

FACILITIES
Mainstage
Seating Capacity: 900
Stage: flexible

Studio Theatre
Seating Capacity: 450
Stage: thrust

FINANCES
Apr. 1, 1988-Mar. 31, 1989
Expenses: $3,024,000

CONTRACTS
AEA TYA

The Empire State Institute for the Performing Arts aspires to nurture

tomorrow's theatre today. By enriching the lives of our youthful and family audiences through an active blending of professional theatre and education, ESIPA strives to develop its audience's critical sensibilities through the discovery of the wonder of the human spirit, as expressed by the inner truth of the theatre. A combination of theatre excellence, a "values education" program complementary to the schools' curricula, cultural exchange and a demonstrated commitment to the development of new works are the hallmarks of ESIPA's mission.
—*Patricia B. Snyder*

PRODUCTIONS 1987–88

Carnival, book: Michael Stewart; music and lyrics: Bob Merrill; (D) Maureen Shea; (S) Alexander Okun; (C) Judy Dearing; (L) Ann G. Wrightson

The Crucifer of Blood, Paul Giovanni; (D) Terence Lamude; (S) Duke Durfee; (C) Gregg Barnes; (L) John McLain

A Christmas Carol, adapt: Amlin Gray, from Charles Dickens; (D) Ed Lange; (S) Duke Durfee; (C) Karen Kammer; (L) Ann G. Wrightson

Hizzoner!, Paul Shyre; (D) John Going; (S) Eldon Elder; (C) Patrizia von Brandenstein; (L) John McLain

Lyle, book, music and lyrics: Charles Strouse; (D) Barbara Siman; (S) Duke Durfee; (C) Judanna Lynn; (L) Ann G. Wrightson

Peter Pan, book: James M. Barrie; music: Mark Charlap; lyrics: Carolyn Leigh; (D) Patricia B. Snyder; (S) Richard Finkelstein; (C) Gregg Barnes; (L) Lloyd S. Riford, III

PRODUCTIONS 1988–89

Once upon a Mattress, book: Jay Thompson, Marshall Barer and Dean Fuller; music: Mary Rodgers; lyrics: Marshall Barer; (D) David Holdgrive; (S) Nancy Thun; (C) William Schroder; (L) John McLain

Peter Pan, book: James M. Barrie; music: Mark Charlap; lyrics: Carolyn Leigh; (D) Patricia B. Snyder; (S) Richard Finkelstein; (C) Gregg Barnes; (L) Lloyd S. Riford, III

Hizzoner!, Paul Shyre; (D) John Going; (S) Eldon Elder; (C) Patrizia von Brandenstein; (L) John McLain

The Penultimate Problem of Sherlock Holmes, John Nassivera; (D) Ed Lange; (S) Victor A. Becker; (C) Brent Griffin; (L) Betsy Adams

A Man for All Seasons, Robert Bolt; (D) Terence Lamude; (S) Harry Feiner; (C) Barbara Forbes; (L) John McLain

The Pied Piper, Adrian Mitchell; conceived: Alan Cohen; (D) John R. Briggs; (S) Victor A. Becker; (C) Gregg Barnes; (L) Victor En Yu Tan

Empire State Institute for the Performing Arts. John Thomas McGuire III and John Corey in *The Crucifer of Blood*. Photo: Timothy Raab/Northern Photo.

The Empty Space Theatre. *The Colored Museum*. Photo: Karen Johanson.

The Empty Space Theatre

M. BURKE WALKER
Artistic Director

MELISSA HINES
Managing Director

Box 1748
Seattle, WA 98111-1748
(206) 587-3737 (bus.)
(206) 467-6000 (b.o.)

FOUNDED 1970
Charles Younger, M. Burke Walker, Julian Schembri, James Royce

SEASON
Nov.-July

FACILITIES
Seating Capacity: 185
Stage: arena

FINANCES
Oct. 1, 1987-Sept. 30, 1988
Expenses: $924,988

CONTRACTS
AEA letter of agreement

The Empty Space Theatre is a home for theatre artists wanting to explore a vigorous, nontraditional mix of new plays, new playwrights, out-of-the-mainstream classics and vulgar (from the Latin vulgaris) low comedy. Peter Handke, Henry Fielding and Sam Shepard happily coexisted in our first season, as did *The Rocky Horror Show*, *Don Juan*, *Aunt Dan and Lemon* and *Drinking in America* more recently. We continue to dedicate ourselves to the development and presentation of new works on our mainstage, such as *Gloria Duplex* by Rebecca Wells and *The Big Bad Wolf and How He Got That Way* by Greg Palmer. We will open our 20th-anniversary season in new quarters across from Seattle's historic Pike Place Market. The theatre will retain its tradition of intimacy and highly energetic and imaginative staging in this new locale.
—*M. Burke Walker*

PRODUCTIONS 1987–88

Scaramouche, adapt: Rex McDowell, James Monitor and Robert Wright, from Raphael Sabatini; (D) M. Burke Walker; (S) William Forrester; (C) Anne Thaxter Watson; (L) Rick Paulsen

Rat in the Skull, Ron Hutchinson; (D) Susan Fenichell; (S) Patti Henry; (C) Morna McEachern; (L) Jeff Robbins

The Overgrown Path, Robert Holman; (D) Jeffrey Steitzer; (S) Scott Weldin; (C) Sally Richardson; (L) Rick Paulsen

The Colored Museum, George C. Wolfe; (D) Tim Bond; (S) Scott

Weldin; (C) Michael Murphy; (L) Collier Woods
The Mystery of Irma Vep, Charles Ludlam; (D) David Ira Goldstein; (S) Michael Olich; (C) Michael Murphy; (L) Phil Schermer

PRODUCTIONS 1988–89

The Puppetmaster of Lodz, Gilles Segal; trans: Sara O'Connor; (D) M. Burke Walker; (S) Karen Gjelsteen; (C) Morna McEachern; (L) Jeff Robbins
Drinking in America, Eric Bogosian; (D) Nikki Appino; (S) Scott Weldin; (C) Morna McEachern; (L) Jeff Robbins
The Big Bad Wolf and How He Got That Way, Greg Palmer; (D) Steve Tomkins; (S) William Forrester; (C) Gene Davis Buck; (L) Richard Devin
In Perpetuity Throughout the Universe, Eric Overmyer; (D) Richard E.T. White; (S) Peggy McDonald; (C) Rose Pederson; (L) Rick Paulsen
Loot, Joe Orton; (D) David Ira Goldstein; (S) William Forrester; (C) Sally Richardson; (L) Phil Schermer
Emerald City, David Williamson; (D) M. Burke Walker; (S) Karen Gjelsteen; (C) Anne Thaxter Watson; (L) Michael Wellborn

Ensemble Studio Theatre

CURT DEMPSTER
Artistic Director

PETER SHAVITZ
Managing Director

549 West 52nd St.
New York, NY 10019
(212) 247-4982 (bus.)
(212) 247-3405 (b.o.)

FOUNDED 1971
Curt Dempster

SEASON
Oct.-June

FACILITIES
Mainstage
Seating Capacity: 99
Stage: flexible

FINANCES
July 1, 1987-June 30, 1988
Expenses: $791,904

CONTRACTS
AEA letter of agreement

Founded in 1971, the Ensemble Studio Theatre remains dedicated to its original mission of nurturing theatre artists, with particular focus on the development and introduction of new American plays by emerging and established playwrights. The Ensemble has been an ecological cause—not just theatre, but a daily challenge to create new plays and keep them alive in an increasingly uncertain environment. The emphasis is on process—whether in the writing of a play or in the creation of a role—rather than product. All the works produced on the Ensemble's main stage are world premieres and have gone through several stages of development including readings, staged readings and workshops. The need of the individual work determines the method and manner of its development. The Ensemble's impact continues to be felt through our annual Marathon festival of new one-act plays and by the more than 360 productions throughout the country of full-length plays first developed at the Ensemble.

—Curt Dempster

PRODUCTIONS 1987–88

House Arrest, Bill Bozzone; (D) Risa Bramon; (S) Kevin Roach; (C) Deborah Shaw; (L) Greg MacPherson

Marathon '88:
Neptune's Hips, Richard Greenburg; (D) Christopher Ashley; (S) Ann Sheffield; (C) Deborah Shaw and Abigail Murray; (L) Greg MacPherson
Buster B and Olivia, Shirley Kaplan; (D) Billy Hopkins; (S) Ann Sheffield; (C) Deborah Shaw and David Sawaryn; (L) Greg MacPherson
Something About Baseball, Quincy Long; (D) Risa Bramon; (S) Ann Sheffield; (C) Deborah Shaw and Abigail Murray; (L) Greg MacPherson
A Poster of the Cosmos, Lanford Wilson; (D) Jonathon Hosan; (S) Ann Sheffield and David Sawaryn; (C) Deborah Shaw and Abigail Murray; (L) Greg MacPherson
Julliet, Romulus Linney; (D) Peter Maloney; (S) Ann Sheffield; (C) Deborah Shaw and David Sawaryn; (L) Greg MacPherson
Door to Cuba, James Ryan; (D) Charles Richter; (S) Ann Sheffield and David Sawaryn; (C) Deborah Shaw and David Swaryn; (L) Greg MacPherson
Human Gravity, Stewart Spencer; (D) Evan Yionoulis; (S) Ann Sheffield; (C) Deborah Shaw and Abigail Murray; (L) Greg MacPherson
Mango Tea, Paul Weitz; (D) Curt Dempster; (S) Ann Sheffield and Shirley Kaplan; (C) Deborah Shaw and David Swaryn; (L) Greg MacPherson
The Man Who Climbed the Pecan Tree, Horton Foote; (D) Curt Dempster; (S) Ann Sheffield; (C) Deborah Shaw and Abigail Murray; (L) Greg MacPherson
Diphthong, Michael B. Kaplan; (D) Lisa Peterson; (S) Ann Sheffield; (C) Deborah Shaw and David Sawaryn; (L) Greg MacPherson
Slaughter in the Lake, Jose Rivera; (D) Joan Yail Thorne; (S) Ann Sheffield; (C) Deborah Shaw and Abigail Murray; (L) Greg MacPherson
Singing Joy, OyamO; (D) Peter Lawless; (S) Ann Sheffield; (C) Deborah Shaw and Abigail Murray; (L) Greg MacPherson

PRODUCTIONS 1988–89

The Promise, Jose Rivera; (D) David Esbjornson; (S) Anne Sheffield; (C) Kia Christina Heath; (L) Greg MacPherson
The Magic Act, Laurence Klavan; (D) Peter Zapp; (S) Brian Martin; (C) David Sawaryn; (L) David Higham

Marathon '89:
The Essence of Morgrovia, Jenny Lombard; (D) Lisa Peterson; (S) Maurice Dana; (C) Deborah Shaw; (L) Greg MacPherson
Self Torture and Strenuous Exercise, Harry Kondoleon; (D) Max Mayer; (S) Maurice Dana; (C) Deborah Shaw; (L) Greg MacPherson
Wink-Dah, William Yellow Robe, Jr.; (D) Richard Lichte; (S) Maurice Dana; (C) Deborah Shaw; (L) Greg MacPherson
Woman Floating Out A Window, Jacklyn Maddux; (D) Charles Karchmer; (S) Linda Giering Balmuth; (C) Teresa Snider-Stein; (L) Greg MacPherson
Pathological Venus, Brighde Mullins; (D) Jimmy Bohr; (S) Linda Giering Balmuth; (C) Teresa Snider-Stein; (L) Greg MacPherson
The Open Boat, Neal Bell; (D) Curt Dempster; (S) Linda Giering Balmuth; (C) Teresa Snider-Stein; (L) Greg MacPherson
Outside The Radio, Kermit Frazier; (D) Oz Scott; (S) Sharon Sprague; (C) David Sawaryn; (L) Gill Danieli
Big Frogs, David Golden; (D) Matthew Penn; (S) Sharon Sprague; (C) David Sawaryn; (L) Gill Danieli
Water Music, Michael Erickson; (D) Beth A. Schachter; (S) Sharon Sprague; (C) David Sawaryn; (L) Gill Danieli

Ensemble Studio Theatre. Barry Sherman and Thomas Kopache in *Big Frogs*. Photo: Felix Kalkman.

Eureka Theatre Company. John Bellucci and Lorri Holt in *Lloyd's Prayer*. Photo: Bob Hsiang.

Eureka Theatre Company

DEBRA J. BALLINGER
Executive Director/Acting Artistic Director

2730 16th St.
San Francisco, CA 94103
(415) 558-9811 (bus.)
(415) 558-9898 (b.o.)

FOUNDED 1972
Robert Woodruff, Chris Silva

SEASON
Sept.-June

FACILITIES
SEATING CAPACITY: 200
STAGE: FLEXIBLE

FINANCES
July 1, 1988-June 30, 1989
Expenses: $600,000

CONTRACTS
AEA BAT

Since its inception, the Eureka Theatre Company has been committed to producing plays that dig deeply into political and social concerns affecting contemporary life. Our productions question oppressive social structures, expose complacency, advocate change, and reflect the cultural and ethnic diversity of our community. The Eureka's repertoire has included plays by Dario Fo, Caryl Churchill, Athol Fugard, Phillip Kan Gotanda, Milcha Sanchez-Scott and George Wolfe as well as such commissions as Emily Mann's *Execution of Justice*, Amlin Gray's *Ubu Unchained* and most recently, Tony Kushner's *Angels in America*. We will continue to commission and develop new plays, adding new music theatre and works from classical and international dramatic literature. In 1989-90, the Eureka will open its late-night series called Heartshouts, emphasizing new and unusual experimental and multicultural theatre. As the Eureka enters its 17th season, we find that our overall aesthetic is in transition. We are in the process of reinventing our organizational structure in order to accommodate the real economic and artistic needs of a mid-sized theatre. This process necessarily involves taking more risks artistically and establishing ties with community and activist organizations.
—*Debra Ballinger*

Note: During the 1987-88 season, Anthony Taccone served as artistic director. During the 1988-89 season, Oskar Eustis served as artistic director.

PRODUCTIONS 1987-88

Roosters, Milcha Sanchez-Scott; (D) Susan Marsden; (S) Kate Edmunds; (C) Jennifer Telford; (L) Ellen Shireman
A Bright Room Called Day, Tony Kushner; (D) Oskar Eustis; (S) Kate Edmunds; (C) Jennifer Telford; (L) Ellen Shireman
A Day Like Any Other, Dario Fo and Franca Rame; trans: Cristina Nutrizio and Sally Schwager; (D) Julie Hebert; (S) Lauren Elder; (C) Gwen Dunham; (L) Ellen Shireman
Road, Jim Cartwright; (D) Anthony Taccone; (S) Barbara Mesney; (C) Gail Russel and Esther Fishman; (L) Ellen Shireman
Kiss of the Spider Woman, Manuel Puig; trans: Allan Baker; (D) Susan Marsden; (S) Bruce Brisson; (C) Jill Whitcroft; (L) Ellen Shireman
The Colored Museum, George C. Wolfe; (D) Claude Purdy; (S) Joe Ragey; (C) Jennifer Telford; (L) Ellen Shireman

PRODUCTIONS 1988-89

Viva, Andy de la Tour; (D) Ken Grantham; (S) Don Weinger and Craig E. Lathrop; (C) Gail Russell; (L) Ellen Shireman
Lloyd's Prayer, Kevin Kling; (D) Oskar Eustis; (S) Joel Fontaine; (C) Jill Whitcroft; (L) Ellen Shireman
In Perpetuity Throughout the Universe, Eric Overmyer; (D) Sharon Ott; (S) Kent Dorsey; (C) Beaver D. Bauer; (L) Kent Dorsey
The Stick Wife, Darrah Cloud; (D) Anthony Taccone; (S) Karen Gjelsteen; (C) Cathleen Edwards; (L) Robert Wierzel
Three Ways Home, Casey Kurtti; (D) Ken Grantham; (S) Barbara Mesney; (C) Cassandra Carpenter; (L) Ellen Shireman
Clown Dreams, Larry Pisoni; (D) Richard Seyd; (S) David Ford; (C) Jill Whitcroft; (L) Dede Moyse

First Stage Milwaukee

ROB GOODMAN
Artistic Director

JANET HARTZELL
Education Coordinator

929 North Water St
Milwaukee, WI 53202
(414) 273-7121 (bus.)
(414) 273-7206 (b.o.)

FOUNDED 1987
Archie Sarazin

SEASON
Sept.-June

FACILITIES
Todd Wehr Theater
Seating Capacity: 500
Stage: thrust

FINANCES
June 30, 1988-July 31, 1989
Expenses: $412,310

CONTRACTS
AEA Guest Artist contract

First Stage Milwaukee is a theatre for all ages, dedicated to producing stories on the stage for the young

First Stage Milwaukee. Robert Barnet in *Huckleberry Finn*. Photo: Mark Avery.

people and families of Wisconsin. Each story is selected to speak to a specific section of our audience, from pre-school to adult, and each is fully mounted with the highest concern for artistic excellence. We at First Stage Milwaukee believe theatre is full of possibilities for today's young people as it takes them beyond the ordinary into a world that engages the imagination in a way that not only stimulates the mind but also deeply touches the heart.

—*Rob Goodman*

PRODUCTIONS 1987–88

The Sleeping Beauty, adapt: Ian Dennis, from Brothers Grimm; (D) Rob Goodman; (S) Sandra Strawn; (C) Ellen Kozak; (L) Peter Pfeil
Huckleberry Finn, adapt: John Leicht, from Mark Twain; (D) Rob Goodman; (S) Pat Doty; (C) Ellen Kozak; (L) Peter Pfeil
Macbeth, William Shakespeare; (D) Rob Goodman; (S) Ken Kloth; (C) Ellen Kozak; (L) Robert Zenoni

PRODUCTIONS 1988–89

Winnie the Pooh, adapt: Rob Goodman, from A.A. Milne; music and lyrics: John Tanner; (D) Rob Goodman; (S) Pat Doty; (C) Ellen Kozak; (L) Peter Pfeil
Terror of the Soul: Tales by Edgar Allan Poe, adapt: K.A. Kern and Edgar Allan Poe; (D) Rob Goodman; (S) Pat Doty; (C) Ellen Kozak; (L) Peter Pfeil
Children of a Lesser God, Mark Medoff; (D) Edmund Waterstreet; (S) David Justin; (C) Cecelia Mason; (L) Robert Zenoni
Beauty and the Beast, adapt: Janne Marie Leprince de Beaumont; music and lyrics: John Tanner and Claude Debussy; (D) Rob Goodman; (S) David Justin; (C) Ellen Kozak; (L) Robert Zenoni

Florida Shakespeare Festival

GAIL DESCHAMPS
Artistic Director

Box 330346
Miami, FL 33233-0346
(305) 358-8648 (bus.)
(305) 446-1116 (b.o.)

FOUNDED 1979
Brian Mullin, Gail Deschamps

SEASON
Oct.-May

FACILITIES
Minorca Playhouse
Seating Capacity: 220
Stage: proscenium

FINANCES
Oct. 1, 1988-Sept. 30, 1989
Expenses: $900,000

CONTRACTS
AEA SPT

Florida Shakespeare Festival is committed to: the work of individual artists and ensemble performance; nontraditional casting; innovative approaches to the classics; artistic risk; actors, directors, designers and musicians who imagine and create beyond the expected; and the continuing development of young audiences for classical theatre. FSF has toured under the auspices of the State of Florida and is part of the Southern Arts Federation touring roster for 1990-92. Our Minorca Playhouse hosts the annual Hispanic Theatre Festival as well as dance and music concerts. Educational programming includes school tours, lectures, workshops and special student matinees, as well as internships in design, performance and technical theatre. FSF is currently developing an apprentice program in technical theatre for minority students.

—*Gail Deschamps*

PRODUCTIONS 1987–88

The Lion in Winter, James Goldman; (D) Mark Brokaw; (S) David Trimble; (C) Teri Beals; (L) Stephen Neal
The Belle of Amherst, William Luce; (D) Kathleen Toledo; (S) Michael Martin; (C) James Greco; (L) Stephen Neal
A Midsummer Night's Dream, William Shakespeare; (D) Gerald Stropnicky; (S) David Trimble; (C) David Trimble; (L) Stephen Neal
Macbeth, William Shakespeare; (D) Thaddeus Motyka; (S) David Trimble; (C) Bobby Pearce; (L) Michael Moody

Private Lives, Noel Coward; (D) Gail Deschamps; (S) David Trimble; (C) Saidah Benjudah; (L) Michael Moody
The Phantom Lady, Pedro Calderon de la Barca; (D) John R. Briggs; (S) Jeff Guzik; (C) Camille; (L) Jeff Guzik

PRODUCTIONS 1988–89

Hamlet, William Shakespeare; (D) John R. Briggs; (S) Allen Cornell; (C) Marilyn Skow; (L) Scott Stipetic
Rosencrantz and Guildenstern Are Dead, Tom Stoppard; (D) Gail Deschamps; (S) Allen Cornell; (C) Marilyn Skow; (L) Scott Stipetic
The Pirates of Penzance, book: W.S. Gilbert; music: Arthur Sullivan; (D) Jerry Ross and James Ewing; (S) David Trimble; (C) Beverly Thomas; (L) Suzanne Jones
The Mystery of Irma Vep, Charles Ludlam; (D) John R. Briggs; (S) John R. Briggs and Todd Sherman; (C) Dolly Quentin and Damaris Rodriguez; (L) Suzanne Jones
Pygmalion, George Bernard Shaw; (D) Gail Deschamps; (S) David Trimble; (C) Damaris Rodriguez; (L) Suzanne Jones
The Taming of the Shrew, William Shakespeare; (D) Nilo Cruz; (S) Beningno Mendez; (C) Jeanne Cerasani; (L) Rolf Rombschick

Florida Shakespeare Festival. Barry Grayson in *The Tempest*.

Florida Studio Theatre

RICHARD HOPKINS
Artistic Director

JOHN JACOBSEN
General Manager

1241 North Palm Ave.
Sarasota, FL 34236
(813) 366-9017 (bus.)
(813) 366-9796 (b.o.)

FOUNDED 1973
Jon Spelman

SEASON
Dec.-June

FACILITIES
Seating Capacity: 165
Stage: modified thrust

FINANCES
July 1, 1988-June 30, 1989
Expenses: $520,000

CONTRACTS
AEA SPT

During the 1970s, Florida Studio Theatre toured original and avant-garde works throughout the southeastern states—to prisons, migrant camps, colleges, hospitals and other nontraditional locales. In 1980, Jon Spelman passed the reins of artistic leadership to Richard Hopkins and the direction of the theatre changed: Touring was minimized, and increased focus and energy were placed on building a resident operation in Sarasota. The basic purpose of presenting alternative, thought-provoking theatre, however, remained intact. Today, nine years later, FST has firmly established itself as a "cutting-edge" theatre in the region. FST executes three primary programs: a mainstage season of four plays dedicated to contemporary writers; a new play development program with emphasis on American works; and an educational program serving the area's avocational needs in addition to a training program for theatre students from around the country. The philosophy and driving vision of a FST are best summed up in the words of James Joyce: "I go for the millionth time to forge in the smithy of my soul the uncreated conscience of the human race."

—*Richard Hopkins*

PRODUCTIONS 1987–88

Tomfoolery, adapt: Cameron MacKintosh and Robin Ray; music and lyrics: Tom Lehrer; (D) Bill Castellino; (S) Kevin Locke; (C) Randall Ouzts; (L) Paul D. Romance

No Way to Treat a Lady, Doug J. Cohen; (D) Richard Hopkins; (S) Alex Polner; (C) Randall Ouzts; (L) Paul D. Romance

Papa, John De Groot; (D) Philip M. Church; (L) Paul D. Romance

Blue Plate Special, book: Tom Edwards; lyrics: Mary L. Fisher; music: Harris Wheeler; (D) David Head; (S) Alex Polner; (C) Randall Ouzts; (L) Paul D. Romance

PRODUCTIONS 1988–89

The Robber Bridegroom, book adapt and lyrics: Alfred Uhry; music: Robert Waldman; (D) Richard Hopkins; (S) Kevin Locke; (C) Robert Horek; (L) Paul D. Romance

Three Postcards, book: Craig Lucas; music and lyrics: Craig Carnelia; (D) Scott Burkell; (S) Jeffrey Dean; (C) Robert Horek; (L) Paul D. Romance

A Hell of a Town, Monte Merrick; (D) Richard Hopkins; (S) Alex Polner; (C) Marla Jurglanis; (L) Paul D. Romance

The Wonder Years, book: David Levy, David Holdgrive, Steve Liebman and Terry La Bolt; music and lyrics: David Levy; (D) Steven Rothman; (S) Kevin Locke; (C) Vicky Small; (L) Paul D. Romance

FMT

MIKE MOYNIHAN
Artistic/Producing Director

Box 07147
Milwaukee, WI 53207
(414) 271-8484

FOUNDED 1973
Mike Moynihan, Barbara Leigh

SEASON
variable

Florida Studio Theatre. Scott Burkell and Kathy Halenda in *The Wonder Years*. Photo: Bill Wisser.

FMT. Ron Anderson, Tom Van Voorhees, Danny Murray, and J. Paul Boehmer in *Ramon and Jules*. Photo: Francis Ford.

FINANCES
Jan. 1, 1988-Dec. 31, 1988
Expenses: $145,957

The primary environment that we live in is made of stories. Human beings are not always able to gain understanding from direct experiences, so we have turned to stories as the main way of exploring our most basic questions: Who are we? Where do we come from? How does the world work? What must we aspire to? Our culture's mass storytelling structures—print, film, video—have largely been transformed into an industry called marketing. Theatre can still reach people in traditional gathering places (parks, schools, churches, festivals, celebrations) and allow each individual, family and community to use metaphor, allegory, irony, burlesque, paradox, myth, satire and ritual as resources of analysis, understanding and celebration. Since 1973 FMT has created and toured over 50 original productions that have told many stories drawn from the life, times and places that we share with our audiences.

—*Mike Moynihan*

PRODUCTIONS 1987–88

Juggling Entertainments, Melinda Boyd and Mike Moynihan; (D) Melinda Boyd and Moynihan Mike

The Longfellow Project, company-developed; (D) Debbie Davis and Ron Anderson

The Cream City Semi-Circus!, Ron Anderson and Mike Moynihan; (D) Ron Anderson and Mike Moynihan; (S) Mike Moynihan; (C) Melinda Boyd

The Meeting, company-developed; (D) Mike Moynihan; (S) Mike Moynihan

Info, Melinda Boyd and Mike Moynihan; (D) Melinda Boyd and Mike Moynihan; (S) Mike Moynihan; (C) Melinda Boyd

Directions, Melinda Boyd and Mike Moynihan; (D) Melinda Boyd and Mike Moynihan; (S) Mike Moynihan; (C) Melinda Boyd

The Body Project, Barbara Leigh

(D) Barbara Leigh; (S) Barbara Leigh
The Snow Queen, adapt: Ann Melchior and Mike Moynihan, from Hans Christian Andersen; (D) Barbara Leigh; (S) Mike Moynihan; (C) Barbara Leigh and Melinda Boyd

PRODUCTIONS 1988–89

The Big Little Show!, Melinda Boyd and Mike Moynihan; (D) Mike Moynihan; (S) Mike Moynihan; (C) Melinda Boyd
The Survival Revival Revue!, Barbara Leigh, Debbie Anderson and Mike Moynihan; (D) Jenny Lerner; (S) Barbara Leigh and Jenny Lerner; (C) Barbara Leigh and Jenny Lerner; (L) Chester Loeffler-Bell
The Cream City Semi-Circus!, Mike Moynihan; (D) Mike Moynihan and Ron Anderson; (S) Mike Moynihan; (C) Cecelia Mason
The Snow Queen, adapt: Ann Melchior and Mike Moynihan, from Hans Christian Andersen; (D) Mike Moynihan; (S) Mike Moynihan
The McKinley Project, company-developed; (D) Melinda Boyd and Mike Moynihan

Ford's Theatre. Steven Crossley in *A Christmas Carol*. Photo: Joan Marcus.

Ford's Theatre

FRANKIE HEWITT
Executive Producer

MICHAEL FOX
Controller

511 Tenth St., NW
Washington, DC 20004
(202) 638-2941 (bus.)
(202) 347-4833 (b.o.)

FOUNDED 1968
Frankie Hewitt

SEASON
Oct.-July

FACILITIES
Seating Capacity: 699
Stage: proscenium

FINANCES
Oct. 1, 1987-Sept. 30, 1988
Expenses: $4,128,331

CONTRACTS
AEA SPT

Holding a unique place in history, Ford's Theatre is one of the oldest working theatres in the United States and the only theatre that presents shows in a national historic site. These productions are designed to celebrate our unique heritage and provide definitive entertainment encasing solid American values. At the core of our artistic plan is rejuvenation of a truly American art form—musical theatre. Ford's Theatre Society has produced numerous world-premiere musicals that might otherwise never have had a chance to attain such national prominence. These include the rousing gospel celebration *Your Arm's Too Short to Box with God*, the beautiful *Amen Corner*, the souped-up *Hot Mikado* and the Broadway-bound *Elmer Gantry*. With the current dearth of exciting new musicals, Ford's Theatre is continuing its long-standing commitment to fulfill a clear responsibility: that of developing and preserving the American musical theatre.
—*Frankie Hewitt*

PRODUCTIONS 1987–88

A Christmas Carol, adapt: David H. Bell, from Charles Dickens; (D) David H. Bell; (S) Daniel Proett; (C) D. Polly Kendrick; (L) David Kissell
Elmer Gantry, book adapt: John Bishop; music: Mel Marvin; lyrics: Robert Satuloff and John Bishop; (D) David H. Bell; (S) Marjorie Bradley Kellogg; (C) David Murin; (L) Pat Collins

PRODUCTIONS 1988–89

A Christmas Carol, adapt: David H. Bell, from Charles Dickens; (D) Mikel Sarah Lambert; (S) Daniel Proett; (C) D. Polly Kendrick; (L) David Kissell

Free Street Theater

DONALD DOUGLAS
Acting Artistic Director

CARROL MCCARREN
General Manager

441 West North Ave.
Chicago, IL 60610
(312) 642-1234

FOUNDED 1969
Patrick Henry, Perry Baer

SEASON
Jan.-Dec.

FINANCES
Apr. 1, 1988-Mar. 31, 1989
Expenses: $283,802

CONTRACTS
AEA TYA

Free Street Theater is an outreach organization dedicated to developing new audiences and participants for the performing arts. We pursue this goal by creating original performance material based on the experiences of the people we seek to engage. Frequently performers are drawn from the community that has inspired the work—such as an inner city neighborhood (*Project!*), or the community of the elderly (the Free Street Too company). Their experiences are interpreted through music, dance and theatre by Free Street's artistic staff. The resultant performance pieces are unique documentaries of an aspect of the contemporary American condition which speak both to and for the community. Some of our companies operate on Actors' Equity contracts, others do not; but all maintain the highest standards. Although the surroundings and trappings may be low-rent, our endeavor is to make the experience high art.
—*Donald Douglas*

Note: The late Patrick Henry served as producer/artistic director from 1969 to 1989.

PRODUCTIONS 1987–88

To Life!, Patrick Henry; (D) Patrick Henry; (S) John Aldridge; (L) John Aldridge
What Do You Want to Be When You Grow Old?, Patrick Henry; (D) Patrick Henry; (S) John Aldridge; (L) John Aldridge
Project!, book and lyrics: Patrick Henry; music and lyrics: Tricia Alexander; music: Doug Lofstrom; (D) Patrick Henry; (S) Rob Hamilton; (L) Denny Clark
Kids from Cabrini, adapt: Patrick Henry; (D) Patrick Henry
Reflections, Patrick Henry; (D) Patrick Henry

PRODUCTIONS 1988–89

What Do You Want to Be When You Grow Old?, Patrick Henry;

Free Street Theater. *Kids from Cabrini.* Photo: Lisa Ebright.

(D) Patrick Henry; (S) John Aldridge; (L) John Aldridge
Project!, book and lyrics: Patrick Henry; music and lyrics: Tricia Alexander; music: Doug Lofstrom; (D) Patrick Henry; (S) Rob Hamilton and Andrea Montag; (L) Denny Clark and Dick Moffat
Kids from Cabrini, adapt: Patrick Henry; (D) Patrick Henry
Reflections, Patrick Henry; (D) Patrick Henry

Fulton Opera House

KATHLEEN A. COLLINS
Artistic Director

DEIDRE W. JACOBSON
Executive Director

12 North Prince St.
Lancaster, PA 17603
(717) 394-7133 (bus.)
(717) 397-7425 (b.o.)

FOUNDED 1963
Fulton Opera House Foundation

SEASON
Oct.-June

FACILITIES
Seating Capacity: 909
Stage: proscenium

FINANCES
Oct. 1, 1987-Sept. 30, 1988
Expenses: $772,753

CONTRACTS
AEA letter of agreement

The Fulton Opera House's mainstage season focuses on classic and contemporary American works. New plays find a home in our playreading series. We also produce an original Theatre for Young Audiences tour that plays to more than 30,000 children annually, and our educational outreach program provides workshops both in the schools and in the theatre space. Having commissioned four new plays in two seasons, we are strongly committed to new works. A National Historic Landmark, the Fulton seeks to keep its legacy alive with a vital regional theatre.
—*Kathleen A. Collins*

PRODUCTIONS 1987-88

The Chimes, Conrad Bishop and Elizabeth Fuller; (D) Conrad Bishop; (S) John F. Whiting; (C) Virginia M. West; (L) Bill Simmons
The Death and Life of Sherlock Holmes, Suzan Zeder; (D) Kathleen A. Collins; (S) James F. Pyne, Jr.; (C) Marla J. Jurglanis; (L) Bill Simmons
This Is Not a Pipe Dream, Barry Kornhauser; (D) Mary Hall Surface; (S) Norman Dodge, Jr.; (C) Beth Dunkelberger; (L) Peter Smith
Children of a Lesser God, Mark Medoff; (D) Kathleen A. Collins; (S) Norman Dodge, Jr.; (C) Beth Dunkelberger; (L) Bill Simmons
The Gin Game, D.L. Coburn; (D) Kathleen A. Collins; (S) John F. Whiting; (C) Virginia M. West; (L) Bill Simmons

PRODUCTIONS 1988-89

Cinderella, book and lyrics: Oscar Hammerstein; music: Richard Rodgers; (D) Kathleen A. Collins; (S) Robert Klingelhoefer; (C) Virginia M. West; (L) Bill Simmons
The Mule and the Milky Way, Susan Kander; (D) Carol M. Tanzman; (S) Robert Klingelhoefer; (C) Beth Dunkelberger; (L) Bill Simmons
Al, Al, et Al: Time and Again, Barry Kornhauser; (D) Barry Kornhauser; (S) Robert Klingelhoefer; (C) Beth Dunkelberger; (L) Peter Smith
The Glass Menagerie, Tennessee Williams; (D) Kathleen A. Collins; (S) Robert Klingelhoefer; (C) Virginia M. West; (L) Bill Simmons
The Nerd, Larry Shue; (D) Kathleen A. Collins; (S) Robert Klingelhoefer; (C) Virginia M. West; (L) Bill Simmons

George Street Playhouse

GREGORY HURST
Producing Director

MICHAEL GENNARO
General Manager

9 Livingston Ave.
New Brunswick, NJ 08901
(201) 846-2895 (bus.)
(201) 246-7469 (b.o.)

FOUNDED 1974
Eric Krebs, John Herochik

SEASON
Oct.-June

Fulton Opera House. Kim Hunter and James Greene in *The Gin Game.*

George Street Playhouse. Peter Jay Fernandez, David S. Howard and William Cain in *Heaven Can Wait*. Photo: Eddie Birch.

FACILITIES
George 367
Seating Capacity: 367
Stage: thrust

George 99
Seating Capacity: 99
Stage: flexible

State Theatre
Seating Capacity: 1,800
Stage: proscenium

FINANCES
July 1, 1988-June 30, 1989
Expenses: $1,930,000

CONTRACTS
LORT (C)

Our 15th-anniversary season was an institutional and artistic watershed. The Playhouse completed the first official season as a resident company of the new $18-million New Brunswick Cultural Center complex, in 1988-89. The Playhouse will realize its goal of providing our audience with a subscription season of 10 plays in three theatres by 1991. Presenting first-class productions of new plays and musicals, rediscovered American classics, and world masterpieces in three vastly different theatre spaces allows the Playhouse to embrace the diversity of its urban audience, foster risktaking and commit to the highest standard of excellence for every production. Increased compensation for artistic and resident personnel is primary to our philosophy. Continuity and freedom for artist and staff are making the Playhouse a fertile place for play and musical development. The 1988-89 season included two world premieres, a revised version of a Pulitzer Prize-winning play, world-class actors, a playwrights' project and statewide outreach program reaching 60,000 students.

—*Gregory Hurst*

Note: During the 1987-88 season, Maureen Heffernan acted as artistic director.

PRODUCTIONS 1987–88

Princess Grace and the Fazzaris, Marc Alan Zagoren; (D) Mary G. Guarldi; (S) Daniel Proett; (C) Jeffrey Ullman and Patricia Sonftner; (L) Kirk Bookman
Nunsense, Dan Goggin; (D) Maureen Heffernan; (S) Daniel Gray; (C) Michael J. Cesario; (L) Daniel Stratman
Max and Maxie, James McLure; (D) D. Lynn Meyers; (S) Eduardo Sicangco; (C) Eduardo Sicangco; (L) Kirk Bookman and David Neville
Lear, adapt: Lee Breuer, from William Shakespeare; (D) Lee Breuer; (S) Alison Xerxa; (C) Ghretta Hynd; (L) Julie Archer
Tracers, Vincent Caristi, Richard Chaves, Rick Gallavan, Merlin Marston, John DiFusco, Eric E. Emerson, Harry Stephens and Sheldon Lettich; (D) John DiFusco; (S) John Falabella; (C) David Navarro Velasquez; (L) Terry Wuthrich
I'm Not Rappaport, Herb Gardner; (D) Maureen Heffernan; (S) Atkin Pace; (C) Patricia Adshead; (L) Donald Holder

PRODUCTIONS 1988–89

Little Shop of Horrors, book and lyrics: Howard Ashman; music: Alan Menken; (D) Allen R. Belknap; (S) Atkin Pace; (C) Barbara Forbes; (L) Donald Holder
The Subject Was Roses, Frank D. Gilroy; (D) Steve Rothman; (S) Atkin Pace; (C) Barbara Forbes; (L) Donald Holder
Tales of Tinseltown, libretto: Michael Colby; music: Paul Katz; (D) Larry Carpenter; (S) Loren Sherman; (C) Lindsay W. Davis; (L) Marcia Madeira
The Eighties, Tom Cole; (D) Lamont Johnson; (S) Atkin Pace; (C) Barbara Forbes; (L) Donald Holder
The Mystery of Irma Vep, Charles Ludlam; (D) Sue Lawless; (S) Deborah Jasien; (C) Barbara Forbes; (L) Spencer Mosse
All My Sons, Arthur Miller; (D) Wendy Liscow; (S) Deborah Jasien; (C) Barbara Forbes; (L) Michael Chybowski
Heaven Can Wait, Harry Segall; (D) Gregory S. Hurst; (S) Atkin Pace; (C) Barbara Forbes; (L) Donald Holder

Germinal Stage Denver

ED BAIERLEIN
Director/Manager

2450 West 44th Avenue
Denver, CO 80211
(303) 455-7108

FOUNDED 1974
Ginger Valone, Jack McKnight, Sallie Diamond, Ed Baierlein

SEASON
Oct.-Aug.

FACILITIES
Seating Capacity: 100
Stage: thrust

FINANCES
Sept. 1, 1988-Aug. 31, 1989
Expenses: $88,500

Germinal Stage Denver is the withered arm of regional theatres, a corner grocery holding its own against the supermarkets, and our supplier's running out of our most popular brand of toilet paper. We're an actors' theatre, semi-rough, vaguely postmodern. We're having less fun than we had two years ago, but more fun than we had six years ago. We bought our own building in 1987, smaller so we couldn't "grow," and have made all our mortgage payments on time. We've been nominated for 30 Denver Critics' Circle awards in the last four years. Recently, we've become aware that, after 16 seasons, we have very little idea of what we're doing. Therefore, we declare ourselves "mainstream," and confidently await the Gulf current.

—*Ed Baierlein*

PRODUCTIONS 1987–88

The Entertainer, John Osborne; (D) Ed Baierlein; (S) Ed Baierlein; (C) Sallie Diamond; (L) Ed Baierlein
Madly in Love, Paul Ableman; (D) Ed Baierlein; (S) Ed Baierlein; (C) Sallie Diamond; (L) Ed Baierlein
The Madman and the Nun, Stanislaw Witkiewicz; (D) Ed Baierlein; (S) Ed Baierlein; (C) Sallie Diamond; (L) Ed Baierlein
My Sister in This House, Wendy Kesselman; (D) Laura Cuetara; (S) Laura Cuetara; (C) Virginia Rossman; (L) Stephen R. Kramer
Village Wooing, George Bernard Shaw; (D) Ed Baierlein; (S) Ed Baierlein; (C) Sallie Diamond; (L) Ed Baierlein
The Man with the Flower in His Mouth, adapt: Ed Baierlein, from Luigi Pirandello; trans: Eric Bentley; (D) Ed Baierlein; (S) Stephen R. Kramer; (C) Sallie Diamond; (L) Stephen R. Kramer
Hughie, Eugene O'Neill; (D) Ed Baierlein; (S) Stephen R. Kramer; (C) Sallie Diamond; (L) Stephen R. Kramer
The Perfect Party, A.R. Gurney, Jr.; (D) Ed Baierlein; (S) Stephen R. Kramer; (C) Sallie Diamond; (L) Stephen R. Kramer

PRODUCTIONS 1988–89

Ferril, Etc., adapt: June Favre and Ed Baierlein, from Thomas Hornsby Ferril; (D) Ed Baierlein; (S) Ed Baierlein;

Germinal Stage Denver. *The Madman and the Nun.* Photo: Strack Edwards.

(C) Sallie Diamond; (L) Ed Baierlein
Miss Margarida's Way, Roberto Athayde; (D) Ed Baierlein; (S) Ed Baierlein; (C) Ed Baierlein; (L) Ed Baierlein
The Caballero's Way, O. Henry; (D) Ed Baierlein; (S) Ed Baierlein; (C) Sallie Diamond; (L) Ed Baierlein
The Darling, Anton Chekhov; (D) Ed Baierlein; (S) Ed Baierlein; (C) Sallie Diamond; (L) Ed Baierlein
Useless Beauty, Guy de Maupassant; (D) Ed Baierlein; (S) Ed Baierlein; (C) Sallie Diamond; (L) Ed Baierlein
Dr. Korczak and the Children, Erwin Sylvanus; (D) Ed Baierlein; (S) Ed Baierlein; (C) Sallie Diamond; (L) Ed Baierlein
The Rainmaker, N. Richard Nash; (D) Ed Baierlein; (S) Stephen R. Kramer; (C) Sallie Diamond; (L) Stephen R. Kramer

GeVa Theatre

HOWARD J. MILLMAN
Producing Director

WILLIAM B. DUNCAN
Managing Director

ANTHONY ZERBE
Associate Artistic Director

75 Woodbury Blvd.
Rochester, NY 14607
(716) 232-1366 (bus.)
(716) 232-1363 (b.o.)

FOUNDED 1972
William Selden, Cynthia Mason Selden

SEASON
Sept.-June

FACILITIES
Richard Pine Theatre
Seating Capacity: 552
Stage: thrust

FINANCES
July 1, 1988-June 30, 1989
Expenses: $3,100,000

CONTRACTS
LORT (B)

GeVa Theatre presents a distinctive variety of theatre experience including the classics of the world and American stage, revivals, musicals, contemporary dramas and comedies. The theatre has a specific commitment to the American playwright, to the production of new plays and to the implementation of those projects that reflect new vision and direction on the part of theatre artists. Newly appointed associate artistic director Anthony Zerbe has specific responsibility for the production of new plays for the main stage. Plays in Progress, a staged reading series, works with playwrights in developing that work. GeVa has also entered upon a new theatre-in-education program designed by the theatre in collaboration with the Rochester City School District. The theatre's ancillary programming enhances the community's knowledge of the process of theatre and includes a noontime lecture series, interpreted performances for the hearing impaired, discussion forums of artists with the audience, play support teams, tours of the renovated landmark theatre facility and an extensive volunteer program. Free-to-the-public outreach efforts include availability of staff for workshops and lectures, and the loan of the theatre's costumes and props.
—*Howard J. Millman*

PRODUCTIONS 1987–88

Charley's Aunt, Brandon Thomas; (D) Walton Jones; (S) Christopher Barreca; (C) Pamela Peterson; (L) Danianne Mizzy
Private Lives, Noel Coward; (D) Walton Jones; (S) Scott Bradley; (C) Pamela Peterson; (L) Danianne Mizzy
The Rose Tattoo, Tennessee Williams; (D) Howard J. Millman; (S) Victor Becker; (C) Pamela Scofield; (L) Phil Monat
A Christmas Carol, adapt: Eberle Thomas, from Charles Dickens; (D) Eberle Thomas; (S) Bob Barnett; (C) Pamela Scofield; (L) Nic Minetor
Stepping Out, Richard Harris; (D) Carl Schurr; (S) Michael Miller; (C) Maria Marrero; (L) Rachael Budin
Alfred Stieglitz Loves O'Keeffe, Lanie Robertson; (D) Allen R. Belknap; (S) William Barclay; (C) Mimi Maxmen; (L) Richard Winkler
The Mystery of Irma Vep, Charles Ludlam; (D) Everett Quinton; (S) Bob Barnett; (C) Everett Quinton; (L) Nic Minetor
Equus, Peter Shaffer; (D) Allen R. Belknap; (S) David Potts; (C) Mimi Maxmen; (L) Richard Winkler

GeVa Theatre. Michael Mauldin and Dan Diggles in *The Mystery of Irma Vep*. Photo: Alan Farkas.

PRODUCTIONS 1988–89
ames at Sea, book and lyrics:
 George Haimsohn and Robin
 Miller; music: Jim Wise;
 (D) Neal Kenyon; (S) Bob
 Barnett; (C) Mary Mease
 Warren; (L) Betsy Adams
il City Symphony, Mark
 Carver, Mark Hardwick, Debra
 Monk and Mary Murfitt;
 (D) Larry Forde; (S) Bob
 Barnett; (C) Dana H. Tinsley;
 (L) Betsy Adams
eel Magnolias, Robert Harling;
 (D) Walton Jones; (S) Victor
 Becker; (C) Pamela Peterson;
 (L) Tina Charney
dith Stein, Arthur Giron;
 (D) Lee Sankowich; (S) Ursula
 Belden; (C) Laura Crow;
 (L) Kirk Bookman
Christmas Carol, adapt: Eberle
 Thomas, from Charles Dickens;
 (D) Eberle Thomas; (S) Bob
 Barnett; (C) Pamela Scofield;
 (L) Nic Minetor
*omfoolery: The Words and
 Music of Tom Lehrer*, adapt:
 Cameron Macintosh and Robin
 Ray, from Tom Lehrer;
 (D) William Roudebush; (S) Bob
 Barnett; (C) Dana H. Tinsley;
 (L) Rachel Budin
Walk in the Woods, Lee
 Blessing; (D) Stephen Rothman;
 (S) Harry Feiner; (C) Dana H.
 Tinsley; (L) Betsy Adams
alian American Reconciliation,
 John Patrick Shanley; (D) Allan
 Carlsen; (S) Loy Arcenas;
 (C) Jim Buff; (L) F. Mitchell
 Dana
'm Not Rappaport, Herb
 Gardner; (D) Howard J.
 Millman; (S) Bob Barnett;
 (C) Pamela Scofield; (L) Nic
 Minetor

Gloucester Stage Company

SRAEL HOROVITZ
rtistic Director

OHN HEDGES
Managing Director

67 East Main St.
Gloucester, MA 01930
(508) 281-4099

OUNDED 1979
srael Horovitz

SEASON
May–Dec.

FACILITIES
Gorton Theatre
Seating Capacity: 150
Stage: flexible

FINANCES
Jan. 1, 1989–Dec. 31, 1989
Expenses: $246,700

CONTRACTS
AEA SPT

The Gloucester Stage Company exists primarily to produce new American and British stage writing that relates thematically to life as it is lived in Gloucester, Massachusetts. The company also embraces actor and director-oriented projects that relate specifically to the Gloucester community. The theatre is especially disposed to linkage with other nonprofit theatres in the development of new work, with a firm dedication to a continuing creative process in the completion of a play prior to its New York City premiere. Further, Gloucester Stage is dedicated to the development and training of future professionals in every aspect of theatre production, and to providing a continuing educational resource to the residents of Cape Ann and the north-of-Boston area.
—*Israel Horovitz*

PRODUCTIONS 1987–88
A Rosen by Any Other Name,
 Israel Horovitz; (D) Richard
 McElvain; (S) Pieter Smit;
 (C) Tracy Pierson; (L) Pieter
 Smit
The Club, David Williamson;
 (D) Grey Cattell Johnson;
 (S) Pieter Smit; (C) Tracy
 Pierson; (L) Pieter Smit
Wenceslas Square, Larry Shue;
 (D) Richard McElvain; (S) Pieter
 Smit; (C) Tracy Pierson;
 (L) Pieter Smit
Henry Lumper, Israel Horovitz;
 (D) Grey Cattell Johnson;
 (S) Pieter Smit; (C) Jeanine
 Burgess; (L) Victor En Yu Tan
Traveling North, David
 Williamson; (D) Roger Curtis;
 (S) Ken Loewit; (C) Tracy
 Pierson; (L) Gil Danieli
Our Town, Thornton Wilder;
 (D) Grey Cattell Johnson;
 (S) Ken Loewit; (C) Rick Kelly;
 (L) Gil Danieli

Gloucester Stage Company. *Henry Lumper.* Photo: Clark S. Linehan.

PRODUCTIONS 1988–89
*Coming Home to Someplace
 New*, Jay O'Callahan;
 (D) Richard McElvain; (L) John
 Ambrosoni
The Chopin Playoffs, Israel
 Horovitz; (D) Richard McElvain;
 (S) Lorilee Coleman; (C) Rick
 Kelly and Mary Wentzel;
 (L) Michael Renken
The Widow's Blind Date, Israel
 Horovitz; (D) Israel Horovitz;
 (S) David Condino and Michael
 Renken; (C) Rick Kelly and
 Janet Irving; (L) Michael
 Renken
Better Days, Richard Dresser;
 (D) Grey Cattell Johnson;
 (S) Jeanine Burgess; (C) Janet
 Irving; (L) Michael Renken
Away, Michael Gow; (D) Grey
 Cattell Johnson; (S) Ken Loewit;
 (C) Esther Doepel; (L) Michael
 Renken
The Hostage, Brendan Behan;
 (D) Michael Allosso; (L) Michael
 Renken

Goodman Theatre

ROBERT FALLS
Artistic Director

ROCHE SCHULFER
Producing Director

FRANK GALATI
MICHAEL MAGGIO
Associate Directors

200 South Columbus Dr.
Chicago, IL 60603
(312) 443-3811 (bus.)
(312) 443-3800 (b.o.)

FOUNDED 1925
Art Institute of Chicago

SEASON
Sept.–July

FACILITIES
Goodman Mainstage
Seating Capacity: 683
Stage: proscenium

Goodman Theatre Studio
Seating Capacity: 135
Stage: proscenium

FINANCES
July 1, 1988–June 30, 1989
Expenses: $5,429,300

CONTRACTS
LORT (B+) AND (D)

The Goodman is Chicago's largest and oldest nonprofit theatre, and we take advantage of its great resources to produce classic and contemporary works of size—large in both imagination and physical scale. Our goal is to infuse the classics with the energy usually reserved for new works, and to treat new plays with the care and reverence usually given to the classics. Working with associate directors Frank Galati and Michael Maggio, I intend to continue our efforts on the Goodman five-play mainstage series. At the same time, we aim to expand our artistic scope, and our audience's, by using our Studio Theatre to introduce new plays and leading theatre artists whose work

59

is rarely seen in Chicago. We will continue to expand auxiliary programming to accompany each production, encouraging our audience into active participation in the theatrical process. We also seek to develop younger audiences through our program of free student matinees and close collaboration with the public school system.

—*Robert Falls*

PRODUCTIONS 1987–88

Red Noses, Peter Barnes; (D) Jeff Steitzer; (S) Scott Weldin; (C) Laura Crow; (L) Rick Paulsen
A Christmas Carol, adapt: Larry Sloan, from Charles Dickens; (D) Michael Maggio; (S) Joe Nieminski; (C) Christa Scholtz; (L) Robert Christen
Passion Play, Peter Nichols; (D) Frank Galati; (S) John Conklin; (C) Jessica Hahn; (L) Kevin Rigdon
Landscape of the Body, book, music and lyrics: John Guare; (D) Robert Falls; (S) George Tsypin; (C) Dunya Ramicova; (L) Jennifer Tipton
A Flea in Her Ear, Georges Feydeau; adapt: Frank Galati; (D) Michael Maggio; (S) John Lee Beatty; (C) Lindsay Davis; (L) Robert Christen
Pal Joey, book: John O'Hara; music: Richard Rodgers; lyrics: Lorenz Hart; (D) Robert Falls; (S) Thomas Lynch; (C) Martin Pakledinaz; (L) Michael S. Philippi

PRODUCTIONS 1988–89

Romeo and Juliet, William Shakespeare; (D) Michael Maggio; (S) Michael Merritt; (C) Nan Cibula; (L) Jennifer Tipton
A Christmas Carol, adapt: Larry Sloan, from Charles Dickens; (D) Michael Maggio; (S) Joseph Nieminski; (C) Julie Jackson; (L) Robert Christen
The Piano Lesson, August Wilson; (D) Lloyd Richards; (S) E. David Cosier, Jr.; (C) Constanza Romero; (L) Christopher Akerlind
The Rover, Aphra Behn; adapt: John Barton; (D) Kyle Donnelly; (S) John Lee Beatty; (C) Lindsay Davis; (L) Judy Rasmuson
The Speed of Darkness, Steve Tesich; (D) Robert Falls; (S) Thomas Lynch; (C) Nan Cibula; (L) Michael S. Philippi
Mill Fire, Sally Nemeth; (D) David Petrarca; (S) Linda Buchanan; (C) Laura Cunningham; (L) Robert Christen
A Funny Thing Happened on the Way to the Forum, book: Larry Gelbart and Burt Shevelove; music and lyrics: Stephen Sondheim and; (D) Frank Galati; (S) Mary Griswold and John Paoletti; (C) Mary Griswold and John Paoletti; (L) Geoffrey Bushor

Goodspeed Opera House. *Oh, Kay!* Photo: Diane Soboleski.

Goodspeed Opera House

MICHAEL P. PRICE
Executive Director

DAN SIRETTA
Associate Artistic Director

SUE FROST
Associate Producer

Goodspeed Landing East Haddam
East Haddam, CT 06423
(203) 873-8664 (bus.)
(203) 873-8668 (b.o.)

FOUNDED 1963
Goodspeed Opera House Foundation

SEASON
Apr.-Dec.

FACILITIES
Goodspeed Opera House
Seating Capacity: 398
Stage: proscenium

Goodspeed-at-Chester/The Norma Terris Theatre
Seating Capacity: 200
Stage: proscenium

CONTRACTS
LORT (B+) and (D)

The Goodspeed Opera House is one of the theatres in the United States dedicated to the heritage, preservation and development of the American musical. Devoted to both classical and contemporary musicals, the Opera House has sent 12 productions to Broadway, including *Annie*, *Shenandoah* and *Man of La Mancha*. The Goodspeed was awarded a special Tony in 1980 for its contributions to thi uniquely American art form. Goodspeed's second stage, Goodspeed-at-Chester/The Norman Terris Theatre, provides an intimate performing space exclusively for new works of musical theatre. Here, writers and creative staff have a rare opportunity to develop a "musical-in-progress" before an audience.

—*Michael P. Price*

PRODUCTIONS 1987–88

Wonderful Town, book: Joseph Fields and Jerome Chodorov; music: Leonard Bernstein; lyrics: Betty Comden and Adolph Green; (D) Thomas Gruenewald; (S) Lowell Detweiler; (C) John Carver Sullivan; (L) Craig Miller
Mr. Cinders, book: Clifford Grey, Greatrex Newman; music: Vivian Ellis and Richard Meyers; lyrics: Leo Robin; (D) Martin Connor; (S) James Leonard Joy; (C) David Toser; (L) Curt Ostermann
Ankles Aweigh, book: Guy Bolton and Eddie Davis; music: Sammy Fain; lyrics: Dan Shapiro; adapt: Charles Busch; (D) Dan Siretta; (S) Eduardo Sicangco; (C) Eduardo Sicangco and Jose Lengson; (L) Allen Lee Hughes
Abyssinia, book: James Racheff; book and music: Ted Kociolek;

Goodman Theatre. Kevin Anderson and Katherine Meloche in *Pal Joey*.

lyrics: James Racheff;
(D) Tazewell Thompson and Ted Kociolek; (S) Lames Leonard Joy; (C) Amanda J. Klein; (L) Allen Lee Hughes

PRODUCTIONS 1988–89

A Connecticut Yankee, book: Herbert Fields; music: Richard Rogers; lyrics: Lorenz Hart; (D) Thomas Gruenewald; (S) Clarke Dunham; (C) Dean Brown; (L) Craig Miller

Madame Sherry, book and lyrics: Otto Harbach; music: Karl Hoschna; (D) Martin Connor; (S) Eduardo Sicangco; (C) Jose Lengson; (L) Kirk Bookman

Oh, Kay!, book: Guy Bolton and P.G. Wodehouse; adapt: James Racheff; music: George Gershwin; lyrics: Ira Gershwin; (D) Martin Connor; (S) Kenneth Foy; (C) Judy Dearing; (L) Craig Miller

A Fine and Private Place, book and lyrics: Erik Haagensen; music: Richard Isen; (D) Robert Kalfin; (S) Fred Kolo; (L) Fred Kolo

Great Lakes Theater Festival

GERALD FREEDMAN
Artistic Director

MARY BILL
Managing Director

1501 Euclid Ave., Suite 250
Cleveland, OH 44115
(216) 241-5490 (bus.)
(216) 241-6000 (b.o.)

FOUNDED 1962
Community members

SEASON
May-Dec.

FACILITIES
Ohio Theatre
Seating Capacity: 643
Stage: proscenium

FINANCES
Feb. 1, 1988-Jan. 31, 1989
Expenses: $2,112,072

CONTRACTS
LORT (B)

Though the Great Lakes Theatre Festival continues to uphold the classical theatre mandate that launched it, we have been challenging our perception of what that responsibility means. We are interested in the whole spectrum of American plays—not only the acknowledged great works, but the culturally significant plays and musicals that placed Broadway in the mainstream of American entertainment from the 1920s through the 1950s. And we are interested in pursuing the special resonance that comes from seeing world classics side by side with new plays. With regard to performance style, I am drawn to actors adept at both classic drama and musicals. I find a kinship between doing Shakespeare, for example, and musical theater. The presentational styles—the soliloquies in one form, the songs in the other—each require a high-energy performance level that forms a visceral relationship with an audience and that is very much my signature.

—*Gerald Freedman*

PRODUCTIONS 1987–88

Love's Labour's Lost, William Shakespeare; (D) Gerald Freedman; (S) John Ezell; (C) James Scott; (L) Natasha Katz

Man and Superman, George Bernard Shaw; (D) Amy Saltz; (S) Bob Shaw; (L) Mary Jo Dondlinger

Lady Day at Emerson's Bar and Grill, Lanie Robertson; (D) Victoria Bussert; (S) Russ Borski; (C) Al Kohout; (L) Mary Jo Dondlinger

A Doll's House, Henrik Ibsen; (D) Richard Hamburger; (S) Christopher Barreca; (C) Catherine Zuber; (L) Stephen Strawbridge

Blood Wedding, Federico Garcia Lorca; (D) Gerald Freedman and Graciela Daniele; (S) John Ezell; (C) Jeanne Button; (L) Peggy Eisenhauer

PRODUCTIONS 1988–89

Hamlet, William Shakespeare; (D) Gerald Freedman; (S) Christopher Barreca; (C) Lawrence Casey; (L) Mary Jo Dondlinger

The Threepenny Opera, Bertolt Brecht and Kurt Weill; trans: Marc Blitzstein; (D) Victoria Bussert; (S) Russ Borski; (C) Jeanne Button; (L) Mary Jo Dondlinger

The Seagull, Anton Chekhov; (D) Gerald Freedman; (S) John Ezell; (C) Lawrence Casey; (L) Thomas Skelton

A Christmas Carol, adapt: Gerald Freedman, from Charles Dickens; (D) Gerald Freedman; (S) John Ezell; (C) Jamie Scott; (L) Mary Jo Dondlinger

Great Lakes Theater Festival. Josie de Guzman and Jane White in *Blood Wedding*. Photo: Roger Mastroianni.

Great North American History Theatre

LYNN LOHR
Producer/Co-Artistic Director

LANCE BELVILLE
Playwright-in-Residence/Co-Artistic Director

TOM BERGER
General Manager

30 East 10th Street
St. Paul, MN 55101
(612) 292-4325 (bus.)
(612) 292-4323 (b.o.)

FOUNDED 1978
Lynn Lohr

SEASON
Sept.-June

FACILITIES
Crawford Livingston Theatre
Seating Capacity: 597
Stage: thrust

FINANCES
July 1, 1988-June 30, 1989
Expenses: $437,800

CONTRACTS
AEA Guest Artist

62 GREAT NORTH AMERICAN HISTORY THEATRE

Great North American History Theatre. Tinia Moulder and Ruth Mackenzie in *Cowgirls*. Photo: Gerald Gustafson.

The Great North American History Theatre is a professional theatre dedicated to commissioning, producing and touring new plays which dramatize the history, folklore and social issues of Minnesota and the Midwest. Occasionally the theatre may develop or feature similar new work about other American regions and seek exchanges with theatres in other countries which have similar missions. The theatre is committed to returning the stories of its region to the people who contributed them. An ever-growing touring, educational, workshop and residency program reaches large and small communities throughout the entire country.

—*Lynn Lohr*

PRODUCTIONS 1987–88

Plain Hearts, book: Lance S. Belville; music and lyrics: Eric Peltoniemi; (D) Lynn Lohr; (S) Thomas Berger; (C) Nayna Rayme; (L) Thomas Berger

Mid-Winter Light, John Louis Anderson; (D) Jacalyn Knight; (S) Chris Johnson; (C) Nayna Rayme; (L) Chris Johnson

Gold in the Streets, Marie Jones; (D) Lynn Lohr; (S) Chris Johnson; (C) Nayna Rayme; (L) Chris Johnson

St. Paul Suite, Thomas Poole; (D) Ron Troutman; (S) Chris Johnson; (C) Nayna Rayme; (L) Chris Johnson

PRODUCTIONS 1988–89

Entertaining Strangers, David Edgar; (D) Lynn Lohr and Pam Nice; (S) Michael Cottom; (C) Nayna Rayme; (L) Nayna Rayme

Tree of Memory, Nancy Bagshaw-Reasoner, Lance S. Belville, David Hawley, Gareth Hiebert and George Sand; (D) George Sand and Belville S. Lance; (S) Steve Griffith; (C) Connie Cadwell; (L) Thomas Berger

A Servants' Christmas, John Fenn; (D) Ron Peluso; (S) Steve Griffith; (C) Thomas Berger; (L) Thomas Berger

Observe the Sons of Ulster Marching Towards the Somme, Frank McGuinness; (D) Derek Campbell; (S) Thomas Berger; (C) Dawn D'Hanson; (L) Thomas Barrett

Queen Clara: Rivers of Blood, Fields of Glory, Lance S. Belville; (D) Lance S. Belville; (S) Chris Johnson; (C) Dawn D'Hanson

Cowgirls, Lance S. Belville; (D) Lynn Lohr; (S) Chris Johnson; (C) Dawn D'Hanson; (L) Chris Johnson

Grove Shakespeare Festival

THOMAS F. BRADAC
Producing Artistic Director

RICHARD STEIN
Managing Director

12852 Main St.
Garden Grove, CA 92640
(714) 636-7214 (bus.)
(714) 636-7213 (b.o.)

FOUNDED 1979
Thomas F. Bradac

SEASON
May–Dec.

FACILITIES
Gem Theatre
Seating Capacity: 172
Stage: proscenium

Festival Amphitheatre
Seating Capacity: 550
Stage: thrust

FINANCES
July 1, 1988–June 30, 1989
Expenses: $620,000

CONTRACTS
AEA SPT and letter of agreement

The Grove Shakespeare Festival utilizes the plays of Shakespeare a the cornerstone for our program, presenting works that challenge both the artist and the audience b addressing our mutual experience beliefs and concerns. In our theatre, whose inspiration is launche by the playwright, the text is the principal source for artistic exploration and vision. Operating with small resident company or actors, the festival strives to provide the finest examples of dramatic literature from both the classical and contemporary theatre. With two working stages, the festival produces 7-10 productions each season for the central Orange

Grove Shakespeare Festival. Debbie Gates, Ferdinand Lewis and Daniel Bryan Cartm in *The Imaginary Invalid*. Photo: Ron Stone.

County area, attracting new directors, actors and designers from the Los Angeles basin. While remaining true to the text, we make every effort to explore the written work with an eye for contemporary, yet meaningful, insights into our complex and challenging world

—*Thomas F. Bradac*

PRODUCTIONS 1987–88

Julius Caesar, William Shakespeare; (D) Jules Aaron; (S) Cliff Faulkner; (C) Shigeru Yaji; (L) Pamela Rank
The Imaginary Invalid, Moliere; (D) Frank Condon; (S) Cliff Faulkner; (C) Karen Weller; (L) Doc Ballard
A Midsummer Night's Dream, William Shakespeare; (D) Thomas F. Bradac; (S) Stanley Meyer; (C) Shigeru Yaji; (L) Pamela Rank
Sherlock's Last Case, Charles Marowitz; (D) Thomas F. Bradac; (S) Gil Morales; (C) Karen Weller; (L) David Palmer
A Child's Christmas in Wales, adapt: Adrian Mitchell and Jeremy Brooks, from Dylan Thomas; (D) Daniel Bryan Cartmell; (S) Gil Morales; (C) Clarice Bessey; (L) David Palmer
Vikings, Stephen Metcalfe; (D) Jules Aaron; (S) Christa Bartels; (C) Sondra Huber; (L) David Palmer
Mrs. California, Doris Baizley; (D) Thomas F. Bradac; (S) Gil Morales; (C) Karen Weller; (L) David Palmer
The Price, Arthur Miller; (D) Jerome Guardino; (S) Gil Morales; (C) Karen Weller; (L) Lawrence Oberman
Pump Boys and Dinettes, John Foley, Mark Hardwick, Debra Monk, Cass Morgan, John Schimmel and Jim Wann; (D) Dean Hess; (S) Gil Morales; (C) Karen Weller; (L) David Palmer

PRODUCTIONS 1988–89

Richard II, William Shakespeare; (D) Jules Aaron; (S) D. Martyn Bookwalter; (C) Claire Marie Verheyen; (L) David Palmer
The Comedy of Errors, William Shakespeare; (D) David Herman; (S) Stanley Meyer; (C) Shigeru Yaji; (L) David Palmer
King Lear, William Shakespeare; (D) Thomas F. Bradac; (S) Stanley Meyer; (C) Shigeru Yaji; (L) Pam Rank
Venus and Adonis, William Shakespeare; (D) Benjamin Stewart; (S) Benjamin Stewart; (C) Benjamin Stewart; (L) David Palmer
And a Nightingale Sang, C.P. Taylor; (D) David Herman; (S) Christa Bartels; (C) Karen J. Weller; (L) Kevin Cook
A Child's Christmas in Wales, adapt: Jeremy Brooks and Adrian Mitchell, from Dylan Thomas; (D) Daniel Bryan Cartmell; (S) Gil Morales; (C) Clarice Bessey; (L) David Palmer
Lily Dale, Horton Foote; (D) Daniel Bryan Cartmell; (S) Gil Morales; (C) Karen J. Weller; (L) David Palmer
Requiem for a Heavyweight, Rod Serling; (D) Thomas F. Bradac; (S) Gil Morales; (C) Karen J. Weller; (L) David Palmer
Tomfoolery, adapt: Robin Ray and Cameron Mackintosh, from Tom Leher; (D) Thomas F. Bradac; (S) Gil Morales; (C) Laura Deremer; (L) David Palmer

The Guthrie Theater

GARLAND WRIGHT
Artistic Director

EDWARD MARTENSON
Executive Director

725 Vineland Pl.
Minneapolis, MN 55403
(612) 347-1100 (bus.)
(612) 377-2224 (b.o.)

FOUNDED 1963
Peter Zeisler, Oliver Rea, Tyrone Guthrie

SEASON
June-Apr.

FACILITIES
Seating Capacity: 1,441
Stage: thrust

FINANCES
Apr. 1, 1988-Mar. 31, 1989
Expenses: $8,524,622

CONTRACTS
LORT (A)

The Guthrie Theater. Daniel Davis and Michael Countryman in *Pravda—A Fleet Street Comedy*. Photo: Michael Daniel.

Theatre is not a place or thing, but an act—an interchange that has consequence. It is the means by which actors and audience choose together to examine and participate in the world—to recognize it, to experience it and, ultimately, to understand it. Theatre reflects the complexity of our reality and, although it is perhaps better at illuminating questions than providing answers, its questioning spirit gives testimony to the seriousness with which it seeks to contribute to the human endeavor. We at the Guthrie firmly commit our efforts to artistic excellence at every level, to the greatest plays of the world repertoire, to the actor as the central communicator of the ideas and poetry within those plays, and to the imagination and its transforming power.

—*Garland Wright*

PRODUCTIONS 1987–88

The Misanthrope, Moliere; trans: Richard Wilbur; (D) Garland Wright; (S) Joel Fontaine; (C) Jack Edwards; (L) Peter Maradudin
The Piggy Bank, Eugene Labiche and Alfred Delacour; trans: Albert Bermel; (D) Garland Wright; (S) John Arnone; (C) Martin Pakledinaz; (L) Frances Aronson
The Bacchae, adapt: Kenneth Cavander, from Euripides; (D) Liviu Ciulei; (S) Liviu Ciulei; (C) Patricia Zipprodt; (L) Marcus Dilliard
The House of Bernarda Alba, Federico Garcia Lorca; trans: Timberlake Wertenbaker; (D) Les Waters; (S) Annie Smart; (C) Martin Pakledinaz; (L) James F. Ingalls
Leon & Lena, Georg Buchner; trans: Henry J. Schmidt; (D) JoAnne Akalaitis; (S) George Tsypin; (C) Adelle Lutz; (L) Jennifer Tipton
A Christmas Carol, adapt: Barbara Field, from Charles Dickens; (D) Richard Ooms; (S) Jack Barkla; (C) Jack

Edwards; (L) Marcus Dilliard
Richard III, William Shakespeare; (D) Garland Wright; (S) Douglas Stein; (C) Ann Hould-Ward; (L) James F. Ingalls

PRODUCTIONS 1988–89

The Glass Menagerie, Tennessee Williams; (D) Vivian Matalon; (S) Desmond Heeley; (C) Ann Hould-Ward; (L) Duane Schuler
The Imaginary Invalid, Moliere; trans: John Wood; (D) Garland Wright; (S) Garland Wright; (C) Jack Edwards; (L) Marcus Dilliard
Frankenstein: Playing with Fire, adapt: Barbara Field, from Mary Shelley; (D) Michael Maggio; (S) John Arnone; (C) Jack Edwards; (L) Marcus Dilliard
Hamlet, William Shakespeare; (D) Garland Wright; (S) Douglas Stein; (C) Ann Hould-Ward; (L) James F. Ingalls
The Wild Duck, adapt: Lucian Pintilie, from Henrik Ibsen; trans: David Westerfer; (D) Lucian Pintilie; (S) Radu Boruzescu; (C) Miruna Boruzescu; (L) Beverly Emmons
A Christmas Carol, adapt: Barbara Field, from Charles Dickens; (D) Richard Ooms; (S) Jack Barkla; (C) Jack Edwards; (L) Marcus Dilliard
Pravda: A Fleet Street Comedy, Howard Brenton and David Hare; (D) Robert Falls; (S) John Arnone; (C) Jane Greenwood; (L) James F. Ingalls

Hartford Stage Company

MARK LAMOS
Artistic Director

DAVID HAWKANSON
Managing Director

50 Church St.
Hartford, CT 06103
(203) 525-5601 (bus.)
(203) 527-5151 (b.o.)

FOUNDED 1964
Jacques Cartier

SEASON
Oct.–June

FACILITIES
John W. Huntington Theatre
Seating Capacity: 489
Stage: thrust

FINANCES
July 1, 1988–June 30, 1989
Expenses: $3,200,000

CONTRACTS
LORT (B)

The work at Hartford Stage reflects the desire to explore every possible kind of theatrical style: new plays, commissioned translations of old plays and adaptations of nontheatrical works. The center of our work is the production of texts from the past—primarily works by Shakespeare, but also plays by Schnitzler, Shaw, Moliere and Ibsen—pieces that are modern, that draw parallels, chart paths and create possibilities. Occasionally, plays from the recent past are also revived, and fully half of each season is devoted to world premieres or to second productions of new plays by U.S. writers. All works, whether written B.C., in the Middle Ages, during the Renaissance, at the turn of the century or yesterday, are presented on a single stage. I believe that the theatre is a place meant for the exploration of dreams; the presentation of mysteries; the seeking of guidance, coherencies, lessons, laughter and wonder. Wonder most of all.

—*Mark Lamos*

PRODUCTIONS 1987–88

Hamlet, William Shakespeare; (D) Mark Lamos; (S) John Conklin; (C) John Conklin; (L) Pat Collins
The Voice of the Prairie, John Olive; (D) Norman Rene; (S) Alexander Okun; (C) Walter Hicklin; (L) Debra Kletter
Hedda Gabler, Henrik Ibsen; trans: Gerry Bamman and Irene B. Berman; (D) Mark Lamos; (S) George Tsypin; (C) Jess Goldstein; (L) Pat Collins
Serenading Louie, Lanford Wilson; (D) Mary B. Robinson; (S) Marjorie Bradley Kellogg; (C) Jess Goldstein; (L) Ken Tabachnick
Principia Scriptoriae, Richard Nelson; (D) James Simpson; (S) Andrew Jackness; (C) Claudia Brown; (L) Stephen Strawbridge
The School for Wives, Moliere; trans: Richard Wilbur; (D) Mark Lamos; (S) John Arnone; (C) Martin Pakledinaz; (L) Peter Kaczorowski

PRODUCTIONS 1988–89

A Midsummer Night's Dream, William Shakespeare; (D) Mark Lamos; (S) Michael H. Yeargan; (C) Jess Goldstein; (L) Pat Collins
Other People's Money, Jerry Sterner; (D) Gloria Muzio; (S) David Jenkins; (C) Jess Goldstein; (L) F. Mitchell Dana
Nothing Sacred, George F. Walker; (D) James Simpson; (S) Michael H. Yeargan; (C) Claudia Brown; (L) Frances Aronson
The Paper Gramophone, Alexander Chervinsky; (D) Yuri Yeremin; (S) Michael H. Yeargan; (C) Micheal H. Yeargan; (L) Ken Tabachnick
Peer Gynt, Henrik Ibsen; trans: Gerry Bamman and Irene B. Berman; (D) Mark Lamos; (S) John Conklin; (C) Merrily Murray-Walsh; (L) Pat Collins
A Moon for the Misbegotten, Eugene O'Neill; (D) Jackson Phippin; (S) Christopher Barreca; (C) Robert Wojewodski; (L) Ken Tabachnick

Hartford Stage Company. *A Midsummer Night's Dream.* Photo: T. Charles Erickson.

Heritage Artists, Ltd. at the Cohoes Music Hall

ROBERT W. TOLAN
Producing Director

ANDREW C. MCGIBBON
General Manager

Box 586
Cohoes, NY 12047
(518) 235-7909 (bus.)
(518) 235-7969 (b.o.)

FOUNDED 1982
John P. Ryan, Jr.

SEASON
Oct.–June

FACILITIES
Cohoes Music Hall
Seating Capacity: 250
Stage: proscenium

FINANCES
July 1, 1988–June 30, 1989
Expenses: $550,000

CONTRACTS
AEA SPT contract

Heritage Artists at the Cohoes Music Hall, upstate New York's professional music theatre, is committed to the development and production of Off-Broadway-scale ensemble musicals. The company is increasingly devoted to mounting new works such as its recent productions of *The Wonder Years*, *Yours Anne*, and *Theda Bara and the Frontier Rabbi*. Revivals of classics of the genre (*The Fantasticks*, *Godspell*) are blended with remountings of rarely produced works of merit and recent commercial hits. While the historic 1874 Cohoes Music Hall is the company's performing home base, its work has been seen Off-Off Broadway, and at The Egg and the Palace Theatre in Albany. Heritage Artists emphasizes productions whose focus is on the performers and the material, and proudly provides opportunities for preprofessional performers (through a vigorous Equity Membership Candidate program), as well as for young authors, composers, directors and designers.

—*Robert W. Tolan*

PRODUCTIONS 1987–88

Nunsense, book, music and lyrics: Dan Goggin; (D) David Holdgrive; (S) Steve Spoonamore; (C) Mary Marsicano; (L) Rachel Bickel

Billy Bishop Goes to War, John Gray and Eric Peterson; (D) William S. Morris; (S) James M. Youmans; (C) Lloyd Waiwaiole; (L) Rachel Bickel

PRODUCTIONS 1988–89

Nunsense, book, music and lyrics: Dan Goggin; (D) David Holdgrive; (S) Steve Spoonamore; (C) Mary Marsicano; (L) Rachel Rickel

The Wonder Years, book: David Holdgrive, David Levy, Steve Liebman and Terry La Bolt; music and lyrics: David Levy; (D) David Holdgrive; (S) Robert Tolan; (C) Jay Herring; (L) Rachel Rickel

Man of La Mancha, book: Dale Wasserman; music: Mitch Leigh; lyrics: Joe Darion; (D) Robert Tolan; (S) Douglas Baloy; (C) Jay Herring; (L) Rachel Rickel

Theda Bara and the Frontier Rabbi, book: Jeff Hochhauser; music: Bob Johnston; lyrics: Bob Johnston, Jeff Hochhauser; (D) David Holdgrive; (S) Michael R. Smith; (C) Jay Herring; (L) Tom Sturge

You're a Good Man Charlie Brown, adapt: Clark Gesner, from Charles Schulz book; lyrics: Clark Gesner; (D) Robert Tolan; (S) Carl J. Sprague; (C) Deb G. Girdler; (L) Carl J. Sprague

I Do! I Do!, book and lyrics: Tom Jones; music: Harvey Schmidt; (D) David Holdgrive; (S) Steven Krahnke; (C) Mary Marsicano; (L) Rachel Bickel

Pump Boys and Dinettes, John Foley, Mark Hardwick, Debra Monk, Cass Morgan, John Schimmel and Jim Wann; (D) William S. Morris; (S) Cynthia Sweetland; (C) Melissa Wayne Skomorowsky; (L) Kenneth Posner

Heritage Artists, Ltd. Deb G. Girdler and Russ Thacker in *I Do! I Do!* Photo: T. Killips.

Hippodrome State Theatre. *Biloxi Blues*. Photo: Gary Wolfson.

Hippodrome State Theatre

MARY HAUSCH
Producing/Artistic Director

25 Southeast Second Pl.
Gainesville, FL 32601
(904) 373-5968 (bus.)
(904) 375-4477 (b.o.)

FOUNDED 1973
Gregory von Hausch, Orin Wechsberg, Marilyn Wall-Asse, Kerry McKenney, Mary Hausch, Bruce Cornwall

SEASON
July-June

FACILITIES
Mainstage
Seating Capacity: 266
Stage: thrust

Second Stage
Seating Capacity: 86
Stage: flexible

FINANCES
June 1, 1988-May 31, 1989
Expenses: $1,200,000

CONTRACTS
LORT (D) and AEA TYA

The Hippodome State Theatre has been nationally recognized for its imaginative theatre that spans contemporary, classic and international boundaries. The Hippodrome was founded as an artistic cooperative 16 years ago. The collective artistic input along with intensely individual visions and stylistic variety, create the theatre's unique premieres, translations, original adaptations of screenplays and classical works. Internationally recognized playwrights, including Tennessee Williams, Adrian Mitchell, Eric Bentley, Lee Breuer, Mario Vargas Llosa and Brian Thomson, have all collaborated with the theatre's company to produce world premieres on the Hippodrome stage. Other programs include touring; an intern/conservatory program; an artistic residency program and a Theatre for Young Audiences that has created 13 original plays and performed for over one million children. The theatre's Gainesville Area Improvisational Teen Theatre utilizes improvisational performances and discussion groups to address problems prevalent among teens, such as drug addiction, sexual abuse, suicide, pregnancy and AIDS.

—*Mary Hausch*

Note: During the 1987-88 season, Gregory von Hausch and Mary Hausch served as co-artistic directors.

PRODUCTIONS 1987–88

Biloxi Blues, Neil Simon; (D) Carlos F. Asse; (S) Carlos F. Asse; (C) Marilyn Wall-Asse; (L) Robert P. Robins

Hair, book and lyrics: James Rado and Gerome Ragni; music: Galt McDermott; (D) James Wren; (S) Carlos F. Asse; (C) Marilyn Wall-Asse; (L) Robert P. Robins

As Is, William Hoffman; (D) Mary Hausch; (S) Carlos F. Asse; (C) Marilyn Wall-Asse; (L) Robert P. Robins
So Long on Lonely Street, Sandra Deer; (D) Gregory von Hausch; (S) Carlos F. Asse; (C) Marilyn Wall-Asse; (L) Robert P. Robins
Rum and Coke, Keith Reddin; (D) Mary Hausch; (S) Carlos F. Asse; (C) Marilyn Wall-Asse; (L) Robert P. Robins
Pump Boys and Dinettes, John Foley, Mark Hardwick, Debra Monk, Cass Morgan, John Schimmel and Jim Wann; (D) Gregory von Hausch; (S) Carlos F. Asse; (C) Marilyn Wall-Asse; (L) Robert P. Robins
Stages, Margaret Bachus and Kevin Rainsberger; (D) Margaret Bachus; (S) Carlos F. Asse; (C) Marilyn Wall-Asse
Captain Jim's Fire Safety Review Revue, Margaret Bachus and Kevin Rainsberger; (D) Margaret Bachus; (S) Carlos F. Asse; (C) Marilyn Wall-Asse
The Water Log, Margaret Bachus and Kevin Rainsberger; (D) Margaret Bachus; (S) Carlos F. Asse; (C) Marilyn Wall-Asse
Just Florida, Margaret Bachus and Kevin Rainsberger; (D) Margaret Bachus; (S) Carlos F. Asse; (C) Marilyn Wall-Asse

PRODUCTIONS 1988–89

I'm Not Rappaport, Herb Gardner; (D) Mary Hausch; (S) Carlos F. Asse; (C) Marilyn Wall-Asse; (L) Robert P. Robins
Blue Plate Special, Tom Edwards; (D) James Wren; (S) Carlos F. Asse; (C) Marilyn Wall-Asse; (L) Robert P. Robins
Talk Radio, Eric Bogosian; (D) Sidney Homan; (S) Carlos F. Asse; (C) Marilyn Wall-Asse; (L) Robert P. Robins
Absent Friends, Alan Ayckbourn; (D) Mary Hausch; (S) Carlos F. Asse; (C) Marilyn Wall-Asse; (L) Robert P. Robins
Broadway Bound, Neil Simon; (D) Carlos F. Asse; (S) Carlos F. Asse; (C) Lisa Martin; (L) Robert P. Robins
A Walk in the Woods, Lee Blessing; (D) Mary Hausch; (S) Carlos F. Asse; (C) Marilyn Wall-Asse; (L) Robert P. Robins
The Energy Carnival, Margaret Bachus and Kevin Rainsberger; (D) Margaret Bachus; (S) Carlos F. Asse; (C) Marilyn Wall-Asse
Nickels, Dimes and Dreams, Margaret Bachus and Kevin Rainsberger; (D) Margaret Bachus; (S) Carlos F. Asse; (C) Marilyn Wall-Asse
Just Florida, Margaret Bachus and Kevin Rainsberger; (D) Margaret Bachus; (S) Carlos F. Asse; (C) Marilyn Wall-Asse

Honolulu Theatre for Youth

JOHN KAUFFMAN
Artistic Director

JANE CAMPBELL
Managing Director

Box 3257
Honolulu, HI 96801
(808) 945-8261

FOUNDED 1955
Nancy Corbett

SEASON
Jan.-Dec.

FACILITIES
McCoy Pavilion
Seating Capacity: 500
Stage: flexible

Leeward Community College Theatre
Seating Capacity: 629
Stage: proscenium

Kaimuki High School Theatre
Seating Capacity: 667
Stage: proscenium

Castle High School Theatre
Seating Capacity: 667
Stage: proscenium

FINANCES
June 1, 1988-May 31, 1989
Expenses: $707,000

Honolulu Theatre for Youth is Hawaii's only professional theatre company. Dedicated to producing high-quality theatre for young audiences, each season offers a broad spectrum of performances adapted from fairy tales, literary classics, contemporary issues and plays celebrating Pacific Rim Cultures. HTY annually tours statewide with one major production. Our education program provides materials, workshops and classes to teachers and students. Additionally, HTY provides assistance to projects such as Very Special Arts Hawaii. We actively encourage the development of new American plays and playwrights by commissioning works and hosting playwrights-in-residence. HTY has provided international outreach programs and has toured to American Samoa, Micronesia and Australia. The ethnic mix of the HTY company is as diverse as the people of Hawaii: nontraditional casting is the norm. The exploration of cultures, values and theatre forms is what HTY is all about.

—*John Kauffman*

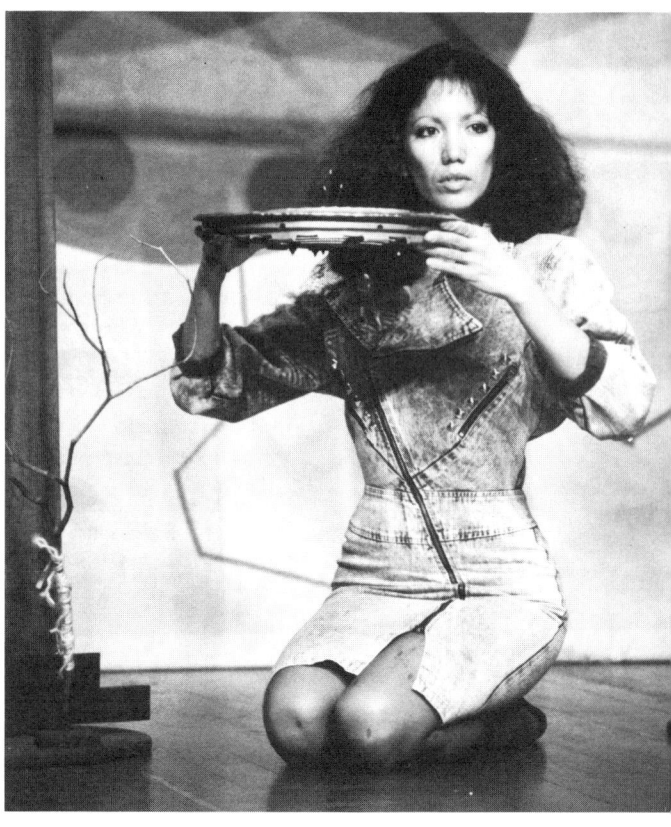

Honolulu Theatre for Youth. Polly Kuulei Sommerfeld in *Oedipus the King*. Photo: Keoni Wagner.

PRODUCTIONS 1987–88

According to Coyote, John Kauffman; (D) John Kauffman; (S) Don Yanik; (L) Jeff Robbins
Dracula, adapt: Nick DiMartino, from Bram Stoker; (D) John Kauffman; (S) Don Yanik; (C) Guy Beuttler; (L) Lloyd S. Riford, III
Maui the Trickster, Wallace Chappell; (D) John Kauffman; (S) Bob Campbell; (C) Ann Asakura Kimura; (L) Lloyd S. Riford, III
Jungalbook, adapt: Edward Mast, from Rudyard Kipling; (D) John Kauffman; (S) Don Yanik; (C) Trudi Vetter; (L) Lloyd S. Riford, III
Seagirl, Francis Elitzig; (D) Phyllis S.K. Look; (S) Joseph Dodd; (C) Joseph Dodd; (L) Douglas McCracken
Oedipus the King, Sophocles; trans: Steven Berg and Diskin Clay; (D) John Kauffman; (S) Douglas McCracken; (C) David Stamsta
The Velveteen Rabbit, adapt: Brian Clark Kenton, from Margery Williams; (D) Brian Clark Kenton; (S) Bill Forrester; (C) Trudi Vetter; (L) Chris Markiewicz

PRODUCTIONS 1988–89

The Sports Show, Arne Zaslove; (D) John Kauffman; (C) Casey Cameron Dinmore
A Wrinkle in Time, adapt: Edward Mast, from Madeleine L'Engle; (D) John Kauffman; (S) Bob Campbell; (C) Trudi Vetter; (L) Lloyd S. Riford, III
Great Expectations, adapt: Barbara Field, from Charles Dickens; (D) John Kauffman; (S) Bill Forrester; (C) Julie James; (L) Lloyd S. Riford, III
James and the Giant Peach, adapt: Richard R. George, from Roald Dahl; (D) Terry Sneed; (S) Don Yanik; (C) Terence Tam

Soon; (L) Lloyd S. Riford, III
Tales from the Dreamtime, John Kauffman; (D) John Kauffman; (S) Joseph Dodd; (C) David Stamsta; (L) Don Ranney
The Inner Circle, Patricia Loughrey; (D) Karen Brilliande; (S) Don Yanik; (C) Gwynne Lee Stormont
Winnie the Pooh, adapt: Kristin Sergel, from A.A. Milne; (D) Pamela Sterling; (S) Paul Guncheon; (C) Hugh Hanson; (L) Sandy Sandelin

Horse Cave Theatre

WARREN HAMMACK
Director

PAMELA WHITE
Associate Director

Box 215
Horse Cave, KY 42749
(502) 786-1200 (bus.)
(502) 786-2177 (b.o.)

FOUNDED 1977
Horse Cave citizens

SEASON
June-Sept.

FACILITIES
SEATING CAPACITY: 347
STAGE: THRUST

FINANCES
Oct. 1, 1987-Sept. 30, 1988
Expenses: $484,831

Horse Cave Theatre. *Noises Off.* **Photo: Gregory Etter.**

CONTRACTS
AEA letter of agreement

Horse Cave Theatre is a professional resident theatre ensemble serving audiences in Kentucky. The theatre presents contemporary plays, new scripts and classics in rotating repertory, and seeks to encourage the development of theatre artists, with a particular commitment to Kentucky playwrights. Under the Kentucky Voices program, the theatre presents plays which combine the unique cultural resources of the region with its own professional resources. Believing that the spark of a live performance is a powerful teaching tool, the theatre provides a wide range of educational programs including workshops, a statewide touring program and, since 1979, a comprehensive outreach program wherein the plays of Shakespeare are presented at the theatre for students. Study guides, discussions and in-service training for teachers supplement the program.
—*Warren Hammack*

PRODUCTIONS 1987–88

Hopscotch, Sallie Bingham; (D) Warren Hammack; (S) Sam Hunt; (C) Rebecca Shouse; (L) Gregory Etter
Noises Off, Michael Frayn; (D) Warren Hammack; (S) Sam Hunt; (C) Rebecca Shouse; (L) Gregory Etter
I'm Not Rappaport, Herb Gardner; (D) Michael Wainstein; (S) Sam Hunt; (C) Rebecca Shouse; (L) Gregory Etter
Anna Christie, Eugene O'Neill; (D) Laura Fine; (S) Sam Hunt; (C) Kelly Ferguson; (L) Gregory Etter
Romeo and Juliet, William Shakespeare; (D) Warren Hammack; (S) Sam Hunt; (C) Rebecca Shouse; (L) Gregory Etter
The Dickens Christmas Carol Show, Arthur Scholey; (D) Warren Hammack; (S) Sam Hunt; (C) Kelly Ferguson; (L) Gregory Etter

PRODUCTIONS 1988–89

Born Yesterday, Garson Kanin; (D) Warren Hammack; (S) Sam Hunt; (C) Amy Hutto; (L) Gregory Etter
Steel Magnolias, Robert Harling; (D) Warren Hammack; (S) Sam Hunt; (C) Amy Hutto; (L) Gregory Etter
The Awakening, adapt: Sallie Bingham, from Kate Chopin; (D) Warren Hammack; (S) Sam Hunt; (C) Amy Hutto; (L) Gregory Etter
Much Ado About Nothing, William Shakespeare; (D) David Shookhoff; (S) Sam Hunt; (C) Amy Hutto; (L) Gregory Etter

Hudson Guild Theatre

GEOFFREY SHERMAN
Producing Director

STEVEN RAMAY
Associate Director

441 West 26th St.
New York, NY 10001
(212) 645-4940 (bus.)
(212) 760-9810 (b.o.)

FOUNDED 1896
John Lovejoy Elliott

SEASON
Sept.-June

FACILITIES
Arthur Strasser Auditorium
Seating Capacity: 135
Stage: proscenium

FINANCES
July 1, 1988-June 30, 1989
Expenses: $387,000

CONTRACTS
AEA letter of agreement

Located in the Chelsea district, in Manhattan's second-oldest settlement house, the Hudson Guild Theatre has grown from a community-based playhouse to one of the leading Off-Broadway theatres in New York City. HGT has been a pioneering force in the introduction of new American and European playwrights, as well as previously unknown actors and directors, to the New York theatre world. The theatre is dedicated to the development of a socially and politically challenging artistic vision that encompasses the finest and most innovative American and international drama. This commitment is implemented through premieres of works by both new and established playwrights; readings and workshops; and an annual festival of new plays by and about minorities.
—*Geoffrey Sherman*

Note: During the 1987-88 season, James Abar served as associate artistic director.

PRODUCTIONS 1987–88

Year of the Duck, Israel Horovitz; (D) Geoffrey Sherman; (S) Paul Wonsek; (C) Mimi Maxmen; (L) Paul Wonsek
The Signal Season of Dummy Hoy, Allen Meyer and Michael Nowak; (D) James Abar; (S) Ron Gottshalk; (C) Karen Hummel; (L) Paul Wonsek
Tapman, Karen Jones Meadows; (D) Samuel P. Barton; (C) Marianne Powell-Parker; (L) Paul Wonsek
The Love Talker, Deborah Pryor; (D) Steven Ramay; (S) Paul Wonsek; (C) Stephanie Handler; (L) Paul Wonsek
In Perpetuity Throughout the Universe, Eric Overmyer; (D) Stan Wojewodski, Jr.; (S) Christopher Barreca; (C) Robert Wojewodski; (L) Stephen Strawbridge

PRODUCTIONS 1988–89

Tea with Mommy and Jack, Sheila Walsh; (D) Lawrence Sacharow; (S) Donald Eastman; (C) Marianne Powell-Parker; (L) Paul Wonsek
Almost Perfect, Jerry Mayer; (D) Geraldine Fitzgerald; (S) James D. Sandefur; (C) Pamela Scofield; (L) Phil Monat
Without Apologies, Thom Thomas; (D) Edgar Lansbury; (S) John Wulp; (C) Karen Hummel; (L) Paul Wonsek
Walkers, Marion Isaac McClinton;

Hudson Guild Theatre. Terry E. Bellamy and James A. Williams in *Walkers*. Photo: Gerry Goodstein.

(D) Steven Ramay and Marion Isaac McClinton; (S) Paul Wonsek; (C) Elsa Ward; (L) Paul Wonsek
Up 'n' Under, John Godber; (D) Geoffrey Sherman; (S) Paul Wonsek; (C) Pamela Scofield; (L) Paul Wonsek

Huntington Theatre Company

PETER ALTMAN
Producing Director

MICHAEL MASO
Managing Director

Boston University Theatre 264
Huntington Ave.
Boston, MA 02115
(617) 353-3320 (bus.)
(617) 266-3913 (b.o.)

FOUNDED 1982
Boston University

SEASON
Sept.-June

FACILITIES
Boston University Theatre
Seating Capacity: 855
Stage: proscenium

Studio 210
Seating Capacity: 99
Stage: flexible

FINANCES
July 1, 1988-June 30, 1989
Expenses: $3,600,000

CONTRACTS
LORT (B)

The Huntington Theatre Company's aim is to produce annual seasons of classics and superior contemporary plays that are acted, directed and designed at a standard of excellence comparable to that of the nation's leading professional companies. We continually seek to devote ourselves to the great masterpieces of dramatic literature; to respond to today's issues and emotions by presenting literate, trenchant comtemporary plays new to Boston; and to be enterprising and cosmopolitan in choosing worthy writing from varied countries and periods. Because we honor the theatre's heritage, we strive to present classic works in their true spirit. In producing plays of any era or style, we enjoy and admire truthful situations, vivid characters, sound dramatic construction, eloquent language, imaginative staging with well-balanced casts and the finest possible level of craftsmanship. We believe that a flexible, allied family of professionals who share this vision will best extend, fulfill and serve our theatre's vision.
—*Peter Altman*

PRODUCTIONS 1987–88

Remembrance, Graham Reid; (D) Munson Hicks; (S) John Falabella; (C) Susan Tsu; (L) Jackie Manassee
The Winter's Tale, William Shakespeare; (D) Sharon Ott; (S) Kate Edmunds; (C) Jess Goldstein; (L) Dan Kotlowitz
The Piano Lesson, August Wilson; (D) Lloyd Richards; (S) E. David Cosier, Jr.; (C) Constanza Romero; (L) Christopher Akerlind
Saturday, Sunday, Monday, Eduardo De Filippo; (D) Jacques Cartier; (S) James Leonard Joy; (C) John Falabella; (L) Roger Meeker
Animal Crackers, book: George S. Kaufman and Morrie Ryskind; music and lyrics: Bert Kalmar and Harry Ruby; (D) Larry Carpenter; (S) James Leonard Joy; (C) Lindsay W. Davis; (L) Marcia Madeira

PRODUCTIONS 1988–89

The American Clock, Arthur Miller; (D) Jackson Phippin; (S) Christopher Barreca; (C) Robert Wojewodski; (L) Stephen Strawbridge
Don Juan, Moliere; trans: Christopher Hampton; (D) Jacques Cartier; (S) John Falabella; (C) Robert Morgan; (L) Roger Meeker
Les Blancs, Lorraine Hansberry; (D) Harold Scott; (S) Karl Eigsti; (C) Marjorie Slaiman; (L) Allan Lee Hughes
All's Well That Ends Well, William Shakespeare; (D) Edward Gilbert; (S) Kate Edmunds; (C) John Falabella; (L) Nick Cernovitch
Candide, book adapt: Hugh Wheeler; music: Leonard Bernstein; lyrics: Richard Wilbur; additional lyrics: Stephen Sondheim and John Latouche; (D) Larry Carpenter; (S) Campbell Baird; (C) John Falabella; (L) Marcia Madeira

Illinois Theatre Center

STEVE S. BILLIG
Artistic Director

ETEL BILLIG
Managing Director

400A Lakewood Blvd.
Park Forest, IL 60466
(312) 481-3693 (bus.)
(312) 481-3510 (b.o.)

FOUNDED 1976
Steve Billig, Etel Billig

SEASON
Oct.-May

FACILITIES
Seating Capacity: 187
Stage: thrust

FINANCES
Sept. 1, 1988-Aug. 31, 1989
Expenses: $250,000

CONTRACTS
AEA CAT

Huntington Theatre Company. *Candide*. Photo: Gerry Goodstein.

Illinois Theatre Center. Todd Zamarripa, Iris Lieberman and Burke Fry in *Yours, Anne*. Photo: Peter LeGrand.

The Illinois Theatre Center was founded in 1976 with the belief that a vigorous artistic and cultural life should be part of all communities. It is through theatre that we hope to enrich the quality of life for all area residents. Through the world of theatre we want our audiences to appreciate man's infinite diversity of expression and the vast range of human invention. Along with our seven-play mainstage season, we have an active outreach program which provides special programming for the elderly, the handicapped and the economically disadvantaged. We also hold an annual free outdoor Classics Festival.
—*Steve S. Billig*

PRODUCTIONS 1987–88

Santa Anita '42, Alan Knee; (D) James Corti; (s) Jonathan Roark; (c) Henriette Swearingen; (L) Richard Peterson
More Fun Than Bowling, Steven Dietz; (D) Steve S. Billig; (s) Jonathan Roark; (c) Pat Decker; (L) August Ziemann
The Robber Bridegroom, book and lyrics: Alfred Uhry; music: Robert Waldman; (D) James Corti; (s) Archway Scenic; (c) Henriette Swearingen; (L) August Ziemann
Handy Dandy, William Gibson; (D) David Perkovich; (s) Jonathan Roark; (c) Pat Decker; (L) August Ziemann
Yours, Anne, book and lyrics: Enid Futterman; music: Michael Cohen; (D) Etel Billig; (s) Archway Scenic; (c) Henriette Swearingen; (L) August Ziemann
The School for Scandal, Richard Brinsley Sheridan; (D) Steve S. Billig; (s) Jonathan Roark; (c) Henriette Swearingen; (L) August Ziemann
Nickel Under My Shoe, Steve S. Billig; (D) Steve S. Billig; (s) Archway Scenic; (c) Pat Decker; (L) August Ziemann
The Tempest, William Shakespeare; (D) Etel Billig; (s) Jonathan Roark; (c) Henriette Swearingen

PRODUCTIONS 1988–89

Bittersuite (Songs of Experience), lyrics: Michael Champagne; music: Elliot Weiss; (D) Steve S. Billig; (s) Archway Scenic; (c) Pat Decker; (L) August Ziemann
Our Lady of the Tortilla, Luis Santeiro; (D) Steve S. Billig; (s) Archway Scenic; (c) Pat Decker; (L) August Ziemann
The Mystery of Edwin Drood, book adapt, music and lyrics: Rupert Holmes; (D) David Perkovich; (s) Archway Scenic; (c) Henriette Swearingen; (L) August Ziemann
Max and Maxie, James McLure; (D) Steve S. Billig; (s) Archway Scenic; (c) Henriette Swearingen; (L) August Ziemann
Amazing Grace, Sandra Deer; (D) Steve S. Billig; (s) Archway Scenic; (c) Pat Decker; (L) August Ziemann
The Musical Comedy Murders of 1940, John Bishop; (D) David Perkovich; (s) Archway Scenic; (c) Henriette Swearingen; (L) August Ziemann
Personals, various; (D) Steve S. Billig; (s) Archway Scenic; (c) Henriette Swearingen; (L) August Ziemann

Illusion Theater

MICHAEL ROBINS
BONNIE MORRIS
Producing Directors

JOHN MONTILINO
Managing Director

528 Hennepin Ave. Suite 704
Minneapolis, MN 55403
(612) 339-4944 (bus.)
(612) 338-8371 (b.o.)

FOUNDED 1974
Michael Robins, Carole Harris Lipschulz

SEASON
Feb.-Aug.

FACILITIES
Hennepin Center for the Arts
Seating Capacity: 220
Stage: thrust

FINANCES
Jan. 1, 1988-Dec. 31, 1988
Expenses: $735,650

CONTRACTS
AEA SPT

We live in a time when much art is involved in the practice of distancing itself from our lives by intellectualizing the human condition. In contrast, Illusion Theater's aesthetic uses the power of theatre to reflect the times we live in by exposing the emotional underside of the same human condition. We do this by consistently producing world and area premieres of new work and rarely produced classics. We maintain a resident company of actors and create new plays collaboratively with writer, director and actor. Encompassed in our aesthetic is a belief that theatre can effect sound change. We demonstrate this belief through our repertoire of plays dedicated to the prevention of sexual abuse, interpersonal violence and HIV/Aids which we tour across the country. We have produced more than 50 new plays and continue to invest in the talent of emerging and established artists as we create a body of plays for the American theatre.
—*Michael Robins, Bonnie Morris*

PRODUCTIONS 1987–88

Orlando, Orlando, adapt: John Orlock, from Virginia Woolf; (D) Michael Robins; (s) Michael Sommers; (c) Sue Haas; (L) Jeff Bartlett
Statements After an Arrest Under the Immorality Act, Athol Fugard; (D) Peter Cantwell; (s) Dean Holzman; (L) David Vogel
Family, Cordelia Anderson, Bonnie Morris, Michael Robins and company; (D) Michael Robins; (s) Dean Holzman; (L) David Vogel
Southern Cross, Jon Klein; (D) David Ira Goldstein; (s) Lori Sullivan; (c) Connie Caldwell; (L) Doug Pippan
Snow, Ping Chong and company; (D) Ping Chong; (s) Dean Holzman and Jim Salen; (c) Richard Thompson; (L) Michael Murnane

PRODUCTIONS 1988–89

The Tower, Matthew Maguire; (D) Matthew Maguire; (s) Dean Holzman; (c) Katie Maurer; (L) Jeff Bartlett
Amazing Grace, Cordelia Anderson, Bonnie Morris, Michael Robins and company; (D) Michael Robins; (s) Linda Cassone; (c) Katie Maurer; (L) David Vogel
Lloyd's Prayer, Kevin Kling; (D) Steven Dietz; (s) Michael Sommers; (c) Sue Haas; (L) Barry Browning
Men Sing, book and lyrics: Michael Robins; music: Gary Rue; (D) Michael Robins; (s) Jim Salen; (c) Katie Maurer; (L) Fred Desbois

Fresh Ink Series:
Letters from Hell, Dane Stauffer; (D) John Richardson; (s) Jim Salen; (c) Katie Maurer; (L) Fred Desbois
Mice, Ben Krielkamp; (D) Ben Krielkamp; (s) Jim Salen; (c) Katie Maurer; (L) Fred Desbois
Interview, Judy McGuire; (D) Judy McGuire; (s) Jim Salen; (c) Katie Maurer; (L) Fred Desbois
Peoria, Jon Klein; (D) Jon Klein; (s) Jim Salen; (c) Katie Maurer; (L) Fred Desbois

ILLUSION THEATER

Illusion Theater. Lester Purry and Lyle Ferguson in *Amazing Grace*. Photo: Bill Carlson.

Fresh Ink Series:
Wild Raspberries, Tom Poole;
  (D) Pamela Nice; (S) Jim Salen;
  (L) Fred Desbois
The Hunger Artist, adapt:
  Michael Sommers, from Franz
  Kafka; (D) Michael Sommers;
  (S) Michael Sommers; (C) Sue
  Haas; (L) Fred Desbois
The Country Doctor, adapt: Ben
  Kreilkamp, from Franz Kafka;
  (D) Ben Kreilkamp; (S) Jim
  Salen; (L) Fred Desbois
Men Sing, book and lyrics:
  Michael Robins; music: Gary
  Rue; (D) Michael Robins;
  (S) Jim Salen; (L) Fred Desbois

FACILITIES
Eye Theatre Works
Seating Capacity: 100
Stage: proscenium

FINANCES
July 1, 1988-June 30, 1989
Expenses: $160,000

The Independent Eye

CONRAD BISHOP
Producing Director

LINDA BISHOP
Associate Producing Director

208 East King St.
Lancaster, PA 17602
(717) 393-9088

FOUNDED 1974
Conrad Bishop, Linda Bishop

SEASON
Sept.-May

PRODUCTIONS 1987–88
Sea Marks, Gardner McKay;
  (D) Gary Smith; (S) Mark Stoner
  and Conrad Bishop; (C) Beth
  Dunkelberger; (L) Jim Jackson
The New Comedy Works,
  company-developed; (D) Camilla
  Schade; (S) Lou Ziegler;
  (L) Archie Wilson
Action News, Conrad Bishop and
  Elizabeth Fuller; (D) Conrad
  Bishop; (S) Conrad Bishop and
  Rick Mazzafro; (L) Conrad
  Bishop
Amazed, Conrad Bishop and
  Elizabeth Fuller; (D) Pat Lemay;
  (S) Richard Whitson;
  (C) Cynthia Haynes; (L) Jim
  Jackson
Shakespeare Now, William
  Shakespeare; (D) Conrad Bishop
  and Gary Smith; (S) Conrad
  Bishop and Gary Smith

PRODUCTIONS 1988–89
Heart's Desire, Conrad Bishop
  and Elizabeth Fuller;
  (D) Conrad Bishop; (S) Conrad
  Bishop; (L) Conrad Bishop
The Lorelei, Ann Chamberlin;
  (D) Gary Smith; (S) Mark
  Stoner; (C) Beth Dunkelberger;
  (L) Conrad Bishop
Billy Bishop Goes to War, John
  Gray and Eric Peterson;
  (D) Terri Mastrobuono;
  (S) Robert A. Nelson; (C) Amy
  Louise Lammert; (L) Peter
  Smith
Limitations, Camilla Schade, D.D.
  Delaney and Lou Ziegler;
  (D) Camilla Schade; (S) Archie
  Wilson; (L) Archie Wilson
Gameshow, Ronlin Foreman,
  Terri Mastrobuono, Judy
  Townsend and Don Kinner;
  (D) Ronlin Foreman;
  (S) Rapitech; (C) Beth
  Dunkelberger, Terri
  Mastrobuono and Judy
  Townsend; (L) Peter Smith
*The Late Lite News Comedy
  Works*, company-developed;
  (D) Camilla Schade; (L) Jim
  Jackson and Archie Wilson

The Independent Eye is a resident theatre and media producer devoted to new work and new visions of classics that reflect deeply felt, commonly shared human experience. The Eye focuses on the sharp incongruities and unsettling mood swings of real life, unabashedly mixing silliness and sentiment with nightmare reality. Styles are extravagantly eclectic: a mask/puppet dreamscape in *Macbeth*, comic-book vignettes in *American Splendor*, puppetry and poetic docudrama in *Marie Antoinette*, lyric realism in *Valentines & Killer Chili*, cabaret in *Families*. In all, the core questions are: Is it true? Do we have a real stake in telling it? Is it surprising? Since 1974, the Eye has toured to 33 states. In 1977, it moved from Chicago to Lancaster, opening the Eye Theatre Works in 1981. Today, it presents a resident season, tours the mid-Atlantic region, distributes radio and videotapes internationally, and hosts poetry and experimental music concerts.
—*Conrad Bishop*

Indiana Repertory Theatre

TOM HAAS
Artistic Director

VICTORIA NOLAN
Managing Director

140 West Washington St.
Indianapolis, IN 46204
(317) 635-5277 (bus.)
(317) 635-5252 (b.o.)

FOUNDED 1972
Edward Stern, Gregory Poggi,
Benjamin Mordecai

SEASON
Oct.-May

FACILITIES
Mainstage
Seating Capacity: 607
Stage: proscenium

Upperstage
Seating Capacity: 269
Stage: proscenium

The Independent Eye. Elizabeth Fuller and Conrad Bishop in *Action News*. Photo: Ma Beach.

Indiana Repertory Theatre. Susan Gabriel and Alan Mixon in *Six Characters in Search of an Author*. Photo: Tod Martens.

Cabaret Club
Seating Capacity: 150
Stage: modified thrust

FINANCES
July 1, 1988-June 30, 1989
Expenses: $2,839,027

CONTRACTS
LORT (C) and (D)

As Indiana's only resident professional theatre, Indiana Repertory Theatre's mission embraces a broad spectrum of activities, addressing an audience extending from those in whom an appreciation of theatre must be awakened to those challenged only by the most innovative. In the mainstage subcription series we dedicate our energies to redefining the classics (both the well known and the forgotten), exploring them stylistically and eliciting fresh perspectives through a core of resident designers, actors and artisans. Juxtaposed against this interest in classicism is our investigation of contemporary work, and our interest in presenting current trends in American playwriting. We also produce up to nine original musical revues in the less formal environment of our Cabaret Theatre. IRT's educational outreach program brings 25,000 students annually to matinees of mainstage productions and to our special program, Classic Theatre for Youth, as our energies turn with increasing vigor to this cultivation of tomorrow's audiences.

—*Tom Haas*

PRODUCTIONS 1987–88

Inherit the Wind, Jerome Lawrence and Robert E. Lee; (D) Tom Haas; (S) Charles McCarry; (C) Bobbi Owen; (L) Stuart Duke
Frankenstein, adapt: Tom Haas and Robert Gross, from Mary Shelley; (D) Tom Haas; (S) G.W. Mercier; (C) Bill Walker; (L) Stuart Duke
A Streetcar Named Desire, Tennessee Williams; (D) Paul Moser; (S) Bill Clarke; (C) Connie Singer; (L) Stuart Duke
The Misanthrope, Moliere; trans: Richard Wilbur; (D) Tom Haas; (S) G. W. Mercier; (C) G. W. Mercier; (L) Rachel Budin
The Cocktail Party, T.S. Eliot; (D) Tom Haas; (S) Ann Sheffield; (C) Connie Singer; (L) Don Holder
Light Up the Sky, Moss Hart; (D) Larry Arrick; (S) Russell Metheny; (C) Gail Brassard; (L) Michael Lincoln

PRODUCTIONS 1988–89

Long Day's Journey into Night, Eugene O'Neill; (D) Tom Haas; (S) Bill Clarke; (C) Bobbi Owen; (L) Dennis Clark
The Great Divide, William Vaughn Moody; (D) Tom Haas; (S) G.W. Mercier; (C) G.W. Mercier; (L) Rachel Budin
The Three Musketeers, adapt: Tom Haas and Robert Gross, from Alexander Dumas; (D) Larry Arrick; (S) G.W. Mercier; (C) Bill Walker; (L) Stuart Duke
Social Security, Andrew Bergman; (D) John David Lutz; (S) David Cosier; (C) Nancy Pope; (L) Don Holder
Macbeth, William Shakespeare; (D) Paul Frellick; (S) Christopher Barreca; (C) Gail Brassard; (L) Stuart Duke
Six Characters in Search of an Author, Luigi Pirandello; trans: Paul Avila Mayer; (D) Tom Haas; (S) Ann Sheffield; (C) Gail Brassard; (L) Rachel Budin
Guys and Dolls, book: Jo Swerling and Abe Burrows; music and lyrics: Frank Loesser; (D) Tom Haas; (S) Charles McCarry; (C) Connie Singer; (L) Don Holder

INTAR Hispanic American Arts Center

MAX FERRA
Artistic Director

JAMES DIPAOLA
Managing Director

Box 788
New York, NY 10108
(212) 695-6134

FOUNDED 1966
Frank Robles, Elsa Ortiz Robles, Gladys Ortiz, Benjamin Lopez, Antonio Gonzalez-Jaen, Oscar Garcia, Max Ferra

SEASON
Sept.-July

FACILITIES
Mainstage
Seating Capacity: 99
Stage: proscenium

Second Stage
Seating Capacity: 99
Stage: proscenium

FINANCES
July 1, 1988-June 30, 1989
Expenses: $1,086,917

CONTRACTS
AEA letter of agreement

INTAR Hispanic American Arts Center identifies, presents and develops contemporary Latin and Hispanic artists living in the U.S. and throughout the world. The INTAR Theatre season is designed to highlight plays that have local and universal appeal. Included in each season is at least one new American work, one musical and the participation of an internationally known artist. INTAR Gallery, one of the most important alternative spaces in New York City for the Latin visual artist, mounts 7 to 10 exhibitions per year, featuring emerging as well as established minority artists. The INTAR Playwrights-in-Residence Laboratory is designed to encourage and support the creative forces that impel talented Hispanic artists from all over the country to write for the stage. INTAR Music Theatre Laboratory, also national in scope, was created to develop new music theatre pieces drawing from the richness and variety of Latin music. Through all its programs, INTAR serves the social and cultural needs of the community and country by nurturing the expressive voices and visions of the Hispanic peoples.

—*Max Ferra*

PRODUCTIONS 1987–88

Tango Apasionado, adapt: Graciela Daniele and Jim Lewis, from Jorge Luis Borges; music: Astor Piazzolla; (D) Graciela Daniele; (S) Santo Loquasto; (C) Santo Loquasto; (L) Peggy Eisenhauer
Welcome Back to Salamanca, book: Migdalia Cruz; music: Fernando Rivas; (D) George Ferencz; (S) Loy Arenas; (C) Sally J. Lesser; (L) Beverly Emmons

INTAR Hispanic American Arts Center. Graciela Daniele, Gregory Mitchell, Tina Paul and John Mineo in *Tango Apasionado*. Photo: Martha Swope.

Alma, book: Ana Maria Simo; music: Fernando Rivas; (D) Paul Zimet; (S) Loy Arcenas; (C) Sally J. Lesser; (L) Beverly Emmons

PRODUCTIONS 1988–89

Suenos, Ruth Maleczech; (D) Ruth Maleczech; (S) Michael Deegan; (C) Toni-Leslie James; (L) Clay Shirky

Don Juan of Seville, Tirso de Molina; trans: Lynne Alvarez; (D) Carey Perloff; (S) Donald Eastman; (C) Gabriel Berry; (L) Frances Aronson

Intiman Theatre Company

ELIZABETH HUDDLE
Artistic Director

PETER DAVIS
Managing Director

Box 19645
Seattle, WA 98109-6645
(206) 626-0775 (bus.)
(206) 626-0782 (b.o.)

FOUNDED 1972
Margaret Booker

SEASON
May-Oct.

FACILITIES
Seating Capacity: 424
Stage: modified thrust

FINANCES
Jan. 1, 1988-Dec. 31, 1988
Expenses: $1,019,787

CONTRACTS
LORT (C)

Intiman's mission is grounded in the classics, but regardless of whether the play is classic or contemporary, our production emphasis is on the actor and the word. Intiman produces the classics because they are exciting, relevant and of tremendous value. People reach to the classics from a fragmented society—for order, for meaning and for spiritual nourishment. At Intiman we work with an ensemble of actors, designers and directors in an intimate setting, and we try to find what a play is saying and to help that meaning resonate with our contemporary audiences.
—*Elizabeth Huddle*

PRODUCTIONS 1987–88

Hard Times, adapt: Stephen Jeffreys, from Charles Dickens; (D) Elizabeth Huddle; (S) Robert Dahlstrom; (C) Anne Thaxter Watson; (L) Jennifer Lupton

Angel Street, Patrick Hamilton; (D) Warner Shook; (S) Scott Weldin; (C) Sally Richardson; (L) Rick Paulsen

The Last Unicorn, book and lyrics: Peter S. Beagle; music: Elaine Lang and June Richards; (D) Elizabeth Huddle; (S) Robert Dahlstrom; (C) Robert Dahlstrom; (L) Robert Dahlstrom

Electra, adapt: Hugo von Hofmannsthal, from Sophocles; trans: Alfred Schwarz; (D) Laird Williamson; (S) Laird Williamson; (C) Rose Pederson; (L) Richard Devin

Blithe Spirit, Noel Coward; (D) Elizabeth Huddle; (S) Jerry S. Hooker; (C) Frances Kenny; (L) Collier Woods

PRODUCTIONS 1988–89

Hamlet, William Shakespeare; (D) Elizabeth Huddle; (S) Michael Olich; (C) Frances Kenny and Michael Olich; (L) Rick Paulsen

Rosencrantz and Guildenstern Are Dead, Tom Stoppard; (D) Warner Shook; (S) Michael Olich; (C) Frances Kenny and Michael Olich; (L) Rick Paulsen

The Road to Mecca, Athol Fugard; (D) Susan Fenichell; (S) Nina Mosier; (L) Rick Paulsen

Born Yesterday, Garson Kanin; (D) Elizabeth Huddle; (S) Robert Dahlstrom; (C) Anne Thaxter Watson; (L) Jennifer Lupton

Frankenstein, adapt: R. N. Sandberg, from Mary Shelley; (D) Andrew J. Traister; (S) Jeff Frkonja; (C) Frances Kenny; (L) Richard Devin

Jean Cocteau Repertory

ROBERT HUPP
Artistic Director

DAVID J. FISHELSON
Managing Director

330 Bowery
New York, NY 10012
(212) 677-0060

FOUNDED 1971
Eve Adamson

SEASON
Sept.-May

FACILITIES
Bouwerie Lane Theatre
Seating Capacity: 140
Stage: proscenium

FINANCES
July 1, 1988-June 30, 1989
Expenses: $300,000

The Cocteau is a resident company of artists performing in rotating repertory those works of world theatre which by their very nature demand to live on a stage. The company is committed to Jean Cocteau's "poetry of the theatre" in which all elements of production—performance, design, music—fuse into a whole that illuminates the heart of the play and elevates it into a "dramatic poem." Whether approaching a classic or a contem-

Intiman Theatre Company. Michael Santo, Susanne Bouchard and Jo Leffingwell in *Blithe Spirit* Photo: Chris Bennion.

Jean Cocteau Repertory. Christopher Oden, Mark Schulte and Coral Potter in *The Trial*. Photo: Gerry Goodstein.

...orporary work of provocative content and structure, the Cocteau strives to create that unique production style appropriate to each play which will engage the audience intellectually and emotionally. Meeting this artistic challenge in rotating repertory requires a disciplined and flexible resident acting company, as well as bold and imaginative designers and directors. Towards that end, the Cocteau has developed and continued to nurture a growing community of repertory-oriented theatre artists.
—Robert Hupp

Note: During the 1987-88 season, Eve Adamson served as artistic director.

PRODUCTIONS 1987–88

No Exit, Jean Paul Sartre; (D) Giles Hogya; (S) Giles Hogya; (C) Susan Young; (L) Giles Hogya
The Trial, trans and adapt: Andre Gide and Jean-Louis Barrault, from Franz Kafka; (D) Eve Adamson; (S) Jan Sawka; (C) Bobby Pearce; (L) Craig Smith
Antigone, Jean Anouilh; trans: Alex Szogyi; (D) Bill Reichblum; (S) Bill Reichblum; (C) Andrea Beeman; (L) Mary Louise Geiger
The Cocktail Party, T.S. Eliot; (D) Eve Adamson; (S) Gary Helm; (C) Barbara Bell; (L) Craig Smith
The Winter's Tale, William Shakespeare; (D) Eve Adamson; (S) Robert Joel Schwartz; (C) David Kay Mikelson; (L) Craig Smith

PRODUCTIONS 1988–89

Break of Noon (Partage de Midi), Paul Claudel; trans: Wallace Fowlie; (D) Eve Adamson; (S) Giles Hogya; (C) Jonathan Bixby; (L) Giles Hogya
Venice Preserv'd, Thomas Otway and Bill Reichblum; (D) Bill Reichblum; (S) Andrea Beeman; (C) Andrea Beeman; (L) Craig Smith
The Three Sisters, Anton Chekhov; (D) Eve Adamson; (S) Christopher Martin; (C) Jonathan Bixby; (L) Christopher Martin
Good, C.P. Taylor; (D) Robert Hupp; (S) Robert Hupp; (C) Jonathan Bixby; (L) Craig Smith
Macbeth, William Shakespeare; (D) Eve Adamson; (S) Jan Sawka; (C) Jonathan Bixby; (L) Craig Smith
On the Verge or The Geography of Yearning, Eric Overmyer; (D) Robert Hupp; (S) George Xenos; (C) Jonathan Bixby; (L) Craig Smith

Jewish Repertory Theatre

RAN AVNI
Artistic Director

344 East 14th St.
New York, NY 10003
(212) 674-7200 (bus.)
(212) 505-2667 (b.o.)

FOUNDED 1974
Ran Avni

SEASON
Oct.-June

FACILITIES
The Irving Brodsky Theatre
Seating Capacity: 200
Stage: proscenium

The Milton Weill Auditorium
Seating Capacity: 100
Stage: flexible

FINANCES
July 1, 1988-June 30, 1989
Expenses: $350,000

CONTRACTS
AEA Mini contract

The Jewish Repertory Theatre is now in its 16th season. JRT has revived such treasured classics as *Awake and Sing!*, *Green Fields*, and *Incident at Vichy*; has rediscovered forgotten American works such as *Me and Molly*, *Unlikely Heroes*, *Success Story* and *Cantorial*; has shed new light on the plays of Chekhov, Pinter, Sartre and de Ghelderode; has produced a series of new musicals including *Vagabond Stars*, *Up from Paradise*, Kuni-Leml, which won four Outer Critics' Awards, including Best Off Broadway Musical, *Pearls*, *The Special*, *The Shop on Main Street* and *Chu Chem*. The JRT Writers' Lab, led by associate director Edward M. Cohen, does readings, workshops and mini-productions aimed at developing the works of young writers. This program has resulted in JRT productions of *Taking Steam*, *Benya the King*, *36*, *Crossing Delancy*, *Bitter Friends* and other plays which are now being produced throughout the country.
—Ran Avni

PRODUCTIONS 1987–88

Sophie, book and lyrics: Rose Leiman Goldemberg; music: Debra Barsha; (D) Louis O. Erdmann; (S) Christian Tucker; (C) Marcy Froehlich; (L) David Weller
Come Blow Your Horn, Neil Simon; (D) Charles Maryan; (S) Atkin Pace; (C) Barbara Bush; (L) Debra Barsha
Yard Sale, Arnold Wesker; (D) Edward M. Cohen; (S) Ray Recht; (C) Karen Hummel; (L) Dan Kinsley
Washington Heights, Larry Cohen; (D) David Saint; (S) Chris Pickart; (C) Edi Giguere; (L) Douglas O'Flaherty

Jewish Repertory Theatre. Anthony Fusco and Lesly Kahn in *Cantorial*. Photo: Martha Swope Associates/Carol Rosegg.

The Grand Tour, music and lyrics: Jerry Herman; book: Michael Stewart and Mark Bramble; (D) Ran Avni; (S) Jeffrey Schneider; (C) Karen Hummel; (L) Dan Kinsley

PRODUCTIONS 1988–89

Cantorial, Ira Levin; (D) Charles Maryan; (S) Atkin Pace; (C) Lana Fritz; (L) Brian Nason
Chu Chem, book: Ted Allen; music: Mitch Leigh; lyrics: Jim Haines and Jack Wohl; (D) Albert Marre; (S) Bob Mitchell; (C) Ken Yount; (L) Jason Sturm
Bitter Friends, Gordon Rayfield; (D) Allen Coulter; (S) Michael C. Smith; (C) Laura Drawbaugh; (L) Dan Kinsley
The Sunshine Boys, Neil Simon; (D) Marilyn Chris; (S) Ray Recht; (C) Karen Hummel; (L) Dan Kinsley
Double Blessing, Brenda Lukeman; (D) Edward M. Cohen; (S) Ray Recht; (C) Karen Hummel; (L) Dan Kinsley

Jomandi Productions, Inc.

TOM JONES
Co-Artistic Director

MARSHA JACKSON
Co-Aritistic Director/Managing Director

144 Mayson St., NE
Atlanta, GA 30324
(404) 876-6346 (bus.)
(404) 892-0880 (b.o.)

FOUNDED 1978
Tom Jones, Marsha Jackson

SEASON
Oct.-July

FACILITIES
Academy Theatre
Seating Capacity: 425
Stage: proscenium

FINANCES
July 1, 1988-June 30, 1989
Expenses: $400,000

CONTRACTS
AEA SPT

At Jomandi's philosophical and aesthetic center is the assertion of the African-American presence in a global community. That presence, while informed by tradition, concurrently acknowledges the present and future possibilities. From this center evolves the design of our programs. Jomandi's upcoming season continues the development of an aesthetic within an ever-changing universe. The company's artistic voice is an articulation of the newest works from established and emerging playwrights. The commitment to tour three productions nationally and internationally this year, while maintaining a schedule of five productions in Atlanta, underscores the company's mission to fulfill the cultural needs of the widest possible community. As architects of the future, Jomandi will continue to redefine the means by which African-American artists examine the values of a new world culture. In this way, the company contributes to a future that encourages cultural pluralism and, specifically, an appreciation of the African-American presence, while capitalizing on the economic and development potentials of theatre in a world marketplace.

—*Marsha Jackson, Tom Jones*

PRODUCTIONS 1987–88

Checkmates, Ron Milner; (D) Woodie King, Jr.; (S) John Harris; (C) Debi Barber; (L) John Harris
Do Lord Remember Me, adapt: James De Jongh; (D) Andrea Frye; (S) John Harris; (C) Andrea Frye and Debi Barber; (L) John Harris
Queen of the Blues, Tom Jones; (D) Tom Jones; (S) John Harris; (C) Gerald Thompson; (L) John Harris
The Boot Dance, Edgar White; (D) Andrea Frye; (S) John Harris; (C) Andrea Frye and Debi Barber; (L) John Harris
That Serious He-Man Ball, Alonzo D. Lamont, Jr.; (D) Marsha A. Jackson; (S) Tony Loadholt; (C) Debi Barber; (L) John Harris

PRODUCTIONS 1988–89

Buried Child, Sam Shepard; (D) Andrea Frye; (S) Elaine Williams; (C) Andrea Frye; (L) Margaret Tucker
Do Lord Remember Me, adapt: James De Jongh; (D) Andrea Frye; (S) John Harris; (C) Andrea Frye and Debi Barber; (L) John Harris

Jomandi Productions. Marsha Jackson, Renee Clark, Thomas W. Jones II and Kah Rahman in *Voices in the Rain*. Photo: Jim Alexander.

El Hajj Malik, N.R. Davidson; (D) Tom Jones; (S) John Harris; (C) Eric Hansen; (L) John Harris
Queen of the Blues, Tom Jones; (D) Tom Jones; (S) John Harris; (C) Eric Hansen; (L) John Harris
The Colored Museum, George C. Wolfe; (D) Andrea Frye; (S) Art Johnson; (C) Goldie Dicks; (L) Margaret Tucker
Sisters, Marsha A. Jackson; (D) Tom Jones; (S) John Harris; (C) Debi Barber; (L) John Harris

La Jolla Playhouse

DES MCANUFF
Artistic Director

ALAN LEVEY
Managing Director

ROBERT BLACKER
Associate Director/Dramaturg

Box 12039
La Jolla, CA 92037
(619) 534-6760 (bus.)
(619) 534-3960 (b.o.)

FOUNDED 1947
Gregory Peck, Dorothy McGuire, Mel Ferrer

SEASON
May-Nov.

FACILITIES
Mandell Weiss Center for the Performing Arts
Seating Capacity: 492
Stage: proscenium

Warren Theatre
Seating Capacity: 248
Stage: thrust

FINANCES
Nov. 1, 1987-Oct. 31, 1988
Expenses: $3,255,761

CONTRACTS
LORT (B) and (C)

The La Jolla Playhouse provides a home for theatre artists to gather, share ideas and extend themselves. At the heart of each project we produce is a director, playwright or performer who can impact the development of our art form and help define the course of American theatre. We encourage a variety of genres and styles, believing that the vitality of the American theatre is bound to our rich and diverse theatrical and cultural heritage. We produce new work and classics side-by-side, because we believe that they inform each other—that working on classics expands contemporary artists' ideas about theatre, and that new works keep classics honest by reminding us that they must be pertinent. This juxtaposition allows artists and au-

ences alike to examine contemporary issues in a historical context.
—Des McAnuff

PRODUCTIONS 1987–88

Once in a Lifetime, Moss Hart and George S. Kaufman; (D) Stephen Zuckerman; (S) Bob Shaw; (C) Susan Denison Geller; (L) Richard Winkler
Two Rooms, Lee Blessing; (D) Des McAnuff; (S) Marjorie Bradley Kellogg; (C) Susan Hilferty; (L) Peter A. Kaczorowski
Lulu, Frank Wedekind; trans and adapt: Roger Downey; (D) Sharon Ott; (S) John Arnone; (C) Deborah M. Dryden; (L) Peter Maradudin
The Fool Show, Geoff Hoyle; (D) Geoff Hoyle; (S) Rob Murphy; (L) Peter A. Kaczorowski
80 Days, book: Snoo Wilson; music and lyrics: Ray Davies; (D) Des McAnuff; (S) Douglas W. Schmidt; (C) Susan Hilferty; (L) David F. Segal

PRODUCTIONS 1988–89

The Grapes of Wrath, adapt: Frank Galati, from John Steinbeck; (D) Frank Galati; (S) Kevin Rigdon; (C) Erin Quigley and Kevin Rigdon; (L) Kevin Rigdon
Nebraska, Keith Reddin; (D) Les Waters; (S) Loy Arcenas; (C) David C. Woolard; (L) Stephen Strawbridge
Dangerous Games, book: James Lewis and Graciela Daniele; music: Astor Piazzolla; lyrics: William Finn; (D) Graciela Daniele; (S) Tony Straiges; (C) Patricia Zipprodt; (L) Peggy Eisenhauer
Down the Road, Lee Blessing; (D) Des McAnuff; (S) Todd Salovey; (C) Susan Hilferty; (L) Peter Maradudin
The Misanthrope, Moliere; adapt: Neil Bartlett; (D) Robert Falls; (S) George Tsypin; (C) Susan Hilferty; (L) James F. Ingalls
Macbeth, William Shakespeare; (D) Des McAnuff; (S) John Arnone; (C) Deborah M. Dryden; (L) Chris Parry

Lamb's Players Theatre. Cynthia Peters, Vicki Smith, Pamela Turner and David Cochran Heath in *The Book of the Dun Cow*. Photo: Nate Peirson.

La Jolla Playhouse. Harris Yulin and Elizabeth Berridge in *Lulu*. Photo: Micha Langer.

Lamb's Players Theatre

ROBERT SMYTH
Producing Artistic Director

Box 26
National City, CA 92050
(619) 474-3385 (bus.)
(619) 474-4542 (b.o.)

FOUNDED 1978
Steve Terrell, Robert Smyth

SEASON
Jan.-Dec.

FACILITIES
Seating Capacity: 175
Stage: arena

FINANCES
Dec. 1, 1987-Nov. 30, 1988
Expenses: $553,437

Lamb's Players Theatre is a year-round ensemble of artists—actors, designers, directors, and playwrights—working in collaboration over an extended period of time, pushing each other toward our best work, seeking to integrate faith and art. While not a "religious" theatre, we are a company that holds the Christian faith as the basis of its artistic vision and its philosophical world view. In addition to our resident theatre we maintain a touring company which performs nationwide on campuses and in prisons as well as in schools with productions dealing with adolescent chemical dependency.
—Robert Smyth

PRODUCTIONS 1987–88

The Foreigner, Larry Shue; (D) Kerry Cederberg; (S) Mike Buckley; (C) Vicki Smith; (L) Mike Buckley
Saint Joan, George Bernard Shaw; (D) Robert Smyth; (S) Mike

Buckley; (C) Vicki Smith; (L) Mike Buckley
The Book of the Dun Cow, adapt: Robert Smyth and Kerry Cederberg, from Walter Wangerin; (D) Robert Smyth; (S) Chris Turner; (C) Vicki Smith and Mike Buckley; (L) Dave Thayer
Kilts, David McFadzean; (D) Robert Smyth; (S) Mike Buckley; (C) Vicki Smith; (L) Mike Buckley
Cotton Patch Gospel, book: Tom Key and Russell Treyz; lyrics and music: Harry Chapin; (D) Deborah Gilmour Smyth; (S) Mike Buckley; (C) Vicki Smith; (L) Brett Kelly
Lamb's Players Festival of Christmas, Kerry Cederberg; (D) Kerry Cederberg and Robert Smyth; (S) Mike Buckley; (C) Vicki Smith; (L) Gerry Enos

PRODUCTIONS 1988–89

Amadeus, Peter Shaffer; (D) Kerry Cederberg; (S) Mike Buckley; (C) Vicki Smith; (L) Brett Kelly
An Inspector Calls, J.B. Priestley; (D) Robert Smyth; (S) Mike Buckley; (C) Vicki Smith; (L) Nathan Peirson
Much Ado About Nothing, William Shakespeare; (D) Sally Smythe; (S) Chris Turner; (C) Vicki Smith; (L) Mike Buckley
The Diary of Anne Frank, Frances Goodrich and Albert Hackett; (D) Robert Smyth; (S) Mike Buckley; (C) Vicki Smith; (L) Robert Smyth
Joseph the Amazing Technicolor Dreamcoat, music and book: Andrew Lloyd Weber; lyrics: Tim Rice; (D) Robert Smyth; (S) Mike Buckley; (C) Vicki Smith; (L) Nathan Peirson
Annual, Kerry Cederberg; (D) Robert Smyth; (S) Mike Buckley; (C) Margaret Nuehoff Vida; (L) Nathan Peirson

L. A. Theatre Works

SUSAN ALBERT LOEWENBERG
Producing Director

SARA MAULTSBY
Associate Producing Director

681 Venice Blvd.
Venice, CA 90291
(213) 827-0808

FOUNDED 1974
Susan Albert Loewenberg, Robert Greenwald, Jeremy Blahnik

SEASON
variable

FINANCES
Oct. 1, 1987-Sept. 30, 1988
Expenses: $368,471

CONTRACTS
LORT (D)

As producing director of L. A. Theatre Works my task has been to guide the evolution of the company—from its beginings as a informally organized group of theatre artists exploring ways to make theatre in unorthodox settings such as prisons and community workshops, to a formal producing organization that develops and presents the work of playwrights from the U.S. and abroad. Our new venture is the L. A. Classic Theatre Works Company, an ensemble of 40 distinguished, classically trained actors who share our ideas about theatre. The company enlarges our artistic scope through innovative presentations of landmark plays both on the stage and for radio. Our commitment is to new work, new forms and the explication of a particular vision. As a post-Brechtian theatre that truly mirrors the "unease" of modern culture, we want our audiences to experience the exhilaration of change, as opposed to the emotional release that comes from artifice. We also support and nurture our theatrical vision through our new play reading series and through collaborations involving conceptual directors, playwrights and designers.
—*Susan Albert Loewenberg*

PRODUCTIONS 1988–89

The Rehearsal, Jean Anouilh; (D) Harris Yulin; (S) Robert Israel; (C) Louise Hayter; (L) Michael Shanman
The Grace of Mary Traverse, Timberlake Wertenbaker; (D) Peggy Shannon; (S) J. Kent Inasy and Ken Booth; (C) Abra Flores; (L) J. Kent Inasy and Ken Booth
Almost Persuaded, Annie Griffin; (D) Annie Griffin; (L) Annie Griffin and Stephen Rolfe

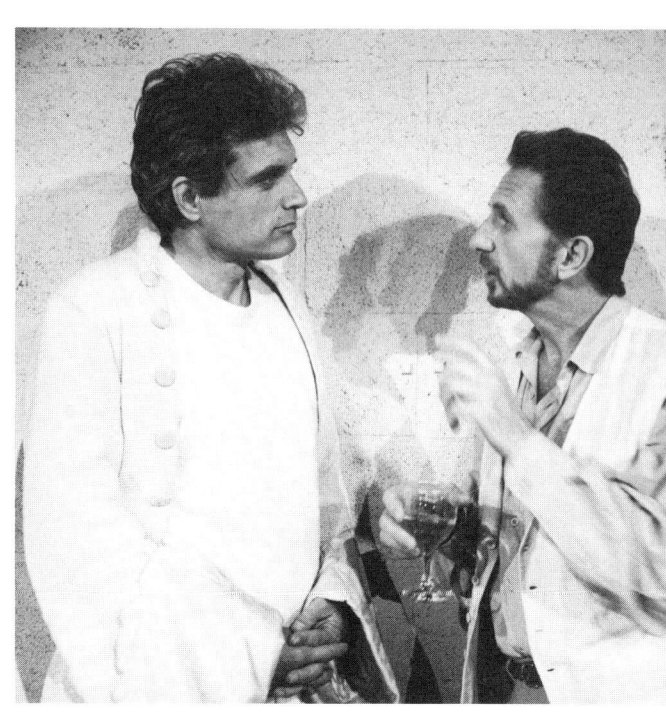

L.A. Theatre Works. David Selby and Rene Auberjonois in *The Rehearsal*. Photo Christopher G. Casler.

Lincoln Center Theater

GREGORY MOSHER
Director

BERNARD GERSTEN
Executive Producer

150 West 65th St.
New York, NY 10023
(212) 362-7600 (bus.)
(212) 239-6200 (b.o.)

FOUNDED 1985
Lincoln Center for the Performing Arts, Inc.

SEASON
Jan.-Dec.

FACILITIES
Vivian Beaumont Theater
Seating Capacity: 1,108
Stage: thrust

Mitzi Newhouse
Seating Capacity: 299
Stage: thrust

FINANCES
July 1, 1988-June 30, 1989
Expenses: $44,808,000

CONTRACTS
LORT (A) and (B)

PRODUCTIONS 1987–88

The Comedy of Errors, William Shakespeare; (D) Robert Woodruff; (S) David Gropman; (C) Susan Hilferty; (L) Paul Gallo
The Regard of Flight, Bill Irwin, Nancy Harrington and company developed; (D) Bill Irwin and Nancy Harrington; (S) Douglas O. Stein; (L) Robert Rosentel
Anything Goes, book: Guy Bolton, P.G. Wodehouse, Howard Lindsay and Russell Crouse; book adapt: Timothy Crouse and John Weidman; music and lyrics: Cole Porter; (D) Jerry Zaks; (S) Tony Walton; (C) Tony Walton; (L) Paul Gallo
Sarafina!, book, music and lyrics: Mbongeni Ngema; music and lyrics: Hugh Masekela; (D) Mbongeni Ngema; (S) Sarah Roberts; (C) Sarah Roberts; (L) Mannie Manim
Boys' Life, Howard Korder; (D) W. H. Macy; (S) James Wolk; (C) Donna Zakowska; (L) Steve Lawnick
Speed-the-Plow, David Mamet; (D) Gregory Mosher; (S) Michael Merritt; (C) Nan Cibula; (L) Kevin Rigdon
I'll Go On, adapt: Gerry Dukes and Barry McGovern, from Samuel Beckett; (D) Colm O'Briain; (S) Robert Ballagh; (C) Robert Ballagh; (L) Rupert Murray

PRODUCTIONS 1988–89

Anything Goes, book: Guy Bolton, P.G. Wodehouse, Howard Lindsay and Russell Crouse; book adapt: Timothy Crouse and John Weidman; music and lyrics: Cole Porter; (D) Jerry Zaks; (S) Tony Walton; (C) Tony Walton; (L) Paul Gallo

Sarafina!, book, music and lyrics: Mbongeni Ngema; music and lyrics: Hugh Masekela; (D) Mbongeni Ngema; (S) Sarah Roberts; (C) Sarah Roberts; (L) Mannie Manim

Speed-the-Plow, David Mamet; (D) Gregory Mosher; (S) Michael Merritt; (C) Nan Cibula; (L) Kevin Rigdon

Road, Jim Cartwright; (D) Simon Curtis; (S) Paul Brown; (C) Paul Brown; (L) Kevin Rigdon

Waiting for Godot, Samuel Beckett; (D) Mike Nichols; (S) Tony Walton; (C) Ann Roth; (L) Jennifer Tipton

Our Town, Thornton Wilder; (D) Gregory Mosher; (S) Douglas Stein; (C) Jane Greenwood; (L) Kevin Rigdon

Measure for Measure, William Shakespeare; (D) Mark Lamos; (S) John Conklin; (C) John Conklin; (L) Pat Collins

Lincoln Center Theater. F. Murray Abraham, Robin Williams, Steve Martin and Bill Irwin *Waiting for Godot*. Photo: Brigitte Lacombe.

Living Stage Theatre Company

ROBERT A. ALEXANDER
Director

CATHERINE IRWIN
Managing Director

6th and Maine Aves., SW
Washington, DC 20024
(202) 554-9066

FOUNDED 1966
Robert A. Alexander

SEASON
Sept.-June

FACILITIES
Seating Capacity: 124
Stage: flexible

FINANCES
July 1, 1988-June 30, 1989
Expenses: $547,660

CONTRACTS
LORT (D)

Our work is, and always has been, intended to impact on the lives of our forgotten young who have been thrown away by society. We turn our audiences on to their own magnificence as artists—their irresistible urge to communicate their deepest feelings and most profound thoughts. The theme of racism runs constant throughout our work—the causes, the results, and the possible means of annihilating this disease which is an intrinsic part of the soil of our land. We have recently been increasing our residencies in other cities and creating larger scripted plays for adult audiences. Our company intends to strengthen our American Sign Language skills and learn to speak Spanish so we can continue to work with deaf audiences and extend our work to Spanish-speaking children and teens. We need to create a school where young actors can be trained in our philosophies and techniques in order to ensure the strength of our ensemble acting company in the future.
—*Robert A. Alexander*

PRODUCTIONS 1987–89

Note: All performances are company-developed from improvisations; dir: Robert A. Alexander.

Living Stage Theatre Company. Ezra Knight during a performance-workshop. Photo: Kelly Jerome.

Long Island Stage

CLINTON J. ATKINSON
Artistic Director

THOMAS M. MADDEN
Managing Director

Box 9001
Rockville Centre, NY
11571-9001
(516) 867-3090 (bus.)
(516) 546-4600 (b.o.)

FOUNDED 1975
Susan E. Barclay

SEASON
Sept.-June

FACILITIES
The Hays Theatre
Seating Capacity: 297
Stage: proscenium

FINANCES
July 1, 1988-Aug. 31, 1989
Expenses: $825,000

CONTRACTS
LORT (D)

Long Island Stage expects its audience to be changed by what it experiences in our theatre. Believing in the primacy of the written word, we also trust in the co-equal power of the visual to create emotional impact. We are interested in works seen to have relevance to the lives of our audience: for example, each season we produce a work by our contemporary, George Bernard Shaw. In any year our repertoire might range from the revival of important classics to the examination of lesser-known works by the major writers to more lightweight fare. We produce one original script a season, allotting it equal weight with more established selections. Working with fine creative talents, we explore the art of the theatre, and our play selections acknowledge the drama's power to

Long Island Stage. Jim Fitzpatrick, David Snizek and Isabella Knight in *In the Beginning*. Photo: Brian M. Ballweg.

affect the moral, political and social fabric. Words and ideas are honored at Long Island Stage: as written, interpreted, spoken, visualized, comprehended and absorbed.

—*Clinton J. Atkinson*

PRODUCTIONS 1987–88

Flights of Devils, Tom McClary; (D) Clinton J. Atkinson; (S) James Singelis; (C) Gail Brassard; (L) John Hickey

Children, A.R. Gurney, Jr.; (D) Terence Lamude; (S) Steven Perry; (C) Don Newcomb; (L) Linda Essig

Back on the Town, John Wallowitch and Bertram Ross; (D) Clinton J. Atkinson; (S) Andrew Earl Jones; (L) John Hickey

Mrs. Warren's Profession, George Bernard Shaw; (D) Clinton J. Atkinson; (S) Steven Perry; (C) Gail Brassard; (L) John Hickey

The Owl and the Pussycat, Bill Manhoff; (D) Clinton J. Atkinson; (S) Daniel Conway; (C) Don Newcomb; (L) John Hickey

Getting the Gold, P.J. Barry; (D) Clinton J. Atkinson; (S) Daniel Conway; (C) Claudia Stephens; (L) John Hickey

PRODUCTIONS 1988–89

The Lion in Winter, James Goldman; (D) Jim Hillgartner; (S) Steven Perry; (C) Gail Brassard; (L) John Hickey

Talley's Folly, Lanford Wilson; (D) Clinton J. Atkinson; (S) Steven Perry; (C) Andrew Earl Jones; (L) John Hickey

Billy Bishop Goes to War, John Gray and Eric Peterson; (D) Clinton J. Atkinson; (S) James Youmans; (C) Andrew Earl Jones; (L) John Hickey

Aftershocks, Doug Haverty; (D) Clinton J. Atkinson; (S) James Youmans; (C) Don Newcomb; (L) John Hickey

In the Beginning, George Bernard Shaw; (D) Clinton J. Atkinson; (S) James Singelis; (C) Gail Brassard; (L) John Hickey

Harvey, Mary C. Chase; (D) Clinton J. Atkinson; (S) Daniel Ettinger; (C) Don Newcomb; (L) John Hickey

Long Wharf Theatre

ARVIN BROWN
Artistic Director

M. EDGAR ROSENBLUM
Executive Director

222 Sargent Drive
New Haven, CT 06511
(203) 787-4284 (bus.)
(203) 787-4282 (b.o.)

FOUNDED 1965
Harlan Kleiman, Jon Jory

SEASON
Sept.-July

FACILITIES
Main Stage
Seating Capacity: 484
Stage: thrust

Stage II
Seating Capacity: 199
Stage: flexible

FINANCES
July 1, 1988-June 30, 1989
Expenses: $4,220,000

CONTRACTS
LORT (B) and (C)

Long Wharf Theatre approaches the end of its first quarter-century with a renewed sense of its goals and responsibilities. We continue to offer imaginative revivals of classic and modern plays, rediscoveries of little-known works from the past, and a variety of world and American premieres. Additionally, we have directed attention to a critical aspect of American theatre today—the fostering of the creative voices that are the theatre's greatest future resource. Long Wharf Theatre has established a series of works-in-process that explore the development of each script rather than the finished products. This project allows emerging playwrights to shape their ideas, while working closely with a director and actors, before an audience. Our productions and workshops represent our continued commitment to maintaining the quality and diversity of the theatrical experience while fulfilling our artistic goal—the presentation of plays of character that examine the human condition and spirit.

—*Arvin Brown*

Long Warg Theatre. Mary McDonnell and Tom Berenger in *National Anthems*. Photo: Charles Erickson.

PRODUCTIONS 1987–88

The Downside, Richard Dresser;
  (D) Kenneth Frankel; (S) Loren
  Sherman; (C) Jess Goldstein;
  (L) Judy Rasmuson
The Laughing Stock, Romulus
  Linney; (D) David Esbjornson;
  (S) Hugh Landwehr; (C) Dunya
  Ramicova; (L) Ronald Wallace
Our Town, Thornton Wilder;
  (D) Arvin Brown; (S) Michael H.
  Yeargan; (C) David Murin;
  (L) Ronald Wallace
Scenes From American Life, A.R.
  Gurney, Jr.; (D) John Tillinger;
  (S) Steve Rubin; (C) Bill Walker;
  (L) David F. Segal
Fathers and Sons, Brian Friel;
  (D) Austin Pendleton; (S) John
  Conklin; (C) David Murin;
  (L) Pat Collins
Fighting Chance, N.J. Crisp;
  (D) Kenneth Frankel;
  (S) Marjorie Bradley Kellogg;
  (C) Jennifer von Mayrhauser;
  (L) David F. Segal
Regina, Lillian Hellman; book,
  music and lyrics: Marc
  Blitzstein; (D) Arvin Brown;
  (S) Michael H. Yeargan; (C) Jess
  Goldstein; (L) Ronald Wallace

PRODUCTIONS 1988–89

Dinner at Eight, George S.
  Kaufman and Edna Ferber;
  (D) Arvin Brown; (S) Hugh
  Landwehr; (C) David Murin;
  (L) Ronald Wallace
Love Letters, A.R. Gurney, Jr.;
  (D) John Tillinger; (L) Judy
  Rasmuson
National Anthems, Dennis
  McIntyre; (D) Arvin Brown;
  (S) Michael H. Yeargan;
  (C) David Murin; (L) Ronald
  Wallace
When We Are Married, J.B.
  Priestley; (D) Kenneth Frankel;
  (S) Hugh Landwehr; (C) Jess
  Goldstein; (L) David F. Segal
Some Sweet Day, Nancy Fales
  Garrett; (D) Seret Scott;
  (S) Michael H. Yeargan;
  (C) David Murin; (L) Pat Collins
Rebel Armies Deep into Chad,
  Mark Lee; (D) John Tillinger;
  (S) John Lee Beatty; (C) Candice
  Donnelly; (L) Marc B. Weiss
The Heiress, Ruth Goetz and
  Augustus Goetz; (D) Kenneth
  Frankel; (S) Loy Arcenas;
  (C) Jess Goldstein; (L) David F.
  Segal

Los Angeles Theatre Center

BILL BUSHNELL
Artistic Producing Director

DIANE WHITE
Producer

514 South Spring St
Los Angeles, CA 90013
(213) 627-6500 (bus.)
(213) 627-5599 (b.o.)

FOUNDED 1985
Diane White, Bill Bushnell

SEASON
Jan.-Dec.

FACILITIES
Tom Bradley Theatre
Seating Capacity: 503
Stage: flexible

Theatre 2
Seating Capacity: 296
Stage: proscenium

Theatre 3
Seating Capacity: 320
Stage: thrust

Theatre 4
Seating Capacity: 99
Stage: flexible

FINANCES
May 1, 1988-Apr. 30, 1989
Expenses: $6,626,000

CONTRACTS
LORT (B), (C) and (D)

The Los Angeles Theatre Center's artistic mission springs from my own cares and concerns: to make theatre which, in its excellence, passion, truth and cultural diversity, reflects and improves the community and the world. The city of Los Angeles—a city of diverse cultures that personifies the social, ethnic and political future—is our inspiration. LATC's four stages and year-round programming serve as "a gathering place" where talented artists from various cultures can propagate brilliant artistic truth that is joyful, beautiful and passionate, while reflecting the toughness and vitality of contemporary life for a multicultural audience. At the heart of LATC's philosophy is the belief that theatre is the synthesizer of all the arts, that all theatre is political in the universal sense and that our role as artists is to agitate and disseminate our perception of the truth.
—*Bill Bushnell*

Los Angeles Theatre Center. Andy Taylor and Karole Foreman in *Minamata*. Photo: Chris Gulker.

PRODUCTIONS 1987–88

Sarcophagus, Vladimir Gobargev;
  trans: Michael Glenny; (D) Bill
  Bushnell; (S) Timian Alsaker;
  (C) Timian Alsaker; (L) Timian
  Alsaker
*Elizabeth: Almost by Chance a
  Woman*, Dario Fo; trans: Ron
  Jenkins; (D) Arturo Corso;
  (S) Arturo Corso and Douglas D.
  Smith; (C) Noel Taylor;
  (L) Arturo Corso and Douglas
  D. Smith
King Lear, William Shakespeare;
  (D) Stein Winge; (S) Timian
  Alsaker; (C) Timian Alsaker;
  (L) Timian Alsaker
What the Butler Saw, Joe Orton;
  (D) Charles Marowitz; (S) D.
  Martyn Bookwalter;
  (C) Christine Hover; (L) Douglas
  D. Smith
Etta Jenks, Marlane Meyer;
  (D) Roberta Levitow; (S) Rosario
  Provenza; (C) Ray Naylor;
  (L) Robert Wierzel
The House of Correction,
  Norman Lock; (D) Bradford
  O'Neil; (S) Douglas D. Smith;
  (C) Sherry Linnell; (L) Douglas
  D. Smith
The Promise, Jose Rivera; (D) Jose
  Luis Valenzuela; (S) Rosario
  Provenza; (C) Tina Navarro;
  (L) Robert Wierzel
Cat's Paw, William Mastrosimone;
  (D) Bill Bushnell; (S) Douglas D.
  Smith; (C) Marianna Elliott;
  (L) Todd A. Jared
*The Kathy and Mo Show:
  Parallel Lives*, Kathy Najimy
  and Mo Gaffney; (D) Carole
  Rothman; (S) Heidi Landesman;
  (L) Frances Aronson
The Jester and the Queen,
  Boleslav Polivka; (D) Boleslav
  Polivka; (S) Leos Janacek and
  Jaromir Tichy
Yankee Dawg You Die, Philip
  Kan Gotanda; (D) Sharon Ott;
  (S) Kent Dorsey; (C) Lydia
  Tanji; (L) Kent Dorsey and
  Douglas D. Smith
Roosters, Milcha Sanchez-Scott;
  (D) Jose Luis Valenzuela;
  (S) Timian Alsaker; (C) Timian
  Alsaker; (L) Douglas D. Smith
The Caretaker, Harold Pinter;
  (D) Alan Mandell; (S) John
  Iacovelli; (C) Ann Bruice;
  (L) Toshiro Ogawa
The Inspector General, Nikolai
  Gogol; trans: Fruma Gottschalk

79

and Milton Ehre; (D) Stein Winge; (S) Pavel Dubrovsky; (C) Marianna Elliott; (L) Pavel Dubrovsky

PRODUCTIONS 1988–89

Kingfish, Marlane Meyer; (D) David Schweizer; (S) Douglas D. Smith; (C) Susan Ninninger; (L) Marianne Schneller
Bopha!, Percy Mtwa; (D) Percy Mtwa; (L) Mannie Manim
The Seagull, Anton Chekhov; trans: Michael Frayn; (D) Charles Marowitz; (S) Ralph Koltai; (C) Noel Taylor; (L) Toshiro Ogawa
The Model Apartment, Donald Margulies; (D) Roberta Levitow; (S) John Iacovelli; (C) Ann Bruice; (L) Liz Stillwell
Stone Wedding, Milcha Sanchez-Scott; (D) Jose Luis Valenzuela; (S) Gronk; (C) David Velasquez; (L) Margaret Anne Dunn
Stars in the Morning Sky, Alexander Galin; adapt: Elise Thoron; (D) Bill Bushnell; (S) Douglas D. Smith; (C) Marianna Elliott; (L) Douglas D. Smith
Demon Wine, Thomas Babe; (D) David Schweizer; (S) Timian Alsaker; (C) Susan Ninninger; (L) Marianne Schneller
A Burning Beach, Eduardo Machado; (D) Bill Bushnell and Jose Luis Valenzuela; (S) John Iacovelli; (C) David Velasquez; (L) Douglas D. Smith
Three Ways Home, Casey Kurtti; (D) Chris Silva; (S) Donald Eastman; (C) Timian Alsaker; (L) Ann Militello
Joe Turner's Come and Gone, August Wilson; (D) Claude Purdy; (S) Scott Bradley; (C) Pamela Peterson and David F. Draper; (L) Ward Carlisle
Minimata, Reza Aboh and Mira-Lani Oglesby; (D) Reza Aboh; (S) Timian Alsaker; (C) Timian Alsaker; (L) Timian Alsaker and Douglas D. Smith
Eden, Steve Carter; (D) Edmund Cambridge; (S) John Iacovelli; (C) Marianna Elliott; (L) Douglas D. Smith
Ten November, Steven Dietz; music and lyrics: Eric Peltoniemi; (D) Steven Dietz; (S) Timian Alsaker and Douglas D. Smith; (C) Ann Bruice; (L) Anne Militello
Boys' Life, Howard Korder; (D) David Beaird; (S) Dean Tschetter; (C) Reve Richards; (L) Douglas D. Smith

Mabou Mines

JOANNE AKALAITIS, LEE BREUER, L.B. DALLAS, ELLEN MCELDUFF, RUTH MALECZECH, GREGORY MEHRTEN, FREDERICK NEUMAN, TERRY O'REILLY AND WILLIAM RAYMOND
Company Members

ANTHONY VASCONCELLOS
Managing Director

150 First Ave.
New York, NY 10009
(212)473-0559

FOUNDED 1970
David Warrilow, Ruth Maleczech, Philip Glass, Lee Breuer, JoAnne Akalaitis

SEASON
Jan.-Dec.

FINANCES
July 1, 1988-June 30, 1989
Expenses: $740,000

CONTRACTS
AEA Guest Artist

Mabou Mines is a nine-member artistic collective based in New York City. The company has produced some 40 works for theatre, film, video and radio during its 20-year history. Combining the visual, aural, musical and sculptural arts with dramatic texts, and synthesizing film, video and live performances through the art of the actor, Mabou Mines has produced experimental theatre pieces that combine aesthetic content and political substance. We have sought to make unembraceable art—art that redefines the culture, punctures holes in what is, pushes the limits of what's thinkable—to raise difficult issues in paradoxical ways and to challenge audiences with new ways of looking at our world. Mabou Mines has performed all over the United States, in Europe, Japan, South America, Israel and Australia. The company has received many awards for its work including the 1984 Brandeis Citation for Creative Arts, the 1986 Village Voice Obie award for sustained achievement and, in 1988, received an Ongoing Ensembles grant from the National Endowment for the Arts. Twenty years is a long time to produce experimental works on the edge of an evermore conservative society. We feel strongly the need to continue working, to gather strength from the global community of artists and to share our vision with a hungry audience.

—*Ruth Maleczech
for the members of Mabou Mines*

PRODUCTIONS 1987–88

Cold Harbor, Dale Worsley; (D) Bill Raymond and Dale Worsley; (S) Linda Hartinian; (C) Gregory Mehrten; (L) B. St. John Schofield
Company, Samuel Beckett; music: Philip Glass; (D) Frederick Neumann and Honora Fergusson; (S) Gerald Marks; (L) Sabrina Hamilton
A Prelude to Death in Venice, Lee Breuer; (D) Lee Breuer; (S) Alison Yerxa and L.B. Dallas; (L) Julie Archer
Flow My Tears, The Policeman Said, adapt: Linda Hartinian, from Philip K. Dick; (D) Bill Raymond; (S) Linda Hartinian; (C) Gabriel Berry; (L) Anne Militello

Mabou Mines. Terry O'Reilly in *Flow My Tears, the Policman Said*. Photo: Carol Rosegg

PRODUCTIONS 1988–89

Suenos, book adapt and lyrics: Ruth Maleczech; music: Herschel Garfein; lyrics: George Emilio Sanchez; (D) Ruth Maleczech; (S) Michael Deegan (C) Toni Leslie James; (L) Clay Shirky
Imagination Dead Imagine, Samuel Beckett; (D) Ruth Maleczech; (S) Linda Hartinian (L) Ann Militello

Madison Repertory Theatre

JOSEPH HANREDDY
Artistic Director

GIAN PAUL MORELLI
Managing Director

11 State St.
Madison, WI 53703
(608) 256-0029 (bus.)
(608) 266-9055 (b.o.)

FOUNDED 1969
Katherine Waack, Vicki Stewart

SEASON
Jan.-Dec.

FACILITIES
Isthmus Playhouse
Seating Capacity: 335
Stage: thrust

FINANCES
July 1, 1988-June 30, 1989
Expenses: $540,000

CONTRACTS
AEA SPT

Embarking on our 21st season, Madison Repertory Theatre has grown from its beginnings in the basement of a local arts center to become a professional theatre company. We look for plays that somehow matter, without restriction of a particular style or theme—plays that are passionate, original, truthful. With the play's text and the vision of the author as our guide, we give it the sharpest, clearest, most exciting production of which we are capable. Our actors, hired for individual productions, often return on a regular basis. We draw largely from our talent pools of Chicago, Minneapolis and Milwaukee. Madison Repertory Theatre's highest priorities are: to improve our level of excellence in all production levels; to consistently challenge ourselves and our audience by producing worthwhile work; to attract the finest talent available by creating a generous, open, hospitable and creative atmosphere.
—*Joseph Hanreddy*

PRODUCTIONS 1987–88

A...My Name Is Alice, Joan Micklin Silver and Julianne Boyd; (D) Fred Weiss; (S) Frank Schneeberger; (C) Mary Neuser; (L) Thomas C. Hase
The Fox, adapt: Allan Miller, from D.H. Lawrence; (D) Joseph Hanreddy; (S) Frank Schneeberger; (C) Mary Neuser; (L) Thomas C. Hase
Strange Snow, Stephen Metcalfe; (D) Joseph Hanreddy; (S) Frank Schneeberger; (C) Mary Neuser; (L) Thomas C. Hase
"Master Harold"...and the Boys, Athol Fugard; (D) Suzanne Allyn and Allan Cook; (S) Frank Schneeberger; (C) Mary Neuser; (L) Thomas C. Hase
The Norman Conquests, Alan Ayckbourn; (D) Joseph Hanreddy; (S) Frank Schneeberger; (C) Mary Neuser; (L) Thomas C. Hase

PRODUCTIONS 1988–89

A...My Name Is Alice, Joan Micklin Silver and Julianne Boyd; (D) Fred Weiss; (S) Frank Schneeberger; (C) Mary Neuser; (L) Thomas C. Hase
Retribution Rag, Buffy Sedlachek; (D) Alma Becker; (S) Frank Schneeberger; (C) Sandra S. Alderman; (L) Thomas C. Hase
The Nerd, Larry Shue; (D) Joseph Hanreddy; (S) Charles Erven; (C) Mary Neuser; (L) Thomas C. Hase
The Common Pursuit, Simon Gray; (D) Leslie Reidel; (S) Frank Schneeberger; (C) Mary Neuser; (L) Thomas C. Hase
Ten November, Steven Dietz; music and lyrics: Eric Peltoniemi; (D) Joseph Hanreddy; (S) Kent Goetz; (C) Mary Neuser; (L) Thomas C. Hase
Pump Boys and Dinettes, John Foley, Mark Hardwick, Debra Monk, Cass Morgan, John Schimmel and Jim Wann; (D) Fred Weiss; (S) Craig Clipper; (C) Mary Neuser; (L) Thomas C. Hase
Woman in Mind, Alan Ayckbourn; (D) Joseph Hanreddy; (S) Scott Bradley; (C) Mary Neuser; (L) Thomas C. Hase

Madison Repertory Theatre. *Ten November*. Photo: Zane Williams.

Magic Theatre

JOHN LION
Artistic Director

HARVEY SEIFTER
Managing Director

Bldg. D, Fort Mason Center
San Francisco, CA 94123
(415) 441-8001 (bus.)
(415) 441-8822 (b.o.)

FOUNDED 1967
John Lion

SEASON
Jan.-Dec.

FACILITIES
Cowell Theatre
Seating Capacity: 399
Stage: proscenium

North Side
Seating Capacity: 165
Stage: thrust

South Side
Seating Capacity: 175
Stage: proscenium

FINANCES
September 1, 1988-Aug. 31, 1989
Expenses: $969,000

CONTRACTS
AEA BAT

The Magic Theatre has grown up around its writers and theatre artists and given the evolving diversity of American theatre, has developed a wide range of interests. We are currently doing a mix of new plays, West Coast premieres and experimental performance works. Most recently, both in response to the changing demographics of the Bay Area and as a result of extensive Pacific Rim travels, the Magic has launched an ambitious new multicultural program that includes an Asian-American Playwrights Festival, a Hispanic Writers Project and a Pacific Rim international theatre festival. With the addition of the part-time use of the new 399-seat Cowell Theatre at Fort Mason, the Magic has created new possibilities for expansion. At the same time, the theatre has redoubled its efforts on behalf of new work with the creation of an annual Springfest. At the core remains our primary aim—superior productions of the finest writing available.
—*John Lion*

PRODUCTIONS 1987–88

Manslaughter, Nicholas Crawford; (D) John Lion and Eli Simon; (S) Ken Ellis; (C) Catherine Verdier; (L) Joe Dignan
Apocalyptic Butterflies, Wendy MacLeod; (D) Julie Hebert; (S) John Mayne; (C) Regina Cate; (L) Novella Smith
Happy Days, Samuel Beckett; (D) Stan Gontarski; (S) Ralph Fetterly; (C) Catherine Verdier; (L) David Welle
Pledging My Love, John Steppling; (D) John Steppling and Robert Glaudini; (S) Barbara J. Mesney; (C) Beaver D. Bauer; (L) Kurt Landisman
A Moon for the Misbegotten, Eugene O'Neill; (D) John Lion; (S) Jeff Rowlings; (C) Regina Cate; (L) David Welle
Fool for Love, Sam Shepard; (D) Andrew Doe; (S) Andy Stacklin; (C) Catherine Verdier; (L) Kurt Landisman

PRODUCTIONS 1988–89

Talk Radio, Eric Bogosian; (D) John Lion; (S) Jeff Rowlings; (C) Regina Cate; (L) Joe Dignan
Breaking the Code, Hugh Whitmore; (D) Albert Takazauckas; (S) John B. Wilson; (C) Kate Irvine; (L) Kurt Landisman
Endgame, Samuel Beckett; (D) Stan Gontarski; (S) Andy Stacklin; (C) Fumiko Bielefeldt; (L) David Welle
The Promise, Jose Rivera; (D) Julie Hebert; (S) John Mayne; (C) Laura Hazlett; (L) Jim Quinn

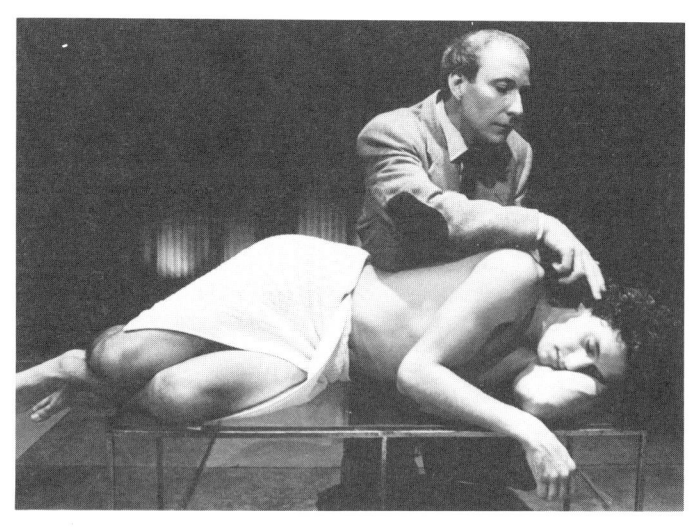

Magic Theatre. Bruce Williams and David Carrera in *Breaking the Code*. Photo: M. Rossi.

Frankie and Johnny in the Clair de Lune, Terrence McNally; (D) Albert Takazauckas; (S) Barbara J. Mesney; (C) Beaver D. Bauer; (L) Kurt Landisman

Springfest:
Speaking in Tongues, Lynne Kaufman; (D) Andrew Doe; (S) Andy Stacklin; (C) Fumiko Bielefeldt; (L) Thomas Kline
Paraguay, Thomas Poole; (D) Chris Brophy; (S) Andy Stacklin; (C) Fumiko Bielefeldt; (L) Thomas Kline
The Poets' Corner, Harry Kondoleon; (D) Jorge Cacheiro; (S) Andy Stacklin; (C) Fumiko Bielefeldt; (L) Thomas Kline

Asian-American Playwrights' Festival:
Holy Food, Jessica Hagedorn; (D) Christina Yao; (S) Joseph W. Redmond; (C) Selina; (L) Jeff Rowlings
Ohio Tip-Off, James Yoshimura; (D) Marc Hayashi; (S) Joseph W. Redmond; (C) Selina; (L) Jeff Rowlings
Barrancas, Rosanna Y. Alfaro; (D) Phyllis S. K. Look; (S) Joseph W. Redmond; (C) Selina; (L) Jeff Rowlings

Manhattan Punch Line Theatre

STEVE KAPLAN
Artistic Director

410 West 42nd St., 3rd Floor
New York, NY 10036
(212) 239-0827 (bus.)
(212) 279-4200 (b.o.)

FOUNDED 1979
Mitch McGuire, Steve Kaplan, Faith Caitlan

SEASON
Oct.-June

FACILITIES
Judith Anderson Theatre
Seating Capacity: 94
Stage: proscenium

INTAR Theatre
Seating Capacity: 94
Stage: proscenium

Samuel Beckett Theatre
Seating Capacity: 99
Stage: proscenium

FINANCES
July 1, 1986-June 30, 1987
Expenses: $313,500

CONTRACTS
AEA showcase code and letter of agreement

Manhattan Punch Line is a theatre dedicated to the spirit of the clown, the gadfly, the satirist. We see laughter as both a curative and a cauterizing agent. We recognize that the ability to laugh at the amazing irrationality of life may be what ultimately makes us most human; in an absurd universe, comedy may be the only rational stance. MPL is a place where actors, directors, designers, comics and playwrights can concentrate on the art of comedy. We are creating the foundation for a vital artistic future through programs such as Comedyworks, our script-development program; Comedy Corps, our in-house script-development acting ensemble; Late Nite Punch Line; and the Comedy Institute. Our mainstage productions introduce new comic voices and performers, and the Festival of One-Act Comedies is the single largest presentation of new comic work in the country. At MPL artists share their comic vision in a creative environment dedicated to excellence, innovation and an appreciation of our comic past.
—*Steve Kaplan*

PRODUCTIONS 1987–88

Fun, Howard Korder; (D) W.H. Macy; (S) James Wolk; (C) Michael Schler; (L) Steve Lawnick

4th Annual Festival of One-Act Comedies, various authors; (D) various; (S) Stanley A. Meyer; (C) Don Newcomb and Michael Schler; (L) Joe Morey
Terry by Terry, Mark Lieb; (D) Mark Brokaw; (S) Derek McLane; (C) Michael Schler; (L) David Noling

PRODUCTIONS 1988–89

New Vaudeville '88, various authors; (D) various; (S) Bernitt Robinson; (L) Ed Morgan
5th Annual Festival of One-Act Comedies, various authors; (D) various; (S) James Wolk; (C) Fontilla Boone and Michael Schler; (L) Danianne Mizzy
An Evening with Wallem and Tolan, book: Linda Wallem and Peter Tolan; music and lyrics: Peter Tolan; (D) Stephen Hollis; (S) James Wolk (C) Paul Patropulos; (L) Danianne Mizzy
Equal 'Wrights, Janet Neipris, Terri Wagener and Grace McKeaney; (D) Steve Kaplan, Robin Saex and Melia Bensusson; (S) Matt Moore; (C) Michael Schler; (L) Brian McDevitt
Friends, Lee Kalcheim; (D) Lee Kalcheim; (S) Richard Meyer; (L) Steve Rust

Manhattan Punch Line Theatre. Elaine Rinehart and Neal Lerner in *One Monday*. Photo Martha Swope Associates, Carol Rosegg.

Manhattan Theatre Club. Zeljko Ivanek and Joseph Maher in *Loot*. Photo: Gerry Goodstein.

Manhattan Theatre Club

LYNNE MEADOW
Artistic Director

BARRY GROVE
Managing Director

453 West 16th St., 2nd Flr.
New York, NY 10011
(212) 645-5590 (bus.)
(212) 581-7907 (b.o.)

FOUNDED 1970
Peregrine Whittlesey, A. Joseph Tandet, George Tabori, Gerard L. Spencer, Margaret Kennedy, A.E. Jeffcoat, Barbara Hirschl, William Gibson, Gene Frankel, Philip Barber

SEASON
variable

FACILITIES
City Center Stage I
Seating Capacity: 299
Stage: proscenium

City Center Stage II
Seating Capacity: 150
Stage: flexible

FINANCES
July 1, 1988-June 30, 1989
Expenses: $3,943,372

CONTRACTS
AEA Off Broadway

Manhattan Theatre Club has a long tradition of developing and presenting important new works by American and international writers. We also produce earlier works we believe have not been fully interpreted or appreciated in the past, as well as New York premieres of plays that originated in American regional theatres. Many of the plays presented at MTC have gone on to be produced on Broadway, in London, in regional theatres nationwide and as major motion pictures. The flexibility of our two spaces enables us to offer greater visibility in a Stage I production, with production standards of the highest possible quality, as well as a more developmental environment in Stage II for new works by emerging and established playwrights, composers and lyricists. MTC's Writers in Performance series has, for nearly 20 years, presented an international array of writers of all genres whose works demonsrate the diversity and power of contemporary literature. Our subscription audience numbers close to 15,000. MTC is accessible to the broadest community through group dicounts; free ticket distribution; sign-interpreted and audio-described performanes; and an eductional outreach program, which combines in-class curriculum with exposure to live theatre for students at the intermediate and high school level.

—*Lynne Meadow*

PRODUCTIONS 1987–88

Frankie and Johnny in the Clair de Lune, Terrence McNally; (D) Paul Benedict; (S) James Noone; (C) David C. Woolard; (L) David Noling
The Day Room, Don DeLillo; (D) Michael Blakemore; (S) Hayden Griffin; (C) Hayden Griffin; (L) Natasha Katz
Woman in Mind, Alan Ayckbourn; (D) Lynne Meadow; (S) John Lee Beatty; (C) Ann Roth; (L) Pat Collins
Emily, Stephen Metcalfe; (D) Gerald Gutierrez; (S) Heidi Landesman; (C) Ann Hould-Ward; (L) Pat Collins
Urban Blight, John Tillinger, et al.; (D) John Tillinger and Richard Maltby, Jr.; (S) Heidi Landesman; (C) C.L. Hundley; (L) Natasha Katz
Tea, Velina Hasu Houston; (D) Julianne Boyd; (S) Wing Lee; (C) C.L. Hindley; (L) Greg MacPherson
One Two Three Four Five, book: Larry Gelbart; music and lyrics: Maury Yeston; (D) Gerald Gutierrez; (S) James D. Sandefur; (L) Michael R. Moody
April Snow, Romulus Linney; (D) David Esbjornson; (S) Hugh Landwehr; (C) C.L. Hundley; (L) Greg MacPherson
The Debutante Ball, Beth Henley; (D) Norman Rene; (S) Loy Arcenas; (C) Walker Hicklin; (L) Debra J. Kletter

PRODUCTIONS 1988–89

Eastern Standard, Richard Greenberg; (D) Michael Engler; (S) Philipp Jung; (C) Candice Donnelly; (L) Dennis Parichy
One Two Three Four Five, book: Larry Gelbart; music and lyrics: Maury Yeston; (D) Gerald Gutierrez; (S) Douglas Stein; (C) Ann Hould-Ward; (L) Pat Collins
What the Butler Saw, Joe Orton; (D) John Tillinger; (S) John Lee Beatty; (C) Jane Greenwood; (L) Ken Billington
Aristocrats, Brian Friel; (D) Robin Lefeure; (S) John Lee Beatty; (C) Jane Greenwood; (L) Dennis Parichy
The Lisbon Traviata, Terrence McNally; (D) John Tillinger; (S) Philipp Jung; (C) Jane Greenwood; (L) Ken Killington
Italian American Reconciliation, John Patrick Shanley; (D) John Patrick Shanley; (S) Santo Loquasto; (C) William Ivey Long; (L) Peter Kaczorowski
The Talented Tenth, Richard Wesley; (D) M. Neema Barnette; (S) Charles McClennahan; (C) Alvin B. Perry; (L) Michael R. Moody
Eleemosynary, Lee Blessing; (D) Lynne Meadow; (S) John Lee Beatty; (C) William Ivey Long; (L) Peter Kaczorowski
The Loman Family Picnic, Donald Margulies; (D) Barnet Kellman; (S) G.W. Mercier; (C) Jess Goldstein; (L) Debra J. Kletter

Marin Theatre Company

WILLIAM MARCHETTI
Artistic Director

TIMOTHY STEVENSON
Acting Managing Director

Box 1439
Mill Valley, CA 94942
(415) 388-5200 (bus.)
(415) 388-5208 (b.o.)

FOUNDED 1966
Sali Lieberman

SEASON
Sept.-June

Marin Theatre Company

FACILITIES
Mainstage
Seating Capacity: 250
Stage: proscenium

Studio Theater
Seating Capacity: 99
Stage: flexible

FINANCES
July 1, 1988-June 30, 1989
Expenses: $704,000

CONTRACTS
AEA SPT

Marin Theatre Company is dedicated to becoming a nationally recognized professional theatre ensemble, presenting audiences with the best current plays and timeless classics. Our seasons are designed to present our audiences with rich theatrical experiences which entertain, reaffirm the positive aspects of the human condition and confront the dangers of self-delusion and false pride. We are committed to the development of an ensemble of actors, directors, designers and technicians, working together with guest artists. As owners and operators of a new performing arts center, we endeavor to supply local artists and community organizations with first-class rehearsal, performance and meeting space. Through our educational programs, we furnish young people and adults with high-quality performing arts training which contributes to building self-esteem, confidence and communication skills, and at the same time develops the future artists and audiences of the American theatre. The stage is set for the future growth of live professional theatre in Marin County.

—*William Marchetti*

PRODUCTIONS 1987–88

The Marriage of Bette and Boo, Christopher Durang; (D) Will Marchetti; (S) Ken Rowland; (C) Dhyanis; (L) Richard Lund
Strange Snow, Stephen Metcalfe; (D) Tom Ramirez; (S) Ken Rowland; (C) Dhyanis; (L) Jim Schelstrate
Uncle Vanya, trans and adapt: James Keller, from Anton Chekhov; (D) Albert Takazauckas; (S) Barbara J. Mesney; (C) Kate Irvine; (L) Kurt Landisman
Artichoke, Joanna M. Glass; (D) Ben Dickson; (S) Ken Rowland; (C) Dhyanis; (L) R.D. Marsan
Hedda Gabler, adapt: Maria Irene Fornes, from Henrik Ibsen; trans: William Archer; (D) Julie Hebert; (S) Steve Coleman; (C) Laura Hazlett; (L) Novella Smith
On the Verge or the Geography of Yearning, Eric Overmyer; (D) Julian Lopez-Morillas; (S) Craig Lathrop and Don Weinger; (C) Ardyss Golden; (L) Craig Lathrop and Don Weinger

PRODUCTIONS 1988–89

Master Harold . . .and the boys, Athol Fugard; (D) Ben Dickson; (S) Ken Rowland; (C) Dhyanis; (L) John Flanders
Noises Off!, Michael Frayn; (D) Richard Seyd; (S) Peggy Snider; (C) Laura Hazlett; (L) Jeff Rowlings
All My Sons, Arthur Miller; (D) Susan Marsden; (S) Ken Rowland; (C) Dhyanis; (L) Kathy Pryzgoda
I Do! I Do!, book and lyrics: Tom Jones; music: Harvey Schmidt; (D) J.D. Trow; (S) Don Weinger; (C) Dhyanis; (L) Jeff Rowlings
Daddy's Dyin' (Who's Got the Will?), Del Shores; (D) Will Marchetti; (S) Andy Stacklin; (C) Dhyanis; (L) Tom Hansen
The Broken Jug, adapt and trans: James Keller, from Albert Takazauckas; (D) Albert Takazauckas; (S) Barbara J. Mesney; (C) Beaver D. Bauer; (L) Kurt Landisman

Marin Theatre Company. Jack Shearer and Nancy Palmer Jones in I Do! I Do!. *Photo: Joe Greco.*

Mark Taper Forum

GORDON DAVIDSON
Artistic Director/Producer

STEPHEN J. ALBERT
Managing Director

135 North Grand Ave.
Los Angeles, CA 90012
(213) 972-7353 (bus.)
(213) 972-7392 (b.o.)

FOUNDED 1967
Gordon Davidson

SEASON
Year-round

FACILITIES
Mark Taper Forum
Seating Capacity: 742
Stage: thrust

Taper, Too
Seating Capacity: 85
Stage: flexible

Itchey Foot Cabaret
Seating Capacity: 99
Stage: flexible

FINANCES
July 1, 1988-June 30, 1989
Expenses: $8,000,000

CONTRACTS
LORT (A) and (B)

Over the past 22 years the Mark Taper Forum has pursued a distinct and vigorous mission: to create and maintain a theatre that is socially and culturally aware, that continually examines and challenges the assumptions of its culture, and that expands the aesthetic boundaries of theatre as an art form while attempting to find the timeliness of the classics in contemporary terms. We continue to attempt to enlighten as well as entertain our audience, to nurture new voices and new forms for the American theatre, to reflect on our stages the rich multi-cultural heritage found in Los Angeles, and to encourage tomorrow's audiences through programming that addresses the concerns and challenges the imaginations of young people. The future of the Mark Taper Forum lies in the pursuit of artistic excellence, aesthetic daring and community service. The challenge of these goals will continue to provide impetus to our broad-based programming as we move toward our second quarter-century.

—*Gordon Davidson*

PRODUCTIONS 1987–88

Babbitt: A Marriage, adapt: Ron Hutchinson, from Sinclair Lewis; (D) Steven Robman; (S) Marjorie Bradley Kellogg; (C) Marianna Elliott; (L) Pat Collins
Hunting Cockroaches, Janusz Glowacki; trans: Jadwiga Kosicka; (D) Arthur Penn; (S) D Martyn Bookwalter; (C) Susan Denison Geller; (L) Paulie Jenkins
A Lie of the Mind, Sam Shepard; (D) Robert Woodruff; (S) Douglas Stein; (C) Nicole Morin; (L) Paulie Jenkins
Made in Bangkok, Anthony Minghella; (D) Robert Egan; (S) John Arnone; (C) Robert Blackman; (L) Peter Maradudin
The Colored Museum, George C. Wolfe and Paulie Jenkins; (D) L. Kenneth Richardson; (S) Brian Martin; (C) Nancy L. Konrardy; (L) Victor En Yu Tan
Lost Highway—The Music and Legend of Hank Williams, Randal Myler and Mark Harelik; (D) Randal Myler; (S) Richard L. Hay; (C) Andrew V. Yelusich; (L) Martin Aronstein

PRODUCTIONS 1988–89

Nothing Sacred, George F. Walker; (D) Michael Lindsay-Hogg; (S) Eugene Lee; (C) Robert Blackman; (L) Natasha Katz

Mark Taper Forum. Margaret Gibson and Tom Hulce in *Nothing Sacred*. Photo: Jay Thompson.

Frankie and Johnny in the Clair de Lune, Terrence McNally; (D) Paul Benedict; (S) D. Martyn Bookwalter; (C) David C. Woolard; (L) Martin Aronstein
Dutch Landscape, Jon Robin Baitz; (D) Gordon Davidson; (S) Heidi Landesman; (C) Ann Bruice; (L) Tharon Musser
Sansei, Hiroshima; (D) Robert Egan; (S) Mark Wendland; (C) Lydia Tanji; (L) Jeff Ravitz
Stand-Up Tragedy, Bill Cain; (D) Ron Link; (S) Yael Pardess; (C) Carol Brolaski; (L) Michael Gilliam
Temptation, Vaclav Havel; trans: Marie Winn; (D) Richard Jordan; (S) John Iacovelli; (C) Csilla Marki; (L) Paulie Jenkins

McCarter Theatre Center for the Performing Arts

NAGLE JACKSON
Artistic Director

JOHN HEROCHIK
Managing Director

91 University Place
Princeton, NJ 08540
(609) 683-9100 (bus.)
(609) 683-8000 (b.o.)

FOUNDED 1972
Daniel Seltzer

SEASON
Oct.-July

FACILITIES
Mainstage
Seating Capacity: 1,078
Stage: flexible

Forbes College Theatre
Seating Capacity: 200
Stage: flexible

Richardson Auditorium
Seating Capacity: 882
Stage: thrust

FINANCES
July 1, 1988-June 30, 1989
Expenses: $4,128,644

CONTRACTS
LORT (B+)

McCarter Theatre Center for the Performing Arts hosts leading dance companies and musical artists, in addition to producing six major dramatic Stage II productions and other projects that the resources of a resident acting company afford. These have ranged form TheatreLabs that are not oriented toward production, to portable productions, one of which traveled to Europe during the 1888-89 season. We aim to offer an alternative type of theatre to an audience brought up on and steeped in the New York commercial product. We tend, therefore, to avoid Broadway—or even off Broadway—reruns, and look for the unusual and the classical. Our large size (1050-plus seats) demands large theatre, and we are pleased to fulfill that expectation.
—*Nagle Jackson*

PRODUCTIONS 1987–88

The Middle Ages, A.R. Gurney, Jr.; (D) Nagle Jackson; (S) John Jensen; (C) Marie Miller; (L) F. Mitchell Dana

Coriolanus, William Shakespeare; (D) Liviu Ciulei; (S) Liviu Ciulei; (C) Smaranda Branescu; (L) Beverly Emmons
Stepping Out, Richard Harris; (D) Nagle Jackson; (S) Patricia Woodbridge; (C) Elizabeth Covey; (L) F. Mitchell Dana
The Dark Sonnets of the Lady, Don Nigro; (D) Robert Lanchester; (S) John Jensen; (C) Gregg Barnes; (L) Victor En Yu Tan
Master Harold…and the boys, Athol Fugard; (D) Jamie Brown; (S) Jeff Modereger; (C) Suzanne Elder; (L) Phil Monat

PRODUCTIONS 1988–89

Born Yesterday, Garson Kanin; (D) Richard Risso; (S) John Jensen; (C) David C. Woolard; (L) Phil Monat
Tartuffe, Moliere; trans: Richard Wilbur; (D) Nagle Jackson; (S) Robert Perdziola; (C) Elizabeth Covey; (L) Phil Monat
Sarcophagus, Vladimir Gubaryev; trans: Michael Glenny; (D) Nagle Jackson; (S) Eduard Kochergin; (C) Eduard Kochergin; (L) F. Mitchell Dana
Dividing the Estate, Horton Foote; (D) Jamie Brown; (S) Jeff Modereger; (C) Pamela Scofield; (L) Phil Monat
A Funny Thing Happened on the Way to the Forum, book: Burt Shevelove and Larry Gelbart; music and lyrics: Stephen Sondheim; (D) Nagle Jackson; (S) Richard Block; (C) Gregg Barnes; (L) F. Mitchell Dana

McCarter Theatre Center for the Performing Arts. Richard Leighton, Elizabeth Hess, Kate Fuglei and Ian Stuart in *The Dark Sonnets of the Lady*. Photo: Clem Fiori.

Merrimack Repertory Theatre. Jonathan Peck and Robert Colston in *Sizwe Bansi is Dead*. Photo: Kevin Karkins.

Merrimack Repertory Theatre

DANIEL L. SCHAY
Producing Director

Box 228
Lowell, MA 01853
(508) 454-6324 (bus.)
(508) 454-3926 (b.o.)

FOUNDED 1979
Mark Kaufman, John R. Briggs

SEASON
Oct.-May

FACILITIES
Liberty Hall
Seating Capacity: 387
Stage: thrust

FINANCES
July 1, 1988-June 30, 1989
Expenses: $762,560

CONTRACTS
LORT (D)

As it begins its second decade, the Merrimack Repertory Theatre has established itself as an important cultural resource for its region and as a contributing participant in the national theatre. Its repertoire has included new plays and musicals as well as distinguished revivals; it has also given voice to native playwrights and has brought Shakespeare, Moliere, Shaw, Fugard and Pinter to a new audience in a unique community. Through its artistic, educational and outreach programs, the MRT has played a major role in the spiritual revitalization that has paralleled the much-heralded economic rebirth of Lowell. The MRT's work is rooted in a recognition of social and historical context, and in a commitment to the centrality of the actor/audience relationship, seeking always to connect the ideas and passions of its art to the lives and aspirations of its demographically diverse audience.
—*Daniel L. Schay*

PRODUCTIONS 1987-88

The Diary of Anne Frank, Frances Goodrich and Albert Hackett; (D) Daniel L. Schay; (S) Alison Ford; (C) Jane Alois Stein; (L) John Ambrosone
A Christmas Carol, adapt: Larry Carpenter, from Charles Dickens; (D) Daniel L. Schay; (S) Leslie Taylor; (C) Amanda Aldridge; (L) David Lockner
Sizwe Bansi is Dead, Athol Fugard, John Kani and Winston Ntshona; (D) Tom Markus; (S) Joseph A. Varga; (C) Jane Alois Stein; (L) David Lockner
Mrs. California, Doris Baizley; (D) Peter H. Clough; (S) Robert Thayer; (C) Lynda L. Salsbury; (L) John Ambrosone
Angel Street, Patrick Hamilton; (D) Richard Rose; (S) Gary English; (C) Amanda Aldridge; (L) Kendall Smith
Bertha, the Sewing Machine Girl, book and lyrics: Robert Emmett; music: Gordon Connell; (D) Maggie Harrer; (S) Jane Clark; (C) Debra Stein; (L) John Ambrosone

PRODUCTIONS 1988-89

As You Like It, William Shakespeare; (D) Daniel L. Schay; (S) David Stern; (C) Jane Alois Stein; (L) John Ambrosone
Noises Off!, Michael Frayn; (D) Michael Allosso; (S) Edwin Chapin; (C) Bradford Wood and Gregory Poplyk; (L) John Ambrosone
A Christmas Carol, adapt: Larry Carpenter, from Charles Dickens; (D) Daniel L. Schay; (S) Alison Ford; (C) Amanda Aldridge; (L) John Ambrosone
Pill Hill Stories, Jay O'Callahan; (D) Richard McElvain; (C) Kelly Reed; (L) John Ambrosone
To Forgive, Divine, Jack Neary; (D) Jack Neary; (S) Leslie Taylor; (C) Jane Alois Stein; (L) John Ambrosone
Betrayal, Harold Pinter; (D) David G. Kent; (S) Gary English; (C) Jane Alois Stein; (L) John Ambrosone
Blithe Spirit, Noel Coward; (D) Richard McElvain; (S) Lorilee Cloeman; (C) Jane Alois Stein; (L) John Ambrosone

Milwaukee Repertory Theater

JOHN DILLON
Artistic Director

SARA O'CONNOR
Managing Director

108 East Wells Street
Milwaukee, WI 53202
(414) 224-1761 (bus.)
(414) 224-9490 (b.o.)

FOUNDED 1954
Mary John

SEASON
Sept.-May

FACILITIES
Powerhouse Theater
Seating Capacity: 720
Stage: thrust

Stiemke Theater
Seating Capacity: 198
Stage: flexible

Stackner Cabaret
Seating Capacity: 116
Stage: proscenium

Pabst Theater
Seating Capacity: 1,392
Stage: proscenium

FINANCES
July 1, 1988-June 30, 1989
Expenses: $3,285,000

CONTRACTS
LORT (A), (C) and (D)

Virtually from its inception, the resident acting company has been at the core of Milwaukee Repertory Theater's identity. Over the years we've enlarged this multiracial troupe to include resident writers, directors, composers and dramaturgs. To challenge the company, we maintain an active program of exchange with theatre: in Japan, Mexico, Ireland and Chile. And to deepen the bonds between the company and the community, we've commissioned works that explore the social and spiritual past and present of our region. Our acting interns work with company members in the Lab, our in-house research and development wing that seeks to develop new works and explore unusual acting styles, while innovative artists like Maria Irene Fornes, Tadashi Suzuki and Ping Chong help us try to keep our artistry on the cutting edge.
—*John Dillon*

PRODUCTIONS 1987-88

The Matchmaker, Thorton Wilder; (D) John Dillon; (S) Hugh Landwehr; (C) Michael Olich; (L) Dan Kotlowitz
The Diary of Anne Frank, Francis Goodrich and Albert Hackett; (D) Kent Stephens; (S) Jeffrey Struckman; (C) Sam Fleming; (L) Spencer Mosse
The Three Sisters, Anton Chekhov; trans: Brian Friel; (D) Kenneth Albers; (S) Victor A. Becker; (C) Sam Fleming; (L) Robert Jared
The Tale of Lear, adapt: Tadashi Suzuki, from William Shakespeare; (D) Tadashi

Suzuki; (S) Arden Fingerhut; (C) Tadashi Suzuki; (L) Arden Fingerhut
The Miracle, Felipe Santander; trans: Amlin Gray; (D) John Dillon; (S) Laura Maurer and Tim Rosman; (C) Sam Fleming; (L) Victor En Yu Tan
The Miser, Moliere; trans: Sara O'Connor; (D) Kenneth Albers; (S) Michael Miller; (C) Charles Berliner; (L) Robert Peterson
A Christmas Carol, adapt: Amlin Gray, from Charles Dickens; (D) Kristine Thatcher; (S) Stuart Wurtzel; (C) Carol Oditz; (L) Robert Shook
The Puppetmaster of Lodz, Gilles Segal; trans: Sara O'Connor; (D) J.R. Sullivan; (S) John Story and Sandra J. Strawn; (C) Ellen Kozak; (L) Robert Zenoni
Loot, Joe Orton; (D) Mary B. Robinson; (S) Ken Kloth; (C) Sam Fleming; (L) Ken Kloth
You Can't Judge a Book by Looking at the Cover: Sayings from the Life and Writings of Junebug Jabbo Jones, Volume II, John O'Neal, Nayo-Barbara Watkins, Steven Kent and Timothy Raphael; (D) Steven Kent; (L) Ken Bowen
Heathen Valley, Romulus Linney; (D) Romulus Linney; (S) Pat Doty; (C) Cecelia Mason; (L) Nancy A. Brunswick
Shue Biz, Larry Shue; (D) Kenneth Albers; (S) John Story; (L) Robert Zenoni
Wholly Moses, Norman Moses and Wesley Savick; (D) Wesley Savick; (S) John Story; (L) Robert Zenoni

PRODUCTIONS 1988–89

The Torch, Alberto Heiremans; trans: Amlin Gray; (D) Guillermo Semler; (S) Laura Maurer; (C) Sam Fleming; (L) Victor En Yu Tan
Precious Memories, Romulus Linney; (D) John Dillon; (S) Loy Arcenas; (C) John Carver Sullivan; (L) Allen Lee Hughes
Talley's Folly, Lanford Wilson; (D) Kenny Leon; (S) Art Johnson; (C) Ellen Kozack; (L) Ann G. Wrightson
She Stoops to Conquer, Oliver Goldsmith; (D) Kenneth Albers; (S) Vicki Smith; (C) Sam Fleming; (L) Robert Zenoni
Wedding Band, Alice Childress; (D) John Dillon; (S) Scott Weldin; (C) Sally Richardson; (L) Kevin Rigdon
Juno and the Paycock, Sean O'Casey; (D) Kenneth Albers; (S) Victor A. Becker; (C) Sam Fleming; (L) Robert Jared
A Christmas Carol, trans: Amlin Gray; (D) Kenneth Albers; (S) Stuart Wurtzel; (C) Carol Oditz; (L) Dan Kotlowitz
Burning Patience, Antonio Skarmeta; trans: Marion Peter Holt; (D) Hector Noguera; (S) Ken Kloth; (C) Terry Donarski; (L) Ken Kloth
Kind Ness, Ping Chong; (D) Ping Chong; (S) Pat Doty; (C) Dawna Gregory; (L) William L. Browning
And What of the Night?, Maria Irene Fornes; (D) Maria Irene Fornes; (S) John Story; (C) Cecelia Mason; (L) LeRoy Stoner
The Chastitute, John B. Keane; (D) J.R. Sullivan; (S) Tamara Turchetta; (C) Peter Gottlieb; (L) Tamara Turchetta
Survival Revival Revue, Barbara Leigh, Mike Moynihan, Debbie Anderson and Jenny Lerner; (D) Jenny Lerner
Laughing Wild, Christopher Durang; (D) Kenneth Albers; (S) John Story and Sandra J. Strawn; (C) Lauri Hartenhoff; (L) Chester Loeffler-Bell
Ain't Nobody's Blues But Mine, Barbara Roberts and Robert Meiksins; (D) Robert Meiksins; (S) John Story and Sandra J. Strawn; (C) Lori Hartenhoff; (L) Chester Loeffler-Bell
Good Evening, Peter Cook and Dudley Moore; (D) Montgomery Davis; (S) John Story and Sandra J. Strawn; (C) Lori Hartenhoff; (L) Chester Loeffler-Bell
The Irish Rascal, David O. Frazier, Joseph Garry and Kathleen Kennedy; (D) Kenneth Albers; (S) John Story and Sandra K. Strawn; (L) Chester Loeffler-Bell

Milwaukee Repertory Theatre. Marie Mathay and Tad Ingram in *Talley's Folly*. Photo: Mark Avery.

Missouri Repertory Theatre

GEORGE KEATHLEY
Artistic Director

JAMES D. COSTIN
Executive Director

4949 Cherry St.
Kansas City, MO 64110
(816) 276-2727 (bus.)
(816) 276-2700 (b.o.)

FOUNDED 1964
Patricia McIlrath, James D. Costin

SEASON
July-Apr.

FACILITIES
Helen F. Spencer Theatre
Seating Capacity: 730
Stage: flexible

Studio 116
Seating Capacity: 99
Stage: flexible

FINANCES
May 1, 1988-Apr. 30, 1989
Expenses: $2,258,098

CONTRACTS
LORT (B)

Theatre has always been a medium through which we can see ourselves and therefore a medium through which we can influence behavior and alter perceptions. This influence is, I hope, in the upward direction of taste, of morality, of ideas. Since theatre both instructs and entertains, the material and style of production must be carefully chosen. The Missouri Repertory Theatre expends a great deal of energy in both these areas. New plays continue to be a high priority for us. We also consider touring to be a vital part of what we do. Last year our tour covered 14,000 miles and we played in states as far afield as Florida and New York. In addition to performing, while on tour we conducted dozens of workshops and master classes.

—*George Keathley*

PRODUCTIONS 1987–88

Dracula, John L. Balderston and Hamilton Deane; (D) Dennis Rosa; (S) Edward Gorey; (C) Edward Gorey; (L) Jackie Manassee
Educating Rita, Willy Russell; (D) George Keathley; (S) John Ezell; (C) Vincent Scassellati; (L) Robert Jared
The Assignment (Formerly: End of the World), Arthur Kopit; (D) Gavin Cameron-Webb; (S) Alison Ford; (C) Vincent Scassellati; (L) Joseph Appelt
A Christmas Carol, adapt: Barbara Field, from Charles Dickens; (D) Beverly Shatto; (S) John Ezell; (C) Baker S. Smith; (L) Joseph Appelt
All My Sons, Arthur Miller; (D) George Keathley; (S) Daniel Robinson; (C) Baker S. Smith; (L) Jospeh W. Clapper
The House of Blue Leaves, John Guare; (D) Beverly Shatto; (S) Herbert L. Camburn; (C) Baker S. Smith; (L) James F. Ingalls
The Curious Adventures of Alice, James D. Costin; (D) George Keathley; (S) John Ezell; (C) Vincent Scassellati; (L) Joseph Appelt

PRODUCTIONS 1988–89

The Great Sebastians, Howard Lindsay and Russell Crouse; (D) George Keathley; (S) Herbert l. Camburn; (C) Vincent Scassellati; (L) Jackie Manassee
The Emperor Jones, Eugene O'Neill; (D) George Keathley; (S) John Ezell; (C) Baker S. Smith; (L) Curt Ostermann
The Immigrant: A Hamilton County Album, Mark Harelik; conceived: Mark Harelik and Randal Myler; (D) Beverly Shatto; (S) David William Wallace; (C) Vincent Scassellati; (L) David Martin Jacques
A Christmas Carol, adapt: Barbara Field, from Charles Dickens; (D) Beverly Shatto; (S) John Ezell; (C) Baker S. Smith; (L) Joseph Appelt
Tons of Money, Will Evans and Valentine; (D) Beverly Shatto; (S) Herbert L. Camburn; (C) Baker S. Smith; (L) David Martin Jacques
The Road to Mecca, Athol Fugard; (D) George Keathley; (S) John Ezell; (C) Vincent Scassellati; (L) Jackie Manassee
The Tempest, William Shakespeare; (D) Dennis Rosa; (S) John Conklin; (C) Virgil Johnson; (L) David Martin Jacques

Missouri Repertory Theatre. Celeste Holm and Rebecca Taylor in *The Road to Mecca*. Photo: Larry Pape.

Mixed Blood Theatre Company. Wayne Evenson, Don Cheadle, Warren C. Bowles and Mike Kissen in *The Boys Next Door*. Photo: Mike Paul, Act Two Photography.

Mixed Blood Theatre Company

JACK REULER
Managing/Artistic Director

1501 South Fourth St.
Minneapolis, MN 55454
(612) 338-0937 (bus.)
(612) 338-6131 (b.o.)

FOUNDED 1976
Jack Reuler

SEASON
Oct.-July

FACILITIES
Seating Capacity: 200
Stage: flexible

FINANCES
July 1, 1988-June 30, 1989
Expenses: $545,000

CONTRACTS
AEA twin cities area

Artistic directors have the rare privilege of smuggling their dreams across the border of reality. We get to show the world not just as it was or as it is, but how we'd like it to be. The Mixed Blood Theatre Company is a prototype and model of a multiracial company and has become a national resource because of its colorblind approach. Recent forums on nontraditional casting have exposed the sad state of casting and race in the theatre. Stalwarts of the American theatre have begun to discuss in theory what Mixed Blood has been doing in practice for 13 years. That theoretical discussion has centered on audience reaction, box office risk, aesthetic integrity, critical reaction and playwright's rights. At Mixed Blood we have proven that colorblind casting works. And contrary to popular misconception, colorblind in not cultureblind. It isn't affirmative action. If we were all to cast in "nontraditional" modes, no one would notice. Nontraditional would become traditional. In such a world, rather than being known as a "mission theatre" or "the place that does colorblind casting," the Mixed Blood Theatre Company would be known to the American theatre, as indeed it is in the Twin Cities, simply as a theatre that does bold new work in an aggressive style.

—*Jack Reuler*

PRODUCTIONS 1987–88

The Colored Museum, George C. Wolfe; (D) Sharon Walton; (S) Bob Fuecker; (C) Anne Ruben; (L) Scott Peters
The Mystery of Irma Vep, Charles Ludlam; (D) Ron Peluso and Jack Reuler; (S) Bob Fuecker; (C) Anne Ruben; (L) Scott Peters
Liquid Skin, Douglas Anderson; (D) David Ira Goldstein; (S) Bob Fuecker; (C) Sue Haas; (L) Scott Peters
I'm Not Rappaport, Herb Gardner; (D) Steve Pearson; (S) Bob Fuecker; (C) Anne Ruben; (L) Scott Peters

PRODUCTIONS 1988–89

Calvinisms, Ken LaZebnik;
(D) Mark Sieve; (S) Michael
Cottom; (C) Anne Ruben;
(L) Scott Peters
The Boys Next Door, Tom
Griffin; (D) John Donahue;
(S) Bob Fuecker; (C) Anne
Ruben; (L) Scott Peters
A...My Name is Alice, Joan
Micklin-Silver and Julianne
Boyd; (D) Sharon Walton and
Brian Grandison; (S) Bob
Fuecker; (C) Anne Ruben;
(L) Scott Peters
Buenavista, Bernardo Solano;
(D) John Donahue; (S) Bob
Fuecker; (C) Anne Ruben;
(L) Scott Peters
Ali!, Graydon Royce and Geoff
Ewing; (D) Jack Reuler;
(S) Colin Tugwell; (C) Anne
Ruben; (L) Scott Peters

Musical Theatre Works

ANTHONY J. STIMAC
Executive Director

440 Lafayette St. 3rd fl.
New York, NY 10003
(212) 677-0040 (bus.)
(212) 688-6022 (b.o.)

FOUNDED 1983
Anthony J. Stimac

SEASON
Sept.-May

FACILITIES
Theatre at St. Peter's Church
Seating Capacity: 164
Stage: flexible

FINANCES
July 1, 1988-June 30, 1989
Expenses: $585,242

CONTRACTS
AEA letter of agreement

Musical Theatre Works is a non-profit producing organization devoted exclusively to developing new musicals and new writers for the musical theatre. Each year MTW presents ten informal readings of new musicals, ten staged readings and three full productions. Since its inception, MTW has presented 92 readings and 26 full productions, of which six have gone on to productions in other venues. MTW was created as a place where composers, lyricists, librettists, directors, choreographers, and actors can learn and develop their craft by going through the whole process. During the run of each production, revisions are made daily and tested on the audience at each performance. Essentially, MTW is seeking to develop a process for creating new works for the American musical theatre in today's inflated economic environment.
—*Anthony J. Stimac*

PRODUCTIONS 1987–88

The No Frills Revue, book, music and lyrics: Martin Charnin, et al.; (D) Martin Charnin;
(S) Evelyn Sakash; (C) Amanda J. Klein; (L) Clarke W. Thornton

A Walk on the Wild Side, book, music, and lyrics: Will Holt;
(D) Pat Birch; (S) Michael Keith;
(C) Amanda J. Klein; (L) Clarke W. Thornton
...After These Messages, book and lyrics: David Curtis, James Hammerstein, Alice Whitfield; music: Ralph Affoumado;
(D) John Driver; (S) Michael Keith; (C) Michael S. Schler;
(L) Clarke W. Thornton
Alias Jimmy Valentine, book: Jack Wrangler; music: Bob Haber; lyrics: Hal Hackady; (D) Charles Repole; (S) Michael Keith;
(C) Stephen L. Bornstein;
(L) Clarke W. Thornton
Ducks, book, music and lyrics: John Driver and Jeffrey Haddow; (D) John Driver;
(C) Victoria Lee; (L) Clarke W. Thornton

PRODUCTIONS 1988–89

Passionate Extremes, book and lyrics: Thayer Q. Burch; music: George Cochran Quincy;
(D) Mark S. Herko; (S) James Noone; (C) Amanda J. Klein;
(L) Kendall Smith
Kiss Me Quick Before the Lava Reaches the Village, book and lyrics: Steve Hayes; music and lyrics: Peter Ekstrom;
(D) Anthony J. Stimac; (S) James Noone; (C) Amanda J. Klein;
(L) Richard Latta
Cradle Song, book and lyrics: Mary Braken Phillips; music: Jan Mullaney; (D) Anthony J. Stimac; (S) Richard Ellis;
(C) Amanda J. Klein; (L) Clarke W. Thornton
Young Rube, book: George W. George; book, music and lyrics: Matty Selman; (D) Mark S. Herko; (S) David Mitchell;
(C) Amanda J. Klein; (L) Richard Latta

Music-Theatre Group

LYN AUSTIN
Producing Director

DIANE WONDISFORD
Managing Director

735 Washington St.
New York, NY 10014
(212) 924-3108 (bus.)
(212) 265-4375 (b.o.)

Lenox Arts Center
Box 128
Stockbridge, MA 01262
(413) 298-5122 (bus.)
(413) 298-3400 (b.o.)

FOUNDED 1971
Lyn Austin

SEASON
Jan.-Dec.

FACILITIES
St. Clement's
Seating Capacity: 136
Stage: flexible

Citizens Hall
Seating Capacity: 75
Stage: flexible

FINANCES
July 1, 1988-June 30, 1989
Expenses: $1,453,314

CONTRACTS
AEA letter of agreement

Music-Theatre Group is a leading pioneer in the development of new works in which theatre, music, dance and the visual arts are combined to create new forms. Music-Theatre Group's work is deliberately eclectic and has been variously termed theatre with music, dance-theatre, opera and musical theatre. Most of the work is developed from an idea rather than a completed score or script. MTG brings together a carefully selected combination of director, composer, writer/lyricist and choreographer and places them in a supportive, collaborative environment. Long-term developmental periods and careful nurturing of the artists are key elements in the organization's artistic approach. We seek to create an atmosphere in which artists can set new sights and take risks, while receiving supporting insight and meaningful critical feedback. The work is fully produced both Off Broadway and in Stockbridge, Mass., and often tours nationally and internationally.
—*Lyn Austin*

PRODUCTIONS 1987–88

The Long Journey of Poppie Nongena, book: Elsa Joubert; music: Sophie Mgcina;
(D) Hilary Blecher; (S) Carl Sprague; (C) Shura Cohen;
(L) William Armstrong
Cinderella/Cendrillon, book: Eve Ensler; music: Jules Massenet; music adapt: Jeff Halpern;
(D) Anne Bogart; (S) Victoria Petrovich; (C) Gregg Barnes;
(L) Carol Mullins

Musical Theatre Works. *Alias Jimmy Valentine.*

Music-Theatre Group. *Juan Darien.* Photo: Donna Gray.

Prison-made Tuxedos, book: George W.S. Trow; music: Frank Morgan; (D) David Warren; (S) John Arnone; (C) David C. Woolard; (L) Debra Dumas
Haddock's Eyes, adapt: David Warren, from Lewis Carroll; music: David Del Tredici; (D) David Warren; (S) John Arnone; (C) David C. Woolard; (L) Debra Dumas
Juan Darien, adapt: Julie Taymor and Elliot Goldenthal, from Horacio Quiroga; music: Elliot Goldenthal; (D) Julie Taymor and Elliot Goldenthal; (S) G.W. Mercier and Julie Taymor; (C) G.W. Mercier and Julie Taymor; (L) Richard Nelson(L)

PRODUCTIONS 1988–89

Out of Order, book: Ben Robinson; music: Mark Bennett; (D) Michael Kantor; (S) Victoria Petrovich; (L) Debra Dumas
The Griffin and the Minor Canon, book: Wendy Kesselman; lyrics: Ellen Fitzhugh; music: Mary Rodgers; (D) Andre Ernotte; (S) Victoria Petrovich; (C) Donna Zakowska; (L) Debra Dumas
Short Takes '89, music: Geri Allen, Denise Delapenha, Leroy Jenkins and Hannibal Peterson; (D) Paul Walker; (L) Debra Dumas
Dangerous Glee Club, book: Charles Moulton; music: Steve Elson; (D) Charles Moulton; (C) Eileen Lynch; (L) Debra Dumas
Ladies, book: Eve Ensler; music: Joshua Shneider; (D) Paul Walker; (S) Victoria Petrovich; (C) Donna Zakowska; (L) Debra Dumas

National Jewish Theater

SHELDON PATINKIN
Artistic Director

FRAN BRUMLIK
Managing Director

5050 West Church St
Skokie, IL 60077
(312) 675-2200 (bus.)
(312) 675-5070 (b.o.)

FOUNDED 1986
Jewish Community Centers of Chicago

SEASON
Oct.-July

FACILITIES
Zollie and Elaine Frank Theater
Seating Capacity: 250
Stage: flexible

FINANCES
July 1, 1988-June 30, 1989
Expenses: $414,900

CONTRACTS
AEA CAT

Although I'm particularly interested in finding new plays and playwrights, the repertoire of the National Jewish Theatre is drawn from everywhere and any time, from Shakespeare to the Marx Brothers to Arthur Miller and beyond. Our audiences are committed to seeing plays and musicals, in English, which deal with the Jewish experience, both present and past. They make their preferences clear by letter, phone and active participation in our twice-a-week postshow discussions; above all, they want variety within the four-show season, as do I. It is therefore my primary goal to present as full a range of theatrical forms and styles as possible, using the best professionals available in the Chicago theatre community. Since artistic merit is my first consideration, the script choices—old and new—are very limited; we therefore accept unsolicited manuscripts, do monthly staged readings of new works, hold a new play contest, and commission playwrights and translators.
—Sheldon Patinkin

PRODUCTIONS 1987–88

Grown Ups, Jules Feiffer; (D) Kyle Donnelly; (S) Jeff Bauer; (C) Jessica Hahn; (L) Rita Pietraszek
The Dybbuk, S. Ansky; (D) Sheldon Patinkin; (S) Gary Baugh; (C) Jordan Ross; (L) Mary Badger
The Magic Barrel, adapt: Arnold Aprill, from Stanley Elkin, Bernard Malamu and I.B. Singer; (D) Arnold Aprill; (S) Richard Penrod and Jacqueline Penrod; (C) Claudia Boddy; (L) Larry Schoeneman
Minnie's Boys, book: Arthur Marx and Robert Fisher; lyrics: Hal Hackady; music: Larry Grossman; (D) Estelle Spector; (S) David S.S. Davis; (C) Jeffrey Kelly; (L) Michael Rourke

PRODUCTIONS 1988–89

The Puppetmaster of Lodz, Gilles Segal; trans: Sara O'Connor; (D) J.R. Sullivan; (S) Gary Baugh; (C) Jessica Hahn; (L) Mary Badger
I Can Get It for You Wholesale, book: Jerome Weidman; music and lyrics: Harold Rome; (D) William Payne; (S) James Dardenne; (C) Jessica Hahn; (L) Rita Pietraszek
After the Fall, Arthur Miller; (D) Sheldon Patinkin; (S) Michael Merritt; (C) Jessica Hahn; (L) Robert Shook
Social Security, Andrew Bergman; (D) B. J. Jones; (S) Mary Griswold; (C) Jessica Hahn; (L) Geoffrey Bushor

Nebraska Theatre Caravan

CHARLES JONES
Founding Director

CAROLYN RUTHERFORD
Managing Director

6915 Cass St.
Omaha, NE 68132
(402) 553-4890 (bus.)
(402) 553-0800 (b.o.)

National Jewish Theater. Jerry Jarrett, Lisa Dodson, Lorna Raver Johnson and Bernard Landis in *The Dybbuk*. Photo: Jennifer Girard.

Nebraska Theatre Caravan. *Man of La Mancha.* Photo: John McIntyre.

FOUNDED 1976
Charles Jones, Omaha
 Community Playhouse

SEASON
Sept.-June

FACILITIES
Omaha Community Playhouse
Seating Capacity: 600
Stage: proscenium

Fonda-McGuire Theatre
Seating Capacity: 250
Stage: flexible

FINANCES
July 1, 1988-June 30, 1989
Expenses: $826,365

CONTRACTS
AEA guest artist contract

The Nebraska Theatre Caravan is the professional touring wing of the Omaha Community Playhouse, the largest community theatre in the nation and the only community theatre to sponsor a national professional touring company. The original mission of the Caravan is to provide high-quality entertainment and educational opportunities to communities where distance, financial limitations or lack of appropriate resources has hindered or prevented such activities. However, we are finding that the company is now providing performances and workshops to all sizes of cities across the U.S. and Canada, as well as in our home state. The 15-member resident company now works together eight months each year. Our dream is to have year-round employment for the professional company that not only performs in our home theatre's Fonda-McGuire Series, but also tours nationally and internationally.
 —*Charles Jones*

PRODUCTIONS 1987–88

Arkansaw Bear, Aurand Harris; (D) Susan Beck; (S) Steven Wheeldon; (C) John Gergel; (L) Steven Wheeldon
Animal Farm, adapt: Peter Hall, from George Orwell; (D) Bill Hutson; (S) Steven Wheeldon; (C) John Gergel; (L) Steven Wheeldon
Over Here!, book: Will Holt; music and lyrics: Richard M. Sherman and Robert B. Sherman; (D) Carl Beck; (S) Steven Wheeldon; (C) John Gergel; (L) Steven Wheeldon
A Christmas Carol, adapt: Charles Jones, from Charles Dickens; (D) Carl Beck; (S) James Othuse; (C) Tom Crisp and Kathy Wilson; (L) James Othuse
Tom Jones, adapt: David Rodgers, from Henry Fielding; (D) Carl Beck; (S) James Othuse; (C) Denise Ervin and John Gergel; (L) James Othuse
The Dragon and St. George, Charles Jones; (D) Charles Jones; (S) James Othuse; (C) Denise Ervin and John Gergel; (L) James Othuse

PRODUCTIONS 1988–89

A Hans Christian Andersen Storybook, book: Charles Jones; adapt and lyrics: Susan Beck; music: Kate Schrader; (D) Susan Beck; (S) Steven Wheeldon; (C) John Gergel; (L) Steven Wheeldon
Julius Caesar, adapt: Charles Jones, from William Shakespeare; (D) Charles Jones; (S) James Othuse; (C) John Gergel; (L) James Othuse
The Fantasticks, book and lyrics: Tom Jones; music: Harvey Schmidt; (D) Carl Beck; (S) Steven Wheeldon; (C) John Gergel; (L) Greg Scheer
A Christmas Carol, adapt: Charles Jones, from Charles Dickens; (D) Charles Jones; (S) James Othuse; (C) Tom Crisp and Kathy Wilson; (L) James Othuse

New American Theater

J. R. SULLIVAN
Producing Director

118 North Main St.
Rockford, IL 61101
(815) 963-9454 (bus.)
(815) 964-8023 (b.o.)

FOUNDED 1972
J.R. Sullivan

SEASON
Sept.-June

FACILITIES
David W. Knapp Theater
Seating Capacity: 282
Stage: thrust

AMCORE Cellar Theater
Seating Capacity: 94
Stage: flexible

FINANCES
July 1, 1988-June 30, 1989
Expenses: $992,916

CONTRACTS
AEA SPT

New American Theater's mission is to produce classical, contemporary and new works in a manner consistent with the high standards of the contemporary American theatre: innovative productions that foster lasting audience and ensemble growth. When New American Theater was founded, its aim was the production of new plays. NAT is now poised to achieve the pursuit of this oft-stated mission with a modern, fully equipped mainstage thrust space designed to feature classic as well as contemporary plays, and a second stage providing workshop and performance space for new work. With a two-season planning process in place, NAT can now pursue workshops of new plays and transfer them to the mainstage, while maintaining an ensemble. Energizing audiences with this mix of theatre has been central to NAT's concept of itself. With our new quarters offering

New American Theater. Lee Ernst in *A Christmas Carol.* Photo: Jon McGinty.

workshops, classes and spaces for affiliate artists and attention to special populations within our community, the promise of consistent and high-quality new work seems on the threshold of fulfillment. To perform with dynamism and to perform with truth, while making every play a new play, remains New American Theater's greatest goal.

—*J. R. Sullivan*

PRODUCTIONS 1987–88

Biloxi Blues, Neil Simon; (D) Francis X. Kuhn; (S) E. Oliver Taylor; (C) Laura Cunningham; (L) David Radunsky
A Streetcar Named Desire, Tennessee Williams; (D) J.R. Sullivan; (S) Michael S. Philippi; (C) Jon R. Accardo; (L) Michael S. Philippi
A Christmas Carol, adapt: Amlin Gray, from Charles Dickens; (D) J.R. Sullivan; (S) James Wolk; (C) Jon R. Accardo; (L) David Radunsky
The Front Page, Ben Hecht and Charles MacArthur; (D) Allan Carlsen; (S) Russel Borski; (C) Laura Cunningham; (L) Cynthia R. Stillings
Strider, adapt: Steve Brown and Robert Kalfin, from Leo Tolstoy; book: Mark Rozovsky; music: Norman L. Berman, Mark Rozovsky and S. Vetkin; lyrics: Steve Brown and Uri Riashentsev; trans: Tamara Bering Sunguroff; (D) Martin deMaat; (S) Jon R. Accardo; (C) Jon R. Accardo; (L) Susan McElhaney
Romeo and Juliet, William Shakespeare; (D) J.R. Sullivan; (S) Michael S. Philippi; (C) Jon R. Accardo; (L) Michael S. Philippi
I'm Not Rappaport, Herb Gardner; (D) Allan Carlsen; (S) Russel Borski; (C) Carla M. Biege; (L) Peter Gottlieb

PRODUCTIONS 1988–89

Long Day's Journey into Night, Eugene O'Neill; (D) J.R. Sullivan; (S) Mary Griswold; (C) John Paoletti; (L) Geoffrey Bushor
The House of Blue Leaves, John Guare; (D) Doug Finlayson; (S) Michael S. Philippi; (C) Jessica Hahn; (L) Susan McElhaney
A Christmas Carol, adapt: Amlin Gray, from Charles Dickens; (D) J.R. Sullivan; (S) James Wolk; (C) Jon R. Accardo; (L) Peter Gottlieb
The Nerd, Larry Shue; (D) Allan Carlsen; (S) Stephen Packard; (C) Jon R. Accardo; (L) Susan McElhaney
Broadway Bound, Neil Simon; (D) J.R. Sullivan; (S) Mary Griswold; (C) John Paoletti; (L) Geoffrey Bushor
Guys and Dolls, book: Jo Swerling and Abe Burrows; music and lyrics: Frank Loesser; (D) Allan Carlsen; (S) Tamara Turchetta; (C) Barbara A. Bell; (L) Thomas Hase

New Dramatists

JEAN PASSANANTE
Executive Director

JOEL K. RUARK
Managing Director

424 West 44th St.
New York, NY 10036
(212) 757-6960

FOUNDED 1949
John Wharton, Richard Rodgers, Michaela O'Hara, Howard Lindsay, Moss Hart, Oscar Hammerstein, II, John Golden

SEASON
Sept.-May

FACILITIES
Mainstage
Seating Capacity: 90
Stage: flexible

Lindsay/Crouse Studio
Seating Capacity: 60
Stage: flexible

FINANCES
July 1, 1988-June 30, 1989
Expenses: $500,000

CONTRACTS
AEA special letter

New Dramatists is entering its fifth decade, firmly establishing it as our country's oldest workshop for playwrights and, indeed, our country's oldest nonprofit service organization for the theatre. In all this time the misssion remains the same: to serve both the artistic and the practical needs of our country's finest emerging playwrights. Our 40 member playwrights, a diverse, nationally based group, are chosen by a panel of their peers to serve five-year terms. During this time they design their own program of working on developing their plays, with the advice and supervision of the artistic staff. In a sense each playwright is "artistic director" of her or his own workshop or reading; each is empowered, respected and assisted. At New Dramatists we believe in powerful playwrights: Our national theatre is still hooked on the word, and the word still belongs to the playwright.

—*Jean Passanante*

Note: During the 1987-88 and 1988-89 seasons, Thomas G. Dunn served as executive director.

PRODUCTIONS 1987–88

A Conversation with Georgia O'Keeffe, Constance Congdon; (D) Greg Leaming
Hunting Down The Sexes, Joan Schenkar; (D) Jean Francois Questiaux
Bargains, Jack Heifner; (D) Diane Kamp
Money in the Bank, David Ives; (D) John Pynchon Holms
Blackie, Y York; (D) Mark Lutwak
Lucy Loves Me, Migdalia Cruz; (D) Janet Murphy
Bovver Boys, Willy Holtzman; (D) John Pynchon Holms
Tales of the Lost Formicans, Constance Congdon; (D) Gordon Edelstein
Lillian, Migdalia Cruz; (D) Pamela Berlin

New Dramatists. Michael Harris and Joy Blackett in *The Tower*. Photo: Steve M. Lillo

Terminal Hip, Mac Wellman
Alone at the Beach, Richard Dresser; (D) Robert Engels
Evenings with Mr. Eddie, Willy Holtzman; (D) Robert Hall
Appointment with a High-Wire Lady, Russell Davis; (D) R.J. Cutler
The Red Address, David Ives; (D) David Esbjornson
Memories of Alphabetical Disorder, Pedro Juan Pietri; (D) Paul Ellis
The Duck Sisters, Sheldon Rosen; (D) Pamela Berlin
Cellophane, Mac Wellman; (D) Jim Simpson
Propaganda, Matthew Maguire; (D) Matthew Maguire
The Classics Professor, John Pielmeier; (D) Susan Gregg
Fire in the Future, Joan Schenkar; music: Christopher Drobny
Butterfly Kiss, Phyllis Nagy; (D) Rosey Hay
Heaven on Earth, Robert Schenkkan; (D) Jim Nicola
All These Blessings, June Jordan; (D) Alma Becker
Zaydok, Dennis Foon; (D) Ted Storey
Courage, John Pielmeier; (D) Susan Gregg
Boys Play, Jack Heifner
Short Pieces, John Pielmeier; (D) Gloria Muzio

One-Act Festival:
Life Gap, Y York; (D) Carey Perloff
White Trash, Willy Holtzman; (D) Mark Lutwak
Nothing is Funnier than Death, Joan Schenkar
Melina's Fish, Y York; (D) Mark Lutwak
Trust and Opening Day, Willy

Holtzman; (D) Liz Diamond
The Tower, Matthew Maguire;
(D) Matthew Maguire
The Stalwarts, OyamO;
(D) Laurie Carlos

No Return, Clairr O'Connor;
(D) Alma Becker
House of Correction, Clairr O'Connor; (D) Rhea Gaisner

PRODUCTIONS 1988–89

The Rowing Machine, Willy Holtzman; (D) John Pynchon Holms
The Cezanne Syndrome, Normand Canac-Marquis; trans: Louison Danis; (D) Liz Diamond
Ted and Edna, Ana Maria Simo; music: Jeffrey Roy; (D) Linda Chapman
Space, David Spencer; (D) Fritz Ertl
Yokohama Duty, Quincy Long; (D) Morgan Jenness
In Living Color, OyamO; (D) Dianne McIntyre
The Duck Sisters, Sheldon Rosen; (D) Gordon Edelstein
Girl Bar, Phyllis Nagy; (D) Rosey Hay
The Sweet Deceit, Joe Sutton; (D) Michael Bloom
All These Blessings, June Jordan; (D) Suzanne Bennett
Pecong, Steve Carter; (D) Arthur French
The Tower, Matthew Maguire; (D) Jennifer McDowall
Bleachers in the Sun, Y York; (D) Mark Lutwak
The Closer, Willy Holtzman; (D) R. J. Cutler
A Knife in the Heart, Susan Yankowitz; (D) Amy Gonzalez
What a Man Weighs, Sherry Kramer; (D) Liz Diamond
Spiele '36, Steve Carter
Whirligig, Mac Wellman; (D) Erin Mee
Bad Penny, Mac Wellman
Accelerando, Lisa Loomer; (D) Liz Diamond
Whole Hearted, Quincy Long; (D) Kathleen Dimmick
Casanova, Constance Congdon; (D) Greg Leaming
The Mysogynist, Michael Harding; (D) R.J. Cutler
Geronimo Jones, OyamO; music: Olu Dara; (D) Liz Diamond

One-Act Festival:
Mere Mortals, David Ives; (D) R.J. Cutler
Variations on the Death of Trotsky, David Ives; (D) R.J. Cutler
Mom Goes to the Party, Y York; (D) Mark Lutwak

Floor Above the Roof, Daniel Therriault; (D) John Pynchon Holms
Proud Flesh, James Nicholson; (D) Kim Sharp
The Old Lady Play, James Nicholson; (D) Liz Diamond
Infinity's House, Ellen McLaughlin; (D) Richard Feldman
...And Howl at the Moon, James Nicholson; (D) R.J. Cutler

New Federal Theatre

WOODIE KING, JR.
Producer

LINDA HERRING
Company Manager

466 Grand St.
New York, NY 10002
(212) 598-0400

FOUNDED 1970
Woodie King, Jr.

SEASON
July-June

FINANCES
July 1, 1987-June 30, 1988
Expenses: $435,958

CONTRACTS
AEA letter of agreement

Growing out of the New York State Council on the Arts Ghetto Arts Program, the New Federal Theatre was officially founded by Woodie King, Jr. at Henry Street Settlement. Now in its 19th season, the New Federal Theatre has carved a much admired special niche for itself in the New York and national theatre worlds. Specializing in minority drama, it has brought the joy of the living stage to the many minority audience members who live in the surrounding Lower East Side community and the greater metropolitan area. It has brought minority playwrights, actors and directors to national attention, and has sponsored a variety of ethnic theatre groups and events.
—*Woodie King, Jr.*

PRODUCTIONS 1987–88

From the Mississippi Delta, Endesha Ida Mae Holland; (D) Ed Smith; (S) Steven Perry; (C) Judy Dearing; (L) William H. Grant
Trinity, Edgar White; (D) Oz Scott; (S) Scott Bradley; (C) C. Jane Epperson; (L) Victor En Yu Tan
After Crystal Night, John Herman Shoner; (D) Max Mayer; (S) Scott Bradley; (C) Judy Dearing; (L) Michael Chybowski
Mr. Universe, Jim Grimsley; (D) Steven Kent; (S) Steven Perry; (C) Michael Keek; (L) Linda Essig

PRODUCTIONS 1988–89

Jika, Maishe Maponay; (D) Maishe Maponay; (S) Terry Chandler; (C) Karen Perry; (L) William H. Grant
Good Black, Rob Penny; (D) Claude Purdy; (S) Ken Ellis; (C) Karen Perry; (L) William H. Grant
Tis the Morning, Ruth Bedford and Ron Stacker Thompson; (D) Ron Stacker Thompson; (S) Kerry Sanders; (C) Rubee Taylor; (L) Ernest Baxter
A Thrill a Moment, music and lyrics: William Stevenson; (D) Edward Love; (S) Richard Harmon; (C) Fontella Boone; (L) William H. Grant

New Federal Theatre. Brenda Denmark, Verneice Turner and June Duell in *From the Mississippi Delta*. Photo: Bert Andrews.

New Jersey Shakespeare Festival

PAUL BARRY
Artistic Director

ELLEN BARRY
Producing Director

Drew University
Route 24
Madison, NJ 07940
(201) 377-5330 (bus.)
(201) 377-4487 (b.o.)

FOUNDED 1963
Paul Barry

SEASON
June-Jan.

FACILITIES
Bowne Theatre
Seating Capacity: 238
Stage: thrust

FINANCES
Jan. 1, 1988-Dec. 31, 1988
Expenses: $719,149

CONTRACTS
LORT (D)

The New Jersey Shakespeare Festival's vision is best explained by the plays produced through 1988 our 26th season: 185 productions from Sophocles to Fugard, including 59

New Jersey Shakespeare Festival. Ed Dennehy and Colleen Flynn-Lawson in *A Moon for the Misbegotten*. Photo: Specialized Photodesign.

mountings of 36 of Shakespeare's plays (we'll soon become one of the few theatres anywhere to complete the cannon). The list is justified by our own aesthetic values, which include a commitment to the preservation of the American classical theatre and to the development of artists for it; a firm preference for proven excellence over newness for its own sake; and devotion to the challenges and resonances of repertory, where related works are juxtaposed for added insights (e.g. the complete *War of the Roses*, *Henry VIII* and *A Man for All Seasons* or *Julius Caesar* and *Anthony and Cleopatra*). If we have accomplished anything, it is this: we are able to choose plays because we believe in them, not because they will turn a dollar—plays of great value that may heal and excite, teach and console. And this brings rare fulfillment to us.

—*Paul Barry*

PRODUCTIONS 1987–88

Hamlet, William Shakespeare; (D) Paul Barry; (S) Bill Motyka; (C) Barbara Bush; (L) David Holcomb
Rosencrantz and Guildenstern are Dead, Tom Stoppard; (D) Paul Barry; (S) David Holcomb; (C) Barbara Bush; (L) David Holcomb
Two Gentlemen of Verona, William Shakespeare; (D) Ronald Martell; (S) Bill Motyka; (C) Sharon Sprague; (L) David Holcomb
All's Well That Ends Well, William Shakespeare; (D) Paul Barry; (S) Bill Motyka; (C) Barbara A. Bell; (L) David Holcomb
A Moon for the Misbegotten, Eugene O'Neill; (D) Paul Barry; (S) Bill Motyka; (C) Julie Abels Chevan; (L) David Holcomb
On the Verge or The Geography of Yearning, Eric Overmyer; (D) Davey Marlin-Jones; (S) Bill Motyka; (C) Sharon Sprague; (L) David Holcomb

PRODUCTIONS 1988–89

Titus Andronicus, William Shakespeare; (D) Paul Barry; (S) James Bazewicz; (C) Kathryn Wagner; (L) Stephen Petrilli
As You Like It, William Shakespeare; (D) Jim Christy; (S) James Bazewicz; (C) Janus Stefanowicz; (L) Stephen Petrilli
Pericles, Prince of Tyre, William Shakespeare; (D) Paul Barry; (S) James Bazewicz; (C) Ann Waugh; (L) Stephen Petrilli
Tom Jones, adapt: John Morrison, from Henry Fielding; (D) Ronald Martell; (S) James Bazewicz; (C) Nanalee Raphael-Schirmer; (L) Stephen Petrilli
Night of the Iguana, Tennessee Williams; (D) Paul Barry; (S) David Stern; (L) Stephen Petrilli
Waiting for Godot, Samuel Beckett; (D) Paul Barry; (S) James Bazewicz; (L) Stephen Petrilli

New Mexico Repertory Theatre

ANDREW SHEA
Artistic Director

Box 789
Albuquerque, NM 87103
(505) 243-4577 (bus.)
(505) 243-4500 (b.o.)

Box 9279
Santa Fe, NM 87504
(505) 983-2382
(505) 984-2226

FOUNDED 1983
Andrew Shea, Steven Schwartz-Hartley, Clayton Karkosh

SEASON
Oct.–May

FACILITIES
KiMo Theatre
Seating Capacity: 755
Stage: proscenium

Santa Fe Armory for the Arts
Seating Capacity: 340
Stage: thrust

FINANCES
July 1, 1988–June 30, 1989
Expenses: $1,250,000

CONTRACTS
LORT (D)

New Mexico Repertory Theatre is in residence in both Albuquerque, an emerging city of 500,000 and the focus of the state's population and business growth, and Santa Fe the cultural center of the Southwest. New Mexico's only professional company, NMRT is committed to a broad and eclectic repertoire, with a special emphasis on playwrights and plays of regional significance. The theatre attempts to address its Hispanic audiences by producing contemporary Hispanic-American plays in the mainstage season, and it has developed extensive outreach, education and humanities programs.

—*Andrew Shea*

PRODUCTIONS 1987–88

Holiday, Philip Barry; (D) Andrew Shea; (S) Brian Jeffries; (C) Clairemarie Verheyan; (L) John Lasiter
The Homage That Follows, Mark Medoff; (D) Mark Medoff; (S) Jim Billings; (C) Deborah L. Brunson; (L) Jim Billings
A Christmas Carol, adapt: David Richard Jones, from Charles Dickens; (D) Andrew Shea; (S) John Malolepsy; (C) Mariel McEwan; (L) John Malolepsy
Once Removed, Eduardo Machado; (D) Melia Beusussen; (S) Tom Kamm; (C) Deborah Shaw; (L) Jason Sturm
Tartuffe, Moliere; trans: Richard Wilbur; (D) Libby Appel; (S) Thomas C. Umfrid; (C) Elizabeth Novack; (L) Jason Sturm
The Road to Mecca, Athol Fugard; (D) Andrew Shea; (S) John Malolepsy; (C) Catherine A. Paxton; (L) John Malolepsy
Bus Stop, William Inge; (D) Philip Killian; (S) Michael C. Smith; (C) Caliremarie Verheyan; (L) John Lasiter

PRODUCTIONS 1988–89

Much Ado About Nothing, William Shakespeare; (D) Andrew Shea; (S) John Malolepsy; (C) David C. Paulin; (L) John Malolepsy
Roosters, Milcha Sanchez-Scott; (D) Roxanne Rogers; (S) Rosario Provenza; (C) Tina Cantu Navarro; (L) Robert Wierzel
When You Comin' Back, Red Ryder?, Mark Medoff; (D) Jules

New Mexico Repertory Theatre. Karmin Murcelo and Rudy Ramos in *Roosters*. Photo: Murrae Haynes.

Aaron; (s) Clayton Karkosh; (c) Maria Wortham; (L) Jim Bilings
A Flea in Her Ear, Georges Feydeau; trans: John Mortimer; (D) Andrew Shea; (s) John Malolepsy; (c) Catherine Zuber; (L) John Malolepsy
Steel Magnolias, Robert Harling; (D) Philip Killian; (s) Michael C. Smith; (c) Elizabeth Novack; (L) Liz Stillwell
A Walk in the Woods, Lee Blessing; (D) Robert Berlinger; (s) Gordon Kennedy; (c) Susan Cox; (L) Gordon Kennedy

New Stage Theatre

JANE REID-PETTY
Producing Artistic Director

CATHEY CROWELL SAWYER
Associate Director

Box 4792
Jackson, MS 39296
(601) 948-3533 (bus.)
(601) 948-3531 (b.o.)

FOUNDED 1966
Jane Reid-Petty

SEASON
Year-round

FACILITIES
Meyer Crystal Auditorium
Seating Capacity: 364
Stage: proscenium

Jimmy Hewes Room
Seating Capacity: 100
Stage: flexible

FINANCES
July 1, 1988-June 30, 1989
Expenses: $585,000

CONTRACTS
AEA letter of agreement

The artist comes first at New Stage Theatre, and our energies are directed toward sustaining a vital environment in which artists can work together to achieve their finest moments on stage. Mississippi audiences are bred on the rich literary heritage of the state that produced William Faulkner, Beth Henley, Eudora Welty, Tennessee Williams and Richard Wright, and they respond to the dramatic event that is rooted in the playwright's word and vision. Our emphasis on new work evolves from this heritage; our special programming of the Eudora Welty New Plays Series, for example, provides the creative meeting of playwright and performing artists that nurtures both the art of the dramatist, and the present and future vitality of the American theatre.
—*Jane Reid-Petty*

PRODUCTIONS 1987–88

So Long on Lonely Street, Sandra Deer; (D) Ivan Rider; (s) Jimmy Robertson and Sonny White; (c) Janet Gray; (L) Morgan Billingsley, Jr.
The Gin Game, D.L. Coburn; (D) Cathey Crowell Sawyer; (s) Janet Gray; (c) Janet Gray; (L) Bill McCarty, III
A Christmas Carol, adapt: Ivan Rider, from Charles Dickens; (D) Ivan Rider; (s) Sandy McNeal and Jimmy Robertson; (c) Janet Gray; (L) Kenneth J. Lewis
Church Key Charlie Blue, Jim Lehrer; (D) Jane Reid-Petty; (s) Roger Farkash; (c) Janet Gray; (L) Roger Farkash
"Master Harold"...and the boys, Athol Fugard; (D) Stephen Hollis; (s) Jimmy Robertson and Sonny White; (c) Janet Gray; (L) Kenneth J. Lewis
The Nerd, Larry Shue; (D) Ivan Rider; (s) Janet Gray; (c) Janet Gray; (L) Kenneth J. Lewis
Greater Tuna, Jaston Williams, Joe Sears and Ed Howard; (D) Ivan Rider; (s) Jimmy Robertson and Sonny White; (c) Nana Kratochvil and Janet Gray; (L) Morgan Billingsley, Jr.
Edna Earle, adapt: Jane Reid-Petty, from Eudora Welty (D) Ivan Rider; (s) Janet Gray; (c) Janet Gray; (L) Kenneth J. Lewis

PRODUCTIONS 1988–89

Noises Off!, Michael Frayn; (D) Terrence Lamude; (s) Janet Gray; (c) Janet Gray; (L) Ann Wrightson
Painting Churches, Tina Howe; (D) Jane Reid-Petty; (s) Roger Farkash; (c) Janet Gray; (L) Roger Farkash
A Christmas Carol, adapt: Ivan Rider, from Charles Dickens; (D) Ivan Rider; (s) Sandy McNeal and Jimmy Robertson; (c) Janet Gray; (L) Bill Kickbush
Long Day's Journey into Night, Eugene O'Neill; (D) Tom Irwin; (s) Janet Gray; (c) Janet Gray; (L) Bill Kickbush
Androcles and the Lion, adapt: Aurand Harris, from George Bernard Shaw; (D) Russell Luke; (s) Janet Gray; (c) Janet Gray; (L) Kathie Stephens
Fallen Angels, Noel Coward; (D) Stephen Hollis; (s) Larry Kadlec; (c) Janet Gray; (L) Ken Hudson
Steel Magnolias, Robert Harling; (D) Ivan Rider; (s) Jimmy Robertson and Sonny White; (c) Janet Gray; (L) Ken Hudson
Oh, Mr. Faulkner, Do You Write?, John Maxwell and Tom Dupree; (D) William Partlan; (s) Jimmy Robertson; (c) Janet Gray; (L) Ken Hudson and Bill McCarty, III

New York Shakespeare Festival

JOSEPH PAPP
Producer

BOB MACDONALD
General Manager

JASON S. COHEN
Associate Producer

425 Lafayette St.
New York, NY 10003
(212) 598-7100 (bus.)
(212) 598-7150 (b.o.)

New Stage Theatre. Ronald Willoughby, Cathey Crowell Sawyer and Susan Blommaert in *Fallen Angels*. Photo: J.D. Schwalm.

NEW YORK SHAKESPEARE FESTIVAL

FOUNDED 1954
Joseph Papp

SEASON
Jan.-Dec.

FACILITIES
Newman Theater
Seating Capacity: 299
Stage: proscenium

Martinson Hall
Seating Capacity: 190
Stage: flexible

LuEsther Hall
Seating Capacity: 150
Stage: flexible

Little Theater
Seating Capacity: 99
Stage: flexible

Susan Stein Shiva Theater
Seating Capacity: 100
Stage: flexible

Anspacher Theater
Seating Capacity: 275
Stage: ¾ arena

FINANCES
Sept. 1, 1988-Aug. 31, 1989
Expenses: $14,000,000

CONTRACTS
AEA Off-Broadway and LORT (B)

Since 1954, the New York Shakespeare Festival has operated in the belief that a theatre with the highest professional standards can attract, and should be made available to, a broadly based public. From this guiding principle a contemporary theatre of extraordinary range and quality has emerged, rooted in the classics but with new American plays as its primary focus. Each summer for the past 32 years, NYSF has presented free outdoor productions of the classics throughout New York City, and for the past 27 years, at the Delacorte Theater in Central Park. NYSF's permanent home is the Public Theater, the landmark Astor Library building. There, a repertoire of new American plays and a generation of American actors, directors and designers have been developed through the Festival's working process. Three programs fully integrated into NYSF's activities are Playwriting in the Schools, which teaches elementary and junior high school students playwriting while introducing them to the world of professional theatre; Festival Latino, an international series of theatre, film, music and dance events; and Film at the Public, an acclaimed year-round forum for both American and international films. The Festival recently embarked on a six-year marathon of Shakespeare's entire works—36 plays with the foremost American actors in the leading roles. In 1983 we broke new ground in the exchange of actors and productions between the U.S. and England when an exchange program between the New York Shakespeare Festival and the Royal Court Theatre was inaugurated.
—*Joseph Papp*

PRODUCTIONS 1987–88

A Midsummer Night's Dream, William Shakespeare; (D) A. J. Antoon; (S) Andrew Jackness; (C) Frank Krenz; (L) Peter Kaczorowski

Julius Caesar, William Shakespeare; (D) Stuart Vaughan; (S) Bob Shaw; (C) Lindsay Davis; (L) Arden Fingerhut

Romeo and Juliet, William Shakespeare; (D) Les Waters; (S) Heidi Landesman; (C) Ann Hould-Ward; (L) Peter Kaczorowski

Much Ado About Nothing, William Shakespeare; (D) Gerald Freedman; (S) John Ezell; (C) Theoni Aldredge; (L) Thomas Skelton

King John, William Shakespeare; (D) Stuart Vaughan; (S) Bob Shaw; (C) Lindsay Davis; (L) John Gleason

Wenceslas Square, Larry Shue; (D) Jerry Zaks; (S) Loren Sherman; (C) William Ivey Long; (L) Paul Gallo

American Notes, Len Jenkin; (D) Joanne Akalaitis; (S) John Arnone; (C) David C. Woolard; (L) Frances Aronson

La Puta Vida, Reinaldo Povod; (D) Bill Hart; (S) Donald Eastman; (C) Gabriel Berry; (L) Anne Militello

Old Business, Joe Cacaci; (D) Joe Cacaci; (S) Richard Meyer; (C) Bill Walker; (L) Richard Meyer

Serious Money, Caryl Churchill; (D) Max Stafford-Clark; (S) Peter Hartwell; (C) Peter Hartwell; (L) Rick Fisher

Talk Radio, Eric Bogosian and Tad Savinar; (D) Frederick Zollo; (S) David Jenkins; (C) Pilar Limosner; (L) Jan Kroeze

Zero Positive, Harry Kondoleon; (D) Ken Elliott; (S) Adrienne Lobel; (C) Susan Hilferty; (L) Natasha Katz

Miracolo d'Amore, Martha Clarke; music: Richard Peaslee; (D) Martha Clarke; (S) Robert Israel; (C) Robert Israel; (L) Paul Gallo

The Death of Garcia Lorca, Jose Antonio Rial; trans: Julio Marzan; (D) Carlos Gimenez; (S) Rafael Reyeros; (C) Rafael Reyeros; (L) Carlos Gimenez

PRODUCTIONS 1988–89

Coriolanus, William Shakespeare; (D) Steven Berkoff; (S) Loren Sherman; (C) Martin Pakledinaz; (L) Steven Berkoff

Love's Labour's Lost, William Shakespeare; (D) Gerald Freedman; (S) John Ezell; (C) James Scott; (L) Natasha Katz

The Winter's Tale, William Shakespeare; (D) James Lapine; (S) John Arnone; (C) Franne Lee; (L) Beverly Emmons

Twelfth Night, William Shakespeare; (D) Harold Guskin; (S) John Lee Beatty; (C) Jeanne Button; (L) Richard Nelson

Titus Andronicus, William Shakespeare; (D) Michael Maggio; (S) John Lee Beatty; (C) Lewis Rampino; (L) Jennifer Tipton

Cymbeline, William Shakespeare; (D) Joanne Akalaitis; (S) George Tsypin; (C) Ann Hould-Ward; (L) Pat Collins

Cafe Crown, Hy Kraft; (D) Martin Charnin; (S) Santo Loquasto; (C) Santo Loquasto; (L) Richard Nelson

Genesis, book and lyrics: A.J. Antoon; book and Lyrics: Robert Montgomery; music: Michael Ward; (D) A.J. Antoon; (S) John Conklin; (C) John Conklin; (L) Jan Kroeze

For Dear Life, Susan Miller; (D) Norman Rene; (S) Loy Arcenas; (C) Walker Hicklin; (L) Arden Fingerhut

Temptation, Vaclav Havel; trans: Marie Winn; (D) Jiri Zizka; (S) Jerry Rojo; (C) Hiroshi Iwasaki; (L) Jerold R. Forsyth

The Forbidden City, Bill Gunn; (D) Joseph Papp; (S) Loren Sherman; (C) Judy Dearing; (L) Peter Kaczorowski

Romance in Hard Times, book, lyrics, and music: William Finn; (D) David Warren; (S) James Youmans; (C) David C. Woolard; (L) Peter Kaczorowski

New York Shakespeare Festival. *Temptation.* Photo: Martha Swope.

New York Theatre Workshop

JAMES C. NICOLA
Artistic Director

NANCY KASSAK DIEKMANN
Managing Director

220 West 42nd St., 18th Floor
New York, NY 10036
(212) 302-7737 (bus.)
(212) 279-4200 (b.o.)

FOUNDED 1979
Stephen Graham

SEASON
Oct.-June

New York Theatre Workshop. Kathleen Chalfant, Isiah Whitlock, Jr., Thom Christopher and Shona Tucker in *The Investigation of the Murder in El Salvador*. Photo: Paula Court.

FACILITIES
Perry Street Theatre
Seating Capacity: 99
Stage: proscenium

FINANCES
July 1, 1988-June 30, 1989
Expenses: $778,600

CONTRACTS
AEA mini

New York Theatre Workshop maintains its commitment to producing works of artistic merit that provide society with a perspective on our history, and on the events and institutions that shape our lives. Each season we present four-to-six fully mounted productions of literate, unconventional plays. These new works are primarily developed from continuing relationships with writers and directors. We seek out artists who can combine an interest in the exploration of theatrical forms with intelligent and substantial content, and who can maintain the highest standards of quality. In addition to the New Works Series, we present the New Directors Series, which provides opportunities for the most promising directors of the next generation, and "O Solo Mio," an annual festival of solo performance art. Our Mondays at Three program provides a forum for presentation of and comment on work in progress, and discussion of current social and artistic issues, thereby creating a sense of community amongst artists and staff.
—*James C. Nicola*

PRODUCTIONS 1987–88
Stella, adapt: Tony Kushner, from Johann Wolfgang von Goethe; (D) Ulli Stephan; (S) Peter Eastman; (C) Barbara Bush; (L) Steven Rosen
Blood Sports, David Edgar; (D) Judy Dennis; (S) Peter Eastman; (C) Barbara Bush; (L) Steven Rosen
Coyote Ugly, Lynn Siefert; (D) Lenora Champagne; (S) Betsy Doyle; (C) Jeffrey Ullman; (L) Mary Louise Geiger
Love Suicides at Amijima, Chikamatsu Monzaemon; (D) Jorge Cacheiro; (S) Norbert Kolb; (C) Jim Buff; (L) Mary Louise Geiger
The Big Love, Brooke Allen; (D) John Tillinger; (S) David Mitchell; (C) Jane Greenwood; (L) Dennis Parichy
Domino, Robert Litz; (D) David Esbjornson; (S) Betsy Doyle; (C) Marianne Powell-Parker; (L) Greg MacPherson

PRODUCTIONS 1988–89
L'Illusion, adapt: Tony Kusher, from Pierre Corneille; (D) Brian Kulick; (S) Stephen Olsen; (C) Claudia Brown; (L) Pat Dignan
Mercedes, Thomas Brasch; trans: Becke Buffalo; (D) Cheryl Faver; (S) Rob Murphy; (C) Marihna Draghici; (L) Pat Dignan
The Nest, Franz Xavier Kroetz; trans: Roger Downey; (D) Bartlett Sher; (S) Rob Murphy; (C) Marina Draghici; (L) Pat Dignan

Emerald City, David Williamson; (D) R.J. Cutler; (S) James Youmans; (C) Michael Krass; (L) Kenneth Posner
The Investigation of the Murder in El Salvador, Charles L. Mee, Jr.; (D) David Schweizer; (S) Tom Kamm; (C) Gabriel Berry; (L) Anne Militello
Nero's Last Folly, Leo Bassi; (D) Leo Bassi; (S) William Lang; (C) Leo Bassi; (L) Brian Aldous

North Carolina Shakespeare Festival

LOUIS RACKOFF
Artistic Director

PEDRO M. SILVA
Managing Director

Box 6066
High Point, NC 27262
(919) 841-6273 (bus.)
(919) 841-6273 (b.o.)

FOUNDED 1977
Stuart Brooks, Mark Woods

SEASON
June-Dec.

FACILITIES
High Point Theatre
Seating Capacity: 820
Stage: proscenium

Second Stage
Seating Capacity: 200
Stage: flexible

FINANCES
Jan. 1, 1988-Dec. 31, 1988
Expenses: $853,000

CONTRACTS
(B) and (D), AEA TYA

The North Carolina Shakespeare Festival serves the people of the Triad area, and a greater regional audience, with the following programs: a mainstage nightly repertory season featuring Shakespeare and other great classics; a Second Stage dedicated to contemporary plays and premieres of new American works; a holiday production of *A Christmas Carol*; and two yearly outreach tours—an eight-state tour of a Shakespeare play and a tour of *Globeworks*, our high school educational program. The Festival produces imaginative plays of social and political relevance in a variety of theatrical forms and styles—theatre that is entertaining, provocative, passionate, and culturally and educationally stimulating. We are committed to nontraditional casting, to the strongest ensemble acting company possible and to a creative, technical and administrative staff working on the highest professional level. NCSF is dedicated to the possibilities of regional theatre as an integral part of our culture.
—*Louis Rackoff*

North Carolina Shakespeare Festival. *Much Ado About Nothing*. Photo: Bill Savage.

PRODUCTIONS 1987–88

Much Ado about Nothing, William Shakespeare; (D) Louis Rackoff; (S) Joseph Flauto; (C) Christine Turbitt; (L) Henry Grillo
The Hostage, Brendan Behan; (D) Imre Goldstein; (S) Bland Wade; (C) Christine Turbitt; (L) Henry Grillo
Macbeth, William Shakespeare; (D) Louis Rackoff; (S) Ray Recht; (C) Madeline Cohen; (L) Henry Grillo
A Christmas Carol, adapt: Michael LaGue, from Charles Dickens; (D) Michael LaGue; (S) Howard Jones; (C) Mark Pirolo and Christine Turbitt; (L) Henry Grillo
Globeworks, adapt: Imre Goldstein, from William Shakespeare; (D) Louis Rackoff; (S) Gary Dartt

PRODUCTIONS 1988–89

Twelfth Night, William Shakespeare; (D) Louis Rackoff; (S) Joseph Flauto; (C) Joseph Flauto; (L) Thomas Hase
An Enemy of the People, adapt: Arthur Miller, from Henrik Ibsen (D) Alex Dmitriev; (S) Ray Recht; (C) Christine Turbitt; (L) Thomas Hase
Arms and the Man, George Bernard Shaw; (D) Geoffrey Hitch; (S) Gary Dartt; (C) Madeline Cohen; (L) Todd Hensley
Waiting for Godot, Samuel Beckett; (D) Louis Rackoff; (S) Gary Dartt; (C) Madeline Cohen; (L) Todd Hensley
A Christmas Carol, adapt: Louis Rackoff, from Charles Dickens; (D) Louis Rackoff; (S) Gary Dartt; (C) Christine Turbitt
Billy Bishop Goes to War, John Gray and Eric Peterson; (D) Louis Rackoff; (S) Richard Smith; (C) Tony French; (L) William Savage
Globeworks, adapt: Imre Goldstein, from William Shakespeare; (D) Louis Rackoff; (S) Gary Dartt

Northlight Theatre

RUSSELL VANDENBROUCKE
Artistic Director

SUSAN MEDAK
Managing Director

2300 Green Bay Rd.
Evanston, IL 60201
(312) 869-7732 (bus.)
(312) 869-7278 (b.o.)

FOUNDED 1974
Gregory Kandel

SEASON
Oct.–May

FACILITIES
Northlight Theatre
Seating Capacity: 298
Stage: proscenium

FINANCES
July 1, 1988–June 30, 1989
Expenses: $1,100,000

CONTRACTS
LORT (D)

In preparing to celebrate its 15th anniversary in 1989-90, Northlight Theatre renews its commitment to ambitious plays that stimulate the imagination and intelligence of both artists and audiences. Eager to explore and expand the allied arts of the theatre, Northlight relies on both local and national artists. The eclectic and distinctive repertoire is composed of contemporary work (including Chicago subjects), fresh interpretations of classics, adaptations, overlooked works of the past, and new plays of scope and substance. Northlight is especially interested in out-of-the-ordinary ideas, characters, language, and settings. A strong sense of Northlight's role in the community informs all choices. The theatre also develops new works through workshops, staged readings and commissions. Each year, more than 265 performances are seen by an audience of 70,000. Many patrons discover theatre through Northlight's extensive outreach programs, which provide special access for students, older adults, veterans and handicapped persons. The theatre also sponsors STAR, a program designed to serve student audiences through ongoing relationships with teachers.
—*Russell Vandenbroucke*

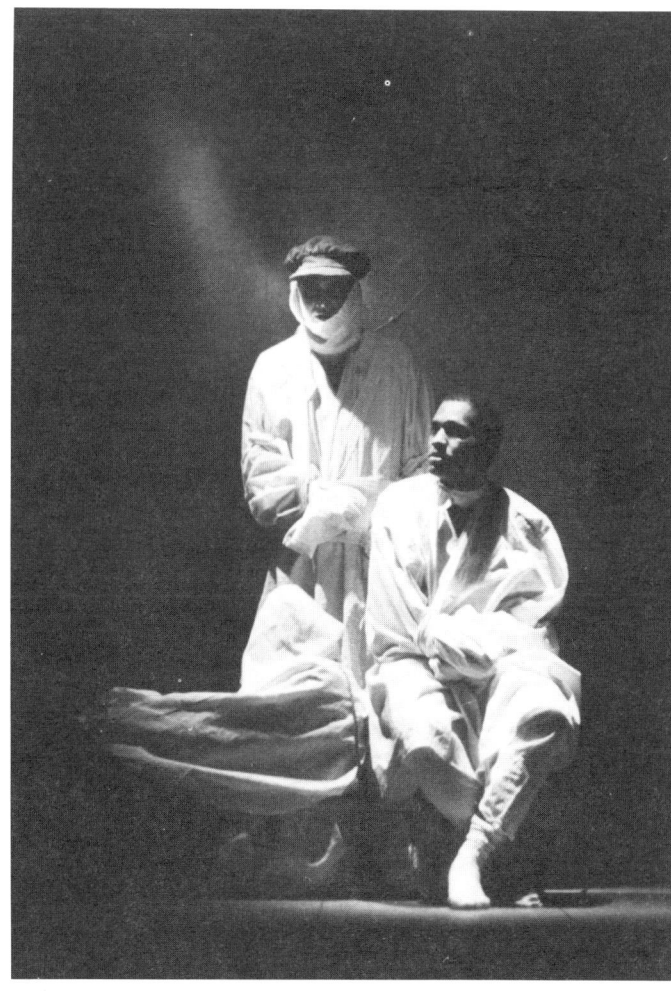

Northlight Theatre. Jack McLaughlin-Gray, Gary Houston and Brent Hendon in *The White Plague*. Photo: Mark Avery.

PRODUCTIONS 1987–88

Two, Ron Elisha; (D) Barbara Damashek; (S) Linda Buchanan; (C) Renee Liepins; (L) Rita Pietraszek
Three Postcards, Craig Lucas; music and lyrics: Craig Carnelia; (D) David Petrarca; (S) Gary Baugh; (C) Jordan Ross; (L) Robert Christen
The Marriage of Figaro, Pierre-Augustin Caron de Beaumarchais; trans: Richard Nelson; (D) Robert Berlinger; (S) Jeff Bauer; (C) Jessica Hahn; (L) Michael S. Philippi
The White Plague, Karel Capek; trans: Michael Henry Heim; (D) Gwen Arner; (S) Michael S. Philippi; (C) Jessica Hahn; (L) Michael S. Philippi
Feiffer's America, adapt: Russell Vandenbroucke, from Jules Feiffer; (D) Russell Vandenbroucke; (S) Jeff Bauer; (C) Ann Jaros; (L) Rita Pietraszek

PRODUCTIONS 1988–89

Talking to Myself, adapt: Paul Sills, from Studs Terkel; (D) Paul Sills; (S) Carol Bleackley; (C) Jessica Hahn; (L) Rita Pietraszek
Love Letters on Blue Paper, Arnold Wesker; (D) Russell Vandenbroucke; (S) Jeff Bauer; (C) Nan Cibula; (L) Robert Christen
Nothing Sacred, George F. Walker; (D) David Petrarca; (S) Michael S. Philippi; (C) Virgil C. Johnson; (L) Robert Christen
The Road to Mecca, Athol Fugard; (D) Thomas Bullard; (S) Linda Buchanan; (C) Renee Liepins; (L) Dennis Parichy
Pastel Refugees, book: Greg Fleming and Jeff Berkson; music and lyrics: Jeff Berkson; (D) Doug Finlayson; (S) Linda Buchanan; (C) Fran Maggio; (L) Ken Bowen

Oakland Ensemble Theatre

BENNY SATO AMBUSH
Producing Director

KERYL E. MCCORD
Managing Director

1428 Alice St., Suite 289
Oakland, CA 94612
(415) 763-7774 (bus.)
(415) 839-5510 (b.o.)

FOUNDED 1974
Ron Stacker Thompson

SEASON
Sept.-June

FACILITIES
Seating Capacity: 500
Stage: flexible

FINANCES
July 1, 1988-June 30, 1989
Expenses: $600,000

CONTRACTS
AEA SPT

Oakland Ensemble Theatre is committed to producing—through the sensibilities and world view of black Americans—insightful, engaging and substantive works of contemporary theatre that explore and illuminate the diverse issues, themes and human dilemmas of the New World experience called America. Steeped in the cultural expressions of black Americans, our voice speaks to an ethnically and culturally diverse audience reflective of Bay Area demographics. Our particular interest is to offer commentary and provide responsible points of view about both the achievements and the problems that emanate from the plural nature of America's national life, as seen from the perspective of black people. We believe in uplifting entertainment, with challenging, relevant ideas, that affirms and celebrates the beauty, strength, dignity and truth about black people and their struggles. We strive to provide theatre that enlightens the conditons and complexities of contemporary living, while conveying a useful understanding of ourselves for the shaping of a more informed, humane world.
—*Benny Sato Ambush*

PRODUCTIONS 1987–88

Ain't Misbehavin', conceived: Murray Horwitz and Richard Maltby, Jr.; music and lyrics: Fats Waller, et al.; (D) Tony Haney; (S) Ken Ellis; (C) Richard Battle; (L) Stephanie Johnson
Tamer of Horses, William Mastrosimone; (D) Benny Sato Ambush; (S) Gene Angell and Ron Pratt; (C) Callie Floor; (L) Kathy Pryzgoda
O. Henry's Christmas, Thomas Edward West; (D) Benny Sato Ambush; (S) Frederic Youens; (C) Suzanne Soxman Raftery; (L) Jeff Boyle

The Meeting, Jeff Stetson; (D) Keryl E. McCord; (S) Richard Battle; (C) Richard Battle; (L) Leslie Siegel

PRODUCTIONS 1988–89

Sisters, Marsha Jackson; (D) Tom Jones; (S) Pamela Peniston; (L) Stephanie Johnson
A Night at the Apollo, Brian Freeman; (D) Benny Sato Ambush; (S) Pamela Peniston; (C) Callie Floor; (L) Stephanie Johnson
Ain't No Use in Goin' Home, Jodie's Got Your Gal and Gone: Sayings from the Life and Writings of Junebug Jabbo Jones, Vol. III, John O'Neal, Nayo-Barbara Malcolm Watkins and Q.R. Hand, Jr.; (D) Steven Kent; (C) Judith Johnson; (L) Patrick Gill

Odyssey Theatre Ensemble

RON SOSSI
Artistic Director

NANCY MCFARLAND
Managing Director

2055 S. Sepulveda Blvd.
Los Angeles, CA 90025
(213) 826-1626

FOUNDED 1969
Ron Sossi

SEASON
Year-round

FACILITIES
Odyssey I
Seating Capacity: 99
Stage: proscenium

Odyssey II
Seating Capacity: 95
Stage: thrust

Odyssey III
Seating Capacity: 91
Stage: thrust

FINANCES
July 1, 1988-June 30, 1989
Expenses: $600,000

CONTRACTS
AEA 99-seat Theatre Plan

The Odyssey Theatre Ensemble's prime *raison d'être* is the production of a six-play mainstage season and a three-play Lab Season of exploration-oriented works drawn from contemporary, classical and original sources, with a strong leaning toward international work. Every Odyssey production is, in some important sense, an adventure in form—an attempt to push outward the boundaries of theatrical possibility. Year-by-year, more Odyssey-evolved work moves out into the larger theatre world. OTE's long-running world-premiere production of Steven Berkoff's *Kvetch* opened Off Broadway; the Home Box Office special based on the Odesssey's *The Chicago Conspiracy Trial* by Ron Sossi and Frank Condon received an ACE award; the Odyssey's *Tracers* by John DiFusco has enjoyed long runs throughout the U.S. and Europe; OTE's version of Elizabeth Swados and Garry Trudeau's *Rap Master Ronnie* enjoyed enormously successful productions (nationwide and in Toronto); *McCarthy*, last season's Odyssey premiere, will be directed at Milwaukee Rep by OTE associate artistic director Frank Condon. The Odyssey continues to build upon its reputation as one of California's leading experimental and process-oriented theatre.
—*Ron Sossi*

PRODUCTIONS 1987–88

Mensch Meier, Franz Xaver Kroetz; trans: Roger Downey; (D) Victor Brandt; (S) Gina Gambill; (C) Susan Braukis; (L) Gina Gambill
Boys and Girls and Men and Women, Gina Wendkos; (D) Gina Wendkos; (S) Eric Warren and Richard Ostroff; (C) Lisa Lovaas; (L) Dawn Hollingsworth
Hunger and Thirst, Eugene Ionesco; (D) Maurice Attias; (S) Ajax Daniels and Stephen Glassman; (C) Joyce Aysta; (L) Dawn Hollingsworth and Suzanne-Michele Northman
The Cage, Rick Cluchey; (D) Rick Cluchey; (S) Brandy Alexander
The Shoemakers, adapt: Kazimierz Braun, from Stanislaw I. Witkiewicz; (D) Kazimierz Braun; (S) Susan Lane; (C) Anna Ungar Herman; (L) Ann M. Archbold
Shakers, John Godber and Jane Thornton; (D) Ron Link; (S) Fred M. Duer; (C) Sivia

Oakland Ensemble Theatre. Gloria Weinstock and Mujahid Abdul Rashid in *Tamer of Horses*. Photo: Fred Speiser.

Odyssey Theatre Ensemble. Andrew Parks and Frances Bay in *Disability: A Comedy*.

Jahnsons; (L) Ann M. Archbold
Three Top Hats, Miguel Mihura; trans: Marcia Cobourn Wellwarth; (D) Ron Sossi; (S) Don Llewellyn; (C) Anne Reghi; (L) Dawn Hollingsworth and Suzanne-Michele Northman
Angry Housewives, book: A.M. Collins; music and lyrics: Chad Henry; (D) David Galligan; (S) Deborah Raymond and Dorian Vernacchiio; (C) Bonnie Stauch; (L) Michael Gilliam
McCarthy, Jeff Goldsmith; (D) Frank Condon; (S) Christa Bartels; (C) Martha Ferrara; (L) Doc Ballard
Flights of Fear and Fancy, Kedrick Robin Wolfe; (D) Scott Kelman
Spring Awakening, Frank Wedekind; trans: Rick Foster; (D) Michael Arabian; (S) Don Llewellyn and Saeed Hedjazi; (C) Betty Berbe; (L) Marianne Schneller

PRODUCTIONS 1988–89

Lady Day, Stephen Stahl; (D) Stephen Stahl; (S) Nancy Eisenman; (C) Nancy Butts; (L) Pieter Smit
Idioglossia, Mark Handley; (D) Ron Sossi; (S) Saeed Hedjazi; (C) Lindsay C. Stewart; (L) Kathi O'Donohue
Symmes' Hole, book and lyrics: Randy Dreyfuss; (D) Carol Corwen; (S) Don Llewellyn; (C) Neal San Teguns; (L) Doc Ballard
Disability: A Comedy, Ron Whyte; (D) Frank Condon; (S) Christa Bartels; (C) Martha Ferrara; (L) Doc Ballard

The Old Creamery Theatre Company

THOMAS P. JOHNSON
Producing Director

MERRITT OLSEN
Associate Producing Director

Company Box 160
Garrison, IA 52229
(319) 477-3925 (bus.)
(319) 477-3165 (b.o.)

FOUNDED 1971
David Berendes, Rita Davis, Mick Denniston, Judy Johnson, Thomas P. Johnson, Steve Kock, Merritt Olsen, Ann Olson, David Olsen, Erica Zaffarano

SEASON
May-Oct.

FACILITIES
Main Stage
Seating Capacity: 260
Stage: thrust

Brenton Stage
Seating Capacity: 130
Stage: proscenium

Amana Visitors Center
Seating Capacity: 260
Stage: proscenium

FINANCES
Jan. 1, 1987-Dec. 31, 1988
Expenses: $590,500

CONTRACTS
AEA SPT

The simple mission of the Old Creamery Theatre Company is to bring theatre of the highest possible quality to the largest possible audience in the rural Midwest. In pursuing this goal the company produces a 156-performance resident season in Garrison, maintains an extensive touring program to rural communities, and has established performance centers on four college campuses in various parts of Iowa. A major objective is the encouragement of developing artists through various internship programs in performance, playwriting and technical theatre. The main element of our artistic vision is to find ways of making all types of theatre palatable to an inexperienced theatre audience by offering a "menu" of theatrical choices. By providing various kinds of fare, the company hopes to broaden its audience base while broadening the tastes of that audience.

—*Thomas P. Johnson*

PRODUCTIONS 1987–88

Warriors of the Mystic Word, company-developed; (D) Thomas P. Johnson
The Cotton Patch Gospel, book: Tom Key and Russell Treyz; music and lyrics: Harry Chapin; (D) Thomas P. Johnson
Extremities, William Mastrosimone; (D) Blaine Stephens
Brighton Beach Memoirs, Neil Simon; (D) Thomas P. Johnson
The Nerd, Larry Shue; (D) Blaine Stephens
The Dining Room, A.R. Gruney, Jr.; (D) Blaine Stephens
The Amorous Flea, Jerry Devine; (D) Thomas P. Johnson
Screw Loose, company-developed

The Old Creamery Theatre Company. Fred Goudy and Ron Tolliver in *The Amorous Flea*.
Photo: Robert A. Lippert.

(D) Blaine Stephens
Theatre in Your Lap, company-developed; (D) Thomas P. Johnson

PRODUCTIONS 1988–89

A Bedfull of Foreigners, Dave Freeman; (D) Richard Lee
I'm Not Rappaport, Herb Gardner; (D) Ron Himes
Pump Boys and Dinettes, John Foley, Mark Hardwick, Debra Monk, Cass Morgan, John Schimmel and Jim Wann; (D) Debra Wicks
Key for Two, John Chapman and Dave Freeman; (D) Richard Lee
A Gentleman and a Scoundrel, Jack Sharkey; (D) Thomas P. Johnson
Playing Doctor, Thomas P. Johnson and Mick Denniston; (D) Mick Denniston
BlueGhost Two-Zero, Bob Drury; (D) Bob Drury
The Boys Next Door, Tom Griffin; (D) Thomas P. Johnson
Billy Bishop Goes to War, John Gray and Eric Peterson; (D) Thomas P. Johnson

Old Globe Theatre

JACK O'BRIEN
Artistic Director

CRAIG NOEL
Executive Director

TOM HALL
Managing Director

Box 2171
San Diego, CA 92112
(619) 231-1941 (bus.)
(619) 239-2255 (b.o.)

FOUNDED 1937
Community members

SEASON
Jan.-Oct.

FACILITIES
Old Globe Theatre
Seating Capacity: 581
Stage: flexible

Lowell Davies Festival Theatre
Seating Capacity: 612
Stage: thrust

Cassius Carter Centre Stage
Seating Capacity: 225
Stage: arena

FINANCES
Nov. 1, 1987-Oct. 31, 1988
Expenses: $7,400,000

CONTRACTS
LORT (B), (B+) and (C)

I believe the network of regional theatres is in transition, moving toward its inevitable emergence as the American National Theatre. The Old Globe Theatre, a bastion of the craft, skill and technique, has kept the classical tradition flourishing in Southern California for 52 years. From the vantage point of this tradition, we offer remarkable venues to writers and artists who formerly flocked to New York for exposure and artistic freedom. Across this country, over the last decade or so, our ability to articulate the classics has shrunk in direct proportion to the influence of film and television, but the Globe still offers an opportunity to actors, directors and designers to stretch their talents and add to their skills in a healthy, competitive market alongside the literature that has sustained theatre for hundreds of years. By juxtaposing the contemporary and the classical we offer audiences the most vigorous, comprehensive theatre experience possible, and we have a wonderful time doing it.
-Jack O'Brien

PRODUCTIONS 1987–88

The Boiler Room, Reuben Gonzalas; (D) Craig Noel; (S) Kent Dorsey; (C) Frank O. Bowers; (L) Kent Dorsey
The Voice of the Prairie, John Olive; (D) Thomas Bullard; (S) Karen Gerson; (C) Karen Gerson; (L) Wendy Heffner
Tea, Velina Hasu Houston; (D) Julianne Boyd; (S) Cliff Faulkner; (C) C.L. Hundley; (L) Peter Maradudin
Holiday, Philip Barry; (D) Jack O'Brien; (S) William Bloodgood; (C) Robert Wojewodski; (L) Robert Peterson
Joe Turner's Come and Gone, August Wilson; (D) Lloyd Richards; (S) Scott Bradley; (C) Pamela Peterson; (L) Michael Giannitti
Suds: The Rocking '60s Musical Soap Opera, Melinda Gilb, Steve Gunderson and Bryan Scott; (D) Will Robertson; (S) Alan K. Okazaki; (C) Gregg Barnes; (L) Daniel J. Corson
Timon of Athens, William Shakespeare; (D) Robert Berlinger; (S) Cliff Faulkner; (C) Robert Wojewodski; (L) Wendy Heffner
Love's Labour's Lost, William Shakespeare; (D) Craig Noel; (S) Richard Seger; (C) Richard Seger; (L) Robert Peterson
White Linen, Stephen Metcalfe; (D) Jack O'Brien; (S) Douglas W. Schmidt; (C) Steven Rubin; (L) Robert Peterson
The Cocktail Hour, A.R. Gurney, Jr.; (D) Jack O'Brien; (S) Steven Rubin; (C) Steven Rubin; (L) Kent Dorsey
Coriolanus, William Shakespeare; (D) John Hirsch; (S) David Jenkins; (C) Lewis Brown; (L) Lewis Brown
Rumors, Neil Simon; (D) Gene Saks; (S) Tony Straiges; (C) Joseph G. Aulisi; (L) Tharon Musser
Jeeves Takes Charge, adapt:

Old Globe Theatre. Chuck Cooper and Byron Jennings in *Coriolanus*. Photo: Will Gullette.

Edward Duke, from P.G. Wodehouse; (D) Edward Duke; (S) Cliff Faulkner; (C) Rosemary Bengele; (L) Wendy Heffner

PRODUCTIONS 1988–89

Alfred Stieglitz Loves O'Keefe, Lanie Robertson; (D) Robert Berlinger; (S) Hugh Landwehr; (C) Christina Haatainen; (L) Peter Maradudin
The Road to Mecca, Athol Fugard; (D) Craig Noel; (S) Joel Fontaine; (C) Joel Fontaine; (L) Barth Ballard
A... My Name Is Alice, Joan Micklin Silver and Julianne Boyd; (D) Julianne Boyd; (S) Cliff Faulkner; (C) Shigeru Yaji; (L) John Forbes
Blood Wedding, Frederica Garcia Lorca; trans: Michael Dewell and Carmen Zapata; (D) Gerald Freedman and Graciela Daniele; (S) John Ezell; (C) Jeanne Button; (L) Peggy Eisenhauer
Romance/Romance, book and lyrics: Barry Harman; music: Keith Herrmann; (D) Barry

Harman; (s) Steven Rubin; (c) Steven Rubin; (l) Craig Miller
Up in Saratoga, Terrence McNally; (d) Jack O'Brien; (s) Douglas W. Schmidt; (c) Robert Wojewodski; (l) David F. Segal
The Piano Lesson, August Wilson; (d) Lloyd Richards; (s) E. David Cosier, Jr.; (c) Constanza Romero; (l) Christopher Akerlind
Romeo and Juliet, William Shakespeare; (d) Richard E.T. White; (s) Steven Rubin; (c) Steven Rubin; (l) Robert Peterson
Driving Miss Daisy, Alfred Uhry; (d) Jack O'Brien; (s) Ralph Funicello; (c) Steven Rubin; (l) Peter Maradudin
Waiting for Godot, Samuel Beckett; (d) Andrew J. Traister; (s) Cliff Faulkner; (c) Shigeru Yaji; (l) John Forbes
The School for Scandal, Richard Brinsley Sheridan; (d) Craig Noel; (s) Steve Rubin; (c) Robert Wojewodski; (l) Robert Peterson
Measure for Measure, William Shakespeare; (d) Adrian Hall; (s) Ralph Funicello; (c) Lewis Brown; (l) Peter Maradudin
Breaking Legs, Tom Dulack; (d) Jack O'Brien; (s) Cliff Faulkner; (c) Robert Wojewodski; (l) John Forbes

Omaha Magic Theatre

JO ANN SCHMIDMAN
Artistic Director

2309 Hanscom Blvd.
Omaha, NE 68105
(402) 346-1227

FOUNDED 1968
Jo Ann Schmidman

SEASON
Year-round

FACILITIES
Seating Capacity: 93
Stage: flexible

FINANCES
June 1, 1988-May 31, 1989
Expenses: $203,880

Living Sculpture. Breathing Words. Fresh Committed Performance. New Music. Resounding Installations. These words describe our work. Our theatre is a mix of words, visual image, performer/artist-created object interaction and music pulsing together into audience consciousness. Now entering our 21st year, the Omaha Magic Theatre is one of America's longest-lived alternative theatres. We produce visually charged, aurally intense, vital, engaging and entertaining performance experiences. We work to impact, impassion and provide an active forum for nurturing audiences in this otherwise passive world. We publish our work and tour, five of our creations are currently being produced by other theatres.
—*Jo Ann Schmidman*

PRODUCTIONS 1987–88

Dinner's in the Blender, book and lyrics: Megan Terry; music: Joe Budenholzer and John J. Sheehan; (d) Jo Ann Schmidman; (s) Diane Ostdiek and Colin Smith; (c) Jo Ann Schmidman; (l) Jim Schumacher
Scar, Murray Mednick; (d) Jo Ann Schmidman and Amy Harmon; (s) Diane Degan; (c) Jo Ann Schmidman; (l) Jim Schumacher
Tenure Track, Joanna Kraus and Greer Woodward; (d) Jo Ann Schmidman and Amy Harmon; (s) Diane Degan; (c) Jo Ann Schmidman; (l) Jim Schumacher
The Progressive Examinations, David Brink; (d) Jo Ann Schmidman and Amy Harmon; (s) Diane Degan; (c) Jo Ann Schmidman; (l) Jim Schumacher
One Person, Robert Patrick; (d) Jo Ann Schmidman; (s) Diane Degan; (c) Jo Ann Schmidman; (l) Jim Schumacher
Chicago, Sam Shepard; (d) Jo Ann Schmidman; (s) Diane Degan; (c) Jo Ann Schmidman; (l) Jim Schumacher
Istanboul, Rochelle Owens; (d) Jo Ann Schmidman; (s) Diane Degan; (c) Jo Ann Schmidman; (l) Jim Schumacher
Jenna's Edge, Laura Cosentino; (d) Jo Ann Schmidman; (s) Diane Degan; (c) Jo Ann Schmidman; (l) Jim Schumacher
David's Red Haired Death, Sherry Kramer; (d) Jo Ann Schmidman; (s) Diane Degan; (c) Jo Ann Schmidman; (l) Jim Schumacher
Sea of Forms, book and lyrics: Megan Terry and Jo Ann Schmidman; music: Joe Budenholzer and John J. Sheehan, Mark Nelson and Ivy Dow; (d) Jo Ann Schmidman; (s) Bill Farmer; (c) Kenda Slavin; (l) Jim Schmacher
Walking Through Walls, book and lyrics: Megan Terry and Jo Ann Schmidman; music: Bill Farber, Mark Nelson and John J. Sheehan; (d) Jo Ann Schmidman; (s) Bill Farmer and Sora Kim; (c) Megan Terry; (l) Chuck St. Lucas
Why Hanna's Skirt Won't Stay Down, Tom Eyen; (d) Jo Ann Schmidman and Ostdiek Diane; (s) Bill Farmer and Sora Kim; (c) Jo Ann Schmidman and Sora Kim; (l) . company
Classics, Carol Flint; (d) Jo Ann Schmidman and Sheehan J. John; (s) Bill Farmer and Sora Kim; (c) Jo Ann Schmidman and Sora Kim; (l) company
Consequence, Kat Smith; (d) Jo Ann Schmidman and Sheehan J. John; (s) Bill Farmer and Sora Kim; (c) Jo Ann Schmidman; (l) company
The Function, Jean-Marie Besset; (d) Jo Ann Schmidman; (s) Bill Farmer and Sora Kim; (c) Jo Ann Schmidman and Sora Kim; (l) company
The Hunter and the Bird, Jean-Claude van Itallie; (d) Jo Ann Schmidman; (s) Bill Farmer and Sora Kim; (c) Megan Terry; (l) company
Amtrak, Megan Terry; (d) Jo Ann Schmidman; (s) Bill Farmer and Sora Kim; (c) Megan Terry; (l) company

Omaha Magic Theatre, *Headlights*. Photo: Megan Terry.

New Age Romance, Lisa Loomer; (d) Jo Ann Schmidman; (s) Bill Farmer and Sora Kim; (c) Jo Ann Schmidman and Sora Kim; (l) company
Kitchenette, Ronald Tavel; (d) Jo Ann Schmidman; (s) Bill Farmer and Sora Kim; (c) Jo Ann Schmidman and Sora Kim; (l) company
And Baby Makes Seven, Paula Vogel; (d) Jo Ann Schmidman; (s) Bill Farmer and Sora Kim; (c) Jo Ann Schmidman and Sora Kim; (l) company
The Birth of Limbo Dancing, Catherine Berg; (d) Jo Ann Schmidman; (s) Bill Farmer and Sora Kim; (c) Jo Ann Schmidman and Sora Kim; (l) company
The Bed Was Full, Rosalyn Drexler; (d) Jo Ann Schmidman; (s) Bill Farmer and Sora Kim; (c) Jo Ann Schmidman and Sora Kim; (l) company
Night Club (Bubi's Hide-Away), Ken Bernard; (d) Jo Ann Schmidman; (s) Bill Farmer and Sora Kim; (c) Jo Ann Schmidman and Sora Kim; (l) company

PRODUCTIONS 1988–89

Babies Unchained, book and lyrics: Megan Terry and Jo Ann Schmidman; lyrics: Keri Kripal; music: John J. Sheehan; (d) Jo Ann Schmidman; (s) Sora Kim and Bill Farmer; (c) Sora Kim; (l) Margaret Mara
My Foetus Lived on Amboy Street, Ronald Tavel; (d) Jo Ann Schmidman; (s) Sora Kim and Jo Ann Schmidman; (c) Jo Ann Schmidman and Sora Kim; (l) Matt Irvin
Alarms, Susan Yankowitz; (d) Jo

Ann Schmidman; (s) Sora Kim and Jo Ann Schmidman; (c) Jo Ann Schmidman and Sora Kim; (L) Matt Irvin
Three Front, Rochelle Owens; (D) Jo Ann Schmidman; (s) Sora Kim and Jo Ann Schmidman; (c) Megan Terry; (L) Matt Irvin
The Heart That Eats Itself, Rosalyn Drexler; (D) Jo Ann Schmidman; (s) Sora Kim and Jo Ann Schmidman; (c) Jo Ann Schmidman and Sora Kim; (L) Matt Irvin
Headlights, book and lyrics: Megan Terry; music: Frank Fong, Rex Gray, Rick Hiatt, Lori Loree, Mark Nelson and Luigi Waites; (D) Jo Ann Schmidman; (s) Sora Kim and Bill Farmer; (c) Kenda Slavin; (L) Jo Ann Schmidman
Lucy Loves Me, Migdalia Cruz; (D) Jo Ann Schmidman; (s) Sora Kim; (c) Jo Ann Schmidman and Sora Kim; (L) Jim Schumacher
Angel Face, Laura Harrington; (D) Jo Ann Schmidman; (s) Sora Kim; (c) Megan Terry; (L) Jim Schumacher
Cut, Terra Daugirda Pressler; (D) Jo Ann Schmidman; (s) Sora Kim; (c) Megan Terry; (L) Jim Schumacher

O'Neill Theater Center

GEORGE C. WHITE
President

LLOYD RICHARDS
Artistic Director, National Playwrights Conference

PAULETTE HAUPT
Artistic Director, National Music Theater Conference

SYLVIA S. TRAEGER
Managing Director

305 Great Neck Rd.
Waterford, CT 06385
(203) 443-5378 (bus.)
(203) 443-1238 (b.o.)

234 W. 44th St.
New York, NY 10036
(212) 382-2790 (bus.)

FOUNDED 1964
George C. White

SEASON
July-Aug.

FACILITIES
Margo and Rufus Rose Barn
Seating Capacity: 200
Stage: flexible

Instant Theater
Seating Capacity: 200
Stage: arena

Amphitheater
Seating Capacity: 300
Stage: thrust

FINANCES
Sept. 1, 1988-Aug. 31, 1989
Expenses: $2,800,000

CONTRACTS
LORT D

The Eugene O'Neill Memorial Theater Center is a collection of allied programs including Creative Arts in Education, Monte Cristo Cottage Museum and Library, National Critics Institute, National Opera/Music Theater Conference, National Playwrights Conference, National Theater Institute, and The American Soviet Theater Initiative, united to foster theatre via exploration, development, training, promotion, conservation and utilization of all aspects of the art form. Named for America's only Nobel Prize-winning playwright, the O'Neill Center pays homage to his memory by initiating and harboring projects of value to the theatre; challenging existing theatrical "truths"; creating an environment for experimentation, deliberation and examination; providing a venue for national and international theatrical interaction, discussion and exchange; and protecting and preserving our native theatrical heritage.
—Lloyd Richards

PRODUCTIONS 1987–88

National Playwrights Conference:
Demon Wine, Thomas Babe; (D) Gitta Honegger; (s) G. W. Mercier; (L) Tina Charney
Gas, Robert Berger; (D) Gitta Honegger; (s) G.W. Mercier; (L) Tina Charney
The Hill-Matheson Affair, Robert Clyman; (D) Gordon Rigsby; (s) Charles H. McClennahan; (L) Tina Charney
Starting Monday, Anne Commire; (D) Amy Saltz; (s) G.W. Mercier; (L) Tina Charney
The Beach, Anthony Giardina; (D) William Partlan; (s) G.W. Mercier; (L) Tina Charney
To My Loving Son, Nancy Gilsenan; (D) Luis Soto; (s) Charles H. McClennahan; (L) Tina Charney
Birdsend, Keith Huff; (D) William Partlan; (s) G.W. Mercier; (L) Tina Charney
Brother Champ, Michael Kassin; (D) Amy Saltz; (s) G. W. Mercier; (L) Tina Charney
Black Holes, Leslie Lyles; (D) Luis Soto; (s) Charles H. McClennahan; (L) Tina Charney
Suffering Fools, Douglas Post; (D) Amy Saltz; (s) G.W. Mercier; (L) Tina Charney
Forgiving Typhoid Mary, Mark St. Germain; (D) Walton Jones; (s) G.W. Mercier; (L) Tina Charney
And the Men Shall Also Gather, Jeffrey Stetson; (D) Dennis Scott; (s) G. W. Mercier; (L) Tina Charney
Sodbusters, Craig Volk; (D) Dennis Scott; (s) G. W. Mercier; (L) Tina Charney
A Slice of Pie, Jeff Wanshel; (D) Walton Jones; (s) G. W. Mercier; (L) Tina Charney
Interrogating the Nude, Doug Wright; (D) Gitta Honegger; (s) G. W. Mercier; (L) Tina Charney

National Music Theater Conference:
Under the Double Moon, book: Deborah Atherton; music:

O'Neill Theater Center. Linda Hunt in a staged reading of *Forgiving Typhoid Mary*. Photo: Vincent Scarano.

Anthony Davis; (D) Rhoda Levine
A Vision, book, music and lyrics: Thomas F. Megan; (D) Leon Major
Swamp Gas and Shallow Feelings, book: Shirlee Strother; book, music and lyrics: Jack Eric Williams; (D) Peter Mark Schifter

PRODUCTIONS 1988–89

National Playwrights Conference
Ready for the River, Neal Bell; (D) William Partlan; (S) G. W. Mercier; (L) Tina Charney
Gulliver, Lonnie Carter; (D) Dennis Scott; (S) G. W. Mercier; (L) Tina Charney
Daylight in Exile, James D'Entremont; (D) Gitta Honegger; (S) G. W. Mercier; (L) Tina Charney
Mapping Uranium, Annie Evans; (D) Amy Saltz; (S) G.W. Mercier; (L) Tina Charney
The Confessions of Franklin Thompson, III, Kermit Frazier; (D) Gitta Honegger; (S) G.W. Mercier; (L) Tina Charney
Rattan, Jeffrey Hatcher; (D) Gordon Rigsby
Have You Seen Road Smith?, Willy Holtzman; (D) Roger Hendricks Simon; (S) Charles H. McClennahan
Mud People, Keith Huff; (D) Megs Booker; (S) G. W. Mercier; (L) Tina Charney
The Cottage, Yuri Knyazev; (S) G. W. Mercier; (L) Tina Charney
Songs Without Words, Jonathan Levy; (D) William Partlan; (S) G. W. Mercier; (L) Tina Charney
Earth and Sky, Douglas Post; (D) Megs Booker; (S) G.W. Mercier; (L) Tina Charney
Heaven and Earth, Robert Schenkkan; (D) William Partlan; (S) G. W. Mercier; (L) Tina Charney
Rust and Ruin, William Snowden; (D) Amy Saltz; (S) G. W. Mercier; (L) Tina Charney

National Music Theater Conference
That Pig of a Molette, book: Sheldon Harnick; music: Thomas Z. Shepard;
Gun Metal Blues, book: Scott Wentworth; music: Craig Bohmler; lyrics: Marion Adler;
Hannah ... 1939, book, music and lyrics: Robert Merrill; *The Real Life Story of Johnny De Facto*, book, music and lyrics: Douglas Post;

Ontological-Hysteric Theater

RICHARD FOREMAN
Artistic Director

GEORGE ASHLEY
Managing Director

c/o Performing Artservices
105 Hudson St.,-Room 200
New York, NY 10013
212-941-8911

FOUNDED 1968
Richard Foreman

SEASON
Year-round

FINANCES
July 1, 1988-June 30, 1989
Expenses: $150,000

Since 1968 I have evolved my own, idiosyncratic theatre language, which is nevertheless applicable to many different moods, subjects and settings. I attempt to stretch the employment of that language further each year, which in itself seems self-evident. But, more important, I try to build into my plays secret reflections upon the inevitable failure involved in pursuing such a goal.
—*Richard Foreman*

PRODUCTIONS 1987–88

Symphony of Rats, Richard Foreman; (D) Richard Foreman; (S) Richard Foreman; (C) Richard Foreman; (L) Richard Foreman
What Did He See?, Richard Foreman; (D) Richard Foreman; (S) Richard Foreman; (C) Richard Foreman; (L) Richard Foreman

PRODUCTIONS 1988–89

Love and Science, Richard Foreman; (D) Richard Foreman; (S) Richard Foreman; (C) Richard Foreman; (L) Richard Foreman

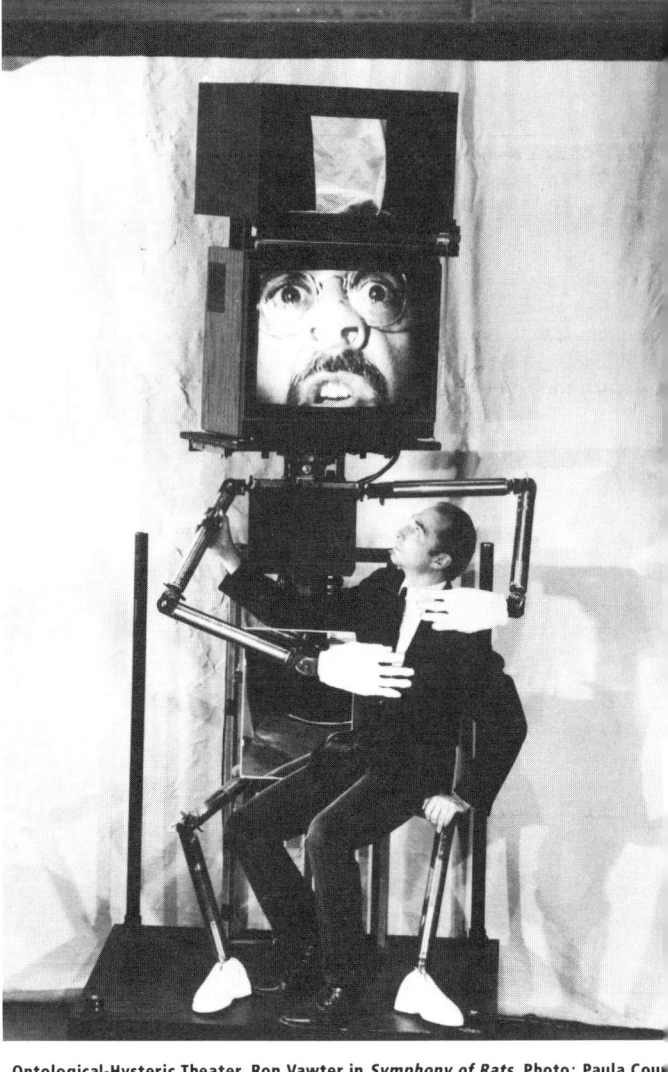

Ontological-Hysteric Theater. Ron Vawter in *Symphony of Rats*. Photo: Paula Cou[...]

The Open Eye: New Stagings

AMIE BROCKWAY
Artistic Director

ADRIENNE J. BROCKWAY
Production/Business Manager

270 West 89th St.
New York, NY 10024
(212) 769-4141 (bus.)
(212) 769-4143 (b.o.)

FOUNDED 1972
Jean Erdman, Joseph Campbell

SEASON
Oct.-June

FACILITIES
Seating Capacity: 104
Stage: proscenium

FINANCES
July 1, 1988-June 30, 1989
Expenses: $335,000

CONTRACTS
AEA letter of agreement

In 1986 we changed our name to The Open Eye: New Stagings to reflect the work we do with new plays and adaptations from classic literature. New Stagings continue the Theater of the Open Eye's commitment to a more theatrical rather than naturalistic—production style that emphasizes the actor-audience relationship. Many plays selected have a mythological quality and incorporate liv[e] music and dance. In 1987 we inaugurated NEW STAGINGS FOR YOUTH, a multi-ethnic ensemble which develops and performs ne[w] plays and adaptations from the classics, specifically for young pe[o]ple and their families. These

oductions are designed for touring as well as performance in our
 n space. Another vital program
 the NEW STAGINGS LAB,
 nich offers opportunities for de-
 lopment of emerging directors
 d playwrights through a program
 rehearsed readings and work-
 op productions.
—*Amie Brockway*

RODUCTIONS 1987–88

 w Stagings for Youth
Circle on the Cross, Thomas
  Cadwaleder Jones; (D) Amie
  Brockway; (S) Adrienne J.
  Brockway; (L) Spencer Mosse
 e *Nightingale*, adapt: William
  Electric Black, from Hans
  Christian Andersen; (D) Gary
  Pollard; (S) Adrienne J.
  Brockway; (C) Adrienne J.
  Brockway
 e *Odyssey*, adapt: Amie
  Brockway, from Homer;
  (D) Amie Brockway;
  (S) Adrienne J. Brockway;
  (C) Adrienne J. Brockway
Folk Tale Quartet, adapt:
  William Electric Black;
  (D) Peter Coy; (S) Adrienne J.
  Brockway; (C) Adrienne J.
  Brockway

 e on Directors
 riah, August Strindberg;
  (D) Donald Brenner

The Unwilling Recruit, adapt:
  Michelle Frenzer Cornell, from
  commedia dell'arte; (D) Michelle
  Frenzer Cornell
Off the Meter, Peter Zablotsky;
  (D) Peter Coy
Daughter of a Soldier, Richard
  Galgano and David Sinkler;
  (D) Richard Galgano
The Bespoke Overcoat, Wolf
  Mankowitz; (D) Lorna Littleway
Asleep on the Wind, Ellen Byron;
  (D) Jeff Mousseau
Hattie's Dress, Walt Vail;
  (D) Gary Pollard
Off to Vegas in a Custom Car,
  Thomas Cadwaleder Jones;
  (D) Kim T. Sharp
The Travelling Man, Lady
  Gregory; (D) Nan Siegmund

PRODUCTIONS 1988–89

Angalak, Walt Vail; (D) Amie
  Brockway; (S) Adrienne J.
  Brockway; (L) Spencer Mosse
The Wall Inside, Thomas
  Cadwaleder Jones; (D) Kim T.
  Sharp; (S) Adrienne J. Brockway;
  (L) Don Gingrasso
A Cricket on the Hearth, adapt:
  Amie Brockway, from Charles
  Dickens; (D) Kim T. Sharp;
  (S) Adrienne J. Brockway
The Odyssey, adapt: Amie
  Brockway, from Homer;
  (D) Amie Brockway;
  (S) Adrienne J. Brockway
A Folk Tale Quartet, adapt:
  William Electric Black;
  (D) Ernest Johns; (S) Adrienne J.
  Brockway
Souvenirs of Old New-York,
  Amie Brockway, Sandra Fenichel
  Asher, Alice Elliot, Tony
  Howarth and Walt Vail;
  (D) Amie Brockway;
  (S) Adrienne J. Brockway

Eye on Directors Festival
The Stronger, August Strindberg;
  trans: Harry G. Carlson;
  (D) Michelle Frenzer Cornell
Fugue in 30 Minutes Flat, Jameel
  Khaja and Doug LaBrecque;
  music: Max Risenhoover;
  (D) Jameel Khaja
The Sicilian or Love the Painter,
  Moliere; trans: John Wood;
  (D) Rebecca Kreinen
Waiting for Lepke, Walt Vail;
  (D) David M. Nevarrez
Kathleen Ni Houlihan, William
  Butler Yeats; (D) Barbara L.
  Rice
Womanchild, Melissa Carey;
  (D) Kim T. Sharp
Bags, Anne McGravie; (D) Nan
  Siegmund
Baby Talk, Chris Glaza Knudsen;
  (D) Sharone Stacy
*The Blind One-armed Deaf
  Mute*, T.S. Gueullete; trans:
  Daniel Gerould; (D) Sherry
  Teitelbaum
Giles in Love, Jan Potocki; trans:
  Daniel Gerould; (D) Sherry
  Teitelbaum

e Open Eye: New Stagings. Oni Faida Lampley and Dan Tubb in *The Wall Inside*.
 oto: Ken Howard.

Oregon Shakespeare Festival

JERRY TURNER
Artistic Director

WILLIAM W. PATTON
Executive Director

DENNIS BIGELOW
Producer, OSF-Portland

Box 158
Ashland, OR 97520
(503) 482-2111 (bus.)
(503) 482-4331 (b.o.)

Box 9008
Portland, OR 97207
(503) 248-6309 (bus.)
(503) 248-4496 (b.o.)

FOUNDED 1935
Angus Bowmer

SEASON
Nov.-Apr.

FACILITIES
Angus Bowmer Theatre
Seating Capacity: 600
Stage: modified thrust

Elizabethan Stage
Seating Capacity: 1,200
Stage: Outdoor

Black Swan Theatre
Seating Capacity: 140
Stage: flexible

OSF Portland Center Stage
Seating Capacity: 657
Stage: proscenium

FINANCES
Jan. 1, 1988-Dec. 31, 1988
Expenses: $7,557,202

CONTRACTS
LORT (B) and AEA SPT

The Oregon Shakespeare Festival operates four theatres in two sites: Portland and Ashland. Most members of the Ashland company work on long-term (10-month) contracts in rotating repertory, producing plays of high literary stature—ancient and modern, classic and contemporary—that have special resonances in our time. Style is dictated primarily by respect for the text, but also by the talent and sensibilities of the artists and the taste and experience of the audience. We serve a large, broad-based audience of disparate backgrounds and interests, but are dedicated uncompromisingly to quality both of text and production. We intend to be bold, innovative and demanding, but we also seek clarity, accessibility and vividness. Shakespeare's work has a special place in our repertoire, not as an icon but representative of a constantly renewable freshness and dramatic power. We aim, in all our work, for the same combination of continuity and immediacy found in the classics.
—*Jerry Turner*

PRODUCTIONS 1987–88

Romeo and Juliet, William
  Shakespeare; (D) Henry
  Woronicz; (S) William
  Bloodgood; (C) Michael Olich;
  (L) Robert Peterson
Boy Meets Girl, Bella Spewack

Oregon Shakespeare Festival. Paul Vincent O'Connor and Matthew Davis in *Henry IV, Part Two*. Photo: Christopher Briscoe.

and Samuel Spewack; (D) Pat Patton; (S) Richard L. Hay; (C) Claudia Everett; (L) James Sale
A Penny for a Song, John Whiting; (D) Craig Latrell; (S) William Bloodgood; (C) Jeannie Davidson; (L) James Sale
Enrico IV, Luigi Pirandello; trans: Robert Cornthwaite; (D) Libby Appel; (S) William Bloodgood; (C) Jeannie Davidson; (L) Robert Peterson
The Iceman Cometh, Eugene O'Neill; (D) Jerry Turner; (S) John Dexter; (C) Jeannie Davidson; (L) James Sale
The Marriage of Bette and Boo, Christopher Durang; (D) Michael Kevin; (S) Richard L. Hay; (C) Jeannie Davidson; (L) Robert Peterson
Ghosts, Henrik Ibsen; trans: Jerry Turne; (D) Jerry Turner; (S) Michael Miller; (C) Michael Olich; (L) Robert Peterson
Orphans, Lyle Kessler; (D) Dennis Bigelow; (S) William Bloodgood; (C) Candice Cain; (L) Robert Peterson
Henry IV, Part 1, William Shakespeare; (D) Pat Patton; (S) William Bloodgood; (C) Sarah Nash Gates; (L) James Sale
Love's Labour's Lost, William Shakespeare; (D) James Edmundson; (S) Richard L. Hay; (C) Deborah Dryden; (L) James Sale
Twelfth Night, William Shakespeare; (D) Bill Cain; (S) Vicki Smith; (C) Jeannie Davidson; (L) James Sale

PRODUCTIONS 1988–89

Cyrano de Bergerac, Edmond Rostand; trans: Anthony Burgess; (D) James Edmondson; (S) William Bloodgood; (C) Deborah Dryden; (L) Robert Peterson
All My Sons, Arthur Miller; (D) Philip Killian; (S) William Bloodgood; (C) Jeannie Davidson; (L) Robert Peterson
And a Nightingale Sang . . . , Cecil P. Taylor; (D) Warner Shook; (S) Richard L. Hay; (C) Frances Kenney; (L) James Sale
Pericles, Prince of Tyre, William Shakespeare; (D) Jerry Turner and Dennis Bigelow; (S) Richard L. Hay; (C) Jeannie Davidson; (L) Robert Peterson
Breaking the Silence, Stephen Poliakoff; (D) Libby Appel; (S) William Bloodgood; (C) Jeannie Davidson; (L) Robert Peterson
Hunting Cockroaches, Janusz Glowacki; trans: Jadwiga Kosicka; (D) Pat Patton; (S) Michael Miller; (C) Deborah Trout; (L) James Sale
Not About Heroes, Stephen McDonald; (D) Kathryn Long; (S) Vicki Smith; (C) Carole Wheeldon; (L) Rick Paulsen
The Road to Mecca, Athol Fugard; (D) Jerry Turner; (S) William Bloodgood; (C) Jeannie Davidson; (L) Robert Peterson
Much Ado About Nothing, William Shakespeare; (D) Pat Patton; (S) John Dexter; (C) Michael Olich; (L) James Sale
Henry IV, Part 2, William Shakespeare; (D) Henry Woronicz; (S) Richard L. Hay; (C) Jeannie Davidson; (L) Robert Peterson
The Two Gentlemen of Verona, William Shakespeare; (D) Bill Cain; (S) William Bloodgood; (C) Jeannie Davidson; (L) James Sale
Heartbreak House, George Bernard Shaw; (D) Jerry Turner; (S) William Bloodgood; (C) Debroah Dryden; (L) James Sale
Steel Magnolias, Robert Harling; (D) Dennis Bigelow; (S) Vicki Smith; (C) Deborah Bruneaux; (L) James Sale
The Miser, Moliere; trans: Sara O'Connor; (D) Dennis Bigelow; (S) Carey Wong; (C) David Mikelson; (L) Rick Paulsen
Terra Nova, Ted Tally; (D) Jeff Steitzer; (S) John Dexter; (C) David Mikelson; (L) Peter Maradudin
Pericles, Prince of Tyre, William Shakespeare; (D) Jerry Turner and Dennis Bigelow; (S) Richard L. Hay; (C) Jeannie Davidson; (L) Robert Peterson

Organic Theater Company

RICHARD FIRE
Artistic Director

RICHARD FRIEDMAN
Executive Director

3319 N. Clark St.
Chicago, IL 60657
(312) 327-2659 (bus.)
(312) 327-5588 (b.o.)

FOUNDED 1969
Carolyn Purdy-Gordon, Stuart Gordon

SEASON
Year-round

FACILITIES
Mainstage
Seating Capacity: 400
Stage: flexible

Lab
Seating Capacity: 80
Stage: proscenium

FINANCES
July 1, 1988-June 30, 1989
Expenses: $413,150

CONTRACTS
AEA CAT

The Organic Theater Company is dedicated to the development and the production of new work and original adaptations. We believe that theatre is for everyone and theatre must be fun. This does not mean that everything we do will please every taste or that we play everything for laughs. It does mean that we seek to reflect the diversity of human experience and deliver the thrill of emotion. We have no hard and fast aesthetic. We seek scripts and ideas with which the writer is passionately involved. Readings and workshops nourish new work. It's risky. Not all projects reach production and not every production succeeds, but the journey of discovery is the greatest adventure that theatre can provide. It is to this process that the Organic Theater is devoted.
—*Richard Fire*

Note: During the 1987-88 season, Thomas Riccio served as artistic director.

PRODUCTIONS 1987–88

A Checkered Carrot, Kathleen Lomardo; (D) L.M. Attea; (S) Susan Attea; (C) Susan Attea; (L) Peter Gottlieb
Pursuit of the Urban Coyote, Joe Larocca; (D) Joe Larocca; (S) Dave Hannah; (C) Dave Hannah; (L) Dave Hannah
Star Crash, Joe Larocca; (D) Mary Linda Moss; (S) Dave Hannah; (C) Dave Hannah; (L) Dave Hannah
Titus Andronicus, William Shakespeare; (D) Thomas Riccio; (S) James Card; (C) Malgorzata Komorowska; (L) James Card
The Danube, Maria Irene Fornes; (D) Blair Thomas; (S) Malgorzata Komorowska; (C) Malgorzata Komorowska; (L) Tom Fleming
The Conduct of Life, Maria Irene Fornes; (D) Thomas Riccio; (S) Barbara H. Niederer; (C) Barbara H. Niederer; (L) Kenneth Moore
Potrait of a Shiksa, Sharon Evans; (D) Sharon Evans; (S) David Lee Csicsko; (C) David Lee Csicsko; (L) James Card

Little Caesar, adapt: Michael
 Miner and Thomas Riccio, from
 W.R. Burnett; (D) Thomas
 Riccio; (S) Greg Mowery;
 (C) Malgorzata Komorowska;
 (L) James Card

PRODUCTIONS 1988–89

*Prayers for the Undoing of
 Spells*, Bryn Magnus; (D) Tom
 Amandes; (S) Bryn Magnus;
 (C) Bryn Magnus; (L) Greg
 Smith
Riffin' with Semple, adapt: Bob
 Curry and Zaid Farid, from
 Langston Hughes; (D) Bob
 Curry; (S) Macee; (C) Macee;
 (L) Macee
The Three Musketeers, adapt:
 David Ruckman, from Alexandre
 Dumas; (D) Warner Crocker;
 (S) Thomas B. Mitchell;
 (C) Susan Anhalt Thetard;
 (L) Walter Reinhardt
Bleacher Bums, Josephine
 Paoletti, Carolyn Purdy-Gordon,
 Dennis Paoli, Michael Saad,
 Keith Szarabajka, and Ian
 Williams; (D) Joe Mantegna;
 (S) Mary Griswold and John
 Paoletti; (C) Mary Griswold and
 John Paoletti; (L) Geoffrey
 Bushor
Swamp Foxes, Laurence Gonzales;
 (D) B.J. Jones; (S) Mary
 Griswold and John Paoletti;
 (C) Mary Griswold and John
 Paoletti; (L) Geoffrey Bushor

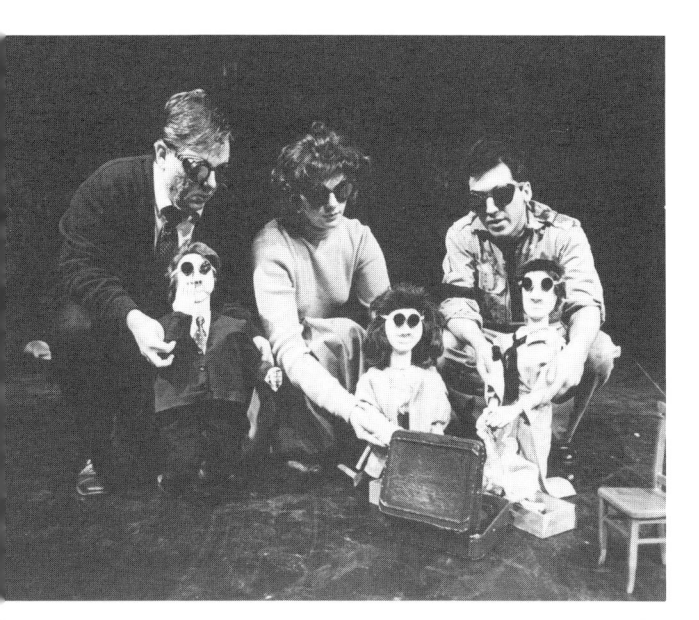

Organic Theater Company. Randy Rakes, Jill Daly, Steve Drukman in *The Danube*.
Photo: J.B. Spector.

Pan Asian Repertory Theatre

TISA CHANG
Artistic/Producing Director

DOMINICK BALLETTA
Producing Associate

47 Great Jones St.
New York, NY 10012
(212) 505-5655 (bus.)
(212) 245-2660 (b.o.)

FOUNDED 1977
Tisa Chang

SEASON
Oct.-June

FACILITIES
Playhouse 46
Seating Capacity: 151
Stage: arena

FINANCES
Sept. 1, 1988-Aug. 31, 1989
Expenses: $516,562

CONTRACTS
AEA letter of agreement

Our 13th season will propel Pan
Asian Rep solidly into the second
decade of championing opportunities
for Asian-American artists.

Pan Asian Repertory Theatre. *The Three Sisters.* Photo: Carol Rosegg, Martha Swope Associates.

With the full implementation of
the Senior Artists program last season,
Pan Asian Rep has achieved
its commitment for significant and
sustained support to artists. In the
next decade we will attempt to resolve
the dilemma of race in art.
For the Asian-American actor new
challenges will mean greater access
and freedom to work on any and
all material without having to justify
race. Regular touring to all
parts of this nation will become a
reality. Dream projects in the near
future include the creation of a
new work about Southeast Asia as
well as the adaptation of the monumental
18th-century Chinese epic
Dream of the Red Chamber. I
know Pan Asian Rep's work will
endure well into the next
millenium.

—*Tisa Chang*

PRODUCTIONS 1987–88

*Boutique Living & Disposable
 Icons*, Momoko Iko; (D) Tisa
 Chang; (S) Jane Epperson;
 (C) Eiko Yamaguchi; (L) Clay
 Shirky
Madame de Sade, Yukio Mishima;
 trans: Donald Keene; (D) Ron
 Nakahara; (S) Alex Polner;
 (C) Eiko Yamaguchi; (L) Victor
 En Yu Tan
Rosie's Cafe, R.A. Shiomi;
 (D) Raul Aranas; (S) Bob
 Phillips; (C) Eiko Yamaguchi;
 (L) Victor En Yu Tan
Shogun Macbeth, adapt: John R.
 Briggs, from William
 Shakespeare; (D) John R. Briggs;
 (S) Atsushi Moriyasu; (C) Eiko
 Yamaguchi; (L) Tina Charney
Yellow Fever, R.A. Shiomi and
 Marc Hayashi; (D) Raul Aranas;
 (S) Bob Phillips; (C) Eiko
 Yamaguchi; (L) Richard
 Dorfman

PRODUCTIONS 1988–89

Noiresque: The Fallen Angel,
 Ping Chong; (D) Ping Chong;
 (S) Ping Chong; (C) Matthew
 Yokobosky; (L) Howard Thies
Play Ball, R.A. Shiomi; (D) Ernest
 H. Abuba; (S) Atsushi Moriyasu;
 (C) Toni-Leslie James; (L) Victor
 En Yu Tan
The Three Sisters, Anton
 Chekhov; trans: Randall Jarrell;
 (D) Margaret Booker; (S) David
 Potts; (C) Eiko Yamaguchi;
 (L) Victor En Yu Tan
Yellow Fever, R.A. Shiomi and
 Marc Hayashi; (D) Raul Aranas;
 (S) Bob Phillips; (C) Eiko
 Yamaguchi; (L) Richard
 Dorfman

Paper Mill Playhouse. Karen Valentine and David Groh in *Beyond a Reasonable Doubt*. Photo: Jerry Dalia.

Paper Mill Playhouse

ANGELO DEL ROSSI
Executive Producer

ROBERT JOHANSON
Artistic Director

Brookside Drive
Millburn, NJ 07041
(201) 379-3636 (bus.)
(201) 376-4343 (b.o.)

FOUNDED 1934
Antoinette Scudder, Frank Carrington

SEASON
Sept.-July

FACILITIES
Paper Mill Playhouse
Seating Capacity: 1,192
Stage: proscenium

Musical Theatre Project Laboratory
Seating Capacity: 80
Stage: flexible

FINANCES
July 1, 1988-June 30, 1989
Expenses: $8,661,910

CONTRACTS
AEA COST

Paper Mill Playhouse produces a wide range of performing arts. Our particular mission is the creation, preservation and production of musical theatre works. In addition to our full-scale productions from the musical theatre repertoire, including American operettas, we give special effort to the creation of new works through our ongoing development program, the Paper Mill Musical Theatre Project. Four musicals and two plays make up our mainstage season for a total of 272 performances. Our productions have transferred to the Kennedy Center in Washington, D.C., and to Broadway. In 1986, we were named "Most Outstanding" in the nationwide showtime's "Search for Excellence in American Theatre" competition, encompassing more than 280 non-profit theatres. Our 1989 production of *Show Boat* was videotaped in performance for international telecast on the Public Broadcasting Service's "Great Performances" series. With our diverse schedule of productions and presented events, we serve more than 400,000 theatregoers annually, attractng a season subscription audience of over 43,000.
— *Angelo Del Rossi*

PRODUCTIONS 1987–88

Sayonara, book: William Luce; lyrics: Hy Gilbert; music: George Fischoff; (D) Robert Johanson; (S) Michael Anania; (C) David Toser and Eiko Yamaguchi; (L) Brian MacDevitt
My One and Only, book: Peter Stone and Timothy S. Mayer; music: George Gershwin; lyrics: Ira Gershwin; (D) Richard Casper; (S) Tony Walton and Adrianne Lobel; (C) Guy Geoly; (L) Marc B. Weiss
Biloxi Blues, Neil Simon; (D) John Going; (S) David Mitchell; (C) Alice S. Hughes; (L) Jeff Davis
Two into One, Ray Cooney; (D) Ray Cooney; (S) Michael Anania; (C) Alice S. Hughes; (L) Jeff Davis
Jesus Christ Superstar, music: Andrew Lloyd Weber; lyrics: Tim Rice; (D) Robert Johanson; (S) Michael Anania; (C) Cecelia A. Friederichs; (L) Jeff Davis
Mack and Mabel, book: Michael Stewart; music and lyrics: Jerry Herman; (D) Robert Johanson; (S) Michael Anania; (C) Guy Geoly and Theoni V. Aldredge; (L) Jeff Davis

PRODUCTIONS 1988–89

La Cage aux Folles, book: Harvey Fierstein; music and lyrics: Jerry Herman; (D) James Pentecost; (S) David Mitchell; (C) Theoni V. Aldredge; (L) Jules Fisher and Natasha Katz
1776, book: Peter Stone; music and lyrics: Sherman Edwards; (D) Robert Johanson; (S) Kevin Rupnik; (C) Guy Geoly; (L) Jeff Davis
Broadway Bound, Neil Simon; (D) Philip Minor; (S) David Mitchell; (C) Alice S. Hughes; (L) David Kissel
Beyond a Reasonable Doubt, Nathan Mayer; (D) Thomas Gruenewald; (S) Michael Anania; (C) Alice S. Hughes; (L) Marilyn Rennagel
Shenandoah, book: James Lee Barrett, Petyer Udell and Philip Rose; music: Gary Geld; lyrics: Peter Udell; (D) Robert Johanson and Rose Philip; (S) Michael Anania; (C) Guy Geoly; (L) Mark Stanley
Show Boat, book and lyrics: Oscar Hammerstein, II; music: Jerome Kern; (D) Robert Johanson; (S) Michael Anania; (C) Bradford Wood and Gregory A. Poplyk; (L) Ken Billington

PCPA Theaterfest

JACK SHOUSE
Managing Artistic Director

THOMAS G. GAFFNEY
Business Manager

Box 1700
Santa Maria, CA 93456
(805) 928-7731 (bus.)
(805) 922-8313 (b.o.)

FOUNDED 1964
Donovan Marley

SEASON
Jan.-Jan.

FACILITIES
Marian Theatre
Seating Capacity: 508
Stage: thrust

Interim Theatre
Seating Capacity: 175
Stage: flexible

Festival Theatre
Seating Capacity: 772
Stage: thrust

FINANCES
Oct. 1, 1987-Sept. 30, 1988
Expenses: $2,450,822

CONTRACTS
AEA U/RTA

We, as theatre artists, performers and craftsmen, share our product with our audience in an attempt entertain and create a heightened awareness of the human condition and to promote a better understanding of what our roles are as individuals and contributors to society. This collaboration is the essence of the theatre. It is the artist who initiates the creative process and the audience who responds, thus maintaining a cycle realization and growth for both. PCPA Theaterfest we create an environment for those artists dedicated to taking that creative initiative. We strive to protect and nurture a theatrical process we feel is vital to our development as individuals and our growth as a civilization. As a performing company and conservatory, we commit ourselves to serving the community, professional staff and student by producing an even wider variety of theatrical works of excellence, while preserving our tradition of offering the classics of world theatre, new plays, contemporary plays, and the new and classic in American musical theatre.
—*Jack Shou*

PRODUCTIONS 1987–88

Charly's Aunt, Brandon Thomas (D) Sandy McCallum; (S) Craig Edelblut; (C) April L. Guttiere (L) Kevin J. Ugar
Here's Love, book, music and lyrics: Meredith Wilson; (D) Brad Carroll; (S) John

Dexter; (C) Mike Chapman; (L) Michael A. Peterson

oming Attractions, Ted Talley; music and lyrics: Jack Feldman; lyrics: Bruce Sussman; (D) Jonathan Gillard Daly; (S) Kate Edmunds; (C) Kitty Murphy; (L) Michael A. Peterson

ump Boys and Dinettes, Mark Hardwick, Debra Monk, Cass Morgan, John Schimmel and Jim Wann; (D) David Kazanjian; (S) Jack Shouse; (C) Jon Olivastro; (L) Candace Brightman

icnic, William Inge; (D) Paul Barnes; (S) John Dexter; (C) April L. Guttierrez; (L) Michael A. Peterson

n the Verge or The Geography of Yearning, Eric Overmyer; (D) Paul Barnes; (S) John Dexter; (C) Fritha Knudsen; (L) Michael A. Peterson

's a Bird . . . It's a Plane . . . It's Superman, book: David Newman and Robert Benton; music: Charles Strouse; lyrics: Lee Adams; (D) Brad Carroll; (S) Carolyn Ross; (C) Sam Fleming; (L) Heather McAvoy

f Mice and Men, John Steinbeck; (D) Sandy McCallum; (S) John Dexter; (C) Dorothy Marshall; (L) Robert Jared

weeney Todd, music and lyrics: Stephen Sondheim; (D) Jack Shouse; (S) D. Martyn Bookwalter; (C) Dorothy Marshall; (L) Robert Jared

he Tempest, William Shakespeare; (D) Kenneth L. Albers; (S) Carolyn Ross; (C) Sam Fleming; (L) Michael A. Peterson

PRODUCTIONS 1988-89

A Christmas Carol, adapt: Cheryl Weiss, from Charles Dickens; (D) Jack Shouse; (S) John Dexter; (C) Ann Bruice; (L) Michael A. Peterson

The Philadelphia Story, Philip Barry; (D) Penny Metropulos; (S) John Dexter; (C) Fritha Knudsen; (L) Michael A. Peterson

Quilters, book: Molly Newman and Barbara Damashek; music and lyrics: Barbara Damashek; (D) Roger DeLaurier; (S) Greg Combs; (C) Kitty Murphy; (L) Jeff White

Romeo and Juliet, William Shakespeare; (D) Paul Barnes; (S) John Dexter; (C) Fritha Knudsen; (L) Michael A. Peterson

Childe Byron, Romulus Linney; (D) Paul Barnes; (C) Deborah Morrison; (L) Jeff Sharp

Eleemosynary, Lee Blessing; (D) Carolyn Keith; (S) Tim Hogan; (C) Bonita Hart; (L) Jeff Sharp

Betrayal, Harold Pinter; (D) Jonathan Gillard Daly; (S) Tim Hogan; (C) Bonita Hart; (L) Jeff Sharp

A Man for All Seasons, Robert Bolt; (D) Kenneth Albers; (S) John Dexter; (C) Dorothy Marshall; (L) Michael A. Peterson

The Fantasticks, book and lyrics: Tom Jones; music: Harvey Schmidt; (D) Roger DeLaurier; (S) Jack Shouse; (C) Dorothy Marshall; (L) Michael A. Peterson

Fiddler on the Roof, book: Joseph Stein; music: Jerry Bock; lyrics: Sheldon Harnick; (D) Paul Barnes; (S) John Iacovelli; (C) Ann Bruice; (L) Jerald R. Enos

The Nerd, Larry Shue; (D) Kenneth Albers; (S) Greg Combs; (C) Ann Bruice; (L) Jerald R. Enos

Evita, music: Andrew Lloyd Webber; lyrics: Tim Rice; (D) Jack Shouse; (S) John Dexter; (C) Dorothy Marshall; (L) Michael A. Peterson

CPA Theaterfest. Teresa Thuman, Cindy Basco and Martha Hawley in *Eleemosynary*. Photo: Tom Smith/Images.

Pennsylvania Stage Company

PETER WRENN-MELECK
Producing Director

LISA HIGGINS
General Manager

837 Linden St.
Allentown, PA 18101
(215) 434-6110 (bus.)
(215) 433-3394 (b.o.)

FOUNDED 1977
Anna Rodale

SEASON
Oct.-June

FACILITIES
J.I. Rodale Theatre
Seating Capacity: 274
Stage: proscenium

FINANCES
July 1, 1988-June 30, 1989
Expenses: $1,265,000

CONTRACTS
LORT (D)

The Pennsylvania Stage Company's artistic purpose is twofold: to continue to build an artistic collective of directors, actors, playwrights, designers and theatrical artisans; and to serve our audience by creating and presenting innovative, relevant and dynamic productions, ranging from American and worldwide classics to contemporary plays, including mainstream and experimental works. As an indispensible cultural resource for eastern Pennsylvania, PSC strives to collaborate with the educational and regional artistic community. We've expanded our resident acting company to four members, who tour *Scenes From Theatre Classics* to more than 10,000 students at 50 schools annually, and who teach multiple levels of acting classes to nearly 200 adults and children each year. As the region's only Equity theatre, the Pennsylvania Stage Company provides a stimulating and supportive environment for national, regional and local artists.

—*Peter Wrenn-Meleck*

Note: During the 1987-88 season, Gregory Hurst served as producing director.

PRODUCTIONS 1987-88

Biloxi Blues, Neil Simon; (D) Martin Herzer; (S) John Falabella; (C) Barbara Forbes; (L) Stuart Duke

Jacques Brel is Alive and Well and Living in Paris, adapt: Eric Blau and Mort Shuman; music and lyrics: Jacques Brel; (D) Gregory S. Hurst; (S) Atkin Pace; (C) Marianne Faust; (L) David Noling

How the Other Half Loves, Alan Ayckbourn; (D) Allen R. Belknap; (S) Linda Sechrist; (C) Kathleen Egan; (L) Donald Holder

Strange Snow, Stephen Metcalfe; (D) Wendy Liscow; (S) Linda Sechrist; (C) Kathleen Egan; (L) Chester Bell

Taking Care of Business, Gil Schwartz; (D) Gregory S. Hurst; (S) Atkin Pace; (C) Barbara Forbes; (L) Donald Holder

A Doll's House, Henrik Ibsen; (D) Wendy Liscow; (S) Linda Sechrist; (C) Barbara Forbes; (L) Curtis Dretsch

I'm Not Rappaport, Herb Gardner; (D) Maureen Heffernan; (S) Atkin Pace; (C) Patricia Adshead; (L) Donald Holder

PRODUCTIONS 1988-89

The Importance of Being Earnest, Oscar Wilde; (D) Gavin Cameron-Webb; (S) Harry Feiner; (C) Gail Brassard; (L) Harry Feiner

Little Shop of Horrors, book and lyrics: Howard Ashman; music: Alan Menken; (D) Allen R. Belknap; (S) Atkin Pace; (C) Barbara Forbes; (L) Donald Holder

The Kiss of the Spider Woman, Manuel Puig; trans: Allan J.

Pennsylvania Stage Company. James Hilbrandt, Victoria Gadsden and Robertson Carricart in *A Moon for the Misbegotten*. Photo: Gregory M. Fota.

Baker; (D) Scott Edmiston; (S) Curtis Dretsch; (C) Kathleen Egan; (L) Curtis Dretsch
The Mystery of Irma Vep, Charles Ludlam; (D) Sue Lawless; (S) Deborah Jasien; (C) Barbara Forbes; (L) Spencer Mosse
A Moon for the Misbegotten, Eugene O'Neill; (D) Donald Hicken; (S) Wally Coberg; (C) Kathleen Egan; (L) Donald Holder
On the Verge or The Geography of Yearning, Eric Overmyer; (D) Veronica Brady; (S) Mike Nichols; (C) Mark Hughes; (L) Spencer Mosse
Broadway Bound, Neil Simon; (D) Scott Edmiston; (S) Curtis Dretsch; (C) Kathleen Egan; (L) Curtis Dretsch

The Penumbra Theatre Company

LOU BELLAMY
Artistic Director

RICHARD D. THOMPSON
General Manager

The Martin Luther King Bld.
270 North Kent St.
St. Paul, MN 55102-1794
(612) 224-4601

FOUNDED 1976
Lou Bellamy

SEASON
Aug.-June

FACILITIES
Hallie Q. Brown Theater
Seating Capacity: 150
Stage: modified thrust

FINANCES
July 1, 1988-June 30, 1989
Expenses: $272,500

CONTRACTS
AEA SPT

Penumbra Theatre Company's mission is to create professional productions that are artistically excellent, thought-provoking, relevant and entertaining. Penumbra's goals are: to increase public awareness of the significant contributions that African Americans have made in creating a diversified American theatrical tradition; to encourage a culturally diverse and all-inclusive American by using theatre to teach, criticize, comment and to provide a model; to use theatre to create an American mythology that includes African Americans and other people of color in every thread of the fabric of our society; to redefine and expand the consciousness of our audiences and our theatrical communities to include a sympathetic and realistic portrayal of people of color; to encourage the staging of plays that address the African-American experience and to continue to stabilize a black performing arts community. Mainstage productions, tours, lectures and conferences contribute to these ends.

—*Lou Bellamy*

PRODUCTIONS 1987–88

Po', Rufus Hill, Phillip Erskine Brown and Keithen Carter; (D) Lewis Whitlock, III; (S) W.J.E. Hammer; (C) Deidrea Whitlock; (L) Scott Peters
Tracers, conceived: John DiFusco; (D) Marion McClinton; (S) Scott Peters; (C) Deidrea Whitlock; (L) Scott Peters
Black Nativity, Langston Hughes; (D) Lewis Whitlock; (S) James P. Taylor; (C) Deidrea Whitlock, III; (L) Mike Wangen
The African Company Presents Richard III, Carlyle Brown; (D) Lou Bellamy; (S) Kenneth Evans; (C) Deidrea Whitlock; (L) Kenneth Evans
Every Night When the Sun Goes Down, Phillip Hayes Dean; (D) Claude Purdy; (S) Gregory Ray; (C) Deidrea Whitlock; (L) Mike Wangen
Malcolm X, August Wilson; (D) Claude Purdy; (S) Kenneth Evans; (C) Deidrea Whitlock; (L) Kenneth Evans

PRODUCTIONS 1988–89

Lost in the Stars, book: Maxwell Anderson; music: Kurt Weill; (D) Lewis Whitlock, III; (S) Gregory Ray; (C) Deidrea Whitlock; (L) Mike Wangen
Brown Silk and Magenta Sunsets, P.J. Gibson; (D) Beverly Smith-Dawson; (S) Gregory Ray; (C) Deidrea Whitlock; (L) Mike Wangen
Black Nativity, Langston Hughes; (D) Lewis Whitlock, III; (S) James P. Taylor; (C) Deidrea Whitlock; (L) Mike Wangen
Major Changes, Karen Jones-Meadows (D) Marion McClinton; (S) W.J.E. Hammer (C) Wayne Murphey; (L) Mike Wangen
Ceremonies in Dark Old Men, Lonne Elder, III (D) Horace Bond; (S) Gregory Ray; (C) Wayne Murphey; (L) Mike Wangen
Malcolm X, August Wilson (D) Claude Purdy; (S) Kenneth Evans; (C) Deidrea Whitlock; (L) Kenneth Evans
George Washington Carver and the Jessup Demonstration Wagon, Carlyle Brown; (D) Beverly Smith-Dawson; (S) Gregory Ray; (C) Gregory Ray; (L) Gregory Ray

The People's Light and Theatre Company

DANNY S. FRUCHTER
Producing Director

GREG T. ROWE
General Manager

39 Conestoga Rd.
Malvern, PA 19355
(215) 647-1900 (bus.)
(215) 644-3500 (b.o.)

The Penumbra Theatre Company. Bruce Thompson and Lou Bellamy in *Major Chang[es]*. Photo: Conie Jerome.

People's Light and Theatre Company. Susan Wilder and Anna Menelaus in *The Middle of the Night*. Photo: Gerry Goodstein.

FOUNDED 1974
Ken Marini, Richard L. Keeler, Danny S. Fruchter, Margaret E. Fruchter

SEASON
Year-round

FACILITIES
Mainstage
Seating Capacity: 400
Stage: flexible

The Steinbright Stage
Seating Capacity: 200
Stage: flexible

FINANCES
Feb. 1, 1988-Jan. 31, 1989
Expenses: $1,366,899

CONTRACTS
LORT (D)

Can a regional theatre be of real use to its community without being both very good, and popular well beyond currently accepted levels of attendance? I think not. We have identified and begun to change some ingrained attitudes and conventional structures which have condemned us and many other regional theatres to the demoralizing limitations of short rehearsals, little planning time and lack of continuous training, often keeping us from truly engaging our audience. By rearranging our internal priorities to maintain a permanent resident company of actors, directors, designers and playwrights, we receive a commitment from theatre workers to be bound to each other and to our community over sufficient time to become more unified in our collective and civic purposes. It is our hope that projects formerly beyond our dreams will now come into focus as artists take up their proper role as partners and family, rather than employees, in this arts institution.

—*Danny S. Fruchter*

PRODUCTIONS 1987–88

Orgasmo Adulto Escapes from the Zoo, Franca Rame and Dario Fo; (D) Ken Marini; (S) Joe Franz; (C) P. Chelsea Harriman; (L) Richard Keeler
A Doll House, Henrik Ibsen; adapt: Lee Devin; (D) Abigail Adams; (S) Joe Ragey; (C) P. Chelsea Harriman; (L) Joe Ragey
Mrs. California, Doris Baizley; (D) Ken Marini; (S) James F. Pyne, Jr.; (C) P. Chelsea Harriman; (L) James F. Pyne, Jr.
Oedipus, adapt: Abigail Adams and Lee Devin, from Sophocles; (D) Abigail Adams; (S) James F. Pyne, Jr.; (C) Marla J. Jurglanis; (L) James F. Pyne, Jr.
Middle of the Night, Paddy Chayefsky; (D) Ken Marini; (S) James F. Pyne, Jr.; (C) P. Chelsea Harriman; (L) James F. Pyne, Jr.

PRODUCTIONS 1988–89

The Voice of the Prairie, John Olive; (D) Ken Marini; (S) James F. Pyne, Jr.; (C) P. Chelsea Harriman; (L) James F. Pyne, Jr.
Zig Zag Zelda, Drury Pifer; (D) Drury Pifer; (S) James F. Pyne, Jr.; (C) P. Chelsea Harriman; (L) James F. Pyne, Jr.
The Temptation of Maddie Graham, Phyllis Purscell; (D) Joan Vail Thorne; (S) James F. Pyne, Jr.; (C) P. Chelsea Harriman; (L) James F. Pyne, Jr.
Traveling Lady, Horton Foote; (D) Abigail Adams; (S) James F. Pyne, Jr.; (C) P. Chelsea Harriman; (L) James F. Pyne, Jr.

Periwinkle National Theatre for Young Audiences

SUNNA RASCH
Executive Director

JUDY LORKOWSKI
Business Manager

19 Clinton Ave.
Monticello, NY 12701
(914) 794-1666

FOUNDED 1963
Sunna Rasch

SEASON
Jan.–Dec.

FINANCES
Aug. 1, 1988-July 31, 1989
Expenses: $325,000

The premise—and promise—of Periwinkle National Theatre for Young Audiences has been to develop theatre programs that communicate with youth, with which young audiences can identify and through which they can expand themselves creatively, intellectually, artistically and emotionally. Periwinkle has developed 25 original productions for every age level, and has toured them to schools and communities nationwide, reaching over two million young people. Programs available for touring reflect our diversity: *The Magic Word*, a play-with-music for primary grades; *The Fabulous Dream of Andrew H. Lupone*, a musical for elementary schools; *Hooray for Me*, a satire for middle schools; and *Halfway There*, a drug education drama for high schools. Periwinkle's productions can stand alone as theatre, but they go beyond, because we believe that theatre is a vital educational tool as well. Periwnkle is committed to the arts in education, and looks forward to reaching even more young people everywhere.

—*Sunna Rasch*

PRODUCTIONS 1987–88

Halfway There, Sunna Rasch; music: Ken Laufer; (D) Michael Dacunto; (S) Michael Daughtry; (C) Marcie Miller; (L) Jay Zion
Hooray For Me!, Scott Laughead, Sunna Rasch and Lynne Graeme; (D) Scott Laughead; (S) Michael Daughtry; (C) Susan Scherer and Megan Hartley
The Ransom of Red-Chief!, Scott Laughead; (D) Scott Laughead; (S) Michael Daughtry; (C) Megan Hartley
The Magic Word, Sunna Rasch; (D) Scott Laughead; (S) Earl Wertheim; (C) Susan Scherer
The Mad Poet Strikes—Again!, Sunna Rasch; (D) Scott Laughead; (S) David Cooper; (C) Scott Laughead

PRODUCTIONS 1988–89

Halfway There, Sunna Rasch; music: Ken Laufer; (D) Michael Dacunto; (S) Michael Daughtry; (C) Marcie Miller and Megan Hartley; (L) Craig Kennedy
Hooray For Me!, book: Scott Laughead, Sunna Rasch and Lynn Graeme; music: Grenoldo Frazier and Eric Rockwell; (D) Eric Rockwell; (S) Michael Daughtry; (C) Susan Scherer and Megan Hartley
America Yes!, Sunna Rasch; (D) Brian Russell; (S) Maude De Angelis and Harry Zierdt;

Periwinkle National Theatre for Young Audiences. Andrei Clark and John Glassman in *Hooray for Me!* Photo: Steven Borns.

(C) Susan Scherer and Megan Hartley
The Ransom of Red-Chief!, Scott Laughead; (D) Richard Sabellico; (S) Michael Daughtry; (C) Megan Hartley

FINANCES
July 1, 1988-June 30, 1989
Expenses: $627,650

Perseverance Theatre

MOLLY D. SMITH
Artistic Director

DEBORAH B. BALEY
Producing Director

914 Third St.
Douglas, AK 99824
(907) 364-2151

FOUNDED 1979
Molly Smith, Kay Smith, Joe Ross, Bill C. Ray, Susie Fowler, Jack Cannon, Kate Bowns

SEASON
Year-round

FACILITIES
Mainstage
Seating Capacity: 150
Stage: flexible

Phoenix Stage
Seating Capacity: 50
Stage: flexible

Elk's Hall
Seating Capacity: 200
Stage: proscenium

Perseverance Theatre is located in Juneau, the capital of Alaska, a community of 28,000 inaccessible by road. Alaska's rich cultural heritage and its environmental and social background contribute profoundly to the artistic direction and scope of Perseverance Theatre. The complex personality of the state draws many kinds of people: winners and losers, people out to get rich quick, Aleuts, Tlingits, Eskimos and whites, oil tycoons and environmentalists looking for the "last frontier." Our major artistic goal is to wrestle with this spirit, this uniquely Alaskan experience, and, using a company of multi-talented performing artists from around the state, develop a voice for it. We produce a full season of classical and contemporary theatre on our mainstage (including at least one new play by an Alaskan playwright), a second stage series and the Great Alaskan Playrush (a statewide playwriting competition). We also tour around the state and offer extensive training programs.

—*Molly D. Smith*

PRODUCTIONS 1987-88

Yerma, Federico Garicia Lorca; trans: James Graham Lujan and Richard L. O'Connell; (D) Roberta Levitow; (S) Dave Hunsaker; (C) Deborah Trout; (L) James Sale
Giving Birth to Thunder, Sleeping with His Daughter: Coyote Builds North America, conceived, adapt and music: John Luther Adams; (D) Molly D. Smith; (S) Bill C. Ray; (C) Bill C. Ray; (L) Vikki Benner
Inherit the Wind, Jerome Lawrence and Robert E. Lee; (D) Jamieson McLean; (S) Pavel M. Dobrusky; (C) Barbara Casement; (L) Pavel M. Dobrusky
Farther West, John Murrell; (D) Molly D. Smith; (S) Dave Hunsaker; (C) Mary Ellen Frank and Lynn Taylor; (L) Brendan Wallace
Our Lady of the Tortilla, Luis Santeiro; (D) Gregg W. Brevoort; (S) Brendan Wallace; (C) Tracey R. Williams; (L) P. Dudley Riggs
Last Frontier Club, Debbie Baley; (D) Kate Bowns; (S) Kathryn Daughhetee; (C) Tracey R. Williams; (L) P. Dudley Riggs
Dancing the Hora in Rubber Boots, Kayla Epstein; (D) Kayla Epstein; (S) Brendan Wallace; (C) Brendan Wallace; (L) Brendan Wallace
The Lady Lou Revue, book and lyrics: Gordon Duffey; music: Alan Chapman; (D) Rita Giomi; (S) Bill C. Ray; (C) Barbara Casement; (L) P. Dudley Riggs

PRODUCTIONS 1988-89

The Tempest, William Shakespeare; (D) Molly D. Smith; (S) Mary Griswold; (C) Mary Ellen Frank and Lynn Taylor; (L) Spencer Mosse
The Night of the Iguana, Tennessee Williams; (D) Robert Rooney; (S) Pavel M. Dobrusky; (C) Deborah Smith; (L) Pavel M. Dobrusky

Le Club Hotzy Totzy, Jack Cannon; (D) Molly D. Smith; (S) Daniel DeRoux; (C) Annie Calkins; (L) Vikki Benner
The Obscene Bird of Night, adapt: Darrah Cloud, from Jos Donoso; (D) Molly D. Smith; (S) Dave Hunsaker; (C) Marta Ann Lastufka; (L) Vikki Benner
Red Noses, Peter Barnes; (D) K Bowns; (S) Jack Cannon; (C) Barbara Casement; (L) Vik Benner
Pure Gold, Susi Gregg Fowler; (D) Kate Bowns; (S) Jack Cannon; (C) Barbara Casemer (L) Vikki Benner
And Baby Makes Seven, Paula Vogel; (D) Annie Stokes-Hutchinson; (S) Jane Terzis an Doug Larson; (C) Sophia Zimmerman; (L) Kay Dickson
The Lady Lou Revue, book and lyrics: Gordon Duffey; music: Alan Chapman; (D) Jack Reule (S) Bill C. Ray; (C) Susan Wilder; (L) P. Dudley Riggs
426 Chandler Street—No Christmas Gelt for Perpetrators, conceived: Lia Gladstone; (D) Lia Gladstone; (S) Kathryn Daughhetee; (C) Sophia Zimmerman; (L) Bruck Bruckman

Perserverance Theatre. Deborah Holmes, Will Shindler, Rick Bundy and Martin Cler ents in *Red Noses*. Photo: Mark Daughhetee.

Philadelphia Drama Guild

GREGORY POGGI
Producing Director

KATHLEEN KUND NOLAN
Business Manager

220 North 17th St.
Philadelphia, PA 19103
(215) 563-7530 (bus.)
(215) 898-6791 (b.o.)

FOUNDED 1956
Sidney S. Bloom

SEASON
Oct.-May

FACILITIES
Zellerbach Theatre
Seating Capacity: 944
Stage: thrust

Harold Prince Theatre
Seating Capacity: 166
Stage: flexible

Studio Theatre
Seating Capacity: 120
Stage: proscenium

FINANCES
June 1, 1988-May 31, 1989
Expenses: $2,226,000

CONTRACTS
LORT (B+)

Great theatre keeps us in touch with a common denominator—the human soul. It compels our imagination and perception and leads us to the unique pleasures of emotional discovery and intellectual revelation. I am attracted to writers who provoke a confrontation and understanding of those distinctly human qualities in which we all share to create a "theatre of involvement"—producing works that are provocative, imaginative and strong on the human condition. Three touchstones inform my play selection at the Philadelphia Drama Guild and motivate their production style: the originality of each writer's world and point of view; the vigor of his or her moral concern for the way we live; and the inherent theatricality of each work, particularly the expressiveness of the playwriting "voice" in filling the playing area of our large Zellerbach Theatre space. Our programming also reflects a conscious effort to attract, entertain and inform young minds. In fulfilling my artistic objectives, this audience of the future remains of paramount importance.

—*Gregory Poggi*

PRODUCTIONS 1987–88

Home, Samm-Art Williams; (D) Walter Dallas; (S) Daniel P. Boylen; (C) Frankie Fehr; (L) Sylvester Nathaniel Weaver, II

The Miracle Worker, William Gibson; (D) Edmund J. Cambridge; (S) Roger Mooney; (C) Frankie Fehr; (L) William H. Grant, III

Division Street, Steve Tesich; (D) Charles Karchmer; (S) R. Mitchell Miller; (C) Gail Brassard; (L) Jeff Davis

Julius Caesar, William Shakespeare; (D) Michael Murray; (S) Karl Eigsti; (C) Karen Roston; (L) Neil Peter Jampolis

Born Yesterday, Garson Kanin; (D) Art Wolff; (S) John Jensen; (C) David Murin; (L) Dennis Parichy

Playwrights of Philadelphia Play Festival

Sad Dance of the Prairie, John Erlanger; (D) Alex Dmitriev; (S) Daniel P. Boylen; (C) Pamela Keech; (L) Jerold R. Forsyth

The Gentlemen of Fifth Avenue, James Penzi; (D) John R. Hawkins; (S) Christopher Nestor; (C) Pamela Keech; (L) Jerold R. Forsyth

PRODUCTIONS 1988–89

The Immigrant: A Hamilton County Album, Mark Harelik; conceived: Randal Myler and Mark Harelik; (D) Charles Karchmer; (S) James Noone; (C) Deborah Shaw; (L) Jeff Davis

An American Journey, Kermit Frazier and John Leicht; (D) John Dillon; (S) Daniel P. Boylen; (C) Sam Fleming; (L) William H. Grant, III

The Boys Next Door, Tom Griffin; (D) Allen R. Belknap; (S) James Fenhagen; (C) Gail Brassard; (L) Richard Winkler

A View from the Bridge, Arthur Miller; (D) Alex Dmitriev; (S) Rosario Provenza; (C) Karen Roston; (L) James Leitner

Rocky and Diego, Roger Cornish; (D) John Henry Davis; (S) John Jensen; (C) Karen Roston; (L) F. Mitchell Dana

Philadelphia Drama Guild. Mark Moses and Julie Hagerty in *Born Yesterday*. Photo: Ken Kauffman.

Philadelphia Festival Theatre for New Plays

CAROL ROCAMORA
Artistic/Producing Director

GRACE E. GRILLET
Administrative Director

3900 Chestnut St.
Philadelphia, PA 19104
(215) 222-5000 (bus.)
(215) 898-6791 (b.o.)

FOUNDED 1981
Carol Rocamora

SEASON
Oct.-June

FACILITIES
Harold Prince Theatre,
Annenberg Center
Seating Capacity: 200
Stage: flexible

FINANCES
July 1, 1988-June 30, 1989
Expenses: $749,000

CONTRACTS
LORT (D)

The Philadelphia Festival Theatre for New Plays is one of the few independent, nonprofit professional theatres in the country dedicated exclusively to the production of new plays by American playwrights. The theatre's mission is twofold: to foster a commitment to new play development and production for the local and national theatre audience, and to make a lasting contribution to American dramatic literature by discovering new plays by established and new writers. In its first 8 years the theatre has produced 60 world premieres from more than 10,000 script submissions. Three-quarters of these premieres have gone on to additional productions or publication. Playwrights' residencies, Curtain Call discussions for playwrights, directors, actors and audiences, new play development seminars, and the Play-Offs reading series are among the programs offered by PFT.

—*Carol Rocamora*

PRODUCTIONS 1987–88

Established Price, Dennis McIntyre; (D) Allen R. Belknap; (S) Hugh Landwehr; (C) Vickie Esposito; (L) Curt Senie
No Stranger, Jule Selbo; (D) Gloria Muzio; (S) Eric Schaeffer; (C) Vickie Esposito; (L) Curt Senie
Magda and Callas, Albert Innaurato; (D) Thomas Gruenewald; (S) Hugh Landwehr; (C) Barbara Forbes; (L) Ann Wrightson
Soulful Scream of a Chosen Son, Ned Eisenberg; (D) Michael Bloom; (S) Eric Schaeffer; (C) Vickie Esposito; (L) Curt Senie
Minor Demons, Bruce Graham; (D) Jim Christy; (S) Eric Schaeffer; (C) Vickie Esposito; (L) Curt Senie
Paco Latto and the Anchorwoman, David Kranes; (D) Gloria Muzio; (S) Eric Schaeffer; (C) Vickie Esposito; (L) Curt Senie
Election '84, Ellen Byron; (D) Jan Silverman; (S) Eric Schaeffer; (C) Vickie Esposito; (L) Curt Senie

PRODUCTIONS 1988–89

A Peep into the Twentieth Century, Christopher Davis; (D) Jim Christy; (S) Phil Graneto; (C) Vickie Esposito; (L) Curt Senie
The Rabbit Foot, Leslie Lee; (D) Walter Dallas; (S) Jim Youmans; (C) Vickie Esposito; (L) Curt Senie
A Piece of My Heart, Shirley Lauro; (D) Walt Jones; (S) Robert Provenza; (C) Barbara Bell; (L) Donald Holder
Moon over the Brewery, Bruce Graham; (D) Jim Christy; (S) James Wolk; (C) Vickie Esposito; (L) Karl Haas
Amorphous George, Glen Merzer; (D) W.H. Macy; (S) James Wolk; (C) Vickie Esposito; (L) Karl Haas
Romance, Ernest Joselovitz; (D) Carol Rocamora; (S) Phil Graneto; (C) Vickie Esposito; (L) Jim Leitner

Philadelphia Festival Theatre for New Plays. Robin Groves, D'Jamin Bartlett and Freda Foh Shen in *A Piece of My Heart*. Photo: Susanne Richelle.

The Philadelphia Theatre Company

SARA GARONZIK
Artistic Director

IRA SCHLOSSER
Managing Director

21 South 5th St., The Bourse
Suite 735
Philadelphia, PA 19106
(215) 592-8333

FOUNDED 1974
Robert Headley, Jean Harrison

SEASON
Oct.–June

FACILITIES
Plays and Players Theater
Seating Capacity: 324
Stage: proscenium

TUCC Stage III
Seating Capacity: 100
Stage: proscenium

FINANCES
Sept. 1, 1988-Aug. 31, 1989
Expenses: $803,000

CONTRACTS
LORT (D) and AEA SPT

The Philadelphia Theatre Company retains a strong commitment to celebrating the vision and variety of the American playwright, producing the emerging as well as the established contemporary voice. This mission permits not only world and regional premiere but the "second look" so critical for writers whose work has had previous viewing. Superior acting and clear, inventive directing are our aesthetic cornerstones, and create an enlightened and suppotive environment where these artists can achieve their best wo Our mission also permits the achievement of great visual and thematic diversity, although we clearly an urban theatre with a strong social and humanitarian conscience. Since 1986, our Stag program has grown into a fulltim laboratory where playwrights an their collaborators can thoroughl explore developing work away fr deadline pressure. From Stages sprung the Mentor Project, whic pairs nationally recognized maste writers with their younger count parts. It has been our recent privilege to have playwright Arth Kopit as our first "mentor."

—*Sara Garon*

PRODUCTIONS 1987–88

Stauf, music and lyrics: Michael Sahl and Eric Salzman; add'l material: Larry Loebell (D) Rhoda Levine; (S) Peter Harrison; (C) Frances Nelson; (L) Karl Haas
Orphans, Lyle Kessler; (D) William Woodman; (S) Lewis Folden; (C) Vickie Esposito; (L) James Leitner
From the Mississippi Delta, Endesha Ida Mae Holland; (D) Ed Smith; (S) Steven Perry (C) Judy Dearing; (L) William H. Grant, III
Sister and Miss Lexie, adapt: David Kaplan and Brenda Currin, from Eudora Welty; (D) David Kaplan; (S) Steven Perry; (C) Susan Hilferty; (L) William H. Grant, III
Hospitality, Allan Havis; (D) William Foeller; (S) Nancy Thun; (C) Nancy Thun; (L) Ka Haas
Out!, Lawrence Kelly; (D) Sara Garonzik; (S) Peter Harrison; (C) Vickie Esposito; (L) James Leitner

Stages New Play Festival '88
Yesterday's Hero, Michael Grady (D) Lynn M. Thompson; (S) M.R. Daniels; (L) James Leitner
Catch!, Jason Katims; (D) Jan Silverman; (S) M.R. Daniels; (L) James Leitner
Tears of Rage, Doris Baizley; (D) Hal Scott; (S) Hiroshi Iwasaki; (L) James Leitner

Philadelphia Theatre Company. Peter Morse and Matthew Penn in *Out!*. Photo: ...rk Garvin.

...RODUCTIONS 1988–89

...ine's Daughter, Mayo Simon; (D) Jules Aaron; (S) Nancy Thun; (C) Frankie Fehr; (L) Karl Haas
...e Voice of the Praire, John Olive; (D) Lynn M. Thompson; (S) M.R. Daniels; (C) Frankie Fehr; (L) Dan Wagner
...ankie and Johnny in the Clare de Lune, Terrence McNally; (D) Sheldon Epps; (S) James Sandefur; (C) Stuart Duke; (L) Nancy Konrardy
...engarry Glen Ross, David Mamet; (D) Gordon Edelstein; (S) Hugh Landwehr; (C) David Murin; (L) Pat Collins
...nnah Senesh, adapt: David Schechter and Lori Wilner, from Hannah Senesh; trans: Marta Cohn and Peter Hay; (D) David Schechter; (S) Peter Harrison; (C) David Woolard; (L) Dan Wagner
...ages New Play Festival '89:
Spike Heels, Theresa Rebeck; (D) Lynn M. Thompson; (S) Dan Boylen; (L) James Leitner
...uats, Martin Jones; (D) Jan Silverman; (S) Dan Boylen; (L) James Leitner
...iku, Kate Snodgrass; (D) Christopher Ashley; (S) Dan Boylen; (L) James Leitner

Ping Chong & Company/The Fiji Company

PING CHONG
Artistic Director

BRUCE ALLARDICE
Managing Director

253 Church St.
New York, NY 10013
(212) 966-0284

FOUNDED 1975
Ping Chong

SEASON
variable

FINANCES
July 1, 1988-June 30, 1989
Expenses: $180,000

Created to address and incorporate the technological and global changes engendered by the communications revolution, The Fiji Company continues to explore the meaning of "contemporary theatre" on a national and international level. The Fiji Company was established to question the syntax of the traditional theatre and to enrich it with an Asian sensibility. We believe that the traditional theatre is a poor imitation of the naturalism that film and television more readily achieve. To survive, paradoxically, the theatre must reconcile its primal purpose as a metaphysical experience with the perceptual syntax of the communications era. In recent years the Fiji Company has expanded into filmmaking, video and visual arts in our continuing dialogue with the art and culture of the late 20th century.

—*Ping Chong*

PRODUCTIONS 1987–88

Snow, Ping Chong; (D) Ping Chong; (S) Ping Chong and Jim Salen; (C) Rich Hampson; (L) Michael Murnane
Quartetto, Henk Van der Mulen; (D) Ping Chong; (S) Tom Vanden Haspel; (C) Willy Smits; (L) Henk de Haas
Angels of Swedenborg, Ping Chong; (D) Ping Chong; (S) Ping Chong; (C) Mel Carpenter; (L) Tina Charney
Maraya, Ping Chong; (D) Ping Chong; (S) Ping Chong and Mark Tambella; (C) Matthew Yokobosky; (L) Ann Militello
Without Law/Without Heaven, Ping Chong and Norman Durkee; (D) Ping Chong; (S) Ping Chong and Carl Smool; (C) Ping Chong and Carl Smool; (L) Gary Vaughn
Astonishment and the Twins, Ping Chong and The Fiji Company; (D) Ping Chong and John Fleming; (S) Ping Chong and Peter Boles; (C) Mel Carpenter; (L) Howard Thies

PRODUCTIONS 1988–89

Skin - A State of Being, Ping Chong and The Fiji Company; (D) Ping Chong; (S) Ping Chong; (C) Matthew Yokobosky; (L) Howard Thies
Noiresque - The Fallen Angel, Ping Chong; (D) Ping Chong; (S) Ping Chong; (C) Matthew Yokobosky; (L) Howard Thies
Kind Ness, Ping Chong and The Fiji Company; (D) Ping Chong; (S) Ping Chong; (C) Mel Carpenter; (L) Howard Thies
Kind Ness, Ping Chong and The Fiji Company; (D) Ping Chong; (S) Pat Doty; (C) Dawna Gregory; (L) William Browning
Angels of Swedenborg, Ping Chong; (D) Ping Chong; (S) Ping Chong; (C) Mel Carpenter; (L) Tina Charney

Pioneer Theatre Company

CHARLES MOREY
Artistic Director

JACK MARK
Managing Director

University of Utah
Salt Lake City, UT 84112
(801) 581-6356 (bus.)
(801) 581-6961 (b.o.)

Ping Chong and Company/The Fiji Company. John Flemin and Louis Smith in *Kind Ness*. Photo: Joe Jefcoat.

Pioneer Theatre Company. Karyn Caplan, Robert Peterson and Kevin Ligon in *A Little Night Music.* Photo: Robert Clayton.

FOUNDED 1962
C. Lowell Lees, University of Utah, local citizens

SEASON
Sept.-June

FACILITIES
Lees Main Stage
Seating Capacity: 1,000
Stage: proscenium

FINANCES
July 1, 1988-June 30, 1989
Expenses: $1,904,937

CONTRACTS
LORT (B) and AEA U/RTA

Pioneer Theatre Company is the resident professional theatre of the University of Utah and draws audiences from four western states. The company's primary concern is to provide our community with an ongoing theatre of the highest professional standards. Secondarily, the company serves an educational purpose as both a cultural resource to the university community and a training ground for aspiring professionals. The educational purpose cannot be fulfilled without first satisfying the primary concern of artistic excellence. The company recently implemented a long-range plan which mandates refocusing the repertoire upon the classics, developing a resident acting ensemble and creating mutually beneficial internships with the university theatre department.
—*Charles Morey*

PRODUCTIONS 1987–88

My One and Only, book: Peter Stone; music: George Gershwin; lyrics: Ira Gershwin; (D) Patti D'Beck; (S) George Maxwell; (C) Elizabeth Novack; (L) Peter L. Willardson and Ariel Baliff
Hamlet, William Shakespeare; (D) Charles Morey; (S) Ariel Baliff; (C) Elizabeth Novack; (L) Peter L. Willardson
You Can't Take It with You, Moss Hart and George Kaufman; (D) Thomas Grunewald; (S) George Maxwell; (C) Ariel Baliff; (L) Kiyono Oshiro
A Flea in Her Ear, Georges Feydeau; trans: John Mortimer; (D) Charles Morey; (S) Peter Harrison; (C) Elizabeth Novack; (L) Peter L. Willardson
The Dining Room, A.R. Gurney, Jr.; (D) Munson Hicks; (S) Ariel Baliff; (C) K.L. Alberts; (L) Karl E. Haas
Death of a Salesman, Arthur Miller; (D) Charles Morey; (S) Ariel Baliff; (C) K.L. Alberts; (L) Karl E. Haas
Singin' in the Rain, adapt: Betty Comden and Adolph Green; music and lyrics: Nacio Herb Brown and Arthur Freed; (D) Darwin Knight; (S) George Maxwell; (C) Elizabeth Novack; (L) Peter L. Willardson

PRODUCTIONS 1988–89

Anything Goes, book: Guy Bolton, P.G. Wodehouse, Howard Lindsay and Russel Crouse; music and lyrics: Cole Porter; (D) Paul Lazarus; (S) George Maxwell; (C) Doug Marmee; (L) Phil Monat
Cyrano de Bergerac, Edmond Rostand and Brian Hooker; (D) Charles Morey; (S) Ariel Baliff; (C) David Paulin; (L) Peter L. Willardson
Room Service, John Murray and Allen Boretz; (D) Charles Morey; (S) Peter L. Harrison; (C) K.L. Alberts; (L) Chika Komura
I'm Not Rappaport, Herb Gardner; (D) Tom Markus; (S) Peter L. Harrison; (C) Linda Sarver; (L) Peter L. Willardson
A Midsummer Night's Dream, William Shakespeare; (D) Charles Morey; (S) George Maxwell; (C) Elizabeth Novack; (L) Peter L. Willardson
Inherit the Wind, Jerome Lawrence and Robert E. Lee; (D) Geoffrey Sherman; (S) Ariel Baliff; (C) K.L. Alberts; (L) Karl E. Haas
A Little Night Music, book: Hugh Wheeler; music and lyrics: Stephen Sondheim; (D) Allen R. Belknap; (S) George Maxwell; (C) Linda Sarver; (L) Peter L. Willardson

Pittsburgh Public Theater

WILLIAM T. GARDNER
Producing Director

DAN FALLON
Managing Director

Allegheny Square
Pittsburgh, PA 15212-5362
(412) 323-8200 (bus.)
(412) 321-9800 (b.o.)

FOUNDED 1975
Ben Shaktman, Margaret Rieck, Joan Apt

SEASON
Sept.-June

FACILITIES
Theodore L. Hazlett, Jr. Theatre
Seating Capacity: 449
Stage: flexible

FINANCES
Sept. 1, 1988-Aug. 31, 1989
Expenses: $2,976,877

CONTRACTS
LORT B

The Pittsburgh Public Theater seeks to present the finest plays of the American and world repertoire to the widest possible audience in a city noted for its cultural diversity. The 1989-90 season represents the 15th anniversary of the theatre and will focus on a celebration of the city's Pulitzer Prize-winning playwrights, George S. Kaufman and August Wilson, as well as including the theatre's first original musical. The 15th season will also mark the theatre's move to a LORT-B status. The following season will feature a new adaptation of Chekhov's *The Three Sisters* by American playwright Corinne Jacker and a major Tennessee Williams work with a notable Pittsburgh actress, Helena Ruoti. Our community of outreach programs include performances for

Pittsburgh Public Theater. *The Hairy Ape.* Photo: Mark Portland.

ident, senior citizen and handicapped constituencies; professional internships; a speakers bureau; programs in schools; and a developing professional affiliation with a number of local educational institutions.
—William T. Gardner

PRODUCTIONS 1987–88

The Hairy Ape, Eugene O'Neill; (D) George Ferencz; (S) Bill Stabile; (C) Sally Lesser; (L) Blu
Dames at Sea, book and lyrics: George Haimson and Robin Miller; music: Jim Wise; (D) Neal Kenyon; (S) Anne Mundell; (C) Mary Mease Warren; (L) Kirk Bookman
Edith Stein, Arthur Giron; (D) Lee Sankowich; (S) Ursula Belden; (C) Laura Crow; (L) Kirk Bookman
The Mystery of Irma Vep, Charles Ludlam; (D) Bruce Bouchard; (S) Rick Dennis; (C) Martha Hally; (L) Jackie Manassee
The Normal Heart, Larry Kramer; (D) Lee Sankowich; (S) Anne Mundell; (C) Craig A. Humphrey; (L) Ann G. Wrightson
My Heart Belongs to Daddy, Laury Marker and Nelsie Spencer; (D) David Warren; (S) John Arnone; (C) David C. Woolard; (L) Kirk Bookman

PRODUCTIONS 1988–89

The Habitation of Dragons, Horton Foote; (D) Horton Foote; (S) Howard Cummings; (C) Van Broughton Ramsey; (L) Kirk Bookman
I'm Not Rappaport, Herb Gardner; (D) Maureen Heffernan; (S) Anne Mundell; (C) Patricia Adshead; (L) Kirk Bookman
The Immigrant: A Hamilton County Album, Mark Harelik; conceived: Randal Myler and Mark Harelik; (D) Howard J. Millman; (S) Kevin Rupnick; (C) Mimi Maxmen; (L) Phil Monat
Fallen Angels, Noel Coward; (D) Philip Minor; (S) Cletus Anderson; (C) David Toser; (L) Kirk Bookman
Hedda Gabler, Henrik Ibsen; trans: Corinne Jacker; (D) Lee Sankowich; (S) Harry Feiner; (C) Laura Crow; (L) Kirk Bookman
Fences, August Wilson; (D) Claude Purdy; (S) James D. Sandefur; (C) Mary Mease Warren; (L) Phil Monat

Players Theatre Columbus

ED GRACZYK
Producing Director

BRUCE B. MAKOUS
Managing Director

Box 18185
Columbus, OH 43218
(614) 644-5300 (bus.)
(614) 644-8425 (b.o.)

FOUNDED 1923
Agnes Jeffrey Shedd

SEASON
Sept.–June

FACILITIES
Capitol Theatre
Seating Capacity: 750
Stage: flexible

Studio I
Seating Capacity: 250
Stage: flexible

Studio II
Seating Capacity: 100
Stage: flexible

FINANCES
July 1, 1988-June 30, 1989
Expenses: $2,268,000

CONTRACTS
LORT (D)

The mission of Players Theatre Columbus is to create a true regional theatre for adult and young audiences alike that examines the nature of the human experience and its implications for Midwestern life. The artistic vision places a strong emphasis on the creation and development of accessible new work which reflects the concerns, conflicts and values of the people of the region. Contemporary American and European classics augment this commitment to new work, ensuring our audiences of diverse exposure to the finest dramatic literature in all of its forms. Being designated the managing tenant for the three-theatre complex in the Vern Riffe Center for Government and the Arts has enabled Players Theatre Columbus to continue our phenomenal growth and broaden our reach to the people of central Ohio.
—Ed Graczyk

Players Theatre Columbus. Debra Ann Draper and Randy Skinner in *Cole*. Photo: Rand Weidenbusch.

PRODUCTIONS 1987–88

The Murder of Crows, Ed Grayzyk; (D) Edward Stern; (S) Ursula Belden; (C) Ruth Boyd; (L) James H. Gage
And a Nightingale Sang, C.P. Taylor; (D) Carter W. Lewis; (S) Carolyn Ott; (C) Ruth Boyd; (L) James H. Gage
Noises Off, Michael Frayn; (D) Dudley Swetland; (S) Gary C. Eckhart; (C) Ruth Boyd; (L) James H. Gage
Cotton Patch Gospel, book adapt: Tom Key and Russell Treyz; music and lyrics: Harry Chapin; (D) Ed Graczyk; (S) Ed Graczyk; (C) Ruth Boyd; (L) Andrew R. Sather
The Incredible Murder of Cardinal Tosca, Alden Nowlan and Walter Learning; (D) Ed Graczyk; (S) James D. Sandefur; (C) Frances Blau; (L) James H. Gage
Benefactors, Michael Frayn; (D) Carter W. Lewis; (S) Rusty Smith; (C) Ruth Boyd; (L) Cynthia R. Stillings
Gypsy, book: Arthur Laurents; music: Jule Styne; lyrics: Stephen Sondheim; (D) Ed Graczyk; (S) Rusty Smith; (C) Rusty Smith; (L) James H. Gage

PRODUCTIONS 1988–89

Babes in Arms, book: George Oppenheimer; music: Richard Rogers; lyrics: Lorenz Hart; (D) Randy Skinner; (S) Linda E. Hacker; (C) Martin Pakledinaz; (L) Allen Lee Hughes
Philadelphia, Here I Come!, Brian Friel; (D) Stephen Hollis; (S) Bill Clarke; (C) Holly Cole; (L) Pete Reader
Steel Magnolias, Robert Harling; (D) Robert Lanchester; (S) Peter B. Harrison; (C) Susan E. Tucker; (L) James H. Gage
Cole, adapt: Alan Strachen and Benny Green; music and lyrics: Cole Porter; (D) Ed Graczyk; (S) Scott Bradley; (C) Doug Fisher; (L) James H. Gage
A Streetcar Named Desire, Tennessee Williams; (D) Edward Stern; (S) David Potts; (C) Dorothy L. Marshall; (L) Robert Wierzel
The Boys Next Door, Tom Griffin; (D) Edward Stern; (S) Scott Bradley; (C) Ruth Boyd; (L) James H. Gage

Playhouse on the Square

JACKIE NICHOLS
Executive Producer

ELIZABETH HOWARD
Administrative Director

51 South Cooper St.
Memphis, TN 38104
(901) 725-0776 (bus.)
(901) 726-4498 (b.o.)

FOUNDED 1968
Jackie Nichols

SEASON
Year-round

FACILITIES
Playhouse on the Square
Seating Capacity: 260
Stage: proscenium

Circuit Playhouse
Seating Capacity: 140
Stage: proscenium

FINANCES
July 1, 1988-June 30, 1989
Expenses: $534,523

Playhouse on the Square, the only professional company in the Memphis/ Mid-South area, serves a broad constituency in a diverse ethnic and cultural community approaching one million people. We produce a varied season and are committed to providing long-term employment to a core acting company and artistic staff. The resident company concept therefore requires us to seek out versatile individuals to support the seasons selected, individuals who are committed to ensemble growth. This philosophy provides artists the opportunity to work and expand their skills with productions for which they may not normally be considered. The manageable size of our organization and dedication to our principles help us maintain our goals in a society that embraces specialization and lack of personal long-term commitment. We also have well-established and highly effective theatre for youth and outreach programs dedicated to the audience of the future.

—*Jackie Nichols*

PRODUCTIONS 1987–88

Sunday in the Park with George, book: James Lapine; music and lyrics: Stephen Sondheim; (D) Terry Sneed; (S) Joe Ragey; (C) Renee Weiss; (L) Joe Ragey

The Member of the Wedding, Carson McCullers; (D) Ken Zimmerman; (S) Lois Mytas; (C) Renee Weiss; (L) John Rankin

Peter Pan, book: James M. Barrie; music: Mark Chapman and Jule Styne; lyrics: Carolyn Leigh (D) Ken Zimmerman; (S) Joe Ragey; (C) Renee Weiss; (L) John Rankin

A Murder is Announced, adapt: Leslie Darbon, from Agatha Christie; (D) Ken Zimmerman; (S) Kathy Haaga; (C) Renee Weiss; (L) Kathy Haaga

Romeo and Juliet, William Shakespeare; (D) Ken Zimmerman; (S) Lois Mytas; (C) Renee Weiss; (L) John Rankin

Glengarry Glen Ross, David Mamet; (D) William Clark; (S) Kathy Haaga; (C) Angela Seymour; (L) John Rankin

Oliver!, book, music and lyrics: Lionel Bart; (D) Ken Zimmerman; (S) Joe Ragey; (C) Angela Seymour; (L) John Rankin

Isn't It Romantic, Wendy Wasserstein; (D) Mindy Moore; (S) Debra Neal; (C) Coleen Duran; (L) Onis McHenry

Scrapbooks, Larry Gray; (D) Willam Clark; (S) William Clark; (C) Renee Weiss; (L) Liz McCraven

The Lion, the Witch, and the Wardrobe, adapt: Jules Tasca, from C.S. Lewis; lyrics: Ted Drachman; music: Thomas Tierney; (D) Jay M. Kinney; (S) Jackie Nichols; (C) Renee Weiss; (L) John Rankin

So Long on Lonely Street, Sandra Deer; (D) Gene Crain; (S) Robert Nowlin; (C) Renee Weiss; (L) Tim Osteen

Daughters, John Morgan Evans; (D) Paul Lormand; (S) Liz McCraven; (C) Angela Seymour; (L) John Rankin

Pump Boys and Dinettes, John Foley, Mark Hardwick, John Schimmel, Debra Monk, Cass Morgan and Jim Wann; (D) Ken Zimmerman; (S) Tim Decker; (C) Angela Seymour; (L) Liz McCraven

A . . . My Name is Alice, Julianne Boyd and Joan Micklin Silver; (D) Carole Ries; (S) Chris Ellis; (C) Angela Seymour; (L) Liz McCraven

Benefactors, Michael Frayn; (D) Tami Hook; (S) Nodie Williams; (C) Angela Seymour; (L) John Rankin

PRODUCTIONS 1988–89

Man of La Mancha, book: Dale Wasserman; lyrics: Joe Darion; music: Mitch Leigh; (D) Philip Giberson; (S) Michael Boyer; (C) Sean O'Casey; (L) Kim Hanson

The Colored Museum, George C. Wolfe; (D) Ruby O'Gray; (S) Joe Ragey; (C) Curtis C.; (L) John Rankin

Peter Pan, book: James M. Barrie; music: Mark Chapman and Jule Styne; lyrics: Carolyn Leigh; (D) Ken Zimmerman; (S) Joe Ragey; (C) Renee Weiss and Elizabeth Miller; (L) John Rankin

Noises Off, Michael Frayn; (D) Laura Fine; (S) Kathy Haaga; (C) Elizabeth Garat; (L) John Rankin

The Taming of the Shrew, William Shakespeare; (D) Ken Zimmerman; (S) Joe Ragey; (C) Kathy Haaga; (L) John Rankin

A Streetcar Named Desire, Tennessee Williams; (D) Ken Zimmerman; (S) Joe Ragey; (C) Elizabeth Garat; (L) John Rankin

Sugar Babies, conceived: Ralph G. Allen and Harry Rigby; (D) Ken Zimmerman; (S) Kathy Haaga; (C) Elizabeth Garat; (L) John Rankin

The Lion, the Witch and the Wardrobe, book adapt: Jules Tasca; lyrics: Ted Drachman; music: Thomas Tierney; (D) Ja M. Kinney; (S) Jackie Nichols; (C) Renee Weiss; (L) John Rankin

The Pied Piper, adapt: Adrian Mitchell, from Robert Browning; music: Dominic Muldowney; (D) Jay M. Kinney; (S) Jackie Nichols; (C) Elizabeth Garat; (L) John Rankin

Hunting Cockroaches, Janusz Glowacki; trans: Jadwiga Kosicka; (D) Sidney Lynch; (S) Henry Swanson; (C) Elizabeth Garat; (L) John Rankin

Remembering the Future, Larry Gray; (D) Tony Isbell; (S) Michael Dempsey; (C) Curt C.; (L) Andrea Hoffman

Woman in Mind, Alan Ayckbour (D) Carole Ries; (C) Elizabeth Garat

The Mystery of Irma Vep, Charles Ludlam; (D) Ken Zimmerman; (S) Henry Swanson; (C) Angela Seymour; (L) Stef Nicovich

Macbett, Eugene Ionesco; trans: Charles Marowitz; (D) Kate Davis; (S) John Rankin; (C) Angela Seymour; (L) John Rankin

Playhouse on the Square. Herman P. Markell and Harry Hood in *Glengarry Glen Ross*. Photo: Saul Rown.

Playmakers at the Ritz. Kathy Grau, Monica Bishop, Shaun Padgett and Jan Carr in *Angry Housewives*. Photo: G. Vogtritter.

Playmakers at the Ritz

MARK HUNTER
Producing Artistic Director

SUSAN PAUL
Executive Director

Box 5745
Tampa, FL 33675
(813) 247-7529 (bus.)
(813) 247-PLAY (b.o.)

FOUNDED 1981
Mark Hunter, Robert Hatch

SEASON
Sept.-June

FACILITIES
Ritz Theatre
Seating Capacity: 275
Stage: proscenium

Wild Side
Seating Capacity: 100
Stage: flexible

FINANCES
July 1, 1988-June 30, 1989
Expenses: $404,000

CONTRACTS
AEA SPT

Theatre, for me, has a touch of holiness about it. It is a means to celebrate our mysteries. Theatre, for me, also has a sense of moral purpose. It is a means of exploring our humanity and allowing for its elevation. Above all, theatre is, I think, a process informed by the sheer joy of collaborative effort and the unique satisfaction of risk rewarded. That is Playmakers' creed: to unite diverse artists in projects that are tinged with risk—the risk of occasional controversy, the risk of provoking powerful thoughts and emotions. To the extent that Playmakers produces contemporary works that are true to that purpose and which also entertain(in the broadest sense of that word), then to that extent Playmakers succeeds.
—*Mark Hunter*

Note: Playmakers at the Ritz was formerly titled Playmakers, Inc.

PRODUCTIONS 1987–88

Old Times, Harold Pinter; (D) Mark Hunter; (S) Patrick Doyle; (L) R.T. Williams
Miss Margarida's Way, Roberto Athayde; (D) Mark Hunter; (S) Mark Hunter; (C) Barbara Smith; (L) Dan Yerman
The Marriage of Bette and Boo, Christopher Durang; (D) Robert Hatch; (S) Alan Reynolds; (C) Loren Bracewell; (L) Alan Reynolds
Danny and the Deep Blue Sea, John Patrick Shanley; (D) Mark Hunter; (S) Steve Mitchell; (C) Claire Joseph; (L) G.B. Stephens
Gift of the Magi, adapt: Peter Ekstrom, from O. Henry; (D) Paul Hughes; (S) Dan Yerman; (C) Loren Bracewell; (L) Paul Hughes
P.S. Your Cat is Dead, James Kirkwood; (D) Neil DeGroot; (S) Barton Lee; (C) Joanne Johnson; (L) G.B. Stephens
Who's Afraid of Virginia Woolf?, Edward Albee; (D) Mark Hunter; (S) Eric Veenstra; (C) Loren Bracewell; (L) Michael Newton Brown
Criminal Minds, Robin Swicord; (D) Ellen Jones; (S) Robert Geitner; (L) Robert Geitner

PRODUCTIONS 1988–89

Jazz, Jam, No Jive, company-developed; (D) Mark Hunter and Barbara Smith; (S) G.B. Stephens; (L) G.B. Stephens
Bent, Martin Sherman; (D) Robert Hatch; (S) Jimmy Humphries; (C) Joanne Johnson; (L) Joseph Oshry
Angry Housewives, book: A.M. Collins; music: Chad Henry; (D) Christopher Steele; (S) Barton Lee; (C) Loren Bracewell; (L) G.B. Stephens
The Road to Mecca, Athol Fugard; (D) Mark Hunter; (S) Jimmy Humphries; (C) Sandra Fox; (L) G.B. Stephens
Woman in Mind, Alan Ayckbourn; (D) Mark Hunter; (S) Jimmy Humphries; (C) Joanne Johnson; (L) G.B. Stephens
Tira Tells Everything There Is to Know About Herself, Michael Weller; (D) Barbara Smith; (S) Barbara Smith; (C) Barbara Smith; (L) Ken Kaczynski
Home Free, Landord Wilson; (D) Barbara Smith; (S) Barbara Smith; (L) Ken Kaczynski
Drinking in America, Eric Bogosian; (D) Mark Hunter; (S) Mark Hunter; (L) Mark Hunter
Tent Meeting, Larry Larson, Levi Lee and Rebecca Wackler; (D) Monica Bishop; (S) Steve Mitchell; (C) Joanne Johnson; (L) Bill Ferrara

PlayMakers Repertory Company

DAVID HAMMOND
Artistic Director

MILLY S. BARRANGER
Executive Producer

REGINA LICKTEIG
Administrative Director

CB# 3235 Graham Memorial Building 052A
Chapel Hill, NC 27599-3235
(919) 962-1122 (bus.)
(919) 962-1121 (b.o.)

FOUNDED 1976
Arthur L. Housman

SEASON
Sept.-May

FACILITIES
Paul Green Theatre
Seating Capacity: 499
Stage: thrust

Playmakers Theatre
Seating Capacity: 285
Stage: proscenium

FINANCES
July 1, 1988-June 30, 1989
Expenses: $774,000

CONTRACTS
LORT (D)

PlayMakers Repertory Company is dedicated to the actor as the center of the performance event. We are committed to the revelation of each play, not by the application of visual metaphor or directorially imposed thematic statement, but through the varying processes applied by the actor in the investigation of the material. Our repertoire is eclectic, and we hope that audiences are unable to anticipate our production "style" from play to play. We aspire to bring to classic and standard works the sense of excitement and discovery too often reserved only for new scripts, and to approach new texts with the discipline, skill and theatrical perceptions of a classically trained company. The interaction of our professional company with students in our training program is a vital aspect of our work: our students carry the results of our efforts to other stages throughout the country.
—*David Hammond*

PRODUCTIONS 1987–88

Romeo and Juliet, William Shakespeare; (D) David Hammond; (S) Sam Kirckpatrick; (C) Sam Kirkpatrick; (L) Robert Wierzel
Orphans, Lyle Kessler; (D) Maureen Heffernan; (S) Dale F. Jordan; (C) Bobbi Owen; (L) Dale F. Jordan
A Child's Christmas in Wales, adapt: Jeremy Brooks and Adrian Mitchell, from Dylan

Playmakers Repertory Company. Demetrios Pappageorge, Kyle MacLachlan and David Whalen in *Romeo and Juliet*. Photo: Keven Keister.

Thomas; (D) Christian Angermann; (S) McKay Coble; (C) McKay Coble; (L) Robert Wierzel
Mourning Becomes Electra, Eugene O'Neill; (D) David Hammond; (S) Bill Clarke; (C) Bill Clarke; (L) Robert Wierzel
On the Verge or The Geography of Yearning, Eric Overmyer; (D) Christian Angermann; (S) Phillip R. Baldwin; (C) Bobbi Owen; (L) Marcus Dilliard
The Beggar's Opera, John Gay; adapt: David Hammond; (D) David Hammond; (S) McKay Coble; (C) Marianne Custer; (L) Robert Wierzel

PRODUCTIONS 1988–89

The Marriage of Figaro, from Pierre-Augustin Caron de Beaumarchais; adapt: Peter Jeffries; (D) David Hammond; (S) McKay Coble; (C) Marianne Custer; (L) Marcus Dilliard
The Road to Mecca, Athol Fugard; (D) Christian Angermann; (S) Michael Miller; (C) Bobbi Owen; (L) Mary Louise Geiger
A Child's Christmas in Wales, adapt: Jeremy Brooks and Adrian Mitchell, from Dylan Thomas; (D) Christian Angermann and Jeffries Peter; (S) McKay Coble; (C) McKay Coble; (L) Robert Wierzel
For Lease or Sale, Elizabeth Spencer; (D) David Hammond; (S) McKay Coble; (C) McKay Coble; (L) Robert Wierzel
Misalliance, George Bernard Shaw; (D) Maureen Heffernan; (S) Anita C. Stewart; (C) Kristine Kearney; (L) Marcus Dilliard
The Taming of the Shrew, William Shakespeare; (D) David Hammond; (S) Bill Clarke; (C) Bill Clarke; (L) Robert Wierzel

Playwrights Horizons

ANDRE BISHOP
Artistic Director

PAUL S. DANIELS
Executive Director

416 West 42nd St.
New York, NY 10036
(212) 564-1235 (bus.)
(212) 279-4200 (b.o.)

FOUNDED 1971
Robert Moss

SEASON
Sept.–June

FACILITIES
Mainstage
Seating Capacity: 156
Stage: proscenium

Studio
Seating Capacity: 74
Stage: flexible

FINANCES
Sept. 1, 1988-Aug. 31, 1989
Expenses: $3,406,000

CONTRACTS
AEA Off Broadway

Playwrights Horizons is dedicated to the support and development of contemporary American playwrights, composers and lyricists and to the production of their work.

—*Andre Bishop*

PRODUCTIONS 1987–88

6th Annual Young Playwrights Festival:
Tiny Mommy, Juliet Garson; (D) Amy Saltz; (S) Derek McLane; (C) Michael Krass; (L) Nancy Schertler
Sparks in the Park, Noble Mason Smith; (D) Gary Pearle; (S) Derek McLane; (C) Michael Krass; (L) Nancy Schertler

Laughing Wild, Christopher Durang; (D) Ron Lagomarsino; (S) Thomas Lynch; (C) William Ivey Long; (L) Arden Fingerhut
Another Antigone, A.R. Gurney, Jr.; (D) John Tillinger; (S) Steve Rubin; (C) Steven Rubin; (L) Kent Dorsey
Lucky Stiff, book and lyrics: Lynn Ahrens; music: Stephen Flaherty; (D) Thommie Walsh; (S) Bob Shaw; (C) Michael Krass; (L) Beverly Emmons
Right Behind the Flag, Kevin Heelan; (D) R.J. Cutler; (S) Loy Arcenas; (C) Candice Donnelly; (L) Debra J. Kletter

New Theatre Wing
Cold Sweat, Neal Bell; (D) John Henry Davis; (S) Randy Benjamin; (C) Donna Zakowska; (L) F. Mitchell Dana
Gus and Al, Albert Innaurato; (D) David Warren; (S) Jim Youmans; (C) David C. Woolard; (L) Robert Jared
Saved from Obscurity, Tom

Playwrights Horizons. Joan Allen and Peter Friedman in *The Heidi Chronicles*. Photo: Gerry Goldstein.

Mardirosian; (D) John Ferraro; (S) Rick Dennis; (C) Marilyn Keith; (L) Jackie Manassee

RODUCTIONS 1988–89

h Annual Young Playwrights Festival:
nd the Air Didn't Answer, Robert Kerr; (D) Christopher Durang; (S) Allen Moyer; (C) Jess Goldstein; (L) Nancy Schertler
niority, Eric Ziegenhagen; (D) Lisa Peterson; (S) Allen Moyer; (C) Jess Goldstein; (L) Nancy Schertler
omen and Wallace, Jonathan Marc Sherman; (D) Don Scardino; (S) Allen Moyer; (C) Jess Goldstein; (L) Nancy Schertler

he Heidi Chronicles, Wendy Wasserstein; (D) Daniel Sullivan; (S) Thomas Lynch; (C) Jennifer von Mayrhauser; (L) Pat Collins
aved from Obscurity, Tom Mardirosian; (D) John Ferraro; (S) Rick Dennis; (C) Marilyn Keith; (L) Jackie Manassee
us and Al, Albert Innaurato; (D) David Warren; (S) Jim Youmans; (C) David C. Woolard; (L) Robert Jared
ankee Dawg You Die, Philip Kan Gotanda; (D) Sharon Ott; (S) Kent Dorsey; (C) Jess Goldstein; (L) Dan Kotlowitz

ew Theatre Wing
ate's Diary, Kathleen Tolan; (D) David Greenspan; (S) William Kennon; (C) Elsa Ward; (L) David Bergstein
ucy's Lapses, book and lyrics: Laura Harrington; music: Christopher Drobny; (D) David Warren; (S) Jim Youmans; (C) David C. Woolard; (L) Debra Dumas

The Playwrights' Center

AVID MOORE, JR.
xecutive Director

301 Franklin Ave., East Minneapolis, MN 55406
612) 332-7481

FOUNDED 1971
John Olive, Jon Jackoway, Barbara Field, Thomas G. Dunn, Eric Brogger, Gregg Almquist

SEASON
Jan.-Dec.

FACILITIES
Mainstage
Seating Capacity: 150
Stage: flexible

FINANCES
July 1, 1988-June 30, 1989
Expenses: $450,000

CONTRACTS
AEA letter of agreement

The Playwrights' Center provides playwrights at all levels services that develop their skills while serving as an advocate for production of their work. To participate in Center programs a playwright can apply for core membership through an annual script submission process or become a general member by paying yearly dues. The Center provides space, professional actors, directors and dramaturgs for "cold" readings, non-performance workshops, staged readings, and special projects. Midwest Playlabs is a two-week development conference for six scripts. The Center awards fellowships and commissions annually to between 16 and 18 writers, most awards ranging in size from $5,000 to $10,000. Jones Awards are one-act play commissions for six Minnesota playwrights. The Center offers information on other opportunities and related services as well. A Young Playwrights unit includes a national, three-week summer writing conference. Storytalers is a professional touring company that performs original works in schools and community centers. The Artist-in-Education program places playwrights in public school residencies. The goal of all Center programs is to provide playwrights of diverse points of view a place to develop their work without the pressure of production.
—*David Moore, Jr*

Note: Seasons are strictly devoted to staged readings, workshops and touring; the listings below are the summer Midwest Playlab's workshops.

The Playwrights' Center. Mark Amdahl, Kathryn O'Malley and Tim Danz in *Briar Patch*. Photo: Melissa Denton.

PRODUCTIONS 1987–88

Briar Patch, Deborah Carol Pryor; (D) Roberta Levitow; (L) Pamela Kildahl
Comfort and Joy, Jeffrey Hatcher; (D) B. Rodney Marriott; (L) Pamela Kildahl
Four Our Fathers, Jon Klein; (D) Oskar Eustis; (L) Pamela Kildahl
Paraguay, Tom Poole; (D) Claude Purdy; (L) Pamela Kildahl
The Virgin Molly, Quincy Long; (D) Morgan Jenness; (L) Pamela Kildahl
Walkers, Marion Clinton; (D) Claude Purdy; (L) Pamela Kildahl

PRODUCTIONS 1988–89

Miriam's Flowers, Migdalia Cruz; (D) Roberta Levitow; (L) Jeff Couture
The Swan Play, Elizabeth Egloff; (D) Morgan Jenness; (L) Jeff Couture
Soundbite, Gary Leon Hill; (D) Roberta Levitow; (L) Jeff Couture
My Dead Wife, Tom Poole; (D) Steven Dietz; (L) Jeff Couture
New Business, Tom Williams; (D) Steven Dietz; (L) Jeff Couture
Mr. Christmas Easter Bunny, Erin Cressida Wilson; (D) Morgan Jenness; (L) Jeff Couture

Portland Repertory Theater

BRENDA HUBBARD
Artistic Director

MARK ALLEN
General Director

NANCY D. WELCH
Producing Director

25 South Salmon St.
Portland, OR
(503) 224-4491

FOUNDED 1980
Mark Allen, Nancy A Welch

SEASON
Oct.-June

FACILITIES
World Trade Center
Seating Capacity: 230
Stage: proscenium

Portland Repertory Theater. Charles Canada, John Morgan and Ron Blair in Master Harold...and the Boys. *Photo: Kevin Haislip.*

FINANCES
Sept. 1, 1988-Aug. 31, 1989
Expenses: $1,000,000

CONTRACTS
AEA SPT

Portland Repertory Theater was so named to reflect the theatre's position as Portland's oldest professional, indigenous theatre company. Performing an eclectic season of six plays ranging from classic to contemporary works, the Rep has a deep commitment to developing a core ensemble of theatre artists who work with the company in an ongoing manner. The company was founded to provide a home for the artist and a forum where a vast world of literary and artistic approaches are explored within the context of an intimate physical setting. Our mission is to create exciting ensemble theatre that explores many facets of humankind to convey far-reaching truths. Plans for 1989-90 include a new play series of staged readings featuring emerging playwrights and a school outreach program that makes performances available to high school students and teachers.

—*Mark Allen*

PRODUCTIONS 1987–88

Artichoke, Joanna M. Glass; (D) Brenda Hubbard; (S) Jeff Seats; (C) Susan L. Bonde; (L) Kobi Enright
"Master Harold" ... and the boys, Athol Fugard; (D) Allen Nause; (S) Mark Loring; (C) Shaune Wunder; (L) Rogue Conn
Oh, Coward, adapt: Roderick Cook; music and lyrics: Noel Coward; (D) David Ira Goldstein; (S) Jeff Seats; (C) Susan L. Bonde; (L) Rogue Conn
Biloxi Blues, Neil Simon; (D) Richard Edwards; (S) Jerry Hooker; (C) Susan L. Bonde; (L) Rogue Conn
The Little Foxes, Lillian Hellman; (D) Brenda Hubbard; (S) Jeff Seats; (C) Susan L. Bonde; (L) Bruce Hopkins
A Pack of Lies, Hugh Whitemore; (D) Cynthia White; (S) Jeff Seats; (C) Shaune Wunder; (L) Jeff Forbes
A ... My Name is Alice, Joan Micklin Silver and Julianne Boyd; (D) Brenda Hubbard; (S) Karen Gjelsteen; (C) Susan L. Bonde; (L) Rogue Conn

PRODUCTIONS 1988–89

Home, David Storey; (D) Brenda Hubbard; (S) Lawrence Larson; (C) Shaune Wunder; (L) Jeff Forbes
A Moon For the Misbegotten, Eugene O'Neill; (D) Tom Ramirez; (S) Karen Gjelsteen; (C) Susan L. Bonde; (L) Rogue Conn
Private Lives, Noel Coward; (D) Brenda Hubbard; (S) D. Martyn Bookwalter; (C) Susan L. Bonde; (L) Lawrence Larson
I'm Not Rappaport, Herb Gardner; (D) Peggy Shannon; (S) Thomas Buderwitz; (C) Susan L. Bonde; (L) Rogue Conn
Dial "M" for Murder, Frederick Knott; (D) Brenda Hubbard; (S) Lawrence Larson; (C) Susan L. Bonde; (L) Rogue Conn
Broadway Bound, Neil Simon; (D) Jon Kretzu; (S) Thomas Buderwitz; (C) Shaune Wunder; (L) Rogue Conn

Portland Stage Company

RICHARD HAMBURGER
Artistic Director

CAROLINE TURNER
Managing Director

Box 1458
Portland, ME 04104
(207) 774-1043 (bus.)
(207) 774-0465 (b.o.)

FOUNDED 1974
Ted Davis

SEASON
Nov.-Apr.

FACILITIES
Portland Performing Arts Center
Seating Capacity: 290
Stage: proscenium

FINANCES
June 1, 1988-May 31, 1989
Expenses: $867,563

CONTRACTS
LORT D

Our common purpose at Portland Stage Company is to nurture the imaginative worlds of gifted writers, actors, directors, designers a composers. Hand in hand with t commitment to artistic expressio and experimentation is our belie that Portland Stage must serve a vital center in the community; a place where people of diverse backgrounds and ages come to learn not only from the plays but also from each other. We believe theatre can be a catalyst for psychologial and social change that encourages artists and audiences alike to ask difficult questions about themselves and their world To this end, we surround each pl with a variety of programs designed to place the work in social political and literary contexts. Pro grams include humanities lecture published essays, a cable televisio series, student matinees and audience discussions. With its uncompromisingly intellectual breadth, our six-play season forms the spiritual spine of the theatre. Portland Stage is dedicated to re terpreting the gloriously rich language and imagery of classic plays as well as to discovering cor temporary work that sharply challenges cherished assumptions. We search for plays where human anxiety, aspiration and behavior a examined with fresh, original and often humorous perspectives.
—*Richard Hamburge*

PRODUCTIONS 1987–88

Seascape, Edward Albee; (D) Tor Prewitt; (S) G.W. Mercier; (C) G.W. Mercier; (L) Jackie Manassee
Tartuffe, Moliere; trans: Donald M. Frame; (D) Michael Engler; (S) Christopher Barecca; (C) Candice Donnelly; (L) Donald Holder

Portland Stage Company. Kimi'Sung and Jacqueline Knapp in Inside Out. *Photo: David A. Rodgers.*

Orphans, Lyle Kessler; (D) Phil
  Killian; (S) Michael Smith;
  (C) Catherine Zuber;
  (L) Stephen Strawbridge
Hard Times, adapt: Stephen
  Jeffreys, from Charles Dickens;
  (D) Richard Hamburger;
  (S) Christopher Barecca;
  (C) Martha Hally; (L) Stephen
  Strawbridge
Painting Churches, Tina Howe;
  (D) Evan Yionoulis; (S) Charles
  McCarry; (C) Ellen McCartney;
  (L) Donald Holder
Sharon and Billy, Alan Bowne;
  (D) Richard Hamburger;
  (S) Derek McLane;
  (C) Catherine Zuber; (L) Robert
  Wierzel

PRODUCTIONS 1988–89

A Walk in the Woods, Lee
  Blessing; (D) Paul Moser;
  (S) Derek McLane;
  (C) Catherine Zuber; (L) Stuart
  Duke
The Hostage, Brendan Behan;
  (D) Richard Hamburger;
  (S) Scott Bradley; (C) Martha
  Hally; (L) Peter Kaczorowski
Benefactors, Michael Frayn;
  (D) Charles Karchmer;
  (S) Michael Miller; (C) Deborah
  Shaw; (L) Robert Wierzel
Ghosts, Henrik Ibsen; trans:
  Christopher Hampton; (D) Mel
  Marvin; (S) Michael H. Yeargan;
  (C) Martha Hally; (L) Donald
  Holder
Inside Out, Willy Holtzman;
  (D) John Pynchon Holms;
  (S) Philipp Jung; (C) Ellen
  McCartney; (L) Michael
  Chybowski
Breaking the Silence, Stephen
  Poliakoff; (D) Richard
  Hamburger; (S) Christopher
  Barecca; (C) Catherine Zuber;
  (L) Stephen Strawbridge

Puerto Rican Traveling Theatre

MIRIAM COLON VALLE
Executive Director

141 West 94th St.
New York, NY 10025
(212) 354-1293 (bus.)
(212) 265-0794 (b.o.)

FOUNDED 1967
Miriam Cologne Balle

SEASON
Jan.-Aug.

FACILITIES
47th Street Theatre
Seating Capacity: 194
Stage: proscenium

FINANCES
Oct. 1, 1987-Sept. 30, 1988
Expenses: $669,500

CONTRACTS
AEA letter of agreement

For 22 years, the Puerto Rican Traveling Theatre's two objectives have been to establish a bilingual theatre emphasizing Hispanic dramatists, both international and U.S.-based, and to make these presentations accessible to the widest possible range of people. Our four programs continue to further these goals: the mainstage season has presented over 50 bilingual productions, the summer tour presents free performances throughout New York City annually, the playwrights' laboratory develops new playwrights through a "page-to-stage" program, and the training unit offers free professional-level classes in the arts to minority students. We perform in Spanish to reaffirm our proud Hispanic heritage while gaining a fuller understanding of the American way of life. We perform in English to provide a bridge which will enhance communication, not only with ourselves, but with a broader segment of the world around us.
—*Miriam Cologne Balle*

PRODUCTIONS 1987–88

Ariano, Richard V. Irizarry; trans:
  Margarita Lopez Chiclana;
  (D) Vicente Castro; (S) James
  Sandefur; (C) Toni-Leslie James;
  (L) Rachel Budin
Senora Carrar's Rifles, Bertolt
  Brecht; trans: Wolfgang
  Sauerlander and Oscar Ferringo;
  (D) Alejandro Quintana;
  (S) Robert Klingelhoefer;
  (C) Laura Drawbaugh; (L) Rick
  Butler
First Class, Candido Tirado;
  trans: Fernando Moreno; (D) A.
  Dean Irby; (S) Robert
  Klingelhoefer; (C) Laura
  Drawbaugh; (L) Rachel Budin
The Garden, Carlos Morton;

Puerto Rican Traveling Theatre. Paul-Felix Montez and Rico Elias in *First Class*.

  trans: Manuel Martin; (D) Jorge
  Huerta; (S) Craig Clipper;
  (C) Laura Drawbaugh

PRODUCTIONS 1988–89

Happy Birthday, Mama, Robert
  Cossa; trans: Myra Gann;
  (D) Vicente Castro; (S) Robert
  Klingelhoefer; (C) Stephen
  Pardee; (L) Bill Simmons
Quintuplets, Luis Rafael Sanchez;
  trans: Alba Oms and Ivonne
  Coll; (D) Alba Oms; (S) Robert
  Klingelhoefer; (C) Laura
  Drawbaugh; (L) Bill Simmons
Conversation Among the Ruins,
  James Sandefur; trans: Myra
  Gann; (D) Alejandra Gutierrez;
  (S) Robert Klingelhoefer;
  (C) Laura Drawbaugh; (L) Bill
  Simmons
Chinese Charade, Manuel
  Pereiras; (D) Susana Tubert;
  (S) Robert Klingelhoefer;
  (C) Maria Ferreira-Contessa

Remains Theatre

AMY MORTON
WILLIAM L. PETERSEN
Co-Artistic Directors

JENNIFER BOZNOS
Producing Director

1300 West Belmont
Chicago, IL 60657
(312) 549-7725 (bus.)
(312) 327-5588 (b.o.)

FOUNDED 1979
Jim Roach, Earl Pastko, David
Alan Novak, D.W. Moffett,
Lindsay McGee

SEASON
Jan.-Dec.

FINANCES
July 1, 1988-June 30, 1989
Expenses: $560,225

CONTRACTS
AEA CAT

Remains Theatre is a group of actors, a stage manager, a small staff, a copier, a fight song and a table at the local bar. In its first seven years Remains explored the work of writers mostly outside the mainstream, such as Franz Xaver Kroetz, Richard Foreman, Spalding Gray, Herman Melville and others. The years were marked by much acclaim and the emergence of exceptional acting, both as an ensemble and individually. We maintain a strong devotion to new works with writers-in-residence and also look to explore more eclectic programming–large but lesser-known plays such as Brecht's *Puntila*, ensemble-developed pieces and collaborations with artists from the other arts. We continue to challenge ourselves as a group, learn from our growing audiences and take an active role in Chicago's strong theatre community.
—Amy Morton,
William L. Petersen

Note: During the 1987-88 season, Larry Sloan served as artistic director.

PRODUCTIONS 1987–88

Big Time, Keith Reddin; (D) Larry Sloan; (S) Kevin Rigdon; (C) Laura Cunningham; (L) Kevin Rigdon

Sneaky Feelings, An Evening of One Act Plays:
The Author's Voice, Richard Greenberg; (D) Lisa Peterson; (S) Mary Griswold; (C) John Paoletti; (L) Geoffrey Bushor
Albert's Bridge, Tom Stoppard; (D) Larry Sloan; (S) Mary Griswold; (C) John Paoletti; (L) Geoffrey Bushor
The Frog Prince, David Mamet; (D) Eric Simonson; (S) Mary Griswold; (C) John Paoletti; (L) Geoffrey Bushor

PRODUCTIONS 1988–89

Lloyd's Prayer, Kevin Kling; (D) David Petrarca; (S) Tamara Turchetta; (C) Frances Maggio; (L) Robert Christen
Speed-the-Plow, David Mamet; (D) Joel Schumacher; (S) Michael S. Philippi and Kevin Rigdon; (C) Laura Cunningham; (L) Kevin Rigdon

Repertorio Espanol

RENE BUCH
Artistic Director

GILBERTO ZALDIVAR
Producer

138 East 27th St.
New York, NY 10016
(212) 889-2850

FOUNDED 1968
Gilberto Zaldivar, Rene Buch

Remains Theatre. Denis O'Hare and Holly Fulger in *Lloyd's Prayer*. Photo: Charles Osgood.

SEASON
Year-round.

FACILITIES
Gramercy Arts Theatre
Seating Capacity: 140
Stage: proscenium

Equitable Tower Auditorium
Seating Capacity: 485
Stage: proscenium

FINANCES
Sept. 1, 1988-Aug. 31, 1989
Expenses: $1,300,000

Artistically, the past few years have brought us great satisfaction, with many advances made possible by our Ongoing Ensembles grant from the Natioinal Endowment for the Arts. The grant gave Repertorio the ability to do several important productions in repertory, while a grant from the Wallace Funds supported the commission of plays by Hispanic-American playwrights, and the Mellon Foundation's support has allowed us to present large-cast productions such as *Granada* and *El Burlador de Sevilla*. A recent grant from the Rockefeller Foundation will bring guest directors from Brazil and Chile for productions which will capture the "magical realism" of Latin American literature and theatre. Our national touring program will expand, taking the company to cities like Phoenix, San Diego and Los Angeles, where there is a natural audience for our work. The company's seasons at the Equitable Tower have fostered a new appreciation for Spanish-language musical and dance events in New York. Our audience grows steadily in size, diversity and sophistication, so the future holds great promise.
—Rene Buch

PRODUCTIONS 1987–88

Padre Gomez y Santa Cecilia, Gloria Gonzalez; (D) Rene Buch; (S) Robert W. Federico; (C) Robert W. Federico; (L) Robert W. Federico
La Celestina, Fernando de Rojas; (D) Rene Buch; (S) Robert W. Federico; (C) Robert W. Federico; (L) Robert W. Federico
Revoltillo, Eduardo Machado; (D) Rene Buch; (S) Robert W. Federico; (C) Robert W. Federico; (L) Robert W. Federico
Don Juan Tenorio, Jose Zorrilla; (D) Rene Buch; (S) Robert W. Federico; (C) Robert W. Federico; (L) Robert W. Federico
El Burlador de Sevilla, Tirso de Molina; (D) Rene Buch; (S) Robert W. Federico; (C) Robert W. Federico; (L) Robert W. Federico
Las Damas Modernas de Guanabacoa, Eduardo Machado; (D) Rene Buch; (S) Robert W. Federico; (C) Robert W. Federico; (L) Robert W. Federico
Cafe Con Leche, Gloria Gonzale (D) Rene Buch; (S) Robert W. Federico; (C) Robert W. Federico; (L) Robert W. Federico
La Generala Alegre, music: Amadeo Vives; lyrics: Perrin y Palacios; (D) Rene Buch; (S) Robert W. Federico; (C) Robert W. Federico; (L) Robert W. Federico
La Corte de Faraon, music: Vicente Lleo; lyrics: Perrin y Palacios; (D) Rene Buch; (S) Robert W. Federico; (C) Robert W. Federico; (L) Robert W. Federico
La Zarzuela, various composers; (D) Rene Buch; (S) Robert W. Federico; (C) Robert W. Federico; (L) Robert W. Federico
Puerto Rico: Encanto y Cancion various composers; (D) Rene Buch; (S) Robert W. Federico; (C) Robert W. Federico; (L) Robert W. Federico
Habana: Antologia Musical, various composers; (D) Rene Buch; (S) Robert W. Federico; (C) Robert W. Federico; (L) Robert W. Federico
Usted Tambien Podra Disfrutar de Ella, Ana Diosdado; (D) Joanne Pottlitzer; (S) Robert W. Federico; (C) Robert W. Federico; (L) Robert W. Federico
Prohibido Suicidasse En Primavera, Alejandro Casona; (D) Delfar Peralta; (S) Robert W. Federico; (C) Robert W. Federico; (L) Robert W. Federico
La Fiaca, Ricardo Talesnik; (D) Delfar Peralta; (S) Robert W. Federico; (C) Robert W. Federico; (L) Robert W. Federico
Yerma, Federico Garcia Lorca; (D) Christopher Martin; (S) Robert W. Federico; (C) Robert W. Federico; (L) Robert W. Federico

PRODUCTIONS 1988–89

Granada, Manuel De Falla and

Repertorio Espanol. *Grenada*. Photo: Gerry Goodstein.

Federico Garcia Lorca; (D) Rene Buch; (S) Robert W. Federico; (C) Robert W. Federico; (L) Robert W. Federico

Puerto Rico: Encanto y Cancion, various composers; (D) Rene Buch; (S) Robert W. Federico; (C) Robert W. Federico; (L) Robert W. Federico

Habana: Antologia Musical, various composers; (D) Rene Buch; (S) Robert W. Federico; (C) Robert W. Federico; (L) Robert W. Federico

La Generala Alegre, music: Amadeo Vives; lyrics: Perrin y Palacios; (D) Rene Buch; (S) Robert W. Federico; (C) Robert W. Federico; (L) Robert W. Federico

La Zarzuela, various composers; (D) Rene Buch; (S) Robert W. Federico; (C) Robert W. Federico; (L) Robert W. Federico

La Corte de Faraon, music: Vicente Lleo; lyrics: Perrin y Palacios; (D) Rene Buch; (S) Robert W. Federico; (C) Robert W. Federico; (L) Robert W. Federico

Cafe Con Leche, Gloria Gonzalez; (D) Rene Buch; (S) Robert W. Federico; (C) Robert W. Federico; (L) Robert W. Federico

El Burlador de Sevilla, Tirso de Molina; (D) Rene Buch; (S) Robert W. Federico; (C) Robert W. Federico; (L) Robert W. Federico

Don Juan Tenorio, Jose Zorrilla; (D) Rene Buch; (S) Robert W. Federico; (C) Robert W. Federico; (L) Robert W. Federico

Revoltillo, Eduardo Machado; (D) Rene Buch; (S) Robert W. Federico; (C) Robert W. Federico; (L) Robert W. Federico

Padre Gomez y Santa Cecilia, Gloria Gonzalez; (D) Rene Buch; (S) Robert W. Federico; (C) Robert W. Federico; (L) Robert W. Federico

La Casa de Bernarda Alba, Federico Garcia Lorca; (D) Rene Buch; (S) Robert W. Federico; (C) Robert W. Federico; (L) Robert W. Federico

Yerma, Federico Garcia Lorca; (D) Rene Buch; (S) Robert W. Federico; (C) Robert W. Federico; (L) Robert W. Federico

La Fiaca, Ricardo Talesnik; (D) Delfar Peralta; (S) Robert W. Federico; (C) Robert W. Federico; (L) Robert W. Federico

La Nonna, Roberto Cossa; (D) Braulio Villar; (S) Robert W. Federico; (C) Robert W. Federico; (L) Robert W. Federico

The Repertory Theatre of St. Louis

STEVEN WOOLF
Artistic Director

MARK D. BERNSTEIN
Managing Director

Box 28030
St. Louis, MO 63119
(314) 968-7340 (bus.)
(314) 968-4925 (b.o.)

FOUNDED 1966
Webster College

SEASON
Sept.-Apr.

FACILITIES
Mainstage
Seating Capacity: 733
Stage: thrust

Studio
Seating Capacity: 125
Stage: flexible

Lab Space
Seating Capacity: 75
Stage: flexible

FINANCES
June 1, 1988-May 31, 1989
Expenses: $3,143,000

CONTRACTS
LORT B and D and AEA TYA

Partnership between audiences, artists and technicians in the joy and wonder of theatre is embraced in the four performance venues of the Repertory Theatre of St. Louis. An eclectic mix of styles gives a widely varied season: Mainstage selections offer work from many sources, giving a wide view of theatre literature to our largest audience; our Studio Theatre explores the new, the old seen in new ways, poetry, music and sometimes season-long themes; the Imaginary Theatre Company is our touring component, playing throughout the state of Missouri using literature as its basis for introducing theatre to younger audiences; the newly formed Lab series focuses on playwrights, giving them a full rehearsal period, professional cast and director to work on a new script. Work in the Lab is open to the public but is not reviewed and has limited production support. Through these activities and others, the Rep seeks to develop an audience that become strong advocates for live performance.

—*Steven Woolf*

PRODUCTIONS 1987–88

Company, book: George Furth; music and lyrics: Stephen Sondheim; (D) Steven Woolf; (S) Carolyn L. Ross; (C) Carolyn L. Ross; (L) Peter E. Sargent

The Little Foxes, Lillian Hellman; (D) Timothy Near; (S) John Ezell; (C) Jim Buff; (L) Max De Volder

Dames at Sea, book and lyrics: George Haimsohn and Robin Miller; music: Jim Wise; (D) Pamela Hunt; (S) John Roslevich, Jr.; (C) Dorothy L. Marshall; (L) Peter E. Sargent

The Immigrant: A Hamilton County Album, Mark Harelik; conceived: Mark Harelik and Randal Myler; (D) Susan Gregg; (S) John Carver Sullivan; (C) John Carver Sullivan; (L) Dale F. Jordan

Julius Ceasar, William Shakespeare; (D) Edward Amor; (S) John Ezell; (C) Dorothy L. Marshall; (L) Max De Volder

How the Other Half Loves, Alan Ayckbourn; (D) Edward Stern; (S) Arthur Ridley; (C) Arthur Ridley; (L) Glenn Dunn

A Quiet End, Robin Swados; (D) Sam Blackwell; (S) Mel Dickerson; (C) Jim Buff; (L) Mark Wilson

Day Six, Martin Halpern; (D) Louis D. Pietig; (S) Larry Biedenstein; (C) Holly Poe Durbin; (L) Peggy Thierheimer

Amazing Grace, Sandra Deer; (D) William Woodman; (S) Richard Tollkuhn; (C) Teri McConnell; (L) Max De Volder

Three Tales of Givers and Their Gifts, Kim Allen Bozark; (D) Wayne Salomon; (S) Kim Wilson; (C) Jana Park-Rogers

The Beauty and the Beast, adapt: Wayne Salomon; (D) Wayne Salomon; (S) Kim Wilson; (C) Jana Park-Rogers

Little Brother, Little Sister, David Campton; (D) Wayne Salomon; (S) Kim Wilson; (C) Jana Park-Rogers

Lady Be Good, the Story of Ella Fitzgerald, Wayne Salomon and Joseph R. Dreyer; (D) Wayne Salomon; (S) Kim Wilson; (C) Jana Park-Rogers

The Repertory Theatre of St. Louis. Marcy DeGonge in *Candide*. Photo: Judy Andrews.

PRODUCTIONS 1988–89

Candide, book adapt: Hugh Wheeler; music: Leonard Bernstein; lyrics: Richard Wilbur; add'l lyrics: Stephen Sondheim and John Latouche; (D) Munson Hicks; (S) John Falabella; (C) Dorothy L. Marshall; (L) Peter E. Sargent
Boy Meets Girl, Bella Spewack and Samuel Spewack; (D) Brian Murray; (S) Derek McLane; (C) Jennifer von Mayrhauser; (L) Stephen Strawbridge
Steel Magnolias, Robert Harling; (D) Susan Gregg; (S) Carolyn L. Ross; (C) Carolyn L. Ross; (L) Max De Volder
Offshore Signals, Roger Cornish; (D) Edward Stern; (S) David Potts; (C) Dorothy L. Marshall; (L) Peter E. Sargent
Saint Joan, George Bernard Shaw; (D) William Woodman; (S) John Ezell; (C) Dorothy L. Marshall; (L) Max De Volder
Noises Off, Michael Frayn; (D) Donald Ewer; (S) James Wolk; (C) Arthur Ridley; (L) Phil Monat
Hannah Senesh, adapt: David Schechter, from Hannah Senesh; (D) David Schechter; (S) Kim Wilson; (C) Bonnie Kruger; (L) Glenn Dunn
The Last Good Moment of Lily Baker, Russell Davis; (D) Tom Martin; (S) Bill Schmiel; (C) Holly Poe Durbin; (L) Mark Wilson
The Voice of the Prairie, John Olive; (D) Steven Woolf; (S) John Roslevich, Jr.; (C) Dorothy L. Marshall; (L) Max De Volder
Dreidels, Wassailing and Other Tails, Kim Allen Bozark; (D) Ron Himes; (S) Kim Wilson; (C) Jana Park-Rogers
Pinocchio, adapt: Sue Greenberg, from Carlo Collodi; (D) Jeffrey Matthews; (S) Kim Wilson; (C) Jana Park-Rogers
The Twilight Room, Kim Allen Bozark; (D) Jeffrey Matthews; (S) Kim Wilson; (C) Jana Park-Rogers

River Arts Repertory

LAWRENCE SACHAROW
Artistic Director

LORI OTT
Company Manager/Marketing Director

Box 1166
Woodstock, NY 12498
(914) 679-5899 (bus.)
(914) 679-2100 (b.o.)

FOUNDED 1979
Lawrence Sacharow, Mrs. Lawrence Webster

SEASON
May-Oct.

FACILITIES
Byrdcliffe Theatre
Seating Capacity: 97
Stage: flexible

Baersville Theatre
Seating Capacity: 220
State: proscenium

FINANCES
Apr. 1, 1988-Mar. 31, 1989
Expenses: $244,700

CONTRACTS
AEA SPT

River Arts Repertory celebrated its 10th-anniverasry season in 1989. To achieve its goal of making contributions to the national theatre network, River Arts has premiered new works by writers including: Len Jenkin, Richard Nelson, Jean-Claude van Itallie, Maria Irene Fornes, Michael Cristofer, Eric Overmyer, Constance Congdon, Janusz Glowacki, Casey Kurtti, Michael Taav and Wendy Hammond. In 1989, River Arts embarked on a major expansion by opening a second theatre in Bearsville, New York. The new facility has 250 seats and affords mainstage possibilities for work that may attract larger audiences. The 125-seat Byrdcliffe Theatre will continue to offer new works and innovative productions of the classics and of contemporary works. Writers in residence in 1989 included Aarienne Kennedy, as well as Anton Shammash, the Palestinian author of Arabesque, and Joshua Sobol, the Israeli author of Ghetto. The mission of River Arts remains a commitment to foster an outstanding community of theatre artists, working together on both finished productions and developmental projects.

—*Lawrence Sacharow*

PRODUCTIONS 1987–88

Once in A Lifetime, George S. Kaufman and Moss Hart; (D) Anne Bogart; (S) Victoria Petrovich; (C) Marianne Powell-Parker; (L) Carol Mullins
Tales of the Lost Formicans, Constance Congdon; (D) Roberta Levitow; (S) Tom Kamm; (C) Marianne Powell-Parker; (L) Frances Aronson
Roots in Water, Richard Nelson; (D) Lawrence Sacharow; (S) Loy Arcenas; (C) Marianne Powell-Parker; (L) Arden Fingerhut

PRODUCTIONS 1988–89

Hair, Ragniano Rado; music: Gal McDermot; (D) Rose Bonczek; (S) Stephen Coles and Victoria Petrovich; (C) Marianne Powell Parker; (L) Mark London
Love Me or Leave Me, adapt: Michael Cristofer; (D) Lawrence Sacharow; (S) Ken Foy; (C) Marianne Powell-Parker; (L) Frances Aronson
Jitterbugging, Richard Nelson; (D) Lawrence Sacharow; (S) Anne Servanton; (C) Marianne Powell-Parker; (L) Mark London
Soul of a Jew, Joshua Sobol; trans: Michael Feingold; (D) Gedalia Besser; (S) George Alison; (C) Marianne Powell-Parker; (L) Frances Aronson

The Road Company

ROBERT H. LEONARD
Artistic Director

LINDA KESLER
General Manager

Box 5278 EKS
Johnson City, TN 37603
(615) 926-7726

FOUNDED 1975
Robert H. Leonard

SEASON
Sept.-June

FACILITIES
The Down Home
Seating Capacity: 150
Stage: flexible

Mountain Home Memorial Theater
Seating Capacity: 650
Stage: proscenium

Gilbreath Theater
Seating Capacity: 375
Stage: thrust

FINANCES
July 1, 1988-June 30, 1989
Expenses: $110,000

I believe theatre is a community event. The Road Company is a working environment for artists who want to apply their skills to the investigation and expression of our community in Upper East Tennessee. The ensemble works on the premise that theatre is a compact between the artists and the audience—artistically and organizationally. The successful theatre event happens when the audience joins the imagination of the production during performance. This belief assumes the enjoyment of theatre is active not passive. It also assumes a long-term relationship between the ensemble and the community. These concepts do not define or restrict subject matter, form or style. These are matters of constant investigation. What subjects are actually of concern? To whom? What style or form is effective within the framework of content and audience aesthetic? These issues and the artistic growth of the ensemble constitute the basis of our dramaturgy. We tour our own works to communities all over Tennessee and the nation.

—*Robert H. Leonard*

PRODUCTIONS 1987–88

Echoes and Postcards, company-developed; (D) Robert H. Leonard; (S) Robert H. Leonard; (C) company; (L) Robert H. Leonard
Happy Days, Samuel Beckett; (D) Robert H. Leonard; (S) Cheri Vasek; (C) Cheri Vasek; (L) Light Impressions

PRODUCTIONS 1988–89

Echoes and Postcards, company-developed; (D) Robert H. Leonard; (S) Robert H. Leonard; (C) company; (L) Robert H. Leonard
Something Entirely New by the Road Company, Margaret Baker, Don Evans, Margaret Gregg, Bob Leonard, Celeste Miller, Christine Murdock and Eugene Wolf; (D) Robert H. Leonard; (S) Margaret Gregg; (C) Margaret Gregg; (L) Light Impressions
Daytrips, Jo Carson; (D) Robert H. Leonard; (S) Donald A. Drapeau; (C) Felice Proctor; (L) Duane P. Becker
A Place with the Pigs, Athol Fugard; (D) Shawn Gulyas; (S) Cheri Vasek; (C) Cheri Vasek; (L) Light Impressions
The Miracle Play, Michael Fields; (D) Robert H. Leonard; (S) Cheri Vasek; (C) Cheri Vasek; (L) Light Impressions

Roadside Theater. Frankie Taylor, Gary Slemp and Don Baker in *Red Fox/Second Hangin'*. Photo: Martha Swope.

Roadside Theater

DUDLEY COCKE
Director

CAROL THOMPSON
Managing Director

306 Madison St.
Whitesburg, KY 41858
(606) 633-0108 (bus.)

FOUNDED 1974
Appalshop, Inc.

SEASON
Year-round

FACILITIES
Appalshop Theater
Seating Capacity: 165
Stage: thrust

FINANCES
Oct. 1, 1987-Sept. 30, 1988
Expenses: $316,500

Roadside is an ensemble of actors, musicians, designers, writers, directors and managers, most of whom grew up in the Appalachian mountains. Appalachia is the subject of the theatre's original plays, and the company has developed its theatrical style from its local heritage of storytelling, mountain music and oral history. In making indigenous theatre and creating a body of native dramatic literature, Roadside sees itself as continuing its region's cultural tradition. Roadside's hometown has 1,200 people; coal mining is the main occupation. The theatre tours year-round, both within and outside the mountains, most often performing for folks who are not in the habit of attending theatre. Roadside is an integral part of the multimedia organization Appalshop, which also produces work about Appalachia through the media of film, television, radio, photography, music and sound recording, and visual art.

—*Dudley Cocke*

PRODUCTIONS 1987–88 AND 1988–89

Mountain Tales and Music, company-adapt; (D) company
Red Fox Second Hangin', Don Baker and Dudley Cocke; (D) Dudley Cocke and Don Baker; (L) Don Baker
South of the Mountain, Ron Short; (D) Ron Short and Dudley Cocke; (L) Ron Short
Pretty Polly, book: Don Baker and Ron Short; music: Ron Short; (D) Ron Short and Dudley Cocke; (L) Jerry McColgan
Leaving Egypt, Ron Short; (D) Dudley Cocke; (L) Jerry McColgan

The Road Company. Eugene Wolf in *A Place with the Pigs*. Photo: Cheri Vasek.

Round House Theatre

JERRY WHIDDON
Artistic Director

TONY ELLIOT
Producing Associate

12210 Bushey Drive
Silver Spring, MD 20902
(301) 217-6770 (bus.)
(301) 468-4234 (b.o.)

FOUNDED 1978
June Allen, Montgomery
County Department of
Recreation

SEASON
Sept.-June

FACILITIES
Seating Capacity: 218
Stage: thrust

FINANCES
July 1, 1988-June 30, 1989
Expenses: $550,000

CONTRACTS
AEA SPT

Looking at music videos, one can get chills seeing how fast our perceptions of this world are changing, even down to the way linear thought is being broken into fragments—prisms that multiply angles and colors. Round House Theatre, though still devoted to the concept of developing and encouraging a company of actors, directors, designers and staff, is beginning to reflect these changes. The past three seasons have been devoted to sharing newer works, newer thoughts, newer voices with our audience. It is that dynamic—a newer challenging and rewarding adventure with the theatregoer—that drives us and that is at work for us on all levels, in all our programs. Indeed it imbues our programs with purpose. We welcome the commitment to make our art accessible through classes and performances in schools and senior citizen centers, and through these programs reacquaint ourselves with that actor's "impulse" toward theatre. Why theatre is needed becomes, simply and wonderfully, obvious. That joy comes full circle in the darkened room where the actor tells a story.

—*Jerry Whiddon*

PRODUCTIONS 1987–88

Rum and Coke, Keith Reddin; (D) Susann Brinkley; (S) Richard H. Young; (C) Rosemary Pardee-Holz; (L) Jane Williams Flank
The Fairy Garden & Self Torture and Strenuous Exercise, Harry Kondoleon; (D) Max Mayer; (S) Jane Williams Flank; (C) Marsha M. LeBoeuf; (L) Joseph B. Musumeci, Jr.
Zastrozzi, George F. Walker; (D) Jerry Whiddon; (S) Joseph B. Musumeci, Jr.; (C) Marsha M. LeBoeuf; (L) Daniel MacLean Wagner
A Hatful of Rain, Michael V. Gazzo; (D) Jeffrey B. Davis; (S) Jane Williams Flank; (C) Rosemary Pardee-Holz; (L) Joseph B. Musumeci, Jr.
On The Verge or The Geography of Yearning, Eric Overmyer; (D) Gillian Drake; (S) Jane Williams Flank; (C) Rosemary Pardee-Holz; (L) Daniel MacLean Wagner

PRODUCTIONS 1988–89

Baby with the Bathwater, Christopher Durang; (D) Kim Rubinstein; (S) Jane Williams Flank; (C) Rosemary Pardee-Holz; (L) Joseph B. Musumeci, Jr.
The Boys Next Door, Tom Griffin; (D) Jim Petosta; (S) Joseph B. Musumeci, Jr.; (C) Rosemary Pardee-Holz; (L) Joseph Ronald Higdon
More Fun Than Bowling, Steven Dietz; (D) Brian Nelson; (S) Jane Williams Flank; (C) Rosemary Pardee-Holz; (L) Daniel MacLean Wagner
Heathen Valley, Romulus Linney; (D) Edward Morgan; (S) Joseph B. Musumeci, Jr.; (C) Jane Schloss Phelan; (L) Jane Williams Flank
American Buffalo, David Mamet; (D) Robert DeFrank; (S) Jane Williams Flank; (C) Rosemary Pardee-Holz; (L) Joseph Ronald Higdon

Round House Theatre. Brigid Cleary, Sarah C. Marshall and Lisa Mathias in *Baby with the Bathwater*. Photo: Geri Olson.

Roundabout Theatre Company

GENE FEIST
Artistic Director

TODD HAIMES
Producing Director

100 East 17th St.
New York, NY 10003
(212) 420-1360 (bus.)
(212) 420-1883 (b.o.)

FOUNDED 1965
Gene Feist

SEASON
Jan.-Dec.

FACILITIES
Christian C. Yegan Theatre
Seating Capacity: 499
Stage: proscenium

Susan Bloch Theatre
Seating Capacity: 152
Stage: arena

FINANCES
Sept. 1, 1988-Aug. 31, 1989
Expenses: $3,050,000

CONTRACTS
LORT (B)

In its 24th year as one of New York's outstanding Off Broadway theatres, the Roundabout Theatre Company continues to take pride in its unique identity as "the home of lost plays" (Walter Kerr), and to devote itself to providing high-quality productions of classic plays from both the traditional and contemporary canon. The basis of Roundabout's repertoire remains the production of familiar plays by internationally known authors, providing residents of the metropolitan area with the rare opportunity to see the world's finest actors give life and passion to plays by Chekhov, Shaw, Pirandello, Strindberg, Ibsen and Goldsmith—plays encountered more often in the classroom than on the stage. Modern stage classics such as John Osborne's *Look Back in Anger*, Harold Pinter's *Old Times*, Lorraine Hansberry's *A Raisin in the Sun* and Carson McCullers' *The Member of the Wedding* have all enjoyed major New York revivals at Roundabout, bringing the company critical acclaim and national attention.

—*Gene Feist*

PRODUCTIONS 1987–88

Of Mice and Men, John Steinbeck; (D) Arthur Storch; (S) Victor A. Becker; (C) Ceceli Eller; (L) Judy Rasmuson
Man and Superman, George Bernard Shaw; (D) William Woodman; (S) Bob Shaw; (C) Andrew B. Marlay; (L) F. Mitchell Dana
Rashomon, Fay Kanin and Michael Kanin; (D) Robert Kalfin; (S) Mina Albergo; (C) Cecelia Eller; (L) F. Mitchell Dana
Dandy Dick, Arthur Wing Pinero; (D) Jimmy Bohr; (S) Daniel

Roundabout Theatre Company. Roma Downey and Daniel Gerroll in *Arms and the Man*. Photo: Martha Swope.

Proett; (C) Andrew B. Marlay; (L) John Hastings
The Mistress of the Inn, Carlo Goldoni; trans and adapt: Mark A. Michaels; (D) Robert Kalfin; (S) Wolfgang Roth; (C) Andrew B. Marlay; (L) F. Mitchell Dana

PRODUCTIONS 1988–89

Ghosts, Henrik Ibsen; trans and adapt: Lars Johannesen; (D) Stuart Vaughan; (S) David Potts; (C) Andrew B. Marlay; (L) F. Mitchell Dana
Enrico IV, Luigi Pirandello; trans: Robert Cornthwaite; (D) J Ranelli; (S) Marjorie Bradley Kellogg; (C) Andrew B. Marlay; (L) John Gleason
The Member of the Wedding, Carson McCullers; (D) Harold Scott; (S) Thomas Cariello; (C) Andrew B. Marlay; (L) Shirley Prendergast
Arms and the Man, George Bernard Shaw; (D) Frank Hauser; (S) Franco Colavecchia; (C) A. Christina Giannini; (L) F. Mitchell Dana
Privates on Parade, book and lyrics: Peter Nichols; music: Denis King; (D) Larry Carpenter; (S) Loren Sherman; (C) Lindsay W. Davis; (L) Marcia Madeira

Sacramento Theatre Company

MARK CUDDY
Producing Director

GLYNIS WOOD-ALBERTS
Associate Producer

1419 H St.
Sacramento, CA 95814
(916) 446-7501 (bus.)
(916) 443-6722 (b.o.)

FOUNDED 1949
Eleanor McClatchy

SEASON
Sept.-May

FACILITIES
McClatchy Mainstage
Seating Capacity: 301
Stage: proscenium

Stage Two
Seating Capacity: 86
Stage: flexible

FINANCES
July 1, 1988-June 30, 1989
Expenses: $992,389

CONTRACTS
AEA Guest Artist

The Sacramento Theatre Company is a young company working toward LORT status. This brings with it several responsibilities including: responding to the city's sociopolitical makeup, taking subscribers on journeys through their hearts and minds, and making contributions to the American theatre both artistically and administratively. We are building a trust with our audience that secures our future and allows them the ownership that they deserve. Our task is to select plays of dramatic stature and present them vividly, clearly and boldly, making demands of ourselves and our audience. We strive to create a cathartic experience which will enhance a sense of community within the theatre. The theatre can be a focal point for the exchange of ideas and emotion among members of a shared community. Above all, we want the Sacramento Theatre Company to be a sane place to work and an adventurous place to visit.
—Mark Cuddy

Note: During the 1987-88 season, Dennis Bigelow served as producing director.

PRODUCTIONS 1987–88

Biloxi Blues, Neil Simon; (D) Dennis Bigelow; (S) William Bloodgood; (C) Debra Bruneaux; (L) Kathryn Burleson
A Moon for the Misbegotten, Eugene O'Neill; (D) Ken Kelleher; (S) Jerry Reynolds; (C) Michael Chapman; (L) Maurice Vercoutere
A Christmas Carol, adapt: Richard Hellesen, from Charles Dickens; (D) Dennis Bigelow; (S) Ralph Fetterly; (C) Debra Bruneaux; (L) Kathryn Burleson
Charley's Aunt, Brandon Thomas; (D) Ken Kelleher; (S) Jeff Hunt; (C) Debra Bruneaux; (L) Kathryn Burleson
Richard III, William Shakespeare; (D) Dennis Bigelow; (S) Paul R. Waldo; (C) Beth Mallette; (L) Kathryn Burleson
Private Lives, Noel Coward; (D) Dennis Bigelow; (S) Jenny Guthrie and Bruce Hill; (C) Debra Bruneaux; (L) Kathryn Burleson
Pump Boys and Dinettes, John Foley, Mark Hardwick, Debra Monk, Cass Morgan, John Schimmel and Jim Wann; (D) Dennis Bigelow; (S) Jenny Guthrie and Bruce Hill; (C) Mark Allen Goff; (L) Maurice Vercoutere

PRODUCTIONS 1988–89

I'm Not Rappaport, Herb Gardner; (D) Mark Cuddy; (S) Jenny Guthrie and Bruce Hill; (C) Sayuri Nina Pinckard;

Sacramento Theatre Company. Tim McDonough, Janice Fuller and Karen Pollard in *Away*. Photo: J. Kenneth Wagner.

(L) Kathryn Burleson
Shooting Stars, Molly Newman; (D) Penny Metropulos; (S) Norm Spencer; (C) Phyllis Kress; (L) Maurice Vercoutere
A Christmas Carol, adapt: Richard Hellesen, from Charles Dickens; (D) Vincent Murphy and Tim Ocel; (S) Ralph Fetterly; (C) Debra Bruneaux and Mark Allen Goff; (L) Kathryn Burleson
The Tempest, William Shakespeare; (D) Mark Cuddy; (S) Jeff Hunt; (C) Michael Chapman; (L) Maurice Vercoutere
A View from the Bridge, Arthur Miller; (D) Tim Ocel; (S) Paul R. Waldo; (C) Patricia Polen; (L) Kathryn Burleson
Tartuffe, Moliere; trans: Richard Wilbur; (D) Vincent Murphy; (S) Leslie Taylor; (C) Leslie Taylor; (L) Kathryn Burleson
Away, Michael Gow; (D) Mark Cuddy; (S) Jeff Hunt; (C) Debra Bruneaux; (L) Maurice Vercoutere

The Salt Lake Acting Company

EDWARD J. GRYSKA
Artistic Director

VICTORIA M. PANELLA
Managing Director

168 West 500 North
Salt Lake City, UT 84103
(801) 363-0526 (bus.)
(801) 363-0525 (b.o.)

FOUNDED 1970
Edward J. Gryska

SEASON
Sept.-June

FACILITIES
The Salt Lake Acting Company
Seating Capacity: 150
Stage: flexible

FINANCES
July 1, 1988-June 30, 1989
Expenses: $496,541

The Salt Lake Acting Company presents a unique and innovative repertoire of plays, including regional premieres, to a city and community rich in traditional art forms; supports new works and new playwrights, particularly Utah writers of national caliber; and endeavors to support and develop a community of professional artists. It is our intent to make a significant contribution to the American professional theatre. The Salt Lake Acting Company is committed to producing theatre of the highest artistic integrity in a protective, nurturing and mutually collaborative environment. The theatre is dedicated to serving our audience, treating them like family, and to making a vital contribution to the cultural life and diversity of our city and state.
—*Edward J. Gryska*

PRODUCTIONS 1987–88

On the Verge or The Geography of Yearning, Eric Overmyer; (D) Hilary Blecher; (S) Bill Beilke; (C) Susan Crotts; (L) Megan McCormick
Saturday's Voyeur: 1978 - 1988 The 10th Anniversary Roadshow, Michael Buttars and Nancy Borgenicht; add'l material: Edward J. Gryska; (D) Edward J. Gryska; (S) Ladd Lambert and Cory Dangerfield; (C) Susan Crotts; (L) Megan McCormick
Sand Mountain, Romulus Linney; (D) Edward J. Gryska; (S) Cory Dangerfield; (C) Susan Crotts; (L) Megan McCormick
Cantrell, David Kranes; (D) David Kirk Chambers; (S) Cory Dangerfield; (C) Susan Crotts; (L) Ingra Draper
Livin' Dolls, book and lyrics: Scott Wittman; music and lyrics: Marc Shaiman; (D) Edward J. Gryska; (S) Cory Dangerfield; (C) Susan Crotts; (L) Megan McCormick

PRODUCTIONS 1988–89

Steel Magnolias, Robert Harling; (D) Edward J. Gryska; (S) Rafael Colon Castenera; (C) Dawnetta Brown; (L) Megan McCormick
Saturday's Voyeur: Christmas Roadshow '88, Nancy Borgenicht and Michael Buttars; add'l Material: Edward J. Gryska; (D) Edward J. Gryska; (S) Ladd Lambert and Cory Dangerfield; (C) Jane Priem; (L) Megan McCormick
Hunting Cockroaches, Janusz Glowacki; trans: Jadwiga Kosicka; (D) Valerie Kittel; (S) Cory Dangerfield; (C) Amy Roberts; (L) Megan McCormick
Beirut, Alan Bowne; (D) Edward J. Gryska; (S) Cory Dangerfield; (C) Amy Roberts; (L) Megan McCormick
1102 and 1103, David Kranes; (D) Kenneth Washington; (S) Michael J. Allman; (C) Amy Roberts; (L) Megan McCormick
Do Black Patent Leather Shoes Really Reflect Up?, book: John R. Powers; music and lyrics: James Quinn and Alaric Jans; (D) Rafael Colon Castenera; (S) Kit Anderton; (C) Jennifer Dehner; (L) Megan McCormick

The Salt Lake Acting Company. Betsy Nagel and Kevin Hassett in *Sand Mountain*. Photo Jess Allen.

Saltworks Theatre Company

GILLETTE ELVGREN, JR.
Artistic Director

LYNN GEORGE
Managing Director

5001 Baum Blvd.
Pittsburgh, PA 15213
(412) 687-8883

FOUNDED 1982
Kate McConnell, Gillette Elvgren

SEASON
variable

FINANCES
July 1, 1988-June 30, 1989
Expenses: $284,365

Saltworks is focused essentially on doing plays that have a direct impact on social needs of the community. This can be seen in our emphasis on touring plays dealing with chemical dependency (*Say No, Max, Finally Fourteen, I Am the Brother of Dragons*), and our new piece on teen sexuality, *All Dressed Up—No Place to Go*, which is scheduled to begin touring in the spring of 1990. In addition there is a strong commitment to producing challenging children's theatre and theatre which deals with Christian values and spiritual issues of our time.
—*Gillette Elvgren, Jr.*

Note: During the 1987-88 season, Kate McConnell served as artistic director.

PRODUCTIONS 1987–88

I Am the Brother of Dragons, Gillette Elvgren; (D) Kate McConnell; (S) Tony Ferrieri
Say No Max, Gillette Elvgren; (D) Kate McConnell; (S) Tony Ferrieri
Finally Fourteen, Gillette Elvgren; (D) Kate McConnell; (S) Tony Ferrieri
Corrie and Papa: A Faith Remembered, Richard Parker; (D) Jill Wadsworth; (S) Jill Wadsworth; (C) Jill Wadsworth
Kings, Patricia Webb; (D) Kate

McConnell; (s) Jack Morgan; (c) Susan Kidd
The Day Boy and the Night Girl, adapt: James Weldon, from George MacDonald; (D) Jill Wadsworth

PRODUCTIONS 1988–89

I Am the Brother of Dragons, Gillette Elvgren; (D) Kate McConnell; (s) Tony Ferrieri; (c) Susan Cologne
Say No Max, Gillette Elvgren; (D) David Bush; (s) Tony Ferrieri; (c) Susan Cologne
Finally Fourteen, Gillette Elvgren; (D) David Bush; (s) Tony Ferrieri; (c) Susan Cologne
Puff the Magic Dragon, adapt: Gillette Elvgren; (D) Brenda Harger
Corrie and Papa: A Faith Remembered, Richard Parker; (D) Jill Wadsworth; (s) Jill Wadsworth; (c) Jill Wadsworth

San Diego Repertory Theatre

DOUGLAS JACOBS
Artistic Director

SAM WOODHOUSE
Producing Director

ADRIAN W. STEWART
Managing Director

79 Horton Plaza
San Diego, CA 92101
(619) 231-3586 (bus.)
(619) 235-8025 (b.o.)

FOUNDED 1976
Sam Woodhouse, Douglas Jacobs

SEASON
May-Dec.

FACILITIES
Lyceum Stage
Seating Capacity: 550
Stage: flexible

Lyceum Space
Seating Capacity: 250
Stage: flexible

Sixth Avenue Playhouse
Seating Capacity: 190
Stage: thrust

FINANCES
Jan. 1, 1988-Dec. 31, 1988
Expenses: $2,200,000

CONTRACTS
AEA letter of agreement

Based on the conviction that theatre continually reinvents itself through an ongoing blending of all the arts, the San Diego Repertory Theatre operates its three theatres as a multidisciplinary, multicultural arts complex. We produce our own season for nine months of the year; during the other three months we book, present or rent our theatre to other artists. Our eclectic programming is based on the belief that the arts should reflect the diversity of the world around and within us, and that the theatre is a uniquely appropriate place to explore the boundaries and borders of life and art. Our seasons emphasize contemporary plays, seldom-seen classics and revivals of well-known classics. We are committed to ensemble development, non-traditional casting, lifelong training for professionals, and to explorations of music, dance, visual arts and poetry, in order to expand and deepen the range of theatrical expression.

—*Douglas Jacobs*

PRODUCTIONS 1987–88

The Mystery of Irma Vep, Charles Ludlam; (D) Will Roberson; (s) Mark Donnelly; (c) Nancy Jo Smith; (L) Kent Dorsey
The Cradle Will Rock, Marc Blitzstein; (D) Robert Benedetti; (s) Nick Reid; (c) Clare Henkel; (L) John Forbes
The Colored Museum, George C. Wolfe; (D) Floyd Gaffney; (s) Rob Murphy; (c) Valeria Watson; (L) Rob Murphy
Red Noses, Peter Barnes; (D) Sam Woodhouse and Jael Weisman; (s) Nick Reid; (c) Nancy Jo Smith; (L) Peter Maradudin
Heathen Valley, Romulus Linney; (D) Douglas Jacobs; (s) D. Martyn Bookwalter; (c) Clare Henkel; (L) Peter Nordyke
Glengarry Glen Ross, David Mamet; (D) Sam Woodhouse; (s) Kent Dorsey and Jane Hinson; (c) Nancy Jo Smith; (L) Brenda Berry
Burning Patience, Antonio Skarmeta; trans: Marion Peter Holt; (D) Douglas Jacobs and Jorge Huerta; (s) Victoria Petrovich; (c) Diane Rodriguez; (L) John Forbes
A Christmas Carol adapt: Douglas Jacobs, from Charles Dickens; (D) Michael Addison; (s) Ron Ranson; (c) Nancy Jo Smith; (L) Craig Wolf

PRODUCTIONS 1988–89

The Marriage of Bette and Boo, Christopher Durang; (D) Walter Schoen; (s) George Suhayda; (c) Nancy Jo Smith; (L) John B. Forbes
Orinoco!, Emilio Carballido; (D) Jorge Huerta; (s) D. Martyn Bookwalter; (c) David Mickelsen; (L) Peter Nordyke
The Scandalous Adventures of Sir Toby Trollope, Ron House and Alan Shearman; (D) Steve Rothman; (s) Fred Duer and Alan Okazaki; (c) David Mickelsen; (L) John B. Forbes
Thin Air, Lynne Alvarez; (D) Sam Woodhouse; (s) D. Martyn Bookwalter; (c) Nancy Jo Smith; (L) Peter Nordyke
Are You Lonesome Tonight, Alan Bleasdale; (D) George Ferencz; (s) Victoria Petrovich; (c) Sally J. Lesser; (L) Brenda Berry
Albanian Softshoe, Mac Wellman; (D) Douglas Jacobs and Michael Roth; (s) Jill Moon; (c) Clare Henkel; (L) Brenda Berry
Slingshot, Nicolai Kolyada; trans: Susan Larsen; (D) Roman Vityuk; (s) Vladimir Boyer; (c) Sally Cleveland; (L) Brenda Berry
A Christmas Carol, adapt: Douglas Jacobs, from Charles Dickens; (D) Walter Schoen; (s) Tom Buderwitz; (c) Catherine Meachem; (L) John B. Forbes
Animal Nation, Steven Friedman; (D) Sam Woodhouse and Jael Weisman; (s) Victoria Petrovich; (c) Nancy Jo Smith; (L) Peter Nordyke

San Jose Repertory Company

TIMOTHY NEAR
Artistic Director

JOHN BROWN
Managing Director

Box 2399
San Jose, CA 95109
(408) 294-7595 (bus.)
(408) 294-7572 (b.o.)

FOUNDED 1980
James P. Reber

SEASON
Oct.-June

FACILITIES
Montgomery Theatre
Seating Capacity: 535
Stage: proscenium

FINANCES
July 1, 1988-June 30, 1989
Expenses: $1,990,000

CONTRACTS
LORT (C)

San Jose Repertory Company performs in the Montgomery Theatre in downtown San Jose, a blossom-

San Diego Repertory Theatre. William Anton, Howard Schechter and Tom Oleniacz in *Glengarry Glen Ross*. Photo: Will Gullette.

San Jose Repertory Company. Mitchell Greenberg and Nancy Frangione in *Talley's Folly*. Photo: Wilson P. Graham, Jr.

ing city that is fast becoming the cultural center of the Santa Clara Valley. The Rep's primary mission is to provide for the computer capital of America a gathering place where people can experience the group-witnessing of the human condition, presented through the work of great playwrights and actors, directors and designers of excellence. The Rep presents a season of six plays, offering a wide range of classic and contemporary drama that speaks to issues pertinent to our culturally and ethnically diverse audience. Each production is cast individually, and we are committed to providing the most creative environment possible for our guest artists. To balance the high-tech influence in this community, the Rep gears its productions towards stimulating the audience's senses emotionally, intellectually, visually and aurally, so that our work includes the exploration of what it is that makes theatre feel truly alive—truly human.

—*Timothy Near*

PRODUCTIONS 1987–88

The Rainmaker, N. Richard Nash; (D) Timothy Near; (S) Jeffrey Struckman; (C) Jeffrey Struckman; (L) Peter Maradudin
Relatively Speaking, Alan Ayckbourn; (D) Skip Foster; (S) Richard R. Goodwin; (C) Beaver D. Bauer; (L) Derek Duarte
Orphans, Lyle Kessler; (D) Skip Foster; (S) Vicki Smith; (C) Cassandra Carpenter; (L) Peter Maradudin
The Unexpected Guest, Agatha Christie; (D) Timothy Near; (S) Jeffrey Struckman; (C) Jeffrey Struckman; (L) Kurt Landisman
Sizwe Bansi Is Dead, Athol Fugard; (D) Claude Purdy; (S) Michael Olich; (C) Michael Olich; (L) Joe Ragey
All My Sons, Arthur Miller; (D) Steven Albrezzi; (S) Jeffrey Struckman; (C) Jeffrey Struckman; (L) Peter Maradudin
A More Perfect Union, Kate Babcock; (D) John McCluggage; (S) Walter Saunders; (C) Deborah Weber Krahenbuhl; (L) Kurt Landisman

PRODUCTIONS 1988–89

Arms and the Man, George Bernard Shaw; (D) Kent Stephens; (S) Kate Edmunds; (C) Jeffrey Struckman; (L) Paulie Jenkins
The 1940's Radio Hour, Walton Jones; (D) Timothy Near; (S) Jeffrey Struckman; (C) Jeffrey Struckman; (L) Peter Maradudin
Benefactors, Michael Frayn; (D) Skip Foster; (S) Joel Fontaine; (C) Deborah Weber Krahenbuhl; (L) Derek Duarte
Talley's Folly, Lanford Wilson; (D) Steven Albrezzi; (S) Jeffrey Struckman; (C) Deborah Weber Krahenbuhl; (L) Derek Duarte
Burning Patience, Antonio Skarmeta; trans: Marion Peter Holt; (D) Tony Curiel; (S) Joel Fontaine; (C) Cassandra Carpenter; (L) Kurt Landisman
A Streetcar Named Desire, Tennessee Williams; (D) Steven Albrezzi; (S) Jeffrey Struckman; (C) Beaver D. Bauer; (L) Paulie Jenkins

Seattle Children's Theatre

LINDA HARTZELL
Artistic Director

THOMAS PECHAR
Managing Director

305 Harrison St.
Seattle, WA 98109
(206) 443-0807 (bus.)
(206) 633-4567 (b.o.)

FOUNDED 1975

SEASON
Sept.-June

FACILITIES
Poncho Theatre
Seating Capacity: 280
Stage: proscenium

FINANCES
July 1, 1988-June 31, 1989
Expenses: $1,200,000

CONTRACTS
TYA

Seattle Children's Theatre, which has a national reputation for producing innovative, thought-provoking professional theatre for young audiences and their families is celebrating its 15th anniversary during the 1989-90 season. SCT has commissioned more than 40 new works for young audiences since its founding in 1975, and its plays have been produced by theatres across the country. In addition to its mainstage season, SCT offers a wide variety of programs to make the theatre accessible to as many children and their families as possible. These include providing classroom workshops, study guides and post play discussions to further enhance the educational experience of the main stage. As part of its mission SCT is committed to providing education and training for young people. The theatre offers year-round classes in acting and theatre skills for grades K-12, which are taught by professional artists. Professional theatre makes a lasting impression on today's youth. Creative discovery inspired by a sophisticated, entertaining theatre experience is my vision of Seattle Children's Theatre.

—*Linda Hartzell*

PRODUCTIONS 1987–88

The Hunchback of Notre Dame, adapt: Greg Palmer, from Victor Hugo; (D) Linda Hartzell; (S) Robert Gardiner; (C) Janet Snyder; (L) Jennifer Lupton
Rocky and Bullwinkle, book, adapt, music and lyrics: Bruce Hurlbut; (D) Linda Hartzell; (S) G. Carr and Rollin Thomas;

Seattle Children's Theatre. *Up the Down Staircase*. Photo: Fred Andrews.

(c) Jan Johnston; (L) Rogue Conn
Most Valuable Player, Mary Hall Surface, et al.; (D) Rex E. Allen; (s) Lynn Graves; (c) Josie Gardner; (L) Lee A. DeLorme
James and the Giant Peach, adapt: Richard R. George, from Roald Dahl; (D) Bruce Hurlbut; (s) Jennifer Lupton; (c) Georgia Becker; (L) Jennifer Lupton
The Death and Life of Sherlock Holmes, adapt: Suzan Zeder, from Arthur Conan Doyle; (D) Linda Hartzell; (s) William Forrester; (c) Janet Snyder; (L) Collier Woods

PRODUCTIONS 1988–89

Up the Down Staircase, adapt: Christopher Sergel, from Bel Kaufman; (D) Rex E. Allen; (s) Charles Walsh; (c) Josie Gardner; (L) Collier Woods
The Hoboken Chicken Emergency, book: Daniel Manus Pinkwater; music and lyrics: Chad Henry; (D) Linda Hartzell; (s) Patti Henry; (c) Josie Gardner; (L) Rogue Conn
The Secret Garden, adapt: Pamela Sterling, from Frances Hodgson Burnett; (D) Linda Hartzell; (s) Robert Gardiner; (c) Sarah Nash Gates; (L) Rogue Conn
According to Coyote, John Kauffman; (D) John Kauffman; (s) Don Yanik; (L) Jeff Robbins
The Would-Be Gentleman, Moliere; (D) Ted D'Arms; (s) William Forrester; (c) Anne Thaxter Watson; (L) Jennifer Lupton

Seattle Group Theatre

RUBEN SIERRA
Artistic Director

4040 Brooklyn Ave., NE
Seattle, WA 98105
(206) 545-4969 (bus.)
(206) 543-4327 (b.o.)

FOUNDED 1978
Gilbert Wong, Ruben Sierra, Scott Caldwell

SEASON
Sept.-June

FACILITIES
Ethnic Theatre
Seating Capacity: 195
Stage: modified thrust

FINANCES
July 1, 1988-June 30, 1989
Expenses: $596,000

CONTRACTS
SPT

The Seattle Group Theatre believes that theatre should be an experience of social, eductional and artistic relevance. We seek to provide the best opportunities for all artists to voice through their art, their dreams, their hopes and their despairs. We want our audience to laugh, to cry—but ultimately we want them to think. We want to serve as a negotiator and a catalyst for playwrights, actors, directors; to open our doors to artists so that they in turn can reach our audience and share that humanity which makes theatre great. We have created programs that go into the elementary and high schools addressing students' need for art and literature. We are in the fifth year of our Multi-Cultural Playwrights' Festival, in which we focus solely on new scripts by American ethnic playwrights. We do one-to-three world premieres during our season by both new and established playwrights. We have toured nationally with such shows as *I Am Celso*, created form the poems of Leo Romero, and *Nappy Edges*, a one-woman show by Tawnya Pettiford-Waites. Finally, we are a theatre that attempts to transform and transcend circumstances, limitations and obstacles—theatre that reflects all of America!
—*Ruben Sierra*

PRODUCTIONS 1987–88

Tracers, John DiFusco; (D) John DiFusco; (s) Patti Henry; (c) Kathleen Maki; (L) Rex Carelton
Division Street, Steve Tesich; (D) John Schwab; (s) Gilbert Wong; (c) Josie Gardner; (L) Darren McCroom
Changing Faces, Nikki Louis; (D) Tim Bond; (s) Rex Carelton; (c) Michael Murphy; (L) Rex Carelton
Kiss of the Spider Woman, Manuel Puig; trans: Allan Baker; (D) Ruben Sierra; (s) Rex Carelton; (c) Patrick Stovall; (L) Rex Carelton
Say, Can you See?, Ruben Sierra; (D) Paul O'Connel; (s) Rex Carelton; (c) Kathleen Maki; (L) Rex Carelton
Voices of Christmas, Ruben Sierra; (D) Ruben Sierra; (s) Patricia Del Campo; (c) Paul Lovey; (L) Collier Woods

PRODUCTIONS 1988–89

Yankee Dawg You Die, Philip Kan Gotanda; (D) Tim Bond; (s) Rex Carelton; (c) Kathleen Maki; (L) Rex Carelton
T Bone N Weasel, Jon Klein; (D) Ruben Sierra; (s) Rex Carelton; (c) Kathleen Maki; (L) Darren McCroom
Voices of Christmas, book: Ruben Sierra; music: Joe Seserko; (D) Ruben Sierra; (s) Patti Henry; (c) Kathleen Maki; (L) Collier Woods
The Meeting, Jeff Stetson; (D) Tim Bond; (s) Rex Carelton; (c) Kathleen Maki; (L) Darren McCroom
Extremities, William Mastrosimone; (D) Ruben Sierra; (s) Charlie Walsh; (c) Kathleen Maki; (L) Rex Carelton
Stealing, lyrics: Ted Sod; music: Suzanne Grant; music: Pamela Gerke; (D) Rita Giomi; (s) Jeff Frkonja; (c) Heather Hudson; (L) Rex Carelton

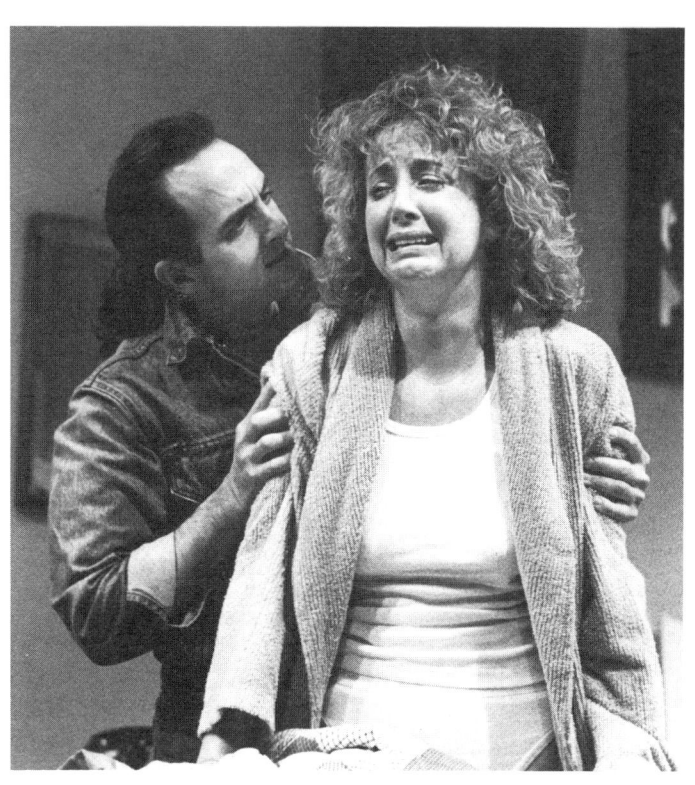

Seattle Group Theatre. Mitch Hale and Kristina Sanborn in *Extremities*. Photo: Fred Andrews.

Seattle Repertory Theatre

DANIEL SULLIVAN
Artistic Director

BENJAMIN MOORE
Managing Director

DOUGLAS HUGHES
Associate Artistic Director

155 Mercer St.
Seattle, WA 98109
(206) 443-2210 (bus.)
(206) 443-2222 (b.o.)

FOUNDED 1963
Bagley Wright

SEASON
Oct.-May

FACILITIES
Bagley Wright Theatre
Seating Capacity: 856
Stage: proscenium

Poncho Forum
Seating Capacity: 142
Stage: flexible

FINANCES
July 1, 1988-June 30, 1989
Expenses: $4,553,716

CONTRACTS
LORT (B+) and (D)

The Seattle Repertory Theatre continues to support a resident acting company, offering long-term employment to members who are cast across a season of six mainstage and three Stage 2 productions. Both the main stage and Stage 2 offer work ranging from the classics to world premieres. Each year we seek to collaborate with other nonprofit theatres to present a special production on the main stage, thus providing extra time for the resident company to prepare subsequent productions. A strong commitment to new work is reflected in workshop productions of four new scripts every spring. Building the resources of a resident acting company and developing new plays remain parallel artistic priorities. Outreach programs include workshops and performances in the schools and a regional tour of one or two mainstage productions to a dozen western state venues.

—*Daniel Sullivan*

PRODUCTIONS 1987–88

The Caucasian Chalk Circle, Bertolt Brecht; trans: Eric Bentley; (D) Daniel Sullivan; (S) Ralph Funicello; (C) Lewis Brown; (L) Pat Collins
Home, David Storey; (D) Geoffrey Sherman; (S) Richard Seger; (C) Robert Wojewodski; (L) Craig Miller
The Garden of Earthly Delights, conceived: Martha Clarke; (D) Martha Clarke; (C) Jane Greenwood; (L) Paul Gallo
Tartuffe, Moliere; trans: Richard Wilbur; (D) Daniel Sullivan; (S) Ralph Funicello; (C) Michael Olich; (L) James F. Ingalls
Hogan's Goat, William Alfred; (D) Douglas Hughes; (S) Ralph Funicello; (C) Michael Olich; (L) James F. Ingalls
Eastern Standard, Richard Greenberg; (D) Michael Engler; (S) Philipp Jung; (C) Candice Donnelly; (L) Donald Holder
Danger: Memory!, Arthur Miller; (D) Thomas Bullard; (S) Robert A. Dahlstrom; (C) Sally Richardson; (L) Robert A. Dahlstrom
The Beauty Part, S.J. Perelman; (D) Douglas Hughes; (S) Hugh Landwehr; (C) Rose Pederson; (L) Peter Maradudin
Hunting Cockroaches, Janusz Glowacki; trans: Jadwiga Kosicka; (D) Peggy Shannon; (S) Scott Weldin; (C) Rose Pederson; (L) Rick Paulsen

PRODUCTIONS 1988–89

The Tempest, William Shakespeare; (D) Daniel Sullivan; (S) Christopher Barreca; (C) Lewis Brown; (L) Pat Collins
Cat on a Hot Tin Roof, Tennessee Williams; (D) Mary B. Robinson; (S) Ralph Funicello; (C) Jess Goldstein; (L) Craig Miller
Largely New York, Bill Irwin; (D) Bill Irwin; (S) Douglas Stein; (C) Rose Pederson; (L) Nancy Schertler
Nothing Sacred, George F. Walker; (D) Douglas Hughes; (S) Richard Seger; (C) Michael Olich; (L) James F. Ingalls
Les Liaisons Dangereuses, adapt: Christopher Hampton, from Choderlos de Laclos; (D) Michael Maggio; (S) Richard Seger; (C) Michael Olich; (L) James F. Ingalls
Truffles in the Soup, adapt: Daniel Sullivan and company, from Carlo Goldoni; (D) Daniel Sullivan; (S) Douglas W. Schmidt; (C) Ann Hould-Ward; (L) Pat Collins
Frankie and Johnny in the Clair de Lune, Terrence McNally; (D) Robin Lynn Smith; (S) Vicki Smith; (C) Rose Pederson; (L) Rick Paulsen
That's It, Folks!, Mark O'Donnell; (D) Douglas Hughes; (S) Scott Weldin; (C) Rose Pederson; (L) Paulie Jenkins
Happy Days, Samuel Beckett; (D) Libby Appel; (S) Scott Weldin; (C) Rose Pederson; (L) Rick Paulsen

Seattle Repertory Theatre. Ken Ruta and Wendell Wright in The Tempest. *Photo: Chris Bennion.*

Second Stage Theatre

ROBYN GOODMAN
CAROLE ROTHMAN
Artistic Directors

DOROTHY MAFFEI
Managing Director

Box 1807, Ansonia Station
New York, NY 10023
(212) 787-8302 (bus.)
(212) 873-6103 (b.o.)

FOUNDED 1979
Carole Rothman, Robyn Goodman

SEASON
Nov.-July

FACILITIES
McGinn/Cazale Theatre
Seating Capacity: 108
Stage: proscenium

FINANCES
July 1, 1988-June 30, 1989
Expenses: $1,094,000

CONTRACTS
AEA letter of agreement

The Second Stage was incorporated in July 1979. Our purpose is to produce plays of the recent past that we believe deserve another chance—including plays that were ahead of their time, not accessible to a wide audience, poorly publicized or obscured by inferior productions. The ability to rewrite is a skill that most playwrights have not had an opportunity to develop. In fostering this talent, the Second Stage is helping them to grow as artists. Thanks to our leadership, the concept of presenting previously produced contemporary plays has become an accepted and frequently imitated part of the theatrical scene. At the same time, we have discovered it is difficult to insist that a playwright have a play produced elsewhere before we can consider it. Therefore, in 1982, we made a commitment to present new plays by our developing corps of writers.

—*Robyn Goodman*
Carole Rothman

PRODUCTIONS 1987–88

Moonchildren, Michael Weller; (D) Mary B. Robinson; (S) Charles McClennahan; (C) Mimi Maxmen; (L) Mal Sturchio
Loose Ends, Michael Weller; (D) Irene Lewis; (S) Kevin Rupnik; (C) Candice Donnelly; (L) Peter Kaczorowski
Spoils of War, Michael Weller; (D) Austin Pendleton; (S) Kevin Rupnik; (C) Ruth Morley; (L) Betsy Adams

Second Stage Theatre. Kate Nelligan and Christopher Collet in *Spoils of War*. Photo: Susan Cook.

The Film Society, Jon Robin Baitz; (D) John Tillinger; (S) Santo Loquasto; (C) Candice Donnelly; (L) Dennis Parichy

PRODUCTIONS 1988–89

The Rimers of Eldritch, Lanford Wilson; (D) Mark Brokaw; (S) Santo Loquasto; (C) Ellen McCartney; (L) Jennifer Tipton
In a Pig's Valise, book and lyrics: Eric Overmyer; music: August Darnell; (D) Graciela Daniele; (S) Bob Shaw; (C) Jeanne Button; (L) Peggy Eisenhauer
Approaching Zanzibar, Tina Howe; (D) Carole Rothman; (S) Heidi Landesman; (C) Susan Hilferty; (L) Dennis Parichy
Shimmer, John O'Keefe; (D) John O'Keefe; (L) Jim Cave

Seven Stages

DEL HAMILTON
Artistic Director

TITO MONTONE
Director of Operations

105 Euclid Ave NE
Atlanta, GA 30307
(404) 522-0911 (bus.)
(404) 523-7647 (b.o.)

FOUNDED 1979
Faye Allen, Del Hamilton

SEASON
Jan.–Dec.

FACILITIES
Seating Capacity: 250
Stage: flexible

Back Door Theater
Seating Capacity: 100
Stage: flexible

FINANCES
Jan. 1, 1988–Dec. 31, 1988
Expenses: $252,000

CONTRACTS
AEA SPT and Guest Artist

Seven Stages produces mostly new plays in a lengthy developmental process involving artists as collaborators. We have produced more than 40 premieres by American and foreign playwrights. Occassionally we produce a classic or modern classic. The content of the plays focuses on spiritual, social and political issues of concern to our audiences and artists. We also present national and international theatre artists and companies in residencies. Our cross-cultural workshop program initiates projects that usually involve artists in several disciplines.

—*Del Hamilton*

PRODUCTIONS 1987–88

Blood on Blood, Rebecca Ranson; (D) Del Hamilton; (S) John Williams; (C) Chris Cook; (L) John Williams
Hondo Gothic, Ted Hayes; (D) Levi Lee; (S) Elaine Williams; (C) Chris Cook; (L) Elaine Williams
Black Cat Bones for Seven Sons, Robert Earl Price; (D) Beryl Jones; (S) Tom Brown; (C) Ida Muldrow; (L) Tom Brown
Zurama, Juli Kearns; (D) Del Hamilton; (S) Juli Kearns; (C) Joe Lester; (L) Eric Jennings
Math and Aftermath, Jim Grimsley; (D) Pam McClure; (S) Bill Georgia; (C) Madeleine St. Romain; (L) Brian Engle
Bananaland, George King and Ruby Lerner; (D) George King and Ruby Lerner; (S) Normando Ismay and Eric Jennings; (C) Eleanor Brownfield; (L) Eric Jennings

PRODUCTIONS 1988–89

Macbeth, adapt: Del Hamilton, from William Shakespeare; (D) Del Hamilton; (S) Del Hamilton; (C) Juli Kearns; (L) Eric Jennings
A Place with the Pigs, Athol Fugard; (D) Levi Lee; (S) Roy McGee; (C) Chris Cook; (L) Eric Jennings
White People, Jim Grimsley; (D) Del Hamilton and Faye Allen; (S) Bill Georgia; (C) Stephanie Kaskel; (L) Eric Jennings
The Heartache Heroine, Celeste Miller; (D) Ian McColl; (S) Mickey More; (C) Mickey More; (L) Ian McColl
The Park, adapt: Christopher Martin and Daniel Waker, from Botho Strauss; (D) Christopher Martin; (S) Steve Olsen; (C) Barbara Bush; (L) Christopher Martin
Cain's Theme, Robert Earl Price; (D) Robert Earl Price; (S) Robert Earl Price; (C) Robert Earl Price; (L) Eric Jennings
Dutchman, Amiri Baraka; (D) Robert Earl Price; (S) Robert Earl Price; (C) Robert Earl Price; (L) Eric Jennings
Mud, Maria Irene Fornes; (D) Carmella Cardina; (S) Carmella Cardina; (C) Carmella Cardina; (L) Eric Jennings

Shakespeare Repertory

BARBARA GAINES
Artistic Director

JAMES JENSEN
Managing Director

2140 North Lincoln Park W
Chicago, IL 60614
(312) 943-2924 (bus.)

FOUNDED 1987
Kathleen Buckley, Barbara Gaines, Susan Geffen, Camilla Hawk, Liz Jacobs, Tom Joyce

SEASON
Oct.–Dec.

FACILITIES
Ruth Page Theatre
Seating Capacity: 250
Stage: flexible

Seven Stages. David Olsen, Charles Dennis, George D. Nikas, Celeste Miller and Del Hamilton in *Heartache Heroine*.

FINANCES
Feb. 1, 1988-Jan. 31, 1989
Expenses: $200,000

CONTRACTS
AEA CAT

Shakespeare Repertory is a theatre for the entire city and all its visitors to enjoy. Accordingly, SR has accepted the responsibility for conducting educational programs for Chicago-area students and training programs for professional actors. In addition, SR considers it a responsibility to reflect Chicago's rich cultural diversity in its artistic and business affairs and, especially, in its casting. Toward that end, the ensemble includes black, Asian, and Hispanic members who are frequently cast in nontraditional roles. The philosophy of the company is that classical training and the ensemble approach are essential to producing Shakespeare well. Only when Shakespeare's verse is well spoken and the actors performances are true to his intent can a theatre company make the plays the rich and powerful experiences that have sustained them for nearly 400 years. Shakespeare Repertory looks forward to a time when residents and visitors to Chicago will consider it one of the major attractions the city has to offer. In the great ensemble theatres of the world, actors spend years training and performing their roles in the company's repertoire. That is the approach to theatre that SR is taking and the kind of cultural institution it is becoming.
—*Barbara Gaines*

PRODUCTIONS 1987–88

Troilus and Cressida, William Shakespeare; (**D**) Barbara Gaines; (**S**) Michael Merritt; (**C**) Kaye Nottbusch; (**L**) Robert Shook

PRODUCTIONS 1988–89

Antony and Cleopatra, William Shakespeare; (**D**) Barbara Gaines; (**S**) Linda Buchanan; (**C**) Frances Maggio; (**L**) Robert Shook

The Shakespeare Theatre at the Folger

MICHAEL KAHN
Artistic Director

MARY ANN DE BARBIERI
Managing Director

301 East Capitol St. SE
Washington, DC 20003
(202) 547-3230 (bus.)
(202) 546-4000 (b.o.)

FOUNDED 1969
O.B. Hardison, Richmond Crinkley, Folger Shakespeare Library

SEASON
Sept.-June

FACILITIES
Seating Capacity: 243
Stage: modified proscenium

FINANCES
July 1, 1988-June 30, 1989
Expenses: $3,200,000

CONTRACTS
LORT (C)

The central issue of the Shakespeare Theatre at the Folger is the development of an American classical style for the 1980s and beyond. Our true challenge is to connect the technical demands made on the classical actor (vocal range, articulation of the text, etc.) and the necessary emotional life (including the larger-than-real-life feelings that Shakespearean characters experience in connecting themselves to the cosmos) to the full use of an actor's intellectual powers and a highly physical acting style. Our other concerns include the need to merge multigenerational artists in all areas of the theatre in a true collaboration; to continue our policy of colorblind casting; to expand our educational outreach programs; to address major social issues as the plays illuminate them; and to connect productively with the complex community in which we work and live.
—*Michael Kahn*

The Shakespeare Theatre at the Folger. Philip Goodwin and Franchelle Stewart Dorn *Macbeth*. Photo: Joan Marcus.

Shakespeare Repertory. Bruce A. Young, Barbara Gaines, Jeannette Schwaba, Tim Gregory and Kevin Gudahl in *Troilus and Cressida*. Photo: Bill Hagen.

PRODUCTIONS 1987–88

The Witch of Edmonton, Thomas Dekker, John Ford and William Rowley; (**D**) Barry Kyle; (**S**) Joe Fontaine; (**C**) Judith Dolan; (**L**) Nancy Schertler
All's Well That Ends Well, William Shakespeare; (**D**) Michael Kahn; (**S**) Russell Metheny; (**C**) Martin Pakledinaz; (**L**) Jim Irwin
Macbeth, William Shakespeare; (**D**) Michael Kahn; (**S**) Michael H. Yeargan; (**C**) Smaranda Branescu; (**L**) Stephen Strawbridge
The Merchant of Venice, William Shakespeare; (**D**) Michael Langham; (**S**) Douglas Stein; (**C**) Susan Hirschfeld; (**L**) Nancy Schertler

PRODUCTIONS 1988–89

Antony and Cleopatra, William Shakespeare; (D) Michael Kahn; (S) Robert Darling; (C) Judith Dolan; (L) Dennis Parichy
Richard II, William Shakespeare; (D) Toby Robertson; (S) Franco Colavechia; (C) Judith Dolan; (L) John McLain
The Beggar's Opera, John Gay; (D) Gene Lesser; (S) Derek McLane; (C) Ellen McCartney; (L) Daniel MacLean Wagner
As You Like It, William Shakespeare; (D) Michael Kahn; (S) Andrew Jackness; (C) Candice Donnelly; (L) Jeff Davis

Snowmass/Aspen Repertory Theatre

GORDON REINHART
Artistic Director

MARCI MAULLAR
Managing Director

Box 6275
Snowmass Village, CO 81615
(303) 923-2618 (bus.)
(303) 923-3773 (b.o.)

FOUNDED 1984
Michael T. Yeager, Ruth Kevan

SEASON
June-Sept.

FACILITIES
Snowmass Performing Arts Center
Seating Capacity: 253
Stage: thrust

FINANCES
Sept. 1, 1988-Aug. 31, 1989
Expenses: $265,160

CONTRACTS
LORT (D)

The Snowmass/Aspen Repertory Theatre is a professional company which operates in true repertory fashion. We are dedicated to the task of providing a home for theatre artists that offers security, encouragement and high standards for creative work. This results in many challenging and exciting experiences for our audience, who in turn fuel further artistic exploration. To help facilitate this interchange between artist and audience we select plays from the full spectrum of dramatic literature, including worthy plays for children, premiere works, and classics from all ages and places. The artistic philosophy that focuses and gives life to these ventures is a respect for the relationship between actor and spectator. All artistic and administrative efforts are geared toward nurturing the intimacy of this bond. The Rep is also expanding through work in education and other outreach programs. Through these and other endeavors we are quickly becoming more than just a series of plays. We are growing into a cultural entity that contributes on a long-term basis to its community and the artists who work here.

—Gordon Reinhart

Note: During the 1987-88 season, Michael T. Yeager served as producing artistic director.

PRODUCTIONS 1987–88

Tom Jones, adapt: Michael T. Yeager, from Henry Fielding; (D) Michael T. Yeager; (S) Tim H. Oien; (C) Erin Quigley; (L) Lloyd Sobel
The Nerd, Larry Shue; (D) Steve Kaplan; (S) Tim H. Oien; (C) Erin Quigley; (L) Lloyd Sobel
I'm Not Rappaport, Herb Gardner; (D) Michael T. Yeager; (S) Tim H. Oien; (C) Erin Quigley; (L) Lloyd Sobel

PRODUCTIONS 1988–89

Angel Street, Patrick Hamilton; (D) Henry Hoffman; (S) Loren Brame; (C) Suzy Campbell; (L) Loren Brame
The Arkansaw Bear, Aurand Harris; (D) Gordon Reinhart; (S) Loren Brame; (C) Suzy Campbell; (L) Loren Brame
Lucy's Play, John Clifford; (D) Gordon Reinhart; (S) Loren Brame; (C) Suzy Campbell; (L) Loren Brame
The Cherry Orchard, Anton Chekhov; trans: Ann Dunnigan; (D) Gordon Reinhart; (S) Loren Brame; (C) Suzy Campbell; (L) Loren Brame

Society Hill Playhouse

JAY KOGAN
Artistic Director

DEEN KOGAN
Managing Director

507 South 8th St.
Philadelphia, PA 19147
(215) 923-0211 (bus.)
(215) 923-0210 (b.o.)

FOUNDED 1959
Deen Kogan, Jay Kogan

SEASON
Jan.-Dec.

FACILITIES
Mainstage
Seating Capacity: 223
Stage: proscenium

Second Space
Seating Capacity: 80
Stage: flexible

FINANCES
July 1, 1988-June 30, 1989
Expenses: $444,402

CONTRACTS
AEA SPT

The primary goal of Society Hill Playhouse was and is to present great contemporary plays to Philadelphians who might not otherwise see them. For years we produced the Philadelphia premieres of such playwrights as Brecht, Genet, Sartre, Frisch, Beckett. England's Arden, Wesker and Pinter first played here. American playwrights like Arthur Kopit and LeRoi Jones were first seen in Philadelphia at this theatre. During the years, many experiments also done by other theatres of the world, were done by us in Philadelphia: public script-in-hand readings, playwrights' workshops, one-act play marathons, street theatre, youth theatre. Our interaction with Philadelphians, not just as spectators but in every aspect of making theatre, produced an expanding commitment and role in the community, affecting many people as an arts institution functioning well beyond just presenting plays. Our continued dedication to our original goals still leads us into new paths of community involvement.

—Jay Kogan

PRODUCTIONS 1987–88

Kiss of the Spider Woman, Manuel Puig; trans: Allan Baker; (D) Randal Hoey; (S) Michael J. Hotopp; (C) Thelma Peake; (L) Michael J. Hotopp
Sex Tips for Modern Girls, Edward Astley, Susan Astley, Kim Seary, John Sereda, Hilary Strang, Christine Willes and Peter Eliot Weiss; (D) Stan Hurwitz; (S) Michael J. Hotopp; (C) Thelma Peake; (L) Stephen Keever
Laughing Wild, Christopher Durang; (D) Deen Kogan; (S) Frederick B. Knight; (C) Susan Turlish; (L) Stephen Keever
Nunsense, Dan Goggin; (D) Dan Goggin; (S) Barry Axtell;

Snowmass/Aspen Repertory Theatre. Jean Tafler and Phil LaDuca in *Little Shop of Horrors*.

Society Hill Playhouse. *Nunsense*. Photo: Paul Sinochman.

(c) Deborah Pokallus;
(L) Morris Cooperman

PRODUCTIONS 1988–89

Nunsense, Dan Goggin; (D) Dan Goggin; (s) Barry Axtell; (c) Deborah Pokallus; (L) Morris Cooperman

Mummers and Mistletoe, Susan Turlish; (D) Susan Turlish; (s) Ray Buffington; (c) Frederick D. Wright; (L) Neil Tomlinson

A Midsummer Night's Dream, William Shakespeare; (D) Renee Dobson; (s) Elizabeth Costello; (c) Elizabeth Costello; (L) Neil Tomlinson

Soho Repertory Theatre

MARLENE SWARTZ
Artistic Director

ALAN SIEGE
Managing Director

80 Varick St.
New York, NY 10013
(212) 925-2588 (bus.)
(212) 226-5620 (b.o.)

FOUNDED 1975
Marlene Swartz, Jerry Engelbach

SEASON
Sept.-June

FACILITIES
Greenwich House
Seating Capacity: 130
Stage: proscenium

FINANCES
July 1, 1988-June 30, 1989
Expenses: $291,175

CONTRACTS
AEA letter of agreement

Those who care about art in the 20th century are forced to worry about its relevance, a problem that did not exist before technology demystified much of the artistic process. Our colleagues who ignore the problem wind up producers not of theatres but museums. There is room for re-creation, but that ought not to be our main function. The creation of a relevant, live, three-dimentional aesthetic in the age of instant video can be a breathtaking challenge, if we regard it, as artists should, as a process more important than box office, community acceptance, and product, and if we refuse to be seduced into mistaking an economically or politically successful diversion for our real purpose. Soho Rep's goals are to re-create the rare dramatic literature of the past without becoming a museum, and to try to develop a theatrical aesthetic with risk-taking new material–maintaining at all times the right to fail.
—*Marlene Swartz*

Note: During the 1987-88 season, Jerry Engelbach served as co-artistic director.

PRODUCTIONS 1987–88

The Racket, Bartlett Cormack; (D) Michael Bloom; (s) Phillip Baldwin; (c) Claudia Stephens; (L) Robert W. Rosentel

The Girl of the Golden West, David Belasco; (D) Julian Webber; (s) Jeffrey David McDonald; (c) Patricia Adshead; (L) Nancy Collings

A Cup of Coffee, Preston Sturges; (D) Larry Carpenter; (s) Mark Wendland; (c) Martha Halley; (L) Stuart Duke

PRODUCTIONS 1988–89

The Blitzstein Project, adapt: Carol Corwen, music and lyrics: Marc Blitzstein; (D) Carol Corwen; (s) Jeffrey David McDonald; (c) G.A. Howard; (L) Donald Holder

The Cezanne Syndrome, Normand Canec-Marquis; trans: Louison Danis; (D) Liz Diamond; (s) Anne Servanton; (c) Sally Lesser; (L) Donald Holder

The Phantom Lady, Pedro Calderon de la Barca; trans: Edwin Honig; (D) Julian Webber; (s) Stephan Olson; (c) Patricia Adshead; (L) Donald Holder

South Coast Repertory

DAVID EMMES
Producing Artistic Director

MARTIN BENSON
Artistic Director

Box 2197
Costa Mesa, CA 92628-1197
(714) 957-2602 (bus.)
(714) 957-4033 (b.o.)

FOUNDED 1964
David Emmes, Martin Benson

SEASON
Sept.-July

FACILITIES
Main Stage
Seating Capacity: 507
Stage: modified thrust

Second Stage
Seating Capacity: 161
Stage: thrust

SCR Amphitheatre
Seating Capacity: 200
Stage: flexible

FINANCES
Sept. 1, 1988-Aug. 31, 1989
Expenses: $5,120,000

CONTRACTS
LORT (B) and (D)

South Coast Repertory commits itself to exploring the most important human and social issues of our time and to testing the bounds of theatre's possibilities. While valuing all elements of theatrical productions, we give primacy to the text and its creators. Through premiere productions and an array of developmental programs we serve, nurture and establish long-term relationships with America's most promising playwrights. Around our core company of actors we have built a large and dynamic ensem-

Soho Repertory Theatre. *The Blitzstein Project*. Photo: Gerry Goodstein.

uth Coast Repertory. Ebbe Roe Smith and Elizabeth Ruscio in *The Geography of Luck*.
oto: Henry DiRocco.

of artists, constantly infusing
ir work with the fresh perspec-
e of artists new to our
llaboration. We devote our finan-
l resources to making theatre a
ble and rewarding profession for
our artists. While striving to ad-
ce the art of theatre, we also
ve our community with a vari-
of educational, multicultural
l outreach programs designed to
pport our artistic mission.
—*Martin Benson*

ODUCTIONS 1987–88

alliance, George Bernard
haw; (D) Martin Benson;
s) Ralph Funicello; (C) Susan
Denison Geller; (L) Tom Ruzika
ngarry Glenn Ross, David
Mamet; (D) David Emmes;
s) Cliff Faulkner; (C) Dwight
Richard Odle; (L) Paulie Jenkins
Christmas Carol, adapt: Jerry
atch, from Charles Dickens;
D) John-David Keller; (S) Cliff
aulkner; (C) Dwight Richard
Odle; (L) Donna Ruzika and
om Ruzika
t Dan and Lemon, Wallace
hawn; (D) Martin Benson;
s) Cliff Faulkner; (C) Susan
Denison Geller; (L) Tom Ruzika
lude to a Kiss, Craig Lucas;
D) Norman Rene; (S) Loy
rcenas; (C) Walker Hicklin;
L) Peter Maradudin
* *School for Scandal*, Richard
Brinsley Sheridan; (D) Paul
Marcus; (S) Cliff Faulkner;
C) Shigeru Yaji; (L) Paulie
enkins

Golden Girls, Louise Page;
(D) David Chambers; (S) Ralph
Funicello; (C) Susan Denison
Geller; (L) Peter Maradudin
Haut Gout, Allan Havis; (D) Jody
McAuliffe; (S) Cliff Faulkner;
(C) Shigeru Yaji; (L) Paulie
Jenkins
Benefactors, Michael Frayn;
(D) Steven Albrezzi; (S) Michael
Devine; (C) Charles Tomlinson;
(L) Tom Ruzika
Marry Me a Little, conceived:
Craig Lucas and Norman Rene;
music and lyrics: Stephen
Sondheim; (D) Jules Aaron;
(S) D. Martyn Bookwalter;
(C) Dwight Richard Odle;
(L) Brian Gale
V & V Only, Jim Leonard, Jr.;
(D) Marshall W. Mason; (S) John
Lee Beatty; (C) Susan Denison
Geller; (L) Tom Ruzika
Dog Logic, Thomas Strelich;
(D) Martin Benson; (S) Michael
Devine; (C) Dwight Richard
Odle; (L) Brian Gale

Educational Touring Production
Mountains and Molehills, Jerry
Patch; (D) John-David Keller;
(S) Dwight Richard Odle;
(C) Dwight Richard Odle

PRODUCTIONS 1988–89

The Crucible, Arthur Miller;
(D) Martin Benson; (S) Susan
Tuohy; (C) Robert Blackman;
(L) Tom Ruzika
At Long Last Leo, Mark Stein;
(D) Steven Albrezzi; (S) Cliff
Faulkner; (C) Walker Hicklin;
(L) Peter Maradudin
A Christmas Carol, adapt: Jerry
Patch, from Charles Dickens;
(D) John-David Keller; (S) Cliff
Faulkner; (C) Dwight Richard
Odle; (L) Donna Ruzika and
Tom Ruzika
The Road to Mecca, Athol
Fugard; (D) Martin Benson;
(S) Michael Devine; (C) Walter
Hicklin; (L) Paulie Jenkins
You Never Can Tell, George
Bernard Shaw; (D) David
Emmes; (S) Cliff Faulkner;
(C) Shigeru Yaji; (L) Peter
Maradudin
Abundance, Beth Henley; (D) Ron
Lagomarsino; (S) Adrienne
Lobel; (C) Robert Wojewodski;
(L) Paulie Jenkins
*Sunday in the Park With
George*, book: James Lapine;
music and lyrics: Stephen
Sondheim; (D) Barbara
Damashek; (S) Cliff Faulkner;
(C) Shigeru Yaji; (L) Tom Ruzika
*In Perpetuity Throughout the
Universe*, Eric Overmyer;
(D) Roberta Levitow; (S) Cliff
Faulkner; (C) Susan Denison
Geller; (L) Paulie Jenkins
Morocco, Allan Havis; (D) David
Emmes; (S) Michael Devine;
(C) Susan Denison Geller;
(L) Brian Gale
Talley's Folly, Lanford Wilson;
(D) Lee Shallat; (S) John
Iacovelli; (C) Shigeru Yaji;
(L) Cam Harvey
Hard Times, adapt: Stephen
Jeffreys, from Charles Dickens;
(D) Robert Goldsby; (S) Ariel
Parkinson; (C) Ariel Parkinson;
(L) Peter Maradudin
Dragon Lady, Robert Daseler;
(D) Jerry Patch; (S) Cliff
Faulkner; (C) Susan Denison
Geller; (L) Tom Ruzika
Geography of Luck, Marlane
Meyer; (D) Roberta Levitow;
(S) Cliff Faulkner; (C) Susan
Denison Geller; (L) Tom Ruzika

Educational Touring Production
When I Grow Up, Jerry Patch;
(D) John David Keller;
(S) Dwight Richard Odle;
(C) Dwight Richard Odle

Stage One: The Louisville Children's Theatre

MOSES GOLDBERG
Producing Director

425 West Market St.
Louisville, KY 40202
(502) 589-5946 (bus.)
(502) 584-7777 (b.o.)

FOUNDED 1946
Sara Spencer, Ming Dick

SEASON
Sept.-May

FACILITIES
*Kentucky Center for the Arts
Bomhard Theater*
Seating Capacity: 626
Stage: thrust

Museum of History and Science
Seating Capacity: 350
Stage: arena

FINANCES
June 1, 1988-May 31, 1989
Expenses: $1,088,050

CONTRACTS
AEA TYA

Stage One: The Louisville Children's Theatre provides theatre experiences for young people and families. Choosing plays for specific age groupings, we attempt to develop the aesthetic sensitivity of our audience, step by step, until they emerge from our program as committed adult theatregoers. We play to both school groups and weekend family audiences. Stage One is also committed to developing professionalism in theatre for young audiences, including upgrading artist compensation to the level of adult theatres our size. We perform an eclectic repertoire, including traditional children's plays, company-created pieces, commissioned plays, plays translated from other cultures and carefully selected works from the adult repertoire. Stage One operates in the belief that the classics (both ancient and modern) of folk and children's literature contain archetypal human relationships which make them compelling subjects for dramatization. We hope to preserve the complexities of these tales, while introducing new audiences to the power of living theatre.

—*Moses Goldberg*

PRODUCTIONS 1987–88

The Brave Little Tailor, Robert G. Miller and Asolo Touring Company; (D) Robert G. Miller; (S) H. Charles Schmidt; (C) Connie Furr; (L) H. Charles Schmidt

Little Women, adapt: Marisha Chamberlain, from Louisa May Alcott; (D) Moses Goldberg; (S) Gary Eckhart; (C) Connie Furr; (L) H. Charles Schmidt

The Wonderful Wizard of Oz, adapt: Virginia Glasgow Koste, from L. Frank Baum; (D) Virginia Glasgow Koste; (S) Robert Barnes; (C) Connie Furr; (L) H. Charles Schmidt

Winnie the Pooh, adapt: Geoffrey Hobin, from A.A. Milne; (D) Geoffrey Hobin

The Emperor's Nightingale, adapt: Laura Amy Schlitz, from Hans Christian Andersen; (D) Moses Goldberg; (S) Connie Furr; (C) Connie Furr

A Wrinkle in Time, adapt: Moses Goldberg, from Madeleine L'Engle; (D) Anne-Denise Ford; (S) Michael Hottois; (C) Connie Furr; (L) H. Charles Schmidt

The Tortoise and the Hare, adapt: Alan Broadhurst, from Aesop; (D) Moses Goldberg; (S) John Michael Roberts; (C) Connie Furr; (L) H. Charles Schmidt

Macbeth, William Shakespeare; (D) Moses Goldberg; (S) F. Elaine Williams; (C) Connie Furr; (L) H. Charles Schmidt

PRODUCTIONS 1988–89

Puss in Boots, adapt: Moses Goldberg; (D) Curt L. Tofteland; (S) Brenda K. Kiefer; (C) Connie Furr

On the Edge, Gennadi Mamlin; (D) Moses Goldberg; (S) Slava Rubanov; (C) Connie Furr; (L) H. Charles Schmidt

The Hobbit, adapt: Moses Goldberg, from J.R.R. Tolkien; (D) Ron Nakahara; (S) Brenda K. Kiefer; (C) Connie Furr; (L) H. Charles Schmidt

The Velveteen Rabbit, adapt: Gail Fairbank, from Margery Williams; (D) Moses Goldberg; (S) Brenda K. Kiefer; (C) Dan Fedie

The Best Christmas Pageant Ever, Barbara Robinson; (D) Geoffrey Hobin; (S) John Michael Roberts; (C) Connie Furr; (L) H. Charles Schmidt

The Sorcerer's Apprentice, Mary Hall Surface; (D) Mary Hall Surface; (S) Brenda K. Kiefer; (C) Connie Furr

The Diary of Anne Frank, Frances Goodrich and Albert Hackett; (D) Moses Goldberg; (S) Kenneth Terrill; (C) Connie Furr; (L) H. Charles Schmidt

The Wind in the Willows, adapt: Moses Goldberg, from Kenneth Grahame; (D) Moses Goldberg; (S) Robert Croghan; (C) Connie Furr; (L) H. Charles Schmidt

Charlotte's Web, adapt: Joseph Robinette, from E.B. White; (D) Moses Goldberg; (S) Sharon Perlmutter; (C) Connie Furr; (L) H. Charles Schmidt

The Odessey, adapt: Kurt Beattie and Gregory Falls; (D) Laura Fine; (S) Brenda K. Kiefer; (C) Connie Furr; (L) Jonathan Sprouse

Stage West

JERRY RUSSELL
Artistic/Managing Director

JAMES COVAULT
Associate Director

Box 2587
Fort Worth, TX 76113
(817) 332-6265 (bus.)
(817) 332-6238 (b.o.)

FOUNDED 1979
Jerry Russell

SEASON
Oct.-Sept.

FACILITIES
Seating Capacity: 155
Stage: thrust

FINANCES
Oct. 1, 1987-Sept. 30, 1988
Expenses: $430,525

CONTRACTS
AEA SPT

Stage West has established the only professional theatre that Fort Worth has ever known. From a beginning with no outside support and only the commitment of our founders, we have grown to over 1,500 subscribers, the second highest annual attendance among the city's performing arts groups, and have gained an enviable reputation in the Dallas-Fort Worth area. Our play selection philosophy is broad-based, with each season containing a mix of contemporary and period pieces, musicals, classical adaptations and original works. We are committed to producing one new work each season. Future objectives include the building of a new 350-seat theatre, the redevelopment of our experimental performing space and advancement to LORT contract status with Actors' Equity Association. To date, budgets have allowed only local casting. The next five years should see an expansion in our casting policies, and possibly a small resident company.

—*Jerry Russell*

PRODUCTIONS 1987–88

Biloxi Blues, Neil Simon; (D) Jerry Russell; (S) Jim Covault; (C) Jim Covault; (L) Michael O'Brien

She Loves Me, book: Joe Masteroff; music: Jerry Bock; lyrics: Sheldon Harnick; (D) Jim Covault; (S) Dale Domm; (C) Jim Covault; (L) Michael O'Brien

Glengarry Glen Ross, David Mamet; (D) Jim Covault; (S) Dale Domm; (C) Jim Covault; (L) Michael O'Brien

Little Lulu in a Tight Orange Dress, John Moynihan; (D) Jerry Russell; (S) Jim Covault; (C) Jim Covault; (L) Michael O'Brien

The Seagull, Anton Chekhov; (D) Jim Covault; (S) Dale Domm; (C) Jim Covault; (L) Michael O'Brien

Pump Boys and Dinettes, John Foley, Mark Hardwick, Debra Monk, Cass Morgan, John Schimmel and Jim Wann; (D) Jerry Russell; (S) Dale Domm; (C) Jim Covault; (L) Michael O'Brien

Housewives, Anne Clayton; (D) Jerry Russell; (S) Michael O'Brien; (C) Jim Covault; (L) Michael O'Brien

The Real Thing, Tom Stoppard; (D) Jerry Russell and Jim Covault; (S) Jim Covault; (C) Jim Covault; (L) Michael O'Brien

PRODUCTIONS 1988–89

On the Verge or The Geography of Yearning, Eric Overmyer; (D) Jerry Russell; (S) Jim Covault; (C) Jim Covault; (L) Michael O'Brien

Rough Crossing, Ferenc Molnar adapt and lyrics: Tom Stoppard; (D) Jim Covault; (S) Nelson Coates; (C) Jim Covault; (L) Suzanne Lavender

Moonshadow, Richard Hellesen; (D) Jerry Russell; (S) Bob Lavallee; (C) Jim Covault; (L) Jay Isham

Relatively Speaking, Alan Ayckbourn; (D) Jim Covault; (S) Jim Covault; (C) Jim Covault; (L) Michael O'Brien

Stepping Out, Richard Harris; (D) Jerry Russell; (S) Dale Domm; (C) Jim Covault; (L) Michael O'Brien

A Day in Hollywood/A Night in the Ukraine, book and lyrics: Dick Vosburgh; music: Frank Lazarus; (D) Jerry Russell; (S) Jim Covault; (C) Jim Covault

Stage One: The Louisville Children's Theatre. Tavis Ross, Brian Russell, Geoffrey Hobin and Art Burns in *The Wind in the Willows*. Photo: Kenneth Hayden.

StageWest. Ojida White and David Poynter in *Rough Crossing*. Photo: Buddy Myers.

StageWest

ERIC HILL
Artistic Director

MARTHA RICHARDS
Managing Director

One Columbus Center
Springfield, MA 01103
(413) 781-4470 (bus.)
(413) 781-2340 (b.o.)

FOUNDED 1967
Stephen E. Hays

SEASON
Sept.-June

FACILITIES
S. Prestley Blake Theatre
Seating Capacity: 447
Stage: thrust

Winnifred Arms Studio Theatre
Seating Capacity: 99
Stage: flexible

FINANCES
July 1, 1988-June 30, 1989
Expenses: $1,889,000

CONTRACTS
LORT (C) and (D)

StageWest's artistic identity is reflected in its commitment to a company of artists whose ongoing collaboration in a varied and expanded repertoire forms the central condition of our work. The goals of the theatre are to develop and cultivate the artists; to present a full range of theatrical works to the broadest possible audience; to promote opportunities for creative individuals of all cultural backgrounds to exercise their artistic and technical skills; to train and develop young talent; and to continue to collaborate with other theatre companies. Ongoing classes for students and special projects in research and development continue through the season. An intern acting company works alongside the Equity company all season, and daily classes in the Suzuki method of actor training are offered to every company member throughout the season.
—*Eric Hill*

Note: During the 1987-88 and 1988-89 seasons, Gregory Boyd served as artistic director.

PRODUCTIONS 1987–88

Dracula, A Musical Nightmare, book and lyrics: Douglas Johnson; music: John Aschenbrenner; (D) Gregory Boyd; (S) Peter David Gould; (C) V. Jane Suttel; (L) Robert Jared
The Odd Couple, Neil Simon; (D) Marcia Milgran Dodge; (S) Rick Dennis; (C) Frances Blau; (L) Robert Jared
Billy Bishop Goes to War, Eric Peterson and John Gray; (D) Gregory Boyd; (S) Sharon Perlmutter; (C) Frances Blau; (L) Robert Jared
Sister Mary Ignatius Explains It All for You, Christopher Durang; (D) Gregory Boyd; (S) Michael Banner; (C) Frances Blau; (L) Robert Jared
The Actor's Nightmare, Christopher Durang; (D) Gregory Boyd; (S) Michael Banner; (C) Frances Blau; (L) Robert Jared
The Real Thing, Tom Stoppard; (D) Gregory Boyd; (S) Peter David Gould; (C) V. Jane Suttel; (L) Robert Jared
Visions of an Ancient Dreamer, adapt: Eric Hill, from Euripides; (D) Eric Hill; (C) Deborah Rosenberg; (L) Clifford E. Berek
The Tale of Lear, adapt: Tadashi Suzuki, from William Shakespeare; (D) Tadashi Suzuki; (S) Arden Fingerhut; (C) Tadashi Suzuki; (L) Arden Fingerhut

PRODUCTIONS 1988–89

A Funny Thing Happened on the Way to the Forum, book: Larry Gelbart and Burt Shevelove; music: Stephen Sondheim; (D) Gregory Boyd; (S) Dale F. Jordan; (C) Michael Krass; (L) Dale F. Jordan
A Christmas Carol, adapt: Gregory Boyd, from Charles Dickens, (D) Eric Hill; (S) Keith Henery; (C) Kristin Yungkurth; (L) Jeff Hill and Clifford E. Berek
Macbeth, William Shakespeare; (D) Gregory Boyd; (S) Keith Henery; (C) Susan Tsu; (L) Robert Jared
Sherlock's Last Case, Charles Marowitz; (D) Eric Hill; (S) Keith Henery; (C) Kristin Yungkurth; (L) Clifford E. Berek
The Nerd, Larry Shue; (D) John Tyson; (S) Keith Henery; (C) Kristin Yungkurth; (L) Jeff Hill
The Dance and the Railroad, David Henry Hwang; (D) Roberta Uno; (S) Keith Henery; (C) Kristin Yungkurth; (L) Clifford E. Berek
Faith Healer, Brian Friel; (D) Eric Hill; (S) Keith Henery; (C) Kristin Yungkurth; (L) Clifford E. Berek
Orestes, adapt: Eric Hill, from Euripides; (D) Eric Hill; (S) Keith Henery; (C) Andrew Carson; (L) Clifford E. Berek

StageWest. *The Tale of Lear*. Photo: Richard Feldman.

(L) Michael O'Brien
The Mighty Methusalah, John Moynihan; (D) Jerry Russell; (S) Dale Domm; (C) Jim Covault; (L) Michael O'Brien
Broadway Bound, Neil Simon; (D) Jim Covault; (S) Jim Covault; (C) Jim Covault; (L) Michael O'Brien

Steppenwolf Theatre Company. Gary Sinise and Terry Kinney in *The Grapes of Wrath*. Photo: Michael Brosilow.

Steppenwolf Theatre Company

RANDALL ARNEY
Artistic Director

STEPHEN B. EICH
Managing Director

2851 North Halsted St.
Chicago, IL 60657
(312) 472-4515 (bus.)
(312) 472-4141 (b.o.)

FOUNDED 1976
Gary Sinise, Jeff Perry, Terry Kinney

SEASON
Year-round

FACILITIES
Seating Capacity: 211
Stage: thrust

FINANCES
Sept. 1, 1988-Aug. 31, 1989
Expenses: $2,110,000

CONTRACTS
AEA CAT

Steppenwolf Theatre is committed to the concept of a community of actors, directors and designers working closely together with a common artistic vision. With a 23-member ensemble of actor-directors producing a wide-ranging repertoire, Steppenwolf aims to provide great theatre through a collective approach to dramatic art–an approach conducive to artistic growth and thus challenging to audience and actor alike. Each artist's commitment to the ensemble approach testifies to its worth: seven of nine original members are still with the group after 11 years. Steppenwolf strives to achieve that rare combination: talented individuals who put the group effort first and simultaneously develop their own individual potential. Steppenwolf now possesses the desire and ability to tackle new challenges—the commissioning of new works, ensemble/playwright residencies, local and national productions, and production exchange. The theatre remains committed to maintaining a permanent resident company in Chicago and to promoting the goals of the ensemble by the presentation of its work to new audiences.

—*Randall Arney*

Note: During the 1987-88 season, Jeff Perry served as co-artistic director.

PRODUCTIONS 1987–88

Burn This, Lanford Wilson; (D) Marshall W. Mason and Beatty John Lee; (S) John Lee Beatty; (C) Laura Crow; (L) Dennis Parichy
Little Egypt, Lynn Siefert; (D) Jeff Perry; (S) Kevin Rigdon; (C) Renee Liepins; (L) Kevin Rigdon
Born Yesterday, Garson Kanin; (D) Frank Galati; (S) Kevin Rigdon; (C) Kevin Rigdon; (L) Kevin Rigdon
The Common Pursuit, Simon Gray; (D) Rondi Reed; (S) Kevin Rigdon; (C) Erin Quigley; (L) Kevin Rigdon
Killers, John Olive; (D) Randall Arney; (S) Kevin Rigdon; (C) Erin Quigley; (L) Kevin Rigdon

PRODUCTIONS 1988–89

The Grapes of Wrath, adapt: Frank Galati, from John Steinbeck; (D) Frank Galati; (S) Kevin Rigdon; (C) Kevin Rigdon and Erin Quigley; (L) Kevin Rigdon
Stepping Out, Richard Harris; (D) Rondi Reed; (S) Kevin Rigdon; (C) Erin Quigley; (L) Kevin Rigdon
A Walk in the Woods, Lee Blessing; (D) Randall Arney; (S) Tim H. Oien; (C) Erin Quigley; (L) Robert Christen
Ring Round the Moon, Jean Anouilh; trans: Christopher Fry; (D) Rondi Reed; (S) Kevin Rigdon; (C) Erin Quigley; (L) Kevin Rigdon
El Salvador, Rafael Lima; (D) Francis Guinan; (S) Kevin Rigdon; (C) Erin Quigley; (L) Kevin Rigdon

St. Louis Black Repertory Company

RONALD J. HIMES
Producing Director

2240 St. Louis Ave
St. Louis, MO 63106
(314) 231-3706

FOUNDED 1980
Ron Himes

SEASON
Oct.-June

FACILITIES
23rd Street Theatre
Seating Capacity: 200
Stage: proscenium

Center of Contemporary Art
Seating Capacity: 480
Stage: proscenium

FINANCES
Jan. 1, 1989-Dec. 31, 1989
Expenses: $307,257

CONTRACTS
AEA SPT

St. Louis Black Repertory Company was founded to heighten the social, cultural and educational awareness of the community—an to create an ongoing arts program for that community. As the community has expanded so have our

St. Louis Black Repertory Company. Ron Himes, Danny Johnson and Ameer Harper *The Little Tommy Parker Celebrated Minstrel Show*. Photo: Maurice Meredith.

ograms: We now produce six
ainstage shows; we have an ex-
nsive educational component that
ludes four-to-six touring shows,
rkshops and residencies, and a
ofessional Intern Program. We
ve also presented dance, music
d film series. Our main stage has
strong commitment to producing
e works of black American and
ird World writers in an environ-
ent that supports not only the
velopment of the work, but also
e actors, directors and designers
olved. As such, the majority of
r productions are area and re-
nal premieres, aimed at artistic
her than commercial success.
—*Ronald J. Himes*

RODUCTIONS 1987–88

ahalia's Song, Vada Butcher;
(D) Ron Himes; (S) Mel
Dickerson; (C) Barbara Vaughan;
(L) Mel Dickerson

ng Time Since Yesterday, P.J.
Gibson; (D) Glenda Dickerson;
(S) Frank Bradley; (C) Barbara
Vaughan; (L) Mel Dickerson

e Colored Museum, George C.
Wolfe; (D) Mike Malone;
(S) Mel Dickerson; (C) Norma
West; (L) Mel Dickerson

*nfinished Women Cry in No
Man's Land While a Bird Dies
in a Gilded Cage*, Aishah
Rahman; (D) Ron Himes;
(S) Frank Bradley; (C) Barbara
Vaughan; (L) Greg Hilmar

eal Away, Ramona King;
(D) Ron Himes; (S) Frank
Bradley; (C) Curtis C. Jackson;
(L) Glenn Dunn

v. Des, Ali Wadud; (D) Debra
Wicks; (S) Jim Burwinkel;
(C) Curtis C. Jackson

RODUCTIONS 1988–89

e Amen Corner, James
Baldwin; (D) Ron Himes;
(S) Frank Bradley; (C) Ron
Himes; (L) Jim Burwinkel

ack Nativity, Langston Hughes;
(D) Ron Himes; (S) Frank
Bradley; (C) Barbara Vaughan;
(L) Kathy Abernathy

*ttle Tommy Parker Celebrated
Colored Minstrel Show*, Carlyle
Brown; (D) James Williams;
(S) Jim Burwinkel; (C) Barbara
Vaughan; (L) Jim Burwinkel

est Memphis Mojo, Martin
Jones; (D) Rhonnie Washington;
(S) Jim Burwinkel; (C) Kim
Perry; (L) Jim Burwinkel

a Rainey's Black Bottom,
August Wilson; (D) Ben Halley,
Jr.; (S) Frank Bradley; (C)
Barbara Vaughan; (L) Jim
Burwinkel

*Dressin Up, Steppin Out, and
Gettin Down*, conceived: Ron
Himes; (D) Ron Himes;
(S) Carol Voelker; (C) Ron
Himes; (L) Kathy Abernathy

The Street Theater

GRAY SMITH
Executive Director

228 Fisher Ave., Room 226
White Plains, NY 10606
(914) 761-3307

FOUNDED 1970
Gray Smith

SEASON
Year-round

FINANCES
June 1, 1988-May 31, 1989
Expenses: $256,000

CONTRACTS
AEA TYA

All Street Theater audience
members—whether in parks,
blocked-off streets, day camps,
schools or other institutions—are
viewed as potential actors. If they
see themselves on stage our work
is validated; if not, we have more
work to do. We try to eliminate
spectacle and to provide little support for "spectators"; whenever
possible our performances lead to
their performances—of pieces developed with our directors through
training and collaboration. Some of
these pieces go on tour, usually
within the school districts where
they originate. All of our work is
original, growing either out of
actor-director collaboration or the
development of commissioned
scripts. Most members of our audience are also "originals": they are
eager to challenge, celebrate and
renew our capacity to tell their
story.   —*Gray Smith*

PRODUCTIONS 1987–88

Me and You, Sara Rubin and
company; (D) Sara Rubin

Turned Around Tales, Sara Rubin
and company; (D) Sara Rubin

PRODUCTIONS 1988–89

Me and You, Sara Rubin and
company; (D) Sara Rubin
Turned Around Tales, Sara Rubin
and company; (D) Sara Rubin

Studio Arena Theatre

DAVID FRANK
Artistic Director

RAYMOND BONNARD
Managing Director

710 Main St.
Buffalo, NY 14202-1990
(716) 856-8025 (bus.)
(716) 856-5650 (b.o.)

FOUNDED 1965
Neal DuBrock

SEASON
Sept.-July

FACILITIES
Seating Capacity: 637
Stage: thrust

FINANCES
July 1, 1988-June 30, 1989
Expenses: $2,997,000

CONTRACTS
LORT (B)

The Street Theater. Harlin Kearsley and J. Michael Reeds in *Me and You*. Photo: Barbara S. Brundage.

Studio Arena Theatre relishes the
special challenge of creating a major theatre in a community with
modest resources. We take joy in
our efforts to create a "popular"
theatre of integrity and ambition,
and conceive of our work as entertainment adventurously enlarged
through the insight of the artist,
rather than as art narrowly defined
and self-righteously distinct from
entertainment. Our work is eclectic
because our taste is so and because
we can afford no self-imposed limitations in the pursuit of our goal,
beyond a determination to choose
work which excites us and which
we believe will also engage our re-
markably large and varied
audience. We aspire to the creation
of an outstanding regional theatre,
dedicated to the audience that has
chosen us, in the belief that this is
the most effective way of making a
contribution of more than regional
significance to the art form as a
whole.
—*David Frank*

PRODUCTIONS 1987–88

The Normal Heart, Larry
Kramer; (D) Donald Driver;
(S) Philipp Jung; (C) Mary Ann
Powell; (L) Heather Carson
Twelfth Night, William
Shakespeare; (D) David Frank;
(S) Joseph A. Varga; (C) Robert
Morgan; (L) Curt Ostermann
Stepping Out, Richard Harris;
(D) Carl Schurr; (S) Michael
Miller; (C) Maria Marrero;
(L) Rachel Budin
Benefactors, Michael Frayn;
(D) Kathryn Long; (S) Loy
Arcenas; (C) Bill Walker; (L) Pat
Collins

Studio Arena Theatre. Susan Gibney in *Abingdon Square*. Photo: Jim Bush.

The Studio Theatre

JOY ZINOMAN
Artistic/Managing Director

KEITH ALAN BAKER
General Manager

1333 P Street, NW
Washington, DC 20005
(202) 232-7267 (bus.)
(202) 332-3300 (b.o.)

FOUNDED 1978
Joy Zinoman

SEASON
Sept.-June

FACILITIES
Mainstage
Seating Capacity: 200
Stage: thrust

Secondstage
Seating Capacity: 50
Stage: flexible

FINANCES
Sept. 1, 19-Aug. 31, 1989
Expenses: $892,500

CONTRACTS
AEA SPT

The Studio Theatre, now in its 12th season, has emerged as a vital and vibrant artistic force, a leader of Washington's professional theatre movement. The Studio marked its 10th anniversary with a move to new facilities at the center of the city's developing theatre district, reaffirming our commitment to the revitalization of the histor 14th Street corridor. Since its founding, the Studio has offered productions, gaining a reputation for innovative and challenging work. The mainstage series offer wide range of plays, primarily Washington-area premieres, emphasizing what is best in contemporary theatre today—productions such as August Wilson's *Ma Rainey's Black Botto* a contemporary adaptation of Eu ripides' *The Bacchae*, Anthony Minghella's *Made in Bangkok*, and William Hoffman's *As Is*. Fulfillir our commitment to providing for the "next generation" of theatre artists, the new developmental S ondstage series offers opportunit for emerging young directors an designers, and the Studio Theatre Acting Conservatory is the area's largest and most comprehensive. The Studio's primary focus is pre enting bold material, which maintains the essence of our work—a highly energetic, eclecti urban theatre focused on performance, intimacy and high production values.
—*Joy Zinom*

PRODUCTIONS 1987-88

North Shore Fish, Israel Horov
(D) Joy Zinoman

Black Play Repertory:
Split Second, Dennis McIntyre;
(D) Samuel Barton
The Colored Museum, George
Wolfe; (D) Samual Barton

Ah, Wilderness!, Eugene O'Nei
D) Joy Zinoman
The Mystery of Irma Vep,
Charles Ludlam; (D) Robert
Fuhrmann

Tintypes, Mary Kyte, Mel Marvin and Gary Pearle; (D) Michael Shawn; (S) Tom Hennes; (C) Mary Ann Powell; (L) Tom Hennes
Isn't It Romantic, Wendy Wasserstein; (D) Kathryn Long; (S) Victor Becker; (C) Mary Grace Froehlich; (L) Nancy Schertler
Hedda Gabler, adapt: Christopher Hampton, from Henrik Ibsen; (D) Rosemary Hay; (S) Robert Morgan; (C) Mary Ann Powell; (L) Dennis Parichy

PRODUCTIONS 1988-89

Men Should Weep, Ena Lamont Stewart; (D) David Frank; (S) John Lee Beatty; (C) Mary Ann Powell; (L) Dennis Parichy
Abingdon Square, Maria Irene Fornes; (D) Maria Irene Fornes; (S) Donald Eastman; (C) Gabriel Berry; (L) Anne Militello
Steel Magnolias, Robert Harling; (D) Walton Jones; (S) Victor A. Becker; (C) Pamela Peterson; (L) Tina Charney
The Boyfriend, Sandy Wilson; (D) David Frank; (S) Paul Wonsek; (C) Mary Ann Powell; (L) Judy Rasmuson
West Memphis Mojo, Martin Jones; (D) Edward G. Smith; (S) Leonard Harman; (C) Catherine F. Norgren; (L) Shirley Prendergast
The Beaux' Strategem, George Farquhar; (D) David Frank; (S) Leonard Harman; (C) Susan Tsu; (L) Curt Ostermann
A Walk in the Woods, Lee Blessing; (D) Ross S. Wasserman; (S) Philipp Jung; (C) Mary Ann Powell; (L) Peter Kaczorowski

The Studio Theatre. Michael Howell and Tomas Kearney in *Split Second*. Photo: Jo Marcus.

PRODUCTIONS 1988-89

Hunting Cockroaches, Janusz Glowacki; trans: Jadwiga Kosicka; (D) Joy Zinoman
Shooting Magda, Joshua Sobol; trans: Miriam Shelesinger; (D) Joy Zinoman
The Gifts of the Magi, book adapt: Mark St. Germain and Randy Courts, from O. Henry; (D) Rob Bowman
Lady Day at Emerson's Bar & Grill, Lanie Robertson; (D) Mike Malone
The Bacchae, adapt: Joy Zinoman and Maynard Marshall, from Euripides; (D) Joy Zinoman
Pooch Music, David Cale
Hard Times, adapt: Stephen Jeffreys, from Charles Dickens; (D) Michael Russotto
The Love Suicide at Schofield Barracks, Romulus Linney; (D) Keith Alan Baker

---

Syracuse Stage

ARTHUR STORCH
Producing Artistic Director

JAMES A. CLARK
Managing Director

820 East Genesee St.
Syracuse, NY 13210
(315) 443-4008 (bus.)
(315) 443-3275 (b.o.)

FOUNDED 1974
Arthur Storch

SEASON
Oct.-Apr.

FACILITIES
John D. Archbold Theatre
Seating Capacity: 510
Stage: proscenium

Experimental Theatre
Seating Capacity: 202
Stage: proscenium

Daniel C. Sutton Pavilion
Seating Capacity: 100
Stage: flexible

Seating Capacity: 0
Stage:

FINANCES
July 1, 1988-June 30, 1989
Expenses: $1,811,282

CONTRACTS
LORT (C)

The principle purpose of Syracuse Stage is to present central New York state residents with a variety of plays selected from the world's dramatic literature as well as American and foreign contemporary playwriting; each season, the theatre strives to present at least one new play. Commitment to the actor in all aspects of his or her stay in Syracuse is a cornerstone of this theatre's policy, and giving the actor the supportive environment to encourage the highest degree of creativity is our goal. Because of the relationship between Syracuse Stage and the Syracuse University drama department, both headed by the same person, there is a mutual commitment to excellence and creativity.

—*Arthur Storch*

PRODUCTIONS 1987-88

Stepping Out, Richard Harris; (D) Carl Schurr; (S) Michael Miller; (C) Maria Marrero; (L) Rachel Budin
Fugue, Leonora Thuna; (D) Arthur Storch; (S) David Potts; (C) Maria Marrero; (L) Marc B. Weiss
The Miser, adapt: Miles Malleson, from Moliere; (D) John Going; (S) William Schroder; (C) William Schroder; (L) F. Mitchell Dana
Hizzoner!, Paul Shyre; (D) John Going; (S) Eldon Elder; (C) Patrizia von Brandenstein; (L) John McLain
7 by Beckett, Samuel Beckett; (D) Arthur Storch; (S) Victor A. Becker; (C) Nanzi Adzima; (L) Natasha Katz
Frankie and Johnny in the Clair de Lune, Terrence McNally; (D) Charles Karchmer; (S) James Noone; (C) Joseph R. McFate; (L) Sandra Schilling

PRODUCTIONS 1988-89

Steel Magnolias, Robert Harling; (D) Walton Jones; (S) Victor A. Becker; (C) Pamela Peterson; (L) Tina Charney
Long Day's Journey into Night, Eugene O'Neill; (D) William Woodman; (S) Gary May; (C) Maria Marrero; (L) Harry Feiner
Look Homeward, Angel, adapt: Ketti Frings, from Thomas Wolfe; (D) Arthur Storch; (S) John Lee Beatty; (C) Nanzi Adzima; (L) Roger Morgan
Another Antigone, A.R. Gurney, Jr.; (D) Robert Berlinger; (S) Victor A. Becker; (C) Maria Marrero; (L) Phil Monat

How the Other Half Loves, Alan Ayckbourn; (D) Tazewell Thompson; (S) James Noone; (C) Judy Dearing; (L) David Noling
Wait Until Dark, Frederick Knott; (D) Arthur Storch; (S) Gary May; (C) Maria Marrero; (L) Phil Monat

---

Tacoma Actors Guild

BRUCE K. SEVY
Artistic Director

KATE HAAS
Managing Director

1323 South Yakima Ave.
Tacoma, WA 98405
(206) 272-3107 (bus.)
(206) 272-2145 (b.o.)

FOUNDED 1978
Rick Tutor, William Becvar

SEASON
Sept.-Apr.

FACILITIES
Seating Capacity: 299
Stage: proscenium

FINANCES
July 1, 1988-June 30, 1989
Expenses: $643,848

CONTRACTS
AEA letter of agreement

Syracuse Stage. P.J. Benjamin and Steven Dennis in *Long Day's Journey into Night*. Photo: Lawrence Mason, Jr.

Tacoma Actors Guild is defined by its name: our theatre is interested in producing plays which provide actors with challenging roles. Although design support is a consideration, the actor is never relegated to a secondary position—it is the actor through which we reach our audience. We provide Northwest talent with appealing roles, while fulfilling our audiences' expectations of professional productions. Our selections reflect a wide diversity in the canon of dramatic literature. We align ourselves with the established play and mount productions that allow new audiences to experience a play whose title is the only known factor, while giving an older audience the opportunity to rediscover an "old friend." In a period when numerous theatres are turning to modern, smaller-cast productions, TAG seeks to develop a reputation for producing plays from a period of time when larger casts were the rule, rather than the exception.

—*Bruce K. Sevy*

PRODUCTIONS 1987-88

Amadeus, Peter Shaffer; (D) Robert Robinson; (S) Peggy MacDonald; (C) Anne Thaxter Watson; (L) Richard Devin
The Belle of Amherst, William Luce; (D) William Becvar; (S) Judith Cullen; (C) Wendela K. Jones; (L) James Verdery
Cole, book: Benny Green and Alan Strachan; music and lyrics: Cole Porter; (D) Rick Tutor; (S) Jerry S. Hooker; (C) Wendela K. Jones; (L) J. Patrick Elmer

Tacoma Actos Guild. Rick Tutor and Stuart Duckworth in *The Caretaker*. Photo: Fred Andrews.

True West, Sam Shepard;
(D) William Becvar; (S) Rob Murphy; (C) Wendela K. Jones; (L) Rob Murphy
Hedda Gabler, Henrik Ibsen; trans: Eva Le Gallienne; (D) Bruce K. Sevy; (S) Rob Murphy; (C) Frances Kenny; (L) J. Patrick Elmer
Same Time, Next Year, Bernard Slade; (D) B.J. Douglas; (S) Rob Murphy; (C) Wendela K. Jones; (L) J. Patrick Elmer

PRODUCTIONS 1988–89

Noises Off!, Michael Frayn; (D) Tom Skore; (S) William Forrester; (C) Sally Richardson; (L) Tammy L. Ray
Sea Marks, Gardner Mc Kay; (D) William Becvar; (S) Jay Hollingsworth; (C) Wendela K. Jones; (L) Rogue Conn
Perfectly Frank, Kenny Solms; music: Frank Loesser, et al.; (S) Patricia Del Campo; (C) Anne Thaxter Watson; (L) Tammy L. Ray
Vikings, Stephen Metcalfe; (D) Rick Tutor; (S) Rollin Thomas; (C) Wendela K. Jones; (L) Tammy L. Ray
The Caretaker, Harold Pinter; (D) William Becvar; (S) Greg Veatch; (C) Wendela K. Jones; (L) Tammy L. Ray
The Foreigner, Larry Shue; (D) Cheri Sorenson; (S) Jeffrey A. Frkonja; (C) Wendela K. Jones; (L) Tammy L. Ray

The Tampa Players

BILL LELBACH
Artistic/Managing Director

601 South Florida Ave.
Tampa, FL 33602
(813) 229-1505 (bus.)
(813) 229-3221 (b.o.)

FOUNDED 1926

SEASON
Sept.-May

FACILITIES
Jaeb Theatre/Tampa Bay Performing Arts Center
Seating Capacity: 300
Stage: flexible

Playhouse/Tampa Bay Performing Arts Center
Seating Capacity: 960
Stage: proscenium

FINANCES
July 1, 1988-June 30, 1989
Expenses: $400,000

CONTRACTS
AEA letter of agreement and SPT

Primary to my work is the belief that through our productions, we can compel the audience to examine the mental, ethical and physical limitations, contradictions and dilemmas facing the individual and society. Through productions which explore limitations placed on the individual, and responses to those limitations, a greater perception evolves of both the individual and the surrounding society. Our production of *Tracers*, performed at the 1988 Piccolo Spoleto Festival, is the type of work which exemplifies our desire to produce classic and contemporary plays of lasting value which collectively examine the individual's world.
—*Bill Lelbach*

PRODUCTIONS 1987–88

Smooth Talk Breakdown, Larry Wright; (D) Bill Lelbach; (S) Bill Lelbach; (C) Leslie Burmeister; (L) R.T. Williams
Terra Nova, Ted Tally; (D) Bill Lelbach; (S) Bill Lelbach; (C) Leslie Burmeister; (L) G.B. Stephens
Biloxi Blues, Neil Simon; (D) T. Newell Kring; (S) Charles T. Parsons; (C) Loren Bracewell; (L) R.T. Williams
A Christmas Carol, adapt: Frank Morse, from Charles Dickens; (D) T. Newell Kring; (C) Loren Bracewell; (L) Alan Pickart
Hedda Gabler, Henrik Ibsen; (D) Bill Lelbach; (S) Charles T. Parsons; (C) Joanne Johnson; (L) G.B. Stephens
The Cry of the Peacock, Jean Anouilh; (D) Bill Lelbach; (S) Kim Edgar Swados; (C) Abby Lillethun; (L) Eric Veenstra
The Colored Museum, George C. Wolfe; (D) Samuel Barton; (S) Eric Veenstra; (C) Bambi-Jeanne Stoll; (L) Eric Veenstra
Tracers, John DiFusco, Vincent Caristi, Richard Caves, Eric E Emerson, Rich Gallavan, Mer Marston, Harry Stephans and Sheldon Lettich; (D) Bill Lelbach; (S) Bill Lelbach; (C) Leslie Burmeister; (L) Charles T. Parsons

PRODUCTIONS 1988–89

Some Things You Need to Kno Before the World Ends (A Final Evening With the Illuminati), Larry Larson and Levi Lee; (D) Bill Lelbach; (S) T.J. Ecenia; (C) Bambi-Jeanne Stoll; (L) G.B. Stephen
Silent Night, Lonely Night, Robert Anderson; (D) Pamela Sanders; (S) Charles T. Parson (C) Loren Bracewell; (L) Char T. Parsons
A Christmas Carol, adapt: Larr Wright, from Charles Dickens (D) Bill Lelbach; (S) Gerry Leahy; (C) Abby Lillethun; (L) Charles T. Parsons
Tomfoolery, adapt: Cameron Mackintosh and Robin Ray, fr Tom Leher; (D) T.Newell Krin (S) Bill Lelbach; (L) David Belcher
Long Day's Journey into Night Eugene O'Neill; (D) Bill Lelbach; (S) David Dusseault; (C) Joanne Johnson; (L) Charle T. Parsons
The Day Room, Don DeLillo; (D) Bill Lelbach; (S) Bill Lelbach; (C) Joanne Johnson; (L) G.B. Stephens

The Tampa Players. Kerry Glamsch and Bret Ancell in *Some Things You Need to Kno Before the World Ends (A Final Evening With the Illuminati.)* Photo: Bill Lelbach.

The Theatre at Monmouth. Maryann Plunkett and Timothy Wheeler in *Jane Eyre*.

The Theater at Monmouth

TED DAVIS
Artistic Director

MARIUS B. PELADEAU
General Manager

Box 385 Cumston Hall
Monmouth, ME 04259
(207) 933-2952 (bus.)
(207) 933-9999 (b.o.)

FOUNDED 1970
Richard Sewell, Robert Joyce

SEASON
June-Sept.

FACILITIES
Cumston Hall
Seating Capacity: 275
Stage: thrust

FINANCES
Oct. 1, 1988-Sept. 30, 1989
Expenses: $204,000

CONTRACTS
AEA SPT

The Theatre at Monmouth presents classical theatre (in rotating repertory) in a beautiful Victorian opera house. Our season is anchored by a basic repertoire of traditional classics mixed with new stage adaptations of literature. We also regularly produce new plays that fit our primary criterion of richly textured and heightened language. As we are primaily an actor's theatre, we cultivate a core company of performers who are comfortable with a variety of writing styles and the demands of an eccentric repertory season. Our high school touring program is designed to introduce young people throughout the state to the works of Shakespeare. And our special children's theatre season provides many area youngsters with their first theatre experience.
—*Ted Davis*

PRODUCTIONS 1987–88

Taking Steps, Alan Ayckbourn;
(D) Ted Davis; (S) Edgar A. Cyrus and Edgar A. Cyrus;
(L) Edgar A. Cyrus
Two Gentleman of Verona, William Shakespeare;
(D) Richard Sewell; (S) Edgar A. Cyrus; (C) Jane Snider;
(L) Edgar A. Cyrus
Richard II, William Shakespeare;
(D) Richard Sewell; (S) Richard Sewell; (C) Jane Snider;
(L) Edgar A. Cyrus
Jane Eyre, adapt: Ted Davis, from Charlotte Bronte; music: David Clark; lyrics: Ted Davis; (D) Ted Davis; (S) Richard Sewell;
(C) Jane Snider; (L) Edgar A. Cyrus

PRODUCTIONS 1988–89

Wenceslas Square, Larry Shue;
(D) Ted Davis; (S) Wayne Merritt; (C) Jane Snider;
(L) Edgar A. Cyrus
All's Well That Ends Well, William Shakespeare; (D) Ted Davis; (S) Wayne Merritt;
(C) Jane Snider; (L) Edgar A. Cyrus
The Country Wife, William Wycherly; (D) Edgar A. Cyrus;
(S) Wayne Merritt; (C) Jane Snider; (L) Edgar A. Cyrus
The Hunchback of Notre Dame, adapt: Timothy Wheeler, from Vicor Hugo; (D) Tim Oman;
(S) Wayne Merritt; (C) Jane Snider; (L) Edgar A. Cyrus

Theatre de la Jeune Lune

BARBRA BERLOVITZ DESBOIS, VINCENT GRACIEUX, ROBERT ROSEN AND DOMINIQUE SERRAND
Artistic Directors

EMILY STEVENS
Business Director

Box 25170
Minneapolis, MN 55458-6170
(612) 332-3968 (bus.)
(612) 333-6200 (b.o.)

FOUNDED 1978
Dominique Serrand, Vincente Gracieux, Barbra Berlovitz Desbois

SEASON
Sept.-July

FACILITIES
Hennepin Center for the Arts
Seating Capacity: 385
Stage: thrust

Guthrie Laboratory
Seating Capacity: 280
Stage: flexible

Southern Theater
Seating Capacity: 220
Stage: proscenium

FINANCES
Aug. 1, 1988-July 31, 1989
Expenses: $518,000

Theatre de la Jeune Lune is a theatre of actors. What is important to us is what the actor puts on the stage when the curtain goes up—what happens in front of the audience. With that end result in mind, we enter into each production. There isn't a play we won't do. We could be interested in a classic, a modern work or an original new play. What we do with it is a different matter. We strive to make the play "ours," to bring across, as our audience would agree, our style. Our heart, passions and emotions open the paths to ideas. We create exactly what we want to,

Theatre de la Jeune Lune. *7 Dwarfs*. Photo: Gerald Gustafson.

within our obvious financial restrictions. Every production is different and each play must be attacked from a new angle with our experience of the past. Pushing ourselves into new areas every year, we want to continue bringing exciting, eventful and important theatre to our community.
—*Dominique Serrand*

PRODUCTIONS 1987–88

Lorenzaccio adapt: Barbra Berlovitz Desbois and Felicity Jones, from Alfred de Musset; trans: Patrick O'Brien; (D) Barbra Berlovitz Desbois; (S) Dominique Serrand and David Coggins; (C) Sonya Berlovitz (L) Frederic Desbois
Cafe Under the Earth, adapt and trans: Vincent Gracieux and Steven Epp, from Alain Gautre; music: Steven Epp; (D) Vincent Gracieux; (S) Dominique Serrand; (C) Steven Epp; (L) Frederic Desbois
Circus, company-developed; (D) Robert Rosen; (S) Tom Rose; (C) Sonya Berlovitz and Margot Curran; (L) Dominique Serrand
Red Noses, Peter Barnes; (D) Dominique Serrand; (S) Vincent Gracieux; (C) Barbra Berlovitz Desbois; (L) Robert Rosen

PRODUCTIONS 1988–89

Ubu for President, Didier Maucort; adapt: David Ball; (D) Barbra Berlovitz Desbois; (S) Michael Sommers; (C) Sue Haas; (L) Jeff Bartlett
The 7 Dwarfs, Kevin Kling; (D) Michael Sommers; (S) Dominique Serrand and Felicity Jones; (C) Kathleen McGee; (L) Frederic Desbois
1789: The French Revolution, Barbra Berlovitz Desbois, Vincent Gracieux, Felicity Jones, Robert Rosen, Christopher Bayes and Paul Walsh; (D) Dominique Serrand; (S) Vincent Gracieux; (C) Andrea McCormack; (L) Mark Sommerfield
Holiday in Kerflooey (Uh Oh, Uh Oh Goes Tralala), company-developed; (D) Robert Rosen; (S) Michael Sommers; (C) Liz Josheff and Catherine Wengler; (L) Vaclav Kucera

Theatre for a New Audience

JEFFREY HOROWITZ
Artistic/Producing Director

220 E. 4th St., 4th Fl
New York, NY 10009
(212) 505-8345

FOUNDED 1979
Jeffrey Horowitz

SEASON
Jan.–June

FACILITIES
CSC Repertory Ltd.
Seating Capacity: 199
Stage: flexible

Perry Street Theatre
Seating Capacity: 95
Stage: proscenium

FINANCES
Sept. 1, 1988-Aug. 31, 1989
Expenses: $550,000

CONTRACTS
AEA letter of agreement and TYA

Theatre for a New Audience's mission is to preserve, enrich and share the dramatic tradition of Shakespeare. It is committed to advancing the American classical and contemporary theatre through vital, inventive productions by our finest artists. The company strives to bring audiences of both adults and young people not only to experience the Bard of Avon, but also the other masters who over the centuries have created a world repertoire of plays that endure as expressions of human condition. The company also advances the dramatic tradition by nurturing contemporary playwrights who fuse language and social conflict, poetry and reality in plays that raise questions important to our time. Governing our classical productions is an aesthetic that focuses on finding the connection between the heightened language of the classics, and the concerns and sensibilites of today's theatre. To challenge the young through serious theatre, all productions play for both students and general audiences.
—*Jeffrey Horowitz*

PRODUCTIONS 1987–88

The Taming of the Shrew, William Shakespeare; (D) Julie Taymor; (S) G.W. Mercier; (C) Catherine Zuber; (L) Beverly Emmons
Evening Star, Milcha Sanchez-Scott; (D) Paul Zimet; (S) G.W. Mercier; (C) G.W. Mercier; (L) M.L. Geiger

PRODUCTIONS 1988–89

Macbeth, William Shakespeare; (D) Nicholas Mahon; (S) G.W. Mercier; (C) G.W. Mercier; (L) Frances Aronson
The Red Sneaks, Elizabeth Swados; (D) Elizabeth Swados; (S) G.W. Mercier; (C) G.W. Mercier; (L) M.L. Geiger
A Midsummer Night's Dream, William Shakespeare; (D) Jeffrey Horowitz; (S) Julie Taymor; (C) Julie Taymor; (L) Daniel Kelly

Theater for the New City

CRYSTAL FIELD
GEORGE BARTENIEFF
Co-artistic Directors

155 First Ave.
New York, NY 10003
(212) 254-1109 (bus.)
(212) 254-1109 (b.o.)

FOUNDED 1971
Larry Kornfeld, Crystal Field, George Bartenieff, Theo Barne

SEASON
Year-round

FACILITIES
Theater 1
Seating Capacity: 99
Stage: flexible

Theatre for a New Audience. Sheila Dabney and Sam Tsoutsouvas in *The Taming of the Shrew*. Photo: Richard Feldman.

Theater II
Seating Capacity: 75
Stage: flexible

Theater III
Seating Capacity: 99
Stage: flexible

Cabaret
Seating Capacity: 50
Stage: flexible

FINANCES
July 1, 1987-June 30, 1988
Expenses: $769,172

CONTRACTS
AEA Showcase Code

Theater for the New City, now in its 18th season, is a center dedicated to the discovery of relevant new writing and the nurturing of new playwrights. TNC has presented 600 new American plays to more than 750,000 audience members, including the premieres of works by Sam Shepard, Maria Irene Fornes, Harvey Fierstein, Hamlin Gray, Jean-Claude van Itallie, Miguel Pinero, Rosalyn Drexler, Robert Patrick, Romulus Linney—the list is practically endless. TNC has also presented many of America's most important theatre companies and artists, among them Richard Foreman, Mabou Mines, Bread and Puppet Theater, Charles Ludlam, and the Talking Band. TNC's commitment to new artists, lesser-known writers and young performers is evidenced by our Emerging Playwrights Program, and a Street Theater Performers Workshop (under our direction). TNC also operate one of the most extensive new play commissioning programs in America. Each year, TNC provides 30,000 free admissions to members of 90 community, senior citizen and youth groups, and creates a free street theatre traveling festival every summer, bringing outdoor performances to New York City's five boroughs. In 1986, after performing in rented spaces, TNC purchased a new home that is being converted into a comminity-based cultural and performance art center.
—Crystal Field, George Bartenieff

PRODUCTIONS 1987–88

Hit the Road, Crystal Field and Mark Hardwick; (D) Crystal Field and Paul Zimet; (S) Myrna Duarte and Joanne Basinger; (C) Edmund Felix and Brian Pride
Why to Refuse, Eduardo Machado; (D) Melia Bensussen; (S) Donald Eastman; (C) David Sawaryn; (L) Anne Militello
Fireworks, (D) Valeria Vasilevski and Ruth Maleczech; (S) Redon Osorio; (C) Laura Lee; (L) Susan Chute
The Talking Band: The Three Lives of Lucie Cabrol, John Berger and Paul Zimet; (D) Paul Zimet; (S) Janie Geiser; (C) Gabriel Berry; (L) Arden Fingerhut
US, Karen Malpede; (D) Judith Malina; (S) Ilion Troya and Judith Malina; (C) Chontik; (L) John P. Dodd
Christmas Pageant, Crystal Field and Mark Hardwick; (D) Crystal Field; (S) Myrna Duarte and Mary Blanchard; (C) company
Explanation of a Christmas Wedding, Robert Patrick; (D) Robert Patrick; (C) Eric Hansen
Love, Oscar, Stephen Holt; (D) Christopher Todd; (C) company; (L) Katie Shaw
Dymphna/Colonial Boy, Ray Dobbins; (D) Bette Bloolips Bourne; (S) Paul Shaw; (C) Paul Shaw; (L) Zdenek Kriz
Thunderbird American Indian Dancers Annual Pow Wow and Dance Concert, (D) Louis Mofsie
Marlene, Marlene, Jiri Schubert; (D) Jiri Schubert; (S) Mark Marcante and Mary Blanchard; (C) Myrna Duarte; (L) Zdenek Kriz
Men in Art, Robert Patrick; (D) Robert Patrick; (S) Patrick Angus; (C) Veronique Cheranich; (L) Katie Shaw
The Rosy Cave, J. Lois Diamond; (D) Rick Lombardo; (S) Olivier Tassin; (C) company; (L) Matt Ehlert
Thighs Like Tina Turner, Larry Myers; (D) John Uecker; (S) Tim Burns; (C) Susan Ruddie; (L) Tim Burns
Chutes and Ladder's Glee, Karen Williams; (D) Susan Sterne; (S) Karen Williams and Tom Andrews; (C) Karen Williams and Tom Andrews; (L) Tom Andrews and Paul Clay
Kamikaze Messenger Service, Eddie DiDonna; (D) Mark Marcante; (S) John Paino; (C) Brian Pride; (L) Tommy Barker
Testimonies of a Rape and Killing, Tony Barsha; (D) Tony Barsha; (S) O. Found; (C) company; (L) John P. Dodd
Musk, Bob Borsodi; (D) Bill Bradford; (S) Myrna Duarte; (C) Myrna Duarte; (L) Tommy Barker
Fanon's People, Toby Armour; (D) Aileen Passeloff; (S) Donald Eastman; (C) Liz Prince; (L) Anne Militello
Beverly's Yard Sale, Sebastian Stuart; (D) Steve Lott; (S) Jamie Leo; (C) Judi Jasinsky; (L) Anne Militello
The Girl Who Swallowed Her Sister, Cora Hook; (D) Lizzie Olesker; (S) Steve Hollow; (C) company; (L) Brian Miller
Reefer Madness, John Mangano; (D) Robert Dahdan; (S) Walter Gurbo; (C) Susan Ruddie; (L) Brian Miller
A Hero of Our Time, Thomas Babe; (D) David Briggs; (S) Jessica Lanier and Nancy Greenstein; (C) Jimmell Mardome; (L) Peter West
The Lodger, Joan Schenkar; (D) Richard Riehle; (S) Jean-Francis Questiaux and Deborah Scott; (C) Tracy Oleinick; (L) Craig Kennedy
Thick Dick, Ronald Tavel; (D) Ronald Tavel; (S) Cliff King; (C) Susan Ruddie; (L) Cliff King
The Poets' Corner, Harry Kondoleon; (D) Betsy Shevey; (S) Mark Wendland and Lynn Hippen; (C) Mark Wendland; (L) Lynn Hippen
Crazy Quilt, Walter Corwin; (D) H. Shep Pamplin; (C) company; (L) Tony Angel
A History of Food, Theodora Skipitares; music: Pat Irwin; lyrics: Andrea Balis; (D) Theodora Skipitares; (S) Tommy Barker and Craig Kennedy; (L) Michael Cummings
Ruzzante Returns from the Wars, Angelo Bealco; (D) Mark Marcante; (L) Zdenek Kriz
The Ride That Never Was, Jiri Schubert; (D) Mark Marcante; (S) Tony Angel; (L) Zdenek Kriz
An Evening of British Music Hall, (D) Mark Marcante; (S) Walter Gurbo; (C) company; (L) Zdenek Kriz
The Heat, Jimmy Camicia; (D) Jimmy Camicia; (S) Tony Angel; (C) company; (L) Mark Hannay
A Circle, Bob Morris; (D) Bob Morris; (S) Tommy Barker; (C) Belinda Rachman; (L) David Birn
Neon Tetra, Sebastian Stuart; (D) Steve Lott; (S) Danianne Mizzy and Jamie Leo; (C) Jamie Leo; (L) Zdenek Kriz

PRODUCTIONS 1988–89

The Coney Island Kid, music: Christopher Cherney; lyrics: Crystal Field; (D) Crystal Field; (S) Myrna Duarte and Mary Blanchard; (C) Brian Pride
Dreamland, Bina Sharif; (D) Rolf Johannmeier; (S) Norbert Kimmel; (C) Gaetano Fazio; (L) Zdenek Kriz
The Fighter, Daniel Keene; (D) Iris James; (S) Robert Cooney; (C) company; (L) Maurice Peralta
Translocation 9:16, Kaja Gam; (D) Kaja Gam; (S) Anne Rochette; (C) Trine Walther; (L) Raymond Dooley and Jane Cocol

Theater for the New City. *One Director Against His Cast.*

Babbling with Joe, Agusto Machado; (D) Agusto Machado; (S) John Edward Hays; (C) John Edward Hays; (L) Tommy Barker
Mainstream, Glynn Vincent; (D) Bart Teush; (S) Tim Burns; (C) Lori Goldstein; (L) Thal Hussey
Family Crest, Alan Roy; (D) John Uecker and Mark Marcante; (S) John Paino; (C) Myrna Duarte; (L) Zdenek Kriz
Why Can't We Talk?, Irving Burton; (D) Irving Burton
Russo & Rucker, Rick Russo; (D) Rick Russo
La Fiaccola Sotto Il Moggio, Gabriele D'Annunzio; (D) Mario Federici
Don Juan in New York City, Eduardo Machado; (D) David Willinger; (S) Donald Eastman; (C) Tracy Ollinick; (L) Ron Burns
Mitzi's Glori, Carl Capatorto; (D) David Briggs; (S) Nancy Greenstein Deren; (C) Nina Carter; (L) Clay Shirky
Safe as Houses, Karen Walker; (D) Melia Bensussen; (S) John Murphy, Jr.; (C) company; (L) John Murphy, Jr.
Gland Motel, Bette Bloolips Bourne and Ray Dobbins; (D) Bette Bloolips Bourne; (S) Bette Bloolips Bourne and Paul Shaw; (C) Bette Bloolips Bourne; (L) Zdenek Kriz
That Crazy Cabaret, John Grimaldi and the New York Lyric Circus; (D) Dan Wagoner
Against the Tide, Jamie Leo; (D) Jamie Leo; (S) Jamie Leo; (C) company; (L) Zdenek Kriz
Heathen Valley, Romulus Linney; (D) Romulus Linney; (S) Mark Marcante; (L) Anne Militello
Vktms, Michael McClure; (D) Judith Malina; (S) Ramm-Ell-Zee; (C) Joanne Freedom; (L) John P. Dodd
Winnetou's Snake Oil Show from Wigwam City, Spiderwoman Theater and Karl May; (D) Muriel Miguel; (S) Spiderwoman Theater; (C) Althea Bodenheim; (L) Zdenek Kriz
Riot '88, Rene Van Gissegem; (D) Rene Van Gissegem; (S) company; (C) company; (L) Rudy D'Hont
The Talking Band: Betty Bends the Blues and The Malady of Death, Ellen Maddow and Marguerite Duras; (D) Paul Zimet; (S) Janie Geiser; (C) Gabriel Berry; (L) Carol Mullins
The Thunderbird American Indian Dancers, (D) Louis Mofsie; (S) Frances Gromley and company; (L) Tommy Barker
Walks of Indian Women, Hortensia and Vira Colorado; (D) Muriel Miguel; (S) Jane Sablow; (C) Hortensia and Vira Colorado; (L) Beau Kennedy
Voodoo Economics, Larry Myers; (D) H. Shep Pamplin; (S) Jamie Leo; (C) Jamie Leo; (L) Tommy Barker
White Boned Demon, Leslie Mohn; (D) Leslie Mohn; (S) Gabriel Backlund; (C) Mary Cricket Smith; (L) Vaclav Kucera
Between the Acts, Joan Schenkar; (D) Joan Schenkar; (S) Donald L. Brooks; (C) Tracy Oleinick; (L) Craig Kennedy and Amy Coombs
Sun of the Sleepless, James Purdy; (D) John Uecker; (S) Wendell Crodtz; (C) Sally J. Lesser; (L) Zdenek Kriz
The Breakaways, Bob Borsodi; (D) Bob Borsodi; (S) Bob Borsodi; (C) company and Onari; (L) Bob Borsodi
Broken Bohemian Hearts, Jiri Schubert and Ron Havern; (D) Jiri Schubert; (S) Anna Frisch; (C) Brian Pride; (L) Zdenek Kriz
One Director Against His Cast, Crystal Field; (D) Crystal Field and Mark Marcante; (S) Myrna Duarte and Mary Blanchard; (C) Brian Pride; (L) Seth Orbach
The Heart Outright, Mark Medoff; (D) Mike Ruttenberg; (S) Peter R. Feuche; (C) Traci DiGesu; (L) K. Robert Hoffman
Empires and Appetites, Theodora Skipitares; lyrics: Andrea Balis; music: Pat Irwin; (D) Theodora Skipitares; (S) Michael Cummings; (L) Pat Dignan
That Old Comedy, Walter Corwin; (D) H. Shep Pamplin; (S) H. Shep Pamplin; (C) company; (L) Juliet Neisser
Bruno's Donuts, Sebastian Stuart; (D) Steve Lott; (S) Jamie Leo; (C) Brian Pride; (L) Zdenek Kriz
Skin, Stone, Positive, Off the Beaten Path Native American Theater Company; (D) Muriel Meguel
Life Forms, June Siegel; (D) Rina Elisha; (S) Peter R. Feuche; (C) John James Hickey; (L) Jason Sturm
24 Lily Pond Lane, Toby Armour; (D) Toby Armour

Theatre IV. John Coleman and Deverell Pedersen in *The Nose*. Photo: Eric Dobbs.

Theatre IV

BRUCE MILLER
Artistic Director

PHILIP WHITEWAY
Managing Director

114 West Broad St.
Richmond, VA 23220
(804) 783-1688 (bus.)
(804) 344-8040 (b.o.)

FOUNDED 1975
Phil Whiteway, Bruce Miller

SEASON
Year-round

FACILITIES
The Empire Theatre
Seating Capacity: 599
Stage: proscenium

The Studio
Seating Capacity: 80
Stage: flexible

Backstage
Seating Capacity: 96
Stage: thrust

FINANCES
July 1, 1988-June 30, 1989
Expenses: $906,000

CONTRACTS
AEA guest artist and SPT

Theatre IV presents contemporary plays and musicals for adults, and original plays and musicals for children, young people and their families. In Richmond we are known primarily as an "alternative" theatre. Our productions of such plays as *The Normal Heart*, *Bosoms and Neglect*, *Do Lord Remember Me* and *5th of July* represent to many in our central Virginia audience the "cutting edge" of American drama. Most of our budget is devoted to youth productions which tour extensively; we present more than 1,200 performances a year from San Juan to Chicago. Our original plays *Hugs and Kisses*, *Runners*, *Walking the Line* and *Dancing in the Dark* deal honestly and effectively with the issues of child sexual abuse, runaways, teenage suicide, substance abuse and teenage pregnancy/sexual responsibility. Our new homes—the grand Empire Theatre and the intimate Studio—opened in 1911, and are the oldest extant theatres in our state.
—*Bruce Miller*

PRODUCTIONS 1987-88

Red Hot and Cole, book: James Bianchi, Muriel McAuley and Randy Strawderman; music and lyrics: Cole Porter; (D) Randy Strawderman; (S) Ron Keller; (C) Jann Paxton; (L) Jefferson Lindquist

Benefactors, Michael Frayn; (D) Bruce Miller; (S) Terrie Powers; (C) Elizabeth Hopper; (L) Bruce Rennie
Biloxi Blues, Neil Simon; (D) Nancy Cates; (S) Brad Boynton; (C) Joan U. Brumbach; (L) Jeff Stroman
Extremities, William Mastrosimone; (D) John Glenn; (S) Terrie Powers; (C) Catherine Szari; (L) Bruce Rennie
Olympus on my Mind, book and lyrics: Barry Harman; music: Grant Sturiale; (D) K Strong; (S) Terrie Powers; (C) Elizabeth Hopper; (L) Lou Szari
Ain't Misbehavin', book adapt: Richard Maltby, Jr.; music and lyrics: Fats Waller, et al.; (D) Bev Appleton; (S) Greg Hilmar and Terrie Powers; (C) Thomas Hammond; (L) Jefferson Lindquist
We the People, Bruce Miller; (D) Bruce Miller; (S) Terrie Powers; (C) Thomas Hammond; (L) Bruce Rennie
Hansel and Gretel, book and lyrics: Douglas Jones; music: Ron Barnett; (D) John Glenn; (S) Terrie Powers; (C) Thomas Hammond; (L) Bruce Rennie
Runners, Bruce Miller and Terry Bliss; (D) Bruce Miller; (S) Terrie Powers; (C) John Glenn; (L) Bruce Rennie
Santa's Holiday Adventure, book, music and lyrics: Richard Giersch; (D) Russell Wilson; (S) Terrie Powers; (C) Joan U. Brumbach; (L) Bruce Rennie
I Have a Dream, Bruce Miller; (D) Bruce Miller; (S) Terrie Powers; (C) John Glenn; (L) Bruce Rennie
Jack and the Beanstalk, book and lyrics: Douglas Jones; music: Ron Barnett; (D) John Glenn; (S) Terrie Powers; (C) Thomas Hammond; (L) Bruce Rennie
Cinderella, book and lyrics: Oscar Hammerstein, II; music: Richard Rogers; (D) Brad Boynton; (S) Terrie Powers; (C) Thomas Hammond; (L) Bruce Rennie
Hugs and Kisses, book and lyrics: Terry Bliss and Bruce Miller; music: Richard Giersch; (D) Bruce Miller; (S) Terrie Powers; (C) John Glenn; (L) Bruce Rennie
The Little Red Hen, book and lyrics: Ford Flannagan; music: Richard Giersch; (D) John Glenn; (S) Terrie Powers; (C) John Glenn; (L) Bruce Rennie
Br'er Rabbit, Bruce Miller; (D) Bruce Miller; (S) Terrie Powers; (C) Thomas Hammond; (L) Bruce Rennie
Walking the Line, Bruce Miller; (D) Bruce Miller; (S) John Glenn; (C) Thomas Hammond; (L) Bruce Rennie

PRODUCTIONS 1988–89

Master Harold ... and the boys, Athol Fugard; (D) Beatrice Bush; (S) Brad Boynton; (C) Carla Binford Jerman; (L) Reed West
Toys for Men, Lee Blessing; (D) Bruce Miller; (S) Terrie Powers; (C) Jennifer Dozier; (L) Terry Cermak
Nice People Dancing to Good Country Music, Lee Blessing; (D) Bruce Miller; (S) Terrie Powers; (C) Jennifer Dozier; (L) Terry Cermak
Lemonade, James Prideaux; (D) Amy Morgan Tysiak; (S) Brad Boynton; (C) Nancy Allen; (L) Reed West
Spittin' Image, Stephen Metcalfe; (D) Gary Hopper; (S) Brad Boynton; (C) Nancy Allen; (L) Reed West
Graceland, Ellen Byron; (D) Denise Simone; (S) Brad Boynton; (C) Nancy Allen; (L) Reed West
Love and How to Cure It, Thornton Wilder; (D) Bruce Miller; (S) Brad Boynton; (C) Elizabeth Hopper; (L) Reed West
How He Lied to Her Husband, George Bernard Shaw; (D) Nancy Cates; (S) Brad Boynton; (C) Elizabeth Hopper; (L) Reed West
Blind Date, Horton Foote; (D) John Welsh; (S) Brad Boynton; (C) Elizabeth Hopper; (L) Reed West
The Nose, Douglas Jones; (D) Carol Coons; (S) Terrie Powers; (C) Thomas Hammond; (L) Terry Cermak
Grandma Duck is Dead, Larry Shue; (D) Keri Wormold; (S) Terrie Powers; (C) John Glenn; (L) Terry Cermak
Walking the Line, Bruce Miller; (D) Bruce Miller; (S) Terrie Powers; (C) John Glenn; (L) Bruce Rennie
Rumplestiltskin, book and lyrics: Douglas Jones; music: Ron Barnett; (D) John Glenn; (S) Terrie Powers; (C) Thomas Hammond; (L) Bruce Rennie
Young Ben Franklin, book and lyrics: Bruce Miller; music: Ron Barnett; (D) Bruce Miller; (S) Terrie Powers; (C) Thomas Hammond; (L) Bruce Rennie
The Magic of Hans Christian Anderson, Terry Snyder; (D) Terry Snyder; (S) Terry Snyder; (C) Terry Snyder; (L) Bruce Rennie
The Mistletoe Moose, Bruce Miller; (D) Bruce Miller; (S) Terrie Powers; (C) Thomas Hammond; (L) Bruce Rennie
Snow White and Rose Red, book and lyrics: Denise Simone; music: Ron Barnett; (D) John Glenn and Lou Szari; (S) Terrie Powers; (C) Thomas Hammond; (L) Bruce Rennie
Virginia Real, David Robbins; (D) Russell Wilson; (S) Terrie Powers; (C) Thomas Hammond; (L) Bruce Rennie
The Maggie Walker Story, Bruce Miller; (D) Bruce Miller; (S) Terrie Powers; (C) John Glenn; (L) Bruce Rennie
The Town Mouse and the Country Mouse, book and lyrics: Douglas Jones; music: Ron Barnett; (D) John Glenn; (S) Terrie Powers; (C) Thomas Hammond; (L) Bruce Rennie
The Golden Goose, book and lyrics: Ford Flannagan; music: K. Strong and Michael Strong; (D) John Glenn; (S) Terrie Powers; (C) John Glenn; (L) Bruce Rennie
Hugs and Kisses, book and lyrics: Terry Bliss and Bruce Miller; music: Richard Giersch; (D) Bruce Miller; (S) Terrie Powers; (C) John Glenn; (L) Bruce Rennie

Theatre Project

PHILIP ARNOULT
Director

CAROL BAISH
Managing Director

45 West Preston St.
Baltimore, MD 21201
(301) 539-3091 (bus.)
(301) 752-8558 (b.o.)

FOUNDED 1971
Philip Arnoult

SEASON
Sept.-June

FACILITIES
Theatre Project
Seating Capacity: 157
Stage: flexible

FINANCES
Jan. 1, 1988-Dec. 31, 1989
Expenses: $615,000

I sit in several hundred theatre seats a year to find work to bring to Theatre Project. I look for work that is small and young—rooted in its own culture, but not bound by it—with a fullness that breaks through the boundaries of language, race, politics. My

Theatre Project. *Anerca.* Photo: Rose Marasco.

commitment to these companies is very personal, and it is as much a commitment to an artistic vision as it is to a particular production. My role as a dramaturg, helping a visiting company fine-tune a work for its American audiences, is a precious one. In my travels everywhere, I see wonderous permutations of the American avant-garde. What is most gratifying is the openness in our selves and in our theatres to presenting these visions, wherever they come from. I have a kind of romantic belief that this special grace will help keep the planet sane.

—Philip Arnoult

PRODUCTIONS 1987–88

Miracles, Phillip MacKenzie and Simon Thorne; (D) Neil Bartlett;
The Bed Experiment I, The Adaptors; (D) Kari Margolis and Tony Brown; (L) Kyle Chepulis
The Edge, David Pownall; (D) Michael Merwitzen;
The Main Event, The Wright Brothers;
Somewhere over the Balcony, Marie Jones; (D) Peter Sheridan; (S) Brian Power andBlaithin Shaerin; (L) Nick McCall
Earrings from "Oral History", Don Baker; (D) Bob Leonard; (C) Ann Beck; (L) Erick Hager
Warsaw Tango, Alberto Felix Alberto; (D) Tulio Stella
As the Piano Plays, Nava Zukerman; (D) Nava Zukerman
Dark Spring, Danstheater Nan Romijn; (D) Robert Broekhuis; (S) Robert Broekhuis; (C) Sarah Moreland; (L) Johan Vonk
The N°gg°r Cafe: A Spooky Show, Judith Jackson; (D) Judith Jackson; (L) Sandra Ross
Assisyai Review, Slava Polunin; (D) The Leningrad Clown Theater
Waiters, Terry Beck; (D) Terry Beck
Lighthouse, Judy Dworin; (D) Judy Dworin

PRODUCTIONS 1988–89

The Power Project, Bob Berkey; (D) Bob Berkey; (L) Frances Aronson
Not for Real, Rinde Eckert and Leonard Pitt; (D) Rinde Eckert; (S) Grant Ditzler and Laurie Polster; (C) Melissa Weaver; (L) Novella T. Smith
Anerca, Figures of Speech Theatre; (D) Philip Arnoult; (L) Stoney Cook
Windowspeak, Daniel Stein; (D) Daniel Stein and Fred Curchack; (S) Paule Stein; (L) Eric Hager
Have You Seen Zandile?, Gcina Mhlophe; (D) Gcina Mhlophe; (S) Brian Beasley; (L) Beth La Joie
Rasputin: The Forbidden Story, Lee Beagley; (D) Lee Beagley; (L) Eric Hager
Icarus, book: Stephen Clark; music: Andrew Peggie; (D) Louis Scheeder; (L) Frances Aronson
Sexual Mythology Part I: The Underworld, Fred Curchack; (D) Fred Curchack
The Dance of the Chickens, Fiona Gordon and Dominique Abel; (D) Fiona Gordon and Dominique Abel

Theatre Project Company

KATHRYN RYBOLT-WHITE
Managing Director

634 North Grand Blvd.
St. Louis, MO 63103
(314) 531-1315 (bus.)
(314) 531-1301 (b.o.)

FOUNDED 1975
Fontaine Syer, Christine E. Smith

SEASON
Sept.-May

FACILITIES
New City School
Seating Capacity: 240
Stage: proscenium

FINANCES
July 1, 1988-June 30, 1989
Expenses: $499,000

CONTRACTS
AEA SPT

Theatre Project Company's major areas of work are our mainstage season: our TYA program—The MUNY/Student Theatre Project, that includes touring productions, classes and storytelling for grades K-12; and Backstage/Onstage—our equivalent to a second stage that offers staged readings, workshop productions, the Performers' Festival and experimental programs. In all areas, the company's work is distinguished by emotional intensity, exploration of contemporary values and maximum interaction between the company and the audience. More than 70 percent of our productions are area premieres. The company's core is a group of artists whose collaboration began 10 years ago. We share a common philosophy and commitment. Our process and an open and supportive working environment are as important as the final product. Development of individual artists is also a prime concern. The theatre experience is a journey shared by many people. We are working to make that journey as interesting, as layered, as challenging and as much fun as we can.

—Kathryn Rybolt-White

Note: During the 1988-89 season, Wayne Salomon served as interim artistic director, during the 1987-88 season, Fontaine Syer served as Artistic director.

PRODUCTIONS 1987–88

Painting Churches, Tina Howe; (D) Fontaine Syer; (S) James J. Burwinkel; (C) Laurie Trevethan; (L) Mel Dickerson
Alice in Concert, book, music and lyrics: Elizabeth Swados; (D) Pamela Sterling; (S) Kim Wilson; (C) Joyce L. Kogut; (L) David Krueger
The Mandrake, adapt and trans: Wallace Shawn; (D) John Grassilli; (S) Mel Dickerson; (C) Teri McConnell; (L) Glenn Dunn
Strange Snow, Stephen Metcalfe; (D) Tom Martin; (S) David Krueger; (C) Laurie Trevethan (L) Katherine C. Abernathy
Arms and the Man, George Bernard Shaw; (D) Wayne Salomon; (S) Mel Dickerson; (C) Elizabeth Eisloeffel; (L) Glenn Dunn

PRODUCTIONS 1988–89

Greater Tuna, Jaston Williams, Jo Sears and Ed Howard; (D) Michael Bollinger; (S) C. Otis Sweezey; (C) Niki Juncker (L) James J. Burwinkel
The Secret Garden, adapt: Pamela Sterling, from Frances Hodgson Burnett; (D) Wayne Salomon; (S) Kim Conway-Wilson; (C) Joyce Kogut; (L) Gregg Hillmar
Eleemosynary, Lee Blessing; (D) Connie I. Lane; (S) James J Burwinkel; (C) Kimberly B. Doyle; (L) James J. Burwinkel
A Coupla White Chicks Sitting Around Talking, John Ford Noonan; (D) Ann Marie Costa; (S) James J. Burwinkel; (C) Kimberly B. Doyle; (L) James J. Burwinkel
Loot, Joe Orton; (D) William Grivna; (S) Mel Dickerson; (C) Laurie Trevethan; (L) Glenn Dunn
Entertaining Mr. Sloan, Joe Orton; (D) John Grassilli; (S) Mel Dickerson; (C) Laurie Trevethan; (L) Glenn Dunn
The Fantasticks, book and lyrics: Tom Jones; music: Harvey Schmidt; (D) Wayne Salomon; (S) James J. Burwinkel; (C) Elizabeth Eisloeffel; (L) James J. Burwinkel

Theatre Project Company. Kari Ely, J. Scott Matthews and Kingsley Leggs in *Loot*. Photo: Pook Pfaffe.

Theatre Rhinoceros. Julia Walter and Lynne Otis in *Lust and Pity*. Photo: Shari Cohen.

Theatre Rhinoceros

KENNETH R. DIXON
Artistic Director

BLAISE BAHARA
Financial Director

FOUNDED 1977
Allan B. Estes, Jr.

SEASON
Jan.-Dec.

FACILITIES
Mainstage
Seating Capacity: 112
Stage: proscenium

Studio
Seating Capacity: 58
Stage: flexible

FINANCES
July 1, 1988-June 30, 1989
Expenses: $371,000

CONTRACTS
AEA SPT

The original and continuing purpose of Theatre Rhinoceros is to produce plays that examine contemporary issues relevant to the gay/lesbian community and the wider society with which it interacts. Theatre Rhinoceros is also dedicated to providing a professional environment where gay/lesbian theatre artists can train and work. The theatre was named for the horned animal which is mild and peace-loving until provoked and is dedicated to creating a culture for, by and about gay and lesbian people.

—*Kenneth R. Dixon*

PRODUCTIONS 1987–88

A Late Snow, Jane Chambers; (D) Linda Wright; (S) Rick Darnell; (C) Barbara Blair; (L) Wendy Gilmore
Poppies, Noel Greig; (D) Nicholas Deutsch; (S) Pamela Peniston; (C) Stephanie Johnson; (L) Mark Jones
Dancing in the Dark, D.R. Andersen; (D) Larry Russell; (S) Rick Darnell; (C) Jean Fredrickson; (L) Joseph Williams
Quisbies, Leland Moss; (D) Barbara Daoust; (S) Edward Gottesman; (C) Jean Fredrickson; (L) Patrick Joseph
Talking to the Sun, John O'Hara; music: Christopher Berg; (D) John F. Karr; (S) Edward Gottesman; (C) Pierre Nadeau; (L) Stephanie Johnson
In Circles, Gertrude Stein; music: Al Carmines; (D) John F. Karr; (S) Edward Gottesman; (C) Pierre Nadeau; (L) Stephanie Johnson
Going to Seed, Eve Powell; (D) Kenneth R. Dixon; (S) Pamela Peniston; (C) Susan Anderson; (L) Stephanie Johnson
In the Summer When It's Hot and Sticky, Doug Holsclaw; (D) Barbara Daoust; (S) Matthew Antnky; (C) Nina Capriolla; (L) Stephanie Johnson
See Rock City, Demece Garepis; (D) Adele Prandini; (S) Andrea Stanley; (C) Mark Jones; (L) Libby Kava

PRODUCTIONS 1988–89

It's Only a Play, Terrence McNally; (D) Leland Moss; (S) Pamela Peniston; (C) Nina Capriolla; (L) Joseph Williams
Life in the Theatre, David Mamet; (D) Kenneth R. Dixon; (S) Edward Gottesman; (C) Mark Jones; (L) Stephanie Johnson
Kudzu, Jane Chambers; (D) Donna Davis; (S) Sandra Howell; (C) Mark Jones; (L) Stephanie Johnson
Passing, Robert Pitman; (D) Kelly Hill; (S) John B. Wilson; (C) Todd Stewart; (L) Joseph Williams
Giving Up the Ghost, Cherrie Muraya; (D) Anita Mattos and Jose Saucedo; (S) Yulanda Lopez; (C) Antonio Chavez; (L) Stephanie Johnson
Queen of Swords, Judy Grahn; (D) Adele Prandini; (S) Pamela Peniston; (C) Karen Schwindt; (L) Stephanie Johnson
The Balcony, Jean Genet; trans: Jean-Claude van Itallie; (D) Leland Moss; (S) Edward Gottesman; (C) Gail Russell; (L) Juell Chartier-Serban
Soul Survivor, Anthony Bruno; (D) Kenneth R. Dixon; (S) Edward Gottesman; (L) Stephanie Johnson

TheatreVirginia

TERRY BURGLER
Executive Artistic Director

KATHLEEN P. BATESON
General Manager

2800 Grove Ave.
Richmond, VA 23221-2466
(804) 367-0840 (bus.)
(804) 367-0831 (b.o.)

FOUNDED 1954
Virginia Museum of Fine Arts

SEASON
Sept.-June

FACILITIES
Main Stage
Seating Capacity: 500
Stage: proscenium

FINANCES
July 1, 1988-June 30, 1989
Expenses: $1,375,000

CONTRACTS
LORT (C)

The medium is the message. For our theatre to make its maximal cultural and aesthetic contribution, we must remember two things: what makes theatre unique and what makes theatre irresistible. Theatre is not a literal event. Its task is not to create a substantive representation of reality but to transform it by imitation. Neither is theatre a literary event (despite the exquisite literature it may contain). Theatre is a dynamic art which melds the collected imaginations of the creators with the collective imagination of the audience. At the moment those imaginations meet, they transform the world in which we live. The theatre, the theatregoer and our culture all emerge enriched. Theatre is a contact art. It must reach its audience. TheatreVirginia's task is to provide arenas for such meetings of the imagination.

—*Terry Burgler*

PRODUCTIONS 1987–88

Noises Off, Michael Frayn; (D) Terry Burgler; (S) Charles Caldwell; (C) Marjorie McGown; (L) Richard Moore
Terra Nova, Ted Tally; (D) Bill Gregg; (S) Ron Keller; (C) Charles Caldwell; (L) Terry Cermak
My Fair Lady, book and lyrics: Alan Jay Lerner; music: Frederick Lowe; (D) Terry Burgler; (S) Joseph A. Varga; (C) Charles Caldwell; (L) Scott Pickney
Beyond the Fringe, Alan Bennet, Peter Cook, Jonathan Miller and Dudley Moore; (D) Terry Burgler; (S) Charles Caldwell; (C) Catherine Szari; (L) Terry Cermak
'Night, Mother, Marsha Norman; (D) Woodie King, Jr.; (S) Charles Caldwell; (C) Catherine Szari; (L) Terry Cermak
'Night, Mother, Marsha Norman; (D) Woodie King, Jr.; (S) Charles Caldwell; (C) Catherine Szari; (L) Terry Cermak
Pump Boys and Dinettes, John Foley, Mark Hardwick, Debra Monk, Cass Morgan, John Schimmel and Jim Wann; (D) Terry Burgler; (S) David Crank; (C) Susan Griffin; (L) Terry Cermak
The Robber Bridegroom, book adapt and lyrics: Alfred Uhry; music: Robert Waldman; (D) Terry Burgler; (S) Charles Caldwell; (C) Catherine Szari; (L) Terry Cermak

153

TheatreVirginia. Lorraine Lannigan and Dan Hamilton in *A Moon for the Misbegotten*.
Photo: Virginia Museum Photography Department.

PRODUCTIONS 1988–89

A Funny Thing Happened on the Way to the Forum, book: Burt Shevelove and Larry Gelbart; music and lyrics: Stephen Sondheim; (D) Terry Burgler; (S) Charles Caldwell; (C) Susan Tsu; (L) Terry Cermak

Camelot, book and lyrics: Alan Jay Lerner; music: Frederick Lowe; (D) Terry Burgler; (S) Charles Caldwell; (C) Charles Caldwell; (L) Terry Cermak

I'm Not Rappaport, Herb Gardner; (D) Terry Burgler; (S) Charles Caldwell; (C) Catherine Szari; (L) Jeff Stroman

A Life in the Theatre, David Mamet; (D) Terry Burgler; (S) Charles Caldwell; (C) Catherine Szari; (L) Terry Cermak

A Moon for the Misbegotten, Eugene O'Neill; (D) Terry Burgler; (S) Charles Caldwell; (C) Catherine Szari; (L) Terry Cermak

Tomfoolery, adapt: Cameron Mackintosh and Robin Raymusic, from Tom Lehrer; (D) Nancy Cates; (S) Charles Caldwell; (C) Charles Caldwell; (L) Terry Cermak

Pump Boys and Dinettes, John Foley, Mark Hardwick, Cass Morgan, Debra Monk, John Schimmel and Jim Wann; (D) Terry Burgler; (S) David Crank; (C) Susan Griffin; (L) Terry Cermak

Greater Tuna, Jaston Williams, Joe Sears and Ed Howard; (D) Terry Burgler; (S) David Crank; (C) Susan Griffin; (L) Jeff Stroman

TheatreWorks

ROBERT KELLEY
Artistic Director

RANDY ADAMS
Managing Director

1305 Middlefield Road
Palo Alto, CA 94301
(415) 424-9441 (bus.)
(415) 329-2623 (b.o.)

FOUNDED 1970
Robert Kelley

SEASON
June-May

FACILITIES
Lucie Stern Theatre
Seating Capacity: 425
Stage: proscenium

Burgess Theatre
Seating Capacity: 275
Stage: proscenium

Appreciation Hall
Seating Capacity: 165
Stage: proscenium

Studio Theatre
Seating Capacity: 100
Stage: flexible

FINANCES
June 1, 1988-May 31, 1989
Expenses: $946,000

CONTRACTS
AEA Guest Artist

TheatreWorks explores and celebrates the human spirit through contemporary plays, musicals of literary merit, new works in development and innovative reinterpretations of the classics, offering audiences in the San Francisco Bay Area a regional theatre of exceptional diversity. We are a theatre for all races and ages, a longtime leader in nontraditional casting and programming. Our mainstage season is selected to expand the social and artistic horizons of a large audience. STAGE II offers world and regional premieres in intimate spaces, and our recently launched Playwrights Forum develops and reads 12 new plays annually, many by our regional writers. As we celebrate 20 years this season, we have focused our financial and artistic efforts on the growth and support of a multiracial company, creating a community that will be a model of diversity and commitment for the larger community we serve.
—*Robert Kelley*

PRODUCTIONS 1987–88

A ... My Name is Alice, conceived: Joan Micklin Silver and Julianne Boyd; (D) Leslie Martinson; (S) Bruce McLeod; (C) Susan E. Tucker; (L) Dan Wadleigh

You Can't Take It with You, Moss Hart and George S. Kaufman; (D) Robert Kelley; (S) W. Truett Roberts; (C) Jill C. Bowers; (L) John G. Rathman

The Rink, book: Terrence McNally; music: John Kander; lyrics: Fred Ebb; (D) Robert Kelley; (S) W. Truett Roberts; (C) Jill C. Bowers; (L) John G. Rathman

The Learned Ladies, adapt: Robert Kelley, from Johanna Dickey; (D) Robert Kelley; (S) John G. Rathman; (C) Fumiko Bielefeldt; (L) John G. Rathman

Benefactors, Michael Frayn; (D) Peter Craze; (S) Joe Ragey; (C) Jill C. Bowers; (L) Bruce McLeod

Drood, book, music and lyrics: Rupert Holmes; (D) Robert Kelley; (S) Bruce McLeod; (C) Fumiko Bielefeldt; (L) Heather McAvoy

Cat's-Paw, William Mastrosimone; (D) Leslie Martinson; (S) Jeffrey M. Gress; (C) Claire Sabo; (L) Jeffrey M. Gress

Peter Pan, book: James M. Barrie; music: Mark Charlap; lyrics: Carolyn Leigh; (D) Robert Kelley; (S) Joe Ragey; (C) Jill C. Bowers; (L) Bruce McLeod

Eleemosynary, Lee Blessing; (D) Anthony J. Haney; (S) Joe Ragey; (C) Mary Ann Flippin; (L) Jeffrey M. Gress

Rough Crossing, adapt: Tom Stoppard, from Ferenc Molnar; (D) Simon Levy; (S) Jasper V. Meerheimb; (C) Susan Archibald Grote; (L) Bruce McLeod

Pacific Overtures, book: John Weidman; music and lyrics: Stephen Sondheim; (D) Robert Kelley; (S) Joe Ragey; (C) Fumiko Bielefeldt; (L) John G. Rathman

In the Sweet Bye and Bye, Donald Driver; (D) David Parr; (S) Jasper V. Meerheimb; (C) Jill C. Bowers; (L) Bruce McLeod

TheatreWorks. Michael McFall and Richard Sherman in *The Two Gentlemen of Verona*.
Photo: Wilson Graham.

PRODUCTIONS 1988–89

Pump Boys and Dinettes, John Foley, Mark Hardwick, Debra Monk, Cass Morgan, John Schimmel and Jim Wann; (D) Rick Simas; (S) John G. Rathman; (C) Susan Anderson; (L) Jeffrey M. Gress

Two Gentlemen of Verona, William Shakespeare; (D) Robert Kelley; (S) Bruce McLeod; (C) Fumiko Bielefeldt; (L) John G. Rathman

Stepping Out, Richard Harris; (D) Leslie Martinson; (S) Ken Ellis; (C) Jill C. Bowers; (L) Bruce McLeod

Dreamgirls, book and lyrics: Tom Eyen; music: Henry Krieger; (D) Anthony J. Haney; (S) Paul Gilger; (C) Richard W. Battle; (L) Kathy Pryzgoda

Bone N Weasel, Jon Klein; (D) Robert Kelley; (S) Joe Ragey; (C) Connie Strayer; (L) Dan Wadleigh

The Front Page, Ben Hecht and Charles MacArthur; (D) Robert Kelley; (S) J.T. von Meerheimb; (C) Jill C. Bowers; (L) John G. Rathman

Peter Pan, book: James M. Barrie; music: Mark Charlap; lyrics: Carolyn Leigh; (D) Robert Kelley; (S) Joe Ragey; (C) Jill C. Bowers; (L) Bruce McLeod

Ma Rainey's Black Bottom, August Wilson; (D) Clinton Turner Davis; (S) Joe Ragey; (C) Richard W. Battle; (L) Bruce McLeod

Rags, book: Joseph Stein; music: Charles Strouse; lyrics: Stephen Schwartz; (D) Robert Kelley; (S) Bruce McLeod; (C) Fumiko Bielefeldt; (L) John G. Rathman

The Boys Next Door, Tom Griffin; (D) Leslie Martinson; (S) John G. Rathman; (C) Alison Connor; (L) Barry Griffith

Theatreworks/USA

JAY HARNICK
Artistic Director

CHARLES HULL
Managing Director

890 Broadway
New York, NY 10003
(212) 677-5959

FOUNDED 1961
Jay Harnick, Robert K. Adams

SEASON
Year-round

FACILITIES
Promenade Theatre
Seating Capacity: 400
Stage: thrust

Town Hall
Seating Capacity: 1,500
Stage: proscenium

FINANCES
Oct. 1, 1987-Sept. 30, 1988
Expenses: $2,520,916

CONTRACTS
AEA TYA

TheatreWorks/USA. Michael David Gordon, Alicia Rene Washington and Ron Bottitta in *Freedom Train*. Photo: Gerry Goodstein.

As we enter our 29th season of creating theatre for young and family audiences, Theatreworks/USA continues to be inspired by the belief that young people deserve theatre endowed with the richness of content demanded by the most discerning adult audience. To that end, we have commissioned an ever-expanding collection of original works from established playwrights, composers and lyricists. Our creative roster includes Ossie Davis, Charles Strouse, Alice Childress, Joe Raposo, Thomas Babe, Albert Hague, Gary William Friedman, Mary Rodgers, Saul Levitt, John Forster and Leslie Lee. We are also dedicated to the development of fresh voices for the American theatre and encourage emerging playwrights to develop projects about issues that concern them and affect the young audiences they seek to address. We currently give over 1,000 performances annually in a touring radius encompassing 49 of the 50 states.

—*Jay Harnick*

PRODUCTIONS 1987–88

Teddy Roosevelt, book: Jonathan Bolt; music: Thomas Tierney; lyrics: John Forster; (D) Greg Gunning; (S) Philipp Jung; (C) Debra Stein

Right in Your Own Backyard, book, music and lyrics: John Forster; (D) Victoria Forster; (S) Philipp Jung; (C) Heidi Hollmann

We the People, book and lyrics: John Allen; music: John Clifton; (D) John Brady; (S) Daniel Conway; (C) Heidi Hollmann

A Charles Dickens Christmas, book: Robert Owens Scott; music: Douglas J. Cohen; lyrics: Tom Toce; (D) Bruce Colville; (S) Robert Edmonds; (C) Sue Ellen Rohrer

Martin Luther King, Jr., book: Leslie Lee; music and lyrics: Charles Strouse; (D) Bob Baker; (S) Kitty Leech; (C) Tom Barnes

Sherlock Holmes and the Red-Headed League, book: John Forster, Greer Woodward and Rick Cummins; music: Rick Cummins; (D) Peter Webb; (S) Bryan Johnson; (C) Kitty Leech

Susan B!, book: Jules Tasca; music: Thomas Tierney; lyrics: Ted Drachman; (D) Greg Gunning; (S) Jack Stewart; (C) David Robinson

The Secret Garden, book: Linda B. Kline, Robert Jess Roth; music: Kim Oler; lyrics: Alison Hubbard; (D) Robert Jess Roth; (S) Stanley A. Meyer; (C) Deborah Rooney

Louis Braille, book: Cynthia L. Cooper and Joel Vig; music: Annie Lebeaux; lyrics: Jane Smulyan; (D) John Henry Davis; (S) Robert Edmonds; (C) Heidi Hollmann

PRODUCTIONS 1988–89

The Play's the Thing, book and lyrics: Thomas Edward West; music: Robert Waldman; (D) R.J. Cutler; (S) James Youmans; (C) Heidi Hollmann

Footprints on the Moon, book and lyrics: Arthur Perlman; music: Jeffrey Lunden; (D) Stuart Ross; (S) Richard Block; (C) Bruce Goodrich

The Amazing Einstein, book: Jules Tasca; music: Thomas Tierney; lyrics: Ted Drachman; (D) Greg Gunning; (S) Tom Barnes; (C) Martha Hally

We the People, book and lyrics: John Allen; music: John Clifton; (D) John Brady; (S) Daniel Conway; (C) Heidi Hollmann

Louis Braille, book: Cynthia L. Cooper and Joel Vig; music: Annie Lebeaux; lyrics: Jane Smulyan; (D) Liz Keene; (S) Robert Edmonds; (C) Heidi Hollmann

The Secret Garden, book: Linda B. Kline and Robert Jess Roth; music: Kim Oler; lyrics: Alison Hubbard; (D) Barbara Pasternack; (S) Stanley A. Meyer; (C) Deborah Rooney

Susan B!, book: Jules Tasca; music: Thomas Tierney; lyrics: Ted Drachman; (D) Greg Gunning; (S) Jack Stewart; (C) David Robinson

A Charles Dickens Christmas, book: Robert Owens; music: Douglas J. Cohen; lyrics: Tom Toce; (D) Bruce Colville; (S) Robert Edmonds; (C) Sue Ellen Rohrer

Freedom Train, book: Marvin Gordon; music: Garrett Morris, Ron Burton; (D) Joy Kelly; (S) Hal Tine; (C) Ben Benson

The Velveteen Rabbit, adapt: James Still, from Margery Williams; (D) Stuart Ross; (S) Richard Block; (C) Debra Stein

Theatre X. John Schneider and Ed Sweet in *My Werewolf*. Photo: Francis Ford.

Theatre X

**DEBORAH CLIFTON
FLORA COKER
JOHN KISHLINE
JOHN SCHNEIDER**
Artistic Directors

JOHN SOBCZAK
Managing Director

Box 92206
Milwaukee, WI 53202
(414) 278-0555 (bus.)
(414) 278-0044 (b.o.)

FOUNDED 1969
Conrad Bishop, Linda Bishop, Ron Gural

SEASON
Year-round

FACILITIES
M K E
Seating Capacity: 74
Stage: flexible

FINANCES
Sept. 1, 1988-Aug. 31, 1989
Expenses: $125,000

To examine the construction of theatre is to examine the construction of reality. At Theatre X, it is possible to reconsider every element of theatre production in light of the issues at hand. Our members, whose association with the company ranges from 10 to 17 years, stay because they want to work that way. Our purpose is to understand and demonstrate the present: in the 1980s, our subject has often been the relationship between our self-understanding and our multiple mediated impressions of the world. We embrace, for the time being, the idea that reality is constructed in significant measure by the linguistic and imagistic representations that saturate our culture, and by the interplay among these representations and the power relations they affirm or conceal. We embrace the idea that these representations can be altered or overthrown in pursuit of an equal distribution of power and an increased autonomy for individuals.

—*John Schneider, Flora Coker*

PRODUCTIONS 1987–88

Happy Days, Samuel Beckett; (D) David Schweizer; (S) James Matson; (C) Sam FLeming; (L) John Kishline

A History of Sexuality, John Kishline, Julia Romansky and John Schneider; (D) David Schweizer; (S) Nina Moser; (C) Nina Moser; (L) Lee DeLorme

PRODUCTIONS 1988–89

I Can't Stop Loving You, John Kishline and Wesley Savick; (D) Wesley Savick; (S) Rick Graham; (C) Sam Fleming; (L) Rick Graham

Under Milk Wood, Dylan Thomas; (D) John Schneider; (S) Marcie Hoffman; (C) Marcie Hoffman; (L) Marcie Hoffman

Poor Folk's Pleasure, Len Jenkin; (D) David Schweizer; (S) James Matson; (C) Carri M. Skoczek; (L) Rick Graham

Jerker, Robert Chesley; (D) Flora Coker; (S) Francis Ullenberg and Scott Schanke; (L) John Kishline and John Starmer

Theatrical Outfit

LEVI LEE
Artistic Director

PIET KNETSCH
Managing Director

Box 7098
Atlanta, GA 30357
(404) 872-0665

FOUNDED 1976
David Head

SEASON
Sept.-June

FACILITIES
Seating Capacity: 200
Stage: flexible

FINANCES
July 1, 1988-June 30, 1989
Expenses: $340,000

CONTRACTS
AEA SPT

Theatrical Outfit provides the cit of Atlanta with an intimate, prof sional theatre, eclectic in scope, producing a broad range of litera ture, fusing various forms and styles. With an emphasis on colla oration, the Outfit's primary goal to nurture a local community of artists and to create an ongoing e change program with artists, bot nationally and internationally.

—*Levi L*

Note: During the 1987-88 season David Head served as artistic director. During the 1988-89 seaso Sharon Levy served as interim a tistic director.

PRODUCTIONS 1987–88

What the Butler Saw, Joe Orto (D) Stuart Culpepper; (S) John Thigpen; (C) Yvonne Lee; (L) Hal McCoy

Michael West: Together At Last

Theatrical Outfit. John Ferguson and Megan McFarland in *Hamlet...The Musical*. Phot Jimmy Robinson.

Michael West; (D) David Head; (S) David Strohauer; (C) Larger than Life Styles; (L) Liz Lee
orpse!, Gerald Moon; (D) Pamela O'Connor; (S) Luis Maza; (C) Jeff Cone; (L) Liz Lee
ashomon, Fay Kanin and Michael Kanin; (D) Sharon Levy; (S) Jeroy Hannah; (C) Stanley Poole; (L) Hal McCoy
he Shaggy Dog Animation, Lee Breuer; (D) Leslie Mohn; (S) Barbara Abramson; (L) Liz Lee

RODUCTIONS 1988–89

amlet . . . The Musical, adapt: Levi Lee and Rebecca Wackler, from William Shakespeare; (D) Rebecca Wackler; (S) Jeroy Hannah; (C) Yvonne Lee; (L) Jeff Nealer
n the Verge or The Geography of Yearning, Eric Overmyer; (D) Sharon Levy; (S) Buck Newman; (C) Stanley Poole; (L) Hal McCoy
'm Not Rappaport, Herb Gardner; (D) Piet Knetsch; (S) Luis Maza; (C) Jeff Cone; (L) Hal McCoy

Touchstone Theatre

WILLIAM GEORGE
Producing Director

SHIRLEY A. THOMAS
Manager

321 East 4th St.
Bethlehem, PA 18105
(215) 867-1689

FOUNDED 1981
William Geoerge and Bridget George

SEASON
Year-round

FACILITIES
Seating Capacity: 72
Stage: flexible

FINANCES
Oct. 1, 1988-Aug. 31, 1989
Expenses: $240,370

Touchstone is an ensemble theatre; creatively, there are five of us. We are theatre artists—not so much actors, playwrights, directors and designers, as a team of people who make theatre. Our repertoire has a consistently distinctive spirit (sometimes described as fantastical), yet it utilizes a broad range of styles. Our work grows from love of the rich beauty found in abstract drama and a history of 15 years performing street theatre in Pennsylvania—a form of drama that naturally emphasizes a more visual and presentational style. In one sense, Touchstone is a modern folk theatre. We take our role in the community very seriously. The ensemble immerses itself in the tide of Bethlehem's diverse cultural spirit (48 different nationalities represented)—its day-to-day fears, joys, aspirations—and responds with a theatre of inner discovery, hope and revelation. Selected ensemble creations, premiered at Touchstone, join our national touring repertory.
—*William George*

PRODUCTIONS 1987–88

Canterbury Tales, adapt: Susan Chase, from Geoffrey Chaucer; (D) Susan Chase; (S) Tyrohne Kontir; (C) Annie-Laurie Wheat; (L) Tyrohne Kontir
No Idea, Mark McKenna; (D) Mark McKenna; (L) Tyrohne Kontir
The Concrete Womb, Jennie Gilrain; (D) Jennie Gilrain; (L) Tyrohne Kontir
Haunting at 905, Bill George; (D) Bill George; (S) Christine Ussler-Trumbull; (L) Tyrohne Kontir
The Seven Mysteries of Life, adapt: Erika Batdorf, from Guy Murchie; (D) Erika Batdorf; (S) Erika Batdorf; (L) Tyrohne Kontir
By the Light of the Silvery Moon, adapt: Jennie Gilrain and Douglas Roysdon, from Nola Langner; (D) Jennie Gilrain; (S) Douglas Roysdon; (C) Annie-Laurie Wheat

PRODUCTIONS 1988–89

Angie's Aching Heart, Janet Ruhe Schoen; (D) Larry Leon Hamilin; (S) Bill Lance; (C) Bill Lance; (L) Bill Lance
Spaces, Jennie Gilrain; (D) Jennie Gilrain; (S) Jennie Gilrain
Sticks and Stones, Sara Zielinska; (D) Sara Zielinska
Virgin Flight, Sara Zielinska; (D) Sara Zielinska
Candide, adapt: company-developed, from Voltaire; (D) Jim Calder; (S) Joan Harmon; (C) Joan Harmon and Barbara Seyda; (L) Joel Giguere
The Three Sillies, Eric Beatty, Jennie Gilrain and Mark McKenna; (D) Mark McKenna; (S) Rosemary Geseck; (C) Rosemary Geseck

Touchstone Theatre. Sara Zielinska and Jennie Gilrain in *Candide*. Photo: B. Stanley.

Trinity Repertory Company

ANNE BOGART
Artistic Director

TIMOTHY LANGAN
Managing Director

201 Washington St.
Providence, RI 02903
(401) 521-1100 (bus.)
(401) 351-4242 (b.o.)

FOUNDED 1963
Adrian Hall

SEASON
Year-round

FACILITIES
Upstairs Theatre
Seating Capacity: 560
Stage: flexible

Downstairs Theatre
Seating Capacity: 297
Stage: thrust

FINANCES
July 1, 1988-June 30, 1989
Expenses: $3,700,000

CONTRACTS
AEA LORT (B) and (C)

Concluding our 25th season, Trinity Repertory Company has earned recognition for its dedication to a resident company of artists, its vigorous ensemble style of production, its long commitment to the development of original works and adaptations, its daring and innovative treatment of world classics

and its fresh approach to traditional material. From the beginning Trinity Rep's two goals have been to provide permanent employment to its resident artists and to engage its audience as participants, rather than spectators, in the theatre experience. The first aim has been supported since we became the first theatre in American history to receive an Ongoing Ensemble grant from the National Endowment for the Arts, enabling us to provide yearly financial security to our artists. The second aim continues to be met with over 20,000 subscribers supporting the company's invigorating theatrical output. Trinity Rep's award-winning humanities program, with essay booklets and post-performance discussions, and the Project Discovery program continue to develop and enhance the audience's theatre experience.
—Anne Bogart

Note: During the 1987-88 and 1988-89 seasons, Adrian Hall served as artistic director.

PRODUCTIONS 1987–88

Lady from Maxim's, Georges Feydeau; trans: John Mortimer; (D) Richard Jenkins; (S) Robert D. Soule; (C) William Lane; (L) John F. Custer
Mourning Becomes Electra, Eugene O'Neill; (D) Edward Payson Call; (S) Robert D. Soule; (C) William Lane; (L) John F. Custer
The House of Blue Leaves, John Guare; (D) David Wheeler; (S) Robert D. Soule; (C) William Lane; (L) John F. Custer
A Christmas Carol, adapt: Adrian Hall and Richard Cumming, from Charles Dickens; (D) Peter Gerety; (S) Robert D. Soule; (C) William Lane; (L) Sid Bennett
Ma Rainey's Black Bottom, August Wilson; (D) William Partlan; (S) Robert D. Soule; (C) William Lane; (L) John F. Custer
The Man Who Came to Dinner, Moss Hart and George S. Kaufman; (D) Phillip Minor; (S) Robert D. Soule; (C) William Lane; (L) John F. Custer
Aunt Dan and Lemon, Wallace Shawn; (D) David Wheeler; (S) Robert D. Soule; (C) William Lane; (L) John F. Custer
Camino Real, Tennessee Williams; (D) Richard Jenkins; (S) Eugene Lee; (C) William Lane; (L) John F. Custer
Mensch Meier, Franz Xaver Kroetz; trans: Roger Downey; (D) Adrian Hall; (S) Eugene Lee; (C) William Lane; (L) Eugene Lee
Sherlock's Last Case, Charles Marowitz; (D) Tony Giordano; (S) Robert D. Soule; (C) William Lane; (L) John F. Custer

PRODUCTIONS 1988–89

Tomfoolery, adapt: Cameron Mackintosh and Robin Ray; music and lyrics: Tom Lehrer; (D) Tony Giordano; (S) Robert D. Soule; (C) William Lane; (L) John F. Custer
Black Coffee, Agatha Christie; (D) Ken Bryant; (S) Robert D. Soule; (C) William Lane; (L) John F. Custer
Hotel Paradiso, Georges Feydeau and Maurice Desvallieres; trans: Peter Glenville; (D) Tony Giordano; (S) Robert D. Soule; (C) William Lane; (L) John F. Custer
The Cherry Orchard, Anton Chekhov; trans: Michael Frayn; (D) Adrian Hall; (S) Eugene Lee; (C) William Lane; (L) Eugene Lee
A Christmas Carol, adapt: Adrian Hall and Richard Cumming, from Charles Dickens; (D) Neal Baron; (S) Robert D. Soule; (C) Marilyn Salvatore; (L) John F. Custer
The Boys Next Door, Tom Griffin; (D) David Wheeler; (S) Robert D. Soule; (C) William Lane; (L) John F. Custer
Volpone, Ben Johnson; (D) Paul Weidner; (S) Robert D. Soule; (C) William Lane; (L) John F. Custer
Joe Turner's Come and Gone, August Wilson; (D) Israel Hicks; (S) Robert D. Soule; (C) William Lane; (L) Michael Giannitti
The Idiot, adapt: Jonas Jurasas, from Fyodor Dostoyevsky; (D) Jonas Jurasas; (S) Alexander Okun; (C) William Lane; (L) John F. Custer
Woman in Mind, Alan Ayckbourn; (D) William Partlan; (S) Robert D. Soule; (C) William Lane; (L) Mark Rippe
Red Noses, Peter Barnes; (D) Adrian Hall; (S) Eugene Lee; (C) William Lane; (L) Eugene Lee

Trinity Repertory Company. *Red Noses.* Photo: Mark Morelli.

Unicorn Theatre

CYNTHIA LEVIN
Artistic Director

WENDY HARDY
Business Manager

3820 Main St.
Kansas City, MO 64111
(816) 531-3033 (bus.)
(816) 531-7529 (b.o.)

FOUNDED 1973
Liz Gordon, Ronald Dennis, James Cairns

SEASON
July-June

FACILITIES
Seating Capacity: 150
Stage: thrust

FINANCES
July 1, 1988-June 30, 1989
Expenses: $291,075

CONTRACTS
AEA SPT

As the artistic director of the Unicorn Theatre, I am dedicated to producing new plays that reflect a social consciousness. I prefer to present works that deal with significant, contemporary issues while creating an intellectual and thought-provoking experience. Our repertoire includes works that have not been previously staged in this area as well as world premieres. Two or three of the plays each season are written by lesser-known playwrights. Several of our premieres have been restaged in Chicago, San Diego, Los Angeles, Denver and Off Broadway in New York. The emphasis at the Unicorn is on the script itself and on the use of local professional artists. The technical aspects of our productions are limited, but we tend to do a lot with very little. Our work is process-centered rather than commercially oriented. Our new space is completely accessible to the handicapped, and offers ongoing theatre classes for people with disabilities as well as for able bodied actors.
—Cynthia Levin

PRODUCTIONS 1987–88

Glengarry Glen Ross, David Mamet; (D) Jim Tibbs; (S) Laura Burkhart; (C) Ron Adler; (L) Art Kent
Kiss of the Spider Woman, Manuel Puig; (D) Cynthia Levin; (S) Atif Rome; (C) Ron Adler; (L) Art Kent
Six Women with Brain Death or Expiring Minds Want to Know book: Christy Brandt, Cheryl Benge, Rosanna Coppedge, Valerie Fagan, Ross Freese, Mark Houston, Sandee Johnson and Peggy Pharr; music: Mark Houston; (D) Cynthia Levin; (S) Don Carlton; (C) Wendy Harms; (L) Randy Cochran

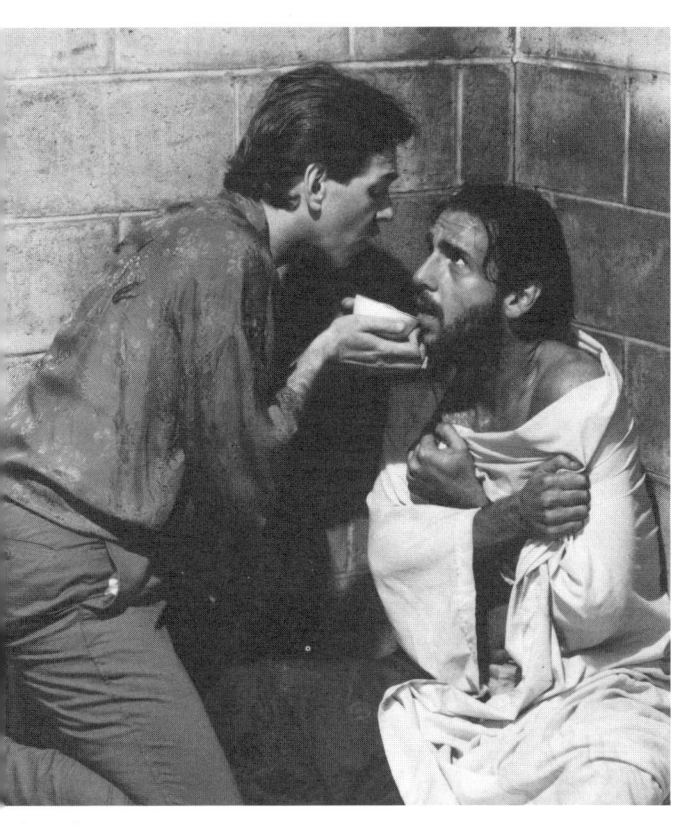

Unicorn Theatre. Jim Tibbs and Blake Stevens in *Kiss of the Spider Woman.*

Julius and Ethel, Loren Rehyer; (D) Lambriny Hedge; (S) Mimi Hedges; (C) Cheryl Benge; (L) Art Kent
Jitters, David French; (D) Francis Cullinan; (S) Laura Burkhart; (C) Cheryl Benge; (L) Joseph Clapper
The Real Thing, Tom Stoppard; (D) Cynthia Levin; (S) Daniel Robinson; (C) Jill Anthony; (L) Art Kent
The Dining Room, A.R. Gurney, Jr.; (D) Carol Blitgen; (S) Atif Rome; (C) Cheryl Benge; (L) Art Kent

PRODUCTIONS 1988–89

Hunting Cockroaches, Janusz Glowacki; trans: Jadwiga Kosicka; (D) Beth Leonard; (S) Laura Burkhart; (C) Cheryl Benge; (L) Art Kent
Talk Radio, Eric Bogosian; (D) Cynthia Levin; (S) Atif Rome; (C) Cheryl Benge; (L) Art Kent
Cat's Paw, William Mastrosimone; (D) Larry Greer; (S) Atif Rome; (C) Cheryl Benge; (L) Jay Wilson
The Rocky Horror Show, Richard O'Brien; (D) Fred Goodson; (S) Mimi Hedges; (C) Wendy Harms; (L) Randy Winder
Veteran's Day, Donald Freed; (D) Charles Gorden; (S) Art Kent; (C) Cheryl Benge; (L) Art Kent

On the Verge or The Geography of Yearning, Eric Overmyer; (D) Ron Schaeffer; (S) Art Kent; (C) Baker S. Smith; (L) Art Kent
Some Things You Need to Know Before the World Ends (A Final Evening with the Illuminati), Levi Lee and Larry Larson; (D) Cynthia Levin; (S) Art Kent; (C) Rit Bardwell; (L) Art Kent
Woman in Mind, Alan Ayckbourn; (D) Beth Leonard; (S) Art Kent; (C) Cheryl Benge; (L) Ruth Cain

Victory Gardens Theater

DENNIS ZACEK
Artistic Director

MARCELLE MCVAY
Managing Director

2257 North Lincoln Ave.
Chicago, IL 60614
(312) 549-5788 (bus.)
(312) 871-3000 (b.o.)

FOUNDED 1974
David Rasche, June Pyskacek, Cecil O'Neal, Mac McGinnes, Roberta Maguire, Stuart Gordon, Cordis Fejer, Warren Casey

SEASON
Sept.–July

FACILITIES
Mainstage
Seating Capacity: 195
Stage: thrust

Studio
Seating Capacity: 60
Stage: proscenium

FINANCES
July 1, 1988-June 30, 1989
Expenses: $845,830

CONTRACTS
AEA CAT

Victory Gardens Theater is a not-for-profit professional developmental theatre unique in the city for its commitment to the Chicago artist, with a special emphasis on the playwright. The theatre features a number of basic programs all geared toward connecting playwright and audience. The mainstage series consists of five diverse multi-ethnic productions, many of which are world premieres. The studio series presents three productions focusing on new work suited to a smaller space. The free Readers Theater series presents works-in-progress on a bimonthly basis. A recently established playwright development fund supports residencies and workshops throughout the year. The training center offers classes in all aspects of theatre and serves over a thousand students a year. The touring program usually features an abbreviated version of one of the mainstage shows, which is seen by more than 10,000 high school students annually. A number of areas interact to produce the same result—developmental theatre.

—*Dennis Zacek*

PRODUCTIONS 1987–88

The Colored Museum, George C. Wolfe; (D) Andre De Shields; (S) William C. Mrkvicka; (C) Kerry Fleming; (L) William C. Mrkvicka
Expectations, Dean Corrin; (D) Dennis Zacek; (S) James Dardenne; (C) John Hancock Brooks, Jr.; (L) Barbara Reeder
Necktie Party, Lonnie Carter; (D) Dennis Zacek; (S) Linda L. Lane; (C) Roger J. Striker; (L) Ellen E. Jones
The Stick Wife, Darrah Cloud; (D) Sandy Shinner; (S) James

Victory Gardens Theater. Yvonne Orona in *Tito*. Photo: Jennifer Girard.

Dardenne; (C) Nan Zabriskie; (L) Michael Rourke
Der Inka Von Peru, Jeffrey M. Jones; (D) Arnold Aprill; (S) Sandra Petrick; (C) Claudia Boddy; (L) Andira L. Fiegel
Chekhov in Yalta, John Driver and Jeffrey Haddow; (D) Arnold Aprill; (S) Rick Paul; (C) Kerry Fleming; (L) Robert Shook
A Joy Forever, Frank Manley; (D) Sandy Shinner; (S) Linda L. Lane; (C) Roger Stricker; (L) Michael Ledger
The Escape Artist, James Sherman; (D) Dennis Zacek; (S) Chris Phillips; (C) John Hancock Brooks, Jr.; (L) Ellen E. Jones

PRODUCTIONS 1988–89

Some Men Need Help, John Ford Noonan; (D) Dennis Zacek; (S) Rick Paul; (C) Patricia L. Hart; (L) Ellen E. Jones
Tamer of Horses, William Mastrosimone; (D) Jonathan Wilson; (S) Maggie Bodwell; (C) Erin Quigley; (L) Chris Phillips
The Long Awaited, Claudia Allen; (D) Sandy Shinner; (S) Jeff Bauer; (C) Claudia Boddy; (L) Michael Rourke
Jelly Belly, Charles Smith; (D) Dennis Zacek; (S) Linda L. Lane; (C) Glenn Billings; (L) Larry Schoeneman
Music from a Locked Room, John Logan; (D) Dennis Zacek; (S) James Dardenne; (C) Kerry Fleming; (L) Ellen E. Jones
Tito, Romolo Arellano; (D) Jose G. Garcia; (S) Jose G. Garcia; (C) Jose G. Garcia; (L) Joseph Anthony Wasson
Woman in Mind, Alan Ayckbourn; (D) Sandy Shinner; (S) Jeff Bauer; (C) Claudia Boddy; (L) Michael Rourke
April Snow, Romulus Linney; (D) Terry McCabe; (S) Sandra Petrick; (C) Kim Schnormeier; (L) Chris Allen

Vineyard Theatre

DOUGLAS AIBEL
Artistic Director

BARBARA ZINN KRIEGER
Executive Director

JOHN NAKAGAWA
Managing Director

108 East 15th Street
New York, NY 10003
(212) 353-3366 (bus.)
(212) 353-3874 (b.o.)

FOUNDED 1981
Barbara Zinn Krieger

SEASON
Jan.–Dec.

FACILITIES
Vineyard Theatre at 26th St.
Seating Capacity: 65
Stage: thrust

Dimson Theatre
Seating Capacity: 150
Stage: flexible

FINANCES
Sept. 1, 1988-Aug. 31, 1989
Expenses: $450,000

CONTRACTS
AEA letter of agreement

The Vineyard Theatre, a multi-art chamber theatre, produces new plays and musicals, music-theatre collaborations and revivals of works that have previously failed in the commercial arena. Over the years, we have attempted to provide a completely supportive and unpressured environment in which our artists can collaborate and experiment. While the range of our programming is eclectic, we've been consistently drawn to young writers with a distinctively poetic style and an affinity for adventurous theatrical forms. Because our organization sponsors several music programs, including early music and classic jazz series, we have also attempted to explore different ways in which music can enhance and enrich a dramatic text. The recent opening of our large new flexible facility at Union Square is the realization of a dream for us, and we look forward to great artistic and technical opportunities there.

—Douglas Aibel

PRODUCTIONS 1987–88

Flora, the Red Menace, book: David Thompson; music: John Kander; lyrics: Fred Ebb; (D) Scott Ellis; (S) Michael J. Hotopp; (C) Lindsay Davis; (L) Phil Monat
The Grandma Plays, Todd Graff; (D) Steve Gomer; (S) William Barclay; (C) Jennifer von Mayrhauser; (L) Phil Monat

Vineyard Theatre. Veanne Cox and Peter Frechette in *Flora, the Red Menace*. Photo: Martha Swope Associates, Carol Rosegg.

PRODUCTIONS 1988–89

Phantasie, Sybille Pearson; (D) John Rubenstein; (S) William Barclay; (C) Deborah Shaw; (L) Phil Monat
The Value of Names, Jeffrey Sweet; (D) Gloria Muzio; (S) William Barclay; (C) Jess Goldstein; (L) Phil Monat
Feast Here Tonight, book: Ken Jenkins; music and lyrics: Daniel Jenkins; (D) Gloria Muzio; (S) William Barclay; (C) Jess Goldstein; (L) Phil Monat

Virginia Stage Company

CHARLES TOWERS
Artistic Director

DEBRA HUMES
Managing Director

Box 3770
Norfolk, VA 23514
(804) 627-6988 (bus.)
(804) 627-1234 (b.o.)

FOUNDED 1979
Comunity Members

SEASON
Oct.-May

FACILITIES
Wells Theatre
Seating Capacity: 675
Stage: proscenium

FINANCES
July 1, 1988-June 30, 1989
Expenses: $1,601,650

CONTRACTS
LORT (C)

At each turn we try to pursue strong theatrical writing—plays by men and women we consider to be genuine stage poets. By working with language that takes on special life only in a stage space, these writers keep alive the art of the spoken word. Because rich text yields subtext, we have a long-term mission to teach our audience how to hear metaphorically instead of concretely. The productions of which we are most proud raise valuable questions and offer perspective instead of diversion. After 10 seasons of operation, we are confident in our ability to maintain a producing institution. Now we are working to enrich the collaborative process by improving the quality of life for everyone who works for and with the company. Significant effort has been put into providing a positive experience for both resident and guest artists, as we strive to build full institutional support for a mission of creation rather than presentation. Both the challenges and the commitment are real.

—Charles Towers

PRODUCTIONS 1987–88

Ah, Wilderness!, Eugene O'Neill; (D) Christopher Hanna; (S) John

Doepp; (c) Candice Cain; (L) Spencer Mosse
Glengarry Glen Ross, David Mamet; (D) Charles Towers; (s) Michael Miller; (c) Candice Cain; (L) Jim Sale
Saltwater Moon, David French; (D) Charles Towers; (s) George Hillow; (c) Candice Cain; (L) Spencer Mosse
Jacques Brel Is Alive and Well and Living in Paris, adapt: Eric Blau and Mort Shuman; music and lyrics: Jacques Brel; (D) Gregory S. Hurst; (s) Atkin Pace; (c) Marianne Faust; (L) David Noling
Play Yourself, Harry Kondoleon; (D) Christopher Hanna; (s) Michael Miller; (c) Candice Cain; (L) Don Holder
Ma Rainey's Black Bottom, August Wilson; (D) Israel Hicks; (s) Lawrence Casey; (c) Lawrence Casey; (L) Kirk Bookman

PRODUCTIONS 1988–89

Les Liaisons Dangereuses, trans and adapt: Christopher Hampton; (D) Charles Towers; (s) Pavel Dobrusky; (c) Candice Cain; (L) Pavel Dobrusky
American Buffalo, David Mamet; (D) Charles Towers; (s) George Hillow; (c) Candice Cain; (L) Spencer Mosse
Fossey, Lois Meredith; (D) Pamela Berlin; (s) Michael Ganio; (c) Candice Cain; (L) Judy Rasmuson
Macbeth, William Shakespeare; (D) Charles Towers; (s) Pavel Dobrusky; (c) Candice Cain; (L) Pavel Dobrusky
Top Girls, Caryl Churchill; (D) Christopher Hanna; (s) Bill Clarke; (c) Candice Cain; (L) Don Holder
A Walk in the Woods, Lee Blessing; (D) Christopher Hanna; (s) George Hillow; (c) Giva Taylor; (L) Don Holder

Whole Theatre

OLYMPIA DUKAKIS
Producing Artistic Director

544 Bloomfield Ave.
Montclair, NJ 07042
(201) 744-2996 (bus.)
(201) 744-2989 (b.o.)

FOUNDED 1973

SEASON
Oct.–May

FACILITIES
Whole Theatre
Seating Capacity: 199
Stage: proscenium

FINANCES
July 1, 1988–June 30, 1989
Expenses: $1,392,500

CONTRACTS
LORT (D)

Virginia Stage Company. Marjorie Lovett and Rose Stockton in *Play Yourself*. Photo: Mark Edward Atkinson.

Whole Theatre. Olympia Dukakis and Louis Zorich in *Better Living*. Photo: Martha Swope.

Whole Theatre's mainstage seaon, school and outreach programs strive, in all respects, to reflect the compelling personal statement and teachings of the company's artists and educators. Long-term commitments to playwrights, actors, directors, designers and theatre educators, as well as affiliations with other state arts organizations, educational institutions, community and social agencies, delineate Whole Theatre's signature and institutional identity. In addition to a five-play season of new work, "new wave" companies, and classics uniquely reconceived and staged, Whole Theatre programs include Thunder in the Light, a company modeled after the Living Stage Theatre Company in Washington, D.C.; "The Gathering," a women writers' project; and an emerging company of comic writers and comedians. Whole Theatre also provides classes for children, teens and adults, as well as residencies at more than 30 sites for groups that include the economically deprived, the disabled, the gifted, the developmentally handicapped, incarcerated women and senior citizens.

—*Olympia Dukakis*

PRODUCTIONS 1987–88

Beautiful Bodies, Laura Cunningham; (D) Vivian Matalon; (s) Michael Miller; (c) Sam Fleming; (L) Richard Nelson (L)
"Adapators" in Autobahn, Tony Brown and Kari Margolis; (D) Tony Brown and Kari Margolis; (c) Kari Margolis; (L) Peter Anderson
The School for Wives, Moliere; trans: Richard Wilbur; (D) Margaret Bard; (s) Lewis Folden; (c) Sam Fleming; (L) Rachel Budin
Tracers, Vincent Caristi, Richard Chaves, John DiFusco, Eric E. Emerson, Rick Gallavan, Merlin Marston, Harry Stephens and Sheldon Lettich; (D) John DiFusco; (s) John Falabella; (c) David Navarro Velasquez; (L) Terry Wuthrich
The Rose Tattoo, Tennessee Williams; (D) Apollo Dukakis; (s) Jack Chandler; (c) Donna Marie Larsen; (L) Phil Monat

PRODUCTIONS 1988–89

Better Living, George F. Walker; (D) Max Mayer; (s) Lewis Folden; (c) Donna Marie Larsen; (L) Rachel Budin
Spare Parts, Elizabeth Page; (D) Susan Einhorn; (s) Ursula Belden; (c) David Murin; (L) Ann Wrightson
Fraternity, Jeff Stetson; (D) Clinton Turner Davis; (s) Jack Chandler; (c) Alvin B. Perry; (L) William H. Grant, III
A Walk in the Woods, Lee Blessing; (D) William Foeller;

(s) Michael Miller; (c) Donna Marie Larsen; (L) Rachel Budin
The World Goes 'Round . . . With Kander & Ebb, book: David Thompson; music: John Kander; lyrics: Fred Ebb; (D) Scott Ellis; (s) Bill Hoffman; (c) Donna Marie Larsen; (L) Phil Monat

Williamstown Theatre Festival

WILLIAM STEWART
Executive Director

PETER HUNT
Artistic Directors

ROBERT ALPAUGH
General Manager

Box 517
Williamstown, MA 01267
(413) 597-3377 (bus.)
(413) 597-3400 (b.o.)

FOUNDED 1955
Nikos Psacharopoulos, Trustees of the Williamstown Theatre Festival

SEASON
June-Aug.

FACILITIES
Adams Memorial Theatre
Seating Capacity: 479
Stage: proscenium

The Extension/Other Stage
Seating Capacity: 96
Stage: flexible

Free Theatre
Seating Capacity: open
Stage: flexible

FINANCES
Dec. /, 197-Nov. 30, 1988
Expenses: $1,300,000

CONTRACTS
AEA CORST (X) and letter of agreement

In its 35th-anniversary year, the Williamstown Theatre Festival is entering a new era, signaled by the death of its longtime artistic director Nikos Psacharopoulos. Nikos helped start a tentative summer-stock troupe in 1955 and transformed it into a theatrical center with a vast reputation. He knew that theatre had to change, that resting on laurels can be dangerous. So he championed many innovations—a vastly expanded Equity company; the additions of an experiential Other Stage, an outdoor Free Theatre, a cabaret, literary events, new play readings. Thanks to him, WTF's identification with ambitious, unusual work is secure. Now, the challenge is to continue, to build on WTF's past identification with modern classics and striking new work. One thing is certain: Williamstown is and always will be a haven for the theatre artist in America.
—*Peter Hunt*

Note: During the 1987-88 and 1988-89 seasons, the late Nikos Psacharopoulos served as artistic/executive director.

Williamstown Theatre Festival. *Arturo VI.* Photo: Richard Termine.

PRODUCTIONS 1987–88
The Legend to Oedipus, adapt: Kenneth Cavander; composer: Adam Guettel; (D) Nikos Psacharopoulos; (s) John Conklin; (c) Merrily Murray-Walsh; (L) Pat Collins
The American Clock, Arthur Miller; (D) Austin Pendleton and Murray-Walsh Merrily; (s) James D. Sandefur; (c) Jeff Goldstein and Merrily Murray-Walsh; (L) Curt Ostermann
The Resistible Rise of Arturo Ui, Bertolt Brecht; (D) Peter Hunt; (s) Michael Ganio and John Conklin; (c) John Dunn; (L) Peter Hunt
Les Liaisons Dangereuses, Christopher Hampton; (D) John Rubenstein; (s) Hugh Landwehr; (c) Claudia Brown; (L) Roger Meeker
The Show-Off, George Kelly; (D) James Simpson; (s) Hugh Landwehr; (c) Yslan Hicks; (L) Arden Fingerhut

PRODUCTIONS 1988–89
John Brown's Body, Stephen Vincent Benet; (D) Peter Hunt; (s) Hugh Landwehr; (c) Rita B. Watson; (L) Peter Hunt
Henry IV, Part I and II, William Shakespeare; (D) Austin Pendleton; (s) Jack Chandler; (c) David Murin; (L) Arden Fingerhut
The Rose Tattoo, Tennessee Williams; (D) Irene Lewis; (s) Hugh Landwehr; (L) Pat Collins
Mother Courage, Bertolt Brecht; (D) Gerald Freedman; (s) Doug Stein; (c) Jeanne Button; (L) Pat Collins
Passion, Peter Nichols; (D) Arvin Brown; (s) Michael Miller; (c) Dunya Ramicova; (L) Scott Zielinski

The Wilma Theater

BLANKA ZIZKA
JIRI ZIZKA
Artistic/Producing Directors

W. COURTENAY WILSON
Managing Director

2030 Sansom St.
Philadelphia, PA 19103
(215) 963-0249 (bus.)
(215) 963-0345 (b.o.)

FOUNDED 1973
Liz Stout, Linda Griffith

SEASON
Oct.-July

FACILITIES
Seating Capacity: 106
Stage: proscenium

FINANCES
Sept. 1, 1988-Aug. 31, 1989
Expenses: $957,000

CONTRACTS
AEA letter of agreement

The Wilma Theatre presents theatre as an art form that engages both audience and artists in an adventure of aesthetic and philosophical reflection on the complexities of contemporary life. We believe that a fine performance of a great play is one of the most rewarding experiences our culture provides. The Wilma relies on the selection of powerful, compelling scripts, to which mixed media add another dimension, allowing each production to evolve beyond the confines of verbal communication into the world of metaphor and poetic vision. Our productions are a synthesis of many artistic disciplines—visual arts, music, choreography, writing, acting; our challenge lies in finding new connections among these disciplines to illuminate the dramatic essence of the script. Our staging utilizes a succession of impermanent images cinematic and three-dimensional, to heighten the inner emotional realities of the characters and create a unique scenic rhythm that captures our age of constant speed, surprise and visual stimulation.
—*Blanka Zizka, Jiri Zizka*

PRODUCTIONS 1987–88
Macbett, Eugene Ionesco; trans: Charles Marowitz; (D) Blanka Zizka; (s) Hiroshi Iwasaki; (c) Hiroshi Iwasaki; (L) Jeff Brown
Philemon, book: Tom Jones; music: Harvey Schmidt; (D) Jiri Zizka; (s) Hiroshi Iwasaki; (c) Hiroshi Iwasaki; (L) Jerold Forsyth
Statements After an Arrest Under the Immorality Act, Athol Fugard; (D) Blanka Zizka; (s) Andrei Efremoff; (c) Donna Lee-Sipple; (L) Jerold Forsyth
Accidental Death of an Anarchist, Dario Fo; trans: Richard Nelson; (D) Jiri Zizka;

The Wilma Theater. David Hurst and Anthony Chisholm in *Incommunicado*.

(S) Hiroshi Iwasaki; (C) Hiroshi Iwasaki; (L) Jerold Forsyth

PRODUCTIONS 1988–89

The Concert at Saint Ovide Fair, Antonio Buero-Vallejo; trans: Marion Peter Holt; (D) Blanka Zizka; (S) Hiroshi Iwasaki; (C) Hiroshi Iwasaki; (L) Jerold Forsyth

The Mystery of Irma Vep, Charles Ludlam; (D) Robert Fuhrmann; (S) Dan Conway; (C) Don Newcomb; (L) Jerold Forsyth

Incommunicado, Tom Dulack; (D) Blanka Zizka; (S) Andrei Efremoff; (C) Lara Ratnikoff; (L) Jerold Forsyth

Temptation, Vaclav Havel; trans: Marie Winn; (D) Jiri Zizka; (S) Jerry Rojo; (C) Hiroshi Iwasaki; (L) Jerold Forsyth

Wisdom Bridge Theatre

JEFFREY ORTMANN
Producing Director

1559 West Howard St.
Chicago, IL 60626
(312) 743-0486 (bus.)
(312) 743-6000 (b.o.)

FOUNDED 1974
David Beaird

SEASON
Sept.-July

FACILITIES
Wisdom Bridge Theatre
Seating Capacity: 196
Stage: proscenium

Coronet Playhouse
Seating Capacity: 440
Stage: proscenium

FINANCES
Aug. 1, 1988-July 31, 1989
Expenses: $1,125,000

CONTRACTS
AEA CAT

Wisdom Bridge Theatre is located on the northernmost edge of Chicago in a second-story loft space. The theatre was named after a painting entitled "The Wisdom Bridge," subtitled "The Bridge to Wisdom lies in the continual asking of questions." The work of the theatre focuses on plays which ask large questions about society, art, the political system, by producing both new works and innovative interpretations of classics. In addition to WBT's main emphasis on producing plays on Howard Street, the theatre also plays a significant role in the community in which it is located. WBT has a nationally recognized outreach program that works with local primary and secondary schools, senior centers, social service agencies, restaurants, the neighborhood (economic) development corporation and community groups. WBT has also toured productions nationally and abroad, and is currently in the planning stages for performances in Australia and the Soviet Union.

—*Jeffrey Ortmann*

Note: During the 1987-88 and 1988-89 seasons, Richard E.T. White served as artistic director.

PRODUCTIONS 1987–88

Ten November, book: Steven Dietz; music and lyrics: Eric Peltoniemi; (D) Richard E. T. White; (S) Michael S. Philippi; (C) Jessica Hahn; (L) Michael S. Philippi

Hard Times, adapt: Stephen Jeffreys, from Charles Dickens; (D) Richard E. T. White; (S) Michael Olich; (C) Kaye Nottbusch; (L) Ken Bowen

Hunting Cockroaches, Janusz Glowacki; trans: Jadwiga Koscika; (D) Douglas Finlayson; (S) Linda Buchanan; (C) Malgorzata Komorowska; (L) Paul Miller

PRODUCTIONS 1988–89

Yankee Dawg You Die, Philip Kan Gotanda; (D) Richard E. T. White; (S) Michael S. Philippi; (C) Jessica Hahn; (L) Michael S. Philippi

The My House Play, Wendy MacLeod; (D) Richard E. T. White; (S) Michael S. Philippi; (C) Pamela Brailey; (L) Ken Bowen

Speed-The-Plow, David Mamet; (D) Joel Schumacher; (S) Michael S. Philippi and Kevin Rigdon; (C) Laura Cunningham; (L) Kevin Rigdon

Traveler in the Dark, Marsha Norman; (D) Ed Kaye-Martin; (S) Michael S. Philippi; (C) Jon Accardo; (L) Michael S. Philippi

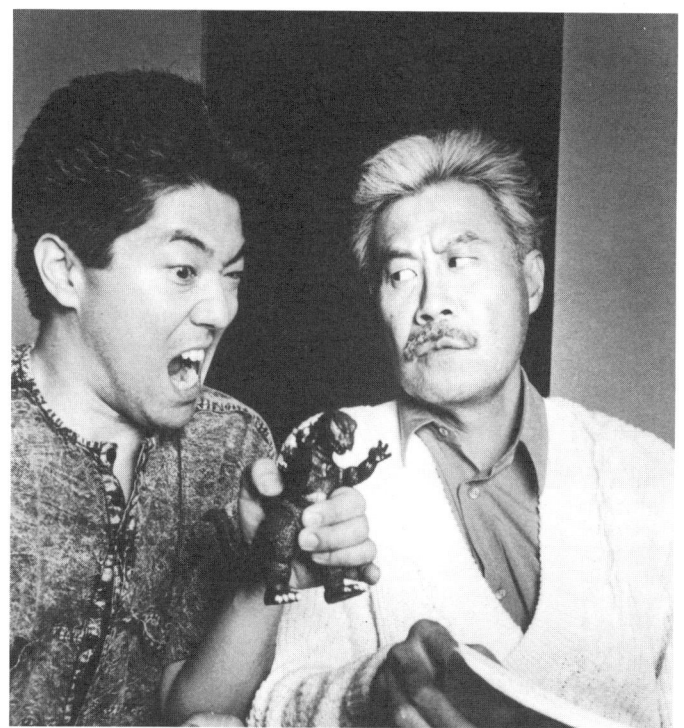

Wisdom Bridge Theatre. Marc Hayashi and Sab Shimono in *Yankee Dawg You Die*. Photo: Jennifer Girard.

The Women's Project and Productions. Helen Stenborg and Frederick Neumann in *Neidecker*. Photo: Martha Holmes.

Women's Project & Productions

JULIA MILES
Artistic Director

SALLY CONGDON
General Manager

220 West 42nd St - 18th Fl
New York, NY 10036
(212) 382-2750 (bus.)
(212) 242-4204 (b.o.)

FOUNDED 1978
Julia Miles

SEASON
Oct.-May

FINANCES
July 1, 1988-June 30, 1989
Expenses: $500,000

CONTRACTS
AEA letter of agreement

The Women's Project and Productions began 11 years ago as a program of the American Place Theatre to encourage women to write for the theatre and to help establish credibility for both women writers and directors in the American theatre. Through a membership structure and developmental readings leading to production, the Project creates an environment where women can work and talents can grow. The aesthetic bias inclines the Project to work with playwrights who, by their use of language, theatricality and original points of view, cause us to examine ourselves and our society. Additionally, the Project has always sought diverse ethnic representation, believing that talents grow where different cultures and races work together. Finally, the Project exists in order to foster a climate that gives equal acceptance to women who choose theatre as their means of questioning and interpreting the world.
—*Julia Miles*

PRODUCTIONS 1987-88

Abingdon Square, Maria Irene Fornes; (D) Maria Irene Fornes; (S) Donald Eastman; (C) Sam Fleming; (L) Anne Militello
Reverend Jenkins' Almost All Colored Orphanage Band, book: Gail Kriegel; music: Luther Henderson; (D) Vernel Bagneris; (S) Max Gorgal; (C) Jo Ann Clevenger; (L) Max Gorgal
Etta Jenks, Marlane Meyer; (D) Roberta Levitow; (S) Rosario Provenza; (C) Ray C. Naylor; (L) Robert Wierzel
Letters to a Daughter from Prison: Indira and Nehru, Lavonne Mueller; (D) Vijaya Mehta; (S) Nancy Harrington and John Kennedy; (L) Sandra L. Ross
Variations on Joan of Arc, Simone Benmussa; (D) Simone Benmussa; (S) Nancy Harrington and John Kennedy; (L) Sandra L. Ross
The Trial of Joan of Arc at Rouen, 1431, Bertolt Brecht; trans: Ralph Manheim and Wolfgang Sauerlander; (D) Marta Luna; (S) Nancy Harrington and John Kennedy; (L) Sandra L. Ross
Viva Reviva, Eve Merriam; (D) Julianne Boyd; (S) Nancy Harrington and John Kenndey; (L) Sandra L. Ross
Voices of Silence, Joan Vail Thorne; (D) Joan Vail Thorne; (S) Nancy Harrington and John Kennedy; (L) Sandra L. Ross
Scenes from Saint Joan, George Bernard Shaw; (D) Lou Nai Ming; (S) Nancy Harrington and John Kennedy; (L) Sandra L. Ross

PRODUCTIONS 1988-89

Ma Rose, Cassandra Medley; (D) Irving Vincent; (S) Phillip Baldwin; (C) Judy Dearing; (L) Pat Dignan
Niedecker, Kristine Thatcher; (D) Julianne Boyd; (S) James Noone; (C) Deborah Shaw; (L) Frances Aronson
Ladies, Eve Ensler; (D) Paul Walker; (S) Victoria Petrovich; (C) Donna Zakowska; (L) Deborah Dumas
O Pioneers!, adapt by Darrah Cloud from Willa Cather; (D) Kevin Kuhlke; (S) John Wulp; (C) Mary Ellen Walter; (L) Jeff Robbins

The Wooster Group

ELIZABETH LECOMPTE, WILLEM DAFOE, SPALDING GRAY, JIM CLAYBURGH, PEYTON SMITH, KATE VALK AND RON VAWTER
Artistic Collective

LINDA CHAPMAN
General Manager

Box 654, Canal Station
New York, NY 10013
(212) 966-9796 (bus.)
(212) 966-3651 (b.o.)

FOUNDED 1967
Richard Schechner

SEASON
variable

FACILITIES
The Performing Garage
Seating Capacity: 100
Stage: flexible

FINANCES
July 1, 1988-June 30, 1989
Expenses: $630,000

The Wooster Group is an ensemble of artists who have worked together for 15 years producing original theatre and media pieces Wooster Group productions are composed by the Group and directed by Elizabeth LeCompte. Their theatre works join an ongoing repertoire and are periodically revived in conjunction with new work. All productions are created and produced at the Group's permanent home, the Performing Garage in New York City. Currently the Wooster Group has seven members: Jim Clayburgh (designer), Willem Dafoe, Spalding Gray, Elizabeth LeCompte (artistic director), Peyton Smith (board president), Kate Valk and Ron Vawter. Wooster Group associates include: Paul Schiff Berman, Scott Breindel, Steve Buscemi, Linda Chapman, Valerie Charles, Denny Dermody, Robin Drummond, Norman Frisch, Paula Gordon, Cynthia Hedstrom, Mary Ann Hestand, Jim Johnson, Michael Kirby, Ken Kobland, Anna Kohler, Christopher Kondek, Michael Nishball, Nancy Reilly, Elion Sacher, James

The Wooster Group. *The Temptation of Saint Anthony.* Photo: Paula Court.

chamus, Jim Strahs, Michael
tumm, Jeff Webster and Mar-
nne Weems.
—*Elizabeth LeCompte*

PRODUCTIONS 1987–88

Frank Dell's the Temptation of St. Antony, company-developed; (D) Elizabeth LeCompte; (S) Jim Clayburgh; (C) company; (L) company
Symphony of Rats, Richard Foreman; (D) Richard Foreman; (S) Richard Foreman; (C) Richard Foreman; (L) Richard Foreman
North Atlantic, Jim Strahs; (D) Elizabeth LeCompte; (S) Jim Clayburgh; (C) company; (L) company
... Just the High Points ...), company-developed; (D) Elizabeth LeCompte; (S) Jim Clayburgh; (C) company; (L) company

PRODUCTIONS 1988–89

Frank Dell's the Temptation of St. Antony, company-developed; (D) Elizabeth LeCompte; (S) Jim Clayburgh; (C) company; (L) company
... Just the High Points ...), company-developed; (D) Elizabeth LeCompte; (S) Jim Clayburgh; (C) company; (L) company

Worcester Foothills Theatre Company

MARC P. SMITH
Executive Producer/Artistic Director

Box 236
Worcester, MA 01602
(508) 754-3314 (bus.)
(508) 754-4018 (b.o.)

FOUNDED 1974
Marc P. Smith

SEASON
Oct.-May

FACILITIES
Foothills Theatre
Seating Capacity: 349
Stage: proscenium

FINANCES
June 1, 1988-May 31, 1989
Expenses: $870,000

CONTRACTS
AEA letter of agreement

The Worcester Foothills Theatre Company was conceived and realized as an artistic extension of a community that is traditional and pragmatic on the one hand, and innovative and daring on the other. The dialogue between the theatre company and its community has shown a mutual responsiveness; each new production expands the dialogue and extends the perimeters of the exchange. The result of this dynamic is constant change, growth and excitement. Examination of universal themes and of the profound problems that confront us in contemporary times do not preclude creating an atmosphere of joy and entertainment. A unity of purpose prevails while embracing a wide range of diversity. Worcester Foothills is truly a theatre company that has demonstrated an impact on a vibrant community and achieved a major voice in that community.
—*Marc P. Smith*

PRODUCTIONS 1987–88

The Foreigner, Larry Shue; (D) Jack Magune; (S) Edwin Chapin; (C) Bradford Wood; (L) Margaret Viverito
The Penultimate Problem of Sherlock Holmes, John Nassivera; (D) Nancy Kindelan; (S) Edwin Chapin; (C) Bradford Wood; (L) Margaret Viverito
Biloxi Blues, Neil Simon; (D) Jack Neary; (S) Edwin Chapin; (C) Bradford Wood; (L) Margaret Viverito
Retrofit, Marc P. Smith; (D) John Grant-Phillips; (S) Edwin Chapin; (C) Bradford Wood; (L) Eric A. Hart
Pack of Lies, Hugh Whitemore; (D) Greg DeJarnett; (S) Edwin Chapin; (C) Gregory A. Poplyk; (L) Margaret Viverito
Dames at Sea, book and lyrics: George Haimsohn and Robin Miller; music: Jim Wise; (D) Lee Roy Reams; (S) Edwin Chapin; (C) Bradford Wood; (L) Eric A. Hart

PRODUCTIONS 1988–89

Noises Off, Michael Frayn; (D) Michael Allosso; (S) Edwin Chapin; (C) Bradford Wood and Gregory A. Poplyk; (L) Eric A. Hart
Deathtrap, Ira Levin; (D) Greg DeJarnett; (S) Edwin Chapin; (C) Bradford Wood and Gregory A. Poplyk; (L) Eric A. Hart
The 1940's Radio Hour, Walton Jones; (D) John Grant-Phillips; (S) Don Ricklin; (C) Bradford Wood and Gregory A. Poplyk; (L) Eric A. Hart
The Diary of Anne Frank, Frances Goodrich and Albert Hackett; (D) Thomas Ouellette; (S) Edwin Chapin; (C) Bradford Wood and Gregory A. Poplyk; (L) Eric A. Hart
I'm Not Rappaport, Herb Gardner; (D) Jack Magune; (S) Edwin Chapin; (C) Bradford Wood and Gregory A. Poplyk; (L) Eric A. Hart
Hedda Gabler, adapt: Marc P. Smith, from Henrik Ibsen; (D) John Grant-Phillips; (S) Lino Toyos; (C) Bradford Wood and Gregory A. Poplyk; (L) David Wiggall
Tomfoolery, adapt: Cameron Mackintosh and Robin Ray; music and lyrics: Tom Lehrer; (D) Michael Allosso; (S) Edwin Chapin; (C) Bradford Wood and Gregory A. Poplyk; (L) Eric A. Hart and David Wiggall

Worcester Foothills Theatre Company. Tom Ouellette and Brian Smith in *The Foreigner.* Photo: Patrick O'Connor.

WPA Theatre

KYLE RENICK
Artistic Director

DONNA LIEBERMAN
Managing Director

519 West 23rd St.
New York, NY 10011
(212) 206-0523

FOUNDED 1977
R. Stuart White, Stephen G. Wells, Kyle Renick, Edward T. Gianfrancesco, Craig Evans, Howard Ashman

SEASON
Year-round

FACILITIES
Seating Capacity: 128
Stage: proscenium

FINANCES
July 1, 1988-June 30, 1989
Expenses: $698,000

CONTRACTS
AEA letter of agreement

The WPA Theatre (Workshop of the Players Art Foundation, Inc.) is dedicated to the creation of a vital and informed American repertoire based on realistic writing, acting, directing and design. The WPA continues to nurture the new generation of American playwrights, to cherish the American theatrical tradition through the revival of neglected plays that have helped to shape the American realistic style, and to develop and produce new works that grow out of this style. The WPA Theatre is an ongoing celebration of the American theatre.

—*Kyle Renick*

PRODUCTIONS 1987–88

The Milk Train Doesn't Stop Here Anymore, Tennessee Williams; (D) Kevin Conway; (S) Edward T. Gianfrancesco; (C) Candice Donnelly; (L) Craig Evans

A Subject of Child, Loren-Paul Caplin; (D) Bill Castellino; (S) Edward T. Gianfrancesco; (C) Don Newcomb; (L) Craig Evans

No Time Flat, Larry Ketron; (D) Peter Maloney; (S) Edward T. Gianfrancesco; (C) Don Newcomb; (L) Craig Evans

Morocco, Allan Havis; (D) Allan Havis; (S) Bill Clarke; (C) Mimi Maxmen; (L) Craig Evans

PRODUCTIONS 1988–89

Just Say No, Larry Kramer; (D) David Esbjornson; (S) Edward T. Gianfrancesco; (C) David C. Woolard; (L) Craig Evans

The Lady in Question, Charles Busch; (D) Kenneth Eliott; (S) B.T. Whitehill; (C) Robert Locke and Jennifer Arnold; (L) Vivien Leone

The Night Hank Williams Died, Larry L. King; (D) Christopher Ashley; (S) Edward T. Gianfrancesco; (C) Jess Goldstein; (L) Craig Evans

The Good Coach, Ben Siegler; (D) Michael Bloom; (S) Edward T. Gianfrancesco; (C) Deborah Shaw; (L) Craig Evans

Early One Evening at the Rainbow Bar & Grille, Bruce Graham; (D) Pamela Berlin; (S) Edward T. Gianfrancesco; (C) Mimi Maxmen; (L) Craig Evans

WPA Theatre. Steve Rankin and Barton Heyman in *The Night Hank Williams Died*. Photo: Martha Swope.

Yale Repertory Theatre

LLOYD RICHARDS
Artistic Director

BENJAMIN MORDECAI
Managing Director

Box 1903A Yale Station
New Haven, CT 06520
(203) 432-1515 (bus.)
(203) 432-1234 (b.o.)

FOUNDED 1966
Robert Brustein

SEASON
Sept.–May

FACILITIES
Yale Repertory Theatre
Seating Capacity: 489
Stage: thrust

University Theatre
Seating Capacity: 656
Stage: proscenium

FINANCES
July 1, 1988 - June 30, 1989
Expenses: $2,802,735

CONTRACTS
LORT (C)

The Yale Repertory Theatre has centered its artistic mission on the playwright, taking its cue from the beginnings of the Yale School of Drama in 1926. Our program has focused on the development of playwrights and the articulate and dramatic presentation of their work. Yale Rep seeks talented voices from the past, present and from those of the future who have a concern for the quality of human existence and the environment in which it is nurtured. We present their work in a variety of formats. To ensure that there is excellence available for every area of theatre in the future, we provide professional, experimental opportunities for the exceptionally talented students of the Yale School of Drama who are studying and practicing al aspects of theatre. We believe that in every area of our work there should be a consciousness of the multinational, multiethnic, multiracial and religious community in which we live, and that this should be reflected on our stage. We love our work and our audience. We are proud to be one with them.

—*Lloyd Richard*

PRODUCTIONS 1987–88

Sarcophagus: A Tragedy, Vladimir Gubaryev; trans: Michael Glenny; (D) David Chambers; (S) Craig Clipper; (C) Teresa Snider-Stein; (L) William B. Warfel

Melons, Bernard Pomerance; (D) Gitta Honegger; (S) Russell Scott Parkman; (C) Dunya Ramicova; (L) Stephen Strawbridge

The Piano Lesson, August Wilson (D) Lloyd Richards; (S) E. David Cosier, Jr.; (C) Constanza Romero; (L) Christopher Akerlind

Winterfest 8:

The My House Play, Wendy MacLeod; (D) Evan Yionoulis; (S) George Denes Suhayda; (C) George Denes Suhayda; (L) Tim Fricker

Chute Roosters, Craig Volk; (D) Donato J. D'Albis; (S) Tamara Turchetta; (C) Tamara Turchetta; (L) Ashley York Kennedy

Neddy, Jeffrey Hatcher; (D) Dennis Scott; (S) James A. Schuette; (C) Russell Scott Parkman; (L) Sarah Lambert

The Wall of Water, Sherry Kramer; (D) Margaret Booker; (S) David Birn; (C) Craig Clipper; (L) Scott Zielinski

Yale Repertory Theatre. Lou Myers in *The Piano Lesson*. Photo: Gerry Goodstein.

The Miser, Moliere; trans: Miles Malleson; (D) Andrei Belgrader; (S) Anita C. Stewart; (C) Marina Draghici; (L) Mark London

Eugene O'Neill Centennial Celebration, in repertory:
Long Day's Journey Into Night, Eugene O'Neill; (D) Jose Quintero; (S) Ben Edwards; (C) Jane Greenwood; (L) Jennifer Tipton
Ah, Wilderness!, Eugene O'Neill; (D) Arvin Brown; (S) Michael H. Yeargan; (C) Jane Greenwood; (L) Jennifer Tipton

PRODUCTIONS 1988–89

Intermezzo, Arthur Schnitzler; trans: Robert David MacDonald; (D) Gitta Honegger; (S) James A. Schuette; (C) Pamela Peterson; (L) Jennifer Tipton
Kiss of the Spider Woman, Manuel Puig and Allan Baker; (D) David Chambers; (S) Michael Yeargan; (C) Joel O. Thayer; (L) Mark London
The Alchemist, Ben Johnson; (D) John Hirsch; (S) David Birn; (C) Wendy A. Rolfe; (L) Christopher Akerlind

Winterfest 9:
Phaedra and Hippolytus, Elizabeth Egloff; (D) Christopher Grabowski; (S) Tony Fanning; (C) Melina Root; (L) Anita C. Stewart
The Beach, Anthony Giardina; (D) Amy Saltz; (S) Michael Loui; (C) Chrisi Karvonides; (L) Mark London
Starting Monday, Anne Commire; (D) Peter Mark Schifter; (S) Sarah Lambert; (C) Nephelie Andonvadis; (L) David Birn
Interrogating the Nude, Doug Wright; (D) Gitta Honegger; (S) James A. Schuette; (C) James A. Schuette; (L) Mark London

Moon Over Miami, John Guare; (D) Andrei Belgrader; (S) Judy Gailen; (C) Candice Donnelly; (L) Scott Zielinski
Cobb, Lee Blessing; (D) Lloyd Richards; (S) Rob Greenberg; (C) Joel O. Thayer; (L) Ashley York Kennedy
Playboy of the West Indies, Mustapha Matura; (D) Dennis Scott; (S) Michael Yeargan; (C) Mary Myers; (L) William B. Warfel

Young Playwrights Festival

NANCY QUINN
Producing Director

SHERI GOLDHIRSCH
Managing Director

234 West 44th St.
New York, NY 10036
(212) 575-7796 (bus.)
(212) 279-4200 (b.o.)

FOUNDED 1982
The Dramatists Guild, Inc.

SEASON
Sept.-Oct.

FINANCES
Oct. 1, 1987-Sept. 30, 1988
Expenses: $431,491

CONTRACTS
AEA Off-Broadway

Since 1982, the Foundation of the Dramatists Guild's Young Playwrights Festival has given professional productions and staged readings to the works of nearly 200 playwrights under the age of 19. The Festival introduces young writers to the profession at its highest level of achievement by involving them in all aspects of production, from design and casting meetings to rehearsals to having their plays reviewed in major publications. Of the 49 playwrights presented in the annual Young Playwrights Festival, 43 have gone on to write another play and/or to see their works produced, developed in workshops or staged readings, commissioned or published. The Festival's education program provides workshops in playwriting taught by theatre professionals to students in grades 4-12, conducts teacher training programs in playwriting techniques, sponsors the annual New York City High School Playwriting Project, and tours Young Playwrights Festival plays to local schools, libraries and youth centers. During the 1988-89 school year, we worked with 5,000 students and 200 teachers.
—*Nancy Quinn*

PRODUCTIONS 1987–88

Tiny Mommy, Juliet Garson; (D) Amy Saltz; (S) Derek McLane; (C) Michael Krass; (L) Nancy Schertler
Sparks in the Park, Noble Mason Smith; (D) Gary Pearle; (S) Derek McLane; (C) Michael Krass; (L) Nancy Schertler

PRODUCTIONS 1988–89

And the Air Didn't Answer, Robert Kerr; (D) Christopher Durang; (S) Allen Moyer; (C) Jess Goldstein; (L) Nancy Schertler
Seniority, Eric Ziegenhagen; (D) Lisa Peterson; (S) Allen Moyer; (C) Jess Goldstein; (L) Nancy Schertler
Women and Wallace, Jonathan Marc Sherman; (D) Don Scardino; (S) Allen Moyer; (C) Jess Goldstein; (L) Nancy Schertler

Young Playwrights Festival. Jill Tasker, Robert Sean Leonard, Richard Council, Jihmi Kennedy, John Augustine in *And the Air Didn't Answer*. Photo: Tess Steinkolk.

THEATRE CHRONOLOGY

The following is a chronological list of founding dates for the theatres included in this book. Years refer to dates of the first public performance or, in a few cases, the company's formal incorporation.

1896
Hudson Guild Theatre

1915
The Cleveland Play House

1925
Goodman Theatre

1926
The Tampa Players

1928
Berkshire Theatre Festival

1933
Barter Theatre

1934
Paper Mill Playhouse

1935
Oregon Shakespeare Festival

1937
Old Globe Theatre

1946
Stage One: The Louisville Children's Theatre

1947
Alley Theatre
La Jolla Playhouse

1949
Emmy Gifford Children's Theater
New Dramatists
Sacramento Theatre Company

1950
Arena Stage

1954
Milwaukee Repertory Theater
New York Shakespeare Festival

1955
Honolulu Theatre for Youth
TheatreVirginia
Williamstown Theatre Festival

1956
Academy Theatre
Philadelphia Drama Guild

1957
Detroit Repertory Theatre

1959
Dallas Theater Center
Society Hill Playhouse

1960
Asolo Theatre Company
Cincinnati Playhouse in the Park

1961
The Children's Theatre Company
Theatreworks/USA

1962
Great Lakes Theater Festival
Pioneer Theatre Company

1963
The Arkansas Arts Center Children's Theatre
Center Stage
Fulton Opera House
Goodspeed Opera House
The Guthrie Theater
New Jersey Shakespeare Festival
Periwinkle National Theatre for Young Audiences
Seattle Repertory Theatre
Trinity Repertory Company

1964
Actors Theatre of Louisville
The American Place Theatre
Hartford Stage Company
Missouri Repertory Theatre
O'Neill Theater Center
PCPA Theaterfest
South Coast Repertory

1965
A Contemporary Theatre
American Conservatory Theatre
Cumberland County Playhouse
East West Players
El Teatro Campesino
Long Wharf Theatre
Roundabout Theatre Company
Studio Arena Theatre

1966
Arizona Theatre Company
The Body Politic Theatre
INTAR Hispanic American Arts Center
Living Stage Theatre Company
Marin Theatre Company
New Stage Theatre
The Repertory Theatre of St. Louis
Yale Repertory Theatre

1967
CSC Repertory Ltd.—The Classic Stage Company
Magic Theatre
Mark Taper Forum
Puerto Rican Traveling Theatre
StageWest
The Wooster Group

1968
AMAS Repertory Theatre
Berkeley Repertory Theatre
The Changing Scene
Ford's Theatre
Omaha Magic Theatre
Ontological-Hysteric Theater
Playhouse on the Square
Repertorio Español

1969
Alliance Theatre Company
Circle Repertory Company
Free Street Theater
Madison Repertory Theatre
Odyssey Theatre Ensemble
Organic Theater Company
Shakespeare Theatre at the Folger
Theatre X

1970
American Theatre Company
BoarsHead: Michigan Public Theater
The Empty Space Theatre
Mabou Mines
Manhattan Theatre Club
New Federal Theatre
The Salt Lake Acting Company
The Street Theater
The Theater at Monmouth
TheaterWorks

1971
The Cricket Theatre
Dell'Arte Players Company
The Ensemble Studio Theatre
Jean Cocteau Repertory
Music-Theatre Group
The Old Creamery Theatre Company
The Playwrights' Center
Playwrights Horizons
Theater for the New City
Theatre Project

1972
The Acting Company
Alabama Shakespeare Festival
Eureka Theatre Company
GeVa Theatre
Indiana Repertory Theatre
Intiman Theatre Company
McCarter Theatre Center for the Performing Arts
Center for The Performing Arts
New American Theater
The Open Eye: New Stagings

1973

Bilingual Foundation of the Arts
City Theatre Company
Florida Studio Theatre
GMT
Hippodrome State Theatre
Unicorn Theatre
Whole Theatre
The Wilma Theater

1974

Berkeley Shakespeare Festival
Clarence Brown Theatre Company
Creative Arts Team
George Street Playhouse
Germinal Stage Denver
Ilusion Theater
The Independent Eye
Jewish Repertory Theatre
L.A. Theatre Works
Northlight Theatre
Oakland Ensemble Theatre
The People's Light and Theatre
　Company
The Philadelphia Theatre
　Company
Portland Stage Company
Roadside Theater
Syracuse Stage
Victory Gardens Theater
Wisdom Bridge Theatre
Worcester Foothills Theatre
　Company

1975

American Stage Festival
Attic Theatre
Caldwell Theatre Company
Ping Chong and Company/The Fiji
　Company
Long Island Stage

Pittsburgh Public Theater
The Road Company
Seattle Children's Theatre
Soho Repertory Theatre
Theatre IV
Theatre Project Company

1976

American Theatre Works
Arkansas Repertory Theatre
California Theatre Center
The CAST Theatre
Empire State Institute for the
　Performing Arts
Illinois Theatre Center
Mixed Blood Theatre Company
Nebraska Theatre Caravan
The Penumbra Theatre Company
PlayMakers Repertory Company
San Diego Repertory Theatre
Steppenwolf Theatre Company
Theatrical Outfit

1977

Actors Theatre of St. Paul
American Players Theatre
Creation Production Company
Horse Cave Theatre
North Carolina Shakespeare
　Festival
Pan Asian Repertory Theatre
Pennsylvania Stage Company
Theatre Rhinoceros
WPA Theatre

1978

A Traveling Jewish Theatre
Bloomsburg Theatre Ensemble
Great North American History
　Theatre

Crossroads Theatre Company
Jomandi Productions
Lamb's Players Theatre
Round House Theatre
Seattle Group Theatre
The Studio Theatre
Tacoma Actors Guild
Theatre de la Jeune Lune
The Women's Project and
　Productions

1979

American Repertory Theatre
American Stage Company
The Back Alley Theatre
Child's Play Touring Theatre
Delaware Theatre Company
Gloucester Stage Company
Grove Theatre Company
Florida Shakespeare Festival
Manhattan Punch Line Theatre
Merrimack Repertory Theatre
New York Theatre Workshop
Perseverance Theatre
Remains Theatre
River Arts Repertory
The Second Stage
Seven Stages
Stage West
Theatre for a New Audience
Virginia Stage Company

1980

The Bathhouse Theatre
Brass Tacks Theatre
Capital Repertory Company
Denver Center Theatre Company
Portland Repertory Theater
San Jose Repertory Company
St. Louis Black Repertory
　Company

1981

The Playmakers
Touchstone Theatre
Vineyard Theatre

1982

Heritage Artists, Ltd.
Huntington Theatre Company
Philadelphia Festival Theatre for
　New Plays
Saltworks Theatre Company
Young Playwrights Festival

1983

Musical Theatre Works
New Mexico Repertory Theatre

1984

Center Theater
Snowmass/Aspen Repertory
　Theatre

1985

Lincoln Center Theater
Los Angeles Theatre Center

1986

Cornerstone Theater Company
National Jewish Theater

1987

Bristol Riverside Theatre
First Stage Milwaukee
Shakespeare Repertory

REGIONAL INDEX

ALABAMA

Alabama Shakespeare Festival

ALASKA

Perseverance Theatre

ARIZONA

Arizona Theatre Company

ARKANSAS

The Arkansas Art Center Children's Theatre
Arkansas Repertory Theatre

CALIFORNIA

American Conservatory Theatre
A Traveling Jewish Theatre
The Back Alley Theatre
Berkeley Repertory Theatre
Berkeley Shakespeare Festival
Bilingual Foundation of the Arts
California Theatre Center
The CAST Theatre
Dell'Arte Players Company
East West Players
El Teatro Campesino
Eureka Theatre Company
Grove Shakespeare Festival
La Jolla Playhouse
Lamb's Players Theatre
L.A. Theatre Works
Los Angeles Theatre Center
Magic Theatre
Marin Theatre Company
Mark Taper Forum
Oakland Ensemble Theatre
Odyssey Theatre Ensemble
Old Globe Theatre
PCPA Theaterfest
Sacramento Theatre Company
San Diego Repertory Theatre
San Jose Repertory Company
South Coast Repertory
Theatre Rhinoceros
TheatreWorks

COLORADO

The Changing Scene
Denver Center Theatre Company
Germinal Stage Denver
Snowmass/Aspen Repertory Theatre

CONNECTICUT

Goodspeed Opera House
Hartford Stage Company
Long Wharf Theatre
O'Neil Theater Center
Yale Repertory Theatre

DELAWARE

Delaware Theatre Company

DISTRICT OF COLUMBIA

Arena Stage
Ford's Theatre
Living Stage Theatre Company
The Shakespeare Theatre at the Folger
The Studio Theatre

FLORIDA

American Stage
Asolo Theatre Company
Caldwell Theatre Company
Florida Shakespeare Festival
Florida Studio Theatre
Hippodrome State Theatre
Playmakers at the Ritz
The Tampa Players

GEORGIA

Academy Theatre
Alliance Theatre Company
Jomandi Productions
Seven Stages
Theatrical Outfit

HAWAII

Honolulu Theatre for Youth

ILLINOIS

The Body Politic Theatre
Center Theater
Child's Play Touring Theatre
Free Street Theater
Goodman Theatre
Illinois Theatre Center
National Jewish Theater
New American Theater
Northlight Theatre
Organic Theater Company
Remains Theatre
Shakespeare Repertory
Steppenwolf Theatre Company
Victory Gardens Theater
Wisdom Bridge Theatre

INDIANA

Indiana Repertory Theatre

IOWA

The Old Creamery Theatre Company

KENTUCKY

Actors Theatre of Louisville
Horse Cave Theatre
Roadside Theater
Stage One: The Louisville Children's Theatre

MAINE

Portland Stage Company
The Theater at Monmouth

MARYLAND

Center Stage
Round House Theatre
Theatre Project

MASSACHUSETTS

American Repertory Theatre
Berkshire Theatre Festival
Gloucester Stage Company
Huntington Theatre Company
Merrimack Repertory Theatre
Music-Theatre Group
StageWest
Williamstown Theatre Festival
Worcester Foothills Theatre Company

MICHIGAN

Attic Theatre
BoarsHead: Michigan Public Theater
Detroit Repertory Theatre

MINNESOTA

Actors Theatre of St. Paul
Brass Tacks Theatre
The Children's Theatre Company
The Cricket Theatre
Great North American History Theatre
The Guthrie Theater
Illusion Theater
Mixed Blood Theatre Company
The Penumbra Theatre Company
The Playwrights' Center
Theatre de la Jeune Lune

MISSISSIPPI

New Stage Theatre

MISSOURI

Missouri Repertory Theatre
The Repertory Theatre of St. Louis
St. Louis Black Repertory Company
Theatre Project Company
Unicorn Theatre

NEBRASKA

Emmy Gifford Children's Theater
Nebraska Theatre Caravan
Omaha Magic Theatre

NEW HEMPSHIRE

American Stage Festival

NEW JERSEY

Crossroads Theatre Company
George Street Playhouse
McCarter Theatre Center for the Performing Arts
New Jersey Shakespeare Festival
Paper Mill Playhouse
Whole Theatre

NEW MEXICO

New Mexico Repertory Theatre

NEW YORK

The Acting Company
AMAS Musical Theatre
The American Place Theatre
Capital Repertory Company
Circle Repertory Company
Creation Production Company
Creative Arts Team
CSC Repertory Ltd.—The Classic Stage Company

Empire State Institute for the
    Performing Arts
The Ensemble Studio Theatre
GeVa Theatre
Heritage Artists, Ltd.
Hudson Guild Theatre
INTAR Hispanic American Arts
    Center
Jean Cocteau Repertory
Jewish Repertory Theatre
Lincoln Center Theater
Long Island Stage
Mabou Mines
Manhattan Punch Line Theatre
Manhattan Theatre Club
Musical Theatre Works
Music-Theatre Group
New Dramatists
New Federal Theatre
New York Shakespeare Festival
New York Theatre Workshop
O'Neill Theater Center
Ontological-Hysteric Theater
The Open Eye: New Stagings
Pan Asian Repertory Theatre
Periwinkle National Theatre for
    Young Audiences
Ping Chong and Company/The Fiji
    Company
Playwright Horizons
Repertorio Español
River Arts Repertory
Roundabout Theatre Company
Second Stage Theatre
Soho Repertory Theatre
The Street Theater
Studio Arena Theatre

Syracuse Stage
Theatre for a New Audience
Theater for the New City
Theatreworks/USA
Vineyard Theatre
The Woman's Project and
    Productions
The Wooster Group
WPA Theatre
Young Playwrights Festival

NORTH CAROLINA

North Carolina Shakespeare
    Festival
PlayMakers Repertory Company

OHIO

Cincinnati Playhouse in the Park
The Cleveland Play House
Great Lakes Theater Festival
Players Theatre Columbus

OKLAHOMA

American Theatre Company

OREGON

Oregon Shakespeare Festival
Portland Repertory Theater

PENNSYLVANIA

Bloomsburg Theatre Ensemble
Bristol Riverside Theatre

City Theatre Company
Fulton Opera House
The Independent Eye
Pennsylvania Stage Company
The People's Light and Theatre
    Company
Philadelphia Drama Guild
Philadelphia Festival Theatre for
    New Plays
The Philadelphia Theatre
    Company
Pittsburgh Public Theater
Saltworks
Society Hill Playhouse
Touchstone Theatre
The Wilma Theater

RHODE ISLAND

Trinity Repertory Company

TENNESSEE

Clerence Brown Theatre Company
Cumberland County Playhouse
Playhouse on the Square
The Road Company

TEXAS

Alley Theatre
Dallas Theater Center
Stage West

UTAH

Pioneer Theatre Company
The Salt Lake Acting Company

VERMONT

American Theatre Works

VIRGINIA

Barter Theatre
Cornerstone Theater Company
Theatre IV
TheatreVirginia
Virgina Stage Company

WASHINGTON

A Contemporary Theatre
The Bathhouse Theatre
The Empty Space Theatre
Intiman Theatre Company
Seattle Children's Theatre
Seattle Group Theatre
Seattle Repertory Theatre
Tacoma Actors Guild

WISCONSIN

First Stage Milwaukee
FMT
Madison Repertory Theatre
Milwaukee Repertory Theater
Theatre X

INDEX OF NAMES

A

Aaron, Jules 6, 30, 63, 95, 115, 139
Abady, Josephine R. 38, 39
Abar, James 67
Abbott, Charles 8
Abbott, George 12
Abbott, Jack Henry 44
Abdoh, Reza 80
Abel, Dominique 152
Abernathy, Kathy 143, 152
Ableman, Paul 57
Abramson, Barbara 157
Abuba, Ernest H. 107
Accardo, Jon 92, 163
Ackerman, Paul 3, 7, 9
Acosta, Belinda 49
Adams, Abigail 111
Adams, Betsy 50, 59, 134
Adams, Randy 154
Adamson, Eve 72, 73
Aday, Gary 21
Addison, Michael 23, 24, 131
Adler, Marion 104
Adler, Ron 158
Adshead, Patricia 57, 109, 117, 138
Adzima, Nanzi 145
Aeschylus 39
Aesop 140
Affoumado, Ralph 89
Ahlin, Lee 13
Aibel, Doublas 160
Akalaitis, JoAnne 63, 80, 96
Akerlind, Christopher 60, 68, 102, 167
Albee, Edward 6, 7, 26, 119, 122
Albergo, Mina 128
Albers, Kenneth L. 39, 86, 87, 109
Albert, Stephen J. 84
Alberto, Alberto Felix 152
Alberts, K.L. 116
Albrezzi, Steven 132, 139
Alcott, Louisa May 35, 140
Alderman, Sandra S. 81
Aldous, Brian 97
Aldredge, Theoni 96, 108
Aldridge, Amanda 13, 86
Aldridge, John 55
Alegria, Alonso 15
Aleskie, Mary Lou 8
Alexander, Brandy 99
Alexander, Robert A. 77
Alexander, Tricia 55
Alexis, Connie L. 36
Alfaro, Rosanna Yamagina 48, 82
Alfred, William 134

Algren, Nelson 20
Alison, George 126
Allardice, Bruce 115
Allen, Chris 160
Allen, Claudia 160
Allen, David 31
Allen, Faye 135
Allen, Geri 90
Allen, John 155
Allen, M. Lynne 21
Allen, Mark 121
Allen, Nancy 151
Allen, Ralph G. 118
Allen, Rex E. 133
Allen, Ruth 47
Allen, Ted 74
Allen, Woody 10
Allman, Michael J. 130
Allosso, Michael 59, 86, 165
Allyn, Suzanne 81
Alpaugh, Robert 162
Alsaker, Timian 79, 80
Altman, Peter 68
Alvarez, Lynne 43, 72, 131
Amandes, Tom 107
Ambrosone, John 30, 59, 86
Ambush, Benny Sato 99
Amdahl, Gary 7
Ammerman, John 3
Anania, Michael 108
Andersen, D.R. 153
Andersen, Hans Christian 55, 105, 140
Anderson, Bradley D. 17
Anderson, Cletus 117
Anderson, Cordelia 69
Anderson, Debbie 55, 87
Anderson, Douglas 88
Anderson, Gary 47
Anderson, George 8
Anderson, John Louis 62
Anderson, Keith 19
Anderson, Linda 3
Anderson, Nels 18, 28
Anderson, Peter 161
Anderson, Phyllis Finton 17
Anderson, Robert 146
Anderson, Ron 54, 55
Anderson, Susan 153, 155
Anderton, Kit 130
Andonvadis, Nephelie 167
Andrews, Tom 149
Andrus, Dee 47
Andrus, T.O. 47
Angel, Tony 149
Angell, Gene 23, 99
Angermann, Christian 120

Angus, Patrick 149
Anouilh, Jean 16, 73, 76, 142, 146
Ansky, S. 19, 90
Anthony, Jill 159
Antnky, Matthew 153
Antoon, A.J. 96
Appel, Libby 16, 106, 134
Appelt, Joseph 88
Appino, Nikki 51
Appleton, Bev 151
Aprill, Arnold 90, 160
Aquilante, Michael 31
Arabian, Michael 100
Aranas, Raul 107
Arcenas, Loy 12, 23, 37, 39, 43, 59, 71, 75, 79, 83, 87, 96, 120, 126, 139, 143
Archbold, Ann M. 99
Archer, Julie 57, 80
Archer, William 84
Arellano, Romolo 160
Aristophanes 10
Armour, Toby 149, 150
Armstrong, Alan 7, 8
Armstrong, William 89
Arner, Gwen 98
Arney, Randall 142
Arnold, Jennifer 166
Arnone, John 16, 63, 64, 75, 84, 90, 96, 117
Arnoult, Philip 151, 152
Aronson, Frances 11, 16, 43, 63, 64, 72, 79, 96, 126, 148, 152
Aronstein, Martin 84, 85
Arrick, Larry 44, 71
Asakura, Setsu 12
Aschenbrenner, John 141
Asher, Sandra Fenichel 105
Ashley, Christopher 115, 166
Ashley, George 104
Ashman, Howard 7, 57, 109
Asion, Julian 11
Asse, Carlos F. 65, 66
Astley, Edward 137
Astley, Susan 137
Aswegan, Jared 16
Athayde, Roberto 25, 36, 58, 119
Atherton, Deborah 103
Atkinson, Clinton J. 78
Atkinson, Susan D. 27, 28
Atkinson, Thomas M. 36
Atlas, Larry 26
Attea, L.M. 106
Attea, Susan 106
Attias, Maurice 99
Aulisi, Joseph 101
Aupperlee, William John 15

Austin, Lyn 89
Averyt, Bennet 18, 19
Avni, Ran 73, 74
Axtell, Barry 28, 137, 138
Ayckbourn, Alan 4, 5, 8, 10, 15, 16, 21, 30, 39, 47, 66, 81, 83, 109, 118, 119, 125, 140, 145, 147, 158, 159, 160
Aysta, Joyce 99

B

Babcock, David 6
Babcock, Kate 132
Babe, Thomas 80, 103, 149
Bachus, Margaret 66
Backlund, Gabriel 150
Badgel, Mary 90
Badger, Mary 33, 90
Baffa-Brill, Diana 7
Bagarella, Sam 20
Bagneris, Vernel 164
Bagnold, Enid 24
Bagshaw-Reasoner, Nancy 62
Bahara, Blaise 153
Baierlein, Ed 57, 58
Bailey, Robert 37
Baird, Campbell 68
Baish, Carol 151
Baisley, Doris 63
Baitz, Jon Robin 85, 135
Baizley, Doris 4, 30, 39, 63, 86, 111, 114
Baker, Allan 18, 52, 133, 137, 167, 110
Baker, Bob 39, 155
Baker, Cliff Fannin 17, 18
Baker, Don 127, 152
Baker, Keith Alan 144, 145
Baker, Margaret 127
Baker, Paul 44
Baker, Steven 40
Balderston, John L. 14, 88
Baldwin, James 143
Baldwin, Philip 164
Baldwin, Phillip 120, 138, 164
Baley, Deborah B. 112
Baliff, Ariel 116
Balis, Andrea 149, 150
Ball, David 148
Ball, Leslie 38
Ball, William 10
Ballagh, Robert 76
Ballard, Barth 101
Ballard, Doc 63, 100
Balletta, Dominick 107

INDEX OF NAMES

Ballinger, Debra 52
Balmuth, Linda Giering 51
Baloy, Douglas 65
Bamman, Gerry 23, 64
Banner, Michael 141
Baraka, Amiri 135
Barber, Debi 74
Barber, Eugene 33
Barclay, William 37, 58, 160
Bard, Margaret 161
Bardwell, Rit 159
Barecca, Christopher 122, 123
Barer, Marshall 50
Barker, Tommy 149, 150
Barkla, Jack 35, 42, 63, 64
Barnes, Gregg 50, 85, 89, 101
Barnes, Paul 109
Barnes, Peter 44, 46, 60, 112, 131, 148, 158
Barnes, Robert 140
Barnes, Theo 148
Barnes, Tom 155
Barnett, Bob 58, 59
Barnett, Ron 151
Barnette, M. Neema 83
Barnhart, Gene 14
Baron, Neal 44, 158
Barranger, Milly S. 119
Barrault, Jean-Louis 73
Barreca, Christopher 9, 32, 58, 61, 64, 67, 68, 71, 134
Barrett, James Lee 44, 108
Barrie, James M. 5, 9, 47, 50, 118, 154, 155
Barry, Ellen 93
Barry, P.J. 78
Barry, Paul 93, 94
Barry, Philip 28, 94, 101
Barsha, Tony 149
Bart, Lionel 49, 118
Bartels, Christa 63, 100
Bartenieff, George 148
Bartlett, Bridget 28, 29
Bartlett, Dan 25
Bartlett, Jeff 40, 69, 148
Bartlett, Kevin 33
Bartlett, Neil 75, 152
Barton, John 60
Barton, Samuel 67, 144, 146
Bassi, Leo 97
Batdorf, Erika 157
Bates, Hank 18
Bateson, Kathy 153
Battle, Richard 99, 155
Battley, Wade 15
Bauer, Beaver D. 10, 11, 23, 52, 81, 82, 84, 132
Bauer, Irvin S. 26
Bauer, Jeff 27, 90, 98, 160
Baugh, Gary 90, 98
Baum, L. Frank 140
Baxter, Ernest 93
Bayes, Christopher 148
Bazarini, Ronald 19
Bazewicz, James 26, 94
Bcker, Victor 9
Beagle, Peter S. 72
Beagley, Lee 152
Beaird, David 80
Bealco, Angelo 149
Beals, Teri 53

Beasley, Brian 152
Beattie, Kurt 140
Beatty, Eric 157
Beatty, John Lee 37, 60, 79, 83, 96, 139, 142, 144
Beaumarchais, Pierre-Augustin de 33, 98, 120
Beck, Ann 152
Beck, Carl 91
Beck, Dennis 33
Beck, Susan 91
Beck, Terry 152
Becker, Alma 81, 92, 93
Becker, Duane P. 127
Becker, Georgia 133
Becker, Victor 9, 50, 58, 59, 87, 128, 144, 145
Beckett, Nancy 33
Beckett, Samuel 7, 23, 26, 47, 76, 77, 80, 81, 82, 94, 98, 102, 127, 134, 145, 156
Becvar, William 145, 146
Bedford, Ruth 93
Beeman, Andrea 73
Beesley, Christopher 35
Behan, Brendan 59, 98, 123
Behn, Aphra 60
Behrman, S.N. 45
Beilke, Bill 130
Belasco, David 138
Belcher, David 146
Belden, Ursula 59, 117, 161
Belgrader, Andrei 43, 166, 167
Belknap, Allen R. 8, 57, 58, 109, 113, 114, 116
Bell, Barbara 73, 114, 92, 94
Bell, Chester 110
Bell, David H. 55
Bell, Neal 51, 104, 120
Ballamy, Lou 110
Belli, Keith 8, 18
Belli, Mary Lou 31
Belville, Lance S. 61, 62
Benedetti, Robert 131
Benedict, Paul 83, 85
Benet, Stephen Vincent 162
Benge, Cheryl 158, 159
Bengele, Rosemary 101
Benjamin, Randy 120
Benjudah, Saidah 53
Benmussa, Simone 164
Benner, Vikki 112
Bennet, Alan 153
Bennett, Frank 28, 29
Bennett, Mark 90
Bennett, Sid 13, 14, 158
Bennett, Suzanne 93
Benson, Ben 155
Benson, Martin 138, 139
Bensussen, Melia 82, 149, 150
Bentley, Eric 57, 134
Berbe, Betty 100
Berc, Shelley 43
Berek, Clifford E. 141
Berezin, Tanya 36
Berg, Catherine 102
Berg, Steven 66
Berger, Sidney 8
Berger, Thomas 61, 62
Bergh, Kate 31
Berglund, John 12

Bergman, Andrew 71, 90
Bergsman, Rolfe 20
Bergstein, David 121
Berkey, Bob 152
Berkoff, Steven 96
Berkson, Jeff 98
Berlin, Irving 15
Berlin, Pamela 92, 161, 166
Berliner, Charles 39, 87
Berlinger, Robert 31, 39, 95, 98, 101, 145
Berlovitz, Sonya 148
Berman, Irene B. 23, 64
Berman, Norman L. 92
Bermel, Albert 12, 63
Bernard, Ken 102
Bernstein, Jeffrey A. 15
Bernstein, Leonard 9, 10, 14, 16, 19, 36, 60, 68, 126
Bernstein, Mark D. 125
Berry, Brenda 131
Berry, Gabriel 43, 72, 80, 96, 97, 144, 149, 150
Besser, Gedalia 126
Besset, Jean-Marie 102
Bessey, Clarice 63
Beusussen, Melia 94
Beuttler, Guy 66
Bewley, David Malcolm 12, 13
Bianchi, James 150
Bickel, Rachel 65
Biedenstein, Larry 125
Biege, Carla M. 92
Bielefeldt, Fumiko 81, 82, 154, 155
Bigelow, Dennis 106, 129, 130
Bill, Mary 61
Biller, Ken 31
Billig, Etel 68, 69
Billig, Steve S 68, 69
Billings, Bryan 33
Billings, Glenn 160
Billings, Jim 94, 95
Billingsley, Jr., Morgan 95
Billington, Ken 83, 108
Bill, Mary 61
Bingham, Sallie 67
Binkley, Howell 12
Birch, Patricia 20
Birk, Raye 30
Birn, David 149, 166, 167
Birturk, Ricia 34, 35
Bishop, Andre 120
Bishop, Conrad 38, 56, 70
Bishop, John 37, 55, 69
Bishop, Linda 70
Bishop, Monica 119
Bixby, Jonathan 26, 73
Black, George 28
Black, William Electric 105
Blacker, Robert 74
Blackman, Michael 18
Blackman, Robert 10, 23, 84, 139
Blackwell, Sam 36, 125
Blackwell, Vera 32
Blair, Barbara 153
Blair, D. Bartlett 36
Blair, Randy 14
Blake, Jeanne 42
Blake, Paul 10
Blakemore, Michael 83
Blanchard, Mary 149, 150

Blase, Linda 44
Blau, Eric 21, 109, 161
Blau, Frances 24, 117, 141
Bleackley, Carol 98
Bleasdale, Alan 131
Blecher, Hilary 90, 130
Blessing, Lee 13, 16, 18, 19, 42, 59, 66, 75, 83, 95, 109, 123, 142, 144, 151, 152, 154, 161, 167
Bliss, Terry 151
Blitgen, Carol 159
Blitzstein, Marc 61, 79, 131, 138
Block, Richard 5, 38, 85, 155, 155
Bloodgood, William 8, 101, 105, 106, 129
Bloom, Michael 9, 93, 114, 138, 166
Blount, Jr., Roy 11
Blu 42, 117
Bluff, Jim 39
Blum, Gregory 3
Blume, Judy 17
Bly, Robert 49
Bochard, Bruce 117
Bock, Jerry 109
Boddy, Claudia 90, 160
Bodenheim, Althea 150
Bodwell, Maggie 160
Boesing, Martha 6, 19
Bogart, Anne 12, 89, 126, 157
Bogosian, Eric 38, 51, 66, 81, 96, 119, 159
Bohmler, Craig 104
Bohr, Jimmy 51, 128
Boles, Peter 115
Bolinger, Don 18
Bollinger, Michael 152
Bolt, Jonathan 5, 155
Bolt, Robert 50
Bolton, Guy 60, 61, 76, 77, 116
Bonczek, Rose 126
Bond, Edward 7
Bond, Tim 50, 133
Bonde, Susan 27, 122
Bones, Pamela Gray 8
Bones, Rebecca Nesbitt 14
Bonnard, Raymond 143
Bonnell, Dan 9
Bontems, Dennis 33
Booker, Margaret 107, 166
Booker, Megs 30, 104
Bookman, Kirk 36, 57, 59, 61, 117, 161
Bookwalter, D. Martyn 63, 79, 84, 85, 109, 122, 131, 139
Boone, Fontella 93
Booth, Ken 76
Borbes, Barbara 13
Borden, Noel 15
Boretz, Allen 116
Borgenicht, Nancy 130
Borges, Jorge Luis 71
Borgeson, Jess 31
Boring, Jeff 13, 14
Bornstein, Stephen L. 89
Borski, Russel 61, 92
Borsodi, Bob 149, 150
Boruzescu, Miruna 15, 64
Boruzescu, Radu 15, 64
Bosakowski, Phil 45
Bostick, Joe 29

INDEX OF NAMES

Boswell, William 47
Bouchard, Bruce 30, 117
Bourne, Bette Bloolips 149, 150
Bowe, Alan 130
Bowen, Ken 87, 98, 163
Bowers, Frank O. 101
Bowers, Jill C. 154, 155
Bowles, Paul 26
Bowne, Alan 8, 123
Bowns, Kate 112
Boyd, George 30
Boyd, Gregory 8, 141
Boyd, Julianne 26, 81, 83, 89, 101, 118, 122, 154, 164
Boyd, Melinda 54, 55
Boyd, Ruth 117
Boyer, Michael 118
Boyer, Vladimir 131
Boyle, Jeff 99
Boylen, Dan 115
Boylen, Daniel P. 113
Boynton, Brad 151
Bozark, Kim Allen 125, 126
Boznos, Jennifer 123
Bozzone, Bill 38, 51
Bracewell, Loren 119, 146
Bradac, Thomas F. 63
Bradberry, Erica 31
Bradberry, Laurence 31
Bradford, Bill 149
Bradley, Frank 143
Bradley, Scott 9, 10, 15, 58, 80, 81, 101, 117, 123
Brady, John 155
Brady, Veronica 18, 110
Brafford, Patrick 13
Brailey, Pamela 163
Brailsford, Pauline 26, 27
Bramble, Mark 74
Brame, Loren 40, 137
Bramon, Risa 51
Brandt, Christy 158
Brandt, Victor 99
Branescu, Smaranda 12, 16, 85, 136
Bras, Steven 25
Brasch, Thomas 97
Brassard, Gail 24, 71, 78, 109, 113
Braukis, Susan 99
Braun, Kazimierz 99
Braverman, Douglas 20
Breault, Michael 39
Brecht, Bertolt 24, 39, 61, 123, 134, 162, 164
Brel, Jacques 21, 109, 161
Brennan, Mary Catherine 4
Brenner, Donald 105
Brenton, Howard 64
Breskin, David 39
Breslin, Jimmy 5
Breuer, Lee 80, 157
Breul, Garry Allan 18, 19
Brevoort, Gregg W. 112
Brewster, Karen 21
Bricaire, Jean-Jacques 38
Briggs, David 149, 150
Briggs, Jody 4
Briggs, John R. 50, 53, 107
Briggs, Raymond 22
Brightman, Candace 109
Brilliande, Karen 67

Brink, David 102
Brisson, Bruce 52
Broadhurst, Alan 140
Brock, Jr., Ed 3
Brockway, Adrienne J. 104, 105
Brockway, Amie 104, 105
Brody, Alan 36
Brody, Leslie 35
Broekhuis, Robert 152
Brogger, Erik 4, 44
Brohan, Paul 20
Brokaw, Mark 53, 82, 135
Brolaski, Carol 85
Bronte, Charlotte 35, 147
Brooke, Haynes 3
Brooks, Jr., John Hancock 159, 160
Brooks, Alfred 33
Brooks, Donald L. 150
Brooks, Jeremy 46, 119, 120
Brophy, Chris 82
Brothers Grimm, 53
Brown, A. Whitney 11
Brown, Arvin 78, 79, 162, 167
Brown, Carlyle 110, 143
Brown, Claudia 40, 64, 97, 162
Brown, Dawnetta 130
Brown, Dean 61
Brown, Jamie 18, 19, 45, 85
Brown, Jeff 162
Brown, John 131
Brown, John Russell 36
Brown, Kent R. 18, 26
Brown, Lewis 101, 102, 134
Brown, Michael Newton 119
Brown, Nacio Herb 116
Brown, Pat 8, 18, 19
Brown, Paul 77
Brown, Phillip Erskine 110
Brown, Steve 92
Brown, Tom 135
Brown, Tony 152, 161
Brown, Zack 16
Brownfield, Eleanor 135
Browning, Barry 34, 35, 69
Browning, Robert 118
Browning, William 87, 115
Bruckman, Bruck 112
Bruice, Ann 79, 80, 85
Brumbach, Joan U. 151
Brumeau, Ainslie G. 18
Brumlik, Fran 90
Bruneau, Ainslie G. 18, 19
Bruneaux, Debra 106, 129, 130
Brune, David 19
Brunet, David 6
Bruno, Anthony 153
Brunson, Deborah L. 94
Brunswick, Nancy 87
Brustein, Robert 11, 12
Bryant, Ken 44, 158
Buch, Rene 11, 124, 125
Buchanan, Linda 60, 98, 136, 163
Buchman, Nanrose 3, 4
Buchner, Georg 63
Buck, Gene Davis 16, 35, 51
Buck, Pearl S. 28
Buckley, Jr., William F. 6
Buckley, Mike 75, 76
Budde, Jordan 8

Budenholzer, Joe 102
Buderwitz, Thomas 16, 122, 131
Budin, Rachel 58, 59, 71, 123, 143, 145, 161, 162
Buero-Vallejo, Antonio 163
Buff, Jim 59, 125
Buffalo, Becke 97
Buffington, Ray 138
Bullard, Thomas 8, 98, 101
Bullock, Beverly 28
Bundy, James 39
Burch, Thayer Q. 89
Burdett, Patricia 28
Burdman, Ralph 24
Burgess, Anthony 106
Burgess, Jeanine 59
Burgler, Terry 153, 154
Burke, Elizabeth 32
Burke, Mary-Claire 21
Burkell, Scott 51
Burkhart, Laura 158, 159
Burleson, Kathryn 129, 130
Burmeister, Leslie 146
Burnell, Peter 33
Burnett, Frances Hodgson 9, 35, 49, 133, 152
Burnett, W.R. 107
Burns, Ron 150
Burns, Tim 149, 150
Burnstein, James 20
Burrows, Abe 71, 92
Burton, Irving 150
Burton, Ron 155
Burwinkel, James J. 143, 152
Busby, Barbara 47
Busch, Charles 60, 166
Bush, Barbara 24, 73, 94, 135
Bush, Beatrice 151
Bush, David 131
Bushnell, Bill 79, 80
Bushor, Geoffrey 60, 90, 92, 107, 124
Bussert, Victoria 61
Butcher, Vada 143
Butler, Eugenia 48
Butler, Rick 123
Butsch, Tom 16, 35
Buttars, Michael 130
Button, Jeanne 61, 96, 101, 135, 162
Butts, Nancy 100
Butts, Tom 29
Byrne, Carolyn 33
Byron, Ellen 105, 114, 151

C

C., Curtis 118
Cacaci, Joe 8, 96
Cacheiro, Jorge 82
Cada, James 6
Cadwell, Connie 62
Cain, Bill 85, 106
Cain, Candice 106, 161
Cain, Ruth 159
Cairns, James 158
Calandra, Dale 32, 33
Calder, Jim 157
Calderon de la Barca, Pedro 12, 53, 138

Caldwell, Charles 7, 8, 36, 153, 154
Caldwell, Connie 69
Caldwell, Scott 133
Caligiuri, Mark 42
Calkins, Annie 112
Call, Edward Payson 16
Cambridge, Edmund 80, 113
Camburn, Herbert L. 88
Cameron-Webb, Gavin 88, 109
Camicia, Jimmy 149
Camille 53
Campbell, Bob 66
Campbell, Clifton 31
Campbell, Jane 66
Campbell, Sarah 4, 22
Campbell, Stancil 39
Campbell, Suzy 137
Campton, David 125
Canac-Marquis, Normand 93, 138
Cannon, Jack 112
Cannon, Rick 18, 19
Cantwell, Peter 7, 69
Capatorto, Carl 150
Capek, Karel 98
Capote, Truman 39, 46
Capriolla, Nina 153
Carballido, Emilio 25, 123, 131
Card, James 106
Cardina, Carmella 135
Cardwell, Betsy P. 39
Carelton, Rex 133
Carey, Alison 39
Carey, Julia 42
Carey, Melissa 105
Cariello, Thomas 128
Caristi, Vincent 57, 146, 161
Carlin, Joy 10
Carlisle, Barbara 36
Carlisle, Ward 80
Carlos, Laurie 93
Carlsen, Allan 59, 92
Carlson, Harry G. 105
Carlton, Don 158
Carlton, Rex 133
Carmines, Al 153
Carnelia, Craig 3, 14, 42, 54, 98
Carney, Kim 26
Carpenter, Cassandra 52, 132
Carpenter, Jack 49
Carpenter, Larry 9, 13, 57, 68, 86, 129, 138
Carpenter, Mel 115
Carr, Charles 18
Carr, G. 132
Carr, Greg 22
Carren, Lois 7
Carroll, Brad 108, 109
Carroll, Lewis 90
Carson, Andrew 141
Carson, Heather 143
Carson, Jo 127
Carter, Christopher 21
Carter, Keithen 110
Carter, Lonnie 104
Carter, Nina 150
Carter, Steve 80, 93
Carter, Thomas G. 31
Cartier, Jacques 68
Cartmell, Daniel Bryan 63
Cartwright, Jim 52, 77

arver, Mark 59
ascio, Anna Theresa 31
asement, Barbara 112
asey, Lawrence 36, 61, 161
asona, Alejandro 124
asper, Richard 108
assone, Linda 69
astellino, Bill 54, 166
astenera, Rafael Colon 130
astro, Robert 49
astro, Vicente 123
ate, Regina 81, 82
ates, Nancy 151, 154
avander, Kenneth 63, 162
ave, Jim 49, 135
aves, Richard 146
awley, Terry 3
ederberg, Kerry 75, 76
entlivre, Susanna 7
crasani, Jeanne 53
ermak, Terry 151, 153, 154
ernovitch, Nick 68
esario, Michael J. 57
hamberlain, Marisha 35, 140
hamberlin, Ann 70
hambers, David 139, 167
hambers, David Kirk 130
hambers, Jane 153
hambliss, Scott 36
hampa, Russell 44
hampagne, Michael 20, 69
hampion, Marge 24
handler, Jack 161, 162
handler, Terrance 11
handler, Terry 93
hang, Tisa 107
hapin, Edwin 86, 165
hapin, Harry 76, 100, 117
hapman, Alan 112
hapman, John 101
hapman, Linda 93, 164
hapman, Mark 118
hapman, Michael 129, 130
hapman, Mike 31, 109
happell, Wallace 66
harbonneau, Nan 26
harlap, Mark 9, 50, 154, 155
harles, David 39
harles, Jill 14, 15
harney, Tina 42, 59, 103, 104, 107, 115, 144, 145
harnin, Martin 44, 89, 96
hartier-Serban, Juell 153
hase, Mary 5, 78
hase, Susan 157
haves, Richard 57, 161
havez, Antonio 153
havez, Josie 48, 49
hayefsky, Paddy 111
hekhov, Anton 7, 12, 15, 22, 38, 43, 44, 58, 61, 73, 80, 84, 107, 137, 140, 158
hepulis, Kyle 152
heranich, Veronique 149
herney, Christopher 149
hervinsky, Alexander 64
hesley, Marie 23
hesley, Robert 156
hevan, Julie Abels 94
hew, Timothy M. 21
hiang, Dawn 35

Chiclana, Margarita Lopez 123
Childress, Alice 87
Chiment, Marie Anne 5
Chin, Glen 48
Chodorov, Jerome 60
Chong, Ping 87, 107, 115
Chontik 149
Chopin, Kate 67
Chow, Jovita 10
Chris, Marilyn 74
Christen, Robert 60, 98, 124, 142
Christian, Kace 14
Christie, Agatha 18, 19, 21, 118, 132, 158
Christina, Kia 51
Christy, Jim 94, 114
Chugg, Eliza 19, 24
Church, Philip M. 54
Churchill, Caryl 23, 24, 36, 96, 161
Chybowski, Michael 57, 93, 123
Cibula, Nan 60, 76, 77, 98
Ciulei, Liviu 12, 16, 63, 85
Clapper, Joseph W. 88, 159
Clark, Bob 21
Clark, David 147
Clark, Dennis 71
Clark, Denny 55, 56
Clark, Helen 28
Clark, James A. 145
Clark, Jane 86
Clark, L.J. 33
Clark, Robert F. 17
Clark, Stephen 152
Clark, Willam 118
Clarke, Bill 7, 12, 71, 117, 119, 120, 161, 166
Clarke, Darren 13
Clarke, Martha 96, 134
Claudel, Paul 73, 73
Clay, Diskin 66
Clay, Paul 149
Clayburgh, Jim 40, 165
Clayton, Anne 140
Cleveland, Rick 20, 39
Cleveland, Sally 131
Clevenger, Jo Ann 164
Clifford, John 137
Clifford, Mikel 23
Clifton, Deborah 156
Clifton, John 155
Clifton, Pamela 33
Clinton, George 43, 44
Clinton, Marion 121
Clipper, Craig 81, 123, 166
Cloeman, Lorilee 86
Cloud, Darrah 27, 52, 112, 159, 164
Clough, Peter 30, 86
Cluchey, Rick 99
Clyman, Robert 103
Coates, Donald 33
Coates, Nelson 140
Cobb, Benajah 40
Coberg, Wally 110
Coble, McKay 120
Coburn, D.L. 56, 95
Cochran, Randy 158
Cochren, Felix E. 20, 42
Cocke, Dudley 127
Cocol, Jane 149
Coggins, David 148

Cohen, Alan 50
Cohen, Douglas J. 54, 155
Cohen, Edward M. 73, 74
Cohen, Gregory 44
Cohen, Jason S. 95
Cohen, Larry 73
Cohen, Madeline 98
Cohen, Michael 69
Cohen, Norman 48
Cohen, Shura 89
Cohn, Marta 115
Coker, Flora 156
Coker, Jerry 45
Colavecchia, Franco 128, 137
Colby, Michael 57
Cole, Bruce W. 11
Cole, Holly 117
Cole, Laurie 29
Cole, Tom 57
Coleman, Christina 14
Coleman, Lorilee 59
Coleman, Steve 84
Coles, Stephen 126
Coll, Ivonne 123
Collings, Nancy 138
Collins, A.M. 100, 119
Collins, Dian 38
Collins, Kathleen A. 56
Collins, Pat 4, 23, 24, 30, 32, 55, 64, 77, 79, 83, 84, 96, 115, 121, 134, 143, 162
Collins, Randi 33
Collodi, Carlo 126
Cologne, Susan 131
Colorado, Vira 150
Colville, Bruce 155
Combs, Greg 109
Comden, Betty 16, 60, 116
Commire, Anne 103, 167
Condino, David 59
Condon, Frank 63, 100
Cone, Jeff 9, 157
Congdon, Constance 6, 24, 34, 35, 92, 93, 126
Congdon, Sally 164
Conger, Trista 33
Conklin, John 0, 5, 32, 60, 64, 77, 79, 88, 96, 162
Conn, Rogue 122, 133, 146
Connell, Gordon 86
Connelly, Mary M. 33
Conner, Bill 34
Connor, Alison 155
Connor, Jim 44
Connor, Martin 60, 61
Conrad, Kathryn K. 21
Conway-Wilson, Kim 152
Conway, Dan 163
Conway, Daniel 78, 155
Conway, Kevin 166
Cook, Allan 81
Cook, Christine 3, 135
Cook, Kevin 63
Cook, Michael 23, 29, 30
Cook, Peter 153
Cook, Roderick 122
Cook, Stoney 152
Cooke, Thomas P. 38
Cooley, Eileen 100
Coombs, Amy 150
Cooney, Ray 108

Cooney, Robert 149
Coons, Carol 151
Cooper, Cynthia L. 155
Cooper, David 111
Cooper, Judith 35
Cooper-Hecht, Gail 11
Cooperman, Morris 138
Coppedge, Rosanna 158
Corin, Robert 3
Cormack, Bartlett 138
Corneille, Pierre 97
Cornelison, Gayle 29, 30
Cornell, Allen 53
Cornell, Michelle Frenzer 105
Cornett, Ewel 5
Cornish, Roger 8, 113, 126
Cornthwaite, Robert 15, 16, 106, 128
Cornwall, Bruce 65
Correa, Stephanie 21
Corrigan, Robert W. 44
Corrin, Dean 159
Corso, Arturo 79
Corson, Daniel J. 101
Corti, James 69
Corwen, Carol 100, 138
Corwin, Walter 149, 150
Corzatte, Clayton 9
Cosentino, Laura 102
Cosier, Jr., E. David 60, 68, 102
Cosier, David 71
Cosler, Charles 36
Coss, Clare 11
Cossa, Roberto 123, 125
Costa, Ann Marie 152
Costello, Elizabeth 138
Costigan, Ken 21
Costin, James D. 87, 88
Cottom, Michael 62, 89
Coulter, Allen 74
Courts, Randy 28
Cousin, Tome 38
Couture, Jeff 121
Covan, Jennie 22
Covault, Jim 140, 141
Covey, Elizabeth 85
Coward, Noel 7, 21, 29, 30, 53, 58, 72, 86, 95, 117, 122
Cox, Douglas 25
Cox, Susan 95
Coy, Peter 105
Crabtree, Abigail 43, 44
Crabtree, Amelie 43, 44
Crabtree, Jim 43, 44
Crabtree, Mary 43, 44
Crabtree, Paul 43
Crain, Gene 118
Crane, Cathy 20
Crank, David 7, 153, 154
Cranney, Jon 34, 35
Crawford, Nicholas 81
Craze, Peter 154
Creevey, Rae 48
Crews, Harry 6
Crinkley, Richmond 136
Crisp, N.J. 79
Crisp, Tom 91
Cristofer, Michael 126
Crocker, Warner 107
Crodtz, Wendell 150
Croghan, Robert 140

176 INDEX OF NAMES

Crotts, Susan 130
Crouse, Russell 76, 77, 88, 116
Crouse, Timothy 76, 77
Crow, Laura 4, 37, 59, 60, 117, 142
Crush, Lance 31
Cruz, Migdalia 71, 92, 103, 121
Cruz, Nilo 53
Crysler, Kevin 3
Csicsko, David Lee 106
Cuddy, Mark 129, 130
Cuetara, Laura 58
Culbert, Bobbi 16
Culbert, John 28
Cullen, Judith 145
Cullinan, Francis 159
Culman, Peter W. 31
Culpepper, Stuart 156
Cumming, Richard 44, 158
Cummings, Howard 117
Cummings, Michael 149, 150
Cummins, Rick 155
Cunningham, Laura 60, 92, 124, 161, 163
Cuomo, Jimmy 31
Curchack, Fred 44, 152
Curiel, Tony 48, 49, 132
Curley, Bill 33
Curran, Keith 37
Curran, Margot 148
Currin, Brenda 114
Curry, Bob 107
Curtis, Burton 17
Curtis, Richard 40
Curtis, Roger 59
Curtis, Simon 77
Custer, John F. 158
Custer, Marianne 38, 120
Cutler, R.J. 24, 92, 93, 97, 120, 155
Cyrus, Edgar A. 147

D

Dacunto, Michael 111
Dahdan, Robert 149
Dahl, Roald 66, 133
Dahlstrom, Robert 72
D'Albis, Donato J. 166
Dalin, Howard 34
Dallas, L.B. 80
Dallas, Walter 42, 113, 114
Dallin, Howard 42
Daly, Jonathan Gillard 109
Damashek, Barbara 5, 98, 139
Damon, Stuart 20
Dana, F. Mitchell 7, 8, 59, 64, 85, 113, 120, 124, 128, 129, 145
Dana, Maurice 51
Dancy, Virginia 5
Danforth, Laurie 20
Danforth, Roger 39
Dangerfield, Cory 130
Daniele, Graciela 61, 71, 75, 101, 135
Danieli, Gil 51, 59
Daniels, Ajax 99
Daniels, M.R. 114, 115
Daniels, Paul S. 120
Danis, Louison 93, 138

Danner, Dorothy 45
D'Annunzio, Gabriele 150
Danstheater Nan Romijn 152
Dante, Nicholas 48
Daoust, Barbara 153
Dara, Olu 93
Darbon, Leslie 118
Dardenne, James 90, 159, 160
Darion, Joe 47, 65, 118
Darling, Robert 137
D'Arms, Ted 22, 133
Darnell, August 135
Darnell, Rick 153
Darnutzer, Don 16
Dartt, Gary 98
Daseler, Robert 139
Daughhetee, Kathryn 112
Daughtry, Michael 111, 112
Davenport, Dennis 43, 44
David, Jeff Cone 9
Davidson, Gordon 85
Davidson, Jeannie 106
Davidson, John B. 17
Davidson, N.R. 74
Davies, Ray 75
Davis, Anthony 104
Davis, Bill C. 15, 18
Davis, Christopher 114
Davis, Clinton Turner 11, 155, 161
Davis, David S.S. 90
Davis, Debbie 54
Davis, Donald 28
Davis, Donna 153
Davis, Eddie 60
Davis, Jeff 9, 24, 39, 108, 113, 137
Davis, Jeffrey B. 128
Davis, John Henry 113, 120, 155
Davis, Kate 118
Davis, Lindsay 9, 57, 60, 96, 129, 160
Davis, Montgomery 87
Davis, Owen 28
Davis, Peter 72
Davis, Rick 45
Davis, Russell 3, 92, 126
Davis, Ted 123, 147
D'Beck, Patti 116
Deal, Dennis 0
De Angelis, Maude 111
Dean, Hamilton 13, 14, 88
Dean, Jeffrey 18, 19, 54
Dean, Phillip Hayes 110
Deardorff, Charlotte 26
Dearing, Judy 42, 50, 61, 93, 96, 114, 145, 164
de Barbieri, Mary Ann 136
de Beaumont, Janne Marie Leprince 53
Debussy, Claude 53
Decker, Gary 20
Decker, Pat 69
Decker, Tim 118
DeCuir, L.J. 38
Deegan, John Michael 35
Deegan, Michael 72, 80
Deer, Sandra 9, 13, 20, 66, 69, 95, 118, 125
De Falla, Manuel 124
De Filippo, Eduardo 68
DeForest, Charles 10
DeFrank, Robert 128

Degan, Diane 102
De Groot, John 54
DeGroot, Neil 119
de Haas, Henk 115
Dehner, Jennifer 130
DeJarnett, Greg 165
De Jongh, James 74
Dekker, Thomas 136
de Laclos, Choderlos 3, 5, 7, 13, 39, 44, 134, 161
Delacour, Alfred 63
Delaney, D.D. 70
Delapenha, Denise 90
de la Tour, Andy 52
DeLaurier, Peter 38
DeLaurier, Roger 109
Del Campo, Patricia 133
del Campo, Patricio 146
DeLillo, Don 146
DeLorme, Lee 133, 156
de Lotbiniere, Christine Jolygn 12
Del Tredici, David 90
Delu, Dahl 34
deMaat, Martin 92
de Maupassant, Guy 58
DeMichele, Mark 18
de Molina, Tirso 43, 124, 125
Dempsey, Michael 118
Dempster, Curt 51
de Musset, Alfred 5, 148
Denhan, Reginald 18
Dennis, Ian 53
Dennis, Rick 117, 121, 141
Denniston, Mick 101
D'Entremont, James 104
dePaola, Tomie 34
dePaul, Gene 43
Depenbrock, Jay 36
De Raey, Daniel 161
Deremer, Laura 63
Deren, Nancy Greenstein 150
de Rojas, Fernando 124
DeRoux, Daniel 112
Desbois, Barbra Berlovitz 147, 148
Desbois, Frederic 69, 70, 148
Deschamps, Gail 53
DeShields, Andre 47, 159
Desvallieres, Maurice 158
Detweiler, Lowell 7, 8, 9, 13, 14, 35, 60
Deutsch, Nicholas 153
Devin, Lee 111
Devin, Richard 51, 72, 145
Devine, Jerry 100
Devine, Michael 139
De Volder, Max 125, 126
Dewell, Michael 25, 101
Dexter, John 46, 47, 106, 109
D'Hanson, Dawn 62
D'Hont, Rudy 150
Dhyanis 84
Diamond, J. Lois 149
Diamond, Liz 27, 93, 138
Diamond, Sallie 33, 57, 58
Diaz, Jorge 25
Dick, Ming 139
Dick, Philip K. 80
Dickens, Charles 3, 4, 5, 7, 10, 14, 16, 18, 29, 30, 39, 44, 50, 55, 58, 59, 60, 61, 63, 64, 66, 69, 72, 86,

87, 88, 91, 92, 94, 95, 98, 105, 123, 129, 130, 131, 139, 141, 146, 158, 163
Dickerson, Glenda 143
Dickerson, Mel 125, 143, 152
Dickey, Johanna 154
Dicks, Goldie 74
Dickson, Ben 84
Dickson, Kay 112
Diderot, Denis 43
DiDonna, Eddie 149
Diekmann, Nancy Kassak 96
Dietz, Steven 4, 6, 27, 38, 69, 80, 81, 121, 128, 163
DiFusco, John 57, 110, 133, 146, 161
DiGesu, Traci 150
Diggs, Elizabeth 30
Dignan, Joe 81
Dignan, Pat 40, 97, 150, 164
Diller, Elizabeth 40
Dilliard, Marcus 63, 64, 120
Dillon, John 87, 113
DiMartino, Nick 66
Dimmick, Kathleen 93
Dinmore, Casey Cameron 66
Diosdado, Ana 124
Dipaola, James 71
Ditzler, Grant 152
Dixcy, Marcia 6
Dixon, Catherine 8
Dixon, Jim 26
Dixon, Kenneth R. 153
Dmitriev, Alex 5, 36, 98, 113
Dobbins, Ray 149, 150
Dobrusky, Pavel 5, 35, 47, 80, 1, 161
Dobson, Renee 138
Dodd, John P. 149, 150
Dodd, Joseph 66, 67
Dodd, Terry 33
Dodge, Jr., Norman 56
Dodge, Marcia Milgran 141
Doe, Andrew 81, 82
Doepel, Esther 59
Doepp, John 161
Doherty, Clayton 29, 30
Doherty, Patricia E. 8
Dolan, Judith 12, 136, 137
Dolas, Theodore M. 23
Domm, Dale 140, 141
Donahue, John 89
Donahue, John Clark 16
Donarski, Terry 87
Donat, Peter 3
Dondlinger, Mary Jo 28, 29, 61
Donnelly, Candice 12, 32, 43, 79, 83, 120, 122, 134, 135, 137, 16
Donnelly, John 38
Donnelly, Kyle 35, 60, 90
Donnelly, Mark 131
Donoso, Jose 112
Dooley, Raymond 149
Dorfman, Richard 107
Dorsey, Kent 16, 23, 52, 79, 101, 121, 131
Dorton, Moses 43
Dostoyevsky, Fyodor 44, 158
Doty, Pat 53, 87, 115
Dougherty, Carol 24
Douglas, B.J. 146

INDEX OF NAMES 177

ouglas, Donald 55
outhit, Lue 33
owd, A. Elizabeth 25
ow, Ivy 102
owney, Reid 20
owney, Roger 25, 39, 75, 97, 99, 158
owse, Sean M, 42
oyle, Arthur Conan 13, 133, 155
oyle, Kimberly B. 152
oyle, Patrick 119
ozier, Jennifer 151
ozortsev, Vladlen 6
rachman, Ted 118, 155
raghici, Marina 97, 166, 167
rake, Gillian 128
rapeau, Donald A. 127
raper, David F. 80
raper, Ingra 130
rawbaugh, Laura 74, 123
recktrah, Anne 31
resser, Richard 5, 42, 59, 79, 92
ressler, Ralph 5, 6
retsch, Curtis 109, 110
rexler, Rosalyn 102, 103
reyer, Joseph R. 125
reyfuss, Randy 100
river, Donald 143, 154
river, John 89, 160
robny, Christopher 92, 121
royan, Alan 19
rury, Bob 101
ryden, Deborah 23, 75, 106
ryer, Joseph R. 125
uarte, Derek 10, 132
uarte, Myrna 149, 150
uBrock, Neal 143
uer, Fred 31, 99, 131
uffey, Gordon 112
ukakis, Apollo 161
ukakis, Olympia 161
uke, Edward 101
uke, Stuart 13, 71, 109, 115, 123, 138
ukes, Gerry 76
ulack, Tom 102, 163
umas, Alexandre 5, 71, 107
umas, Deborah 164
umas, Debra 90, 121
uncan, Susan G. 23
uncan, William B. 9, 58
unham, Clarke 61
unham, Gwen 52
unkelberger, Beth 56, 70
unlap, Richard 24
unn, Glenn 125, 126, 143, 152
unn, Margaret Anne 80
unn, Thomas 35
unnigan, Ann 137
unning, Philip 12
upree, Tom 95
uran, Coleen 118
urang, Christopher 4, 18, 24, 33, 44, 84, 87, 119, 120, 121, 128, 131, 137, 141, 167
uras, Marguerite 150
urbin, Holly Poe 125, 126
urfee, Duke 50
urkee, Norman 115
urrenmatt, Friedrich 44

Dusseault, David 146
Dworin, Judy 152
Dyer, Tom 29, 30

E

Earle, Edward 28
Eastman, Donald 11, 43, 67, 72, 80, 96, 144, 149, 150, 164
Eaton, Jonathan 36
Ebb, Fred 154, 160, 162
Ecenia, T.J. 146
Eckert, Rinde 152
Eckhart, Gary 140
Eckstrom, Peter 20
Edelblut, Craig 108
Edelen, Terri 33
Edelstein, Gordon 24, 30, 92, 93, 115
Edens, Cooper 17
Edgar, David 62
Edgerton, Earle 7
Edmiston, Scott 110
Edmondson, James 106
Edmonds, Robert 155
Edmunds, Kate 23, 68, 109, 132
Edwards, Ben 167
Edwards, Cathleen 10, 23, 52
Edwards, Jack 63, 64
Edwards, Richard 122
Edwards, Shannon 29, 30
Edwards, Sherman 108
Edwards, Tom 54, 66
Efremoff, Andrei 162, 163
Egan, Kathleen 26, 109, 110
Egan, Robert 84, 85
Eglar-Bilsky, Tere 38
Egloff, Elizabeth 121, 167
Ehlert, Matt 149
Ehre, Milton 80
Eicher, Chris 8
Eich, Stephen B. 142
Eigsti, Karl 15, 16, 68, 113
Einhorn, Susan 161
Eisenberg, Ned 114
Eisenhauer, Peggy 61, 71, 75, 101, 135
Eisenman, Nancy 100
Eisloeffel, Elizabeth 152
Eister, Karen 12
Ekstrom, Peter 5, 6, 89, 119
Elder, Eldon 50, 145
Elder, Lauren 52
Elder, III, Lonnie 11
Elder, Suzanne 85
Elice, Eric 9
Eliot, T.S. 71, 73
Eliott, Kenneth 166
Elisha, Rina 150
Elisha, Ron 98
Elitzig, Francis 30, 66
Elkin, Stanley 90
Eller, Cecelia 128
Ellington, Duke 42
Elliot, Alice 105
Elliot, Kenneth 166
Elliot, Tony 128
Elliott, Holly 3
Elliott, Ken 96

Elliott, Marianna 79, 80, 84
Ellis, Chris 118
Ellis, Ken 81, 93, 99, 155
Ellis, Paul 92
Ellis, Richard 14, 89
Ellis, Scott 160, 162
Ellis, Vivian 60
Elmer, J. Patrick 145, 146
Elson, Steve 90
Elvgren, Jr., Gillette 130, 131
Emerson, Eric E. 57, 146, 161
Emerson, Jonathan 31
Emmes, David 138, 139
Emmett, Robert 86
Emmons, Beverly 15, 39, 43, 64, 71, 85, 96, 120, 148
Emonts, Ann 37
Engle, Brian 135
Engler, Michael 12, 32, 83, 122
Engles, Robert 92
English, Gary 13, 14, 86
Enos, Gerry 76
Enos, Jerald R. 109
Enquist, Per Olov 33
Enright, Kobi 122
Ensler, Eve 89, 90
Epp, Steven 148
Epperson, Jane 93, 107
Epps, Sheldon 13, 38, 115
Epstein, Kayla 112
Epstein, Sabin 10
Epton, Paul 20
Erdman, Nikolai 25
Erickson, David Michael 31
Erickson, Michael 51
Erlanger, John 113
Ernotte, Andre 90
Ertl, Fritz 24, 93
Erven, Charles 81
Ervin, Denise 91
Esbjornson, David 51, 79, 83, 92, 166
Eshelman, M.A. 38
Esparza, Phil 48
Esposito, Vickie 114
Essad, Michael 29, 30
Essen, B.J. 47
Essig, Linda 78, 93
Esslin, Martin 32
Esslin, Renata 32
Estes, Jr., Allan B. 153
Etter, Gregory 67
Ettinger, Daniel 21, 78
Euckert, Kyle 26
Euripides 19, 63, 141
Eustis, Oskar 23, 52, 121
Evans, Annie 104
Evans, Craig 166
Evans, Don 42, 127
Evans, John Morgan 118
Evans, Kenneth 110
Evans, Sharon 106
Evans, Will 88
Everett, Claudia 46, 106
Eves, Caroline 22
Ewer, Donald 126
Ewing, Geoff 89
Ewing, James 53
Eyen, Tom 102, 155
Ezell, John 18, 61, 88, 96, 101, 126

F

Fagan, Valerie 158
Fagles, Robert 39
Fain, Sammy 60
Fairbank, Gail 140
Falabella, John 9, 13, 13, 24, 57, 68, 109, 126, 161
Fallon, Dan 116
Falls, Gregory 3, 4, 13, 14, 140
Falls, Robert 60, 64, 75
Fanning, Tony 167
Farid, Zaid 107
Farkash, Roger 95
Farley, Robert J. 9
Farmer, Bill 102, 103
Farquhar, George 144
Farrington, Lynn 42
Faulkner, Cliff 63, 101, 102, 139
Faust, Marianne 109, 161
Faver, Cheryl 97
Favre, June 57
Fayos, Manena 100
Fazio, Gaetano 149
Federici, Mario 150
Federico, Robert W. 124, 125
Fedie, Dan 140
Fehr, Frankie 113, 115
Feiffer, Jules 20, 22, 28, 90, 98
Fein, Judith 5
Feiner, Harry 50, 59, 109, 117, 145
Feingold, Michael 126
Feist, Gene 128
Feldman, Richard 93
Felix, Edmund 149
Fell, Marion 43
Fenhagen, James 113
Fenichell, Susan 50, 72
Fenn, John 62
Ferber, Edna 27, 79
Ferencz, George 5, 23, 39, 42, 71, 117, 131
Ferguson, John Forrest 3
Ferguson, Kelly 67
Ferguson, Margaret 3
Fergusson, Honora 80
Ferra, Max 71
Ferrara, Bill 119
Ferrara, Martha 100
Ferraro, John 121
Ferreira-Contessa, Maria 123
Ferrieri, Tony 38, 130, 131
Ferril, Thomas Hornsby 57
Ferringo, Oscar 123
Fetterly, Ralph 81, 82, 129, 130
Fetterman, Bob 36
Feuche, Peter R. 150
Feydeau, Georges 32, 33, 60, 95, 116, 158
Fichandler, Thomas C. 15
Fichandler, Zelda 15
Fiegel, Andira L 160
Field, Barbara 5, 16, 63, 64, 66, 88
Field, Crystal 148, 149, 150
Fielding, Henry 20, 33, 91, 94, 137
Fields, Herbert 61
Fields, Joseph 60
Fields, Michael 45, 46, 127
Fierstein, Harvey 108
Figures of Speech Theatre 152
Fine, Laura 67, 118, 140

Fingerhut, Arden 16, 23, 87, 96, 126, 141, 149, 162
Finkelstein, Richard 50
Finlayson, Doug 92, 98, 163
Finlay, Suzanne 47
Finn, William 4, 75, 96
Fire, Richard 106
Fischer, Corey 19
Fischoff, George 108
Fishelson, David J. 72
Fisher, Doug 117
Fisher, John 31
Fisher, Jules 108
Fisher, Mary L. 54
Fisher, Rick 96
Fisher, Robert 90
Fishman, Esther 52
Fitzgerald, Geraldine 67
Fitzhugh, Ellen 90
Fitzsimmons, Margaret 33
Fjelde, Rolf 32
Flaherty, Stephen 120
Flanders, John 84
Flank, Jane Williams 128
Flannagan, Ford 151
Flauto, Joseph 98
Fleming, Greg 98
Fleming, John 115
Fleming, Kerry 27, 159, 160
Fleming, Sam 87, 113, 156, 161, 164
Fletcher, John C. 10
Fletcher, Robert 10
Flint, Carol 102
Flippin, Mary Ann 154
Flood, Peter 31
Floor, Callie 99
Flores, Abra 76
Flores, Ramon 49
Fo, Dario 52, 79, 111, 162
Foeller, William 32, 114, 161
Fokin, Valerie 7
Folden, Lewis 28, 45, 114, 161
Foley, John 18, 63, 65, 66, 81, 101, 118, 140, 153, 154, 155
Fong, Frank 103
Fontaine, Joel 10, 24, 52, 63, 101, 132, 136
Foon, Dennis 92
Foote, Horton 45, 51, 63, 85, 111, 117, 151
Forbes, Barbara 14, 50, 57, 109, 110, 114
Forbes, Jeff 122
Forbes, John 0, 101, 102, 131
Ford, Alison 86, 88
Ford, Anne-Denise 4, 140
Ford, David 52
Forde, Larry 59
Ford, John 136
Foreman, Richard 12, 104, 165
Foreman, Ronlin 70
Fornes, Maria Irene 43, 84, 87, 135, 144, 164
Forrest, Donald 45, 46
Forrester, Bill 66
Forrester, William 4, 51, 133, 146
Forster, John 155
Forster, Victoria 155
Forsyth, Jerold 28, 96, 113, 162, 163

Foster, Michael 46
Foster, Rich 6
Foster, Rick 100
Foster, Skip 9, 132
Found, O. 149
Found, Stephen 3
Fowler, Susi Gregg 112
Fowlie, Wallace 73
Fox, Michael 55
Fox, Sandra 119
Foy, Kenneth 61, 126
Frame, Donald M. 122
Frances, Aronson 11
Frank, David 143, 144
Frank, Mary Ellen 112
Frank, Melvin 43
Frankel, Kenneth 79
Frankish, Leslie 39
Franz, Joe 111
Frayn, Michael 6, 7, 9, 18, 21, 67, 80, 84, 86, 95, 117, 118, 123, 126, 132, 139, 143, 146, 151, 153, 154, 158, 165
Frazer, Shauna 22
Frazier, David O. 87
Frazier, Kermit 51, 104, 113
Frazier, Shauna 22
Fredrickson, Jean 153
Fredrik, Burry 8
Freed, Arthur 116
Freed, Donald 46, 47, 159
Freedman, Gerald 61, 96, 101, 162
Freedom, Joanne 150
Freeman, Brian 99
Freeman, Dave 101
Freese, Ross 158
Frellick, Paul 71
French, Arthur 93
French, David 159, 161
French, Marc 17
French, Tony 98
Friederichs, Cecelia A. 108
Friedman, Richard 106
Friedman, Steven 131
Friel, Brian 5, 79, 83, 117, 141
Frings, Ketti 145
Frisch, Anna 150
Fritz, Lana 74
Frkonja, Jeffrey A. 72, 133, 146
Froehlich, Mary Grace 144
Fromer, Robert 25
Frost, Sue 60
Fruchter, Danny S. 110
Fry, Christopher 16, 142
Fry, Ray 5
Frye, Andrea 74
Fuecker, Bob 88, 89
Fugard, Athol 7, 8, 9, 14, 16, 23, 26, 36, 38, 45, 69, 72, 81, 84, 85, 86, 88, 94, 95, 98, 101, 106, 119, 120, 122, 127, 132, 135, 139, 151, 162
Fuhrmann, Robert 144, 163
Fuller, Dean 50
Fuller, Elizabeth 56, 70
Funicello, Ralph 10, 11, 23, 46, 102, 134, 139
Furr, Connie 140
Furth, George 4, 47, 125
Futterman, Enid 69
Fyfe, Joe 40

G

Gaffney, Floyd 131
Gaffney, Mo 79
Gaffney, Thomas G. 108
Gage, James H. 117
Gailen, Judy 167
Gainer, Fred 49
Gaines, Barbara 135, 136
Gaines, Frederick 32
Gaisner, Rhea 93
Galati, Frank 60, 75, 142
Galban, Margarita 24
Gale, Brian 139
Gale, Zona 33
Galgano, Richard 105
Galin, Alexander 80
Gallagher, Larry 5
Gallavan, Rick 57, 146, 161
Galli, Allen 22
Galligan, David 100
Gallo, Paul 76, 77, 96, 134
Galvin, Helen 41
Gam, Kaja 149
Gambill, Gina 99
Ganio, Michael 161
Gann, Myra 123
Gant, Richard 42
Garat, Elizabeth 118
Garcia, Jose G. 160
Gardiner, Robert 4, 132, 133
Gardner, Herb 13, 14, 15, 16, 18, 36, 47, 57, 59, 66, 67, 88, 92, 101, 109, 116, 117, 122, 129, 137, 154, 157, 165
Gardner, Josie 133
Gardner, William T. 116
Gardner, Worth 36
Garepis, Demece 153
Garfein, Herschel 80
Garonzik, Sara 114
Garrett, Nancy Fales 79
Garry, Joseph 87
Garson, Juliet 120, 167
Garza, Michele 47
Gates, Sarah Nash 106, 133
Gautre, Alain 148
Gay, John 8, 45, 120, 137
Gazzo, Michael V 128
Geerdes, Sherri 49
Geiger, Mary Louise 73, 120, 148
Geiser, Janie 149, 150
Geitner, Robert 119
Gelbart, Larry 11, 12, 60, 83, 85, 141, 154
Geld, Gary 44, 108
Gelger, Paul 155
Geller, Susan Denison 37, 75, 139
Genet, Jean 153
Gennaro, Jane 11
Gennaro, Michael 56
Gentry, Judith 26
Geoly, Guy 108
George, George W. 89
George, Lynn 130
George, Richard R. 66, 133
George, William 157
Georgia, Bill 135
Georgianna, Frank 46, 47
Gerdes, Rich 17
Gerety, Peter 158

Gergel, John 91
Gerke, Pamela 133
Gerlach, Robert 28
Gerould, Daniel 105
Gershwin, George 61, 108
Gershwin, Ira 61, 108
Gerson, Karen 101
Gersten, Bernard 76
Geseck, Rosemary 157
Gesner, Clark 65
Gianfrancesco, Edward T. 166
Giannini, A. Christina 128
Giannitti, Michael 15, 101, 158
Giardina, Anthony 103, 167
Gibboney, Mary 30
Gibson, P.J. 143
Gibson, William 8, 69, 113
Gide, Andre 73
Giersch, Richard 151
Giguere, Edi 11, 73
Giguere, Joel 157
Gilb, Melinda 101
Gilbert, Edward 68
Gilbert, Hy 108
Gilbert, Meg 20
Gilbert, W.S. 53
Gilbert, William S. 5
Gilger, Paul 155
Gill, Patrick 99
Gilles, D.B. 45
Gillette, William 13
Gilliam, Michael 85, 100
Gillman, Robert A. 45
Gilmore, Wendy 153
Gilrain, Jennie 157
Gilroy, Frank D, 57
Gilsenan, Nancy 103
Gimenez, Carlos 96
Gingrasso, Don 105
Giomi, Rita 112, 133
Giordano, Tony 44, 158
Giovanni, Paul 5, 50
Girdler, Deb G. 65
Giron, Arthur 59
Gisselman, Gary 16
Gitomer, Dan 28
Gjelsteen, Karen 9, 23, 51, 52, 125
Gladden, Dean R. 38
Gladstone, Lia 112
Glass, Joanna M. 122
Glass, Philip 80
Glasser, D. Scott 6,7
Glassman, Stephen 99
Glaudini, Robert 31, 81, 82
Glazer, Peter 13, 20
Gleason, John 96, 128
Glenn, David M 15, 16
Glenn, John 151
Glenny, Michael 79, 85, 166
Glenville, Peter 158
Glowacki, Janusz 8, 84, 106, 118, 130, 134, 145, 159, 163
Gobargev, Vladimir 79
Godber, John 68, 99
Goetz-Sankiewicz, Marketa 6
Goetz, Augustus 18, 79
Goetz, Kent 81
Goetz, Ruth 18, 79
Goff, Mark Allen 129, 130
Goggin, Dan 18, 57, 65, 137, 138
Gogol, Nikolai 79

INDEX OF NAMES

oing, John 5, 50, 108, 145
oins, Luther 36
oldberg, Moses 139, 140
oldemberg, Rose Leiman 73
olden, Ardyss 84
olden, David 51
oldenthal, Elliot 90
oldhirsch, Sheri 167
olding, William 17
oldman, James 53, 78
oldoni, Carlo 29, 129, 134
oldsby, Robert 139
oldsmith, Jeff 100
oldsmith, Oliver 87
oldstein, David Ira 4, 16, 51, 69, 88, 122
oldstein, Imre 98
oldstein, Jess 5, 64, 68, 79, 83, 121, 134, 160, 166, 167
oldstein, Lori 150
oldstone, Bruce 13, 14
omer, Steve 160
ontarski, Stan 81, 82
onzales, Laurence 107
onzalez, Amy 93
onzalez, Gloria 124, 125
oodman, Rob 52, 53
oodman, Robyn 134
oodrich, Bruce 155
oodrich, Frances 76, 86, 140, 165
oodson, Fred 159
oodwin, Richard R. 132
orden, Charles 159
ordon, Fiona 152
ordon, Marvin 155
ordon, Richard 26
orey, Edward 88
orgal, Max 164
otanda, Philip Kan 23, 79, 121, 133, 163
ottesman, Edward 153
ottlieb, Peter 87, 87, 92, 106
ottschalk, Fruma 79
ottschalk, Ron 67
ould, Barney 30
ould, Peter David 141
ould, Richard 39
ow, Michael 59, 130
ozzi, Carlo 12
rabowski, Christopher 167
race, Daniel 17
racieux, Vincent 147, 148
raczyk, Ed 117
rady, Michael 16, 114
raeme, Lynn 111
raff, Todd 160
raham, Bruce 36, 114, 166
rahame, Kenneth 140
raham, Rick 156
rahn, Judy 153
randison, Brian 89
raneto, Phil 114
rant, Micki 10
rant, Suzanne 133
rant, William H. 11, 42, 93, 113, 114
rant-Phillips, John 165
rantham, Ken, 23, 24, 52
rassilli, John 152
raves, Kevin 31
raves, Lynn 22, 133

Gray, Amlin 50, 87, 92
Gray, Dan 21
Gray, Daniel 21, 57
Gray, Janet 95
Gray, John 65, 70, 78, 98, 101, 141
Gray, Kathy 18
Gray, Larry 118
Gray, Rex 103
Gray, Simon 39, 81, 142
Greanier, Mary-Ann 40
Greco, James 7, 8, 53
Greco, Jim 7
Green, Adolph 16, 60, 116
Green, Benny 117, 145
Greenberg, Albert 19
Greenberg, Richard 83, 124
Greenberg, Rob 167
Greenberg, Stanley R. 10
Greenberg, Sue 126
Greenburg, Richard 51
Greenspan, David 121
Greenstein, Nancy 149
Greenwood, Jane 39, 64, 77, 83, 134, 167
Greer, Larry 159
Gregg, Bill 7, 153
Gregg, Margaret 127
Gregg, Susan 92, 125, 126
Gregory, Dawna 13, 39, 87, 115
Gregory, Lady 105
Greif, Michael 24, 44
Greig, Noel 153
Gress, Jeffrey M. 154, 155
Grey, Clifford 60
Griegel, Gail 164
Griffin, Annie 76
Griffin, Brent 50
Griffin, Hayden 83
Griffin, Susan 153, 154
Griffin, Tom 19, 39, 44, 89, 101, 113, 117, 128, 155, 158
Griffith, Barry 155
Griffith, Steve 62
Griffiths, Trevor 39
Grillet, Grace E. 113
Grillo, Henry 98
Grimaldi, John 150
Grimsley, Jim 93, 135
Griswold, Mary 60, 90, 92, 107, 112, 124
Grivna, William 152
Gromley, Frances 150
Gronk 80
Gropman, David 76
Gross, Robert 71
Grossman, Larry 90
Grossman, Suzanne 32
Grote, Susan Archibald 154
Grove, Barry 83
Gruber, Don 20, 21
Gruenewald, Thomas 60, 61, 108, 114
Grunen, Gerta 9
Grunewald, Thomas 116
Gryska, Edward J. 130
Guardino, Jerome 63
Guare, John 38, 44, 60, 88, 92, 167
Guarldi, Mary G. 57
Gubaryev, Vladimir 85, 166
Guettel, Adam 162
Gueullete, T.S. 105

Guinan, Francis 142
Gulley, John 18, 19
Gulyas, Shawn 127
Guncheon, Paul 67
Gunderson, Steve 101
Gunn, Bill 96
Gunning, Greg 155
Gurbo, Walter 149
Gurney, Jr., A.R. 24, 29, 57, 78, 79, 85, 100, 101, 116, 145, 159
Guskin, Harold 96
Guthrie, Jenny 129, 130
Guthrie, Tyrone 63
Guthrie, Woody 20
Gutierrez, Alejandra 123
Gutierrez, Carole 32
Gutierrez, Gerald 4, 83
Guttierez, April L. 108, 109
Guyer, Murphy 3, 5
Guzik, Jeff 53

H

Haaga, Kathy 118
Haagensen, Erik 61
Haas, Karl 114, 115, 116
Haas, Kate 145
Haas, Sue 69, 88, 148
Haas, Tom 70, 71
Haatainen, Christina 101
Haber, Bob 89
Haber, John 8
Hackaday, Hal 89, 90
Hacker, Linda E. 117
Hackett, Albert 76, 86, 140, 165
Haddow, Jeffrey 89, 160
Hadley, Jennifer 42
Hadley, Michael 42
Hagedorn, Jessica 82
Hager, Eric 152
Hahn, Jessica 35, 60, 90, 92, 98, 163
Haimes, Todd 128
Haimsohn, George 165
Haines, Jim 74
Hale, Pamela 21
Hall, Adrian 15, 44, 102, 158
Hall, Bob 36
Hall, David 31
Hall, Michael 28, 29
Hall, Peter 3, 91
Hall, Robert 92
Hall, Tom 101
Halley, Jr., Ben 143
Halley, Martha 138
Halliday, Jimm 26
Hally, Martha 30, 117, 123, 155
Halpern, Martin 125
Halpern, Michael 3
Hamburger, Richard 61, 122, 123
Hamilin, Larry Leon 157
Hamilton, Del 135
Hamilton, Patrick 72, 86, 137
Hamilton, Rob 0, 33, 55
Hamilton, Sabrina 80
Hamlisch, Marvin 48
Hammack, Warren 67
Hammer, W.J.E. 110
Hammerstein, II, Oscar 43, 47, 49, 56, 108, 151

Hammes, Lynne 133
Hammond, David 119, 120
Hammond, Thomas 151
Hampson, Rich 115
Hampton, Christopher 3, 5, 7, 13, 39, 44, 68, 123, 134, 144, 161, 162
Hamson, Rich 6, 7, 42
Hand, Jr., Q.R. 99
Handel, Beatrice 44
Handler, Stephanie 67
Handley, Mark 100
Handman, Wynn 11
Haney, Anthony J. 154, 155
Haney, Tony 99
Hanighen, Bernard 24
Hanna, Christopher 160, 161
Hannah, Dave 106
Hannah, Jeroy 157
Hannah, Michael 42
Hannay, Mark 149
Hanreddy, Joseph 80, 81
Hansberry, Lorraine 15, 47, 68
Hansen, Eric 15, 74, 149
Hansen, Tom 84
Hanson, Erik 31
Hanson, Hugh 67
Hanson, Kim 118
Hanson, Rik 31
Hantula, Tim 49
Hara, Lillian 48
Harbach, Otto 61
Hard, Randi Collins 33
Harden, Richard 36
Harding, Michael 93
Hardison, O.B. 136
Hardman, Cathy 25
Hardwick, Mark 18, 59, 63, 65, 66, 81, 101, 118, 129, 140, 149, 153, 154, 155
Hardy, Wendy 158
Hare, David 64
Harelik, Mark 9, 10, 30, 39, 84, 88, 113, 113, 117, 125
Harger, Brenda 131
Harley, Margot 4
Harling, Robert 6, 7, 8, 9, 14, 15, 16, 18, 21, 36, 59, 67, 95, 106, 117, 126, 130, 144, 145
Harman, Barry 101, 102
Harman, Leonard 44, 144
Harmon, Amy 102
Harmon, Joan 157
Harmon, Leonard 38
Harmon, Richard 93
Harms, Wendy 158, 159
Harnick, Jay 155
Harnick, Sheldon 104, 140
Harrer, Maggie 86
Harrie, Marten 30
Harrigan, Peter 38
Harriman, P. Chelsea 111
Harrington, Laura 103, 121
Harrington, Nancy 76, 164
Harris, Aurand 91, 95, 137
Harris, Gary 43, 44
Harris, Jed Allen 38
Harris, Joel Chandler 29
Harris, John 74
Harris, Richard 8, 24, 36, 58, 85, 140, 142, 143, 145, 155

INDEX OF NAMES

Harrison, Margaret Keyes 43
Harrison, Peter 20, 114, 115, 116, 117
Harrison, Tony 43
Hart, Bill 96
Hart, Bonita 109
Hart, Eric A. 165
Hart, Lorenz 60, 61, 117
Hart, Moss 15, 26, 71, 75, 116, 126, 126, 154, 158
Hart, Patricia L 160
Hartenhoff, Lauri 87
Hartinian, Linda 80
Hartley, Megan 111, 112
Hartwell, Peter 96
Hartzell, Janet 52
Hartzell, Linda 132, 133
Harvey, Cam 139
Hase, Thomas 81, 92, 98
Hasson, Bruce 19
Hastings, Edward 10
Hastings, John 39, 129
Hastings, Paul 45
Hatcher, Jeffrey 7, 104, 121, 166
Hatch, Robert 119
Haupt, Paulette 103
Hausch, Mary 65, 66
Hauser, Frank 128
Havel, Vaclav 32, 85, 96, 163
Havern, Ron 150
Haverty, Doug 78
Havis, Allan 24, 114, 139, 166
Hawkanson, David 64
Hawkins, John R. 113
Hawley, David 62
Hay, Peter 114
Hay, Richard L. 46, 47, 84, 106
Hay, Rosemary 144
Hay, Rosey 92, 93
Hayashi, Marc 82, 107
Hayes, Steve 89
Hayes, Ted 135
Haynes, Cynthia 70
Hays, John Edward 150
Hays, Stephen E. 141
Hazlett, Laura 81, 84
Head, David 54, 157
Heath, Heather 3
Heath, Kia Christina 51
Hebert, Julie 52, 81, 82, 84
Hecht, Ben 92, 155
Hedge, Eleanor 31
Hedge, Lambriny 159
Hedges, John 59
Hedges, Mimi 159
Hedjazi, Saeed 100
Heelan, Kevin 120
Heeley, Desmond 35, 64
Heffernan, Maureen 57, 109, 117, 119, 120
Heffner, Wendy 101
Heifner, Jack 18, 92
Heim, Michael Henry 98
Heintzman, Michael 11
Heiremans, Alberto 87
Heister, Dan 33
Heister, Phillippe 33
Hellesen, Richard 129, 130, 140
Hellman, Lillian 79, 122, 125
Helm, Gary 73
Hempleman, Terry 11

Henderson, Luther 164
Henery, Keith 39, 141
Henkel, Clare 131
Henley, Beth 8, 83, 139
Hennes, Tom 144
Henry, Chad 100, 119, 133
Henry, O. 20, 28, 58, 119
Henry, Patrick 55, 56
Henry, Patti 22, 50, 133
Hensley, Charlie 9
Hensley, Todd 6, 98
Hent, Peter 162
Herbert-Slater, Marilee 5
Herko, Mark 89
Herman, Anna Ungar 99
Herman, David 63
Herman, Jerry 74, 108
Herochik, John 85
Herrera, Shizuko 48
Herrick, Jack 8
Herring, Jay 65
Herring, Linda 93
Herrmann, Keith 101
Herzer, Martin 109
Hess, Dean 63
Hess, Ivan 46
Hess, Jeff 33
Hewitt, Jr., Kenneth R. 47
Hewitt, Frankie 55
Heymann, Henry 38
Hiatt, Rick 103
Hicken, Donald 110
Hickey, John
Hickey, John James 150
Hicklin, Walker 23, 37, 83, 96, 139
Hicks, Israel 13, 36, 158, 161
Hicks, Munson 9, 13, 68, 116, 126
Hicks, Yslan 162
Hiebert, Gareth 62
Higdon, Joseph Ronald 128
Higgins, David 31
Higgins, Lisa 109
Higgins, Steve 31
Higham, David 51
Higle, Laura S. 47
Hilferty, Susan 11, 23, 75, 76, 96, 114, 135
Hill, Bruce 129
Hill, Eric 141
Hill, Frederick 26
Hill, Gary Leon 121
Hill, Jeff 141
Hill, Kelly 153
Hill, Lucienne 8
Hill, Martha 43, 44
Hill, Rufus 110
Hill, Terrance S. 19
Hillgartner, Jim 78
Hillow, George 161
Hilmar, Greg 143, 151
Himes, Ron 101, 126, 142, 143
Hindley, C.L. 83
Hines, Melissa 50
Hinkle, Wendall S. 26
Hinson, Jane 131
Hippen, Lynn 149
Hird, Tom 30
Hiroshima 85
Hirsch, John 9, 101, 167
Hirschfeld, Susan 9, 13, 136
Hitch, Geoffrey 21, 98

Hobin, Geoffrey 140
Hochhauser, Jeff 65
Hockenberry, Gaye 38
Hoeger, Mark 49
Hoey, Randal 137
Hoffman, Andrea 118
Hoffman, Bill 162
Hoffman, Henry 137
Hoffman, K. Robert 150
Hoffman, Marcie 156
Hoffman, William 39, 66
Hofsiss, Jack 39
Hogan, Frank X. 46
Hogan, Tim 0
Hogya, Giles 73
Hohanshelt, Laura 35, 35
Holden, Vicki S. 18
Holder, Don 14, 71, 161
Holder, Donald 57, 109, 110, 114, 122, 123, 138
Holder, Laurence 11
Holdgrive, David 50, 54, 65
Holland, Endesha Ida Mae 93, 114
Hollingsworth, Dawn 99, 100
Hollingsworth, Jay 146
Hollis, Jesse 10
Hollis, Stephen 7, 95, 117
Hollmann, Heidi 20, 155
Holloway, Victoria L. 12, 13
Hollow, Steve 149
Hollywood, Danielle 24
Holman, Robert 50
Holmes, Rupert 18, 69, 154
Holmgren, Norah 7
Holms, John 30
Holms, John Pynchon 30, 92, 93, 123
Holsclaw, Doug 153
Holt, Marion Peter 87, 131, 132, 163
Holt, Stephen 149
Holt, Will 20, 29, 91
Holtzman, Willy 39, 92, 93, 104, 123
Holzman, Dean 40, 69, DEAN
Homan, Sidney 66
Homer 105
Honea, Marc 3
Honegger, Gitta 103, 104, 167
Honig, Edwin 12, 138
Hook, Cora 149
Hook, Tami 118
Hooker, Brian 7, 116
Hooker, Jerry 4, 72, 122, 145
Hopkins, Billy 51
Hopkins, Bruce 122
Hopkins, Richard 12, 45, 54
Hopper, Elizabeth 151
Hopper, Gary 151
Horek, Robert 54
Horner, John 38, 43
Horovitz, Israel 28, 59, 67, 144
Horowitz, Jeffrey 148
Hortensia 150
Horwitz, Murray 99
Hosan, Jonathon 51
Hoschna, Karl 61
Hoshi, Shizuko 48
Hotopp, Michael J. 137, 160
Hottois, Michael 140
Hough, Paul 48

Hould-Ward, Ann 4, 64, 83, 96, 134
House, Ron 131
Houseman, John 4
Houston, Mark 158
Houston, Velina Hasu 83, 101
Hover, Christine 79
Howard, Bette 42
Howard, Ed 18, 21, 95, 152, 154
Howard, Elizabeth 118
Howard, G.A. 138
Howard, Sidney 24
Howarth, Tony 105
Howe, Tina 7, 15, 27, 95, 123, 13, 152
Howell, Sandra 153
Howell, Steven 31
Hoyle, Geoff 75
Hubbard, Alison 155
Hubbard, Brenda 122
Hubbard, Coleen 33
Hubbell, Jeffrey 10
Huber, Sondra 63
Huddle, Elizabeth 72
Huddleston, Will 29, 30
Hudson, Heather 133
Hudson, Katherine 26
Hudson, Ken 95
Huerta, Jorge 123, 131
Huff, Keith 103, 104
Hughes, Alice S. 108
Hughes, Allen Lee 6, 15, 16, 61, 68, 87, 117
Hughes, Douglas 133, 134
Hughes, Langston 107, 110, 143
Hughes, Mark 17, 18, 110
Hughes, Patrick 8
Hughes, Paul 119
Hugo, Victor 132, 147
Hull, Anne 13
Hull, Charles 155
Hume, Michael 30
Humes, Debra 160
Hummel, Karen 67, 73, 74
Humphrey, Craig A. 117
Humphries, Jimmy 13, 119
Hundley, C.L. 39, 83
Hunsaker, Dave 112
Hunt, Jeff 129, 130
Hunt, Jim 33
Hunt, Peter 162
Hunt, Sam 67
Hunter, Mark 119
Hupp, Robert 72, 73
Hurlbut, Bruce 132, 133
Hurst, Gregory 13, 14, 57, 109, 161
Hussey, Thal 150
Hutchinson, Ron 50, 84
Hutson, Bill 91
Hutzler, Laurie H. 47
Hwang, David Henry 141
Hynd, Ghretta 57

I

Iacovelli, John 79, 80, 85, 109, 139
Ibsen, Henrik 23, 32, 61, 64, 84, 98, 106, 109, 111, 117, 123, 129, 144, 146, 165

INDEX OF NAMES **181**

...ko, Momoko 107
...asy, J. Kent 76
...ngalls, James F. 12, 32, 34, 63, 64, 75, 88, 134
...nge, William 94, 109
...nnaurato, Albert 114, 120, 121
...onesco, Eugene 39, 47, 99, 118, 162
...rby, A. Dean 42, 123
...rizarry, Richard V. 123
...rvin, Matt 102, 103
...rvine, Kate 23, 81
...rving, Janet 59
...rwin, Bill 76, 134
...rwin, Catherine 77
...rwin, Jim 136
...rwin, Pat 149, 150
...rwin, Tom 95
...rwin, Will 24
...sbell, Tony 118
...sen, Richard 61
...sham, Jay 140
...sherwood, Christopher 39
...smay, Normando 135
...srael, Robert 76, 96
...to, Robert 48
...ves, David 92, 93
...wasaki, Hiroshi 96, 114, 162, 163

J

Jacker, Corinne 117
Jackness, Andrew 64, 96, 137
Jackson, Charles. 47
Jackson, Curtis C. 143
Jackson, Damone Paul 31
Jackson, Jim 70
Jackson, Judith 152
Jackson, Julie 60
Jackson, Marsha 74, 99
Jackson, Nagle 85
Jackson, Suzanne 49
Jacobs, Douglas 131
Jacobs, Michelle 19
Jacobsen, John 53, 54
Jacobson, Deidre W. 56
Jacques, David Martin 88
Jagim, Jay Michael 8
Jahnsons, Sivia 100
James, Iris 149
James, Julie 66
James, Toni-Leslie 72, 80, 107
Jampolis, Neil Peter 113
Jamson, Rich 6
Janacek, Leos 79
Jankousky, Steve 26
Jans, Alaric 130
Jared, Robert 8, 87, 88, 109, 120, 121, 141
Jared, Todd A. 79
Jaros, Ann 98
Jarrell, Randall 107
Jasien, Deborah 57, 110
Jasinsky, Judi 149
Jauchem, Esquire 31
Jeff, Gail Brassard 24
Jeffers, Robinson 19
Jeffreys, Stephen 72, 123, 139, 145, 163
Jeffries, Lynn 39, 40

Jeffries, Peter 120
Jenkin, Len 96, 156
Jenkins-Evans, Hollis 5
Jenkins, Daniel 160
Jenkins, David 39, 64, 96, 101
Jenkins, Ken 160
Jenkins, Leroy 90
Jenkins, Paulie 4, 84, 85, 132, 134, 139
Jenkins, Richard 158
Jenkins, Ron 79
Jenness, Morgan 93, 121
Jennings, Eric 135
Jennings, Gary 3
Jensen, James 135
Jensen, John 85, 113
Jensen, Julie 30
Jerman, Carla Binford 151
Jerome, Chodorov 60
Jody, Allan 139
Johannesen, Lars 129
Johannmeier, Rolf 149
Johanson, Robert 108
Johns, Andrew 26
Johns, Bill 3
Johns, Ernest 105
Johnson, Art 74, 87
Johnson, Ben 158, 167
Johnson, Bernard 42
Johnson, Bryan 155
Johnson, Chris 6, 42, 62
Johnson, Cindy Lou 37
Johnson, Douglas 141
Johnson, Eric M. 20
Johnson, Grey Cattell 59
Johnson, Joanne 13, 119, 146
Johnson, Judith 99
Johnson, Kathleen 31
Johnson, Ken 42
Johnson, Lamont 57
Johnson, Laura 25
Johnson, Myron 35
Johnson, Sandee 158
Johnson, Stephanie 99, 153
Johnson, Thomas P. 100, 101
Johnson, Virgil 88, 98
Johnston, Bob 65
Johnston, Jan 133
Jonas, Jerry 28
Jone, Ken 47
Jones, Andrew Earl 78
Jones, B.J. 90, 107
Jones, Beryl 135
Jones, Cathi 26
Jones, Charles 91
Jones, David Richard 94
Jones, Dawn Renee 6, 7
Jones, Douglas 151
Jones, Ellen 119, 160
Jones, Felicity 148
Joncs, Howard 98
Jones, Jeffrey M. 40, 160
Jones, Ken 47
Jones, Marie 62, 152
Jones, Mark 153
Jones, Marshall 41
Jones, Martin 115, 143, 144
Jones, Robert A. 18
Jones, Steven 36
Jones, Suzanne 53
Jones, Thomas Cadwaleder 105

Jones, Tom 48, 65, 74, 84, 91, 99, 152, 162
Jones, Walt 114
Jones, Walton 9, 14, 58, 59, 103, 132, 144, 145, 165
Jones, Wendela K. 145, 146
Jonson, Ben 167
Jordan, Dale F. 30, 119, 125, 141
Jordan, June 92, 93
Jordan, Richard 85
Jory, Jon 5, 6, 78
Joselovitz, Ernest 114
Joseph, Claire 119
Joseph, Fields 60
Joseph, Patrick 153
Josheff, Liz 148
Joubert, Elsa 89
Joy, James Leonard 9, 16, 60, 61, 68
Joyce, John Liam 28
Joyce, Robert 147
Juncker, Niki 152
Jung, Philipp 12, 13, 20, 83, 123, 143, 144, 155
Jurasas, Jonas 44, 158
Jurglanis, Marla 45, 54, 56, 111
Juster, Norton 5
Justin, David 53

K

Kaczorowski, Peter 23, 64, 75, 83, 96, 123, 134, 144
Kaczynski, Ken 119
Kading, Charles S. 8
Kadlec, Larry 95
Kafka, Franz 13, 69, 73
Kageyama, Rodney 48
Kahn, Michael 4, 136, 137
Kahn, Rick 42
Kalcheim, Lee 82
Kalfin, Robert 61, 92, 128, 129
Kalmer, Bert 9, 68
Kammer, Karen 50
Kamm, Tom 94, 97, 126
Kandel, Gregory 98
Kander, John 154, 160, 161
Kander, Susan 56
Kandert, John 162
Kani, John 16, 86
Kanin, Fay 128, 157
Kanin, Garson 28, 39, 67, 72, 85, 113, 142
Kanin, Michael 128, 157
Kantor, Michael 90
Kantrowitz, Jason 9, 13
Kaplan, David 114
Kaplan, Howard Tsvi 8, 19
Kaplan, Michael B. 51
Kaplan, Steve 137
Kaplon, Shirley 51
Karchmer, Charles 6, 51, 113, 123, 145
Karkosh, Clayton 94, 95
Karvonides, Chrisi 167
Kashiwagi, Hiroshi 48
Kaskel, Stephanie 135
Kasner, Rose 24
Kassin, Michael 103
Katims, Jason 114

Katz, Natasha 39, 44, 61, 83, 84, 96, 108, 145
Katz, Paul 57
Kauffman, John 66, 67, 133
Kaufman, Bel 133
Kaufman, George 9, 15, 27, 68, 75, 79, 116, 126, 154, 158
Kaufman, Lynne 82
Kaushansky, Larry 49
Kava, Caroline 12, 18, 20
Kava, Libby 153
Kawolsky, Chris. 8
Kaye-Martin, Ed 163
Kazanjian, David 109
Keane, John B. 87
Kearney, Kristine 7, 120
Kearns, Juli 135
Keathley, George 88
Keating, Barry 13
Keech, Pamela 113
Keek, Michael 93
Keeler, Richard 111
Keene, Daniel 149
Keene, Donald 107
Keene, Liz 155
Keever, Tom 40
Keith, Carolyn 109
Keith, Marilyn 121
Keith, Michael 89
Kelleher, Ken 129
Keller, James 30, 84
Keller, John David 139
Keller, Ron 44, 150, 153
Kelley, Robert 154, 155
Kellman, Barnet 83
Kellogg, Marjorie Bradley 36, 55, 64, 75, 79, 84, 128
Kelly, Brett 76
Kelly, Daniel 148
Kelly, George 162
Kelly, Jeffrey 90
Kelly, Joy 155
Kelly, Lawrence 114
Kelly, Rick 59
Kelly, Susan 13
Kelman, Scott 100
Kendrick, D. Polly 55
Kenndey, John 164
Kennedy, Ashley York 166, 167
Kennedy, Beau 10, 150
Kennedy, Craig 111, 149, 150
Kennedy, Dennis 38
Kennedy, Gordon 95
Kennedy, Holly J. 33
Kennedy, John 164
Kennedy, Kathleen 87
Kennedy, Steve 6
Kennedy, Steven 34, 35
Kenney, Frances 106
Kenney, Pamela Stross 33
Kennon, William 121
Kenny, Frances 4, 72, 146
Kent, Art 158, 159
Kent, David G. 86
Kent, Steven 87, 93, 99
Kenton, Brian Clark 66
Kern, Jerome 108
Kern, K.A. 53
Kerr, Robert 121, 167
Kersels, Martin 100
Kerwick, Danny 33

INDEX OF NAMES

Kesler, Linda 126
Kesselman, Wendy 58, 90
Kessler, Lyle 106, 114, 119, 123, 132
Ketron, Larry 166
Kevan, Ruth 137
Key, Eugene 41
Key, Tom 9, 76, 100, 117
Khaja, Jameel 105
Khan, Rick 42
Kibble, David 33
Kickbush, Bill 95
Kidd, Susan 131
Kiefer, Brenda K, 140
Kildahl, Pamela 121
Kilian, Jr., Charles J. 7
Killian, Phil 123
Killian, Philip 94, 95, 106
Killington, Ken 83
Kilty, Jerome 21
Kim, Mara 9
Kim, Sora 102, 103
Kimball, Carol 33
Kimmel, Norbert 149
Kimura, Ann Asakura 66
Kinard, Jeff 17
Kindelan, Nancy 165
Kindley, Jeffrey 14
Kindlon, Peter 30
King, Carole 36
King, Cliff 149
King, Denis 129
King, George 135
King, Larry L. 18, 166
King, Ramona 143
King, Jr., Woodie 11, 15, 74, 153
Kinney, Jay M. 118
Kinney, Terry 37, 142
Kinnier, Don 70
Kinsley, Dan 30, 73, 74
Kinter, Richard 21
Kipling, Rudyard 29, 66
Kirkham, Scott 13
Kirkman-Beck, Susan 33
Kirkpatrick, Sam 23, 23, 119
Kirkwood, James 48, 119
Kishline, John 156
Kissel, David 55, 108
Kissman, Lee 31
Kittel, Valerie 130
Klapperich, Laurie 33
Klavan, Laurence 51
Kleban, Edward 48
Klein, Amanda J. 16, 61, 89
Klein, Jon 6, 9, 69, 70, 121, 133, 155
Kletter, Debra J. 23, 37, 83, 120
Kline, Linda B. 155
Kline, Thomas 82
Klingelhoefer, Robert 5, 56, 123
Kling, Kevin 5, 52, 69, 124, 148
Kloth, Ken 53, 87
Knee, Alan 69
Knetsch, Piet 156, 157
Knight, Darwin 116
Knight, Frederick B. 137
Knight, Jacalyn 62
Knott, Frederick 21, 122, 145
Knouse, Lorin Blane 7
Knudsen, Chris Glaza 105
Knudsen, Fritha 10, 109

Knyazev, Yuri 104
Kochergin, Eduard 85
Kociolek, Ted 16, 60
Koerner, Michael 35
Kogan, Deen 137
Kogan, Jay 137
Kogut, Joyce 152
Kohout, Al 61
Kohout, Pavel 6
Kolo, Fred 11, 61
Koltai, Ralph 80
Kolyada, Nicolai 131
Komorowska, Malgorzata 26, 107, 163
Komura, Chika 116
Kondoleon, Harry 51, 82, 96, 128, 149, 161
Konrardy, Nancy 32, 37, 42, 84, 115
Kontir, Tyrohne 157
Kopit, Arthur 6, 9, 10, 88
Korder, Howard 12, 76, 80, 82
Kornfeld, Larry 148
Kornhauser, Barry 56
Kosicka, Jadwiga 84, 106, 118, 130, 134, 159, 163
Koste, Virginia 49, 140
Kotlowitz, Dan 23, 68, 87, 121
Kottenstett, David 33
Kozak, Ellen 53, 87
Kraft, Hy 96
Krahenbuhl, Deborah Weber 132
Krahnke, Steven 65
Krakower, Bob 5
Kramer, Larry 9, 117, 143, 166
Kramer, Sherry 93, 102, 166
Kramer, Stephen R. 33, 57, 58
Kranes, David 114, 130
Krass, Michael 6, 97, 120, 141, 167
Kratochvil, Nana 95
Kraus, Joanna 102
Kreilkamp, Ben 69
Kreinen, Rebecca 105
Krenz, Frank 96
Kreppel, Paul 31
Kress, Donna 8, 44
Kress, Phyllis 130
Kretzu, Jon 122
Kriegel, Gail 164
Krieger, Barbara Zinn 160
Krieger, Henry 155
Krielkamp, Ben 70
Kring, T. Newell 146
Kripal, Keri 102
Kriz, Zdenek 149, 150
Kroetz, Franz Xaver 25, 97, 99, 158
Kroeze, Jan 96
Krueger, David 152
Kruger, Bonnie 126
Kubota, Warren Sumio 48
Kucera, Vaclav 148, 150
Kuhlke, Kevin 164
Kuhn, Francis X, 92
Kuhn, Marguerite 11
Kulick, Brian 97
Kurta, Kay 39
Kurtti, Casey 52, 80
Kurtz, Ken 18
Kushner, Tony 52, 97
Kwiat, David M. 6, 7

Kyle, Barry 136
Kyte, Mary 144

L

Labiche, Eugene 63
La Bolt, Terry 54, 65
LaBrecque, Doug 105
Lach, Mary Ann 10
Ladenson, Michael 28
Lagomarsino, Ron 23, 37, 139
LaGue, Michael 98
LaJoie, Beth 38, 158
Lambert, Jane 29, 30
Lambert, Ladd 130
Lambert, Sarah 55, 167
Lambie, Lauren K. 8
Lammert, Amy Louise 70
Lamont, Jr., Alonzo D. 11, 74
LaMorte, Dan 32, 33
Lamos, Mark 64, 77
Lamude, Terence 50, 78, 95
Lance, Bill 157
Lanchester, Robert 85, 117
Landau, Tina 12
Landesman, Heidi 79, 83, 85, 96, 135
Landisman, Kurt 23, 24, 81, 82, 84, 132
Landrum, Sherry 43, 44
Landsbergis, Algirdas 44
Landwehr, Hugh 24, 30, 32, 39, 79, 83, 101, 114, 115, 134, 162
Lane, Connie I. 152
Lane, Linda L. 27, 160
Lane, Scott 21
Lane, Susan 99
Lane, William 158
Lang, Elaine 72
Lang, Tony 11
Lang, William 97
Langan, Timothy 157
Lange, Ed 50
Langham, Michael 136
Langley, Jr., William 12
Langner, Nola 157
Lanier, Jessica 149
Lanier, Sidney 11
Lansbury, Edgar 15, 67
Lapine, James 96, 118, 139
Larice, Lisa 49
Larocca, Joe 106
Larsen, Donna Marie 161, 162
Larsen, Rick 48, 49
Larsen, Susan 131
Larson, Doug 112
Larson, James 49
Larson, Larry 9, 119, 146, 159
Larson, Lawrence 122
Larson, Roberta 49
Lasaygues, Maurice 38
Lascelles, Kendrew 46, 47, 108
Lasiter, John 94
Lastufka, Marta Ann 112
Lathrop, Craig 52, 84
Latouche, John 9, 16, 36, 68, 126
Latrell, Craig 106
Latta, Richard 25, 26, 89
Laufer, Ken 111, 111
Laughead, Scott 111, 112

Laurents, Arthur 14, 117
Lauro, Shirley 114
Lavallee, Bob 140
Lavender, Suzanne 140
Lavery, Byrony 41
Lawless, Peter 51
Lawless, Sarah 46
Lawless, Sue 39, 57, 110
Lawnick, Steve 76, 82
Lawrence, D.H. 21, 81
Lawrence, Jerome 71, 112, 116
Lazarus, Frank 28, 140
Lazarus, Paul 37, 116
LaZebnik, Ken 89
Leahy, Gerry 146
Leaming, Greg 92, 93
Learning, Walter 117
Leathers, Scott 44
Lebeaux, Annie 155
LeBoeuf, Marsha M. 128
Lebow, Barbara 3, 8
LeCompte, Elizabeth 165
Ledger, Michael 160
Lee-Sipple, Donna 162
Lee, Barton 119
Lee, Dana 48
Lee, Eugene 44, 84, 158
Lee, Franne 96
Lee, Leslie 42, 114, 155
Lee, Levi 3, 9, 119, 135, 146, 157, 159
Lee, Liz 9, 157
Lee, Mark 79
Lee, Ming Cho 6
Lee, Richard 101
Lee, Robert E. 71, 112, 116
Lee, Victoria 89
Lee, Wing 83
Lee, Yvonne 9, 156, 157
Leech, Kitty 155
Leerhoff, Dick 6, 7
Lefeure, Robin 83
Le Gallienne, Eva 146
Lehrer, Jim 95
Lehrer, Tom 5, 8, 18, 37, 54, 59, 63, 146, 154, 158, 165
Leibert, Michael W. 22
Leicht, John 113
Leigh, Barbara 54, 55, 87
Leigh, Carolyn 9, 50, 118, 154, 155
Leigh, Mitch 47, 65, 74, 118
Leitner, James 113, 114, 115
Lelbach, Bill 12, 13, 146
Lemay, Pat 70
L'Engle, Madeleine 9, 66, 140
Lengson, Jose 60, 61
Leningrad Clown Theater 152
Lennon, Ken 20
LeNoire, Rosetta 9
Leo, Jamie 149, 150
Leon, Kenneth 9, 89
Leonard, Jr., Jim 139
Leonard, Beth 159
Leonard, Bob 127, 152
Leonard, Jim 37
Leonard, Robert H. 126, 127
Leone, Vivien 166
Lerner, Alan Jay 153, 154
Lerner, Gene 18, 21
Lerner, Jenny 55, 87
Lerner, Ruby 135

errhoff, Dick 7
esser, Gene 137
esser, Sally 11, 23, 42, 71, 117, 131, 138, 150
essor, Sally J. 40
ester, Joe 135
ettich, Sheldon 57, 146, 161
evans, Daniel 22
evey, Alan 74
evidow, Nancy 19
evin, Cynthia 158, 159
evin, Ira 74, 165
evine, Rhoda 104, 114
evingood, William S. 37
evitow, Roberta 6, 79, 80, 121, 126, 139, 164
evy, David 54, 65
evy, Jonathan 104
evy, Sharon 157
evy, Simon 154
ewis, C.S. 118
ewis, Carter W. 117
ewis, Colleen Troy 29, 30
ewis, Irene 23, 32, 134, 162
ewis, James 75
ewis, Jim 71
ewis, Kenneth J. 95
ewis, Scott 33
ewis, Sinclair 55, 84
ichte, Richard 51
ickteig, Regina 119
ieb, Mark 12, 82
ieberman, Donna 166
iebman, Steve 54, 65
iepins, Renee 27, 98, 142
ight, Mark 6
illethun, Abby 13, 146
im, Paul Stephen 48
ima, Rafael 37, 142
imosner, Pilar 96
incoln, Michael 71
indgren, Astrid 35
indquist, Jefferson 150, 151
indsay-Hogg, Michael 84
indsay, Howard 76, 77, 88, 116
infante, Michele 46
inger, Diana 33
ink, Ron 85, 99
innell, Sherry 79
inney, Romulus 6, 18, 20, 51, 79, 83, 87, 109, 128, 131, 145, 150, 160
ion, John 81
iscow, Wendy 57, 109, 110
Lisner, Stephen 11
Littleway, Lorna 105
Littman, Michael 41
Lleo, Vicente 124, 125
Llewellyn, Don 100
Loadholt, Tony 74
Lobel, Adrianne 16, 96, 108, 139
Lobel, Arnold 49
Lock, Keven 18, 19
Lock, Kevin 18
Lock, Norman 20, 79
Locke, Robert 166
Lockner, David 86
Loebell, Larry 114
Loeffler-Bell, Chester 55, 87
Loesser, Frank 71, 92, 146
Loewit, Ken 59

Lofstrom, Doug 55
Logan, John 160
Lohr, Lynn 62
Lomardo, Kathleen 106
Lombard, Jenny 51
Lombardo, Rick 149
London, Mark 126, 167
Lonf, Quincy 51
Long, Adam 31
Long, Kathryn 106, 143, 144
Long, Quincy 51, 93, 121
Long, William Ivey 39, 83, 96
Look, Phyllis S.K. 66, 82
Loomer, Lisa 93, 102
Lopez-Morillas, Julian 23, 24, 29, 84
Lopez, Barry 112
Lopez, Josephina 49
Lopez, Yulanda 153
Loquasto, Santo 71, 83, 96, 135, 135
Lorca, Federico Garcia 3, 25, 61, 63, 101, 112, 124, 125
Lord, Robert 15
Lorden, Terry C. 13
Loree, Lori 17, 103
Lorkowski, Judy 111
Lormand, Paul 118
Lortz, James 22
Lott, Steve 149, 150
Loughrey, Patricia 67
Loui, Michael 167
Louis, Nikki 133
Lovaas, Lisa 99
Love, Edith H. 9
Love, Edward 93
Lovey, Paul 133
Lowe, Frank 21
Lowe, Frederick 153, 154
Lowell, Robert 45
Loy, Myrna 11
Lucas, Craig 3, 6, 18, 23, 37, 42, 54, 98, 139
Lucas, Greg 16
Lucas, John M. 11
Luce, William 8, 53, 108, 145
Ludlam, Charles 12, 13, 51, 53, 57, 58, 88, 110, 117, 118, 131, 163
Lujan, James Graham 112
Luke, Russell 95
Lukeman, Brenda 74
Lummis, Suzanne 31
Luna, Marta 164
Lunden, Jeffrey 155
Lupton, Jennifer 4, 72, 132, 133
Luster, Tina 31
Lutwak, Mark 92, 93
Lutz, Adelle 63
Lutz, John David 71
Lyall, Susan 37
Lyden, James E. 17
Lyles, Dale 3
Lyles, Leslie 103
Lynch, Eileen 90
Lynch, Michael 31
Lynch, Patty 27
Lynch, Sidney 118
Lynch, Thomas 15, 60, 121
Lynn, Judanna 50
Lyon, Milton 85
Lyons, Andi 30

Lysander, Per 30

M

MacArthur, Charles 92, 155
MacDevitt, Brian 11, 108
MacDonald, Bob 95
MacDonald, Christine 33
MacDonald, George 131
MacDonald, Heather 15
MacDonald, Peggy 145
MacDonald, Robert David 167
Macee, 107
Mace, Mimi 46, 46
Machado, Agusto 150
Machado, Eduardo 11, 80, 94, 124, 125, 149, 150
Machiavelli, Niccolo 152
Macintosh, Cameron 59
MacIntyre-Fender, Ron 17
MacKaye, Percy 33
MacKenzie, Phillip 152
Mackintosh, Cameron 5, 8, 18, 38,54,63,146,165
Mackintosh, Robert 10
MacLeod, Charles 46, 47
MacLeod, Wendy 6, 81, 163, 166
MacNicholas, John 38
MacPherson, Greg 51, 83
Macy, W.H. 76, 82, 114
Madden, Thomas M. 77
Maddow, Ellen 150
Maddux, Jacklyn 51
Madeira, Marcia 9, 13, 57, 68, 129
Maffei, Dorothy 134
Maggio, Fran 98
Maggio, Frances 124, 136
Maggio, Michael 5, 60, 64, 96, 134
Magnus, Bryn 107
Maguire, Matthew 40, 69, 92, 93
Magune, Jack 165
Mahon, Nicholas 148
Major, Leon 104
Major, Richard 21, 21, 21
Maki, Kathleen 133, 133, 133, 133
Mako, 48, 48, 48, 48
Makous, Bruce B. 117
Makushenko, Vladimir 7
Malamud, Bernard 90
Malamud, Marc D. 11
Malcolm, Deborah 39
Maleczech, Ruth 72, 80, 149
Malina, Judith 149, 150
Malinowski, John 12
Malleson, Miles 145, 167
Malolepsy, John 94, 95
Malone, Mike 143
Maloney, Peter 51, 166
Malpede, Karen 149
Maltby, Jr., Richard 83, 99, 151
Mamet, David 4, 12, 24, 30, 36, 44, 47, 76, 77, 115, 118, 124, 128, 131 ,140, 153, 154, 158, 161, 163
Mamlin, Gennadi 140
Manassee, Jackie 30, 68,88, 117, 121, 122
Mandell, Alan 79
Mandich, Christopher 8, 8
Manganaro, Eileen 32

Mangano, John 149
Manheim, Ralph 39, 164
Manhoff, Bill 78
Manim, Mannie 76, 77, 80
Manke, Art 30
Mankowitz, Wolf 105
Manley, Frank 160
Manning, E. Hugh 33
Mantegna, Joe 107
Margulies, Donald 20
Maponay, Maishe 93
Mara, Margaret 102
Maradudin, Peter 23, 46,47, 63, 75, 101, 102, 106, 131, 132, 134, 139
Marcante, Mark 149, 150
Marchetti, Will 84, 84
Marchetti, William 83
Marcus, Paul 139
Mardirosian, Tom 121
Mardome, Jimmell 149
Margolis, Kari 152, 161, 161, 161, 161
Margulies, Donald 20, 80, 83
Marini, Ken 111
Mark, Jack 115
Marker, Laury 117
Marki, Csilla 85
Markiewicz, Chris 66
Marks, Gerald 80
Markus, Tom 86, 116
Marlay, Andrew B. 128, 129
Marley, Donovan 46, 47, 108
Marlin-Jones, Davey 94
Marmee, Doug 116
Marowitz, Charles 14, 63, 79, 80, 118, 141, 158, 162
Marr, Douglas 49
Marre, Albert 74
Marrero, Maria 58, 143, 145, 145, 145, 145
Marriott, B. Rodney 6, 26, 37, 37, 121
Marsan, R.D. 84
Marsden, Susan 52, 52, 84, 84
Marsh, Bernard J. 42
Marsh, Frazier W. 5
Marshall, Dorothy 109, 117, 126
Marshall, Rob 18, 19
Marsicano, Mary 15, 65
Marston, Merlin 57, 146, 161
Martell, Ronald 20, 20, 94
Martenson, Edward 63
Martin, Brian 5 ,32
Martin, Christopher 42, 73, 124, 135
Martin, James 8
Martin, Jane 18
Martin, Lisa 66
Martin, Manuel 123
Martin, Michael 53
Martin, Patricia 3
Martin, Rick 37
Martin, Tom 126, 152
Martinson, Leslie 154, 155
Marton, Laszlo 5
Marvin, Mel 55, 123, 144
Marx, Arthur 90
Maryan, Charles 74
Marzan, Julio 96
Masekela, Hugh 76, 77

Maso, Michael 68
Mason, Bruce 17
Mason, Cecelia 53, 55, 87
Mason, Marshall W. 36, 37, 139, 142
Mason, Timothy 34, 35, 37
Mast, Edward 66
Masterson, Marc 37, 38
Mastrobuono, Terri 70
Mastrosimone, William 20, 26, 38, 79, 99, 100, 133, 154, 159, 160
Matalon, Vivian 64, 161
Materson, Marc 37
Mathieson, Paul 39
Mathis, Mindy 38
Matson, James 156
Matthews, Jeffrey 126
Matthews, Tenna 18, 19
Mattos, Anita 153
Matura, Mustapha 16, 42, 167
Maucort, Didier 148
Maullar, Marci 137
Maultsby, Sara 76
Maurer, Katie 27, 40, 69, 70
Maurer, Laura 87
Mawtell, Mark 31
Maxmen, Mimi 30, 39, 58, 58, 67, 117, 134, 166, 166
Maxwell, George 116
Maxwell, John 95
May, Gary 145
May, Karl 150
Mayer, Jerry 67
Mayer, Max 16, 51, 93, 128, 161
Mayer, Nathan 108
Mayer, Paul Avila 71
Mayer, Timothy S 108
Mayhew, Henry 5
Mayne, John 81, 82
Maza, Luis 157
Mazzafro, Rick 70
McAnuff, Des 75
McAuley, Muriel 150
McAuliffe, Jody 139
McAvoy, Heather 154
McCabe, Terry 27, 160
McCall, Nick 152
McCallum, Sandy 108, 109
McCants, Laurie 25, 26
McCarroll, Jr., Earl 18
McCarry, Charles 71, 123
McCarthy, Nobu 48
McCartney, Ellen 12, 123, 135, 137
McCarty, III, Bill 95
McClary, Tom 78
McClatchy, Eleanor 129
McClellan, Cathie 16
McClennahan, Charles 11, 42, 83, 103, 104, 134
McClinton, Marion Isaac 67, 68, 134
McCluggage, John 132
McClure, Michael 150
McClure, Pam 135
McColgan, Jerry 127
McColl, Ian 135
McConnell, Kate 130, 131
McConnell, Teri 125, 152
McCord, Keryl E. 99

McCormack, Andrea 148
McCormick, Megan 130
McCoy, Hal 156, 157
McCoy, Scott 0
McCracken, Douglas 66
McCraven, Liz 118
McCray, Jennifer 5
McCroom, Darren 133
McCullers, Carson 128
McDaniel, William F. 42
McDonald, Bob 95
McDermott, Galt 65, 126
McDonald, Heather 15
McDonald, James 28
McDonald, Jeffrey David 138
McDonald, Peggy 51
McDonald, Stephen 106
McDougall, Gordon 38
McDowell, Jennifer 40, 93
McDowell, Rex 50
McEachern, Morna 50, 51
McElduff, Ellen 80
McElhaney, Susan 92
McElroy, Evie 39
McElvain, Richard 59, 86
McEwan, Mariel 94
McFadzean, David 76
McFarland, Nancy 99
McFate, Joseph R. 145
McGarty, Michael 44
McGee, Kathleen 148
McGibbon, Andrew C. 64
McGovern, Barry 76
McGown, Marjorie 153
McGravie, Anne 105
McGuire, Judy 70
McGurl, Mimi 14
McHenry, Onis 118
McIntyre, Dennis 79, 114
McIntyre, Dianne 93
McKay, Gardner 29, 70, 146
Mc Kay, Gardner 146
McKay, W. Colin 48
McKeaney, Grace 82
McKenna, Mark 157
McKenney, Kerry 65
McKinney, Larry 14
McLain, John 50, 137, 145
McLane, Derek 4, 5, 12, 20, 32, 82, 120, 123, 123, 126, 137, 167
McLaughlin, Ellen 93
McLean, Jamieson 112
McLeod, Bruce 154, 155
McLure, James 36, 57, 69
McNally, Terrence 8, 19, 38, 42, 82, 85, 102, 115, 134, 145, 153, 154
McNeal, Sandy 95
McVay, Marcelle 159
Meachem, Catherine 131
Meadow, Lynne 83
Meadows, Karen Jones 67
Medak, Susan 98
Medley, Cassandra 164
Mednick, Murray 102
Mednikov, Vera 42
Medoff, Mark 28, 43, 53, 56, 94, 150
Mee, Jr., Charles L. 97
Mee, Erin 93
Meehan, Thomas 44

Meeker, Roger 68, 162
Meerheimb, Jasper V. 154, 154
Megan, Thomas F. 104
Meguel, Muriel 150
Mehrten, Gregory 80
Mehta, Vijaya 164
Meiksins, Robert 87
Melano, Graziano 30
Melchior, Ann 55
Melchitzky, Diane 38
Menchell, Ivan 39
Mendez, Beningno 53
Menken, Alan 7, 57, 109
Mercier, G.W. 42, 71, 83, 90, 103, 104, 122, 148
Meredith, Lois 161
Merer, Johnny 43
Merrell, Amy 36
Merriam, Eve 18, 164
Merrick, Monte 45, 54
Merrill, Bob 9, 39, 50
Merrill, Robert 104
Merritt, Michael 60, 76, 77, 90, 136
Merwitzen, Michael 152
Merzer, Glen 114
Mesney, Barbara 10, 24, 52, 84, 81, 82, 84
Metcalfe, Stephen 12, 63, 81, 83, 101, 109, 146, 151, 152
Metheny, Russell 71, 136, 144
Metropulos, Penny 109, 130
Meunier, Gilberte 100
Meyer, Allen 67
Meyer, Marlane 79, 80, 139, 164
Meyer, Peter 5
Meyer, Richard 96
Meyer, Stanley 63, 82, 155
Meyers, Bruce 19
Meyers, D. Lynn 36, 57
Meyers, Richard 60
Mgcina, Sophie 89
Mhlohpe, Gcina 152
Michaels, Mark A. 129
Micheels, Lisa 21
Michel, Marilouise 43, 44
Mickelsen, David 16, 131
Mickey, Susan E. 9
Micklin-Silver, Joan 89, 118
Miguel, Muriel 150
Mihura, Miguel 100
Mikelson, David Kay 73, 106
Miles, Julia 164
Militello, Anne 80, 96, 97, 115, 144, 149, 150, 164
Millan, Bruce E. 47
Miller, Allan 20, 21, 21, 81
Miller, Arthur 8, 9, 23, 38, 46, 57, 63, 68, 84, 88, 90, 98, 106, 113, 116, 130, 132, 134, 139, 162
Miller, Bob 20, 21
Miller, Brian 149
Miller, Bruce 150, 151
Miller, Celeste 127, 135
Miller, Craig 60, 61, 102, 134, 134
Miller, Debra 35
Miller, Jason 29
Miller, Elizabeth 118
Miller, Jonathan 153
Miller, Marcie 111

Miller, Michael 58, 87, 106, 106, 120, 123, 143, 145, 161, 162
Miller, Paul 163
Miller, R. Mitchell 113
Miller, Robert 18, 140
Miller, Robin 165
Miller, Susan 96
Miller, Tim 31
Millman, Howard J. 30, 58, 59, 11
Milne, A.A. 49, 53, 67, 140
Milner, Ron 15, 74
Miner, Michael 6, 107
Miner, Michael Andrew 6, 7
Minetor, Nic 58, 59
Ming, Lou Nai 164
Minghella, Anthony 84
Minor, Philip 108, 117, 158
Minskoff, Lee 10
Mirrione, Jim 4, 41
Mishima, Yukio 107
Mitchell, Adrian 3, 46, 50, 63, 118, 119, 120
Mitchell, Bob 74
Mitchell, David 89, 108
Mitchell, Ivan 39
Mitchell, Mark 22
Mitchell, Steve 119
Mitchell, Thomas B. 107
Mizzy, Danianne 58, 82, 149
Modereger, Jeff 85
Moffat, Dick 56
Mofsie, Louis 149, 150
Mohn, Leslie 150, 157
Moliere, 12, 23, 25, 30, 39, 46, 63, 64, 68, 71, 75, 85, 87, 94, 105, 106, 122, 130, 133, 134, 145, 161
Molnar, Ferenc 27, 140, 154
Monat, Phil 30, 37, 58, 67, 85, 116, 117, 126, 145, 160, 161, 162
Mongold, Mark 26
Monitor, James 50
Monk, Debra 18, 59, 63, 65, 66, 81, 101, 118, 129, 140, 153, 154, 155
Monroe, Betty 26
Montag, Andrea 56
Montgomery, Robert 96
Montilino, John 69
Montone, Vito 135
Moody, Michael 53, 83
Moody, William Vaughn 71
Moon, Gerald 157
Moon, Jill 131
Mooney, Roger 113
Moore, Benjamin 133
Moore, Dudley 153
Moore, Jr., David 121
Moore, Mindy 118
Moore, Richard 153
Morales, Gil 63
Mordecai, Benjamin 70, 166
More, Mickey 135
Moreland, Sarah 152
Morelli, Gian Paul 80
Morell, Richard 33
Moreno, Fernando 123
Morey, Charles 13, 14, 115, 116
Morey, Joe 82
Morgan, Cass 18, 63, 65, 66, 81, 101, 118, 129, 140, 153, 154, 155

INDEX OF NAMES   **185**

Morgan, Charles 13, 14, 39
Morgan, Edward 82, 128
Morgan, Jack 131
Morgan, James 28, 29
Morgan, Robert 10, 68, 143, 144
Morgan, Roger 145
Morin, Nicole 84
Moritz, Susan T. 3
Moriyasu, Atsushi 107
Morken, Linda 33
Morley, Ruth 134
Morris, Bob 149
Morris, Bonnie 69
Morris, Bruce 45
Morris, Cleveland 45
Morris, Garrett 155
Morris, Janet S 46, 47
Morris, William S. 65
Morrison, John 15, 20, 33, 94
Morrison, Malcolm 46, 47
Morriss, Bruce 45
Morse, Frank 146
Mortimer, John 95, 116, 158
Morton, Amy 124
Morton, Carlos 123
Mosakowski, Susan 40
Moser, Nina 156
Moser, Paul 36, 71, 123, 153
Moses, Norman 87
Mosher, Gregory 76, 77
Mosier, Nina 72
Mosrgan, Charles 13
Leland Moss 153
Moss, Mary Linda 106
Moss, Sylvia 20
Mosse, Spencer 57, 105, 110, 161
Moss, Leland 153
Moss, Mary Linda 106
Motyka, Bill 94
Motyka, Thaddeus 53
Moulton, Charles 90
Mousseau, Jeff 105
Mowery, Greg 107
Moyer, Allen 121, 167
Moyer, Lavinia 19, 20
Moynihan, John 140, 141
Moynihan, Mike 54, 55, 87
Moyse, Dede 52
Mrkvicka, William C. 159
Mrozek, Slawomir 47
Mtwa, Percy 20, 42, 80
Mueller, Harold 39
Mueller, Lavonne 164
Muirhead, Jim 27
Mula, Tom 27
Muldowney, Dominic 118
Muldrow, Ida 135
Mullaney, Jan 89
Mullin, Brian 53
Mullins, Brighde 51
Mullins, Carol 89, 126, 150
Mumpton, Lisa 33
Mundell, Anne 117
Munt, Maxine 33
Muraya, Cherrie 153
Murbach, John 33
Murchie, Guy 157
Murdock, Christine 127
Murfitt, Mary 59
Murin, David 24, 30, 55, 79, 113, 115, 161, 162

Murnane, Michael 16, 27, 34, 35,
Murphy, Jr., John 150
Murphy, Kitty 109
Murphy, Michael 51, 133
Murphy, Rob 75, 97, 131, 146
Murphy, Tom 27
Murphy, Vincent 130 EP
Murray-Walsh, Merrily 5, 64
Murray, Abigail 51
Murray, Brian 5, 126
Murray, Dan 33
Murray, Daniel 46, 47
Murray, John 116
Murray, Michael 113
Murray, Rupert 76
Murrell, John 112
Muson, Eve 13, 14
Musser, Tharon 85, 101
Musumeci, Joseph B. 128
Muszynski, John P. 26
Muzio, Gloria 5, 6, 64, 92, 114, 160
Myers, Dinna 30
Myers, Larry 149, 150
Myers, Mary 167
Myler, Randal 9, 10, 30, 46, 47, 84, 88, 113, 117, 125
Mytas, Lois 118

N

Nadeau, Pierre 153
Nagy, Phyllis 92, 93
Nail, J. Paul 43
Najimy, Kathy 79
Nakagawa, Jon 160
Nakahara, Ron 107
Nakamura, Yuki 48
Nall, Roger 44
Nanus, Susan 5
Nash, Betty 100
Nash, N. Richard 14, 29, 58
Nason, Brian 74
Nassivera, John 15, 50, 165
Navarro, David 57
Navarro, Tina Cantu 94
Naylor, Ray 79, 164
Ndlovu, Duma 42
Neal, Debra 118
Neal, Marilyn 14
Neal, Stephen 53
Near, Timothy 125, 132
Nealer, Jeff 3, 157
Neary, Jack 86
Neilson, Peter 33
Neipris, Susan 82
Neisser, Juliet 150
Nelson, Brian 128
Nelson, Frances 114
Nelson, Ken 14
Nelson, Marjorie 22
Nelson, Mark 102, 103
Nelson, Richard (lighting designer) 90, 96, 161, 162
Nelson, Richard (playwright) 4, 24, 25, 38, 98, 126
Nelson, Robert A. 70
Neman, Caryn 24
Nemeth, Sally 60
Nemiroff, Robert 15

Nestor, Christopher 113
Neumann, Frederick 80
Neuser, Mary 81
Nevarrez, David M. 105
Neville, David 36, 57
Newcomb, Claudia 33
Newcomb, Don 78, 82, 163, 166
Newman, Naomi 19
Newman, Buck 3, 157
Newman, David 109
Newman, Greatrex 60
Newman, Molly 130
Newton, Michael 119
Newton-Brown, Michael 12, 13
Ngema, Mbongeni 42, 76, 77
Nice, Pamela 62, 69
Nichols, Jackie 118
Nichols, Mike 18, 77, 110
Nichols, Peter 6, 60, 129, 162
Nicholson, James 93
Nicholson, Jeffrey 33
Nicola, James C. 92, 96
Nicovich, Stef 118
Niederer, Barbara H. 106
Nielson, Peter 33
Nieman, Sheryl 33
Nieminski, Joseph 60
Nigro, Don 85
Ninninger, Susan 80
Noel, Craig 101, 102
Noguera, Hector 87
Nolan, Kathleen Kund 113
Nolan, Victoria 70
Noling, David 13, 20, 109, 145, 161
Noonan, John Ford 18, 152, 160
Noone, James 24, 83, 89, 113, 145
Nordyke, Peter 131
Norgren, Catherine F. 144
Norman, Marsha 5, 153, 163
Northman, Suzanne-Michele 99, 100
Nottbusch, Kaye 136, 163
Novack, Elizabeth 94, 95, 116
Novack, Ellen 42
Nowak, Achim 4
Nowak, Michael 67
Nowlan, Alden 117
Nowlin, Robert 118
Ntshona, Winston 16, 86
Nutrizio, Cristina 52
Nwankwo, Nkeonye 31

O

Oberman, Lawrence 20, 31, 63
O'Briain, Colm 76
O'Brien, Jack 101, 102
O'Brien, Madeline Walker 33
O'Brien, Michael 140, 141
O'Brien, Patrick 148
O'Brien, Richard 5, 36, 159
O'Callahan, Jay 59, 86
O'Casey, Sean 87, 118
Ocel, Tim 130
O'Connell, Richard L. 112
O'Connel, Paul 133
O'Connor, Clairr 93
O'Connor, Pamela 157
O'Connor, Sara 51, 86, 90, 106

Odets, Clifford 10, 26, 30, 32
Oditz, Carol 87
Odle, Dwight Richard 139
Odle, Robert 14
Odom, Bary Allen 22
O'Donnell, Mark 134
O'Donnell, William 38
O'Donohue, Kathi 31, 100
Odorisio, Robert T. 6
O'Flaherty, Douglas 73
Ogawa, Toshiro 79, 80
Oglesby, Mira-Lani 80
O'Gray, Ruby 118
O'Hara, John 60, 153
Oien, Tim H. 137, 142
Okazaki, Alan 131, 101
O'Keefe, John 135
Okun, Alexander 32, 44, 50, 158
Oleinick, Tracy 149, 150
Oler, Kim 155
Olesker, Lizzie 149
Olich, Michael 4, 9, 51, 72, 105, 106, 132, 134, 163
Olivastro, Jon 109
Olive, John 4, 8, 13, 21, 26, 30, 38, 101, 111, 115, 126, 142
Ollinick, Tracy 150
Olsen, Merritt 100
Olsen, Stephen 97 135, 138
Olson, Thomas W. 9, 17, 35
Olszewski, Mary Lou 20
Oman, Tim 147
Oms, Alba 123
Onari, 150
O'Neal, John 87, 99
O'Neil, Bradford 79
O'Neil, Tom 29
O'Neill Eugene 3, 6, 10, 20, 22, 23, 36, 44, 46, 57, 64, 67, 71, 81, 88, 92, 94, 95, 106, 110, 117, 120, 122, 129, 145, 146, 154, 160, 167
O'Neill, Raymond 38
O'Neill, Robert K. 27
O'Neill, Sue 37
Ooms Richard 63, 64
Oppenheimer, George 117
Orbach, Seth 150
Orchard, Robert J. 11
O'Reilly, Maureen 29
Ore, John E. 8
Orlock, John 69
Orr, Cyndi 21, 21, 21
Ortmann, Jeffrey 163
Orton, Joe 23, 51, 79, 83, 87, 152, 156
Orwell, George 3, 91
Osborn, Paul 17
Osborne, John 57
Osborne, Kerrie 3
Oshiro, Kiyono 116
Oshry, Joe 12, 13
Oshry, Joseph 18, 119
Osteen, Tim 118
Oster, Al 21
Oster, Suzanne 30
Ostermann, Curt 60, 88, 143, 144
Ostroff, Richard 99
Ostrovsky, Alexander 4, 44
Oswald, George 3
Othuse, James 91

INDEX OF NAMES

Ott, Carolyn 117
Ott, Lori 126
Ott, Sharon 22, 23, 52, 68, 75, 79, 121,
Otway, Thomas 73
Ouellette, Thomas 165
Ouzounian, Richard 7
Ouzts, Randall 54
Overmyer, Eric 7, 16, 18, 32, 36, 51, 52, 67, 73, 84, 94, 110, 128, 130, 135, 139, 140, 157, 159
Owen, Bobbi 71, 119, 120
Owen, Paul 5, 6
Owens, Robert 155
Owens, Rochelle 102, 103
Owens, Romell Foster 31
OyamO, 51, 93

P

Pace, Atkin 13, 14, 57, 74, 109
Pacha, Melinda 20
Packard, Stephen 92
Page, Elizabeth 161
Page, Louise 139
Paino, John 149, 150
Painter, Estelle 39
Pakledinaz, Martin 15, 60, 63, 64, 96, 117, 136
Palacios, Perrin y 124, 125
Palm, Thom 12
Palmer, David 63
Palmer, Greg 51, 132
Pamplin, H. Shep 149, 150
Panam, Norman 43
Panella, Victoria M. 130
Panoff, Kathleen 36
Paoletti, John 60, 92, 70, 124
Paoletti, Josephine 107
Paoli, Dennis 107
Papp, Joseph 96
Pardee-Holz, Rosemary 128
Pardee, Stephen 123
Pardess, Yael 85
Pardon, Ricky 31
Parichy, Dennis 4, 23, 7, 37, 83, 98, 113, 135, 137, 142, 144,
Parker, Richard 130, 131
Parker, Wayne David 20
Parkinson, Ariel 139
Parkman, Russell 5, 49
Park-Rogers, Jana 125, 126
Parr, David 154
Parry, Chris 75
Parson, Charles 33
Parsons, Charles T. 146
Parsons, Tim 146
Partington, Rex 21
Partington, Tony 21
Partlan, William 7, 41, 42, 95, 103, 104, 158
Partyka, John 43, 44
Passanante, Jean 92
Passeloff, Aileen 149
Passos, John Dos 22
Pasternack, Barbara 155
Patch, Jerry 139
Patinkin, Sheldon 90
Patrick, Robert 102, 149

Patton, Eleanor 48
Patton, Pat 106
Patton, William W. 105
Paulin, David 116, 94
Paul, Rick 160
Paulsen, Rick 4, 46, 50, 51, 60, 72, 106, 134
Paul, Susan 119
Paxton, Catherine A. 94
Paxton, Jann 150
Payne, Darwin L. 38
Payne, Jeff 13, 14
Payne, Jim 24
Payne, William 90
Peakes, John 26
Peake, Thelma 137
Pearce, Bobby 53, 73
Pearl, Jamie 165
Pearle, Gary 120, 144, 167
Pearson, Steve 88
Pearson, Sybille 160
Peaslee, Richard 3, 96
Pechar, Thomas 132
Pederson, Rose 4, 51, 72, 134
Peet, Bill 49
Pegg, Scott 13, 14
Peggie, Andrew 152
Pehlivanian, Raffi 10
Peirson, Nathan 76
Peladeau, Marius B. 147
Peltoniemi, Eric 80, 81, 163
Peluso, Ron 62, 88
Pendleton, Austin 79, 134, 162
Penfield, Derek 100
Peniston, Pamela 99, 153
Penn, Arthur 84
Penn, Matthew 51
Pennel, Nicholas 39
Penny, Rob 93
Penrod, Jacqueline 90
Penrod, Richard 90
Penzi, James 113
Peralta, Delfar 124, 125
Peralta, Maurice 149
Percy, Edward 18
Perdziola, Robert 35, 85
Pereiras, Manuel 123
Perelman, S.J. 134
Perkovich, David 69
Perlman, Arthur 155
Perlman, Elizabeth 12
Perlmutter, Sharon 140, 141
Perloff, Carey 42, 43, 72, 92
Perry, Alvin 42, 83, 161
Perry, Jane 12
Perry, Jeff 142
Perry, Karen 93
Perry, Kim 143
Perry, Shauneille 11
Perry, Steven 78, 93, 114
Peters, James 26
Peters, Scott 88, 89, 110
Petersen, William L. 123
Peterson, Robert 87, 101, 102, 105, 106
Peterson, Eric 65, 70, 78, 98, 101, 141
Peterson, Hannibal 90
Peterson, Lisa 51, 121, 124, 167
Peterson, Mark Allen 33
Peterson, Michael A. 109

Peterson, Pamela 9, 10, 15, 58, 59, 80, 101, 144, 145, 167
Petlock, Martin 18, 19
Petosta, Jim 128
Petrarca, David 60, 98, 124
Petrick, Sandra 160
Petrilli, Stephen 94
Petrovich, Victoria 23, 48, 49, 89, 90, 126, 131, 164
Pfeil, Peter 53
Pharr, Peggy 158
Phelan, Jane Schloss 128, 144
Phetteplace, Gordon 26
Philippi, Michael S. 60, 92, 98, 124, 163
Phillips, Bob 107
Phillips, Chris 33, 160
Phillips, M. Michele 49
Phillips, Mary Braken 89
Phillups, J. 31
Phippin, Jackson 23, 32, 64, 68
Piazzolla, Astor 72, 75
Pickart, Alan 146
Pickart, Chris 73
Pickney, Scott 153
Pielmeier, John 92, 93
Pierson, Tracy 59
Pietig, Louis D. 125
Pietraszek, Rita 90, 98
Pietri, Pedro Juan 92
Pifer, Drury 111
Pinckard, Sayuri Nina 129
Pinero, Arthur Wing 128
Pinkney, Scott 28
Pinkwater, Daniel Manus 133
Pinter, Harold 24, 43, 44, 79, 86, 119, 146
Pintilie, Lucian 15, 64
Pipan, Doug 6, 7, 69
Pirandello, Luigi 12, 15, 16, 57, 71, 106, 128
Pirolo, Mark 98
Pisoni, Larry 52
Pitman, Robert 153
Pitt, Leonard 152
Platt, Martin L. 7, 8
Plymale, Trip 21
Podagrosi, June 35
Podagrosi, Victor 35
Poe, Edgar Allan 53
Poggi, Gregory 113
Pokallus, Deborah 138
Polen, Patricia 130
Polenek, Rick 42
Poliakoff, Stephen 106, 123
Polivka, Boleslav 79
Pollack, Jane 19
Pollard, Gary 105
Pollock, Suann 26
Polner, Alex 45, 54, 107
Polster, Laurie 152
Polunin, Slava 152
Ponomarov, Sergei 38
Poole, Stanley 157
Poole, Thomas 35, 62, 69, 82, 121
Pope, Nancy 71
Poplyk, Gregory 86, 108, 165
Porter, Cole 76, 77, 116, 117, 145, 150
Posner, Kenneth 24, 65, 97
Posnick, Michael 19

Post, Douglas 103, 104
Potocki, Jan 105
Pottlitzer, Joanne 124
Potts, David 5, 16, 37, 39, 58, 107, 117, 126, 129, 145
Pound, Ezra 43
Povod, Reinaldo 96
Powell-Parker, Marianne 67, 126
Powell, Eve 153
Powell, Mary Ann 143, 144
Power, Brian 152
Powers, Dennis 10
Powers, John R. 130
Powers, P. J. 17
Powers, Terrie 151
Pownall, David 152
Prandini, Adele 153
Pratt, Ron 23, 99
Prendergast, Shirley 42, 128, 144
Pressler, Terra Daugirda 103
Prewitt, Tom 122
Price, Michael 60
Price, Paul 48
Price, Robert Earl 135
Price, Viveca 31
Prida, Dolores 25
Pride, Brian 149, 150
Prideaux, James 24, 151
Priebe, James F. 4
Priem, Jane 130
Priestley, J.B. 10, 30, 76, 79
Prince, Liz 149
Proctor, Felice 127
Proett, Daniel 42, 55, 57, 129
Provenza, Robert 114
Provenza, Rosario 79, 94, 113, 164
Pryor, Deborah 3, 16, 67, 121
Pryzgoda, Kathy 84, 99, 155
Puig, Manuel 52, 109, 133, 137, 158, 167
Pullin, Judy 49
Purdy-Gordon, Carolyn 107
Purdy, Claude 10, 52, 80, 93, 110, 117, 121, 132
Purdy, James 150
Purscell, Phyllis 111
Pyne, Jr., James F. 45, 56, 111

Q

Qizhi, Huang 18
Quan, Dori 48
Queen, Jim 14
Quentin, Dolly 53
Questiaux, Jean-Francis 149
Quigley, Erin 75, 137, 142, 160
Quincy, George Cochran 89
Quinn, James 130
Quinn, Jim 19, 81
Quinn, Nancy 167
Quintana, Alejandro 123
Quintero, Jose 167
Quinton, Everett 58
Quiroga, Horacio 90

R

Rabin, Arnold 33
Racheff, James 16, 60, 61

Rachman, Belinda 149
Racine, Jean 43
Rackoff, Louis 97, 98
Rado, James 65
Rado, Ragniano 126
Radunsky, David 92
Raftery, Suzanne Soxman 99
Ragey, Joe 52, 111, 118, 132, 154, 155
Ragni, Gerome 65
Rahman, Aishah 42, 143
Rainsberger, Kevin 66
Ralston, Teri 21
Ramay, Steven 67, 68
Rame, Franca 52, 111
Ramey, Nayna 6, 7, 42
Ramicova, Dunya 23, 60, 79, 162
Ramirez, Tom 29, 122
Ramm-Ell-Zee, 150
Ramont, Mark 15, 26, 37
Ramos, Richard Russell 7
Rampino, Lewis D. 5, 6, 96
Ramsey, Van Broughton 117
Ramuz, C.F. 18

Ranelli, J. 128
Rank, Pamela 63
Rankin, John 118
Ranney, Don 67
Ranson, Rebecca 135
Ranson, Ron 131
Raphael-Schirmer, Nanalee 94
Raphael, Jay E. 36
Raphael, Timothy 87
Rapitech, 70
Rappoport, David Steven 37
Rasch, Sunna 111
Rasmuson, Judy 7, 9, 60, 79, 128, 144, 161
Rasmussen, Rick 29
Rathman, John G. 154, 155
Ratner, Bonnie Lee Moss 42
Ratnikoff, Lara 163
Rauch, Bill 39, 40
Ravitz, Jeff 85
Ray, Bill C. 112
Ray, Gregory 110
Ray, Leslie 31
Ray, Robin 5, 8, 18, 38, 54, 59, 63, 146, 154, 158, 165
Ray, Tammy L. 146
Rayfield, Gordon 74
Rayme, Nayna 62
Raymond, Bill 80
Raymond, Deborah 21, 100
Reader, Pete 117
Reams, Lee Roy 165
Rea, Oliver 63
Reave-Phillips, Sandra 42
Rebeck, Theresa 115
Reber, James P. 131
Recht, Ray 30, 72, 73, 74, 98, 98
Reddin, Keith 12, 66, 75, 124, 128
Redick, Charlene 6
Redmond, Joseph W. 81, 82
Reed, Brian Alan 29
Reed, Kelly 86
Reed, Rondi 142
Reese, Kevin 29
Rees, Roger 9
Regal, David 20

Reghi, Anne 100
Rehyer, Loren 159
Reichblum, Bill 73
Reid, Graham 68
Reid, Nick 46, 131
Reid-Petty, Jane 95
Reidel, Leslie 81
Reiffel, David 39
Reilly, Charles Nelson 8
Reinhardt, Walter 107
Reinhart, Gordon 20, 137
Reise, Brian 31
Rene, Norman 18, 23, 37, 83, 96, 139, 139
Renick, Kyle 166
Renken, Michael 59
Rennagel, Marilyn 108
Rennie, Bruce 151
Reno, Cindy 3
Repole, Charles 89
Reuler, Jack 88, 89, 112
Revuelta, Pilar 25
Reyeros, Rafael 96
Reynolds, Alan 119
Reynolds, Jerry 129
Rhode, Mary 18
Rhys, William 39
Rial, Jose Antonio 96
Riashentsev, Uri 92
Ribblet, Beth 42
Riccio, Thomas 106, 107
Rice, Barbara L. 105
Rice, Michael 18
Rice, Tim 76, 108
Richards, Barbara 13
Richards, June 72
Richards, Lloyd 15, 60, 68, 101, 102, 103, 167
Richards, Martha 141
Richards, Reve 80
Richards, Robert 13
Richardson, John 42, 70
Richardson, L. Kenneth 32, 42
Richardson, Sally 4, 9, 50, 51, 72, 87, 134, 146
Richmond, David 36
Richter, Charles 51
Rickel, Rachel 65
Ricklin, Don 165
Riddell, Richard 12
Rider, Ivan 95
Ridley, Arthur 125, 126
Riehle, Richard 149
Ries, Carole 118
Riford, III, Lloyd S. 50, 66
Rigby, Harry 118
Rigdon, Kevin 60, 75, 76, 77, 87, 124, 142, 163
Riggs, P. Dudley 112
Rigsby, Gordon 103, 104
Riherd, Mark 41
Rippe, Mark 158
Risberg, Del W. 32
Risenhoover, Max 105
Risso, Richard 85
Rivas, Fernando 71, 72
Rivera, Jose 51, 79, 81
Roach, Kevin 51
Roark, Jonathan 69
Robbins, David 151
Robbins, Jeff 50, 51, 66, 133, 164

Robe, Jr., William Yellow 51
Roberson, Will 131
Roberts, Amy 130
Roberts, Barbara 87
Roberts, John Michael 140
Roberts, Kitty 14
Roberts, Sarah 76, 77
Roberts, W. Truett 154
Robertson, Jimmy 95
Robertson, Lanie 8, 20, 42, 58, 101, 145
Robertson, Toby 137
Robertson, Will 101
Robinette, Joseph 17, 49, 140
Robin, Leo 60
Robin, Steven 101
Robins, Michael 69, 70
Robins, Robert P. 65, 66
Robinson, Andre 42
Robinson, Ben 90
Robinson, Bernitta 82
Robinson, Daniel 88, 159
Robinson, David 155
Robinson, Mary B. 64, 86, 87, 134
Robinson, Robert 145
Robman, Steven 84
Rocamora, Carol 113, 114
Rochette, Anne 149
Rockwell, Eric 111
Rockwell, Thomas 49
Rodgers, David 91
Rodgers, Mary 19, 50, 90
Rodgers, Richard 43, 49, 56, 60
Rodriguez, Damaris 53
Rodriguez, Diane 131
Rodriguez, John 25
Roemer, Rick 20
Rogers, Mary 10
Rogers, Richard 10, 19, 47, 61, 117, 151
Rogers, Roxanne 94
Rohrer, Sue Ellen 25, 155
Rojo, Jerry 96, 163
Rolfe, Stephen 76
Rolfe, Wendy A. 167
Romance, Paul D. 54
Romansky, Julia 156
Rombschick, Rolf 53
Rome, Atif 158, 159
Rome, Harold 90
Romero, Constance 5
Romero, Constanza 38, 60, 68, 102
Rooney, Deborah 155
Rooney, Robert 24, 112
Rose, Leslie 20
Rose, Philip 44, 108
Rose, Rich 20, 21
Rose, Richard 13, 14, 86
Rose, Tom 148
Rosen, Robert 147, 148
Rosen, Sheldon 92, 93
Rosenberg, Deborah 141
Rosenblum, M. Edgar 78
Rosengarten, Theodore 42
Rosentel, Robert W. 138
Rosenthal, Robert 76
Rosenthal, Sandy 16
Roslevich, Jr., John 126
Rosman, Tim 87
Ross, Bertram 78

Ross, Carolyn 47, 109, 125, 126,
Ross, Jerry 53
Ross, Jordan 90, 98
Ross, Sandra 42, 152, 164
Ross, Stuart 13, 155
Rossman, Virginia 58
Rostand, Edmond 7, 19, 106, 116
Roston, Karen 113
Roth, Ann 39, 77, 83
Roth, Michael 131
Roth, Robert Jess 155
Roth, Wolfgang 28, 129
Rothman, Carole 79, 134, 135
Rothman, Stephen 20, 54, 57, 59, 131
Roudebush, William 5, 59
Rourke, Michael 27, 90, 160
Rowe, Greg T. 110
Rowland, Ken 84
Rowley, William 136
Rowlings, Jeff 81, 82, 84
Rowlings, John 84
Roy, Alan 150
Royce, Graydon 89
Roy, Jeffrey 93
Roysdon, Douglas 157
Rozovsky, Mark 92
Ruark, Joel 92
Rubanov, Slava 140
Ruben, Anne 88, 89
Rubenstein, John 162
Rubin, Sara 143
Rubin, Steven 79, 101, 102
Rubinstein, John 160
Rubinstein, Kim 128
Rubio, Isabel 28
Ruby, Harry 9, 68
Ruckman, David 107
Rudd, Enid 31
Ruddie, Susan 149
Rue, Gary 38, 70
Rupert, Michael 45
Rupnick, Kevin 117
Rupnik, Kevin 30, 108, 134
Russel, Gail 52
Russell, Brian 111
Russell, Gail 52, 153
Russell, Jerry 140, 141
Russell, Larry 153
Russell, Norman 38
Russell, Willy 18, 88
Russo, Rick 150
Russo, Ronald G. 10
Russoto, Michael 145
Rust, Steve 82
Rustin, Dan 28
Ruth, Anita 35
Rutherford, Carolyn 90
Ruttenberg, Mike 150
Ruzika, Donna 139
Ruzika, Tom 139
Ryan, Denise 13
Ryan, James 51
Ryan, Michael 8
Ryan, Ralph J. 29, 30
Ryan, Rand 31
Ryan, Thomas M. 27
Ryan, Tim 31
Rybolt-White, Kathryn 152
Ryskind, Morrie 9, 68

S

Saad, Michael 107
Saar, David 13, 14
Sabatini, Raphael 50
Sabellico, Richard 112
Sablow, Jane 10, 150
Sabo, Claire 154
Sacharow, Lawrence 67, 126
Sadowski, Joseph 27
Saex, Robin 82
Sage, Jefferson 39
Sahl, Michael 114
Saint, David 73
Sakamoto, Edward 48
Sakash, Evelyn 35, 89
Sakren, Jared 47
Saks, Gene 101
Sale, James 8, 106, 161
Salen, Jim 69, 70
Sales, Mitzi 22
Salisbury, Lynda L. 30
Salomon, Wayne 125, 152
Salovey, Todd 75
Salsbury, Lynda 24, 30, 86
Saltz, Amy 61, 103, 104, 120, 167
Salvatore, Marilyn 158
Salzman, Eric 114
Samkowich, Lee 117
Samuels, Mark 19
Sanchez, George Emilio 80
Sanchez, Luis Rafael 123
Sanchez-Scott, Milcha 49, 52, 79, 80, 94, 148
Sandberg, Lynn 33
Sandberg, R.N. 72
Sandefur, James D. 67, 83, 115, 117
Sandelin, Sandy 67
Sanders, Kerry 93
Sanders, Pamela 146
Sand, George 42, 62
Sanford, Beth 8, 39
Sankowich, Lee 59, 117
Santander, Felipe 87
Santeiro, Luis 25, 69, 112
Sargent, Michael 31
Sargent, Peter E. 125, 126
Sartre, Jean-Paul 26, 73
Sarver, Linda 116
Sather, Andrew R. 117
Sato, Shozo 4
Satuloff, Robert 55
Saucedo, Jose 153
Sauerlander, Wolfgang 123, 164
Saunders, Anne 20
Saunders, Walter 132
Savage, William 98
Savick, Wesley 87, 156
Savinar, Tad 96
Sawaryn, David 51, 149
Sawka, Jan 73
Sawyer, Cathey Crowell 12, 13, 18, 95
Scardino, Don 121, 167
Scassellati Vincent 88
Schachter, Beth A. 51
Schachter, Steven 6, 12
Schade, Camilla 70
Schaefer, George 24
Schaefer, Louis 6

Schaeffer, Eric 45, 114
Schaeffer, Ron 159
Schaffer, Matt 37
Schanke, Scott 156
Schario, Christopher 7
Schay, Daniel L. 86
Schechter, David 115, 126
Scheeder, Louis 152
Scheer, Greg 91
Schelstrate, Jim 84
Schenkar, Joan 92, 149, 150
Schenkkan, Robert 92, 104
Scherer, Susan 111
Schermer, Phil 4, 51
Schermer, S.H. 22
Schermer, Shelley Henze 4, 22
Schertler, Nancy 15, 16, 120, 121, 134, 136, 144, 167
Schifter, Peter Mark 104, 167
Schilling, Sandra 145
Schimmel, John 18, 63, 65, 66, 81, 101, 118, 129, 140, 153, 154, 155
Schirle, Alain 46
Schirle, Joan 45, 46
Schler, Michael 82
Schlitz, Laura Amy 26, 140
Schlosser, Ira 114
Schmidman, Jo Ann 102, 103
Schmidt, Douglas W. 10, 75, 101, 102, 134
Schmidt, H. Charles 140
Schmidt, Harvey 48, 65, 84, 91, 152, 162
Schmidt, Henry J. 63
Schmiel, Bill 126
Schmitt, Anthony 20
Schmitt, Ted 31
Schneeberger, Frank 81
Schneider, Jeffrey 74
Schneider, John 156
Schneller, Marianne 80, 100
Schnitzler, Arthur 21, 167
Schnormeier, Kim 160
Schoeneman, Larry 90, 160
Schoen, Janet Ruhe 157
Schoen, Walter 131
Schofield, B. St. John 80
Scholey, Arthur 67
Scholtz, Christa 60
Schons, Alain 46
Schrader, Kate 91
Schrock, Robert 31
Schroder, William 50, 145
Schroeter, Jeff 33
Schubert, Jiri 149, 150
Schuette, James A. 166, 167
Schuetz, Kathleen 27
Schulberg, Budd 39
Schuler, Duane 64
Schulfer, Roche 59
Schull, Rebecca 31
Schulte, Sandra Nei 6
Schulz, Charles 65
Schumacher, Jim 102, 103
Schumacher, Joel 124, 163
Schurr, Carl 58, 143, 145
Schwab, Brenda 43, 44
Schwab, John 133
Schwab, Terry 43, 44
Schwager, Sally 52

Schwartz, Gil 109
Schwartz, Robert Joel 73
Schwartz, Stephen 155
Schwarz, Alfred 72
Schweizer, David 80, 97, 156, 156
Schwindt, Karen 153
Scofidio, Ricardo 40
Scofield, Pamela 58, 59, 67, 68, 85
Scott, Bryan 101
Scott, Deborah 149
Scott, Dennis 103, 104, 166, 167
Scott, Hal 114
Scott, Harold 15, 68, 128
Scott, James 30, 61, 96
Scott, Jamie 61
Scott, Oz 51
Scott, Raymond 24
Scott, Robert Owens 155
Scott, Seret 42, 79
Scully, Patrick J. 7
Sears, Joe 18, 21, 95, 152, 154
Seary, Kim 137
Seats, Jeff 122
Sechrist, Linda 26, 38, 109
Sedlachek, Buffy 81
Segal, David F. 75, 79, 102
Segal, Gilles 51, 87, 90
Segall, Harry 13, 14, 57
Seger, Richard 10, 101, 134
Seibert, John 6, 7
Seifer, Bobbie 12
Seifter, Harvey 81
Selbo, Jule 114
Selby, Curt 14
Selden, Cynthia 58
Selden, William 58
Selig, Paul 31
Selina 82
Sellers, Barbara E. 46
Selman, Matty 89
Semans, William 41
Semler, Guillermo 87
Senesh, Hannah 115
Senie, Curt 45, 114
Senske, Rebecca 36
Serban, Andrei 12
Serban, Joelle 19
Sereda, John 137
Sergel, Christopher 133
Sergel, Kristin 49, 67
Serling, Rod 63
Serrand, Dominique 147, 148
Servanton, Anne 126, 138
Seserko, Joe 133
Seuss, Dr. 35
Sevy, Bruce K. 46, 47, 145, 146
Sewell, Richard 147
Seyda, Barbara 157
Seyd, Richard 23, 52, 84
Seymour, Angela 118
Shaerin, Blaithin 152
Shaffer, Jay 33
Shaffer, Matt 38
Shaffer, Peter 9, 36, 38, 58, 76, 145
Shaiman, Marc 130
Shakespeare, William 4, 5, 6, 7, 8, 10, 13, 16, 18, 19, 20, 21, 22, 23, 24, 26, 27, 29, 32, 33, 36, 39, 44, 47, 53, 57, 60, 61, 63, 64, 66, 67,

68, 69, 70, 71, 72, 73, 75, 76, 7 79, 86, 88, 91, 92, 94, 96, 98, 101, 102, 105, 106, 107, 112, 113, 116, 118, 119, 120, 125, 129, 130, 134, 135, 136, 137, 138, 140, 141, 143, 147, 148, 155, 157, 161, 162
Shallat, Lee 4, 139
Shange, Ntozake 42
Shanley, John Patrick 18, 31, 39, 42, 59, 83, 119
Shanman, Michael 76
Shannon, Peggy 24, 76, 122, 134
Shapiro, Dan 60
Shapiro, Mel 15, 16
Sharif, Bina 149
Sharkey, Jack 101
Sharkey, Richard 13
Sharp, Jeff 109
Sharp, Kim 93, 105
Sharp, Michael 28
Sharp, Pat 14
Shatto, Beverly 88
Shavitz, Peter 51
Shaw, Bob 61, 75, 96, 120, 128, 135
Shaw, Deborah 9, 13, 20, 51, 94, 113, 123, 160, 166
Shaw, George Bernard 7, 11, 16, 21, 38, 53, 57, 61, 75, 76, 78, 9 98, 106, 120, 126, 128, 132, 15 152, 164
Shaw, Katie 149
Shaw, Paul 149, 150
Shawn, Michael 144
Shawn, Wallace 32, 44, 139, 152, 158
Shea, Andrew 94, 94, 95
Shea, Maureen 50
Shearman, Alan 131
Sheehan, John 102
Sheffield, Ann 35, 51, 71
Shelley, Mary 36, 64, 71, 72
Shell, Martin 26
Shepard, Nona 41
Shepard, Sam 3, 4, 6, 10, 16, 32, 38, 46, 74, 81, 102, 146
Shepard, Thomas Z. 104
Sher, Bartlett 97
Sheridan, Peter 152
Sheridan, Richard Brinsley 23, 69 102, 139
Sherman, Geoffrey 67, 68, 116, 134
Sherman, James 160
Sherman, Jonathan Marc 121, 167
Sherman, Loren 32, 57, 79, 96, 129
Sherman, Martin 119
Sherman, Richard M. 29, 91
Sherman, Robert B. 91
Sherman, Todd 53
Shevelove, Burt 11, 60, 85, 141, 154
Shevey, Betsy 149
Shideler, Ross 33
Shinn, P. Hamilton 9
Shinner, Sandy 159, 160
Shiomi, R.A. 107
Shireman, Ellen 52
Shirky, Clay 72, 80, 107, 150

hneider, Joshua 90
honer, John Herman 93
hookhoff, David 67
hook, Robert 87, 90, 136, 160
hook, Warner 72, 106
hores, Del 84
hort, Ron 127
horter, Alan 35
hort, Ron 127
hortt, Paul 36
house, Jack 108
house, Rebecca 67
hue, Larry 5, 8, 14, 18, 27, 30, 30, 44, 45, 56, 59, 75, 76, 81, 87, 92, 95, 96, 100, 137, 141, 146, 147, 151, 165
human, Mort 21, 109
hur, Paulina 7
hyre, Paul 22, 50, 145
icangco, Eduardo 36, 57, 61
iddons, Bruce 12, 13
iebert, John 6
iefert, Lynn 142
iege, Alan 138
iegel, Betty 16
iegel, June 150
iegel, Leslie 99
iegler, Ben 166
iegmund, Nan 105
ierra, Ruben 133
ieve, Mark 89
ills, Paul 98
ilva, Chris 80
ilva, Pedro M. 97
ilver, Joan Micklin 26, 81, 101, 122, 154
ilverman, Jan 114, 115
ilverman, Judd Lear 31
ilverman, Stan 39
ilverman, Stephanie 11
iman, Barbara 50
imas, Rick 155
immons, Bill 56, 123
imo, Ana Maria 72, 93
imon, Barney 42
imon, Eli 81
imon, Mayo 115
imon, Neil 4, 14, 30, 65, 66, 74, 92, 100, 101, 108, 109, 110, 122, 129, 140, 141, 146
imon, Roger Hendricks 104
imone, Denise 151
imonson, Eric 124
impson, Bland 8
impson, James 6, 64, 162
impson, Jim 27, 92
ingelis, James 78
inger, Connie 37, 71
inger, Daniel 31
inger, I.B. 90
inise, Gary 142
inkkonin, Eric 23
inkler, David 105
inks, Doris 38
iretta, Dan 60
joberg, Margaret 33
karmeta, Antonio 87, 131, 132
kelton, Thomas 61, 96
kinner, Randy 117
kipitares, Theodora 149, 150
klar, Roberta 11

Skoczek, Carri M. 156
Skomorowsky, Melissa Wayne 65
Skore, Tom 146
Skow, Marilyn 53
Slade, Bernard 146
Slaiman, Marjorie 15, 16, 68
Slavin, Kenda 102
Sloane, Hilary 21
Sloan, Larry 60, 124
Small, Vicky 54
Smart, Annie 63
Smit, Pieter 56, 70
Smith, Alan Keith 17
Smith, Baker S. 88, 159
Smith, Barbara 119
Smith, Bradley Rand 33
Smith, Charles 160
Smith, Christine E. 152
Smith, Craig 73
Smith, Deborah 112
Smith, Douglas D. 79, 80
Smith, Ed 93, 114
Smith, Edward G. 144
Smith, Gary 70
Smith, Gray 143
Smith, Greg 107
Smith, Kat 102
Smith, Ken 13, 14
Smith, Kendall 20, 26, 86, 89, 20
Smith, Marc P. 165
Smith, Mary Cricket 150
Smith, Michael 74, 94, 95, 123
Smith, Michael R. 65
Smith, Molly D. 112
Smith, Nancy Jo 23, 24, 46, 131
Smith, Noble Mason 120, 167
Smith, Novella 81, 82, 84, 152
Smith, Patrick 19
Smith, Peter 56, 70
Smith, Richard 98
Smith, Robin Lynn 134
Smith, Rusty 117
Smith, Vicki 16, 23, 47, 76, 87, 106, 132, 134
Smith-Dawson, Beverly 6, 110
Smits, Willy 115
Smool, Carl 115
Smtih, Alan Keith 17
Smuin, Michael 11
Smulyan, Jane 155
Smyth, Deborah Gilmour 76
Smyth, Robert 75, 76
Sneed, Terry 18, 66, 118
Snider-Stein, Teresa 51
Snider, Jane 147
Snider, Keith 29
Snider, Peggy 84
Snodgrass, Kate 115
Snowden, William 104
Snyder, Janet 133
Snyder, Patricia B. 50
Snyder, Terry 151
Sobel, Lloyd 137
Sobol, Joshua 126, 145
Sod, Ted 133
Soeder, Fran 5, 9
Solano, Bernardo 89
Solis, Jeffrey 9
Solms, Kenny 146
Sommerfield, Mark 148
Sommers, Michael 27, 69, 148

Sondheim, Stephen 4, 9, 10, 11, 12, 13, 14, 16, 18, 19, 36, 47, 60, 68, 85, 116, 117, 118, 125, 126, 139, 139, 141, 154, 154
Sonftner, Patricia 57
Soon, Terence Tam 48, 67
Sophocles, 43, 66, 72, 111, 140
Sorenson, Cheri 146
Sossi, Ron 100
Soto, Luis 103
Soule, Robert 158
Spahn, Karen S. 7, 8
Spector, Estelle 90
Speer, Alexander 5
Spencer, David 93
Spencer, Elizabeth 120
Spencer, Nelsie 117
Spencer, Norm 130
Spencer, Sara 139
Spencer, Stewart 51
Spewack, Bella 4, 15, 105, 126
Spewack, Samuel 5, 15, 126
Spoonamore, Steve 65
Sprague, Carl 24, 65, 89
Sprague, Sharon 20, 51, 94
Sprankle, Mary Beth 12, 13
Sprouse, Jonathan 140
St. Germain, Mark 28, 103
St. Lucas, Chuck 102
St. Romain, Madeleine 135
Stabenow, Steve 49
Stabile, Bill 39, 42, 117
Stacklin, Andy 46, 81, 82, 84
Stacy, Sharone 105
Stafford-Clark, Max 96
Stahl, Stephen 100
Stames, Penny 33
Stamsta, David 66, 67
Stanley, Andrea 153
Stanley, Mark 108
Starmer, John 156
Starr-Liepins, Renee 33
Stauch, Bonnie 100
Stauffer, Dane 70
Stauffer, Michael 3, 7, 9
Stecker, Sr., Robert D. 44
Steele, Christopher 119
Stefanowicz, Janus 94
Stein, Daniel 152
Stein, Debra 28, 86, 155
Stein, Douglas 4, 15, 64, 76, 77, 83, 84, 134, 136, 162
Stein, Gertrude 153
Stein, Jane 86
Stein, Joseph 155
Stein, Mark 139
Stein, Paule 152
Stein, Richard 62
Steinbeck, John 18, 75, 142
Steineck, Bob 37
Steitzer, Jeff 3, 4, 50, 60, 106
Stella, Tulio 152
Stenberg, Peter 6
Stephans, Harry 146
Stephen, G.B. 146
Stephens, Blaine 100, 101
Stephens, Claudia 78, 138
Stephens, G.B. 119, 146
Stephens, Harry 57, 161
Stephens, John 3
Stephens, Kathie 95

Stephens, Kent 6, 7, 27, 42, 132
Steppling, John 31, 81, 82
Sterling, Pamela 67, 133, 152
Stern, David 86, 94
Stern, Edward 7, 117, 125, 126
Sterne, Susan 149
Sterner, Jerry 64
Stetson, Jeff 99, 103, 133
Stevens, Debra 13
Stevens, Emily 147
Stevenson, George 33
Stevenson, Robert Louis 9
Stevenson, Timothy
Stevenson, William 93
Stewart, Adrian W. 131
Stewart, Anita 32, 43, 120, 166, 167
Stewart, Benjamin 63
Stewart, Elva 8
Stewart, Ena Lamont 144
Stewart, Jack 155
Stewart, Lindsay C. 100
Stewart, Michael 9, 39, 50, 74, 108
Stewart, Scott 23, 24
Stewart, Todd 153
Stewart, Vicki 81
Stewart, William 162
Still, James 49, 155
Stillings, Cynthia R. 92, 117
Stillwell, Liz 80, 95
Stimac, Anthony J. 89
Stipetic, Scott 53
Stock, R. 146
Stockard, Carrie L. 3
Stocker, Margarita 25
Stoker, Bram 17, 29, 66
Stoker, Margarita 25
Stokes-Hutchinson, Annie 112
Stoll, Bambi-Jeanne 146
Stoltzfus, Helen 19
Stone, Edward 5
Stone, Ewin 13
Stone, Peter 108
Stoner, LeRoy 87
Stoner, Mark 70
Stoppard, Tom 5, 27, 45, 53, 72, 124, 140, 141, 154, 159
Storch, Arthur 128, 145
Storey, David 122, 134
Storey, Ted 92
Stormont, Gwynne Lee 67
Story, John 87
Stovall, Patrick 133
Stowell, Jim 27
Strachen, Alan 117, 145
Strahs, Jim 165
Straiges, Tony 75, 101
Straine, Robert 8
Strand, Mark 35
Strand, Richard 6
Strang, Hilary 137
Stratman, Daniel 57
Strauss, Botho 135
Stravinsky, Igor 18
Strawbridge, Stephen 5, 32, 61, 64, 67, 68, 75, 122, 123, 126, 136
Strawderman, Randy 150
Strawn, Sandra J. 87
Strayer, Connie 155
Strelich, Thomas 139
Stricker, Roger 160

INDEX OF NAMES

Strimbeck, Leigh 25, 26
Strindberg, August 105
Strockenstrom, Truda 35
Strohauer, David 157
Stroman, Jeff 154
Strong, K. 151
Strong, Michael 151
Stropnicky, Gerald 26, 53
Strother, Shirlee 104
Strouse, Charles 44, 50, 155
Struckman, Jeff 23, 24, 132
Stuart, Kelly 31
Stuart, Sebastian 149, 150
Sturchio, Mal 134
Sturge, Tom 26, 65
Sturges, Preston 138
Sturm, Jason 74, 94, 150
Styne, Jule 10, 19, 117, 118
Suddeth, Greg 31
Suhayda, George Denes 131, 166
Sullivan, Alice 7, 8
Sullivan, Arthur 53
Sullivan, Daniel 121, 133, 134
Sullivan, Greg 47
Sullivan, J.R. 87, 90, 91, 92
Sullivan, John 10
Sullivan, John Carver 60, 87, 125
Sullivan, Lori 6, 27, 69
Sunde, Karen 4
Sunguroff, Tamara Bering 92
Surface, Mary Hall 29, 30, 56, 133, 140
Sussman, Bruce 109
Sutowski, Anthony 39
Suttel, V. Jane 141
Sutton, Joe 93
Suzuki, Tadashi 16, 23, 86, 87, 141
Swados, Elizabeth 148, 152
Swados, K. Edgar 12, 13, 146
Swados, Robin 125
Swan, Jon 32
Swanson, Henry 118
Swartz, Marlene 138
Swaryn, David 51
Swaw, Deborah 51
Swearingen, Henriette 69
Sweet, Jeffrey 160
Sweetland, Cynthia 65
Sweezey, C. Otis 152
Swerling, Jo 71, 92
Swetland, Dudley 39, 117
Swicord, Robin 119
Swiggart, Lisa 14
Syer, Fontaine 152
Sylvanus, Erwin 58
Symonds, Alan P. 12
Synge, John Millington 7, 22
Szarabajka, Keith 107
Szari, Catherine 153, 154
Szari, Lou 151
Szogyi, Alex 73

T

Taa, Gone 48
Tabachnick, Ken 64
Taccone, Anthony 23, 52
Takazauckas, Albert 10, 11, 23, 30, 81, 82, 84
Talesnik, Ricardo 124, 125
Tally, Ted 26, 106, 146, 154
Tambella, Mark 115
Tan, Victor En Yu 6, 12, 30, 32, 42, 44, 50, 59, 84, 85, 87, 107
Tanji, Lydia 10, 23, 48, 79, 85
Tanner, John 53
Tanner, Tony 18
Tanzman, Carol M. 56
Tardieu, Jean 33
Tasca, Jules 26, 118, 155
Taschetta, Sal-Thomas 40
Tashima, Chris 48
Tassin, Olivier 149
Tauffer, Michael 9
Tavel, Ronald 102, 149
Taylor, C.P. 63, 73, 117
Taylor, Cecil P. 106
Taylor, Clifton 39
Taylor, Dorie Rush 48
Taylor, E. Oliver 92
Taylor, Giva 161
Taylor, James P. 110
Taylor, Leslie 30, 86, 130
Taylor, Lynn 112
Taylor, Noel 8, 24, 79, 80
Taylor, Rubee 93
Taymor, Julie 12, 90, 148
Teguns, Neal San 100
Teitelbaum, Sherry 105
Telford, Jennifer 52, 84
Terkel, Studs 9, 16, 98
Terrill, Kenneth 140
Terry, Megan 102, 103
Terzis, Jane 112
Tesich, Steve 60, 113, 133
Teush, Bart 150
Thatcher, Kristine 87, 164
Thayer, Dave 76
Thayer, Joel O. 167
Thayer, Robert 30, 86
Thero, Jennifer 33
Therriault, Daniel 93
Thetard, Susan Anhalt 107
Thierheimer, Peggy 125
Thies, Howard 107, 115
Thigpen, Johnny 9, 156
Thirkield, Robert 36
Thomas, Beverly 53
Thomas, Brandon 58, 108, 129
Thomas, Dylan 16, 21, 46, 63, 119, 120, 156
Thomas, Eberle 8, 58, 59
Thomas, Rollin 132, 146
Thomas, Shirley A. 157
Thomas, Thom 15, 67
Thompson, Bryan 3
Thompson, Carol 127
Thompson, David 160, 162
Thompson, Ernest 43
Thompson, Jay 50
Thompson, Kent 7
Thompson, Lynn M. 114, 115
Thompson, Richard 34, 35, 110
Thompson, Rod 33
Thompson, Ron Stacker 93
Thompson, Tazewell 16, 39, 61, 145
Thompson, Tommy 8
Thomson, Jeff 16
Thorne, Joan Vail 8, 51, 111, 164
Thorne, Simon 152
Thornton, Carey 35
Thornton, Clarke W. 89
Thornton, Jane 99
Thoron, Elise 6, 80
Thun, Nancy 50, 114, 115
Thuna, Leonora 145
Tichenor, Austin 13, 14
Tichenor, John 13
Tichy, Jaromir 79
Tierney, Thomas 118, 155
Tilford, Joseph P. 36
Tillinger, John 79, 83, 135
Tine, Hal 155
Tinsley, Dana H. 59
Tipton, Jennifer 12, 32, 60, 63, 77, 96, 135, 167
Tirado, Candido 123
Tobar, Rene 25
Toce, Tom 155
Todd, Christopher 149
Tofteland, Curt L. 17, 140
Tolan, Kathleen 121
Tolan, Michael 11
Tolan, Robert 64, 65
Toledo, Kathleen 53
Tolkien, J.R.R. 140
Tollkuhn, Richard 125
Tolstoy, Leo 92
Tomkins, Steve 51
Tomlinson, Charles 139
Tomlinson, Neil 138
Torrey, Dee 22
Toser, David 60, 108, 117
Towers, Charles 160, 161
Townsend, Christopher 16
Townsend, Judy 70
Toyos, Lino 165
Trader, Beverly 3
Traeger, Sylvia S. 103
Traister, Andrew J. 30, 72, 102
Travis, Warren 10, 24
Traylor, David O. 9
Traynor, Brian 27
Tredici, David 90
Trevethan, Laurie 152
Treyz, Russell 9, 76, 100, 117
Trillin, Calvin 11
Trimble, David 53
Trimble, Susan 45
Tripp, Peter 31
Tristan, Anne Marie 37
Trout, Deborah 106
Troutman, Ron 62
Trow, George W.S. 90
Trow, J.D. 84
Troya, Ilion 149
Truss, Tori 26
Tschetter, Dean 80
Tsu, Susan 68, 141, 144, 154
Tsypin, George 11, 16, 60, 63, 64, 75, 96
Tubert, Susana 123
Tucker, Margaret 74
Tucker, Susan E. 117, 154
Tugwell, Colin 42, 89
Tully, Richard Walton 49
Tuohy, Susan 139
Turbitt, Christine 98
Turchetta, Tamara 87, 92, 124, 166
Turgenev, Ivan 7
Turlish, Susan 137, 138
Turne, Jerry 106
Turner, Caroline 122
Turner, Chris 76
Turner, Jerry 105, 106
Tutor, Rick 145, 146
Tvardovskaya, Olga 7
Twain, Mark 21, 26
Tyler, Royall 22
Tyree, Dianne 13, 14
Tysiak, Amy Morgan 151
Tyson, John 141

U

Udell, Peter 44, 108
Uecker, John 149, 150
Ugar, Kevin J. 108
Uhry, Alfred 9, 28, 43, 54, 69, 102, 153
Ullenberg, Francis 156
Ullman, Jeffrey 57
Ulmer, John 18, 19
Umfrid, Thomas C. 94
Uno, Roberta 141

V

Vaden, Doyle 43
Vagin, Nicolai 38
Vail, Walt 105
Valdez, Luis 48, 49
Valentine, 88
Valentino, Luca 30
Valenzuela, Jose Luis 79, 80
Valle, Miriam Colon 123
Vallerga, Paul 29, 30
Vampilov, Alexander 7
Van Bridge, Tony 7
Vance, Nina 8
Vandenbroucke, Russell 98
Van Gissegem, Rene 150
van Itallie, Jean-Claude 15, 102, 153
Van Keyser, William 21
Van Landingham, Michael 30
Varga, Joseph 28, 43, 45, 86, 143, 153
Vasek, Cheri 127
Vaughan, Barbara 143
Vaughan, Stuart 96, 129
Vaughn, Garry 115
Vaules, G. Todd 28
Veatch, Greg 146
Veenstra, Eric 119, 146
Velasco, Joseph 49
Velasquez, David Navarro 57, 80, 161
Venberg, Lorraine 38
Vercoutere, Maurice 129, 130
Verdery, James 145
Verdier, Catherine 81, 82
Verheyen, Claire Marie 63, 94
Verheyen, Marianne 9
Vernacchio, Dorian 21, 100
Vetkin, S. 92
Vetrie, Michael 33

Vetter, Trudi 66
Vida, Margaret Nuehof 76
Vig, Joel 155
Villar, Braulio 125
Vincent, Glynn 150
Vincent, Irving 164
Vityuk, Roman 131
Viverito, Margaret 165
Vives, Amadeo 124, 125
Voelker, Carol 143
Vogel, David 69
Vogel, Paula 102, 112
Vogt, Michael 28
Volk, Craig 103, 166
Voltaire, 16, 36, 68, 126
Volz, Jim 7
von Brandenstein, Patrizia 50, 145
von Goethe, Johann Wolfgang 97
von Hausch, Gregory 65, 66
von Hofmannsthal, Hugo 72
von Horvath, Odon 32
Vonk, Johan 152
von Kleist, Heinrich 32, 84
von Mayrhauser, Jennifer 5, 37, 79, 121, 126, 160
von Meerheimb, J.T. 155
Vosburgh, Dick 28, 140
Vox, David 28
Vreeke, John 18
Vukich, Bob 38
Vyzga, Bernard 47

W

Waack, Katherine 81
Wackler, Rebecca 119, 157
Wade, Bland 98
Wadleigh, Dan 154, 155
Wadsworth, Jill 130, 131
Wadud, Ali 143
Wagener, Terri 82
Wager, Douglas C. 15, 16
Wagner, Dan 115
Wagner, Daniel MacLean 128, 137, 144
Wagner, Jane 30
Wagner, Kathryn 94
Wagoner, Dan 150
Wainstein, Michael 67
Waites, Luigi 103
Waiwaiole, Lloyd 65
Waker, Daniel 135
Waldman, Robert 28, 43, 54, 69, 153, 155
Waldo, Paul R. 129, 130
Waldron, Peter 26
Walker, Bill 71, 79, 96, 143
Walker, George F. 11, 16, 64, 84, 98, 128, 134, 161
Walker, Karen 150
Walker, M. Burke 23, 50, 51
Walker, Paul 15, 90, 164
Wallace, Basil 30
Wallace, Brendan 112
Wallace, Ronald 79
Wall-Asse, Marilyn 65, 66
Waller, Fats 99, 151
Wallowitch, John 78
Walsh, Charles 133
Walsh, Paul 148

Walsh, Sheila 67
Walsh, Thommie 120
Walter, Mary Ellen 164
Walther, Trine 149
Walton, Sharon 89
Walton, Tony 76, 77, 108
Wangen, Mike 110
Wangerin, Walter 76
Wann, Jim 8, 18, 63, 65, 66, 81, 101, 118, 129, 140, 153, 154, 155
Wanshel, Jeff 42, 103
Ward, Elsa 68, 121
Ward, Michael 96
Warfel, William B. 167
Warik, Joe 21
Warner, Lee 18
Warren, David 90, 96, 117, 120, 121
Warren, Eric 99
Warren, Mary Mease 59, 117
Warren, Robert Penn 15
Warrington, Marian 42
Washington, Ken 5
Washington, Kenneth 130
Washington, Rhonnie 143
Washington, Von H. 20
Wasserman, Dale 47, 65, 118
Wasserman, Ross S. 144
Wasserstein, Wendy 118, 121, 144
Wasson, Joseph Anthony 160
Waters, Les 63, 75, 96
Waterstreet, Edmund 53
Watkins, Nayo-Barbara Malcolm 87, 99
Watson, Anne Thaxter 50, 51, 72, 133, 145, 146
Watson, Rita B. 162
Watson, Valeria 131
Waugh, Ann 94
Wayne, Melissa 65
Weatherly, Gary 3
Weaver, II, Sylvester Nathaniel 113
Weaver, Melissa 152
Webb, Elmon 5
Webb, Patricia 130
Webb, Peter 28, 155
Webber, Julian 138
Weber, Andrew Lloyd 76, 108
Weber, Debbie 18
Wedekind, Frank 75, 100
Weeldon, Steven 91
Weidman, Jerome 90
Weidman, John 76, 77, 154
Weidner, Paul 16, 158
Weill, Kurt 18, 21, 61
Weinger, Don 52, 84
Weisman, Jael 45, 46, 131
Weiss, Cheryl 109
Weiss, Elliot 20, 69
Weiss, Fred 81
Weiss, Julie 39
Weiss, Marc B. 79, 108, 145
Weiss, Mark 39
Weiss, Peter Eliot 137
Weiss, Renee 118
Weist-Hines, Marsha 35
Weitz, Paul 51
Welch, Nancy D. 121
Weldin, Scott 4, 50, 51, 60, 72, 87, 134

Weldon, James 131
Wellborn, Michael 51
Welle, David 81, 82
Weller, Karen 63
Weller, Michael 119, 134
Wellman, Mac 27, 92, 93, 131
Wells, Cathy 49
Wells, Rebecca 21
Wellwarth, Marcia Cobourn 100
Welsh, John 151
Welty, Eudora 43, 95, 114, 153
Wenck, Robert 13
Wendel, Kent 30
Wendkos, Gina 31, 99
Wendland, Mark 13, 85, 138, 149
Wengler, Catherine 148
Wentworth, Scott 104
Wentzel, Mary 59
Wertenbaker, Timberlake 63, 76
Wertheim, Earl 111
Wesker, Arnold 73, 98
Wesley, Richard 83
Westerfer, David 64
West, Greg A. 7
West, Jeff 44
West, Mae 10
West, Michael 157
West, Norma 143
West, Peter 12, 149
West, Reed 151
West, Thomas Edward 99, 155
West, Virginia M. 56
Wetherall, Jack 33
Whaley, Russell 30
Wheat, Annie-Laurie 157
Wheeldon, Carole 106
Wheeldon, Steven 49, 91
Wheeler, David 12, 158
Wheeler, Harris 54
Wheeler, Hugh 9, 16, 36, 68, 116, 126
Wheeler, Timothy 147
Whiddon, Jerry 128
Whipple, Karen 3
Whipple, Rand 26
Whitcroft, Jill 52
White, Cynthia 122
White, Diane 79
White, E.B. 17, 49, 140
White, Edgar 30, 74, 93
White, George C. 103
White, Jeff 109
White, Pamela 67
White, Richard E.T. 24, 51, 102, 163
White, Sonny 95
White, Susan A. 42
Whitehead, Paxton 32
Whitehill, B.T. 166
Whitelock, Patricia 46, 47
Whitemore, Hugh 39, 122
Whiteway, Philip 150
Whiting, John 56, 106
Whitlock, III, Deidrea 42, 110
Whitlock, III, Lewis 110
Whitmore, Hugh 81
Whitson, Richard 70
Whyte, Ron 100
Wicks, Debra 143
Wierzel, Robert 23, 32, 43, 52, 79, 94, 119, 120, 123, 164

Wiggall, David 165
Wilbur, Richard 9, 16, 23, 25, 63, 64, 68, 71, 85, 94, 126, 130, 134, 161
Wilde, Oscar 26, 29, 30, 32, 109
Wilder, Susan 112
Wilder, Thornton 47, 59, 77, 79, 151
Wilkerson, C.J. 33
Wilkins, George 8
Willardson, Peter L. 116
Willes, Christine 137
Williams, Bruce 29
Williams, Edmond 7
Williams, Elaine 74, 135
Williams, F. Elaine 3, 140
Williams, Ian 107
Williams, Jack 104
Williams, James 143
Williams, Jaston 18, 21, 95, 152, 154
Williams, John 135
Williams, Joseph 153
Williams, Karen 149
Williams, Margery 35, 66, 140, 155
Williams, Nodie 118
Williams, R.T. 119, 146
Williams, Samm-Art 113
Williams, Tennessee 4, 7, 16, 25, 39, 44, 47, 56, 58, 64, 71, 92, 94, 112, 117, 118, 132, 134, 158, 161, 162, 166
Williams, Tom 121
Williamson, David 51, 59, 97
Williamson, Laird 10, 46, 47, 72
Williams, Tracey R. 112
Willinger, David 150
Willis, Jack 44
Willis, Susan 8
Wilner, Lori 115
Wilson, Archie 70
Wilson, August 9, 10, 15, 32, 36, 60, 68, 80, 101, 102, 110, 117, 143, 155, 158, 158, 161
Wilson, Erin Cressida 121
Wilson, Jay 159
Wilson, John B. 23, 81, 153
Wilson, Jonathan 160
Wilson, Kathy 91
Wilson, Kim 125, 126, 152
Wilson, Lanford 6, 19, 36, 51, 64, 78, 87, 119, 132, 135, 139, 142
Wilson, Mark 125, 126
Wilson, Meredith 44, 108
Wilson, Richard 14
Wilson, Russell 151
Wilson, Sandy 144
Wilson, Seth 33
Wilson, Snoo 75
Wilson, W. Courtney 162
Wimer, Jo 14
Winder, Randy 159
Winge, Stein 79, 80
Winkler, Richard 39, 58, 113
Winn, Marie 85, 96, 163
Winograd, Judy 3
Wise, Jim 165
Wiseman, Frederick 12
Witkiewicz, Stanislaw 57, 99
Witten, Matthew 42
Wittman, Scott 130

Wittow, Frank 3
Wittstein, Ed 24
Wodehouse, P.G. 61, 76, 77, 101, 116
Woerner, Catherine 20
Wohl, Jack 72, 74
Wojewodski, Jr., Stan 32, 67
Wojewodski, Robert 32, 64, 67, 68, 101, 102, 134, 139
Wolcott, Judy 22
Wolf, Craig 131
Wolf, Eugene 127
Wolfe, George C. 32, 36, 47, 50, 52, 74, 88, 118, 131, 143, 146, 159
Wolfe, Kedrick Robin 100
Wolfe, Thomas 29, 145
Wolff, Art 113
Wolff, Jurgen 26
Wolk, James 9, 76, 80, 92, 114, 126
Wollard, David C. 24
Wolpe, David 11
Wolshonak, Derek 28, 45
Wondisford, Diane 89
Wong, Carey 23, 106
Wong, Gilbert 48, 133
Wonsek, Paul 67, 68, 144
Wood, Bradford 86, 108, 165
Wood, John 64, 105
Wood-Alberts, Glynis 129
Woodall, Oliver 29
Woodall, Sandra 11
Wood, Bradford 86, 108, 165
Woodbridge, Patricia 30, 85
Woodhouse, Sam 46, 131
Woodman, William 45, 114, 125, 126, 128, 145
Woodruff, Robert 11, 76
Woods, Collier 51, 72, 133
Woodward, Greer 155
Woolard, David 24, 30, 75, 83, 85, 90, 96, 115, 117, 120, 121, 166
Woolf, Steven 125, 126
Woolf, Virginia 69
World, Ronnie 31
Wormold, Keri 151
Woronicz, Henry 105, 106
Worsley, Dale 80
Wotham, Maria 95
Wren, James 65, 66
Wrenn-Meleck, Peter 109
Wright, Bagley 133
Wright Brothers, 152
Wright, Doug 103, 167
Wright, Frederick D. 138
Wright, Garland 16, 63, 64
Wright, Larry 146
Wright, Linda 153
Wright, Robert 50
Wrightson, Ann 9, 50, 87, 95, 114, 117, 161
Wulp, John 164
Wunder, Shaune 122
Wurtzel, Stuart 87
Wuthrich, Terry 57, 161
Wycherly, William 147

X

Xenos, George 73
Xerxa, Alison 57

Y

Yabuku, Reuben 47
Yaji, Shigeru 63, 101, 102, 139
Yamaguchi, Eiko 107, 108
Yanez, Rene 49
Yanik, Don 66, 67, 133
Yankowitz, Susan 93, 102
Yao, Christina 29, 82
Yashima, Momo 48
Yeager, Michael T. 137
Yeargan, Michael 12, 64, 79, 123, 136, 167
Yeats, William Butler 105
Yelusich, Andrew V. 46, 47, 84
Yeremin, Yuri 64
Yergan, David 30
Yerman, Dan 119
Yerxa, Alison 80
Yesh, Sharon 47
Yeston, Maury 83
Yesulich, Andrew V. 46
Yionoulis, Evan 51, 123
Yokobosky, Matthew 107, 115
York, Will 7, 8
York, Y. 92, 93
Yoshimura, James 82
Youens, Frederic 99
Youmans, James 24, 65, 96, 97, 114, 120, 121, 155
Young, Jean 46
Young, Susan 73
Yount, Ken 74
Yulin, Harris 76
Yungkurth, Kristin 141
Yunker, Don 35
Yurgaitis, Daniel 20

Z

Zablotsky, Peter 105
Zabriskie, Nan 160
Zacek, Dennis 159, 160
Zagoren, Marc Alan 57
Zakowska, Donna 76, 90, 120, 164
Zaks, Jerry 76, 77, 96
Zaldivar, Gilberto 124
Zapata, Carmen 24, 25, 101
Zapp, Peter 51
Zaslove, Arne 22, 66
Zeder, Suzan 49, 56, 133
Zeisler, Peter 63
Zenoni, Robert 53, 87
Zerbe, Anthony 58
Ziegenhagen, Eric 121, 167
Ziegler, Lou 70
Zielinska, Sara 157
Zielinski, Scott 162, 166, 167
Ziemann, August 69
Zierdt, Harry 111
Zimet, Paul 72, 148, 149, 150
Zimmerman, Ken 118
Zimmerman, Lynda 41
Zimmerman, Sophia 112
Zindel, Paul 37
Zinoman, Joy 144, 145
Zion, Jay 111
Zipprodt, Patricia 12, 63, 75
Zizka, Blanka 162, 163
Zizka, Jiri 96, 162, 163

Zollo, Frederick 96
Zorrilla, Jose 124, 125
Zuber, Catherine 12, 23, 32, 61, 95, 123, 148
Zucker, Laura 20
Zuckerman, Stephen 75
Zuker, David 31
Zukerman, Nava 152

INDEX OF TITLES

A

Abingdon Square, 144, 164
Absent Friends, 66
Abundance, 139
Abyssinia, 16, 60
Accelerando, 93
Accidental Death of an Anarchist, 162
According to Coyote, 66, 133
Action News, 70
Actor's Nightmare, The, 141
Adventures of Huckleberry Finn, The, 26
Adventures of Tom Sawyer, The, 34
African Company Presents Richard III, The, 110
After Crystal Night, 93
Aftershocks, 78
After the Fall, 90
. . . After These Messages, 89
Against the Tide, 150
Ah, Wilderness!, 23, 44, 144, 160, 167
Ain't Misbehavin', 99, 151
Ain't Nobody's Blues But Mine, 87
Ain't No Use in Goin' Home, Jodie's Got Your Gal and Gone: Sayings from the Life and Writings of Junebug Jabbo Jones, Vol. III, 99
Al, Al, et Al: Time and Again, 56
Alarms, 102
Albanian Softshoe, 131
Albert's Bridge, 124
Alchemist, The, 167
Alfred Stieglitz Loves O'Keeffe, 8, 42, 58, 101
Ali!, 89
Alias Jimmy Valentine, 89
Alice in Concert, 152
Alice Through the Looking Glass, 13
All God's Dangers, 42
All My Sons, 9, 14, 57, 84, 88, 106, 132
All's Well That Ends Well, 68, 94, 136, 147
All the King's Men, 15
All the Queen's Men, 15
All These Blessings, 92, 93
Alma, 72
Almost Perfect, 67
Almost Persuaded, 76
Alone at the Beach, 5, 92
Amadeus, 9, 38, 76, 145
Amazed, 70

Amazing Einstein, The, 155
Amazing Grace, 20, 69, 69, 125
Amelia Earhart: Flights of Fancy, 29
Amen Corner, The, 143
American Buffalo, 36, 128, 161
American Century, The, 3
American Clock, The, 68, 162
American Dream, The, 7
American Dreams: Lost and Found, 9
American Notes, 96
American Pie, 31
America Yes!, 111
Amorous Flea, The, 100
Amorphous George, 114
Amtrak, 102
Amulets Against the Dragon Forces, 37
A . . . My Name Is Alice, 26, 81, 89, 101, 118, 122, 154
An Afternoon at Willie's Bar, 48
An American Journey, 113
Ancient Memories, Modern Dreams, 29, 30
And a Nightingale Sang, 63, 110, 117
And Baby Makes Seven, 102, 112
. . . And Howl at the Moon, 93
Androcles and the Lion, 95
And the Air Didn't Answer, 121, 167
And the Men Shall Also Gather, 103
And What of the Night?, 87
An Enemy of the People, 98
Anerca, 152
An Evening of British Music Hall, 149
Angalak, 105
Angel Face, 103
Angels of Swedenborg, 115, 115
Angel Street, 72, 86, 137
Angie's Aching Heart, 157
Angry Housewives, 100, 119
Animal Crackers, 9, 68
Animal Farm, 3, 91
Animal Nation, 131
Animal Tales and Dinosaur Scales, 35
An Inspector Calls, 76
Ankles Aweigh, 60
Anna Christie, 22, 67
Annie, 44
Annual, 76
An Old Fashion Holiday, 30
An Old Time Movie, 30

Another Antigone, 29, 120, 145
Antigone, 73
Antony and Cleopatra, 136, 137
Anything Goes, 76, 77, 116
Apartment/Across The Way, 31
Apocalyptic Butterflies, 81
Apollo to the Moon, 29
Appetite, 31
Appointment with a High-Wire Lady, 92
Approaching Zanzibar, 135
April Snow, 83, 160
Are You Lonesome Tonight, 131
Ariano, 123
Aristocrats, 83
Arkansaw Bear, The, 91, 137
Arms and the Man, 16, 98, 129, 132, 152
Artichoke, 84, 121
Artificial Jungle, The, 13
As Is, 39, 66
Asleep on the Wind, 105
Assignment (Formerly: End of the World), The, 88
Assisyai Review, 152
As the Piano Plays, 152
Astonishing World of Benjamin Franklin, The, 17
Astonishment and the Twins, 115
As You Like It, 7, 19, 86, 94, 137
At Long Last Leo, 139
At The Back of My Head, 11
Aunt Dan and Lemon, 31, 45, 139, 158
Author's Voice, The, 124
Autobahn, 161
Autumn Elegy, 6
Awake and Sing!, 26
Awakening, The, 67
Away, 59, 130
A. Whitney Brown's The Big Picture, 11

B

Babbitt: A Marriage, 84
Babbling with Joe, 150
Babel on Babylon, 41
Babes in Arms, 117
Babies Unchained, 102
Baby Talk, 105
Baby with the Bathwater, 24, 128
Bacchae, The, 46, 63, 144
Back on the Town, 78
Bad Penny, 93
Bags, 105

Bait Shop, 3
Balcony, The, 153
Bananaland, 135
Bargains, 92
Barrancas, 82
Beach, The, 103, 167
Beach of Dreams, 30
Beatrix Potter's Christmas, 35
Beautiful Bodies, 161
Beauty and the Beast, 9, 14, 17, 30, 53, 125
Beauty Part, The, 134
Beaux' Strategem, The, 144
Bed Experiment I, The, 152
Bedfull of Foreigners, A, 101
Bed Was Full, The, 102
Beehive, 5
Beggar's Opera, The, 8, 45, 120, 137
Behind You, 31
Beirut, 130
Belle of Amherst, The, 53, 145
Benefactors, 117, 118, 123, 132, 139, 143, 151, 154
Benito Cereno, 45
Bent, 119
Berlin, Jerusalem and the Moon, 19
Berlin to Broadway with Kurt Weill, 18, 21
Bertha, the Sewing Machine Girl, 86
Bespoke Overcoat, The, 105
Best Christmas Pageant Ever, The, 140
Best of the Big Broadcast, The, 22
Betrayal, 24, 86, 109
Betrothal, A, 6
Better Days, 59
Better Living, 161
Between the Acts, 150
Beverly's Yard Sale, 149
Beyond a Reasonable Doubt, 108
Beyond the Fringe, 153
Big Bad Bruce, 49
Big Bad Wolf and How He Got That Way, The, 51
Big Boy, 31
Big Frogs, 51
Big Knife, The, 30
Big Little Show!, The, 55
Big Love, The, 97
Big Time: Scenes from a Service Economy, 12, 124
Billy Bishop Goes to War, 65, 70, 78, 98, 101, 141
Biloxi Blues, 4, 14, 18, 30, 65, 92, 108, 109, 122, 129, 140, 146, 151, 165

INDEX OF TITLES

Biography, 45
Birdsend, 103
Birthday Party, The, 43, 45
Birth of Limbo Dancing, The, 102
Bitter Friends, 74
Bittersuite: Songs of Experience, 20, 69
Blackamoor, 10
Black Cat Bones for Seven Sons, 135
Black Coffee, 158
Black Holes, 103
Blackie, 92
Black Nativity, 110, 143
Bleacher Bums, 107
Bleachers in the Sun, 93
Blessing, The, 11
Blind Date, 151
Blind One-armed Deaf Mute, The, 105
Blithe Spirit, 21, 72, 86
Blitzstein Project, The, 138
Blood Issue, 6
Blood Knot, The, 36
Blood on Blood, 135
Blood Sports, 97
Blood Wedding, 61, 101
BlueGhost Two-Zero, 101
Blue Plate Special, 54, 66
Blues in the Night, 38
Blue Window, 6
Body Project, The, 54
Boiler Room, The, 101
Bold Stroke for a Wife, A, 7
Bombshells, 26
Bone-the-Fish, 6
Boob Story, The, 11
Book of the Dun Cow, The, 76
Boot Dance, The, 74
Bopha!, 20, 80
Borderlines, 37
Born Yesterday, 39, 67, 72, 85, 113, 142
Boutique Living & Disposable Icons, 107
Bovver Boys, 39, 92
Boyfriend, The, 144
Boyle, 34
Boy Meets Girl, 4, 105, 126
Boys and Girls and Men and Women, 099
Boys' Life, 76, 80
Boys Next Door, The, 19, 39, 45, 89, 101, 113, 117, 128, 155, 158
Boys Play, 92
Brand New Beat, 44
Brave Little Tailor, The, 30, 149
Break, 33
Breakaways, The, 150
Breakfast with Strangers, 6
Breaking Legs, 102
Breaking the Code, 39, 81
Breaking the Silence, 106, 123
Break of Noon (Partage de Midi), 73
Br'er Rabbit, 151
Briar Patch, 16, 121
Bride/Bachelor Trilogy, 41
Brighton Beach Memoirs, 100
Bright Room Called Day, A, 52
Brilliant Traces, 37
Broadway, 12
Broadway Bound, 14, 66, 92, 108, 110, 122, 141
Broken Bohemian Hearts, 150
Broken Jug, The, 84
Broken Pitcher, The, 31
Brother Champ, 103
Bruno's Donuts, 150
Buddy Systems, 31
Buenavista, 89
Bug, The, 6
Bulldog and the Bear, 26
Buried Child, 74
Burkie, 36
Burning Beach, A, 11, 80
Burning Patience, 87, 131, 132
Burn This, 19, 142
Business at Hand, The, 6
Bus Stop, 94
Buster B and Olivia, 51
Butterfly Kiss, 92
By the Light of the Silvery Moon, 157

C

Caballero's Way, The, 58
Cabinet of Dr. Caligari, The, 40
Cafe Con Leche, 124, 125
Cafe Crown, 96
Cafe Under the Earth, 148
Cage, The, 099
Cain's Theme, 135
Calvinisms, 89
Calvin Trillin's Uncle Sam, 11
Camelot, 154
Camille, 5
Camino Real, 158
Candida, 7, 28
Candide, 9, 16, 36, 68, 126, 157
Canned Laughter, 31
Canterbury Tales, 157
Cantorial, 74
Cantrell, 130
Caprices of Marianne, 5
Captain Jim's Fire Safety Review Revue, 66
Caretaker, The, 79, 146
Carnival!, 9, 39, 50
Carousel, 47
Casanova, 93
Cash Flow, 45
Catch!, 114
Cat on a Hot Tin Roof, 16, 44, 47, 134
Cat's-Paw, 26, 79, 154, 159
Caucasian Chalk Circle, The, 133
Cave Life, 37
Celebrate the Pacific Basin, 29
Celebration, 11
Cellophane, 92
Cemetery Club, The, 39
Ceremonies in Dark Old Men, 110
Cezanne Syndrome, The, 93, 138
Chalk Garden, The, 24
Changing Faces, 133
Channels, 5
Charles Dickens Christmas, A, 155
Charley's Aunt, 58, 108, 129
Charlie, 47
Charlotte's Web, 17, 49, 140
Chastitute, The, 87
Checkered Carrot, A, 106
Checkmates, 15, 74
Chekhov in Yalta, 160
Cherry Orchard, The, 15, 137, 158
Chicago, 102
Childe Byron, 109
Child of Luck, 47
Children, 78
Children of a Lesser God, 43, 53, 56
Child's Christmas in Wales, A, 46, 63, 119, 120
Child's Play!, 35
Chimes, The, 56
Chinamen, 7
Chinese Charade, 123
Chopin Playoffs, The, 28, 59
Chorus Line, A, 48
Chorus of Disapproval, A, 4, 16
Christmas Carol, A, 3, 4, 5, 7, 10, 14, 25, 29, 30, 39, 44, 50, 55, 58, 59, 60, 61, 63, 64, 86, 87, 88, 91, 92, 94, 95, 98, 129, 130, 131, 139, 141, 146, 158
Christmas Memory, A, 39, 46
Christmas Pageant, 149
Chu Chem, 74
Church Key Charlie Blue, 95
Chute Roosters, 166
Chutes and Ladder's Glee, 149
Cinderella, 13, 17, 29, 49, 56, 151
Cinderella/Cendrillon, 89
Circle, A, 149
Circle on the Cross, A, 105
Circus, 148
Cities Out of Print, 40
Class 'C' Trial in Yokohama, A, 8
Classics, 102
Classics Professor, The, 92
Clear Liquor and Coal Black Nights, 36
Cleveland, 27
Closer, The, 93
Cloud Nine, 9, 24, 36
Clown Dreams, 52
Club, The, 18, 59
Coastal Disturbances, 27
Cobb, 167
Cocktail Hour, The, 101
Cocktail Party, The, 71, 73
Cocoanuts, The, 15
Cold Harbor, 80
Cold Sweat, 120
Cole, 117, 145
Colored Museum, The, 31, 36, 47, 50, 52, 74, 84, 88, 118, 131, 143, 144, 146, 159
Come Blow Your Horn, 73
Comedy of Errors, The, 13, 22, 23, 63, 76
Comfort and Joy, 121
Coming Attractions, 109
Coming Home to Someplace New, 59
Common Pursuit, The, 39, 81, 142
Company, 47, 80, 125
Concert at Saint Ovide Fair, The, 163
Concrete Womb, The, 157
Conduct of Life, The, 106
Coney Island Kid, The, 149
Confessions of an Actor, 7
Confessions of Franklin Thompson III, The, 104
Connecticut Yankee, A, 61
Conrack, 10
Consequence, 102
Contents of Her Purse, The, 34
Contrast, The, 22
Conversation Among the Ruins, 123
Conversation with Georgia O'Keeffe, A, 92
Coriolanus, 85, 96, 101
Cornstalk Wine, 44
Corpse!, 157
Corrie and Papa: A Faith Remembered, 130, 131
Cost of Living, 34
Cottage, The, 104
Cotton Patch Gospel, 9, 76, 100, 117
Country Cops, 15
Country Doctor, The, 69
Country Wife, The, 147
Coupla White Chicks Sitting Around Talking, A, 14, 152
Courage, 92
Cowgirls, 62
Coyote Ugly, 97
Cradle Song, 89
Cradle Will Rock, The, 131
Crazy Quilt, 149
Cream City Semi-Circus!, The, 54, 55
Cricket on the Hearth, A, 105
Criminal Minds, 119
Crossing Niagara, 15
Crossin' The Line, 45
Crucible, The, 139
Crucifer of Blood, The, 50
Cry in the Distance, A, 25
Cry of the Peacock, The, 146
Cup of Coffee, A, 138
Curious Adventures of Alice, The, 88
Cymbeline, 96
Cyrano de Bergerac, 7, 19, 106, 116

D

Daddy's Dyin' (Who's Got the Will?), 84
Dalton's Back, 37
Dames at Sea, 59, 117, 125, 165
Dance and the Railroad, The, 14
Dance of Exile, 19
Dance of the Chickens, The, 152
Dancing in the Dark, 153
Dancing on the Ceiling, 14
Dancing the Hora in Rubber Boots, 112
Dandy Dick, 128
Danger: Memory!, 38, 134
Dangerous Games, 75
Dangerous Glee Club, 90
Danny and the Deep Blue Sea, 1, 31, 119

INDEX OF TITLES   195

Danube, The, 106
Darkside, 47
Dark Sonnets of the Lady, The, 85
Dark Spring, 152
Darling, The, 58
Daughter of a Soldier, 105
Daughters, 118
David's Red Haired Death, 102
Day Boy and the Night Girl, The, 131
Day in Hollywood/A Night in the Ukraine, A, 28, 140
Day in the Death of Joe Egg, A, 6
Daylight in Exile, 104
Day Like Any Other, A, 52
Day Room, The, 83, 146
Day Six, 125
Daytrips, 127
Deal, The, 42
Dear Liar, 21
Death and Life of Sherlock Holmes, The, 49, 56, 133
Death of a Salesman, 116
Death of Garcia Lorca, The, 96
Deathraft, 39
Deathtrap, 165
Debutante Ball, The, 83
Deja Vu, 38
Demon Wine, 80, 103
Der Inka Von Peru, 160
Dial "M" for Murder, 122
Diamond Cut Diamond, 42
Diamond Lil, 10
Diary of Anne Frank, The, 76, 86, 86, 140, 165
Diary of a Scoundrel, The, 4, 44
Dickens Christmas Carol Show, The, 67
Dining Room, The, 100, 116, 159
Dinner at Eight, 79
Dinner's in the Blender, 102
Dinner with the Undertaker, 33
Dinosaurs, 31
Diphthong, 51
Directions, 54
Disability: A Comedy, 100
Divider, The, 41, 41
Dividing the Estate, 85
Division Street, 113, 133
Do Black Patent Leather Shoes Really Reflect Up?, 130
Does This Hurt?, 33
Dog Beneath the Skin: An Epidemic Epic, The, 39
Dog Lady, 49
Dog Logic, 139
Dogman's Last Stand, 20
Doll House, A, 111
Doll's House, A, 61, 109
Do Lord Remember Me, 74
Domino, 97
Don Juan, 68
Don Juan In Hell, 21
Don Juan in New York City, 150
Don Juan of Seville, 43, 72
Don Juan Tenorio, 124, 125
Don't Quit Your Day Job, 31
Door to Cuba, 51
Double Blessing, 74
Double Double, 9
Downside, The, 42, 79

Down the Road, 75
Dr. Korczak and the Children, 58
Dr. M. Kurtz's Christian Radio Hour, 27
Dracula, 14, 17, 29, 66, 88
Dracula, A Musical Nightmare, 141
Dragon and St. George, The, 91
Dragon Lady, 139
Dramatization of Richard Warren, 33
Dreamers of the Day, 16
Dreamgirls, 155
Dreamland, 149
Dreidels, Wassailing and Other Tails, 126
Dressin Up, Steppin Out, and Gettin Down, 143
Drinking in America, 51, 119
Driving Around the House, 19
Driving Miss Daisy, 9, 102
Drood, 154
Dubliners, 161
Ducks, 89
Duck Sisters, The, 92, 93
Dust, 33
Dutch Landscape, 85
Dutchman, 135
Dybbuk, The, 19, 90
Dymphna/Colonial Boy, 149

E

Early Girl, The, 12, 18, 20
Early One Evening at the Rainbow Bar & Grille, 166
Earrings from "Oral History", 152
Earth and Sky, 104
Eastern Standard, 83, 133
Echoes and Postcards, 127
Eddie and the Ecclectics, 14, 14
Eden, 80
Edge, The, 152
Edith Stein, 59, 117
Edna Earle, 95
Educating Rita, 18, 88
Eighties, The, 57
80 Days, 75
Elaine's Daughter, 115
El Burlador de Sevilla, 124, 125
Election '84, 114
Electra, 72
Eleemosynary, 19, 42, 83, 109, 152, 154
Elektra, 43
El Fin del Mundo, 48
El Hajj Malik, 74
Elizabeth: Almost by Chance a Woman, 79
Elmer Gantry, 55
1102 and 1103, 130
El Salvador, 37, 142
Elsie's Kitchen, 6
Emerald City, 51, 97
Emily, 83
Emperor's New Clothes, The, 13, 29
Emperor's Nightingale, The, 149
Emperor Jones, The, 88
Empires and Appetites, 150
Enchanted Night, 47

Endgame, 81
End of the World with Symposium to Follow, 9, 10
Energy Carnival, The, 66
Engaged, 7
Enrico IV, 15, 106, 129
Entertainer, The, 57
Entertaining Mr. Sloan, 152
Entertaining Strangers, 62
Equal Rights, 82
Equus, 36, 58
Escape Artist, The, 160
Essence of Morgrovia, The, 51
Established Price, 114
Etta Jenks, 79, 164
Evening Star, 148
Evenings with Mr. Eddie, 92
Every Night When the Sun Goes Down, 110
Evita, 109
Exclusive Circles, 47
Exit the King, 39
Expectations, 159
Explanation of a Christmas Wedding, 149
Extremities, 100, 133, 151

F

Fairy Garden & Self Torture and Strenuous Exercise, The, 128
Faith Healer, 5, 141
Fallen Angels, 29, 95, 117
Fall of the House of Usher, The, 12
Family, 69
Family Crest, 150
Fanon's People, 149
Fantasticks, The, 39, 48, 91, 109, 152
Farther West, 112
Fat, 103
Fathers and Sons, 79
Feast Here Tonight, 160
Feathers, 10
Feiffer's America, 98
Fellow Travellers, 7
Fences, 117
Ferril, Etc., 57
Feu la Mere de Madame, 33
Fiddler on the Roof, 109
Fighter, The, 149
Fighting Chance, 79
Figure and Other Short Works, The, 31
Film Society, The, 135
Finally Fourteen, 130, 131
Fine and Private Place, A, 61
Fine Line, A, 31
Fire in the Basement, 6
Fire in the Future, 92
Fireworks, 149
First Class, 123
First Olympics, The, 13
First Time Anywhere!, 18
Five by Ten, 4
500 Hats of Bartholomew Cubbins, The, 35
Flea in Her Ear, A, 60, 95, 116
Flight, 33
Flights of Devils, 78

Flights of Fear and Fancy, 100
Floating Light Bulb, The, 10
Floor Above the Roof, 93
Flora, the Red Menace, 160
Flow My Tears, The Policeman Said, 80
Folk Tale Quartet, A, 105
Fool for Love, 31, 81
Foolin' Around with Infinity, 27
Fool Show, The, 75
Fools Rush In, 26
Footprints on the Moon, 155
Forbidden City, The, 96
For Dear Life, 96
Foreigner, The, 14, 18, 45, 75, 146, 165
Forgiving Typhoid Mary, 103
For Lease or Sale, 120
Fossey, 161
Four Our Fathers, 6, 121
426 Chandler Street, 112
Fox, The, 21, 81
Frank Dell's the Temptation of St. Antony, 165
Frankenstein, 71, 72
Frankenstein: Playing with Fire, 64
Frankenstein: The Modern Prometheus, 36
Frankie and Johnny in the Clair de Lune, 8, 19, 38, 42, 82, 83, 85, 115, 134, 145
Fraternity, 161
Freedom Train, 155
French Delights, 34
Friends, 82
Frog and Toad, 49
Frog Prince, The, 124
From Off the Streets of Cleveland Comes . . . American Splendor, 15
From the Mississippi Delta, 93, 114
Front Page, The, 92, 155
Fugue, 145
Fugue in 30 Minutes Flat, 105
Fun, 12, 82
Fun!, 35
Function, The, 102
Funny Thing Happened on the Way to the Forum, A, 11, 60, 85, 141, 154

G

Gameshow, 70
Garden, The, 123
Garden of Earthly Delights, The, 133
Gas, 103
Genesis, 96
Gentleman and a Scoundrel, A, 101
Gentlemen of Fifth Avenue, The, 113
Geography of Luck, 139
George Washington Carver and the Jessup Demonstration Wagon, 110
Geronimo Jones, 93
Getting the Gold, 78
Getting the Hell Out of Dodge, 7

INDEX OF TITLES

Getting Through, 41
Ghosts, 106, 123, 129
Gift of the Magi, The, 5, 5, 6, 20, 28, 119, 145
Giles in Love, 105
Gillette, 12
Gin Game, The, 56, 95
Gingerale Afternoon, 31
Girl Bar, 93
Girl of the Golden West, The, 138
Girl Who Swallowed Her Sister, The, 149
Giving Birth to Thunder, Sleeping with His Daughter: Coyote Builds North America, 112
Giving Up the Ghost, 153
Gland Motel, 150
Glass Menagerie, The, 39, 56, 64
Glengarry Glen Ross, 4, 30, 44, 47, 115, 118, 131, 139, 140, 158, 161
Globeworks, 98
Gloria Duplex, 21
Goat Singers, The, 34
God's Country, 4, 6
Going to Seed, 153
Golden Boy, 10
Golden Girls, 139
Golden Goose, The, 151
Golden Shadows Old West Museum, The, 18
Gold in the Streets, 62
Gone to Glory, 47
Good, 73
Good Black, 93
Good Coach, The, 166
Good Earth, The, 28
Good Evening, 87
Good Person of Long Creek, The, 40
Good Woman of Setzuan, The, 12
Gospel According to Gramps, 33
Graceland, 151
Grace of Mary Traverse, The, 76
Granada, 124
Grandma Duck Is Dead, 151
Grandma Plays, The, 160
Grand Tour, The, 74
Grapes of Wrath, The, 75, 142
Greasepaper, 3
Great Divide, The, 71
Greater Tuna, 18, 21, 95, 152, 154
Great Expectations, 16, 66
Great Sebastians, The, 88
Griffin and the Minor Canon, The, 90
Grown Ups, 90
Gulliver, 104
Gun Metal Blues, 104
Gurley and the Finn, 6
Gus and Al, 120, 121
Guys and Dolls, 46, 71, 92
Gypsy, 117

H

Habana: Antologia Musical, 124, 125
Habeas Corpus, 26
Habitation of Dragons, The, 117
Haddock's Eyes, 90
Haiku, 115
Hair, 65, 126
Hairy Ape, The, 23, 117
Halfway There, 111
Hamlet, 7, 31, 53, 61, 64, 72, 94, 116
Hamlet ... The Musical, 157
Handy Dandy, 69
Hannah ... 1939, 104
Hannah Senesh, 115, 126
Hans Christian Andersen Storybook, A, 91
Hansel and Gretel, 151
Happy Birthday, Mama, 123
Happy Days, 81, 81, 127, 134, 156
Happy Ending, 28
Hard Times, 72, 123, 139, 144, 163
Harriet the Spy, 35
Harvey, 5, 78
Hatful of Rain, A, 128
Hattie's Dress, 105
Haunting at 905, 157
Haut Gout, 139
Have You Seen Road Smith?, 104
Have You Seen Zandile?, 152
Hay Fever, 7, 30
Headlights, 103
Headlines, 3
Heartache Heroine, The, 135
Heartbreak House, 106
Heart of the Nation, 3
Heart of the World, 19
Heart Outright, The, 150
Heart's Desire, 70
Heart That Eats Itself, The, 103
Heat, The, 149
Heathen Valley, 87, 128, 131, 150
Heaven and Earth, 104
Heaven Can Wait, 14, 57
Heaven on Earth, 92
Heaven's Hard, 8
Hedda Gabler, 23, 64, 84, 117, 144, 146, 165
Heidi Chronicles, The, 121
Heiress, The, 18, 79
Hell of a Town, A, 45, 54
Henceforward ..., 8
Henry IV, Part 1, 106
Henry IV, Part 2, 106
Henry IV, Part I and II, 162
Henry Lumper, 59
Here's Love, 108
Hero of Our Time, A, 149
Hill-Matheson Affair, The, 103
History of Food, A, 149
History of Sexuality, A, 156
Hit the Road, 148
Hizzoner!, 50, 50, 145
Hobbit, The, 140
Hoboken Chicken Emergency, The, 133
Hogan's Goat, 133
Holiday, 94, 101
Holiday Cabaret: Expectations, 20
Holiday in Kerflooey (Uh Oh, Uh Oh Goes Tralala), 148
Holy Food, 82
Homage That Follows, The, 94
Home, 113, 122, 133
Home Court, 41
Home Free, 119
Homestead Album, A, 43
Hondo Gothic, 135
Hooray For Me!, 111
Hopscotch, 67
Hospitality, 114
Hostage, The, 59, 98, 123
Hotel Paradiso, 158
Hot for You, Baby, 33
House Arrest, 51
House of Bernarda Alba, The, 3, 63
House of Blue Leaves, The, 38, 44, 88, 92, 158
House of Correction, The, 20, 79, 93
House on Walker River, The, 40
Housewives, 140
How He Lied to Her Husband, 151
How the Other Half Loves, 109, 125, 145
How to Eat Fried Worms, 49
Huckleberry Finn, 53
Hughie, 6, 57
Hugs and Kisses, 151
Human Gravity, 51
Hunchback of Notre Dame, The, 132, 147
Hunger and Thirst, 99
Hunger Artist, The, 69
Hunter and the Bird, The, 102
Hunting Cockroaches, 8, 84, 106, 118, 130, 134, 159, 163
Hunting Down The Sexes, 92

I

I Am the Brother of Dragons, 130, 131
I Can Get It for You Wholesale, 90
I Can't Pay the Rent, 40
I Can't Stop Loving You, 156
Icarus, 152
Icarus's Mother, 6
Iceman Cometh, The, 106
Idioglossia, 100
Idiot, The, 45, 158
I Do! I Do!, 65, 84
If I Had a Dinosaur for a Pet, 35
If I'm Traveling on a Moving Train ..., 7
I Have a Dream, 151
I'll Go On, 76
Imaginary Invalid, The, 63, 64
Imagination Dead Imagine, 80
Imagine, 29, 30
Immigrant: A Hamilton County Album, The, 9, 10, 30, 39, 88, 113, 117, 125
I'm Not Rappaport, 13, 14, 16, 18, 36, 47, 57, 59, 66, 67, 88, 92, 101, 109, 116, 117, 122, 129, 137, 154, 157, 165
Importance of Being Earnest, The, 26, 29, 30, 31, 109
In a Pig's Valise, 135
In Circles, 153
Incommunicado, 163
Increased Difficulty of Concentration, The, 31
Incredible Murder of Cardinal Tosca, The, 117
Independence, 13
Infinity's House, 93
Info, 54
Inherit the Wind, 71, 112, 116
In Living Color, 93
Inner Circle, The, 67
In Perpetuity Throughout the Universe, 23, 31, 51, 52, 67, 139
Inside Out, 123
Inspector General, The, 79
Intelligent Life, 6
Intermezzo, 167
Interrogating the Nude, 103, 167
Interview, 70
In the Beginning, 78
In the Belly of the Beast, 45
In the Memory of Trees, 3
In the Summer When It's Hot and Sticky, 153
In the Sweet Bye and Bye, 154
In Twilight: Tales from Chekhov, 12
Invention for Fathers and Sons, 30
Investigation of the Murder in El Salvador, The, 97
Invictus, 47
Irish Rascal, The, 87
Irresistible Urge, The, 34
Isn't It Romantic, 118, 144
Istanbul, 102
Is There Life After High School?, 14
Italian American Reconciliation, 39, 59, 83
It's a Bird ... It's a Plane ... It's Superman, 109
It's Only a Play, 153

J

Jack and the Beanstalk, 17, 29, 30, 49, 151
Jacques Brel Is Alive and Well and Living in Paris, 20, 21, 109, 16
James and the Giant Peach, 66, 133
Jamie 22, 29
Jane Eyre, 147
Jazz, Jam, No Jive, 119
Jeeves Takes Charge, 101
Jelly Belly, 160
Jenna's Edge, 102
Jerker, 156
Jester and the Queen, The, 79
Jesus Christ Superstar, 108
Jika, 93
Jitterbugging, 126
Jitters, 159
Joe Turner's Come and Gone, 9, 10, 15, 31, 80, 101, 158
Jog, 33
John Brown's Body, 162
Johnny Got His Gun, 33
Joseph and the Amazing Technicolor Dreamcoat, 76
Journey Into The Whirlwind, 31
Joy Forever, A, 160
Juan Darien, 90

INDEX OF TITLES 197

Judgment Day, 31
Juggling Entertainments, 54
Julius and Ethel, 159
Julius Caesar, 23, 63, 91, 96, 113, 125
Julliet, 51
June 8, 1968, 31
Jungalbook, 66
Juno and the Paycock, 87
Just Florida, 66
Just Say No, 166
. . . Just the High Points . . .)165
Just So Stories, 29

K

K2, 39
Kabuki Macbeth, 4
Kamikaze Messenger Service, 149
Kate's Diary, 121
Kathleen Ni Houlihan, 105
Kathy and Mo Show: Parallel Lives, The, 79
Keepers, The, 3
Key for Two, 101
Kids for President, 35
Kids from Cabrini, 55, 56
Kids in the Dark, 39
Killers, 142
Kilts, 76
Kind Ness, 87, 115
King and I, The, 43
Kingfish, 80
King John, 96
King Lear, 10, 27, 47, 63, 79
Kings, 130
King Stag, The, 12
Kiss Me Quick Before the Lava Reaches the Village, 89
Kiss of the Spider Woman, 18, 52, 109, 133, 137, 158, 167
Kitchenette, 102
Kleinhoff Demonstrates Tonight, 34
Knife in the Heart, A, 93
Knock Knock, 20, 28
Koozy's Piece, 46
Krapp's Last Tape, 26
Kudzu, 153

L

Labor Relations, 33
La Cage aux Folles, 108
La Casa de Bernarda Alba, 125
La Celestina, 124
La Corte de Faraon, 124, 125
Ladies, 90, 164
Ladies in Retirement, 18
Lady Be Good, the Story of Ella Fitzgerald, 126
Lady Day, 100
Lady Day at Emerson's Bar and Grill, 20, 29, 42, 42, 61
Lady from Maxim's, 158
Lady from the Sea, The, 31
Lady I & Lady II Talk Like Pigeons, They Dooooo . . . They Dooooo . . ., 33
Lady in Question, The, 166

Lady Lou Revue, The, 112
La Fiaca, 124, 125
La Fiaccola Sotto Il Moggio, 150
La Generala Alegre, 124, 125
Lamb's Players Festival of Christmas, 76
Landscape of the Body, 60
La Nonna, 125
La Pastorela, 48, 49
La Puta Vida, 96
Largely New York, 134
La Ronde, 21
Las Damas Modernas de Guanabacoa, 124
Last Flapper, The, 8
Last Frontier Club, 112
Last Good Moment of Lily Baker, The, 126
Last Summer in Chulimsk, 7
Last Unicorn, The, 72
Last Yiddish Poet, The, 19
Late Great Ladies of Blues and Jazz, 42
Late Lite News Comedy Works, The, 70
Late Snow, A, 153
Laughing Stock, The, 79
Laughing Wild, 44, 87, 120, 137
Laughter and False Teeth, 48
La Virgen de Tepeyaca, 49
La Zarzuela, 124, 125
Lear, 57
Learned Ladies, The, 154
Learn to Fall, 20
Leaving Egypt, 127
Le Club Hotzy Totzy, 112
Legend of Sleepy Hollow, The, 49
Legend to Oedipus, The, 162
Le Mariage de Figaro, 34
Lemonade, 151
Leon & Lena, 63
Les Blancs, 15, 47, 68
Le Senorita Margarita, 25
Les Liaisons Dangereuses, 3, 5, 7, 13, 39, 44, 134, 161, 162
Letters from Hell, 70
Letters to a Daughter from Prison: Indira and Nehru, 164
L'Histoire du Soldat, 18
Liars Poker, 31
Lie of the Mind, A, 3, 4, 10, 16, 46, 84
Life and Fate, 12
Life Forms, 150
Life Gap, 92
Life in the Theatre, A, 153, 154
Life Is a Dream, 12
Lighthouse, 152
Light Up the Sky, 15, 26, 71
Like Them That Dream, 30
Li'l Abner, 43
Lillian, 92
Lily Dale, 63
Limitations, 70
Lion, the Witch and the Wardrobe, The, 118
Lion in Winter, The, 53, 78
Liquid Skin, 88
Lisbon Traviata, The, 83
Little Brother, Little Sister, 125
Little Caesar, 107

Little Egypt, 142
Little Footsteps, 26
Little Foxes, The, 122, 125
Little Lulu in a Tight Orange Dress, 140
Little Murders, 22
Little Night Music, A, 116
Little Prince, The, 31
Little Princess, The, 49
Little Red Hen, The, 151
Little Red Riding Hood, 14
Little Shop of Horrors, 7, 57, 109
Little Tommy Parker's Celebrated Colored Minstrel Show, 143
Little Women, 35, 149
Livin' Dolls, 130
Living Skills, 26
Lloyd's Prayer, 5, 52, 69, 124
Local Menace, 3
Lodger, The, 149
Loman Family Picnic, The, 83
Lone Ranger, The, 14
Long Awaited, The, 160
Long Day's Journey into Night, 7, 23, 36, 46, 71, 92, 95, 145, 146, 167
Longfellow Project, The, 54
Long Journey of Poppie Nongena, The, 89
Long Time Since Yesterday, 143
Look Homeward, Angel, 29, 145
Loose Ends, 134
Loot, 51, 87, 152
Lord of the Flies, 17
Lorelei, The, 70
Lorenzaccio, 148
Lost Colony, The, 6
Lost Highway—The Music and Legend of Hank Williams, 84
Louis Braille, 155
Love, Oscar, 149
Love and How to Cure It, 151
Love and Science, 104
Love Letters, 79
Love Letters on Blue Paper, 98
Love Me or Leave Me, 126
Love's Labour's Lost, 5, 61, 96, 101, 106
Love Suicide at Schofield Barracks, The, 145
Love Suicides at Amijima, 97
Love Talker, The, 3, 67
Lucky Spot, The, 8
Lucky Stiff, 120
Lucy Loves Me, 92, 103
Lucy's Lapses, 121
Lucy's Play, 137
Lulu, 75
Lusty and Comical History of Tom Jones, The, 20, 33
Lute Song, 24
Lyle, 50

M

Mee and You, 143
Macbeth, 53, 71, 73, 75, 98, 135, 136, 141, 148, 149, 161
Macbett, 118, 162
Mack and Mabel, 108

Madame de Sade, 107
Madame Sherry, 61
Made in Bangkok, 84
Madly in Love, 57
Madman and the Nun, The, 57
Mad Poet Strikes—Again!, The, 111
Magda and Callas, 114
Maggie Walker Story, The, 151
Magic Act, The, 51
Magic Barrel, The, 90
Magic of Hans Christian Anderson, The, 151
Magic Word, The, 111
Mahalia's Song, 143
Main Event, The, 152
Mainstream, 150
Majestic Kid, The, 28
Major Changes, 110
Malcolm X, 31, 110
Malignancy of Henrietta Lacks, The, 34
Malpractice or Love's the Best Doctor, 46
Man and Superman, 61, 128
Mandrake, The, 152
Man for All Seasons, A, 50, 109
Mango Tea, 51
Man of La Mancha, 47, 65, 188
Man of Mode, The, 38
Manslaughter, 81
Man Who Came to Dinner, The, 158
Man Who Climbed the Pecan Tree, The, 51
Man Without a Contra, 31
Man with the Flower in His Mouth, The, 57
Mapping Uranium, 104
Ma Rainey's Black Bottom, 36, 143, 155, 158, 161
Maraya, 115
March of the Falsettos, 4
Marco Millions, 10
Mariana Pineda, 25
Marlene, Marlene, 149
Ma Rose, 164
Marriage Gambol, 31
Marriage of Bette and Boo, The, 4, 33, 84, 106, 119, 131
Marriage of Figaro, The, 98, 120
Marry Me a Little, 18, 139
Martin Luther King, Jr., 155
Marvels of Modern Medicine, 33
Mass Appeal, 15, 18
Mastergate, 12
Master Harold . . . and the boys, 26, 38, 45, 81, 84, 85, 95, 122, 151
Matchmaker, The, 47, 86
Math and Aftermath, 135
Maui the Trickster, 66
Max and Maxie, 36, 57, 69
McCarthy, 100
McKinley Project, The, 55
Me and You, 143
Measure for Measure, 20, 24, 33, 77, 102
Medea, 19
Meeting, The, 54, 99, 133
Melina's Fish, 92

INDEX OF TITLES

Melons, 166
Member of the Wedding, The, 118, 129
Memories of Alphabetical Disorder, 92
Men in Art, 149
Mensch Meier, 99, 158
Men Should Weep, 144
Men Sing, 69
Merchant of Venice, The, 136
Mere Mortals, 93
Merrily We Roll Along, 4
Merry Christmas, Strega Nona, 34
Merry Wives of Windsor, Texas, The, 8
Metaphor, The, 5
Mice, 70
Michael West: Together At Last, 156
Mickey's Teeth, 6
Mid-Winter Light, 62
Middle Ages, The, 24, 85
Middle of the Night, 111
Middle Passage, The, 28
Midsummer Night's Dream, A, 26, 40, 53, 63, 64, 74, 96, 116, 138, 148
Mighty Methusalah, The, 141
Milk Train Doesn't Stop Here Anymore, The, 166
Mill Fire, 60
Mine Enemies, 31
Minimata, 80
Minnie's Boys, 90
Minor Demons, 114
Miracle, The, 87
Miracle Play, The, 127
Miracles, 152
Miracle Worker, The, 8, 13, 113
Miracolo d'Amore, 96
Miriam's Flowers, 121
Misalliance, 120, 139
Misanthrope, The, 23, 63, 71, 75
Miser, The, 12, 30, 87, 106, 145, 167
Mishima, 48
Miss Edwina, 13
Miss Lulu Bett, 33
Miss Margarida's Way, 36, 58, 119
Mistletoe Moose, The, 151
Mistress of the Inn, The, 129
Mitzi's Glori, 150
Model Apartment, The, 80
Mojo and the Sayso, The, 42
Mom Goes to the Party, 93
Money in the Bank, 92
Monkey Man, The, 33
Month in the Country, A, 7
Moonchildren, 134
Moon for the Misbegotten, A, 20, 64, 81, 94, 110, 122, 129, 154
Moonlight Daring Us to Go Insane, 27
Moon Over Miami, 167
Moon over the Brewery, 114
Moonshadow, 140
More Fun Than Bowling, 69, 128
More Perfect Union, A, 132
Morning's at Seven, 47
Morocco, 24, 139, 166
Most Valuable Player, 29, 133
Mother Courage, 162

Mother Goose, 49
Mother Tongue, 48
Mountains and Molehills, 139
Mountain Tales and Music, 127
Mourning Becomes Electra, 120, 158
Mousetrap, The, 18
Mr. Christmas Easter Bunny, 121
Mr. Cinders, 60
Mr. Universe, 93
Mrs. California, 4, 30, 63, 86, 111
Mrs. Warren's Profession, 78
Much Ado About Nothing, 4, 7, 22, 24, 36, 39, 67, 76, 98, 106, 94, 96
Mud, 135
Mud People, 104
Mule and the Milky Way, The, 56
Mummers and Mistletoe, 138
Murder Is Announced, A, 118
Murder of Crows, The, 117
Muscles of Hands, 33
Musical Comedy Murders of 1940, The, 69
Music from a Locked Room, 160
Music Man, The, 44
Musk, 149
My Dead Wife, 121
My Fair Lady, 153
My Foetus Lived on Amboy Street, 102
My Heart Belongs to Daddy, 117
My House Play, The, 163, 166
My One and Only, 108, 116
My Sister in This House, 57
Mysoginist, The, 93
Mystery of Edwin Drood, The, 18, 69
Mystery of Irma Vep, The, 12, 13, 51, 53, 57, 58, 88, 110, 117, 118, 131, 144, 163
Myth of Consequence, A, 34
My Three Angels, 15

N

N°gg°r Cafe: A Spooky Show, The, 152
Names Have Been Changed to Protect the Innocent, The, 34
National Anthems, 79
Nebraska, 75
Necktie Party, 159
Neddy, 166
Neon Tetra, 149
Neptune's Hips, 51
Nerd, The, 5, 8, 18, 30, 44, 56, 81, 92, 95, 100, 109, 137, 141
Nero's Last Folly, 97
Nest, The, 25, 97
New Age Is Dawning, A, 29
New Age Romance, 102
New Business, 121
New Comedy Works, The, 70
New Voices, 35
Nice People Dancing to Good Country Music, 151
Nickels, Dimes and Dreams, 66
Nickel Under My Shoe, 69
Niedecker, 164

Night at the Apollo, A, 99
Night Club (Bubi's Hide-Away), 102
Night Hank Williams Died, The, 166
Nightingale, The, 29, 30, 105
'Night, Mother, 153, 153
Night of the Iguana, The, 94, 112
Night of the Tribades, The, 33
1918, 45
1940's Radio Hour, The, 14, 132, 165
Nobody, 12
No Exit, 26, 73
No Frills Revue, The, 89
No Idea, 157
Noiresque: The Fallen Angel, 107, 115
Noises Off, 6, 7, 9, 18, 21, 67, 84, 86, 95, 117, 118, 126, 146, 153, 165
No Mercy, 24
No Return, 93
Normal Heart, The, 9, 117, 143
Norman Conquests, The, 81
North Atlantic, 165
North Shore Fish, 144
Nose, The, 151
No Stranger, 114
Not About Heroes, 106
Not for Real, 152
Nothing Is Funnier than Death, 92
Nothing Sacred, 11, 16, 64, 84, 98, 134
Not I, 7
No Time Flat, 166
No Way to Treat a Lady, 54
Nunsense, 18, 57, 65, 137, 138

O

Obscene Bird of Night, The, 112
Observe the Sons of Ulster Marching Towards the Somme, 62
October 22, 4004 B.C., Saturday, 31
Odd Couple, The, 141
Odd Jobbers, 11
Odyssey, The, 105
Oedipus, 111
Oedipus the King, 66
Offshore Signals, 126
Offstage Voices, 21
Off the Meter, 105
Off to Vegas in a Custom Car, 105
Of Mice and Men, 18, 109, 128
Oh, Coward, 122
O. Henry's Christmas, 99
Oh, Kay!, 61
Oh, Mr. Faulkner, Do You Write?, 95
Ohio Tip-Off, 82
Oil City Symphony, 59
Old Business, 96
Old Lady Play, The, 93
Old Times, 119
Oliver!, 49, 118
Olympus on My Mind, 151
Omalingwo, 31

Once in a Lifetime, 75, 126
Once Removed, 94
Once upon a Mattress, 50
One Director Against His Cast, 150
One Laugh to Live, 26
One Monster After Another, 35
One Person, 102
One Two Three Four Five, 83
On Golden Pond, 43
Only You, 37
On the Edge, 140
On the Town, 16
On the Verge or The Geography of Yearning, 7, 16, 18, 36, 73, 84, 94, 109, 110, 120, 128, 130, 140, 157, 159
On the Waterfront, 39
Open Boat, The, 51
O Pioneers!, 164
Orange Pentheus, 33
Orestes, 141
Orgasmo Adulto Escapes from the Zoo, 111
Orinoco!, 131
Orlando, Orlando, 69
Orphans, 106, 114, 119, 123, 132
Other People's Money, 64
Our Lady of the Tortilla, 25, 69, 112
Our Town, 59, 77, 79
Out!, 114
Out at Sea, 47
Out of Order, 90
Outside The Radio, 51
Overgrown Path, The, 50
Over Here!, 91
Owl and the Pussycat, The, 78
Ozma of Oz, 14

P

P.S. Your Cat is Dead, 119
Pacific Overtures, 154
Pack of Lies, A, 122, 165
Paco Latto and the Anchorwoman, 114
Padre Gomez y Santa Cecilia, 124, 125
Pageant, 18
Painting Churches, 7, 15, 95, 123, 152
Painting It Red, 38
Pal Joey, 60
Papa, 54
Paper Gramophone, The, 64
Paradise Lost, 31
Paraguay, 82, 121
Parenting Class, Scene 4, 33
Pariah, 105
Park, The, 135
Passage to America, 26
Passing, 153
Passing Through, 34
Passion, 162
Passionate Extremes, 89
Passion Play, 60
Passion Play: The Way of the Cross, The, 49
Pastel Refugees, 98

INDEX OF TITLES   **199**

athological Venus, 51
econg, 93
eep into the Twentieth Century, A, 114
eer Gynt, 64
enny for a Song, A, 106
enultimate Problem of Sherlock Holmes, The, 50, 165
eoria, 70
erfectly Frank, 146
erfect Party, The, 57
erformance Anxiety, 46
ericles, Prince of Tyre, 8, 94, 106
erils of Pinocchio, The, 43
ersonals, 69
eter Pan, 5, 9, 47, 50, 118, 154, 155
haedra and Hippolytus, 167
haedra Britannica, 43
hantasie, 160
hantom Lady, The, 53, 138
hantom Tollbooth, The, 5
hiladelphia, Here I Come!, 18, 117
hiladelphia Story, The, 28, 109
hilemon, 162
hysicists, The, 44
iano Lesson, The, 60, 68, 102, 166
icnic, 109
iece of My Heart, A, 114
ied Piper, The, 50, 118
iggy Bank, The, 63
ill Hill Stories, 86
inocchio, 126
ippi Longstocking, 35
irates and Pinafores, 44
irates of Penzance, The, 53
lace with the Pigs, A, 127, 135
lain Hearts, 62
latanov, 12
lay Ball, 107
layboy of the Western World, The, 7, 22
layboy of the West Indies, 16, 42, 167
laygroup, 34
laying Doctor, 101
lay's the Thing, The, 155
lay Yourself, 161
ledging My Love, 81
o', 110
oets' Corner, The, 82, 149
oor Folk's Pleasure, 156
oppies, 153
ortrait of a Shiksa, 106
oster of the Cosmos, A, 51
ower Project, The, 152
ravda: A Fleet Street Comedy, 64
rayers for the Undoing of Spells, 107
recious Memories, 87
relude to a Kiss, 23, 139
relude to Death in Venice, A, 80
retty Polly, 127
rice, The, 24, 46, 63
rince and the Pauper, The, 21
rince Free from Sorrows, 30
rincess and the Pea, The, 14
rincess Grace and the Fazzaris, 57

Principia Scriptoriae, 4, 38, 64
Prison-made Tuxedos, 90
Private Lives, 53, 58, 122, 129
Privates on Parade, 129
Prizes, 10
Progressive Examinations, The, 102
Prohibido Suicidasse En Primavera, 124
Project!, 55, 56
Promise, The, 51, 79, 81
Propaganda, 92
Proud Flesh, 93
Providing, 33
Puerto Rico: Encanto y Carcion, 124, 125
Puff the Magic Dragon, 131
Pump Boys and Dinettes, 18, 63, 65, 66, 81, 101, 109, 118, 129, 140, 153, 154, 155
Puppetmaster of Lodz, The, 51, 87, 90
Pure Gold, 112
Pursuit of the Urban Coyote, 106
Pushcart War, The, 14
Puss in Boots, 140
Pygmalion, 38, 53

Q

Quarry, 19
Quartet, 12
Quartetto, 115
Queen Clara: Rivers of Blood, Fields of Glory, 62
Queen of Swords, 153
Queen of the Blues, 74
Queen of the Leaky Roof Circuit, The, 5
Quiet End, A, 125
Quilters, 109
Quintuplets, 123
Quirks, 31
Quisbies, 153

R

Rabbit Foot, The, 42, 114
Racket, The, 138
Raggedy Ann and Andy, 34
Rags, 155
Rainmaker, The, 14, 29, 58, 132
Rameau's Nephew, 43
Ransom of Red-Chief!, The, 111
Rapunzel and the Witch, 30
Rashomon, 128, 157
Rasputin: The Forbidden Story, 152
Rat in the Skull, 50
Rattan, 104
Ready for the River, 104
Real Dreams, 39
Realists, The, 3
Real Life Story of Johnny De Facto, The, 104
Real Thing, The, 5, 140, 141, 159
Rebel Armies Deep into Chad, 79
Reckless, 37
Red Address, The, 92
Red Fox Second Hangin', 127

Red Hot and Cole, 150
Red Hot Holidays, 42
Redmoon Waxing, 33
Red Noses, 45, 46, 60, 112, 131, 148, 158
Red Sneaks, The, 148
Reduced for Quick Sale, 26
Reduced Shakespeare, 31
Reefer Madness, 149
Reflections, 55, 56
Regard of Flight, The, 76
Regina, 79
Rehearsal, The, 76
Relatively Speaking, 21, 132, 140
Rembrandt Takes a Walk, 35
Remembering the Future, 118
Remembrance, 68
Requiem for a Heavyweight, 63
Resistible Rise of Arturo Ui, The, 162
Retribution Rag, 81
Retrofit, 165
Return of Pinocchio, The, 24
Rev. Des, 143
Reverend Jenkins' Almost All Colored Orphanage Band, 164
Revoltillo, 124, 125
Rhinoceros, 47
Richard II, 63, 137, 147
Richard III, 64, 129
Ride That Never Was, The, 149
Riffin' with Semple, 107
Right Behind the Flag, 120
Right in Your Own Backyard, 155
Right You Are (If You Think You Are), 12
Rimers of Eldritch, The, 135
Ring Round the Moon, 5, 16, 142
Rink, The, 154
Riot '88, 150
Rivals, The, 23
Rivers and Ravines, The, 15
Road, 52, 77
Road to Mecca, The, 7, 8, 9, 14, 23, 72, 85, 89, 94, 98, 101, 106, 119, 120, 139
Robber Bridegroom, The, 28, 43, 54, 69, 153
Robin Hood, 35
Robin Hood of Sherwood Forest, 17
Robin's Band, 10
Rocky and Bullwinkle, 132
Rocky and Diego, 113
Rocky Horror Show, The, 5, 36, 159
Romance, 114
Romance/Romance, 101
Romance in Hard Times, 96
Romeo and Juliet, 7, 18, 24, 40, 60, 67, 92, 96, 102, 105, 109, 118, 119
Room Service, 116
Roosters, 52, 79, 94
Roots in Water, 126
Rose Cottages, 38
Rosen by Any Other Name, A, 59
Rosencrantz and Guildenstern Are Dead, 45, 53, 72, 94
Rose of the Rancho, The, 49
Rose Tattoo, The, 58, 161, 162

Rose with Two Aromas, A, 25
Rosewood Bed, The, 34
Rosie's Cafe, 107
Rosy Cave, The, 149
Rotary Notary and His Hot Plate, The, 40
Rough Crossing, 27, 140, 154
Round and Round the Garden, 30
Rounds, 31
Rover, The, 60
Rowing Machine, The, 93
Royal Family, The, 27
Roy Blount's Happy Hour & a Half, 11
Rucker & Russo, 150
Rudolph Goes Hollywood, 35
Rum and Coke, 66, 128
Rumors, 101
Rumplestilskin & Kalulu and His Money Farm: Two African Tales, 35
Rumplestiltskin, 14, 151
Runaways, 3
Runners, 151
Rust and Ruin, 104
Ruzzante Returns from the Wars, 149

S

Sad Dance of the Prairie, 113
Safe as Houses, 150
Saint Florence, 30
Saint Joan, 11, 75, 126
Sally's Gone, She Left Her Name, 3
Saltwater Moon, 161
Samantha, 3
Same Time, Next Year, 146
Sand Mountain, 20, 130
Sansei, 85
Santa & Company, 35
Santa Anita '42, 69
Santa's Holiday Adventure, 151
Santa's Secret, 30
Sarafina!, 76, 77
Sarah and Abraham, 5
Sarcophagus, 79, 85, 166
Saturday, Sunday, Monday, 68
Saturday's Voyeur: 1978–1988 The 10th Anniversary Roadshow, 130
Saturday's Voyeur: Christmas Roadshow '88, 130
Savage in Limbo, 31, 42
Saved from Obscurity, 120, 121
Say, Can you See?, 133
Say It with Music, 22
Say No Max, 130, 131
Sayonara, 108
Scandalous Adventures of Sir Toby Trollope, The, 131
Scar, 102
Scaramouche, 50
Scarecrow, The, 33
Scenes From American Life, 79
Scenes from Saint Joan, 164
School for Scandal, The, 69, 102, 139
School for Wives, The, 64, 161
Scrapbooks, 118
Screw Loose, 100

INDEX OF TITLES

Sea, The, 7
Seagirl, 7, 66
Seagull, The, 61, 80, 140
Sea Marks, 29, 70, 146
Sea of Forms, 102
Search for Signs of Intelligent Life in the Universe, The, 30
Seascape, 122
Second Shepherd's Play, 6
Secret Garden, The, 9, 35, 133, 152, 155
Secret of Body Language, 31
See Rock City, 153
Self Defense, 8
Self Torture and Strenuous Exercise, 51, 128
Seniority, 121, 167
Senora Carrar's Rifles, 123
Serenading Louie, 64
Serious Money, 23, 96
Serpent Woman, The, 12
Servant of Two Masters, 29
Servants' Christmas, A, 62
Seven Mysteries of Life, The, 157
7 by Beckett, 145
7 Dwarfs, The, 148
1789: The French Revolution, 148
1776, 108
Sex Tips for Modern Girls, 137
Sexual Mythology Part I: The Underworld, 152
Shadow, 34
Shaggy Dog Animation, The, 157
Shakers, 099
Shakespeare Now, 70
Shall We Dance?, 22
Sharon and Billy, 8, 123
Shayna Maidel, A, 8
She Loves Me, 140
Shelter, 34
Shelter Me, 33
Shenandoah, 44, 108
Sherlock Holmes, 13
Sherlock Holmes and the Baker Street Irregulars, 35
Sherlock Holmes and the Red-Headed League, 155
Sherlock Holmes and the Shakespeare Solution, 30
Sherlock's Last Case, 14, 27, 63, 141, 158
She Stoops to Conquer, 87
Shimmer, 135
Shoemakers, The, 099
Shoes, 33
Shogun Macbeth, 107
Shooting Magda, 145
Shooting Stars, 130
Short Pieces, 92
Short Takes '89, 90
Show-Off, The, 162
Show Boat, 108
Shue Biz, 87
Sicilian or Love the Painter, The, 105
Side by Side by Sondheim, 10, 12, 19
Signal Season of Dummy Hoy, The, 67
Signs, 34
Silent Night, 6
Silent Night, Lonely Night, 146
Simply Maria/Food for the Dead, 49

Singing Joy, 51
Singin' in the Rain, 116
Sister and Miss Lexie, 114
Sister Mary Ignatius Explains It All for You, 18, 141
Sisters, 26, 74, 99
Six Characters in Search of an Author, 12, 16, 71
Six Women with Brain Death or Expiring Minds Want to Know, 158
Sizwe Bansi Is Dead, 16, 86, 132
Skin, Stone, Positive, 150
Skin—A State of Being, 115
Slaughter in the Lake, 51
Sleeping Beauty, The, 53
Slice of Pie, A, 103
Slides of Our Trip, 40
Slingshot, 131
Slowly I Turn, 46
Smoky Mountain Suite, 43, 44
Smooth Talk Breakdown, 146
Snake Talk: Urgent Messages from the Mother, 19
Snow, 69, 115
Snow Queen, The, 55
Snow White and Rose Red, 151
Social Security, 71, 90
Sodbusters, 103
Soul of a Jew, 126
So Long on Lonely Street, 13, 66, 95, 118
Some Golden States, 31
Some Men Need Help, 160
Some Sweet Day, 79
Something About Baseball, 51
Something Entirely New by the Road Company, 127
Something's Afoot, 28
Some Things You Need to Know Before the World Ends (A Final Evening with the Illuminati), 146, 159
Somewhere over the Balcony, 152
Songs Without Words, 104
Sophie, 73
Sophisticated Ladies, 42
Sorcerer's Apprentice, The, 140
Soulful Scream of a Chosen Son, 114
Soul Survivor, 153
Soundbite, 121
Southern Cross, 69
South of the Mountain, 127
Souvenirs of Old New-York, 105
Space, 93
Space and Light, 34
Spaces, 157
Spare Parts, 161
Sparks in the Park, 120, 167
Speaking in Tongues, 82
Special Occasions, 21
Speed-the-Plow, 76, 77, 124, 163
Speed of Darkness, The, 60
Spell #7, 42
Spiele '36, 93
Spike Heels, 115
Spittin' Image, 151
Splendid Mummer, 11
Split Second, 144
Spoils of War, 134

Spooks, 42
Sports Show, The, 66
Spring Awakening, 100
Squats, 115
St. Paul Suite, 62
Stages, 66
Stained Glass, 6
Stalwarts, The, 93
Stand-Up Tragedy, 85
Standard of the Breed, 31
Starcleaner Reunion: Tales of Wonder, The, 17
Star Crash, 106
Starmites, 13
Stars in the Morning Sky, 80
Starting Monday, 103, 167
Statements After an Arrest Under the Immorality Act, 69, 162
Stauf, 114
Steal Away, 143
Stealing, 133
Steel Magnolias, 6, 7, 8, 9, 14, 15, 16, 18, 21, 36, 59, 67, 95, 106, 117, 126, 130, 144, 145
Stella, 97
Step into My World, 10
Stepping Out, 8, 24, 36, 58, 85, 140, 142, 145, 155
Stew Rice, 48
Sticks and Stones, 157
Stick Wife, The, 23, 27, 52, 159
Stone Wedding, 80
Stories of the Golden West, 29
Storybook Theatre, 14
Strange Snow, 81, 84, 109, 152
Streetcar Named Desire, A, 7, 25, 71, 92, 117, 118, 132
Strider, 92
Stronger, The, 105
Struttin', 10
Subject of Child, A, 166
Subject Was Roses, The, 57
Suds: The Rocking '60s Musical Soap Opera, 101
Suenos, 72, 80
Suffering Fools, 103
Sugar Babies, 118
Suicide, The, 25
Summer of the Dance, The, 33
Sunday in the Park with George, 118, 139
Sun of the Sleepless, 150
Sunshine Boys, The, 74
Survival Revival Revue!, The, 55, 87
Susan B!, 155
Swamp Foxes, 107
Swamp Gas and Shallow Feelings, 104
Swan Play, The, 121
Sweeney Todd, 109
Sweet-Talker, 26
Sweet Deceit, The, 93
Symmes' Hole, 100
Symphony of Rats, 104, 165

T

Table Manners, 47
Takedown, 34
Taking Care of Business, 109

Taking Steps, 5, 15, 16, 21, 39, 14
Talented Tenth, The, 83
Tale of Lear, The, 16, 23, 86, 141
Tales from the Dreamtime, 67
Tales of a Fourth Grade Nothing, 17
Tales of Brer Rabbit, 29
Tales of the Holiday, 29, 30
Tales of the Lost Formicans, 6, 92, 126
Tales of Tinseltown, 57
Talking Band: Betty Bends the Blues and The Malady of Death, The, 150
Talking Band: The Three Lives of Lucie Cabrol, The, 149
Talking Pictures, 27
Talking to Myself, 98
Talking to the Sun, 153
Talking With . . . , 18
Talk Radio, 38, 66, 81, 96, 159
Talley's Folly, 78, 87, 132, 139
Tallulah Tonight, 11
Tamer of Horses, 20, 38, 99, 160
Taming of the Shrew, The, 24, 53, 118, 120, 148
Tango Apasionado, 71
Tapestry, 36
Tapman, 67
Taproot, 31
Tartoof, or an Imposter in Norcatur—and at Christmas!, 4
Tartuffe, 25, 85, 94, 122, 130, 133
T Bone N Weasel, 9, 133, 155
Tea, 83, 101
Teamsters Basement, 31
Tears of Rage, 114
Tea with Mommy and Jack, 67
Ted and Edna, 93
Teddy Roosevelt, 155
Tempest, The, 6, 13, 16, 29, 31, 4, 69, 88, 109, 112, 130, 134
Temporary Place, A, 31
Temptation, 85, 96, 163
Temptation of Maddie Graham, The, 111
Ten November, 6, 20, 80, 81, 163
Tent Meeting, 119
Tenure Track, 102
Terminal Bar, 31
Terminal Hip, 92
Terra Nova, 106, 146, 153
Terror of the Soul: Tales by Edgar Allan Poe, 53
Terry by Terry, 82
Testimonies of a Rape and Killing, 149
Tete a Tete, 24
Texarkana, 33
That Championship Season, 29
That Crazy Cabaret, 150
That Old Comedy, 150
That Pig of a Molette, 104
That Serious He-Man Ball, 11, 74
That's It, Folks!, 134
Theater, 26
Theatre in Your Lap, 101
Theda Bara and the Frontier Rabbi, 65
There's One in Every Marriage, 3
Thick Dick, 149

INDEX OF TITLES 201

highs Like Tina Turner, 149
hin Air, 131
his Is Not a Pipe Dream, 56
housand Clowns, A, 15
hree S, The, 73
hree Front, 103
  Guys Naked From the Waist
    Down, 45
hree Little Pigs and Three Billy
  Goats Gruff, The, 17
hree Musketeers, The, 71, 107
hreepenny Opera, The, 61
hree Postcards, 3, 42, 54, 98
hree Sillies, The, 157
hree Sisters, The, 22, 73, 86, 107
hree Tales of Givers and Their
  Gifts, 125
hree Top Hats, 100
hree Ways Home, 52, 80
hrill a Moment, A, 93
hunderbird American Indian
  Dancers Annual Pow Wow and
  Dance Concert, 149
hursday's Child, 30
ime and the Conways, 30
imon of Athens, 23, 101
intypes, 144
iny Mommy, 120, 167
ira Tells Everything There Is to
  Know About Herself, 119
is Pity She's a Whore, 12
is the Morning, 93
ito, 160
itus Andronicus, 8, 94, 96, 106
oday's Special, 31
oe to Toe, 31
o Forgive, Divine, 86
o Gleam It Around, To Show My
  Shine, 42
o Life!, 55
omfoolery, 5, 8, 18, 38, 54, 59,
  63, 146, 154, 158, 165
om Jones, 91, 94, 137
om Sawyer, 13, 21
om's Coffee Dog, 34
o My Loving Son, 103
ons of Money, 88
op Girls, 161
orch, The, 87
ortoise and the Hare, The, 149
orture, 33
ouch of the Poet, A, 3
owards Zero, 19
ower, The, 40, 41, 69, 93
own Mouse and the Country
  Mouse, The, 151
oys for Men, 151
racers, 57, 110, 133, 146, 161
ransitions in Time and Space, 33
ranslocation 9:16, 149
raveler in the Dark, 163
raveling Lady, 111
raveling North, 59
ravelling Man, The, 105
reasure Island, 9
ree of Memory, 62
rial, The, 73
rial of Joan of Arc at Rouen,
  1431, The, 164
rinity, 93
roilus and Cressida, 23, 136

Trophy Hunters, 46
Troubles: Children of Belfast, The,
  35
True West, 38, 146
Truffles in the Soup, 134
Trust and Opening Day, 92
Turned Around Tales, 143
Tusitala, 24
Twelfth Night, 21, 22, 96, 98, 106,
  143
24 Lilly Pond Lane150
Twilight Room, The, 126
Two, 98
Two Gentlemen of Verona, 46, 94,
  106, 147, 155
Two into One, 108
Two Lous, 33
Two Many Bosses, 33
Two Rooms, 75

U

U.S.A., 22
Ubu for President, 148
Uncle Vanya, 12, 38, 43, 44, 84
Under Milk Wood, 16, 21, 156
Under One Sun, 29
Under the Double Moon, 103
Une Heureuse Rencontre, 33
Unexpected Guest, The, 21, 132
Unfinished Women Cry in No
  Man's Land While a Bird Dies in
  a Gilded Cage, 143
Unguided Missile, The, 11
Unwilling Recruit, The, 105
Up in Saratoga, 102
Up 'n' Under, 68
Up the Down Staircase, 133
Urban Blight, 83
Urges, 33
US, 149
Useless Beauty, 58
Usted Tambier Podra Disfrutar de
  Ella, 124

V

V & V Only, 37, 139
Vacancy, 48
Value of Names, The, 160
Variations on Joan of Arc, 164
Variations on the Death of Trotsky,
  93
Velveteen Rabbit, The, 35, 66, 140,
  155
Venus and Adonis, 63
Veteran's Day, 46, 159
View from the Bridge, A, 8, 23,
  113, 130
Vikings, 12, 63, 146
Village Wooing, 57
Virgin Flight, 157
Virginia Real, 151
Virgin Molly, The, 121
Vision, A, 104
Visions of an Ancient Dreamer, 141
Visions of Don Juan, 40
Viva, 52

Viva Reviva, 164
Vktms, 150
Voice of the Prairie, The, 4, 8, 13,
  21, 26, 30, 38, 64, 101, 111, 115;
  126
Voices of Christmas, 133
Voices of Silence, 164
Volpone, 158
Voodoo Economics, 150
Voyage of Sinbad the Sailor, The,
  17

W

Waiters, 152
Waiting for Godot, 23, 47, 77, 94,
  98, 102
Waiting for Lepke, 105
Wait Until Dark, 21, 145
Walkers, 67, 121
Walking Fire, 34
Walking the Line, 151
Walking Through Walls, 102
Walk in the Woods, A, 16, 18, 59,
  66, 95, 123, 142, 144, 161
Walk on the Wild Side, A, 20, 89
Walks of Indian Women, 150
Wall Inside, The, 105
Wall of Water, The, 166
Waltz of the Toreadors, The, 8
Warriors of the Mystic Word, 100
Warsaw Tango, 152
Washington Heights, 73
Water Engine, The, 24
Water Log, The, 66
Water Music, 51
Water Torture, 6
Wedding, The, 24
Wedding Band, 87
Webster Street Blues, 48
Welcome Back to Salamanca, 71
Wenceslas Square, 27, 59, 96, 147
West Memphis Mojo, 42, 143,
  144
West Side Story, 14
Wet Carpets, 42
We the People, 151, 155
What a Man Weighs, 93
What Did He See?, 104
What Do You Want to Be When
  You Grow Old?, 55
What Part Will I Play, 29
What's Wrong with This Picture?,
  20
What the Butler Saw, 23, 79, 83,
  156
When I Grow Up, 139
When the Wind Blows, 22
When We Are Married, 10, 79
When You Comin' Back, Red
  Ryder?, 94
Whereabouts Unknown, 5
Where Nobody Belongs, 48
Whirligig, 93
Whistle in the Dark, A, 27
White Boned Demon, 150
White Death, 31
White Linen, 101
White People, 135
White Plague, The, 98

White Trash, 92
Whole Hearted, 93
Wholly Moses, 87
Whore and the h'Empress, The, 5
Who's Afraid of Virginia Woolf?,
  26, 119
Why Can't We Talk?, 150
Why Can't You Be Him?, 18
Why Hanna's Skirt Won't Stay
  Down, 102
Why the Lord Come to Sand
  Mountain, 6
Why to Refuse, 149
Widow's Blind Date, The, 59
Wild Duck, The, 64
Wild Honey, 7
Wild Raspberries, 69
Wind in the Willows, The, 140
Windowspeak, 152
Wink-Dah, 51
Winnetou's Snake Oil Show from
  Wigwam City, 150
Winnie the Pooh, 49, 53, 67, 149
Winter's Tale, The, 8, 68, 73, 96
Wintertime, 28
Wipeout, 40, 41
Witch of Edmonton, The, 136
Without Apologies, 15, 67
Without Law/Without Heaven, 115
Womanchild, 105
Woman Floating Out A Window,
  51
Woman in Mind, 10, 81, 83, 118,
  119, 158, 159, 160
Women and Wallace, 121, 167
Wonderful Town, 60
Wonderful Wizard of Oz, The, 149
Wonder Years, The, 54, 65
Woody Guthrie's American Song,
  13, 20
World Goes 'Round . . . With
  Kander & Ebb, The, 162
Would-Be Gentleman, The, 133
Woza Albert!, 42
Wreck of the Hesperus, 27
Wrinkle in Time, A, 9, 66, 149
Write On!, 35
Write On, Chicago!, 35
Writing Is . . . Child's Play!, 35

Y

Yankee Dawg You Die, 23, 79, 121,
  133, 163
Yard Sale, 73
Year of the Duck, 67
Yellow Fever, 107
Yerma, 112, 124, 125
Yesterday's Hero, 114
Yokohama Duty, 93
You Can't Judge a Book by
  Looking at the Cover: Sayings
  from the Life and Writings of
  Junebug Jabbo Jones, Volume II,
  87
You Can't Take It with You, 116,
  154
You Never Can Tell, 7, 21, 139
Young Ben Franklin, 151
Young Jane Eyre, 35

Young Rube, 89
You're a Good Man Charlie Brown, 65
Yours, Anne, 69

Z

Zastrozzi, 128
Zaydok, 92
Zero Positive, 96
Zig Zag Zelda, 111
Zoo Story, The, 6
Zora Neale Hurston, 11
Zurama, 135

ABOUT TCG

Theatre Communications Group is the national organization for the nonprofit professional theatre. Since its founding in 1961, TCG has developed a unique and comprehensive support system that addresses the artistic and management concerns of theatres, as well as institutionally based and freelance artists nationwide.

TCG provides a national forum and communications network for a field that is as aesthetically diverse as it is geographically widespread. Its goals are to foster the cross-fertilization of ideas among the individuals and institutions comprising the profession; to improve the artistic and administrative capabilities of the field; to enhance the visibility and demonstrate the achievements of the American theatre by increasing public awareness of the theatre's role in society; and to encourage the development of a mutually supportive network of professional companies and artists that collectively represent our "national theatre."

TCG's centralized services and programs facilitate the work of thousands of actors, artistic and managing directors, playwrights, literary managers, directors, designers, trustees and administrative personnel, as well as a constituency of hundreds theatre institutions across the country.

THEATRE COMMUNICATIONS GROUP

Peter Zeisler, Director
Lindy Zesch and Arthur Bartow
Associate Directors

Board of Directors

Robert Falls, President
Anthony Taccone, Vice President
Jennifer von Mayrhauser, Secretary
Sarah Lawless, Treasurer

JoAnne Akalaitis
Anne Bogart
Ping Chong
John Conklin
Olympia Dukakis
Maria Irene Fornes
Barry Grove
Laura J. Hardman
Jeffrey Horowitz
David Henry Hwang
Kevin Kline
Mel Marvin

Ronald L. Merriman
Jack O'Brien
L. Kenneth Richardson
Harold Scott
Douglas Stein
William Stewart
Megan Terry
Charles Towers
Stan Wojewodski, Jr.
Garland Wright
Peter Zeisler